The Birth of an Ideology

The Birth of an Ideology

Myths and Symbols of Nation in Late-Medieval France

Colette Beaune

Translated by Susan Ross Huston
Edited by Fredric L. Cheyette

UNIVERSITY OF CALIFORNIA PRESS
Berkeley · Los Angeles · Oxford

University of California Press
Berkeley and Los Angeles, California

University of California Press
Oxford, England

Copyright © 1991 by The Regents of the University of California
Originally published in French by Edition Gallimard, Paris, © 1985.

Library of Congress Cataloging-in-Publication Data

Beaune, Colette.
    [Naissance de la nation France. English]
    The birth of an ideology : myths and symbols of nation in late
-medieval France / Colette Beaune ; translated by Susan Ross Huston
; edited by Fredric L. Cheyette.
        p.   cm.
    Translation of: Naissance de la nation France.
    Includes bibliographical references and index.
    ISBN 0-520-05941-7 (alk. paper)
        1. France—Social life and customs—1328–1600.   2. France-
-History—Medieval period, 987–1515.   3. France—Church history-
-Middle Ages, 987–1515.   4. France—Kings and rulers—Biography.
I. Cheyette, Fredric L.   II. Title.
    DC33.2.B413   1991
944'.02—dc20   90-24687
                                                                          CIP

Printed in the United States of America

1 2 3 4 5 6 7 8 9

The paper used in this publication meets the minimum requirements
of American National Standard for Information Sciences—Permanence
of Paper for Printed Library Materials, ANSI Z39.48-1984 ⊗

Contents

Translator's Note

The following is a translation of Colette Beaune, *Naissance de la Nation France*, published by Gallimard in Paris in 1985. The work has been revised for this translation. Chapters have been rearranged, new introductory materials and a new section on the *oriflamme* added, and some minor errors corrected. The editor wishes to thank Colette Beaune for her willingness to make these changes.

General Introduction

The origins of the Nation is a subject that has blessed us with much theorizing but little information.[1] One reason is that nationhood is more than just a historical problem; it is—and long has been—a vital political problem as well. Historians have therefore commonly taken some pre-defined notion of the nation and attempted to determine when it first appeared. And what a multitude of definitions there have been. In the historical literature, these definitions have generally been of three types:

1. The Nation is based on race, on ethnic purity; it is identical with a people and is determined by blood ties. Such a definition was often adopted by nineteenth-century German scholars.

2. The Nation is the fruit of a shared history that has led a group of people to share common customs, a common spirit, and a desire to live together. Most French historians of the nineteenth century thought along these lines.

3. The development of nations is linked to the rise of the bourgeoisie, which hoped to find in nationalism a guarantee for the hegemony that set it apart from, and eventually placed it at odds with, both monarchy and the nobility. This is the Marxist point of view. To make matters more complicated, in later nineteenth-century France, the ideology of nationhood was strongly associated with the right. The left favored other concepts of community, those of social class and the international proletarian movement. In the Middle Ages, of course, neither had yet been thought of.

If we play theoretical games of this sort, we could find the birth date for the French nation in almost any period at all: in classical antiquity, in the narrow confines of the Gallic *civitates* where some claim to have found a vague notion of the Gallic fatherland; in the eighteenth century if we chose to identify the nation with hostility toward the monarchy and the idea of liberty; or we could insist that the nation is a contemporary phenomenon, belonging only to nineteenth- and twentieth-century history. Eugen Weber, for example, has argued that the French nation was a product of the mandatory, secular schooling promoted by the Third Republic; in this sense, the idea of France, a wholly republican France, only began to take shape on the eve of World War I.

Historians have most often, however, discovered the birth of the French nation in the Middle Ages. Since the early nineteenth century, this has been the position of traditional political historians. Sensitized by three wars, generations of French scholars made the medieval birth of the nation one of their grandest themes. The war of 1870 prompted Georges Guibal to write his *History of National Feeling in France* and Charles Lenient his *Patriotic Poetry in France;* World War II inspired Marie Madeleine Martin's *History of French Unity* and the articles of Ferdinand Lot on the same theme.[2] They all used the most traditional forms of political history to shape their arguments. Royal reigns and glorious battles showed forth their patriotic deeds. Republican historians expatiated on the stories of Le Grand Ferré and Joan of Arc, son and daughter of the People; monarchist versions insisted on the dynasty and its centralization of government. In the former, France was made by the people, in the latter, by the king; but in each case, France was the child of events.

In the earlier part of this century, Vidal de la Blache and Charles Seignobos looked at the problem from very different and far more ambitious vantage points.[3] Vidal's *Systematic View of the Geography of France* formed the first volume of Ernest Lavisse's monumental history of France, a masterwork of positivist scholarly history. Seignobos's *A Truthful History of the French Nation* came out in at least ten different editions between 1933 and 1940. Both works were popularized in textbooks and helped to shape several generations of scholars, readers, and students. They appeared thirty years apart and expressed somewhat different points of view. Vidal de la Blache sought the reason for the development of France's political unity in its geography. He found rooted in its soil a harmony, variety, and equilibrium that combined to form a common political destiny. For him, the French people were the

fruit of their land. Though Seignobos also gave the land much importance, he stressed the unitary thread that ran through its culture. Institutional and economic structures, literary and artistic creations, had created the common lifestyle that had forged a French identity and the
glories of the French Republic.

Both Vidal and Seignobos went beyond the mere recitation of the
Capetian success story to seek the reasons for it. Like their predecessors,
however, neither had the slightest doubt that this evolution toward a
nation-state was a good thing. The history of France had a meaning.
Centuries of lived experiences had flowed together to form a nation.
France was the inevitable fruit of time.

Traditional political history made this a story of events. Vidal and
Seignobos went beyond the events to emphasize such factors of cohesion as institutions and the spread of the use of the French language. But
these were all still histories of deeds. In the recent studies that have
continued this tradition, France may no longer be the child of events,
but she is still the child of historical deeds.

A new tendency began in 1927 with the appearance of Marc Bloch's
The Royal Touch.[4] Drawing his inspiration from the work of contemporary German historians (especially P. E. Schramm), Bloch created a
history of political mentalities. His approach would eventually transform the political history of the later Middle Ages. Soon after its appearance, however, he and the "*Annales* school" dropped this line of inquiry
and turned to problems of economic history. During the 1950s, although many important theses on the seignorial economy of the late
Middle Ages appeared, political history fell from fashion in France and
was abandoned by the country's medievalists. It reappeared only slowly.

In 1958, Raymond Cazelles—a historian who belonged to no established "school"—published his *Political Society in the Reign of Philip
of Valois* (with a sequel appearing nearly twenty-five years later).[5]
Cazelles skillfully focused on the members of the royal government,
their social background, and the regions from which they came, examining the way different governing groups succeeded one another and their
various political agendas. Around the same time, Bernard Guenée began
work on his *Tribunals and Judicial Personnel in the Bailliage of Senlis,* a
model social analysis of a provincial judiciary.[6] Guenée's work created a
large following in a way that Cazelles's had not. His student, Françoise
Autrand, published her thesis on the Parlement and its members in the
late Middle Ages;[7] Jacques Krynen's *Princely Ideals and Royal Power in
France Under Charles VI* was indirectly inspired by Guenée's work and

owed much to it.[8] Politics, once again in fashion, began to invade French medieval historiography.

In English-speaking countries, studies of late-medieval France have developed along similar lines. Oxford's Peter S. Lewis stands at the center of this renaissance, since his *Later Medieval France: The Polity* (1968) has served as a model for Michael Jones, Malcolm Vale, and above all Christopher Allmand.[9] In the United States, Ralph Giesey, with his examination of the rituals of power during the waning years of the Middle Ages and the beginning of the modern era, has been the principal innovator. Drawing inspiration from the teachings of Ernst Kantorowicz, he has in turn been followed by Sarah Hanley and Lawrence Bryant.[10] Gabrielle Spiegel's studies of the Saint-Denis chronicles have focused more especially on the Middle Ages, as has Elizabeth Brown's work on the last Capetians and Andrew Lewis's on the royal family.[11]

The work that follows is intended to take its place in this new program of political history. It does not begin with any a priori notion of what the nation is. I am interested in examining how people thought of France, what they said about it, and how they expressed their love for it. Mental images, images of the collective imagination, will be my primary focus. Readers should not be surprised when they find that these medieval images hardly coincide with eighteenth- and nineteenth-century ideas of nationhood.

There are two more questions we need to put aside. First, was the historical development that led to nation-states a good thing or a bad thing? That question belongs to moral philosophers to answer, not historians. Nor is it meaningful to ask whether a national ideology is based on truth. Every ideology consists of myths; every ideology presents itself as the truth. What is genuinely important about an ideology is its ability to generate allegiances, not its relationship to truth. Every study of ideology is a study of falsehood, or of truths that have been molded into a given point of view. On this point, earlier times were neither more nor less naive than ours.

QUESTIONS OF VOCABULARY

The terms we now use to speak of nationhood and beliefs associated with it are of recent vintage.[12] The French word *nationalisme* (nationalism) only appeared in 1812; *patriotisme* (patriotism) shortly before, in the eighteenth century; *patriote* (patriot) first surfaced in literature in 1568 and in the *Dictionnaire de l'Académie* only in 1762, though Suger had used *compatriota* (fellow inhabitant of a region) as early as the second half of the twelfth century.[13] *Patrie* (fatherland) and *nation* (nation) have similar stories. The Latin word *patria* has been used in its modern sense off and on since the end of the twelfth century, but the French equivalent, *patrie*, was unknown prior to 1530–1540. *Pays* (country) was used instead. Only the educated used the word *patrie*, for they were imbued with classical culture and Italian humanism, and the usage remained pedantic until around 1550. "He who has a *pays*, has no need of a *patrie*," wrote Charles Loyseau to Joachim du Bellay.[14] As for *natio*, from the Latin verb *nasci* (to be born), in the Middle Ages it referred to many different kinds of groups: ethnic (as in the *natio* of Bretons); academic (as in the four nations of the University of Paris—the Picards, Normans, English, and Germans); ecclesiastical (the nations of the College of Cardinals, of the Order of Malta, and the four nations of the Church councils—France, Germany, Aragon, and England);[15] mercantile (the nation of London was the corporation of London merchants). References to the "French nation," however, were rare before the end of the fifteenth century,[16] and the expression *sentiment national* (national feeling) did not make its appearance until the eighteenth. People spoke about "France" or the "kingdom" or the "Crown," rather than the "nation." They spoke about *amour du pays* or *charité du pays* (both of which mean "love for one's country" or "for one's region"). The inappropriateness of modern vocabulary to medieval reality probably indicates that our modern ideas are a poor match for a time and place so profoundly different from our own.

TIME AND PLACE

The Capetian kingdom was an outgrowth of what the treaties of 843 called *Francia occidentalis;* it consisted of the western part of the empire of Charlemagne (771–814), which became the portion of his grandson Charles the Bald (843–877). After shaky beginnings rocked by invasions, private wars, and feudal turmoil, this region experienced a rapid development of centralized authority. This trend toward consolidation, launched during the reign of Louis VI (1108–1137), eventually brought the *regnum* all the way to the shores of the Atlantic with the conquest of Normandy and other Angevin lands in 1204. The death of Alphonse of Poitiers, successor to the counts of Toulouse, in 1271, and the absorption of his lands into the royal domain, extended it to the Mediterranean. Two important battles waged against foreign coalitions had ma-

jor political and psychological consequences. In 1124 Louis VI confronted the Emperor Henry V; in 1214 Philip Augustus defeated the
allied Imperial, English, and Flemish forces at Bouvines.[17] As a result, by
1300 the king was obeyed nearly everywhere within a territory bounded
by the Atlantic, the Mediterranean, and the four rivers that came to
mark the traditional eastern boundary of the kingdom: the Escaut,
Meuse, Saone, and Rhone.[18]

Covering 350,000 square kilometers, it was one of the largest kingdoms of the time and one of the best organized. From the late-twelfth to
the early fourteenth century, it boasted great numbers of royal officials;
its central institutions (the Chambre de comptes, the Parlement) were
precociously effective.[19] In a country such as this, where Paris by the
thirteenth century had already begun to function as undisputed capital,
the state most definitely preceded and supported the development of the
nation, contrary to the experiences of Italy and Germany, both of them
nations before they were states. Thus by the time the thirteenth century
was drawing to a close, the kingdom had acquired a degree of territorial
stability that it maintained until the end of the fifteenth, when rapid
growth began again as Burgundy, Provence, and Brittany were absorbed. No longer solely feudal, France now constituted a territorial
state. Its inhabitants were all subjects of the king, whether or not they
were his vassals, and every region, even if it was not held of the king as a
fief, depended on him. When, in 1307, the bishop of Mende proclaimed
that his bishopric was not part of the kingdom, he was leading a
rearguard attack.[20] Although France remained highly diversified and
fragmented, it belonged to a single political structure, to a state. As a
result, national sentiment emerged within a unique set of circumstances.
In that development, the dynasty played an essential role.

The period 1300 to 1500—the timespan of my study—was one of
the most tumultuous of European history. Economic and demographic
crises led to a continuous cycle of famine and plague. To this the Hundred Years War (1338–1450) added a multitude of military defeats
(Poitiers in 1356, Agincourt in 1415) that completed the sinister trilogy.
Only the reconquest of 1430 to 1450 gradually won back what had
been lost, and then only slowly.

The great plague of 1348 and its sequels killed from a quarter to a
third of the total French population; this we can estimate from the
household census of 1328 to have been around 18,000,000. The decline
was aggravated by widespread famine and losses due to war and
scorched earth tactics. As 90 percent of the population were peasants,

the instability that affected them lasted for several generations. The royal dynasty, the one organized political force in the kingdom, also suffered a blow, its prestige struck to the core when the king of England challenged the legitimacy of the Valois by taking the name and arms of France and claiming closer kinship with Saint Louis. The French nobility, who lost at Courtrai, Crécy, and Verneuil, stood accused of incompetence and treason. The nobility suffered more than any other social group except the Church. When their fixed incomes collapsed with monetary changes and inflation they tried to mitigate their difficulties by tendering service to the king. As for the clergy, their prestige was tarnished when the papacy took up residence at Avignon (1306–1378) and further darkened by the Great Schism from 1378 to 1439, when there were first two and then three popes.

Beyond the frontiers of the kingdom, great institutions of power were falling all around: the Empire had broken under the strain of its conflict with the papacy and was forced to accept the independent status of new states within its bounds; the papacy lost its theocratic pretensions in the course of its conflict with Philip the Fair (1285–1314). But internal disarray was every bit as strong. The equilibrium that had once held the various social groups in place had disappeared; political consensus had collapsed in the crises of 1356–1358 and the civil war between the Armagnacs and Burgundians. Traditional values disappeared. But the idea of nationhood, evolving since the beginning of the twelfth century, surged into the vacuum and eventually brought whatever was left of the old values under its own sway. It was these new values that allowed a profoundly shaken society to set itself aright, to create a different set of allegiances better adapted to the problems of the day.

I have defined the spatial and temporal dimensions of my study to match the parameters of the subject. The Capetian kingdom of the late Middle Ages is a relatively coherent and stable nation-state. The period of the late Middle Ages is large enough to allow us to see both change and continuity. And, since boundaries—whether temporal or geographical—are only heuristic, nothing will prevent us from moving back before 1100 or forward beyond 1550 or making comparisons with other medieval nations when the subject demands it.

THE SUBJECT

This book seeks to examine the mental representations of a collectivity, mythic representations that surface in the course of time. I have purposely avoided making the kingdom's political ups and downs, its institutions and administrative bodies, my primary subject of study. They are the frame, not the picture. Rather than being a political history, this is a history of ideologies, though even to use this word is misleading since *ideology* is too abstract, rational, and text-based for the subject at hand. The word *mythology* probably corresponds better to a love of country that is felt far more than it is thought. Mythology is better suited to convey the idea of a web of themes that are constantly in flux, now joining together, now transmogrifying into something else, often in ways that defy logic. But as nontextual sources are so important in studies of the national symbols of societies where oral tradition coexists with the written, the term *symbolism* would also seem appropriate. Let us say therefore that I have written a book about the myths and symbols of nationhood, about the perspectives and the discourses people constructed around it.

I have divided the material into two major sections. The first part of the book deals with the relationship of France with God. Geographically, France belonged to Latin Christendom, which the Turkish incursion had reduced to a "small corner of the world." France also belonged mentally to Latin Christendom, for the notion of Europe did not yet have sufficient substance to serve as an adequate alternative frame. The French believed their country was the best and the most ardently faithful of all Christian kingdoms. The mission it had to accomplish was a Christian mission. From it sprang saints, not heroes; the latter were mere counterfeit figures who followed after. The hero's role was to glorify the nation, increase its prestige (still more religious than cultural), and serve as intermediary between the nation and its divine judge. Alternately, Saint Denis, Saint Clovis, Saint Louis, and Saint Michael were surrounded by popular fervor, depending on the era and what notion it favored of the relationship between France and God.

Sources are quite disparate on this matter. I have chosen to complete what historians have said by drawing on the work of theologians and jurists. I have used accounts of miracles, papal bulls, prayer texts, and liturgies for the king and kingdom along with the *Great Chronicles of France,* the official account of the reigns of French kings that the monks of Saint-Denis produced generation after generation.[21] For these authors, Christian and French were nearly synonymous. Since the Middle Ages believed the sacred was the only feasible source of identity, France rooted itself in the sacred tradition, found justification for its existence through that tradition, and sought in it a sense of self that transcended the temporal.

The second part of this book is devoted to signs and symbols. In the same way that modern French people associate Marianne, the Phrygian bonnet, and the blue, white, and red of the flag with France, medieval France was symbolized by the white cross, the winged deer, and the three lilies, signs richly endowed with connotations that all observers understood more or less clearly. What medieval people said about their history, its meaning, and the virtues it revealed, and how that history was used, is also informative. Learned circles dealt in other national signs: for servants of the state and those who were well-educated, the Trojan origins of France, the Salic Law, and the French language were all richly endowed with meaning. In addition to particularizing metaphors like these, there were also overarching projections of the nation as well. These included the Tree and the Garden of Paradise, evocative of the territory of France; the Voice and eventually the Body of France stood for the French people as a whole. I will also examine the relationship between France and the French people, the ties that bound the people to their country, their profession of love for it, and their willingness to sacrifice themselves for it.

In larger terms, the book deals with how France looked at itself and what image it had of itself. As I have been careful to eliminate topics not integral to the subject at hand, the question of what images France had of other countries will not appear here. These images, as we know, were often xenophobic, an easily understandable thing where the English were concerned, though less so when it comes to Germans and Italians.[22]

Insofar as possible, I have tried to give the dates and specify the geographical and social origins of the texts I refer to. This should afford an insight into what groups were touched by the propaganda of nationhood, though it leaves us in the dark as to how the information was received. Any form of effective propaganda certainly has a deep-seated link to shared sentiments, and the success of this French propaganda has long since been demonstrated. Although the English won the Hundred Years War militarily in 1338–1360 and in 1415, they never won the hearts and minds of their enemy.[23] The term *propaganda* should not be interpreted pejoratively here. Medieval governments were all too aware of how to manipulate opinion. But I have chosen to use *propaganda* in reference to all those projections France made of itself, whether or not they rang with truth and sincerity and whether or not people were paid to create them. In some cases these were unconscious projections, in some they were shared beliefs. Such beliefs did more during the fourteenth and fifteenth centuries to shore up the unsteady trusses of the state than any institutions. This would seem justification enough to examine the changing and multiple world of shared medieval opinion. For that world too has a history.

PART I

Introduction

To men and women of the Middle Ages, the visible world corresponded in many ways to the invisible: both were the creation of God, and their continued existence depended on Him. Since prayers served as the invisible thread that bound the two together, it seemed only fitting to pray for the king and kingdom which the Maker had created and which participated in the grand design of His Church. Prayers were offered for the king from the early Middle Ages onward. They slowly evolved from those given in the royal chapel for the souls of those privileged believers—the kings—to specific liturgies, then, by the thirteenth century, to prayers that all good folk were to offer for their king, and then, within a hundred years, to prayers they were called upon to offer for the entire nation.

In the last centuries of the Middle Ages, the king's subjects prayed for him on any number of occasions. Coronation masses and royal funerals involved but small numbers of attendants drawn from the upper nobility and episcopacy. Their liturgy, hardly disinterested, charts the evolution of this group's conceptions of royalty.[1] But these ceremonies had limited influence: the paucity of contemporary manuscript *ordines*—liturgical texts for such occasions—attests to that. There were, however, more frequent if not necessarily more regular occasions when many more people were involved. The king's ceremonial entries into his "good towns," for example, culminated with the celebration of a mass. The liturgical text would be based on the ordinary one for the day, but the sermon itself was specially written for the event.[2] Both clergy and town governments discovered further reasons to hold public prayers, whether or not they were ordered by royal command. People in different regions might honor with a *Te Deum* the king's victory in battle.[3] Defeats in turn were marked by ritual observances for the dead, as they were in Dauphiné for the soldiers of Agincourt and Verneuil.

There were also public forms of prayer more closely linked to the king himself—held at times of birth, marriage, or sickness. Whenever Charles VI (1380–1422) was gripped with insanity, the streets of Paris filled with processions of agitated crowds. There were the festivals that were a regular part of the liturgical calendar, like the birthdays of the saints honored by the royal family—Dagobert on January 19; Charlemagne on January 28; Saint Louis at the end of August; the Blessed Charles of Blois, nephew of Philip VI,[4] on September 29; and Saint Louis of Anjou on August 19—all times when people prayed for their king.

The public involved in these rituals varied from one observance to the next. With few exceptions, only churches founded by the Merovingian king Dagobert (623–639) celebrated his feast day for example,[5] whereas none but the sanctuaries of the Parisian basin honored August 11 as the day of Holy Crown, commemorating Saint Louis's translation of the Crown of Thorns to the Sainte Chapelle. But the whole kingdom joined in for the celebration of the feast day of Saint Louis himself. Many abbeys purportedly founded or sustained by members of the royal house also held ceremonies to pay homage to their benefactors. The liturgical calendar of the abbey of Saint-Denis was replete with ceremonial observances of royal deaths; the same was true to a lesser extent for other abbeys. Privileges and gifts bestowed on churches drew prayers for the donor kings, their ancestors, and their families. Grants of royal safeguard to churches and abbeys encouraged this most strongly. Thus areas of special prayers began to grow within the kingdom.

In addition to public prayer on official occasions, from the early thirteenth century on, private supplications on behalf of the king were also encouraged. From 1247 to 1249, while the king was on crusade, Pope Innocent IV offered four days of indulgence to all who prayed daily for Louis IX (1226–1270).[6] This was not new, for the diocese of Paris had already prayed for Philip Augustus (1180–1223) when he departed on crusade. In both cases the prayers were for a successful outcome to the king's holy voyage rather than for the king himself. But at Easter 1252, Innocent gave the Dominicans permission to announce

in their sermons that ten days of indulgence would be granted to everyone who prayed for the king who was then held captive in the Holy
Land.[7] Alexander IV reinstituted the crusading indulgences in 1255.
Later in the century, Saint Thomas asserted that those who prayed daily
for the king, in whatever time or place, would have ten days of indulgence. To this he added only the following conditions: the believer must
show proof of faith and reverence and offer the prayers in the name of a
holy and spiritual cause.[8] Though indulgences drew criticism from some
quarters, they were useful in strengthening the bond of affection between the king and his people. Prayers for the king reinforced the idea of
national unity; it was a sacred and spiritual cause, an example of the
amor generalis, the love of all, which theologians placed high on their
list of virtues. Praying for the king opens heaven's gates, said Saint
Thomas. The phrase became famous. At the end of the fifteenth century,
Cosme Guimier and Jean Ferrault were still quoting it.

    In the fourteenth century indulgences spread into newer and different
spheres of activity. The Avignon papacy spared nothing for the benefit
of the monarchy it depended on so heavily. Pope Clement V was particularly generous. He offered personal plenary indulgences to all who
prayed for the deceased relatives of the royal family and thereby helped
their souls pass from purgatory into heaven. But the most interesting
indulgences are those that were clearly political: forty (and later a hundred) days of indulgence and pardon, he told the king, would be given
to those who pray for "you, the kings and queens who will succeed you,
and the eternal salvation of your soul," and also to those who "pray for
true peace in the kingdom."[9] The indulgences of Clement V reflected a
warming of relations following the tensions between Boniface VIII and
Philip the Fair. They also combined traditional elements—like concern
for the soul of the king and the fate of the dead—with newly formulated
desires for the future of the lineage and for peace in the kingdom.
Prayers were meant to serve not only the king as an individual but the
past and future house of France as well, and—beyond it—the nation as
a whole. When Philip VI ascended the throne in 1328, his agents
worked to have the indulgences confirmed for the new dynasty: the
Valois were a contested house and much in need of prayers and support.
Clement V's bulls, which encouraged "daily prayers for the king or the
kingdom," brought Philip the confirmation he sought, though no prayer
text was specified and the words as well as the place of prayer were
probably left to the discretion of the supplicant.

    From 1400 onward, private prayers for the king and kingdom were rechanneled toward the foundation of chantries. Here the prayers were more frequent and more numerous and were offered by the clergy; they were prayers that the benefactors hoped would have greater potency than those of individual laymen. But because these were costly undertakings, only powerful people could afford them. People of an earlier age had founded chantries for themselves and their close relatives. Now the king belonged to every family in the kingdom. The same phenomenon occurred in the principalities, particularly in Burgundy, but on a much smaller scale.[10]

An interesting example of such a foundation has come down to us in a liturgical text written sometime between 1465 and 1468 at the behest of Charles of Melun, baron of Landes and Normanville and Grand Master of France.[11] The Grand Master had been governor of Paris during the War of the Public Weal in 1465; as his loyalties had been none too consistently royalist, in order to clear his name he requested that a series of daily prayers be dedicated to Louis XI (1461–1483). The liturgy, composed by a cleric, was to be performed by twelve priests and four choirboys of the Augustinian house of Saint-Amand-Montrond, which was part of the commandery of Landes.[12] It called for weekly recitation of the 150 psalms of David, divided according to the canonical hours, and included anthems, hymns, and canticles from the Scriptures similar to those in the psalter of Charles V,[13] but the prayers themselves were quite new. Related in subject matter to the hourly psalms, they combined concerns for the king and for the kingdom:

> May you keep the king you have placed above us safe and secure. May he be spared enemy ambushes, treacheries, sickness, and poison. At the end of his long and prosperous life, may you open heaven to him. May his kingdom remain faithful to him, may it be deaf to the foolish words of agitators, sure in its administration of peace, justice, and harmony, and may the great and the small carry out their duty with love for one another.

The nation that God preferred above all others would thus be blessed and saved by the works of its leader and all its members. "May God save the king and us all here in this world and may the king live in eternity with us at his side. May the king reign and France rejoice!" With these words each of the liturgical sequences was to end. We have no way of knowing whether this in fact was ever carried out. For, despite his foundation, Charles of Melun was executed anyway, at Les Andelys in 1468.

These were thoroughly Christian prayers. The king's soul ascended to heaven through the collective support of his people, (who also contributed to his virtues in the here and now). He partook of the communion of the saints and participated in the exchange of merits and prayers which were part of it. But these prayers were also political. No one other than the pope could have rightfully drawn such widespread daily Christian support. As people made no distinction between the king's political merits and his religious qualities, they were praying for their king, for the peace and stability of their kingdom, and for themselves as members of the Christian nation all at once. Religion lent support to the idea of national unity and made it palpable to all. Nationhood was still a new value that had not yet begun to seek recognition in secular terms. Instead, it bid for incorporation into the world of the sacred, it sought to share in that world's prestige.

These prayers were not necessarily addressed directly to God or the Virgin Mary; they were not always so universal. Intermediary patrons were often called on to intervene with the Divine Power at the behest of the nation. Early medieval forms of saintly patronage commonly tied a people to its evangelizers. Since Saint Martin, Saint Remigius, and Saint Denis had all played important roles in the conversion of Gaul, they were chosen to continue their service as patrons of the Frankish and then of the French kingdoms.

As the alliance the Capetian dynasty had forged with the abbey of Saint-Denis was a particularly sturdy one from the reign of Louis VI onward, it assured that the abbey's namesake would win out over the others. Though the salient facts about Denis's life were historically obscure, he nonetheless became the patron saint of the king and eventually of the kingdom and the Crown. French kings willingly chose to be buried at the abbey of Saint-Denis; they carried its banner into battle; it was there that they housed the *regalia* of their coronation. But at the beginning of the fifteenth century, when this favored abbey passed into the hands of the English, relations became strained. Saint Denis was transformed into the guardian of the double monarchy of England and France, and his reputation recovered from this betrayal only with great difficulty.

The patronage of Louis IX suffered a similar fate for similar reasons. Accounts of the life of this pious ancestor, ideal king of the Mendicant orders, had always been ambiguous. They allowed oppositional factions such as the Navarre party and later the Burgundian party to preempt for their own ends the memory of his resistance to taxes and his defense of local freedoms. The ruler of the double monarchy asserted he was a more direct descendant of Louis than were the kings of the house of Valois, and he claimed he would reenact Louis's policies of governance. Consequently, not until the seventeenth century would this saint, whose reputation had become so tarnished, succeed in becoming a model Christian ruler.

Neither Saint Louis nor Saint Denis managed to acquire a sphere of influence that spread much beyond the Parisian basin. Around 1415, however, the centers of royal religion located in and around the capital began spreading southward. The world of the king, the court, and the central administration shifted to Bourges, Poitiers, and the Loire Valley, and remained there for more than a century. Parisian nationalism was uprooted and relocated in more central parts of the country and in areas skirting the borders. The frontier of Gascony was soon dotted with royal sanctuaries, as were the Loire and Brittany frontiers. Charles VII (1422–1461) exchanged the patronage of Denis and Louis for Saint Michael, making him chief saint of the Kingdom of Bourges and eventually the entire nation. It was important now that heavenly protection should come in the form of the military force needed to ensure survival, and the image that the Archangel Michael projected was one of a youthful knight dedicated to saving those who were imperiled. He protected the sanctuary of Mont-Saint-Michel from the assaults of the English. French troups took to making processions behind the banner of Michael's white cross, like masses of reverent pilgrims. And from time to time, the Archangel made appearances along the most threatened parts of the battle front. Thus, when the country was liberated at last around 1450, Saint Michael became its guardian angel. Louis XI paid homage to him, making him the patron of a chivalric order.

The France of the Middle Ages entertained different kinds of relations with its heavenly patrons. The converted were linked to those who had converted them; kings bore in their veins the blood of Saint Louis and Saint Charlemagne; Saint Michael inspired the spiritual aspirations of the faithful. Each expressed a different notion of the role of the patron saint of the kingdom.

Other European nations went through similar changes, and by the end of the Middle Ages almost all were blessed with celestial protectors. Heaven was mapped by the balance of European powers. In France, indeed, the sacred had been parceled out to such a degree that each political faction had its celestial representative. Traces of this remained visible even at the end of the fifteenth century, when, despite the great prestige of the official saints of royalty, Saint André still defended the

Duchy of Burgundy and the ambiguous Charles of Blois still watched over Brittany. Religious unity and political unity still went hand in hand, and neither was yet fully realized.

Nations are particularistic; Christianity is universal. One might have expected that Christianity itself would have tempered the growth of nationalism. But this did not happen. Most European nations in the Middle Ages had little difficulty projecting their sense of nationhood in religious terms. This was especially true with France, which emerged into nationhood particularly early. France fashioned a religious image for itself and claimed a choice role in the Divine Plan. The French made themselves the second Chosen People, replacing the Hebrews in their alliance with God. France also became the most Christian nation: it had never known schism or heresy. Already at the end of the twelfth century Robert the Monk wrote of "the holy race of the Franks whom God has chosen as his people and his heritage."[14] The memory of the many crusading kings from Charlemagne to Saint Louis transformed every French king into a protector of holy places, a ruler predestined to lead all crusades. The most Christian king of France was safe from the threat of excommunication. He ascended into heaven automatically, often enhanced by the privileged cloak of sainthood. His blood was holy; it elevated him above the ranks of other rulers, liberating him, some said, even from the obligation to be crowned or knighted and giving him the power to create the symbols of kingship and to work miracles. For God had approved this single line of legitimate French kings, which stretched from one century to the next. Thus, in France, kings ruled even if they were insane or mere infants. This is how God wanted it to be.

These beliefs endowed French kings with an unusual degree of power. And at the end of the fifteenth century, the idea of most Christian rulership was further aggrandized. Now, more than just an expression of the will of God, it became a manifestation of the uniqueness of French nationhood. To be most Christian was to be different from other nations and kings, and that difference was a superiority. France showed its specificity in other domains as well—cultural, for example; but its religious specificity continued to be mentioned first. Often it was the only form of national identity that came to mind.

CHAPTER 1

Saint Denis

PATRON SAINTHOOD ASSERTED AND QUESTIONED

Saint Denis was the earliest and for a long time the only major patron saint of France and its kings. From the Carolingian era to the beginning of the fifteenth century the spiritual affinities between the lands that had once been Gaul and its evangelizer remained undisputed. But Denis's protectorship was not without problems. Those who wrote about him could not agree on his identity, his life, his dates, the works attributed to him, or the place where he was buried. The authoritative voice of Hilduin, abbot of Saint-Denis (814–842), asserted around 835 that Denis the Areopagite, converted by Saint Paul to become bishop of Athens, was one and the same with Denis, the bishop of Paris. But well-reasoned doubts were constantly heard outside of the Paris area. During the twelfth and thirteenth centuries, however, the monarchy endorsed Hilduin's view as the official version of the saint's life, and thereafter it stood almost undisputed, though interested scholars might well have brought together from scattered sources all the elements needed to discredit it. No one made such a case, for challenging Saint Denis was akin to challenging the king. The abbey of Saint-Denis had linked itself with the dynasty and served it in indispensable ways. Saint Denis was the patron saint of the king, of the kingdom, and of the Crown.

As the king's guardian, Denis protected him bodily from wounds and sickness; he shielded his soul from evil and ministered to him at the hour of death. A long line of kings, from Dagobert (623–639), to Charles Martel (714–741), Charlemagne (751–814), Charles the Bald (843–877), and Philip Augustus (1180–1223), all had visions attesting to this. Through the help of the Areopagite, the king escaped hell and even purgatory and, by the end of the Middle Ages, he was guaranteed entry into heaven, due as much to the new royal death rites as to divine intervention.

Saint Denis was also the patron saint of the kingdom, for he had evangelized it in its entirety. The number of companions said to have accompanied him grew. And according to the fourteenth-century account of the monk Yves de Saint-Denis, the country Denis and his fellow missionaries converted was the whole kingdom, bounded by the borders of 1317. Denis was credited with having worked from Paris outward to establish most of the episcopal sees in the French lands north of the Loire. From the time of Abbot Suger (1122–1151), he was also said to be patron saint of the Crown, and his abbey housed all of the royal regalia, the symbols of the monarchy, including the oriflamme, the crown of Saint Louis, and the crown of Charlemagne.

Nonetheless, after 1415, breaks appeared in the tradition, breaks whose importance should not be underestimated. Though Charles VII (1422–1461) continued to use the Holy Ampulla, he also created new regalia. A number of legends were invented to cover his new practices, affirming he had indeed used the regalia of Saint-Denis, whereas the English had been unable to do so. But Charles's innovations had consequences nevertheless: the white cross replaced the oriflamme, and a new coronation *ordo* was composed. The abbey's role as royal necropolis was also profoundly altered. Saint-Denis, which had served specifically as the cemetery of kings until 1300 and during the reign of Charles V (1364–1380) had become the resting place of all those of royal blood and the pantheon of heroes, now relinquished this role until the middle of the sixteenth century. One French king was not even buried there. Despite efforts to restore the abbey's preeminence toward the end of the fifteenth century, from this time on, the roles were reversed: it was now the kings who watched over the abbey of Saint-Denis.

A WAVERING TRADITION

Saint Denis was an evolving creation of intellectuals of the early Middle Ages. This third-century bishop of Paris had, in the course of time, come to be confused with a first-century bishop of Athens, converted by Saint

Paul. Slowly, spectacular miracles and hermetic Greek writings—most notably the *De hierarchia*—were attributed to him. Let us see how this illustrious unknown was created.

The most decisive step in the process came around 835 when Hilduin, the abbot of Saint-Denis, wrote his *Life of Saint Denis*.[1] Up until the seventh century, the only sources available on the life of the bishop of Paris had been passages from Eusebeus of Caesarea (265–339), the late fifth-century *Gloriosae* (the first *Life* of Saint Denis), and Gregory of Tours (538–594). Eusebeus in his *Ecclesiastical History*[2]—a work on the history of the early Church which was widely available as a reference in all monastic libraries—clearly distinguished between Denis the Areopagite, whose conversion by Saint Paul is related in the *Book of Acts*,[3] and the third-century Denis, the bishop of Corinth, who wrote many epistles to the churches of Greece and the Middle East. Gregory of Tours, for his part, wrote of seven bishops sent from Rome to evangelize Gaul in the days of the Emperor Decius (249–251) and Pope Sixtus II (257–258). "We learn from the story of the holy martyr Saturninus," he wrote, "[that] . . . when Decius and Gratus were consuls . . . the seven Bishops were sent to their sees: Bishop Gatianus to the men of Tours; Bishop Trophimus to the men of Arles; Bishop Paulus to Narbonne; Bishop Saturninus to Toulouse; Bishop Dionysius to the men of Paris; Bishop Stremonius to the men of Clermont-Ferrand; and Martialis was made Bishop of Limoges. Of these Saint Dionysius, Bishop of Paris, suffered repeated torture in Christ's name and then ended his earthly existence by the sword."[4] The *Gloriosae* added two companions, Rusticus and Eleutherius, who joined Denis in martyrdom. It placed the martyrdom under a Pope Clement (Clement I? c. 91–100), though it did not attribute any date to the event and did not identify Denis as an apostle. Neither did it say that Denis was Greek in origin or that he was the author of the *De hierarchia*.[5]

At the beginning of the eighth century, the prolific English writer, the Venerable Bede (673–735), took on all three Denises of the tradition: the bishop of Corinth, the bishop of Athens, and the bishop of Paris. The version he drew from these sources was the following: "Denis the Areopagite, who was converted by Saint Paul in Athens, became the bishop of Corinth and wrote a number of remarkable works."[6] This is why Bede quite logically registered only two feast days of Saint Denis in his martyrology instead of three,[7] launching a tradition that would later be adapted by Hilduin. According to Bede, October 3 was the feast day of Denis, Areopagite and bishop of Corinth; October 9 the day of

Denis, bishop of Paris, who was martyred along with Rusticus and Eleutherius under the rule of Domitian (81–96).

FROM HILDUIN TO ABELARD

When Abbot Hilduin of Saint-Denis was officially commissioned to write a *Life* to glorify Denis, the patron saint of the Carolingian dynasty, a Byzantine mission had recently arrived in Western Europe with Greek manuscripts of the *De hierarchia*.[8] Hilduin enjoyed marked advantages over his predecessors: he benefited not only from the haziness of the tradition, but also from his solid knowledge of Greek and from the access he had to the remarkable library at the abbey of Saint-Denis. Using an intermediate *Life* as a model, Hilduin had no difficulty in composing a life of the saint that was different from the *Gloriosae*, one that would defend the interests of his abbey. He turned into one and the same person the Areopagite who was converted by Saint Paul, the bishop of Athens who wrote the *De hierarchia*, and the evangelizer whom Pope Clement sent to christianize Gaul, where he became bishop of Paris and was martyred, carrying his head from the place where he was killed to his burial site. All of these events Hilduin now situated in the first century.

Hilduin thus managed to bring together all the elements of the tradition into one single figure: Denis, the bishop of Paris, became an apostle and also the author of an enormous and well-respected work. With this story the abbot of Saint-Denis won imperial protection, but his transformations were soon noticed and drew the attention of adversaries as well as supporters.

From a letter that Hilduin wrote to Emperor Louis the Pious (814–840), we can get some idea of the arguments his opposition raised.[9] None of what he said had appeared in Latin texts known at the time—not in the *Life* of Saint Saturninus, not in Gregory of Tours, not in Bede. No Greek texts referred to Denis's mission to Gaul or to his martyrdom. Fortunatus's *Hymn to Denis*,[10] written in the sixth century, mentioned neither his life in Greece nor his writing the *De hierarchia*.

Hilduin responded to these objections by attacking his adversaries. They were "blind men, driven by a perverse spirit." He dismissed Gregory's account: was the bishop not poorly educated, simple, indulgent, lacking all experience with texts? As for Fortunatus, Hilduin admitted that he was unaware of Denis's life in Greece and his status as the Areopagite but argued that he never actually denied them. The core of

Hilduin's argument, however, lay in proofs he claimed to find in Greek texts, proofs he could supposedly show anyone interested in seeing them, since "they [were] in the archives of [his] monastery." Other texts, he said, "lacked authority," because the authority of his own was superior. He was bringing "to the light of Christ" the story of Denis that was known in the Greek world but not in the Latin, "a true account according to true sources."

Not all the bishops and abbots of the empire rallied around this new version.[11] Ado of Vienne, who composed a popular *Martyrology* around 870, shortly after Hilduin's death, was one of those who opposed the abbot.[12] In his argument, however, he used the same fundamental strategy: he created an earlier Greek source that contradicted what Hilduin had said. Ado claimed to build his case on the *Apologia for Christianity*,[13] written about 145 by Aelius Aristides for Hadrian, a work that was reputed in the early Middle Ages to be a good source for the Church history of the first century. To heighten the authority of the *Apologia*, Ado wrote in his *Martyrology* for August 31: "[Death of] the blessed Aristides, who wrote the *Apologia*, a text worthy of belief, and one of the oldest in Greek." Ado's appeal to this text, however, was pure subterfuge. Ninth-century authors had no copies of the *Apologia* available to them, and the text itself does not in fact ever mention Denis the Areopagite. Ado nevertheless claimed to have found a crucial passage from the *Apologia* in a text he called the *Little Roman Martyrology*, which, he asserted, predated his own. But here too there was sleight of hand; for this *Little Roman Martyrology* was in fact Ado's first version of his own work. Ado insisted that it was necessary to distinguish between October 3, the feast day of Denis the Areopagite, the bishop of Athens who was converted by Saint Paul and martyred under the rule of Hadrian (as recounted, he said, by Aristides), and October 9, dedicated to Denis, Rusticus, and Eleutherius, who were sent to Gaul by an unknown pope to preach the faith and then martyred in Paris after the intervention of Provost Sissinus (one of Hilduin's inventions).

Around 875, Usuard's *Martyrology* presented Ado's arguments in abridged form. All subsequent martyrologies retained traces of this same argument, hostile to the idea that the first bishop of Paris had been one and the same with the Areopagite.

Another skeptic on the matter was John Scotus Erigena, a contemporary of Ado, who was commissioned by Charles the Bald to translate the *De hierarchia*. "It is said that there were two Denis's," Erigena wrote in his preface, "the Areopagite, converted by Saint Paul, and the bishop of

Corinth, referred to in Eusebeus's work and in the homilies of Pope Gregory the Great. Certain authors claim the two are not the same. Some in our own time nevertheless hold that, according to a saint's life translated by men worthy of faith, Saint Clement sent Denis the Areopagite to Gaul, and that he was martyred in Paris."[14] Despite the respect John Scotus here paid to Hilduin, he clearly had reservations, reservations that he confirmed in the preface to his translation of Anastasius Bibliothecarius. There he noted that no pontifical text had made reference to Denis before the end of the fifth century. "Perhaps heretics hid these books [i.e. the works Hilduin claimed to draw from] and the codex was only later miraculously rediscovered."

The Carolingian era thus drew to a close without reaching agreement on Hilduin's history of the saint.

Outside of the Parisian sphere of influence people continued to have reservations until about 1120. Their hesitations were visible in oblique references made to Saint Denis in the *Lives* of Denis's saintly companions—except, of course, where those *Lives* made equivalent claims for the apostolicity of their heroes.

The *Life* of Saint Stremonius,[15] written in Clermont around 900, had this holy companion sent to Gaul by Saint Clement (c. 88–97), but martyred under the rule of Decius (249–251). (Later lives resolved this chronological impossibility by simply omitting the reference to Decius.) According to Letaldus of Micy's tenth-century *Life* of Saint Julianus,[16] that saint and Denis were both sent by Rome and martyred during the era of Decius and Pope Sixtus. They could not have been sent by Saint Clement, Letaldus argued, because Clement died during the reign of Trajan, and several emperors separated Trajan from Decius. (Trajan, in fact, reigned from 98 to 117.) Consequently, they were not apostles, even if they were the first to convert Le Mans and Paris.

In 1028, the Italian monk Benedict of Chiusa raised questions about another of Denis's companions, Saint Martialis of Limoges, whose apostolicity the chronicler Adhemar of Chabannes (988–1034) had recently defended.[17] Benedict argued that it was not until the third century that Martialis, like Denis, went to Gaul, pointing out that no ancient text referred to the apostolicity of either saint and maintaining that these men were simple evangelists, not apostles. For his troubles, the unfortunate Benedict was labeled an "ignorant, irascible Lombard" and, following a contentious meeting with Adhemar of Chabannes, he was banished from Toulouse.

At Chartres, a prestigious intellectual center at this time, and well apart from the Parisian royal sphere, Bishop Fulbert (1007–1029) dared to claim in his *Life* of Saint Piaton that Piaton, the first bishop of Tournai (who had also preached at Chartres), was decapitated and ascend d into heaven—like Saint Denis—during the reign of the Emperor Maximian (286–305): "Maximian was made co-emperor by Diocletian [in 285] and he was assigned to Gaul in order to solve the problem of the revolt of the Bagaudae there. He lived in Gaul and set in motion a generalized campaign of persecution of the Christians . . . and Saint Piaton was killed at Tournai and Saint Denis at Paris."[18]

Ivo of Chartres (1091–1116) continued to be skeptical of the apostolicity of the bishop of Paris and his identification with the Areopagite. Following in the tradition of Bede and Eusebeus of Caesarea, Ivo wrote that "Denis the Areopagite was the bishop of Athens who governed this church gloriously and wrote a number of remarkable books."[19] And when he dealt in his *Decretum* with the question of transfers of episcopal sees, he asserted that these were very rare in the first century, and the listing he made of them did not include the name of Denis. In fact, not a single papal decree prior to the tenth century alluded to Denis's having been sent from Athens to Paris.

ABELARD

Though Abelard (1079–1142), the master of dialectic, was the only one of his generation to voice doubts about Bishop Denis of Paris being the same as Denis the Areopagite, as he did in 1121, he had not discovered something new in doing so: his doubts were the culmination of a long tradition. But the alliance between the king and the abbey of Saint-Denis at the beginning of the twelfth century had done much to suppress objections. The chronicler Sigebert of Gembloux (1030–1112) had affirmed that Denis the bishop of Paris was indeed the Areopagite[20] and expressed astonishment that neither Saint Jerome nor Gennadius (d. 496) included him in their lists of ecclesiastical authors. (He knew that Gregory the Great in a homily dated about 590 was the first to cite the *De hierarchia.*) Hugh of Saint-Victor's *Commentary* on the *De hierarchia*,[21] written on royal commission for the young Louis VII (1137–1180), likewise showed no trace of skepticism about the patron saint of the dynasty. Abelard, in contrast, had deduced from his readings of Bede and Eusebeus of Caesarea that the Areopagite was the third-century bishop of Corinth. In so doing, he chose to favor Bede and Eusebeus over Hilduin.[22] Abelard's misfortune in this case was to voice his doubts at the abbey of Saint-Denis itself. The infuriated monks forced him to retract.

Abelard's retraction in a letter to Abbot Adam[23] was typical of methods used in the twelfth century to get at historical truth. He moved from a critical examination of dates to an explicit confrontation of authorities.[24] He contrasted the authority of Bede, who had made the Areopagite bishop of Corinth, with more accepted sources that said the Areopagite was bishop of Athens. Saint Jerome, for his part, in his book *On Famous Men,* had indeed spoken of a third-century Denis as bishop of Corinth, but Jerome merely said he wrote many epistles. Bede and Saint Jerome thus disagreed on whether this third-century bishop of Corinth was the Areopagite or not. Abelard pointed out that Eusebeus's *Ecclesiastical History* had also distinguished between two Denises: the first-century bishop of Athens and the third-century bishop of Corinth. The first of these witnessed the teachings of Saint Paul in Athens, as told in the *Book of Acts.* At least 160 years separated the two bishops, "according to the calculations of the chronicles of the emperors of Rome." Therefore, the two had to be different, he argued, and it was the chronology of *Acts* and the *Ecclesiastical History* that had to be heeded, rather than Bede's. "It is well known," he wrote, "that Eusebeus of Caesarea was Bede's principal source and also the source for all those who wrote later histories of the origins of the Church." Either Bede was wrong or he had introduced a new judgment in his reading of Eusebeus's *Ecclesiastical History.* Or then again, supposing he had been right, there must have been two bishops of Corinth named Denis, one in the first century and the other in the third, one later appointed bishop of Athens and sent to Gaul by Saint Clement, the other living in the way recounted by Saint Jerome. Thus, all the sources were reconciled in Abelard's argument.

This kind of reasoning was very cunning and not very different from the syllogisms Abelard was then working with in *Sic et non,* but it was also more than mildly sophistic. For he focused the debate on the Corinth-Athens dispute, whereas the real queston—was it the Areopagite who was buried at the abbey of Saint-Denis?—he carefully avoided.

Abelard's detour was characteristic of the new state of affairs created by the alliance between the monarchy and the abbey in the twelfth century. Before 1120, it was already difficult to deny that Denis was the Areopagite; afterward it became impossible. Hilduin himself had said that his adversaries "were trying to work against the glory of their country."[25] Archbishop Hincmar of Reims (806–882) had claimed they were bad Christians. "And if there are still some who deny that our patron Saint Denis is in fact the Areopagite," he wrote, "let them follow the proof of the Greek texts, the assertion of the Holy See, and the common knowledge of Gaul, and may this truth, all too often contested, shine forth."[26] Around 875, the *Miracles of Saint-Denis* had affirmed that "unbelievers who try to blot out the fame of Denis the Areopagite are as much his assassins as was Sissinus. They are acting out of jealousy, and he who hates his brother is guilty of murder."[27] But by 1120, the sins of which Abelard was accused appeared to be more secular: "He attacked the honor of the kingdom and the Crown." (As late as the seventeenth century, the two accusations could be brought together: "He who does not believe that Saint Denis is one and the same with the Areopagite, bishop of Athens, despite the fact that the Church and the king, Saint Louis, have stated this to be so, is a poor Frenchmen and he is an ingrate toward the one who gave him faith. He is neither agreeable in the eyes of God nor can he be saved.")[28] Doubters were thus subject to punishment by both the nation and the Church. Expression of skepticism, as a result, became more and more rare and did not really reappear until the Crusade of 1204—and then only in the background.

FROM THE THIRTEENTH CENTURY TO YVES DE SAINT-DENIS

The Greek world had always been skeptical of assertions that the Areopagite had become bishop of Paris. And the conquest of Constantinople opened the West to their skepticism in many ways.

There were scholarly problems, first of all. Around 1250, a Byzantine monk discovered marked similarities between the *De hierarchia* and a text of the neoplatonic philosopher Proclus (412–485), leading him to the conclusion that the *De hierarchia* was written sometime after Proclus's death in 485.[29] This idea, however, was not accepted in the Greek world for a long time, and it took even longer for the West to agree to it. The real problem for Saint-Denis was not texts but bones.

The monks of Saint-Denis claimed to possess the body of the saint absolutely whole, but new relics of Denis the Areopagite were discovered in the East. Thus, although criticisms of the historical tradition dried up in the thirteenth century, competing bits of skeleton flooded the West. Innocent III (1198–1216) gave voice to the new doubts in 1216,[30] as did the *Chronicle of Tournai* in 1227.[31] After the fourth Lateran Council, the pope sent the abbey the body of Bishop Denis of Corinth, which crusaders had brought to Rome. "The glorious martyr and bishop Denis," he wrote to the monks, "whose body is in your abbey, is he in fact the Areopagite converted by Saint Paul? There are differing opinions on this question. Some say that he died and was buried in Greece and that he and the Apostle of Gaul are not the same person. Others disagree, saying he was sent to Gaul by Saint Clement." It was for safety's sake that the pope sent the new relic to Saint-Denis. In this way, both bodies would be housed there. For its part, the *Chronicle*—a summary of world history—noted in its account of the third century that, "according to Gregory of Tours and the legend of Saint Sixtus, the persecutions of Decius were carried out in those days, and the *Life* of Saint Saturninus relates that the seven bishops who had been sent to Gaul were martyred. They included Gatianus, martyred in Tours, and Denis, killed in Paris."

Two more relics remained beyond the abbey's reach: the skull at Notre-Dame of Paris, which we will discuss in a moment, and the head at the Cistercian abbey of Longpont. The latter was brought back from Byzantium by Nivelon de Chierzy, bishop of Soissons and advisor to Baldwin of Flanders, the first Latin emperor of Constantinople (1204–1205). It had once belonged to the treasury of the Byzantine emperors and was attributed to the bishop of Athens. Obviously, this relic implied that even if the Areopagite had preached in Gaul, it was in Greece that he died. For Saint-Denis, Longpont was a serious competitor: a number of great families were buried there, and many kings came on pilgrimage at important moments in their lives—Saint Louis in 1226 at the time of his coronation, Charles of Valois, Philip the Fair, and Philip V (1316–1322) again immediately following his coronation.

Thus, when the *Life and Works* was composed at Saint-Denis between 1223 and 1233—the first work since Hilduin's to present the life of the saint, the history of the monastery, its relics, and the miracles that had taken place there—both the abbey and the monarchy were in difficulty: the abbey as a consequence of the Crusades, the monarchy because King Louis IX was only a child. The *Life and Works* was written to shore up both of them. To the debate on Denis's identity, however, it brought nothing new.[32] Later, the glory of Louis IX cloaked all these problems in a mantle of respect and silence. After his death, the abbey served as a cult site for Saint Louis as much as for Saint Denis, from whom all uncertainty was banished.

In 1317, following another dynastic crisis when Philip of Poitiers brutally blocked his niece's ascension to the throne, abbot Gilles de Pontoise (1305–1325) asked the monk Yves de Saint-Denis to write a book that would be more complete than the *Life and Works*, one that

would, among other things, tell the story of the continuing relationship
throughout history of the kings of the Franks to Saint Denis. This he did
in his third book.[33] Yves drew on Hilduin's earlier version of the martyrdom, then from the three books of miracles, and finally arrived at his
description of the works of the Areopagite. There he ran into serious
trouble. Not satisfied with the traditional summaries, he opened up the
Latin translation of the *De hierarchia* that he found in his abbey's
library.

As a skilled reader, Yves discovered that the *De hierarchia* quoted
texts not yet written in A.D. 96, the supposed date of Denis's death. But
it was ideologically impossible for him to admit the obvious—that the
De hierarchia was written after the latest texts it used. So taking as his
point of departure a single, very simple premise, he launched into an
extraordinarily complicated argument.[34] "Denis quotes the *Gospel of
John* in both the *De hierarchia* and in his epistles," he began. "But the
Gospel was written after A.D. 96." According to Jerome,[35] he continued, Saint John was first exiled to Patmos during the rule of Domitian.
There he wrote the *Apocalypse* in the fourth year after the persecutions
of Nero. It was during the rule of Nerva (96–98) that he went to
Ephesus, remaining there during the rule of Trajan (98–117). There he
preached and there too he wrote his gospel. He died in Ephesus sixty-
eight years after the crucifixion of Christ, in the year A.D. 101. Therefore, Yves concluded from Jerome's account, the *Gospel of John* was
written between the years A.D. 98 and 101. Yet Denis was supposed to
have died during the rule of Domitian (in A.D. 96 at the latest). At the
same time, according to Hilduin's *Life*, he was supposed to have been
twenty-five years old in A.D. 33. This would have made him about
ninety under Domitian, a very late age at which to undertake the composition of an enormous work.

Thus, chronology presented Yves with an impossible choice. There
was a conflict between tradition and the regnal dates of the Roman
emperors, and there were anachronisms within the tradition itself. If
Denis began his work at the age of ninety, his life would have been
unbelievably long. Yet, if Yves held that the work was written around
A.D. 50–60 in Greece, as all of his predecessors had, then how could he
explain the fact that it contained texts written between A.D. 98 and A.D.
101? How could he resolve this problem without violating either the
authority of Saint Jerome, a Father of the Church, or the affirmations of
Hilduin? He found a possible way out in the *History* of Eusebeus of
Caesarea, who wrote that Saint John preached the gospel all his life.

Perhaps, Yves reasoned, he wrote a first version of his gospel very early and held it back, reading it only to his friends. Denis might have become acquainted with this version in Greece before his departure for Gaul.

Yves's was the obverse of the reasoning of Anastasius Bibliothecarius and Ivo of Chartres when they realized that the work of Denis had never been cited in papal texts before the sixth century (an objection that Yves de Saint-Denis seems to have been unaware of). Instead of asking who knew the texts of the Areopagite, he asked what texts did the Areopagite know. Poor Yves de Saint-Denis! In order to reconcile the arguments of Saint Jerome and Hilduin, he was forced to set the composition of one of the Gospels at least forty years earlier than its conventional date.

Something very important came out of Yves's difficulties nevertheless: he had focused on a crucial problem of internal coherence within the tradition. The *De hierarchia* and the epistles of Denis contained unspecified references to works dating later than A.D. 96. Since most of the truly problematic references were drawn from Greek texts that were largely or entirely unknown in the Latin West at his time, Yves, in fact, had uncovered the only flaw that his material would allow him to find.

All the pieces of the puzzle had thus been assembled by 1317. Ado and his followers had demonstrated that Eusebeus and Gregory of Tours placed the Parisian Denis in the third century and distinguished him from the Areopagite, bishop of Athens. Anastasius and Ivo of Chartres had revealed that the *De hierarchia* was not cited before the sixth century, and Yves de Saint-Denis discovered it included texts dating from after A.D. 96. The arguments of Abelard, in contrast, served little more than to show that there was a great deal of obscurity and contradiction in the tradition.

None of these commentators, however, brought all the diverse critical elements together. This was not because they were incapable of doing so but because no one wanted to strike such a massive blow to the prestige of the monarchy. Belief in Saint Denis the Areopagite had become an official false truth, like those known to every state. As a result, later adaptations of Yves de Saint-Denis's work suppressed the skeptical passages. They continued to have Denis compose his *De hierarchia* in Gaul at the end of his life. The most they would say was that "some raise questions . . ."

It was not until the sixteenth century that the problem of the *De hierarchia* was honestly dealt with in France. And yet, already in the

first half of the fifteenth century, the Florentine humanist Lorenzo Valla
had demonstrated in the course of his *Commentary on the Acts of the
Apostles*[36] that Denis, the bishop of Paris, was not the Areopagite. "This
surname means 'judge' in Greek, not 'philosopher,' " he wrote. "Therefore it cannot be used to support the argument that someone bearing it
has written a philosophical work." He knew that Greek scholars had
shown the *De hierarchia* to be an anonymous fifth-century work. Valla
passed this thirteenth-century Greek demonstration on to the Latin
world. Knowing Greek, he was able to pick out first-century references
that derived from other Eastern texts. Erasmus, Luther, and Calvin all
took up his arguments, though neither Cardinal Bessarion (1403–1472)
nor many French writers before the seventeenth century were convinced
by it. Not until 1722 did a bishop of Paris officially renounce the claim
that Saint Denis was the Areopagite.

FOURTEENTH- AND FIFTEENTH-CENTURY DOUBTS

In the fourteenth and fifteenth centuries, although a few people continued to call their tradition into question, the abbey of Saint-Denis still
had a prestigious patron saint. The abbey attempted to lessen its vulnera-
bility by being as supportive of the monarchy as possible.

First it began to collect relics that were thought to be undeniably
authentic, relics other than those of Saint Denis. Since the eleventh
century, the abbey had had in its possession a number of relics from the
Crucifixion: the Holy Nail and the Crown of Thorns. The *Descriptio
qualiter*[37] told how Charlemagne had brought these back from the eastern Mediterranean to his palace in Aix. Charles the Bald later had them
transferred to Saint-Denis. But by the thirteenth century, they were in
competition with the relics that Saint Louis had brought back from
Byzantium—the relics for which he built the Sainte-Chapelle. Nonetheless, there were apparently no disputes over them. Saint Louis gave
some of the new relics to the abbey of Saint-Denis and the two sets were
considered two parts of a whole. The relics of the Crucifixion had been
"discovered" at the abbey soon after the abbey of Saint-Emmeran at
Regensburg claimed in 1059 to possess the body of Saint Denis.[38] They
helped to divert competition that was coming from the Empire and to
guarantee the Dionysian aura surrounding the Capetians. Then, toward
the end of the eleventh century, the abbey added the body of Saint
Peregrinus and the relics of its own miraculous consecration: the window through which Christ himself had come and the face of the leper he

cured that night.[39] The abbey treasury of the relics grew further with contributions by Philip Augustus, which included a piece of the True Cross that he donated sometime after 1204. In the thirteenth century, the bodies of Saint Denis of Corinth and of Saint Eustachius were added. Those of Saint Hippolytus and Saint Eugenius had come earlier, in the twelfth century.

The abbey made little use of the bodies of Denis, Rusticus, and Eleutherius, other than during the ceremonial taking up of the oriflamme. Most healings came through the Holy Nail or the Crown of Thorns, while the body of Saint Hippolytus was used to predict flooding on the Seine and other natural disasters. By now, the abbey of Saint-Denis had vastly enlarged its repertory.

During the next period, however, it spent a good deal of time fending off competitors. With the ruin of the abbey of Longpont around 1350, its principal source of competition became the object that the clergy of Notre-Dame of Paris claimed to be the top of Saint Denis's skull. Notre-Dame had had possession of this relic since at least 1186,[40] though later it was claimed that it had actually been found in 1217 at Saint-Etienne-des-Grecs (one of the three Parisian churches that Saint Denis had supposedly founded) and that it had been given to the cathedral by Philip Augustus. Three times the abbey displayed its relic of Saint Denis before the king, the bishops, and the court—in 1191, 1368, and 1406—in order to prove that it was whole. But this was in vain. The canons and the bishop of Paris refused to give up their claims. From 1398 on, they were supported by John, duke of Berry, to whom they had given a part of the relic. Conciliation by Chancellor Gerson (1363–1429) and Abbot Philippe de Villette brought momentary respite. In 1410, the Parlement of Paris tried the dispute. The monks defended themselves by challenging the recent date of the canons' claims and insisting on the wholeness of all of their relics (apart from the bone fragments they had given long before to Pope Stephen II and to the church of Vergy). They pointed out that every version of the story of Saint Denis said that the saint had been decapitated; none claimed that the top of his skull had been removed.[41] The abbey enjoyed the support of Charles VI and his brother, Louis, duke of Orléans.[42] Even as late as 1408, it tried to acquire the saint's belt and sandals from an imposter who claimed to be a Byzantine bishop. These clashes, replete with comic interludes (rival processions, reciprocal prohibitions on preaching) demonstrated that the memory of Saint Denis was slowly dissassociating itself from the abbey and becoming firmly embedded in the Parisian landscape. And this was happening despite the abbey's efforts to regain control over everything in any way associated with Saint Denis.

At the same time, memory of the saint was becoming entwined with the history of the nation. Although Denis's apostolicity did not interest the fourteenth century very much, his involvement in the origins of the nation remained ideologically necessary. Under the circumstances, what was more logical than to make him a contemporary of Clovis (c. 481–511), the first Christian king? Saint Remigius, the evangelist, had already been assigned to Clovis. But who converted Clotilda, Clovis's wife? Why not Denis? This idea was already implicit in the versified *Floovant* of the twelfth century,[43] which placed Denis in the days

> Du premier roi de France qui chrétien vint
> Cil eut nom Clovis et fut roi sarrasin,
> Et ne trouvait nul homme qui à Dieu crut
> Qu'il ne voulut l'occire . . .[44]

> [Of the first king of France who became a Christian
> He had for name Clovis and was a Saracen king
> Who had never met a man believing in God
> That he didn't want to kill . . .]

Around 1250, Philippe Mouskès of Tournai became acquainted with a more explicit version of the *Floovant* in which Denis converted Clotilda and was decapitated during the rule of Clovis.[45]

All references to these events then disappeared until the time of Charles V, around 1356, when the poem "Florent et Octavien" recounted how Saint Denis had converted Clotilda before he was martyred. Denis's head was placed in Notre-Dame; the church of La Châtre memorialized the place he was held prisoner.[46] Indirect evidence of the same belief can be found in texts where Saint Denis is depicted carrying lilies to Clovis: most often these scenes portray not a vision but rather a literal encounter that purportedly took place between two contemporaries. At the end of the fifteenth century, a life of Saint Denis written in alexandrines still placed him at the beginning of the French monarchy[47] and the *Octosyllabic Life* still housed Denis's head at Notre-Dame.[48]

Thus the tradition carried along a great many uncertainties about the bishop's life, works, and burial place. Neither the truth nor the falsity of Hilduin's claims had been proven, despite doubts that were raised on several occasions. The strategy of focusing on other relics, the attempt to found a different tradition, one centered in Paris and inscribed not in the story of Christianity but in that of the monarchy, succeeded more or less in covering up the problem. It was not through any intrinsic power of his own that Saint Denis managed to survive difficult times. It was rather that the abbey of Saint-Denis played many roles that were indispensable to the monarchy. As long as the abbey continued to fill these roles, no questions about its patron saint could be openly debated.

SAINT DENIS AND THE LIFE AND DEATH OF THE KING

PATRONUS REGIS: THE PATRON SAINT OF THE KING

Bodily Health   Saint Denis was the principal patron saint of most of the Merovingian dynasty from the time of Dagobert on, as he was for the Carolingians from Charlemagne to Charles the Bald and for the Capetians beginning with Hugh Capet. For a long time, Denis retained characteristics that were related to his function of protector of the royal person. First of all, he watched over the physical well-being of the king—"Our Integrity" as King Louis VI called it.

All the kings from Louis VI (in 1111, 1135, and 1137) through Louis XI (in 1482) beseeched Saint Denis to guarantee their health and the health of their family. They had prayers said at the abbey of Saint-Denis on their behalf. In 1135, for example, when Louis VI was gravely ill at Châteauneuf, he called for Saint Denis's help;[49] when he was well again, he went to the abbey to give thanks and many gifts. In July 1191, while Philip Augustus was away, his successor, the future Louis VIII, became ill.[50] He was cured when the monks of Saint-Denis processed to Paris and placed the relics of the martyrdom on the ailing part of Louis's body. At the same time, Philip Augustus was cured of dysentery far off in the Holy Land. In 1244, Saint Louis fell so ill that he vowed to go on a crusade. The reliquaries of Denis, Rusticus, and Eleutherius were placed on the abbey's main altar for him, as the oriflamme would have been during times of great public danger.

According to Guillaume de Nangis,[51] although the health of a king might constitute a public danger, that of a successor did not and would not justify recourse to this solemn ritual. When did this distinction come about?

The reliquaries were most certainly brought out in 1191, since Philip Augustus had taken the oriflamme before leaving on crusade. Suger's commentary is too vague to determine whether the bodies of the saints were actually raised up onto the altar when the king was ill in 1135: "He asked . . . to be brought before the holy bodies. He reverently lay down before them and humbly thanked them." If by this we are meant to understand that the reliquaries were placed on the altar on this occasion, then the two rituals—the ceremonial taking out of the oriflamme while the bodies of the saints rested on the altar (such as we know took place from 1124 on) and the raising of the relics to heal the king—were invented at the same time. If this is so, from the twelfth century on, royal illness would have been considered as great a threat as invasion. In 1335, the duke of Normandy, the future King John II (1350–1364), fell gravely ill.[52] The same rites as those used in 1191, this time with the added relics of Saint Louis, succeeded in curing the prince. But at the end of the fourteenth century, the efficacity of the relics of Saint Denis were unfortunately insufficient to restore Charles VI's sanity, despite the fact that he often visited the abbey. Sources from this period no longer allow a distinction to be drawn between the rites used for a king and those applied to a dauphin. Possibly, the solemn ceremony of taking up the reliquaries was renounced in times of chronic, nonfatal illness like insanity. Another hypothesis is that the deaths of kings and dauphins were no longer considered grave public dangers when the continuity of the dynasty was fully assured. Ceremonies were then limited to prayers and processions.

In 1392, when Charles VI was momentarily cured, he offered a reliquary in memory of Saint Louis. In 1394, he fell sick again; a special mass said for him at Saint-Denis seemed to have no effect. In 1396, he gave another reliquary in thanks for the temporary remission of his illness—it was meant to encase the Holy Nail. The same thing occurred in 1400. In January of 1401, despite three processions between Paris and Saint-Denis, the king's son, the Dauphin Charles, died.[53] But Charles VI continued to pray to the saint for his own health in 1402 and 1403, though the monastic chronicler of Saint-Denis made no note of any special ceremonies held in his behalf.

Louis XI was the last medieval king to ask that prayers for his health be said at Saint-Denis, in 1480 and 1482.

Visions of the Afterlife   Parallel to the world of physical health lay that of moral health. Keeping the king from vice, making him a good Christian, and staying by his side at the moment of death were tasks that normally fell to an evangelist. This idea helped guarantee the monks of Saint-Denis nearly exclusive rights as royal confessors. In this respect, Denis's role toward the king was no different from the role he might play toward any of the faithful; there was nothing exceptional about it. From Louis VI—who "wanted the eternal crown of glory to insure the salvation of his soul," to John II—"who wanted to receive heavenly recompense just as those we come after and piously imitate," to Louis XI,[54] kings wanted to secure the saint's help above all at that final accounting when all their earthly deeds would be judged. In the hour of his death, Saint Louis called on Saint Denis; so did Philip IV.

This quite commonplace role was illustrated in a spectacular way in a series of visions invented between the Carolingian era and the twelfth century, visions designed to prove the saint's effectiveness when souls were weighed in the balance.

The first three visions concerned Dagobert, Charles Martel, and Charlemagne. They all followed the same narrative scheme: through lust or greed, the king fails to be wholly virtuous and at the moment of death risks being condemned to hell, but through the aid of Saint Denis he is sent to heaven instead. These three visions from the Carolingian era show a ready belief that a king who had not led a Christian life should suffer in hell. They passed no judgments on the political actions of the rulers but focused instead on their moral values. The only good king was a good Christian king.

The vision concerning Dagobert appeared in the *Deeds of Dagobert* written by a member of Hilduin's circle in celebration of the founding of the abbey. In it, Dagobert's soul is seized by devils as he makes his way toward hell. The hermit John of Lipari learns of this through a dream and notifies Bishop Ansoaldus, who is then on a mission to Italy.[55] Saint Denis, called by the king for help, intercedes on the king's behalf and he is saved. In later versions, the help of Saint Maurice was sometimes invoked. The texts do not say why Dagobert, who had been so generous toward churches, was threatened with hell.

Beyond the walls of the abbey of Saint-Denis, the Dagobert vision was particularly favored by Aimoin of Fleury (965–1008), Sigebert of Gembloux, and Jacobus de Voragine (1228–1298) and, from the thirteenth century on, a picture of the vision also stood for all to see within the abbey itself, in the niche above Dagobert's tomb.

The vision concerning Charles Martel was the exact opposite of the Dagobert vision. It described the damnation of the king rather than his entry into heaven and, although the damned king lay buried at the abbey of Saint-Denis, its saint played no role. In order to protect the property of the Church from royal ambitions, Archbishop Hincmar of Reims sketched out its basic lines in a letter to Louis the German and in his prologue to the *Life of Remigius* written at the time of the Synod of Quierzy (858).[56]

In this vision, Eucherius, the bishop of Orléans, sees Charles Martel in hell. The king has been sufficiently brazen to give away the goods of the Church. Eucherius talks about what he has seen to Saint Boniface (680–755), converter of the Holy Roman Empire, and to Fulrad, abbot of Saint-Denis (752–757). They arrange to have Charles's tomb opened, whereupon a dragon comes flying out of the sepulcher and traces of fire appear on the tombstone. These signs reveal that the king has been "lost forever."

The faults this vision condemns were political. They were not easily categorized as sinful, and the vision, critical as it was of his government, met with no more than local success. It appeared only at Orléans and Reims. Some textual interpolations of the life of Saint Eucherius[57] modified it only to the extent of making demons rather than a dragon spring from the coffin. Around 870, at Fleury-sur-Loire, the monk Adrevaldus proved to be less severe: though Charles still appeared as a condemned man, one of his sons, Carloman, was shown choosing to become a monk, and the other, Pepin, demonstrating great generosity toward the Church, both of them going to heaven.[58] In Reims, Eucherius's vision was inserted into the life of Saint Rigobertus, "so that the just condemnation of this person might be known to all readers."[59] Later, it was also integrated into the work of Flodoard, the historian of Reims (894–966), who wrote, "This bastard son of a servant woman showed himself to be audacious only in his desire to hurt the churches of Christ."[60]

Only in much later texts did this judgment on Martel's life begin to change. During the thirteenth and fourteenth centuries, though his soul was still damned in the *Deeds of the Frankish People* of the anonymous author of Béthune in 1217, and in the work of Philippe Mouskès in 1250,[61] the works about Saint Denis—the *Life and Works,* the Latin chronicle of Saint Denis, and the *Great Chronicles*—all painted a subtle, nuanced picture of Charles Martel and made no mention of the vision. Then Yves de Saint-Denis brought it back in 1317. Yves took up the "vision of Eucherius" as he had found it,[62] but he interpreted Charles's tortured stay in hell as transitory, claiming that he was saved by the restitutions that his son Pepin made to the churches. And around 1360, the author of the third continuation to the *Deeds of the Bishops of St.-Trond*[63] (Saint-Trond was the abbey where Saint Eucherius was buried) held that Charles's misdeeds were compensated for by the generosity of Pepin and by Carloman's monastic vows at Monte Cassino. Of course, Yves de Saint-Denis was the only one to claim that Saint Denis himself had intervened on behalf of the Carolingian and shortened his stay in purgatory. It thus took an especially long time for the concepts of purgatory and intergenerational compensation to be applied to Charles Martel. But with the canonization of Louis IX in 1297, the condemnation of a dynastic ancestor to hell had become unacceptable.

In the third cycle of visions, Charlemagne's soul suffered the same trials and tribulations as had Dagobert's.

The earliest version was soon forgotten. The *Vision of Wettin* of Walahfrid Strabo (c. 826)[64] depicts Charlemagne hounded in hell by a horrible beast in punishment for his libertinage, though, in the end, he is destined to enjoy everlasting glory attained without the help of any mediator.

It was only in the later part of the twelfth century that the emperor's posthumous fate was shaped definitively in a vision added to the Pseudo-Turpin:[65] Archbishop Turpin of Reims kneels to pray and sees troops of demons heading toward Aix-la-Chapelle. They are on their way to attend the emperor on his deathbed, hoping to gain possession of his soul. When they later return, they are dejected, for Charlemagne's soul has gotten away: at the crucial moment, a headless Galician (Saint James) placed on the balance all the churches that Charlemagne had built, and he was saved.

In the translations of this passage made at the abbey of Saint-Denis, a "decapitated Frenchman" (Saint Denis) interceded along with Saint James. The *Life and Works,* Yves de Saint-Denis, and the *Great Chronicles* all adopted this story,[66] which closely resembled the Dagobert vision: the same sins are present, the same act of intercession, and the same happy ending. But Charlemagne is not carried all the way to hell as Dagobert had been. His is a sweetened fate. Though people might say in the twelfth century that a king deserved to go to hell, in visionary practice, he was spared.

The problem of the king's posthumous destiny appeared again in 1223 on the death of Philip II, for the immense glory he took with him to the grave bore the blot of bigamy and excommunication. It is reasonable to think that the "Visions of Philip" that sprang up so rapidly after his death were a defensive tactic staged by the abbey and the royal family.[67] The *Philippide* of Guillaume Le Breton (1169–1224) was created within the circle of Louis VIII; Etienne de Bourbon (d. 1262) drew his story from Sibylle de Hainaut, sister-in-law of the king; Richer de Senones (d. 1264) heard his from monks of an abbey near Senones, dependent on the abbey of Saint-Denis, and later heard it again at Saint-Denis itself. The vision appeared in the *Life and Works,* written between 1223 and 1233, and in Philippe Mouskès's *Chronique rimée* (1282).[68] Thus, at least five different accounts appeared immediately after Philip's death. In contrast, the visions of Dagobert, Charles Martel, and Charlemagne were all written from one to three centuries after the deaths of the kings concerned.

The kind of text chosen for the Philip vision was already well known. It had been used frequently in propaganda for kings and for Saint Denis. Like Dagobert's, the story is set in Italy—in Perugia, or Segni, or Rome. The man who receives the vision, however, is neither a saint, a bishop, nor a well-known figure; he is a knight. His name differs from one version to another and he is unfamiliar with both France and the king. In some versions, he enjoys powerful affiliations: he is a Frangipani, for example, or a relative of a king or of the pope. At other times, he has no such relations. He is sick and dying, and, were he to be cured, it would be symbolic of the truthfulness of his mission. Though this particular aspect had not been seen before in accounts of visions, it was a recurrent motif in accounts of miracles.

The characters in the knight's vision vary from account to account. Saint Denis is always present, appearing as an old man with a miter and a shepherd's staff. In Richer de Senones's version, he is accompanied by Rusticus and Eleutherius, and in the *Philippide,* by angels. King Philip figures either at Denis's side, dressed as he was when still alive, or on horseback (*Life and Works*) or holding a lance (*Chronicle of Tournai*). In the *Philippide,* he has already been transformed and wears luminous white clothes. Philippe Mouskès imagined his soul in the form of a crowned child being carried in the arms of Saint Denis. Going where? According to the Dominican Etienne de Bourbon, he is traveling to purgatory and from there on to paradise. The few venial sins still clinging to his soul will disappear. *Life and Works* sends him directly to the Valley of Jehoshaphat.[69] Both Philippe Mouskès and the *Philippide* explain this by saying that God wished to enjoy the company of his soul as soon as possible.

So the chroniclers were all optimistic about Philip's fate. Of course, the pope's sanction was also needed. But because Philip had been excommunicated, this was problematic. In the thirteenth century, it was the Church that decided who was to be canonized and who was to be damned. Popular will no longer carried the weight it once had. Thus, at the end of every vision, it was the pope who appeared to carry out the funeral rites for the king and chant the "Absolve eum, Domine," though the stories stopped short of having him actually absolve Philip. They simply noted he was saved, for "the keys to heaven belong to God and to the pope, and those who die in the grace of God will indeed be saved, but they must also be surrounded by the prayers of the Church."

In its many forms, the visions of Philip spread far.[70] With an anonymous King Philip it even appeared in many collections of moralized tales that were put together for the use of preachers.[71]

Thus, the power of Saint Denis always proved effective at the moment of final judgment. During the period when the afterlife was divided between two regions, the soul of the king of France was always saved from hell. After purgatory was invented, he was spared that place as well. This was true even for kings who had been excommunicated and were therefore in principal destined to suffer eternal damnation. The newfound security, which, according to the monks, the kings owed to Saint Denis, would assure the blessing of their entire dynastic line and its eternal right to the throne.

The Vision of Charles the Fat and Charles the Bald   The vision of Charles the Fat, written around 901,[72] gave yet another version of God blessing the dynastic line. Charles the Fat was the grandson of Louis the Pious and the great-grandson of Charlemagne. He was first the king of Germany and then, from 885 to 888, emperor, and the vision concerned the rights of succession to the Empire. It took the form of a visit to the next world. A man dressed in white comes to the sleeping emperor and offers him a shining thread to guide him through the world of the afterlife. The emperor first visits hell, where he sees tormented prelates and royal rulers, including his own father, Louis the German (843–876). Then he goes to heaven where he finds his uncle Lothaire and Lothaire's son, Louis, both of whom have been saved by Saint Peter and Saint Remigius and who ask Charles to pass the throne on to Louis the Child, Lothaire's grandson through the female line, since the king has no direct heirs of his own. At the end of the story Charles dies, shortly after his fantastic journey ends, but, since he has been blessedly informed about how to avoid hell, his soul is saved.

In contrast to the other visions this one joined together two distinct issues: it linked a ruler's merit to the questions of whether or not he had a lineal successor to the throne. A king who was damned might cause his son to lose his right to rule or have no direct descendant and see his power pass to a cousin through the female line. This vision had stronger political implications than any of the others. Since it concerned the Empire and not the Frankish kingdom, it did not mention Saint Denis.

Remigius, "patron of the Empire and of the *gens Francorum*," was its central saintly figure.

This vision reappeared at the beginning of the twelfth century in the works of Hariulf of Saint-Ric 1ier (1060–1143) and William of Malmesbury (1095–1139), each of whom found their source in a Carolingian manuscript from the abbey of Saint-Wandrille.[73] Both Hariulf and William retained Charles the Fat as the voyager and Saint Remigius and Saint Peter as the intercessors. And in the second half of that century, the universal chronicle of Helinand of Froidmont (d. 1215) and the chronography of Guy de Bazoches (d. 1203) remained faithful to the Flemish tradition of Hariulf.[74]

In the reign of Philip Augustus, however, there were sporadic attempts to change the identity of the ruler to whom the vision appeared in order to make it pertinent to the French kingdom. As early as 1150, a Parisian manuscript collection of the lives of the Carolingian saints and texts from Saint-Denis[75] attributed the vision of Charles the Fat to Charlemagne at the moment of his coronation, without correcting the dynastic incoherence that resulted. The point of the story—that God alone has the power to give and take away the *imperium*—was kept, though it hardly applied to Charlemagne, who reigned for many years and was succeeded by generations of direct descendants. Yet, for the first time, the vision had been recast to apply to the kingdom of France. From the reign of Philip Augustus onward, French kings thought of themselves as Carolingians.[76] As a result, the meaning of the vision was transformed. Charles the Bald now replaced Charles the Fat.

The monk Helinand had read somewhere that the soul of Charles the Bald, who died and was buried at Nantua, appeared before a monk at Saint-Denis named Erencharius and also to a cleric at Saint-Quentin, and that he asked that his body be brought to Saint-Denis, the abbey to which he had given many gifts during his lifetime.[77] Though this version tells us that Charles the Bald's soul was saved, it says nothing about the successors to his throne.

One of the two manuscripts of the *Deeds of the Franks Up to 1180*, the last historical work written at Saint-Denis before that of Abbot Suger, gave an account of the vision of Charles the Bald that was homologous to the vision of Charles the Fat.[78] It recounted Charles the Bald's appearance to Erencharius, to whom the king revealed that his soul had been saved through the intercession of Saint Denis and therefore asked to be buried at the abbey.

In this version, the Carolingian line is not threatened: Louis the

Stammerer (877–879) follows his father to the throne. By transforming Charles the Fat into Charles the Bald—a king whose son became *rex Francorum*—it gave flesh to the belief that the Carolingians always had been and always would be the kings of France. This version reappeared in the *Life and Deeds,* in the *Great Chronicles of France,* and in the *Latin Chronicle* of Saint-Denis.[79] In 1317, Yves de Saint-Denis faithfully copied it from the *Deeds of the Franks.* Charles gives the throne to his son Louis the Stammerer—who is "not to be confused with Louis the Child, King of Provence and Italy, for the kings of France pass the throne from father to son within the Carolingian line of descent."[80] Pope Stephen II promised it would be so forever.

During the reign of Charles V, the Carmelite friar Jean Golein wrote in his *Treatise on the Coronation* (1364)[81] that the vision of Charles the Bald proved that "the monarchy [was] given over to Charlemagne's descendants, following the male line of descent, for all time." It had come to affirm the Salic Law, where its first version—as the vision of Charles the Fat—had actually justified succession to the throne through women.

The vision reappeared yet again in the fifteenth century in a collection by Goezwin Kemp, with every intercessor connected to the Saint Denis legend: Saint Denis himself, Saint Hippolytus, and Saint Patroclus. So too in the version of Guillaume Lemaire in 1482, where Charles is saved by the intercession of Saint Denis—by the prayers of him who was made "apostle of the king and the Franks by God, without whose warnings the *genealogia* of the kings would long since have ceased to wield power and rule over the kingdom."[82] Finally, in the book given to Charles VIII in 1495 by the monks of Saint Denis,[83] the vision of Charles the Bald and the vision of Erencharius were united once again, and it was the prayers of both Saint Remigius and Saint Denis that saved the king, whose descendants had ruled ever since.

Thus, the *Vision of Charles the Bald* assured not only the salvation of the king but also the dynastic continuity of a single royal line—the Carolingian house. As it guaranteed the survival of the ruling family it also assured the prosperity and stability of the kingdom. Its promise was similar to the one Saint Remigius had made to Clovis: as long as he and the kingdom remained good Christians, their successors would rule forever. The vision of Charles the Bald was a special example of this promise, for it covered over the crisis of 987, the most marked rupture in royal succession in French history. From the beginning of the thirteenth century on, it was no more admissible that the kings of France—

having become Carolingians once again—could lose their power than it was for them to be condemned to hell.

Royal Death Rites   The fourteenth and fifteenth centuries produced no new visions of royal souls in danger of damnation. In order to emphasize the new certainties about the king's salvation and the continuity of power, royal deaths were increasingly ritualized. Greater numbers of witnesses were at hand. Accounts of the king's death were spread abroad.

Prior to Suger's account of the death of Louis VI, there are almost no detailed descriptions of royal deaths, apart from references to the pious death of Robert I (996–1031), which was a monk's death more than a king's.[84] The ritual transfer of the royal crown at the moment of the king's death was not instituted until the death of Philip Augustus in 1223. Before then, the successor had always been crowned during his father's lifetime. Thus, we are largely limited to texts that date from after 1270. Even then, the funerary ritual did not always occur. It did not take place, for example, if the king died a violent death. He had to die in or near Paris, and his successor had to be present for the ceremonial practices to be observed.

The deaths of Saint Louis in 1270, of Philip the Fair in 1314, Charles V in 1380, and Louis XI in 1483 are all excellent examples of the royal death ritual,[85] which from one occurrence to the next fluctuated between the very Christian and the very royal. When the king's impending death was organized in a Christian fashion, he made his confession, asked for forgiveness from all, received communion and extreme unction, kissed the cross or the relics, and gave responses to litanies until the very last moment; he died either with his arms crossed on his chest (as did Philip IV) or else lying on a bed of ashes (as did both Louis VI and Saint Louis). These gestures were aimed at conveying the image of a king who was an exemplary Christian to a broad public of counselors, prelates, monks, and local people.

To this was added a series of rites to transfer the power of the king.

The king instructed his son on how to govern. Saint Louis's *Instructions to His Son* is a famous text. Philip IV counseled his son at the last moment as well, telling him of his secret cure for scrofula. Philip VI (1328–1350) gave his son the principal arguments against the rights of the English kings to the French throne. Charles V spoke to his son about the Schism; Louis XI spoke to his about the structure of the regency and recommended that he be generous with the abbey of Saint-Denis.

Then too, there were transfers of the visible signs of power. Louis VI gave his eldest son his ring. Philip IV and Charles V meditated on the difference between the two crowns—the Crown of Thorns (Saint-Denis's or the Sainte-Chapelle's) and the royal crown. The Crown of Thorns was present at the deaths of Saint Louis, Philip V, and Charles V. Philip IV referred to the royal crown when he said to his son: "Louis, you will go to Reims and wear this crown." Drawing from the first-century Roman historian Valerius Maximus, Charles V spoke of the two crowns as "the crown of vain glory and the crown of eternal glory." Though it was the Holy Ampulla and the Cross of Charlemagne from the Sainte-Chapelle that Louis XI had near his side when he died, rather than the crowns, the symbolism was the same. The two objects represented the transition soon to be accomplished: the father would exchange the earthly for the heavenly crown; the son, blessed by his father in the manner of Abraham, would assume the coronation crown.

The hour of death was also the time when Kings Philip IV (1314), Philip V (1322), and Charles V (1380) chose to abolish unpopular taxes.

The king's death had indeed become a ritual. The *Anonymous Account of the Death of Charles V* stated that there were "sacrosanct rules for the death of most-Christian kings." Even if all prerequisite conditions could not be met, the ritual was to be observed. So it was, for instance, in 1380, when the young dauphin was absent. The ritual benediction and review of the previous government—which was to serve as a basis for the development of the dauphin's own policies— took place nonetheless, according to custom, and those attending were asked to communicate the results to the dauphin. The desire to imitate the death of Saint Louis probably often played an important role. It is hardly surprising that Philip IV and the first Valois rulers—whose rights to the throne were contested—agreed to submit to this ceremony, for, as constraining as it was, the ritual was necessary. It foreshadowed great royal death scenes to come, like the death of Louis XIV in 1715.

One of the most moving and least known of these ceremonies was the death of Philip IV, as told by Yves de Saint-Denis.[86] The king died at a difficult moment: his counselor Enguerran de Marigny had been discredited, his nobles were in revolt, and oppressive taxes were provoking the people beyond measure. The succession to the throne was not assured, for the marriages of the king's three sons had been beclouded with uncertainty when their wives were condemned for adultery. The Grand Master of the Knights Templar, before being burned at the stake, had

called for Philip to be judged in heaven. Yves, in response, composed
three full pages on Philip's most perfect and politically useful death. He
told how the king instructed his son, Louis X (1314–1316), blessed
him, and delivered a complete philosophy of government that justified
the politics of Marigny. Then he died with his arms crossed upon his
chest, meditating on the vanity of the crowns of this world. "This is how
his life ended and this is how his glory began," wrote Yves, despite the
fact that Philip IV, during his lifetime, had been threatened with excommunication, just as Philip Augustus was, though for very different reasons. It was the holiness of Philip IV's death that guaranteed him salvation and assured the transfer of power to his son.

A century earlier, these things would have been secured through a
vision instead. Now it could no longer be said, as Robert the Pious did
in 1008, that "all kings who have honored Saint Denis have ruled
happily and gone to heaven; the others have lost both life and crown."[87]
From this time on, every French king went to heaven and passed on his
crown, whether Saint Denis intervened for him or not. The virtues of
royal blood had come to be held in greater esteem than the virtues of the
patron saint.

PATRONUS REGNI: THE PATRON SAINT OF THE KINGDOM

The Carolingians had made Saint Denis the patron saint not just of their
kings, but of their empire and their people as well. In the words of a
much later royal document, those who had been protectors of a given
territory during their lifetime retained "the right to conduct and petition
for the needs of that country" in heaven.[88] Those who were converted,
and all their descendants, were united in the same faith with him who
had brought the Gospel to them. They served as its defenders and
intercessors before God. Although in the tenth and eleventh centuries
this patronage had gone into eclipse, it had not been forgotten. In the
eleventh and twelfth century, the abbey of Saint-Denis forged a number
of documents to demonstrate that Denis was the most prized patron
saint of the Gauls from the time of Dagobert to Charlemagne. Then
came Abbot Suger who applied the patronage of Saint Denis exclusively
to the Capetian monarchy.[89]

Because Denis was guarantor of the faith in the territories he had
converted, it was important to define what area that was. What lands
had Pope Clement assigned to Denis? Was it Gaul? The Western world

in general? France? And what specific region had he converted? Though the kingdom could be defined as Paris and its environs in the time of Louis VI, this was no longer true by the end of the Middle Ages. Consequently, two adjustments to the story had to be made: either a number of companion evangelizers had to be enlisted to help Denis serve France in its entirety, or the principle had to be asserted that whatever applied to Paris, the heart and soul of the kingdom, applied to France as a whole.

The Creation of Yves de Saint-Denis   Adjustments of the first sort can be found in the work of Yves de Saint-Denis, who in 1317 first projected a comprehensive vision of the conversion of all French territory to Christianity.[90] To do this, however, he first had to resolve a certain number of problems.

Yves had great difficulties identifying the companions of Saint Denis for two reasons. First, his sources disagreed on the number of bishops who went out from Rome. Gregory of Tours, drawing from the *Life* of Saint Saturninus, listed seven bishops.[91] But two later lists in circulation when Yves was writing named twelve; still others told of seventy-two disciples sent to Gaul.[92] The texts of the abbey of Saint-Denis, however, mentioned only two companions to Denis—Rusticus and Eleutherius. The second problem was that Yves's sources disagreed on which pope had had the honor of sending the mission. Sometimes Saint Peter was named, sometimes Saint Clement, and at other times it was Saint Sixtus. There was no information at all about the organization of the mission. Did individuals work independently? Was there a preestablished hierarchy? Yves's overall conception of how the region was converted to Christianity depended on how he answered these technical questions.

Let us look more closely at the source material available to him.

The first three lives of Saint Denis—the fifth-century *Gloriosae,* Hilduin's ninth-century *Life,* and the tenth-century *Life*[93]—did not list the same companions as did Gregory of Tours. They mentioned neither Trophimus in Arles, Gatianus in Tours, Stremonius in Auvergne, nor Martialis in Limoges, though the *Gloriosae* did refer to Saturninus, Sanctinus of Meaux, and Paul of Narbonne, most likely drawing its information from the *Life* of Saint Saturninus.

Hilduin's *Life* retained Rusticus and Eleutherius from the *Gloriosae,* and Clement as the pope who sent them. But where the *Gloriosae* had made Gaul their destination, Hilduin made it the Carolingian Empire. For Hilduin, Denis was the apostle of the entire Western world, who had established himself in Paris because that was the crossroads of the Germanic and Gallic peoples.

The tenth-century *Life* drew from both Hilduin and the *Gloriosae*. Here the apostle of the Western world was accompanied by Rusticus, Eleutherius, Saint Marcellus (the apostle of Spain), Saint Saturninus (bishop of Toulouse), and Saint Lucianus (bishop of Beauvais). This last companion was borrowed from the third *Life* of Saint Lucianus, written by Odo of Beauvais sometime after 860,[94] in which Lucianus was portrayed as a double of Hilduin's Denis, after his martyrdom carrying his head to his place of burial.

Thirteenth-century versions of Denis's life were all derived from the *Life and Works* of 1233, which in succeeding centuries was often revised, abbreviated, translated, and even brought out in illustrated editions.[95] The great innovation of this work was to dismiss the idea that Denis had evangelized the entire Western world; apart from passing references to Eugenius and Marcellus, apostles to Spain, it portrayed a mission entirely circumscribed by the boundaries of the Capetian kingdom.[96] Denis's companions were the same as those in the Carolingian lives: Lucianus (of Beauvais), Sanctinus and Antoninus (of Meaux). It told the story, taken from Hincmar of Reims, of their miraculous voyage to Rome to give the pope news of Denis's death. The only other companion named in *Life and Works* was Saint Regulus, bishop of Arles and Senlis, who, it related, while celebrating mass in Senlis learned of the deaths of Denis, Rusticus, and Eleutherius through a vision of three doves. To comfort the faithful at their loss, Regulus went to Paris and Beauvais before establishing himself in Senlis.[97] Not content merely to cite names, the *Life and Works* told the stories of these companions, inserting summaries of their *Lives* into the story of Saint Denis. Thus, on close examination, the image of the conversion of the kingdom in the *Life and Works* proves to be specifically Parisian. Paris, Beauvais, Senlis, and Meaux all enjoy glorious stories of the founding of their episcopal sees. In contrast, Saturninus—the apostle of Aquitaine— appears only as a name, his story ignored. France, as yet, has made only a timid foray south of the Loire.

Following the *Life and Works,* there were no new accounts of the conversion of the kingdom until Yves de Saint-Denis set to work in 1317. Where this subject was concerned, both the *Latin Chronicles* of Saint-Denis and the *Great Chronicles* did nothing more than narrate the baptism of Clovis.

For Yves de Saint-Denis, however, the kingdom existed before its first king was baptized, and it had the right to its own global conversion, one in which Paris figured as the summit and the center for propagation of the faith. To accomplish this, Yves made Saint Denis the apostle "of the Western world and of all of France," and credited him with founding six archbishoprics and about twenty bishoprics—about half the episcopal sees in the kingdom—as well as three episcopal sees outside of France.[98] How did he arrive at such numbers?

First, Yves took all the sees named in the *Life and Works:* Beauvais, Senlis, Meaux, and Arles. To these, he added the entire list cited by Gregory of Tours: Tours, Narbonne, Auvergne, Limoges, and Toulouse. Gregory's list had also been given in the tenth century by Abbot Letaldus of Micy[99] and by the anonymous *Chronicle of Tournai*.[100] The dating of their missions no longer presented insuperable difficulty, for some of them—Saint Martialis for example—had meanwhile been made apostles. He added Saint Ursinus of Bourges, whom Gregory of Tours had presented as disciple of the seven in the following generation.[101] Finally, the twelve disciples named in the ninth-century *Life of Saint Memmius*[102] (presented there as companions to Denis, sent by Saint Peter) furnished him with the additional names of the sees of Chalon, Reims, Soissons, and Trier.

For the remainder of the kingdom, however, Yves had no guides on whom to draw. Though Normandy had been part of the kingdom since 1204, it had not yet been linked to Saint Denis. The *Ecclesiastical History* of Ordericus Vitalis (1075–1142), which Yves must have come across in some way, supplied him with the names of two saints who supposedly lived during the first century—Nicasius of Rouen and Saint Taurinus of Evreux.[103] But the regions to the south and east of the Parisian basin still remained untouched. Fortunately, the great *Passio* of Sens,[104] written around the middle of the eleventh century in support of the claim of the archbishop of Sens to primacy over Gaul, provided Yves with a solution. Paris belonged to the archdiocese of Sens. According to the *Passio*, Saint Peter had sent Saints Savinianus, Potentianus, and Ceraunus on a mission to Sens; they had also founded the sees of Troyes, Orléans, and Chartres. In addition, well before Denis, they had preached in Paris. Yves, in an audacious move, deflected this story to the profit of Paris. Not until fifty years later during the reign of Charles V, did the bishop of Paris, with the king's support, make an attempt to escape from the archdiocese of Sens, doubtless by enlisting the same kind of arguments as Yves had used. After all, if Paris rather than Sens had converted the kingdom, then it was logical to confer on the capital

both the archiepiscopal primacy and its symbol, the pallium.[105] To
complete his argument, Yves called on several individual lives already
linked to Saint Denis by others: Saint Piaton of Tournai and Saint
Julianus of Le Mans, whose names had appeared in the lists of the seven
disciples cited by Letaldus of Micy and Fulbert of Chartres.[106] He also
picked up Saint Ionus, since he was Greek and, like Denis, was also
represented carrying his head.[107] Though Yves was silent on most lands
outside the kingdom, he paid particular attenton to the conversion of
Flanders, from Cambrai to Tournai. Contemporary politics was not
without its power.

Thus, Yves proceeded in a very simple way. He used the tradition of
his own abbey and other preexisting lists. To these he annexed the rival
tradition of Sens, adding to it all the head-carrying Greek saints he
could find. The documents on which he drew spanned the period from
the end of the ninth century to the middle of the eleventh and had been
composed either under the protective umbrella of Hilduin's *Life* or
written to attack it in favor of Sens. He readily adapted these sources to
fit his own needs. He deleted several sees named in the lists or in the
Passio, including Lyon and Toul, for example, which were situated
outside of the kingdom. He also omitted the name of Saint Peregrinus of
Auxerre, whose rival of the same name was buried at Saint-Denis. And
he left out Saint Fronto of Périgueux.

But Yves's version of Christian France was still incomplete. It included little of the region south of the Loire, little of the western part of
the kingdom, none of Brittany, and none of the area east of the Escaut,
Meuse, Saône, and Rhône. Though he had not caught up with the actual
growth of the kingdom (with the exception of his reference to Flanders),
he did make Paris the center of power. His account was therefore ideologically acceptable.

Yves's assiduous gathering went beyond the bounds of the usual
collection of texts. He gave the first comprehensive account of the kingdom's conversion to Christianity, in the tradition of Gregory of Tours,
but quite opposed to the official version, which (in the thirteenth-
century *Great Chronicles,* for example) focused that story on the baptism of Clovis. Yves's work here bore witness to the rediscovery of
Gaul. Its influence was durable. At the end of the fifteenth century, the
Octosyllabic Life took over his hierarchical and centralized schema,
adding only Saint Exuperius of Bayeux to Yves's list.[108] In the seventeenth century, Doublet rounded out Yves's list with Nantes and
Vannes in the west, Metz, Toul, Verdun, and Strasbourg in the east, and

a few locations to the south, including Périgueux.[109] Thus, under the aegis of Denis's first-century mission, Doublet managed to create nearly all of the episcopal sees that existed in the kingdom of the seventeenth century and even anticipated what was to come with the Treaty of Westphalia.

Taking the Part for the Whole   An alternative to Yves's approach was to reason by synecdoche. Saint Denis had begun with Paris in his effort to christianize the kingdom and had converted it in the most miraculous and orthodox fashion. "The faith in other parts of the land grew out of this," a speaker exclaimed at the Estates-General of 1484. "Denis exalted the faith so well," said a royal act of 1482, "that our entire kingdom was thereby baptized."[110] In other words, the part stood for the whole. Paris was the center of France, its heart, as men said in the fourteenth century.[111] There, martyrs had spilled their blood; there they chose to lie buried. Converting Paris they converted the whole kingdom.[112]

All of this served to glorify Paris: from the twelfth century on, the ideal center of the kingdom—though in this case, the ideal long preceded reality.[113] In the thirteenth and fourteenth centuries, it was further magnified: it became Paris without equal, Paradise Paris, the Pillar of Faith, the Fountain of Wisdom and Learning, the Seat of All Justice, and above all, the Home of the Kings. Founded by the Trojans (see chap. 8) and the first city in the kingdom to become Christian, Paris was the mother of all French towns.

Referred to alternately as New Athens, Rome, or Jerusalem, the *civitas Parisius* was the common fatherland, *communis patria*, of all who lived in the kingdom.[114] In Roman law, the expression *communis patria* signified that each citizen of the Roman Empire belonged both to his own particular fatherland and to the common fatherland—the city of Rome—as well. Copying this, French legal texts from 1280 to 1400 affirmed that, as the most excellent of cities and the home of the kings, Paris was the common fatherland of all who lived within the kingdom. Parisians, moreover, were the king's most faithful subjects: so it was said in 1124 and again at Bouvines in 1214. The *Great Chronicles* praised them for being "ready to die to defend the Crown." Among them the king took his stand, for (the *Chronicles* had him say) "I know very well they would not abandon me to my enemies either dead or alive."[115]

Despite all the official affirmation that Paris remained the administrative capital and the common fatherland, however, the privileged rela-

tionship of the city to the king grew weaker following the crisis of
1355–1358 and disappeared totally in the fifteenth century, after the
city betrayed the king in 1418 by opening its gates to the Burgundians.
From 1418 to 1435, it was only the government of the English regent,
John, duke of Bedford, which sang praises to Paris and its evangelist
Saint Denis.[116] Genealogies posted in Anglo-Burgundian France around
1422 showed Saint Denis and Saint George presenting the Lancastrian
king, Henry VI, to the Virgin Mary. And when Henry formally entered
Paris for his coronation in December 1431, the city welcomed him with
a dramatization of the life of Saint Denis.

Consequently, the propaganda that came from the circle of the future
King Charles VII took a dim view of Paris and the Parisians, and it made
no mention of Saint Denis at all. The saint did not appear in any of the
visions of Joan of Arc. In 1435, a plaintive ballad that began "Hélas
Paris, noble cité" ("Alas Paris, noble city")[117] described an earlier city,
prosperous, noble, and at peace, replete with prestigious relics, home of
governing bodies, the residence of kings. Compare what it has become:
exhausted, full of dilapidated and decaying houses; its churches have
been defiled; justice has vanished among the debauchery of its inhabitants. "You have lost all your honor, you have fallen into poverty. . . .
Everyone wants to desert you, princes have abandoned you." For by
now, the kings had taken up residence in the Loire Valley and came to
Paris only to visit. As the centers of power were no longer Parisian, the
image of Saint Denis, bishop of Paris, suffered significantly.

There was, of course, an enormous gap between real history and the
manner in which the authors we have considered represented it. The
conversion of the kingdom to Christianity in the first century was presented as fact, even though there had been no Christian community in
Gaul prior to A.D. 150 and few bishoprics existed there much before
A.D. 250.[118] As the story was told, conversion had come to Paris from
Rome and then had spread from Paris outward, systematically traveling
down the lines of hierarchy. First came the bishops, then came the
community. The decisive contributions that Lyon, Provence, and the
Rhone Valley made in propagating the faith were entirely overlooked.
We now know that it was Lyon that played the role attributed to Paris;
but because it was still located within the Holy Roman Empire, medieval authors could not accept it as the place from which conversion had
come. The late-medieval account respected fourteenth- and fifteenth-
century ecclesiastical structures and justified their existence. It recog-

nized the borders of the kingdom for which the story was invented. It discarded the imperial framework in favor of one that was purely French. Despite the fact that in 1300 the boundaries of dioceses did not yet match the borders of the kingdom, and the hierarchy of the ecclesiastical sees did not yet correspond to those of the royal government, the idea of the kingdom was so compelling to fourteenth-century minds that their image of the process of conversion to Christianity was entirely molded to fit its shape.

This representation of the conversion of the kingdom had one major flaw: it was too heavily focused on Paris and its role as capital. When the centers of power moved south of the Loire, it became more burdensome than useful. In its favor was the fact that it described the birth of the most Christian nation, and it did this in tandem with the story of the rise of the monarchy. But when the French nation reconstructed its foundations in the fifteenth century, Saint Denis would not be the patron saint of the Kingdom of Bourges.

PATRONUS CORONAE: THE PATRON SAINT OF THE CROWN

Patronus coronae: Abbot Suger invented this mysterious term to refer to the two different functions of the abbey of Saint-Denis: the abbey preserved the regalia among its treasures; it also served as royal necropolis. The two functions were closely related, for the oriflamme, the crowns, the scepters, and the staff of justice which it housed were central to the ceremony of coronation, and the men and women who lay within its tombs had once been adorned with those same ritual objects.

The Oriflamme   The story of the oriflamme begins in 1124, when Suger asked Louis VI, as advocate of the abbey of Saint-Denis, to carry the abbey's flag—a piece of red sendal cloth attached to the end of a golden lance—when he went into battle to defend its county of Vexin.[119] Over the succeeding century and a half, Louis VII, Philip Augustus, and Saint Louis all carried the flag on crusade, and it flew at the decisive battle of Bouvines in 1214.

At the beginning of the thirteenth century it was said to be the oriflamme that Charlemagne carried against the Saracens. The Emperor Constantine, so the tale went, had a dream in which Charlemagne appeared with the banner and announced that he was leaving to free Jerusalem. In the second half of the fourteenth century, Raoul de

Presles, the *Romance of the Fleur-de-lys,* and Jean Golein changed its origin to a dream of the Byzantine Emperor Manuel. In their story, a savior from the Western world, announced by an angel, appears before Manuel carrying the banner that was destined to be kept at the abbey of Saint-Denis. And as Charlemagne was the true embodiment of the imperial ideal, at the beginning of the fifteenth century Abbot Philippe de Villette attributed the dream directly to him: Charlemagne is preparing to leave for Constantinople, when Saint Denis appears and gives him the protective flag.

Not all writers agreed that the oriflamme was Charlemagne's, however. Guillaume Guiart attributed it to Dagobert, the founder of the abbey. And from the middle of the fifteenth century, preference was generally given to Clovis, around whom by then all material symbols of the monarchy were accumulating.

Although the myth of the oriflamme steadily grew larger, the historical events surrounding the real flag followed a more uncertain path.

In contrast to the clear victories for the oriflamme in the thirteenth-century the results of fourteenth-century battles were disquieting. When the French engaged the Flemings at Mons-en-Pévèle in 1304, King Philip IV remained in control of the field but, in the course of the battle, the oriflamme was apparently thrown to the ground and torn, and at some point was lost. Whereas the Flemish sources give a straightforward account of this part of the battle, the French narratives either prudently say nothing or are curiously circumspect. The event suggested that a new way had to be found to use the banner. Soon, duplicate banners were being produced before each military campaign, while the original stayed behind in the abbey treasury. So regularly were the copies used in the fourteenth century that the abbey composed a liturgy of the oriflamme for their consecration.

This liturgy was most fully elaborated between 1364 and 1422, during the reigns of Charles V and Charles VI. On the night before the ceremony, the king would come to Saint-Denis. The next day, accompanied by the abbot, he would process into the abbey, to be greeted there by the reliquaries of Denis, Rusticus, and Eleutherius, and sometimes also the relics of Saint Louis, which would be sitting on the altar of the martyred saints at the back of the choir. Reverently, the relics would be lifted out of their reliquaries and the newly made oriflamme touched to them. This was followed by a mass, whose sermon was devoted to the duties of the king and the guardian of the oriflamme, both of whom took communion. Next, the oriflamme was blessed in the name of Saint

Denis, "so that he would work to defend the faith and the kingdom." Finally, the guardian would take an oath and, while kneeling, receive the oriflamme directly from the hands of the king before turning to show it to the people. A reverse ritual was held each time the oriflamme was returned to the abbey at the end of a military campaign.

The charge of guardian of the oriflamme was awarded for life and paid well, but it was a weighty responsibility. In battle, the guardian was entrusted to carry it above all other banners in the front line. It was thus a risk-filled role, for raising the oriflamme was a call to wage "mortal battle," in which no prisoners should be taken. It was used only in important battles, those that would determine the outcome of war, those that represented the judgment of God. For this reason, the guardians were all experienced soldiers and mature men, and drawn from chivalric families—such as the Noyers, the Charnys, and the Villiers de l'Isle Adam—from whose ranks came many officials of the Crown.

At Crécy in 1346 the oriflamme was lost; ten years later at Poitiers it was as well, when its guardian Geoffroi de Charny was killed. Even though it brought victory over the Flemish weavers at Roosebeke in 1382, its reputation began to waver, its moral force to weaken. Though all agreed that it should be carried against the infidels, as had been the case in the first days of its glory, and that it should be unfurled before schismatics if need be, this proved meaningless when, at the beginning of the fifteenth century, it was used in the labyrinth of the civil war. After 1418, the oriflamme no longer appeared very often. As Charles VII was deprived of access to Saint-Denis during most of his reign, he was obliged to fight under the protection of different symbols. And though his successors through the end of the sixteenth century continued to go to the abbey before each military expedition to pray before the reliquaries of the martyrs, the oriflamme itself was no longer used.

The Crowns and Other Regalia   From 1120 on, the abbey also housed the coronation crowns of the kings and the queens who were buried there:[120] the heavy crown used for the ceremony itself, and the lighter, personal crown, worn during the festivities surrounding it. It never laid claim to crowns other than those that served in the coronation. It showed no interest, for example, in the twenty or more crowns that Charles V possessed (according to his *Inventory*) and which he used for royal entries, for *lits de justice* (judicial ceremonies), and for diplomatic receptions. In its treasury were two male crowns, dating from the thirteenth century; and the last crown of any kind to enter its possession in the

Middle Ages was that which Joan of Navarre, wife of Charles IV (1322–1328), wore for the festive celebrations surrounding the coronation. In the late Middle Ages, when the same crowns were repeatedly used for the coronation, the collection at Saint-Denis stopped growing.[121]

In the beginning, a new crown may have been made for each coronation, and it seems that it always remained acceptable to do this. But little by little the crowns of Charlemagne and Saint Louis took on special value and became particularly favored.

The origin of the crown of Saint Louis—a tall circlet of a single piece, with a large central stone and four incurved, deeply cut trefoils—presents few difficulties. Art historians date it from the first half of the thirteenth century, so it is entirely possible that Louis himself had it made and wore it. It is a reliquary crown, encasing thorns from Christ's crown as well as some of his hair, and is therefore sometimes called the Holy Crown (sainte couronne) or the Crown of Thorns (couronne d'épines).

The crown of Charlemagne, by contrast, presents a number of nearly insoluble problems. Sometime between 1160 and 1165, the abbey of Saint-Denis apparently forged a capitulary of Charlemagne, which it dated 813, stating that on his departure for the Crusades, Charlemagne left his crown on the abbey's altar. The fabrication of this capitulary makes it likely that the abbey then had a crown in its possession that it claimed to have been the emperor's. It is possible that this was the crown used at Saint-Denis in 1179 for the coronation of Philip Augustus, the first Capetian to claim Carolingian descent. The modern historian Hervé Pinoteau advances such a theory,[122] though there are no accounts dating from the period itself that affirm it. It has been claimed that, with the exception of John II, Charles VII, and Henry IV (1589–1610), all the kings of France until the Revolution wore Charlemagne's crown. But here again, textual evidence is lacking. No mention of the crown appeared until 1340, when a royal edict of Philip VI referred to it as "the great imperial crown." In 1450, the Italian humanist Antonio Astesano called it "the crown of Charlemagne," but we cannot be certain that it was worn in a coronation until 1515. After this, it was used regularly for royal coronations.[123]

Art historians who have studied representations of this crown, with its four hinged sections and deeply notched fleurs-de-lys, think it comes from the second half of the thirteenth century. It is possible that an earlier crown was reshaped to produce it. The jurist Guglielmus Benedicti, who saw it at Saint-Denis at the beginning of the sixteenth century, reported that the monks of the abbey informed him that it was remade during the reign of Philip III (1270–1285) and placed in the abbey treasury by Louis X.[124] Some historians say the crown disappeared during the religious wars of the sixteenth century, leaving kings of the seventeenth and eighteenth centuries to wear the ancient crown of queens, identical to the male crown though smaller;[125] but as no original crowns from the abbey treasury have survived, it is difficult to draw any firm conclusions.

We might conjecture that from 1300 on, French kings had two crowns at their disposal, both prestigious, and that they chose to use one or the other according to their needs. When it was politically useful for a king to appear to be a descendant of Saint Louis (as was the case with John II and Charles VII, both of whom had to fend off the rival pretensions of English kings), the king might choose Saint Louis's crown. If, however, he had imperialistic ambitions, a king might wear the crown of Charlemagne (as did both Charles V and Charles VI on certain occasions). From the end of the fifteenth and the beginning of the sixteenth centuries, all kings coveted the Empire. Thus, Charlemagne's crown eventually won out over Saint Louis's, which from the sixteenth century on was considered little more than a relic.

The other ritual objects used for the coronation were rarely attributed to Charlemagne prior to the thirteenth century. The sword "Joyeuse" (Joyful) was carried before Philip III in 1271, though earlier it had been referred to only as "the sword of justice."[126] In 1380, it was used in the coronation of Charles VI, and in 1422 it was carried before the duke of Bedford. As for the scepter topped with a miniature figure of Charlemagne, this did not appear until 1364, when it was produced on command for Charles V.

The Abbey as Guardian   During the later Middle Ages, the abbey's guardianship of the regalia was seriously challenged. In July 1429, while Saint-Denis lay in the hands of the English, Charles VII was crowned at Reims. For the coronation, the Holy Ampulla provided its chrism, but none of the other ritual objects were available. Since the Holy Ampulla had been a gift from heaven, the king could not produce a second one. He could certainly create new regalia, however, and in 1429 he did.

Charles arrived in Reims on the evening of Saturday, July 16. His council deliberated all night to organize the ceremony.[127] "And it was marvellous, because we found all the great things that we needed in this very city, even though we could not have those which are kept at Saint-

Denis in France."[128] The *ordo* (the liturgical text of the ritual) was the last Capetian ordo. A manuscript of this text, called the "Blue Book," had been housed in the library of Saint-Remi since 1330.[129] Care was taken to summon the lay peers of the realm and to find substitutes for those then in the enemy camp: the duke of Alençon replaced the duke of Burgundy; the counts of Clermont, Vendôme, and Laval played the roles of the other peers. Renaud de Chartres—the archbishop of Reims who was Charles's chancellor—officiated at the ceremony. Joan of Arc participated. Gilles de Rais went to retrieve the Holy Ampulla. The ancient customs were observed: Charles VII was crowned "as his father and the other kings of France had been crowned . . . according to the liturgical ceremonies proper to the coronation."[130] Coronation festivities followed, ample though markedly less costly than Louis XI's would later be.[131] The king then left for Saint-Marcoul-de-Corbény and Saint-Denis along the route traditionally followed after coronations. The return had also by tradition ended with the new sovereign's first royal entry into his capital; but in Charles VII's case, it had to end at Saint-Denis.

Finding certain of the objects needed for Charles's coronation in the city of Reims itself—things like wall hangings, offertory bread, and ritual objects for the altar—was probably not difficult, for kings had customarily given gifts to the cathedral on the occasion of their coronations, and Charles V, three-quarters of a century before, had been particularly generous.[132] The tasks of organizing the festivities and preparing the site for the event were taken care of by the local citizenry, who also provided lodging for the court, according to protocol dating back to the beginning of the fourteenth century.

The knottiest problem, however, was probably to locate a crown. According to the *Chronicle of the Maid*, it was found in the city of Reims itself.[133] But we do not know for certain where. All known representations of Charles VII's coronation, and particularly those in the Reims tapestries, come from a much later period and thus are not very useful in helping us answer this question. Given the press of time, it must have been taken either from the cathedral's treasury or from the abbey of Saint-Remi, which housed the Holy Ampulla and the ordo. It was most probably from the latter.

Saint-Remi had been the site of the consecration, coronation, and burial of two of the last Carolingians, Louis (d. 954) and Lothaire (d. 986), as well as of two queens, Gerberga and Frederun. Statues of the two kings, which had stood in the abbey since the middle of the thirteenth century, showed them seated on thrones and wearing crowns. In the center of the abbey, there was a monumental tomb of the Apostle of the Gauls, within it a reliquary whose decoration represented the baptism of Clovis, the Holy Ampulla, the Pastoral Staff, and Saint Remigius's ring. At some unspecified date, a crown was added—possibly Carolingian—for when the baptism of Clovis began to be conceived of as both a consecration *and* a coronation, the abbey had to produce one. Our only knowledge of the existence of such a crown, however, comes from sixteenth-century and later inventories,[134] but it is quite possible that an ancient crown was used for the coronation of Charles VII, a crown that was housed at Saint-Remi and attributed either to Clovis or to Lothaire.

The king must have kept the crown, for in 1437 he made his royal entry into Paris wearing a very curious one, described as "bearing a double fleur-de-lys in front."[135] An illumination in the dedication to the manuscript of the *Armorial Berry* shows the same crown being used for the royal entry into Rouen.[136] It was a narrow circlet decorated with four small fleurs-de-lys flaring out at the top, and it had an enormous double fleur-de-lys in the center that looked rather more like a Cross of Lorraine than a heraldic fleur-de-lys. Such an unusual crown might well have come from the early Middle Ages.

Let us now look at Charles's strange stay at Saint-Denis from August 23 to September 13, 1429. When he took possession of Saint-Denis, he had masses said in memory of his father, imitating more or less what the duke of Bedford had done in 1422. Then, according to Thomas Basin (1412–1491), bishop of Lisieux, "he had himself crowned there, as [is] the custom for a new king."[137] Basin considered the ceremony held earlier at Reims to have been primarily a consecration. During the masses that preceded the first royal entries into Paris—as they had been celebrated at Saint Denis since 1223—kings appeared in royal robes and wore crowns. But though in Charles's case no royal entry occurred because Paris was not in his hands, we have no reason to doubt Basin's account of what took place.[138] Charles reclaimed the regalia at Saint-Denis. He then took Saint Louis's crown and the Holy Nail away with him and placed them in the Sainte-Chapelle in Bourges.[139] We can assume it was the crown of Saint Louis that Charles used for the ceremonies at Saint-Denis, for documents make no mention of the crown of Charlemagne, or of Charlemagne's sword "Joyeuse." These two objects may actually have been in Paris, where the duke of Bedford was developing plans for the coronation of the young English king, Henry VI, plans that in the end had to be canceled because Paris was not safe enough.

They did not reappear until after the army of Charles VII recaptured Paris in 1435.

In July of 1445, Charles returned the jewels and relics to Abbot Philippe de Gamaches of Saint-Denis, who had remained faithful to him through the hardest of times. Solemn processions were held to accompany the treasures on their way from Paris back to Saint-Denis.[140] But it is important to note that the abbey had been deprived of its relics for fifteen years and that during this time other regalia were used in their stead.

There were other problems with the regalia of Saint-Denis. Continuity in their use could be as troublesome as the lack thereof. In 1422, "Joyeuse" was carried before the English regent, the duke of Bedford, on his return from the funeral of Charles VI.[141] As we have seen, the crown of Charlemagne may have been similarly involved. In December 1431, Henry VI was crowned at Notre-Dame in Paris as successor to Charles VI. The ceremony was arranged by Henry Beaufort, the English cardinal who opposed the duke of Bedford's regency and, since he knew nothing of how these things were done in France, he used an English-style coronation ordo and two crowns. One was the crown of England, used at the coronation that had taken place earlier in London. The other, the crown of France, may have been one brought from England, or it may have been inherited from Charles VI. Then again, it may have been the famous crown of Charlemagne—though no English propaganda maintained that Charlemagne's crown had been used[142] and, unfortunately, the three accounts of this event—by the "Bourgeois of Paris," the Burgundian chronicler Enguerran de Monstrelet (1400–1453), and the *Great Chronicle of London*[143]—do not give us the information we need to resolve the issue.

Several legends developed to conceal this history. One went as follows: "A long time ago, during the period when the English ruled over the kingdom, a monk from Saint-Denis took the Holy Nail and the crown away from the abbey, so the English could not seize them and take them to their country, and he carried them to Bourges in the Berry."[144] This tale presupposed, of course, that Charles VII had the regalia of Saint-Denis at his disposal in July 1429. He did not. It also implied that the English had never made use of them. This may be true, but it has not been proven. Another story was told at the abbey around 1450, according to which the regalia spent the entire war buried beyond everyone's reach.[145] When an English soldier tried to dig them up, he was suddenly struck blind, and the sacred objects remained hidden.

Both stories showed that the abbey was acutely aware of the consequences of 1429 and 1431 and deemed it necessary to try to mask them. Rumors also circulated about the use of the Holy Ampulla in 1429. Some maintained that the Anglo-Burgundians were not able to take it from Reims because it was protected by God, that the sacred liquid had dried up for the English pretender to the throne (Henry V, Henry VI, or the duke of Bedford, depending on which account one reads) and then had suddenly rematerialized in abundance to fulfill the needs of the true king of France.[146]

What were the consequences of this partial break in the traditions associated with Saint Denis?

As far as the coronation rituals are concerned, the American historian Richard A. Jackson has demonstrated that the break was quite significant.[147] Whereas Charles V and Charles VI had been crowned using the ordo of 1364, Charles VII's ceremony was built around the last Capetian ordo. Later, in 1461 and again in 1484, both the ordo of Charles V and the last Capetian ordo were used. The form of the resulting liturgy was mixed, and it was used as such from then on. Charles VII's choice in 1429 had had long-term consequences.

It is harder, however, to evaluate the significance of what happened with the regalia. Charles VII used the regalia of Saint-Denis as well as other symbolic objects; he showed that kings far removed from the abbey could create regalia of their own. The flag with the white cross that he used definitively replaced the oriflamme, whereas the chrism from the Holy Ampulla, conserved at Saint-Remi in Reims, proved to be irreplaceable. But Charles VII began using the title of king in 1422, before his coronation, dating the start of his reign from the death of his father. Though Joan of Arc referred to him as the Dauphin from 1422 to 1429, lawyers called him King of France. That is to say, an entire generation in the middle of the fifteenth century adopted the attitude that the king could bypass the regalia and the ceremony of the coronation. Heredity was what counted. Only royal blood could create what was sacred, and no ceremony in and of itself could give this to the king.

The result was that kings no longer needed Saint-Denis. To the contrary, it was the abbey that needed the kings, and it remained scrupulously faithful to them for the rest of the century.

The abbey of Saint-Denis, however, acquired new privileges at the end of the Middle Ages, though these lay in a secondary realm. At the end of the fifteenth century, for example, it began to monopolize the coronation of the queens of France.

Queens had been consecrated and crowned since the days of Charles the Bald. From 1092 on, Capetian queens were crowned at Reims at the same time as their husbands if their marriage had preceded their husbands' accession to the throne: Joan of Navarre (the wife of Philip IV), Joan of Burgundy (wife of Philip V), Clemence of Hungary (wife of Charles IV), Joan of Boulogne (wife of John II), and Joan of Bourbon (wife of Charles V) were all anointed and crowned at Reims—in 1285, 1317, 1324, 1350, and 1364 respectively. When their marriages were to crowned monarchs, their own coronations took place at the time and place of their weddings. Special ceremonies had to be arranged for Maria of Brabant, the wife of Philip III, for Maria of Luxembourg and Joan of Evreux, wives of Charles IV, and for Blanche of Navarre, wife of Philip VI. The coronations of queens were thus celebrated in many different places and by many different prelates. There was no need to go to Reims, because the Holy Ampulla housed there was not used for queens; and between 1285 and 1389, ceremonies for the queens who were not crowned with their husbands were held in the Sainte-Chapelle in Paris.

At the end of the Middle Ages, other practices began to evolve. First, the coronation of queens was separated from their marriage ceremonies; the two events came to be held at different times and different places (four years after her marriage in the case of Isabelle of Bavaria), and the coronations progressively became associated with their first royal entries into Paris—the earliest example is again the coronation of Isabelle of Bavaria. Charles VI had Blanche of Navarre, widow of Philip VI, search in the archives of the abbey of Saint-Denis for information on how queens were to be crowned, but she found nothing concerning their entry processions.[148] Isabelle's entry in 1389 may thus have been the first such ceremony observed for a woman. Following her ritual entry, Isabelle was crowned at the Sainte-Chapelle, just as her predecessors had been. The ordo used was that of 1364 as it was found in the Saint-Denis manuscript.

As the fifteenth century went on, practice became increasingly irregular. Blanche of Navarre (d. 1398) was buried at Saint-Denis with royal honors even though she had never been crowned.[149] Neither Maria of Anjou, wife of Charles VII, nor Charlotte of Savoy, wife of Louis XI, was crowned with her husband at Reims, because of circumstances surrounding the coronations. There may have been coronation ceremonies for them at the time of their entries into Paris in 1437 and 1467, in which case the ceremonies may have been held in the Sainte-Chapelle at the very end of the royal entries; or they may have been held at Saint-Denis, before the entry processionals began. But although both were fully considered queens, there is no sure evidence that such ceremonies were actually held for them. Anne of Brittany (the wife first of Charles VIII and then of Louis XII) was crowned at Saint-Denis in 1491. She was crowned there again in 1504, before her royal entry into Paris. The same was true of Maria of England, the second wife of Louis XII, for by this time the abbey had evidently become the predominant choice for a ceremony, which, though its pomp and pageantry had continued to grow, enjoyed little constitutive importance of its own.

Saint-Denis housed the regalia and the holy chrism and was large enough for an occasion that brought together a great number of people. The coronation of queens was only one part of the larger ceremony of the royal entry—which had grown to be crucially important in the late Middle Ages. It was more logical to hold the coronation of a queen before the entry, rather than after it, for this allowed spectators the pleasure of applauding a true queen during the entry. As the queens were not of French royal blood, the coronation was more important to them than it was to the kings, unless their having given birth to a successor to the throne had already compensated for that lack. All fifteenth-century queens were pregnant or had given birth by the time of their coronation; they were either carrying the sacred blood during the coronation or had already done so. Perhaps for queens as for kings, the idea of royal blood had likewise begun to hold greater significance than the coronation itself.

The Tombs of the Royal Family   The abbey of Saint-Denis was also the cemetery of kings. Many visitors came there to pay homage to the royal tombs as well as to the relics of the saints. For their benefit, French and Latin inscriptions concerning the history of France were inscribed on each tomb; the texts that Guillaume Rigord recorded in 1196 and the Latin and French inscriptions recorded by the monk Guillaume de Nangis, who died in 1300, have survived to this day.[150]

During the late Middle Ages, visits to the royal tombs were considered an essential part of the normal round of official tours. As one account reported: "On the following Monday [in 1378], the Holy Roman Emperor Charles IV of Luxemburg had himself brought before the bodies of the saints and he kissed the relics, the skull, the Holy Nail, and the crown. When the devotions were over, he asked to see the tombs of the kings, above all those of Charles IV and Philip VI, in whose courts he had been raised, and he also asked to see the tomb of King John."[151] Emperor Charles's son, Emperor Sigismund, paid a similar visit in 1405.

The initial arrangement of the tombs at the abbey was established between 1263 and 1264, when Abbot Matthieu de Vendôme undertook to demonstrate visually that the Capetians were descended from the Carolingians, and that the abbey of Saint-Denis was the only fitting burial place for them. The Cistercians were dangerous rivals to the abbey at that time, for they housed the tomb of Louis VII at Barbeaux and held a series of tombs at Royaumont in reserve for the royal house.[152] In 1306—in an attempt to demonstrate that all who had reigned from the Merovingians onward belonged to a single dynasty, rather than there having been a *reditus*, a passing on of rulership, from the Carolingians to the Capetians—Philip the Fair had the tombs at the abbey of Saint-Denis again rearranged. He had Philip Augustus and Louis VIII placed in the center to symbolize the union of Carolingians and Capetians. Saint Louis was then added, near Philip Augustus and Louis VIII, without much attention given to order. Later kings, the last of the Capetians and the Valois, came to be massed together in similar fashion to the right.

Charles V made another innovation when in 1373 he endowed a memorial in the chapel of Saint John the Baptist, the first chapel on the right near the chancel. Throughout the fifteenth century, this chapel would serve as the burial place for all kings save Louis XI, who asked to be buried at Cléry. Charles V's endowment serves as a useful example to help us understand the role of Saint-Denis at the end of the Middle Ages. Up until then, the abbey had served exclusively as "the kings' cemetery,"[153] that is, only rarely were their royal remains joined in death by their wives and children. In the thirteenth century, the burial sites for members of the royal families had been at Royaumont and Poissy. The first queens to be interred at Saint-Denis were the wives of Philip VI; from then until sometime after 1500, all were buried there as long as they had been reigning queens. Whereas Bonne of Luxemburg (d. 1348), for example, the first wife of John II, was buried at Saint-Laon-de-Thouars because she died before her husband ascended to the throne; Blanche of Navarre, though never crowned, was buried at Saint-Denis because she was the wife of an annointed king. Increasingly, the tombs of kings and queens were coupled: beside Philip VI lay his first wife; beside Louis XII lay Anne of Brittany.[154] Thus, the change that brought queens into the abbey preceded Charles V's rearrangement of the tombs. His new design merely implanted it in the chapel of Saint

John the Baptist, where the series of coupled tombs continued to grow through the end of the fifteenth century.

The problem presented by the burial of royal children is more complex. We need first to disregard the cases of daughters who were married out of the family and younger sons who were awarded land of their own in *apanage*, since they were destined for other burial sites: the daughters were laid to rest next to their husbands, the sons in the lands they had received. Only the children who died young or without having been married concern us. Among them we must make distinctions of gender and age.

Until the mid-fourteenth century, female children were normally excluded from the royal necropolis. Most were buried at Poissy, Maubuisson, or the Parisian convents of the mendicant orders. From 1340 on, some princesses were buried at the abbey of Saint-Denis, though their tombs were placed in side chapels: Maria and Blanche, daughters of Charles IV, in the chapel of Notre-Dame-la-Blanche; Blanche and Joan of Navarre in the chapel of Saint-Hippolytus, and the daughters of Philip V in the chapel of Saint-Michel. The first princess to be buried at Saint-Denis was probably Joan of France, the child of Louis X who had been prevented by her uncle from ascending the throne. Later, a daughter of John II, as well as two of Charles V (Joan, who died at one year of age, and Isabelle, who died at five) were buried alongside their fathers rather than in the side chapels. Whereas daughters during the first half of the fourteenth century only had the right to be buried at Saint-Denis if they had no brothers and therefore stood in line for the throne themselves, from the reign of Charles V on, it sufficed for them to be of royal blood to merit burial in the most honorable place in the necropolis.

The same was true of the firstborn males, whether actual or only virtual dauphins: they were not buried at Saint-Denis before the time of Charles V. Louis, the son of Louis X, who died in 1316, was buried at the Franciscan house; Philip and Louis, sons of Charles IV, were buried at Pont-aux-Dames and Montargis respectively. The three oldest sons of Philip VI, who died between 1328 and 1333, were buried at the Franciscan house and at Poissy. Charles V lost only one young son, John, who died before the endowment of the chapel of Saint John the Baptist, but we do not know where he was buried. The sons of Charles VI—a first Charles, who was less than a year old when he died in 1386, and a second, who died at nine in 1400—were buried at Saint-Denis beside their grandfather, Charles V. So was their brother Philip, who lived less than a day in November 1407. However, Louis of Guyenne and John of

Touraine, the older brothers of Charles VII, who died in 1415 and 1416 respectively, were buried in Notre-Dame and in Compiègne, because times were too troubled for them to be taken to Saint-Denis. By and large, Charles V's endowment in 1373 nonetheless marked the beginning of a new way of thinking, and as a result, the abbey of Saint-Denis became the burial place for nearly all the royal blood of France, regardless of age and gender. From this point on, queens and children were put to rest beside the ruling kings.

Around this same time, the idea arose to turn the chapel of Saint John the Baptist into a kind of pantheon. Already in the thirteenth century, Pierre le Chambellan had been buried at the feet of Saint Louis and, in the fourteenth century, Charles V willed that the Constable Bertrand Du Guesclin (d. 1380), the most famous soldier of his day, the "equal of the mythic knights of old," be buried at his side. Du Guesclin was memorialized in 1388 by Charles VI. Also placed alongside of Charles V were Bureau de la Rivière, chamberlain to both Charles V and VI, who died in 1400, and Louis de Sancerre, constable of France and hero of the reconquest in 1403. During the reign of Charles VII, Arnaud Guilhem de Barbazan, the "blameless knight" who had lost his life for the king at Nancy in 1432, and Guillaume du Chatel, killed while fighting at the king's side during the siege of Pontoise in 1436, were buried in the chapel. In the time of Louis XI, Louis de Pontoise, killed by the Burgundians at Crotoy in 1475, was buried in the abbey, though outside of the chapel itself, because by then there was no room. It is worth noting that those chosen to be buried beside the royal family were all men and that, for the most part, they were soliders who had been killed in battle.

The era of Charles V thus brought about two changes: the abbey of Saint-Denis had become the necropolis of the entire French royal house and the pantheon of heroes. The later fifteenth century broke completely with both traditions. The sons and daughters of Charles VII and Charles VIII (1483–1498) were buried at Tours; the children of Louis XI at Amboise and Tours. Not even the young Charles-Orland, son of Anne of Brittany and Charles VIII, who had been the recognized dauphin until his death at five, was buried at Saint-Denis. Nor was his brother, François. This change refleced a decline in the status of the abbey as a burial site rather than any loss in the popular appeal of the idea of the royal blood of France. The break would be felt at the abbey from 1415 to at least the middle of the sixteenth century.

Montjoies *and Funerary Rituals*   Nine little commemorative cairns, called *montjoies*, stood like stations of the cross along the route that led from Paris to the abbey and its tombs.[155] Each consisted of a pedestal bearing a cross and containing three niches that held statues of kings: Philip Augustus, Louis VIII, and Saint Louis were in some; Philip appeared alone in others. They were erected in two separate construction campaigns, in 1223 and in 1270. The first was projected to go from Mantes to Paris and Saint-Denis for, as its official chronicler, Guillaume Le Breton, explained: "Each time the casket was set down, a cross was made." The second series was initiated at the death of Saint Louis, when King Philip III helped carry Louis's coffin to the abbey.

Small chapels similar to the montjoies had long existed in many parts of the kingdom—at places where miracles had occurred and which often became small monastic sites; but they were all dedicated to saints rather than to kings. It was the special role of the montjoies—like the gallery of kings in cathedrals and the large hall of the royal palace—to pay homage to kings rather than to Saint Denis. Their task was to delineate the sacred path that linked the abbey with the capital.

Funerary liturgies were composed around the royal tombs and the montjoies,[156] in the Carolingian period, with the commemoration of the death of Charles the Bald, and again in the twelfth century, when Abbot Adam arranged the commemoration of Dagobert—linked to the anniversary of the dedication of the abbey. In 1140, Abbot Suger introduced another liturgy and a series of special rituals in memory of Charles the Bald; this was soon followed by a ceremony in honor of Robert the Pious and a liturgy in memory of Louis VI composed by Suger himself.

From Philip Augustus on, almost all the kings established chaplaincies themselves, providing for regular masses to be said in their memory. Charles V's 1373 endowment called for the celebration of two masses in his name each day, four solemn memorial masses each year—on the anniversary of his death, at Pentecost, and on the feast days of Saint Denis and Saint John the Baptist—and asked that a lamp be kept burning continuously by his tomb. To provide for this, he furnished five hundred pounds per year and provided the cost of clothing for twenty monks.[157] Even without this, the monks of Saint-Denis were continuously intoning prayers for the royal house. Though Louis VII found this bothersome—fearing his memory would be lost in the midst of so many great kings—most Capetians saw the advantage to these rituals of eternal praise to the monarchy. It was in their favor that in the heart of their land prayers were constantly proffered—for them, for their dynasty, and for the kingdom that God had given them.

And so it was that Saint Denis served as the ancient and powerful patron saint for the kings, the kingdom, and the Crown.

The Language of Patronage   It is interesting to note, however, that Denis's relationship with those he looked after was couched neither in theological terms nor in terms of kinship, but in terms of law. There are few references in this literature to the communion of saints or to the reciprocal bonds between the living and the dead, though, admittedly, such things were not clearly conceptualized before 1200. References to the bond between proselytizer and converts, to the French being the spiritual offspring of Denis, did appear from time to time, but they were not fully developed. Although Ernst Kantorowicz has claimed that much of medieval political reality was conceived of in theological terms,[158] in the case of Saint Denis, we find instead a theological reality cast in the language of the laity and, most particularly, in the language of Roman and feudal laws, which furnished a vocabulary of contract between unequal partners.

Roman law provided the concepts of *tutela* and *confederatio*. *Tutela*—the legal guardianship of minors—gave the *tutor* more or less the same authority as a legal defender had when an adult was absent or unable to defend himself. To Saint Denis—represented in Parisian iconography as an old man—was attributed a tutela over the king and kingdom as minors: he managed their goods and instructed them, and through his constant presence led them toward salvation. Such a relationship between Saint Denis and the royal house was perpetual, for the king and kingdom were always minors in the life of the here and now.

From the twelfth century on, writers also claimed they were "*confederati* of Saint Denis."[159] In the ancient world, confederati—"federated tribes"—had been tied to Rome through treaties of unequal partnership: in return for land, they were required to do military service for Rome. In the same way, Saint Denis's conversion of the kingdom to Christianity was imagined as a contractual pact. Converts received the faith, and they in turn took on duties toward God. Charlemagne's gift of the kingdom to Saint-Denis could thus be interpreted as one that sealed a lasting confederation between the royal house and the abbey. As a *socius,* of course, the king constituted a more active contractual partner than he did as a minor under Denis's tutela.

Feudal law, for its part, contributed the concepts of vassalage and servitude. In 1124, at the very moment when invasion threatened, Louis VI came to Saint-Denis as a vassal would have done, to carry the abbey's banner in a war over the border territory of the Vexin. In consequence, the Vexin came to be attributed to Saint Denis in theory and to the king in fact.[160] The false diploma of 813, which gave the kingdom in fief to Saint Denis, was another exercise of the same genre. It is not certain whether or not Louis VI followed Abbot Suger's direction as stringently as a vassal would have done, but the *Lives* of Louis VI and Louis VII, and the royal decrees issued during their reigns, often spoke of Saint Denis as if he were their Lord. Denis was depicted pledging to give the king help and counsel, while the king vowed to protect his lord's goods and his honor. Clearly, the abbey had a great deal to gain from this kind of thinking.

The supposed royal "head tax" illustrates how the relationship could be imagined as one of royal servitude. Just as each of their serfs owed them four pennies in head tax, Philip Augustus and Saint Louis were said in turn to have placed four Byzantine gold coins on Denis's altar to serve as the head tax that, according to the Pseudo-Turpin, kings owed the saint.[161] Though there may have been additional examples of this practice after the time of Saint Louis, it had few practical consequences.

All this changed, however, after 1350. Then a king could no longer be considered either a vassal or a serf, even of the supernatural. The language and its associated practices disappeared. For better or worse, these kinds of relationship were now outdated. To glorify the royal house, more fitting guardianships were invented: those of the ancestral Clovis, Saint Charlemagne, and Saint Louis. Saint Michael furnished a spiritual kinship. The people of France were spoken of as children to the kings. The relationship between France and its heavenly protectors became progressively warmer and more equal. Little by little, the distance between this world and the next grew smaller.

In the end, kings escaped the guardianship of Saint Denis entirely. They created their own regalia and eventually showed they could do without both the coronation ritual and the use of the royal necropolis. Between 1300 and 1500, the relationship between the king and Saint Denis reversed itself completely: French kings, having come of age, began to exercise their guardianship over the abbey of Saint-Denis.

CHAPTER 2

Saint Clovis

THE TRANSFORMATION OF THE HISTORICAL CLOVIS

The historiography of the first Christian Merovingian king, Clovis (481–511), has not always been given the attention that it deserves. The accounts from Gregory of Tours and the seventh-century Fredegar, from Carolingian and later chronicles through the thirteenth century, are relatively well known,[1] but one would guess from modern historians that the fourteenth and fifteenth centuries were an historiographical void, when nothing new was said about Clovis and nothing old was called into question. This impression is quite false. Historians of the fourteenth and fifteenth century did on the whole preserve the picture of Clovis that their predecessors had created, but human imagination did not stop working on it; for though the story was nearly a thousand years old, it was the beginning of the nation's history.

In the historical imaginings of the late Middle Ages, Clovis's military exploits were thinned and simplified to allow them to become more noble and meaningful. His victories served as justification for the contemporary boundaries of the French kingdom. He took on the visage either of a heroic knight or of someone very much like a monk. Because his destiny was to serve as model for every French king to come, he was cast as the first ruler to have all the royal attributes possible. In the fourteenth and fifteenth centuries, a Clovis cycle appeared, in which the era of the first Christian king grew into a political ideal, an island of peace and justice.

The late-medieval transformation of Clovis turned him into a saint, the most holy founder of the French monarchy: it allowed him to play the same role in France that Saint Olaf had played in Norway and Saint Stephen in Hungary. How unlikely a candidate, this deceitful and violent barbarian! Yet, by the end of the fourteenth century, the cushion of ten centuries had allowed him a kind of sanctification. During the fifteenth century, references to Clovis as a saint grew more frequent, appearing even in official texts. Clovis as a saintly founder of his country is a peculiar example of continuity in a waning Middle Ages so often thought to have been awash with secularism.

Saints are invariably surrounded by cults of worship; but it is difficult to gain much information about those that might have been devoted to Clovis since he was not recognized as a saint by the institutional Church, which by the fourteenth century had a monopoly on deciding who officially was one. However many cults there may have been, they were more a form of folkloric than of official veneration. Though we can identify some sanctuaries where he was honored, we will probably never be able to locate all of them, nor will we be able to map their spread chronologically as can be done with the cults of other dynastic saints. But some of the references that we do have from late-medieval iconography and oral legends allow us nonetheless to capture some of the aura of "royal religion" that surrounded the first king of France.

PORTRAITS OF CLOVIS PREDATING 1300

The earliest depictions of Clovis made one point clearly: they praised his skills as a warrior. Gregory of Tours, Fredegar, Hincmar of Reims, and Aimoin of Fleury (tenth century) all agreed on this; in the thirteenth century, the *Great Chronicles* gave this quality privilege of place: "He was noble in battle and glorious in victory."[2] By this time, a few of his military campaigns had clearly become the chroniclers' favorites: the wars that he fought against Syagrius near Soissons, at the beginning of his reign; the campaign he waged against the Alemanni, when he promised to be baptized; the battle against Alaric's Aryan Goths, when God worked numerous miracles; and those that came at the end of his rule, when he pitted his skills against Chararic and Ragnachar of Cambrai. But even these stories were not without their ambiguities. Three similar legends competed with one another concerning a vase taken as booty: one about the vase of Soissons, another about Saint Maixent, and a third about Saint Lehire of Tournai.[3] In all of them Clovis appeared as a plunderer—or king of plunderers—as well as a benefactor: from the booty he won in battle he gave a portion to the churches.

Early texts had attested to his relations with holy bishops and monks—and some of these stories may possibly be historically true. Gregory of Tours mentioned Saint Martin of Tours, Saint Remigius, Saint Genovefa, Saint Hilary of Poitiers, Saint Maxentius, Saint Melanius, and Saint Vedastus; Fredegar added Saint Paternus; Carolingian authors contributed Saint Maximinus and Saint Severinus of Agaune, Saint Deodatus, Saint Eleutherius, Saint Fridolinus, Saint Gothardus of Rouen, and Saint Solina of Chartres; yet later authors added Saint Regalus of Senlis, Saint Sacerdos of Limoges, and especially Saint Leonard. Most of these associations enjoyed only a brief and very localized fame. By 1300, the only ones still linked to Clovis were those listed in the *Great Chronicles* and in the great historical encyclopedia, the *Mirror of History* by the Dominican Vincent of Beauvais (d. 1264), which, along with the early fourteenth-century *Miracles of Our Lady,* provided the classic portrait of the king.[4]

A nearly perfect family circle surrounded this somewhat dubious hero. Almost everyone seems to have known the story of how Aurelian presented the king's ring to the Burgundian princess Clotilda when he went to seek her as a bride for Clovis. Before the wedding night, it was said, Clotilda spoke to Clovis of the wonders of the Christian faith but, after the marriage, she had not only to endure the death of her first son, but also her husband's continued refusal to believe in Christ. Some of her prayers were rewarded when her second son was cured through her devotion; she was able to have him baptized, and eventually she played an active role in the conversion of Clovis. For this, she was quickly canonized and came to be venerated at Sainte-Geneviève in Paris, at Les Andelys, and elsewhere. A number of the king's and queen's grandsons and nephews also rose to sainthood, including Dagobert of Metz, Clodulphus, Radegond, and Théodechild.

In the fourteenth century, the story of Clotilda's life was spread mainly by the *Miracles of Our Lady,* which credited the Virgin Mary with saving the life of Clotilda's second child. Up until then Clovis was portrayed as frequenting the saints—saints from both inside and outside the family. Later, when it no longer sufficed for him merely to be surrounded with saints, he would be sanctified in his own right.

THE SIMPLIFICATIONS OF THE FOURTEENTH AND FIFTEENTH CENTURIES

During the fourteenth and fifteenth centuries, Clovis continued to appear as a warrior, but epic distancing gradually had an effect on his image. Little by little, he was given a more active and personal part to play in battles. Sometimes, it was said that he killed the Alamannic king Candat, or else the king of the Wisigoths; sometimes, he was credited with both. Where earlier authors had given leadership in the Languedocian campaigns to his eldest son, late-medieval authors attributed it to him. As accounts of Clovis's military exploits grew more simplistic and imprecise, some authors began to indulge in pure fantasy. Around 1461, the *Abbreviated History of the Kings of France* listed among Clovis's exploits the capture of Lorraine and of Melun, in order to endow the indispensable Aurelian—Fredegar's creation—with land.[5] Accounts of the siege of Verdun were equally popular thanks to the promotional efforts of the monks of Saint-Mesmin of Orléans.[6] At the beginning of the sixteenth century, the *Antiquities of Gaul* even went so far as to portray Clovis as the triumphant conqueror of all "the Saxons, Goths, Turonois[?], Burgundians, Lorrainers, and other neighboring peoples."[7] This simplified the vision of his wars dramatically. Now, few mentioned the siege of Soissons with its story of the vase, despite the fact that it would have made a forceful moral anecdote for late-medieval preachers. The Burgundian wars were also forgotten—except during the reign of Louis XI, when they served the king in his political struggle with Charles the Bold. Even more interesting is the disappearance of the wars against Chararic and Ragnachar of Cambrai, still well known around 1300; the dramatic scenes from the last part of Clovis's reign, filled as they were with so many atrocities, vanished from all but the handful of historical accounts that remained faithful to the *Great Chronicles*. Apparently, it had become expedient to forget these questionable episodes: having occurred after Clovis's baptism, their inclusion certainly would have raised doubts about the quality of his conversion. The story of the vase, by contrast, could be included if need be, both because it was ambiguous and because it occurred at the beginning of his reign, before his baptism.

As the late wars disappeared, two types of narratives emerged. One—the most common—reduced his military activity to two symmetrical battles that framed on either side the culminating point of his reign, his baptism-coronation: both were organically tied to this central event, for the first, when Clovis made his vow to convert, was the cause of the baptism, while in the second he demonstrated the fervor of his new-found faith. This was the narrative of the Dominican Bernard Gui (1261–1331) in his *Flower of Chronicles*, of Jehan Mansel (a mid-fifteenth-century Burgundian compiler) in his *Flower of Histories*, and of the anonymous authors of the *Rosebush of Wars*, commissioned by Louis XI, and the *Mirror of History*, written in the middle of the fifteenth century;[8] in almost all of them, the Germans played his first enemies. A second kind of narrative appeared in brief, allusive texts, lacking in the interpretive richness of those just mentioned. Here the only battle was that of the vow, against the Alemanni/Germans; no later one demonstrated the strength of his conversion. This was the form adopted in the *Origin of the French Kingdom*, the *Sea of Histories*, the work of Olivier de la Marche, and in the early sixteenth-century chronicle of Philippe de Vigneulles of Metz.[9] Texts recounting the legend of Joyenval all followed this second narrative pattern,[10] with the imaginary Candat replacing the king of the Alemanni; here there was an added ambiguity, for even before Clovis went off to the battle during which he made his vow, he was given the sacred lilies, symbols of the Christian faith. In these accounts, the battle functioned doubly, as both the cause and the effect of the king's conversion: it encompassed both the war against the Alemanni and the war against the Goths. Though such accounts had little to do with actual historical events, they are excellent examples of the art of simplification and the making of potent symbolic images.

At the same time as his campaigns were reduced in number, Clovis's military activity was being ennobled. No one any longer remembered the remark of Hugues of Fleury (d. 1114) in his universal chronicle that "Clovis, the king of France, invaded Aquitaine, because he wanted to enlarge his kingdom."[11] To the contrary, he put aside his personal ambitions to work to realize God's plan for France, while God in turn rewarded him with many miracles. Every writer told of the miracles of the doe who showed the way to the ford in the river Vienne, of the miraculous pillar of fire at Poitiers, and of the walls at Angoulême that collapsed like the walls of Jericho—all placed in the war against Alaric, which consciously or unconsciously became the prototype for the crusades of the kings of France. To underscore his zeal, the *Miracles of Our Lady* sang "He was the noble champion of the Holy Church,"[12] and the *Rosebush of Wars* specified that "with the help of God and lord Saint

Martin, Clovis chased King Alaric, the Spanish Saracen, away from the Gauls."[13] The *Mirror of History* described his "steadfast faith, his exemplary courage in exalting Christianity," which won him victories "by the grace of Our Lord, to whose care he entrusted himself."[14] Jehan Mansel ended each story of victory with the refrain, "and this came to pass through divine will," and Guillaume Crétin (at the beginning of the sixteenth century) with "this was a miracle and a sign that Clovis was a friend of God."[15]

Medieval authors may have seen God at work everywhere, but these were signs that Clovis was truly engaged in a crusade. As the leader of the chosen people and the recipient of obvious signs of heavenly assistance, Clovis, aided by the Church, was engaged in a struggle against impiety. So much did the Crusades still inform the idea of royalty in the fourteenth and fifteenth centuries that one writer— Aimery de Peyrac, abbot of Moissac (1377–1407)—went so far as to imagine Clovis going off to Jerusalem after the battle of Vouillé.[16] Legend had much earlier—and with great success—created a comparable destiny for Charlemagne and, in apocalyptic legends, the king of France of the Last Days was also fated to go to the Holy Land to carry on exploits begun at home. The question Aimery de Peyrac's invention thus raised was whether it was fitting for Clovis to be sent off to the Holy Land or whether, true to his place at the beginning of royal history, he should have stayed behind in France to pursue his royal— but incomplete—career.

As the nature of Clovis's military exploits changed, so too did their consequences. No longer were they painted in the dry geographical terms of a Sigebert de Gembloux or the *Great Chronicles* (which had charted the growth of the kingdom from its tiny and ineffectual beginnings, expanding first to the Seine and then to the Loire); Clovis became the architect of the territorial boundaries of the kingdom—as they were and would be for eternity. Under his rule, "Francia" and "Gallia" began to coincide, for he "expanded his kingdom across all the lands of Gaul."[17] The *Rosebush of Wars* propelled him to the southernmost border as "he conquored all the land from the Loire to the Mount Pyrenees that separate France from the kingdoms of Spain." The *Abbreviated History of the Kings of France* spoke of the border in Lorraine,[18] and the *Antiquities of Gaul* insisted that "his kingdom stretched from Lyon to Brittany and from Cambrai to the Pyrenees."[19] The history of Clovis served to justify not only the current boundaries of the kingdom but its future territorial ambitions as well. At the end of the fifteenth century, he was at work on the eastern frontier, where an earlier conjuring of "Charlemagne" had created more problems than it had solved. "The great king Clovis I, who was never called the Duke of Bar but only and solely King of France . . . , enjoyed by that title the rights to the said lands and territories," declared an anonymous *Remonstrance* on the lands of Lorraine and Bar.[20] French national history thus began with Clovis, for during his reign the Franks took possession of a territory that was clearly defined. Aside from the illustrated genealogies of the kings of France, which implied as much when they depicted Clovis in his baptismal font preceding Dagobert holding Saint Denis and Charlemagne of the flowing beard, there were direct affirmations. "[Clovis] was the principal founder and augmenter of the kingdom,"[21] "under whose rule, the reign of the Franks began to grow and flourish."[22]

This early focus of French national history on the reign of the first Merovingian king was helped not only by the new conception of his military exploits, but also by the gradual idealization of his persona. Limited by the absence of source material on his personality, historians drew his portrait from one or the other of two ideal types or fit the two together. Some compared Clovis to the legendary Charlemagne, depicting him as a great example of heroism and chivalry. These emphasized his physical qualities: his physical attractiveness (in the work of the humanist Robert Gaguin (1425 or 1433–1501 or 1502), his noble countenance and proud gaze (in the *Great Chronicles*); or they emphasized his moral character: magnanimous and courageous, said Vincent of Beauvais; full of glory and skill and endowed with great gifts of speech, said Guillaume Crétin.[23] The other alternative was to make him like a monk. At Saint-Mesmin, they clothed him in holy virtues: a fervent devotee of God and Christianity, he grew in probity and integrity. The *Mirror of History* depicted him as a gentle and sensitive king who fed the poor and paid respect to the clergy, a pious and good-willed man who "believed in praising and loving people"[24]—attributes more suited to the eleventh-century king, Robert the Pious, than to Clovis. Because of his personal virtues, Clovis was an excellent king, bringing peace and justice to France; for the best Christians made the best kings. Vincent of Beauvais, Bernard Gui, the *Rosebush of Wars,* and the Veronese historian Paulus Aemilius agreed: the kingdom enjoyed true peace under his rule. The Sire de La Bouquechardière was even more explicit: "Clovis reigned well, and judged all in good faith; he kept his people bound by good reason and the public weal by equity."[25]

SAINT CLOVIS AS MODEL AND ARCHETYPE OF THE MOST CHRISTIAN KING

These fourteenth- and fifteenth-century transformations of Clovis's character and deeds created two complementary images: he was ideal king and ideal Christian. Though late-medieval writers did not speak of "the days of Clovis" as often as they did of "the days of Saint Louis," they spoke of both in the same terms—military glory, peace, and justice. Peace in Clovis's time had been "certain and ongoing"; he had demanded neither general taxes nor salt taxes; he had used the most judicious means to name clergy to office.[26] For them, the France of Clovis prefigured that of their own days. In their remonstrances to Louis XI, the judges of the Parlement of Paris drew on Vincent of Beauvais's account of the Council of Orléans to make of Clovis the ancestral guarantor of the Pragmatic Sanction.[27] When the Pragmatic Sanction of Saint Louis was forged around 1450, Clovis and Louis joined hands as the models of rulers who had established good relations among the French monarchy, the pope, and the Church of France.

The honesty, goodness, and chastity of Clovis were held up as a model for the edification of all Christians, and particularly for King Charles VII. Two *Mirrors of History,* the one written at Orléans in 1429 and the other from 1450, as well as the last prologue to the *Life of Saint Mesmin,* all elaborated on the parallel between Charles and Clovis:[28] until the time of Charles, Clovis was the king whom God had most helped, for he was most in need of God's assistance in building a great kingdom from a small beginning. Faced with the similar challenge of keeping peace and justice in the kingdom, Charles became a second Clovis, who with God's help made himself the second founder of his country.

Clovis was also a model for every King Louis to come. "Louis," in fact the same name as "Clovis," was taken to be its Christian transformation; so the *Miracles of Our Lady* had Clotilda say to her husband on the occasion of his baptism: "Louis . . . that is a beautiful name, my lord."[29] Clovis was the first Louis; the numbering began with him, and Louis X, XI and XII thought of him as their predecessor. Every Louis felt a strong unity with the others:

> Et des Clovis les clercs gestes toucher,
> Voulant vivifier leurs mémoires et exemplifier
> A tous futurs . . .
> [And clerks relate the deeds of the Clovises,
> To revivify their memory and display them as examples
> For all those yet to come . . .][30]

So securely did authors identify Clovis with his successors that we must
beware of their confusion when we read their texts, especially of confus-
ing Clovis with Saint Louis.

We can readily understand how the Merovingian Clovis became a
prototype—"Kings must learn to seek refuge and help in the Lord, as
King Clovis did in his age," said the *Mirror of History*[31]—for in
addition to being a model king, Clovis was France's first Christian
king. He had all the attributes. And he was called "Most Christian."
Rarely used before the middle of the fifteenth century, the epithet
was attached to Clovis even as it emerged in the official title of the
king.[32]

Clovis, it was said, was the first to be anointed from the Holy
Ampulla: every *Mirror of History* told the story of how the special oil
descended from heaven to be housed thereafter at Reims and used in all
the sacrings and crownings to come. The legend, supported by the
authority of Archbishop Hincmar and passed through the *Great Chronicles*, became for the late Middle Ages the heart of the history of Clovis.
Here no fantasies were allowed, for the story was an obligatory truth of
French patriotism, and any embellishment would have been lèse-
majesté. For this reason, the accounts of Clovis's baptism are highly
stereotyped. About the only exceptions to this uniformity were the explanations offered for the traditional anecdote that the Holy Chrism
arrived late for the ceremony. Some blamed it on the press of the crowd.
Others told how the Ampulla was dropped and broken—a terrible
omen, and how the Holy Spirit immediately intervened to make it whole
again.[33] The arrival of the Holy Ampulla was interpreted in two ways.
One quite simply said it showed how God confirmed, established, and
approved the creation of the kingdom; on that day, "in the person of
Clovis, the power of the kings of France was constituted, established,
and approved by God."[34] The second was more complex. Inspired by
the coronation oath, it took the episode to mean "that it [was] the duty
of the king of France to be a good and faithful Christian . . . a defender
of the Holy Church, [and] an upright and righteous wielder of the
sword of justice."[35]

Clovis, it was said, was also the first to bear the oriflamme. Both
the Norman Robert Blondel, in his fifteenth-century *Treatise on the
Rights of the Crown of France,* and the *Debate of the Heralds of
France and England* made the claim[36]—a curious claim, for though
the oriflamme was then still prestigious, it was no longer much used.

Perhaps the story went further back in time. A funeral orator in 1350 asserted that Clovis was the first to receive the banner, and the *Universal Chronicle Up to the Year 1422* did the same.[37] But such references were rare until the end of the fifteenth century, when they suddenly began to proliferate. They appeared in the works of Robert Gaguin and Maitre Guilloche of Bordeaux, in Philippe de Vigneulle's *Chronicle*, in the *Antonine History*, the *Antiquities of Gaul*, and the *Panegyric of the Kings of France* by the early sixteenth-century jurist, Jean Bonaud de Sauset.[38]

Clovis's shield also bore the sacred lilies of France. The story of how they came as a gift from heaven was already abroad at the beginning of the fourteenth century.[39] Around 1330, the monastery at Joyenval— prosperous but still new—began to elaborate new details in order to glorify its own name.[40] Shortly before Clovis went into battle against a Saracen king at Conflans-Sainte-Honorine between the hill of Montjoie and the fountain at Joyenval, so their story went, a hermit had given the Frankish king the lily-adorned coat of arms after receiving it from an angel of the Lord. To show his thanks for winning the battle, Clovis converted to Christianity and founded the abbey of Joyenval on the site where the miracle had taken place. The story was popularized at the court of Charles V by Raoul de Presles, Jean Golein, and the *Dream in the Pleasure Garden*. Around 1400 a competing version, influenced by the abbey of Saint-Denis, appeared in the works of Etienne de Conti and the Chancellor Gerson, who conflated the unknown hermit of Joyenval with Saint-Denis, the apostle of Gaul; but their story met with little success: in the fifteenth century, without new additions, the legend of Joyenval appeared intact in the works of Robert Gaguin, Nicole Gilles, Guillaume Crétin, and all the other authors of Frankish histories. As a final touch, two manuscript illuminations of the late-fifteenth century gave Clovis the power to cure scrofula.[41]

All these miraculous attributes of the monarchy came together to form a cycle of Clovis, the founder of the French monarchy. Latent among the jurists of Charles V in the second half of the fourteenth century, it was complete by the reign of Charles VII. The first visual representation appeared in 1430.[42] After his seemingly miraculous expulsion of the English from the kingdom, Charles VII ended his reign in glory—the second founder of the monarchy, a second Clovis. By reflection, the image of Clovis grew brighter, and he received the sacred symbols and attributes of his distant successor.

THE CULT OF SAINT CLOVIS

SAINTHOOD

The first unequivocal examples of belief in the sainthood of Clovis date
from the end of the fourteenth century, though even the Carolingians
had taken it for granted that his conversion had won him paradise:[43] an
anonymous thirteenth-century epitaph on Clovis's tomb at Sainte-
Geneviève asserted as much; so too did the *Great Chronicles*. But it was
not until the late Middle Ages that people fully considered him a saint
and graced him with all the requisite attributes: he became a miracle
worker with the power to intercede on behalf of others who were in
need of help.

Aimery de Peyrac, abbot of Moissac from 1371 to 1407 and author
of a universal chronicle, incorporated into his larger narrative of
France's first Christian king a number of local tales concerning Clovis's
supposed founding of the abbey of Moissac. Aimery firmly believed that
the ruler he held to be the patron and founder of his monastery was
indeed a saint: "Undefeated king, bearer of the glorious sword of Christianity, you are the one who precedes all the other kings of France in the
army of Christ . . . you will be rewarded with heaven." "It was Saint
Clovis," he continued, "who called together the Council of Orléans
where many useful laws were made. . . . After being baptized, he became Most Christian and he is honored as one of the saints. . . . We all
believe that King Clovis went to heaven . . . a victorious, wise and
saintly king."[44]

The contemporary *On the Subcelestial Hierarchy*, written in 1396,
emphasized the virtues of "the Most Christian Saint Clovis."[45] Clovis is
already the indefatigable right arm of the Church, but now he is transformed from a king helped by God into a king who achieved miracles of
his own through prayer and personal merit. Soon after, Chancellor
Gerson—in a sermon dedicated to "Saint Louis" (Clovis or Louis
IX?)—spoke of the gift of the lilies.[46] The association also appeared in a
widely known poem, *Lilia crescant!* ("May the lilies grow"),[47] which
linked the glory of Saint Louis to both Clovis and Saint Remi. Eventually, even a royal edict issued by King Louis XI in 1481 expressed belief
in the sainthood of Clovis: "Clovis, our predecessor, who during his
lifetime was a true and perfect friend of the God who granted him so
much grace and so many victories . . . was sanctified and glorified after
his death along with the glorious saints of paradise, and his name and

his memory were filled with great miracles wrought daily by God, as prayed for by this glorious and saintly king."[48] The ordinance issued at the founding of the collegiate church at Tarascon in 1483 is equally interesting, for it affirmed that Clovis was the protector of all kings who came after.[49] Thus, we find Clovis portrayed as an intercessor and miracle worker in both life and death.

At the end of the fifteenth century, references to his sainthood began to multiply. To the Italian humanist Boniface Symoneta, Clovis was notable for his holiness, his religiosity, and the heavenly protection God accorded him.[50] The jurist Jacques Almain expressed similar sentiments: "Clovis was a saint and . . . the banners of the Gauls were brought to him."[51] The Veronese historian Paulus Aemilius—despite his reputation as a destroyer of legends—likewise remained sensitive to the pious zeal of this "saintly and just" king, protector of the faith and the founder of the French religion.[52] We may therefore consider it normal that Clovis often appeared in collections of saints' lives during this period—under the ambiguous title, *Vita Ludovici,* "The Life of Saint Louis."[53]

PLACES OF WORSHIP

Though saints automatically imply the existence of cults, the cult of Clovis raises considerable difficulties. First of all, Clovis was never accepted as a saint by ecclesiastical authorities; though he was venerated, he was not legally canonized and, for this reason, it is difficult to locate the cult sites dedicated to him. Worshippers sometimes mistook him for Saint Louis, who had been honored through an officially sanctioned cult since the beginning of the fourteenth century. The confusion that grew out of their names was compounded by similarities in the ways they were depicted. Like Louis, Clovis was portrayed in the ceremonial dress of the coronation; his countenance was perfect, surrounded by striking, flowing hair; he wore a crown and held the scepter and the staff of Justice; the golden-lily motif decorated either his shield or his robe.[54] In some cases, the aura of Clovis outshone the saint to whom a given sanctuary was officially dedicated, regardless of whether or not Clovis had any ties to this saint or had founded the monastery; consequently, the list of sanctuaries that may have had links to Clovis is quite long. It included Saint-Martin in Tours, Saint-Vaast in Arras, Saint-Hilaire in Poitiers, Saint-Séverin in Chateau-Landon, and Saint-Lehire in Tournai, all of which had early associations with Clovis. To these we can add the monasteries with forged diplomas of foundation or gift from Clovis: Saint-Pierre-le-

Vif in Sens, Saint-Mesmin in Orléans, Saint-Jean in Réomé, and the grotto-church of Our Lady in Bethléem.[55] Though Sainte-Geneviève in Paris, where Clovis was buried, was in fact the only church he actually established, most of these churches continued to extol Clovis as their founder throughout the fourteenth and fifteenth centuries.

For most of these churches, there is evidence only that they honored Clovis as their founder or benefactor. There are two exceptions, however: at Saint-Mesmin in Orléans, special prayers were dedicated to Clovis during the reign of Charles VII;[56] and at Sainte-Geneviève, late in the fifteenth century, "the Gauls [i.e. the French] established a round-the-clock ritual to honor the king venerated there as a saint."[57] The latter, in all likelihood, refers to ceremonies once held during a pilgrimage to Clovis's tomb on November 27, the anniversary of his death. Rome may well have tolerated such a ceremony at Sainte-Geneviève because Clovis's wife, Clotilda, an officially canonized saint, lay buried there alongside him.

Sanctuaries that waited until the beginning of the fifteenth century to associate themselves with Clovis provide us with more interesting examples, for we generally have a greater quantity of information about them: accounts of what happened there were written down, whereas his veneration earlier at other places may have existed in practice but left no evidence behind. Let us take a look here at three of the cult sites dedicated to Clovis in the fifteenth century: Moissac, Saint-Pierre at Dorat, and Sainte-Marthe at Tarascon. We will examine what happened at Joyenval in chapter 7.

The Abbey of Moissac   As early as the eleventh century, the monastery at Moissac had laid claim to Clovis as its founder: the dedication of the new church, reconstructed by the monks of Cluny on the pilgrimage road to Santiago de Compostello, already mentions it; but this account of Moissac's founding did not often appear before the thirteenth century, before, that is, the abbey received the protection of the kings of France in return for assisting their entry into the conquered territory of the counts of Toulouse. From Philip III onward, kings in their grants of safeguard regularly alluded to Clovis as the abbey's founder.[58] Administrative rights to the town of Moissac were divided between the royal house and the abbey. And the king—as vassal to the abbey—had a gold *obolus* coin placed on the altar of Saint-Pierre each year.

The first detailed legend of the founding of the monastery appeared only in the fourteenth century, when the abbey still enjoyed the status of a royal stronghold, now against the English. Our knowledge of that legend comes principally from the work of Aymery de Peyrac, a frequent visitor at the royal court, where he went to secure privileges that would allow him to reconstruct and restore the abbey after the long trials of war and plague. Aymery was knowledgeable in both history and theology; he knew Bernard Gui's *Flower of Chronicles,* the *Great Chronicles,* the writings of Vincent of Beauvais, and Moissac's own *Life of Saint Cyprianus;* to write his *Chronicle of the Kings of France, of the Counts of Toulouse, and of the Abbots of Moissac* he probably also drew on a number of charters that had been part of the abbey's collections since at least the early fourteenth century. Here Aymery referred to Clovis several times.[59]

In Aymery's version, Clovis—following his defeat of Alaric—was on his way from Bordeaux to Toulouse when he stopped along the Tarn to build an oratory. There he had a dream of griffins piling stones one upon the other, a vision that led him to build a great monastery rather than just a simple oratory and to bestow important privileges upon it. Another version (of unknown date) claimed that during the march from Bordeaux to Toulouse, Clovis's army was ambushed and a thousand of his soldiers killed. That night, Saint Peter appeared to him and ordered him to build a monastery where one thousand monks would pray for the dead soldiers. So Clovis shot an arrow into the air, and Moissac was constructed on sturdy pilings in the lake where the arrow fell.[60] Aymery alluded to this story as well. The story of the lake in the midst of the woods he drew from the *Life of Saint Cyprianus;* all the other elements, except for the dream and the ambush (reminiscent of Roncevaux), came from Gregory of Tours, who had used them in his account of the founding of Saint-Pierre (the future Sainte-Geneviève) in Paris. They played the same role in the story of Moissac as they had in the story of Saint-Pierre: in both, an arrow marked the spot where the church was to be built, and both were dedicated to Saint Peter. There was also the surprising assimilation of Moissac, a city on the water, to Lutèce-Paris, the city on the marsh. Thus, the new Clovis legend skillfully imitated a preexisting historical narrative.

The legend was also given expression in visual form. A fourteenth-century mosaic once set in the floor at Moissac, near the great altar, depicted the scene of the griffins. Although it was destroyed by the abbot Pierre de Carman (1449–1485) when he built a new chancel, Aymery de Peyrac's written description of it has survived.[61] There is also a bas-relief, dating from the time of Pierre de Carman and still extant, in which Clovis is shown reclining as he listens to Saint Peter's request to build a monastery. An inscription below reads, *Clovis rex pius christ. 506*, "Clovis pious Christian king, [A.D.] 506."[62] Two other representations also existed, but our only knowledge of them comes through an act of authentification drawn up by a Moissac judge in 1553, when six bourgeois of the town—chosen from among the elders—testified that they "had always seen these pictures" at Moissac; they must therefore date back to the fifteenth century.[63] One picture portrayed Clovis and an angel and bore the inscriptions "Clovis received the lilies from the angel" and "Clovis founded this monastery." The second showed the daily distribution of alms, which the monastery claimed had been founded by Clovis and which is already attested in the thirteenth century. The local inhabitants also apparently thought that the figure of the Christ of the Apocalypse in the tympanum over the central portal of the abbey church was Clovis: from the middle of the fourteenth century to the end of the nineteenth, the figure was called the "Reclobis" (Rex Clovis). The twenty-four elders surrounding the central figure may have lent themselves to interpretation as his court or guard.[64] The monastery pavement and the arms of the town also bore the lilies that symbolized the royal safeguard. Once this royal origin was forgotten, the gift of the lilies could easily have been attributed to Moissac. Both Aymery de Peyrac's skepticism about Joyenval[65] and the way the sixteenth century told the story lead us to this conclusion; but the chances of such an attribution having any real impact were small, for it would have come too late in the evolution of the Clovis legend to have had a lasting effect, and Moissac enjoyed only marginal importance compared to other late-medieval centers of power.

As for the cult of Clovis, it seems that Aymery de Peyrac, who believed firmly in the sainthood of the supposed founder of his abbey, was almost convinced that Moissac should be dedicated to the saint-king: "And I learned," he wrote, "that in certain regions, there were churches dedicated to Saint Clovis, who had called together the Council of Orléans."[66] Every day, the monks of Moissac burned two wax crowns on the main altar, gave alms to the poor in honor of Clovis, and said prayers for his successors.

Saint-Pierre-de-Dorat　　　The abbey of Dorat in the county of La Marche, twenty kilometers north of Bellac, never enjoyed the widespread fame of Moissac. It entered the royal domain along with La Marche at the beginning of the fourteenth century. Of the seven extant privileges that the kings of France issued to Dorat between 1281 and 1481, only the last made reference to Clovis.[67] The 1281 document held the founder of the abbey to be Hugh Capet, who had acted on behalf of Boso, count of La Marche. Documents of Charles V and his immediate successors named no founder, though they did speak loudly of Dorat's inviolable fidelity to the monarchy: from 1360 to 1371—when, as a result of the treaty of Brétigny, the Limousin had become English—the abbey was located on the frontier of the French Kingdom, as it was again later during the so-called Kingdom of Bourges. The royal privilege of 1481, by contrast, is voluble on the subject of Clovis. What it tells is confirmed by an act of the keeper of the royal seal of Limoges, authenticating a book that contained the legend of Clovis.[68]

According to these two documents, during the rule of Alaric, the region around Dorat was devastated and the inhabitants tortured by the heretical Goths. Clovis, having recently been baptized and anointed, wanted to devote all his energy to fighting them. When he came face to face with the enemy ten kilometers from Poitiers, he killed Alaric, and the whole region was converted to the "true faith." In order to memorialize his victory, Clovis had a small oratory built at Dorat in honor of Saint Peter and granted many privileges to its clergy, including seignorial rights over the town. A stone engraved with the year 501 stood in the church as a testimony to all this.

Because there are no conclusive texts, we can only conjecture about the date when the cult first appeared at Dorat. By 1481, however, it had already existed for a long time; that much is certain, for the privilege of 1481 described the text of the legend as "old and written in an old hand." We know it must have postdated 1350—the date of the last document naming Hugh Capet founder of the abbey. The period from 1360 to 1370 would have been the most favorable moment for the spread of this kind of belief, for the legend portrayed the enemy Aryan Goths in the guise of English torturers who persecuted all good subjects of the king, men and women alike.

Dorat's chief competitor—and perhaps its model—was Saint-Léonard, about fifty kilometers away, at Noblat. The principal festival at each sanctuary was November 6, and Saint-Peter-in-Chains, to whom the church at Dorat was dedicated, had things in common with Saint Leonard, the liberator of prisoners. The story of how Clovis founded the monastery at Noblat after the campaign at Vouillé was comparable to the story invented at Dorat, though older and more widely known. But from 1360 to 1370, Noblat lay in the hands of the

English, and Dorat began to play the role of a substitute. The year 1430 must have marked the end of Dorat's period of influence, when its status as a fortified stronghold on the edge of the kingdom—which had allowed the legend to take shape—was no longer useful.[69]

It seems reasonable to conclude that the cult of Clovis grew up at Dorat sometime between 1360 and 1430. It included a pilgrimage held every November 6 (of which we have only later descriptions) during which an armed procession wound its way through sixteen villages surrounding the abbey, traveling at least fifteen kilometers from one village to the next. Even as late as the fifteenth century, miracles were said to take place during the pilgrimage—cures and the release of prisoners, as at Noblat.[70]

The case of the abbey of Dorat was rather different from that of Moissac. Dorat was located in a part of the kingdom where royal influence, though strong, was threatened. It stood for the kind of border patriotism prevalent at the beginning of the reign of Charles V and during the early days of the so-called Kingdom of Bourges. The idea of liberation was probably closely tied to the cult at the abbey, for Clovis, the liberator of Aquitaine, was prefigured by Saint-Peter-in-Chains. The subjects of Charles V and Charles VII hoped their kings would likewise be liberators, and we shall see further on that the so-called Kingdom of Bourges was likewise filled with liberator-saints.

Sainte-Marthe of Tarascon   For Sainte-Marthe of Tarascon we have two particularly instructive manuscripts. The first bears the title: *Report to the king on the mission he charged me with concerning the church of Sainte-Marthe.*[71] It was drawn up by a royal official (most likely a member of either the Chamber of Accounts or the Parlement) who had been sent to Sainte-Marthe to see what could be done about requests it had made. The church had apparently claimed a right to the income from land within a radius of about three miles around, asserting that this land had been a gift from Clovis, and the income paid in Merovingian currency. The flustered official reported that he could not find any coins from Clovis's time in the region and advised the king to have the sum evaluated and paid in florins! The second document, the foundation charter of the collegiate church of Tarascon in 1482, adds further details on the cult of Clovis there, and the grants of lands and rights which purported to match those awarded by Clovis.[72]

Two iconographic documents add something to these. The first is an inscription of unknown date still visible on the steps leading to the church crypt, beginning with the words *Rex Clodoveus beatae Marthae* . . . The second is a figure of Clovis that apparently comprised one of the twelve miracles of Saint Martha represented on the base of a reliquary that Louis XI presented to the church in 1478. (It no longer exists: it was melted down during the French Revolution.)

The legend linking Clovis to Saint Martha was quite conventional. It appeared in the larger context of a little-known, possibly imaginary event—the war against Gundobad and the siege of Avignon—and fit the traditional two-part sequence of healing and donation. Another story like this, the celebrated one of Saint Severinus, was already part of the Clovis corpus. Clovis, who was ill at the time of the siege, was cured, it was said, by the intercession of Saint Martha. The story must have been invented rather late, in the second half of the fifteenth century.

It is impossible to trace the legend's early history. Martha was the sister of Lazarus in the New Testament, who, so it was claimed, finished her life in the Rhone Valley and Provence. The first church was dedicated to her at Tarascon in the sixth century. Both Gregory of Tours and Fredegar included long and confused accounts of an episode involving Clovis and Saint Martha, whereas the *Great Chronicles* and Vincent of Beauvais ignored it, and none of the lives of Saint Martha referred to it. There were two factors involved in the coupling of Clovis with the church of Sainte-Marthe. First, the cult of Saint Martha and all the religious manifestations associated with it—such as the Sainte-Baume, a cult site to the east in the mountains of Provence, and the Tarasque, a representation of the dragon from which Saint Martha had supposedly freed the town of Tarascon—were spreading rapidly throughout Provence in the later fifteenth century, when Martha had become the protector of the Angevins, the younger line of the Capetian dynasty. Some of the Angevins were buried in the church of Sainte-Marthe, alongside the great officers of the Kingdom of Provence; but in addition to being a dynastic church, Sainte-Marthe was also the center of widespread popular devotion. The earliest reference to the Feast of Saint Martha dates to 1452, and the sculpting of Tarasques for religious processions first began in 1465. King René of Anjou seems to have favored these celebrations. French kings, on their side, wanted to profit from the associated religious fervor: both immediately before and after Louis XI officially took possession of Provence he gave gifts in honor of Saint Martha.[73] The churches that he chose as pilgrimage sites or to receive his gifts were hardly the result of personal whim; in place of churches in the Paris basin, still tainted by its collaboration with the English and Burgundians, he preferred sanctuaries in the Loire Valley (Notre-Dame at Cléry, for example, or Saint-Julien at Le Mans), or else in Lorraine, Brittany, and (with Sainte-Marthe of Tarascon) in Provence, all of them areas coveted by the French royal house.

The rituals of the cult at Sainte-Marthe were quite traditional. Pilgrimages led the faithful into the crypt to file around the tomb of Saint Martha, the reliquary, and the stone dedicated to the memory of Clovis. Prayers and regular masses were said "so that, through his intervention, the Savior might create and send forth from the heavens eternal peace, tranquility, and union to our kingdom."[74] But the function of the cult at Sainte-Marthe was different from Moissac and Dorat. As the church was situated far from the center of a kingdom that was in the process of being integrated, it needed a history and shared figures of worship. The cult of Clovis at Tarascon was more than just a frontier cult; it was a cult of integration.

The sanctuaries honoring Clovis have elements in common which allow us to establish a typology of these royal cult sites. The dedication of these churches varied, though Saint Peter—to whom Clovis dedicated a church in Paris—and Saint Louis seem to have some preference; but there were others, and neither Saint Bartholomew nor Saint Martha had any obvious connection to Clovis. Aside from the simple commemoration of Clovis as supposed founder or donor, there were no special cults devoted to him before 1300. But during the fourteenth and fifteenth centuries, rituals slowly began to develop hand in hand with the transformation of his character and history. They were still flourishing at the end of the fifteenth century—so richly endowed with legendary accounts—and they continued to survive into the seventeenth.

Geographically speaking, the important cult sites changed from one period to the next. In the fourteenth century, centers like Joyenval in the Parisian Basin predominated. But in the fifteenth century, their influence was replaced by centers in more outlying areas because the southern and central regions of France were becoming more powerful. The cult tended to follow shifts in the royal centers of power.

Of course, we have only limited insight into the nature of the worshippers each sanctuary served. We do know that at times they were primarily local, as was the case with Dorat. At other times however the sphere of worship spread to cover an entire province: Tarascon, for example, served all of Provence. Sometimes it was even larger. Both Moissac and Sainte-Geneviève—Paris's old Saint-Pierre—functioned as important sites for pilgrimages. Probably the only thing all the people whom these churches served had in common was their lack of literacy. Nonwritten references characterize all of the sites. At Moissac, there were five nonwritten references and only two textual references. Worshippers knew little of learned culture—of Gregory of Tours and the Apocalypse—and they tended to interpret all that they saw, whether it was a rusty shield like the one at Joyenval, a section of pavement decorated with the lily motif, or an unusual statue of Christ, as a statement in favor of the royal house. The Clovis cult—more aptly called popular belief in the sainthood of the first king of France—is difficult for us to grasp in its entirety because we do not necessarily associate all of these objects with Clovis. The written texts, in contrast, are only legends interpolated into the history of Clovis, the work of monastic clerks who were skilled at keeping alive the memory of their purported founder or donor and ready to put to profit anything that might serve the interests of their house.

But it is not difficult for us to determine the overall role of the cult of Clovis. It enjoyed the protection of the royal house and was spoken of in royal ordinances. French kings were naturally interested in seeing that their earliest ancestor be honored as a saintly king, one who possessed all the characteristics of a king of France and of a saint as well. It is also revealing that these beliefs, which had first appeared within the royal domain, spread to the border regions, to the southern areas that had only recently become part of the kingdom. Clovis, king of the Aquitanians as well as the Franks, served as historical guarantor of the legitimacy of the royal house in the south. The sanctuaries dedicated to him there helped in their own way to carry to those newly acquired regions a feeling of belonging. And that feeling, which must have been difficult for some to grasp, so vast as it was, was in fact a nascent sense of French nationhood.

CHAPTER 3

Saint Louis

"In the said year [1478], the King [Louis XI], who held the holy deeds of Saint Louis and Saint Charlemagne in high esteem, ordered their images which were placed long ago in the niches of the pillars of the big hall of the Palace in Paris to be taken down so they could be placed at the far end of the Great Hall on the upper floor, alongside the chapel."[1] This link between the two saints—Louis and Charlemagne—had already been forged by Joan of Arc when in her vision on the eve of the attack on Orléans she saw "Saint Louis and Saint Charlemagne praying to God for the salvation of the king and the city."[2]

What could have been more logical, indeed, than for a medieval dynasty to choose one of its own as its heavenly representative, someone who was glorious, famous, and far removed in time. Other nations had already done so in Scandinavia and Central Europe, where they venerated the saintly kings who had converted their kingdoms to Christianity or had found some other cause to canonize an ancestor of the ruling house. The German emperors could count on Henry II and Charlemagne, both canonized by an antipope in 1165. But for a long time the kings of France found no such privileged ancestor, despite the fact that most of its thirteenth-century kings had at one time or another been candidates for canonization.

From the time that French kings began calling themselves Carolingians as well as Capetians, Saint Charlemagne could well have filled the role of the dynastic saint but, until the end of the Middle Ages, French kings insisted on thinking of Charlemagne as the legendary white-bearded emperor of the *chansons de geste* rather than as an actual, historical person. Although Charlemagne appeared as early as 1280 in additions to the *Golden Legend* of the Dominican Jacobus de Voragine, he was never to be considered validly canonized in the French kingdom. Because the status of Charlemagne—both emperor and king—was ambiguous, the popularity of his cult was limited to periods of amity between France and the Empire. For this reason, there were only two brief periods when the cult of Charlemagne managed to set down a few roots west of the Rhine. Charles V, the son of Bonne of Luxemburg, sister of Emperor Charles IV, celebrated the feast of Charlemagne at the royal chapel, drawing the liturgy from that of Aachen. A century later in 1475, Louis XI, allied with the Emperor in his struggles against Charles the Bold, duke of Burgundy, tried to have January 28 established throughout the kingdom as Charlemagne's feastday, but his efforts were successful only with the University of Paris and a few churches, such as Reims, and the Mathurins, Saint-Jacques, and Saint-Germain-des-Prés in Paris, all of which had particular historical ties to the great Charles. Elsewhere, the cult of Charlemagne was hardly visible before the seventeenth century, for an Emperor was an inconvenient ancestor for a king to have.

Saint Louis, by contrast, as a king and a Capetian, presented no such obstacles. He was canonized early, and his sanctity remained undisputed. Although his sainthood was modeled on the Mendicant ideal and thus served less as a royal than as a spiritual model, it had an astounding success through the reign of Philip the Fair. After that it began to adopt different shapes: Louis became the symbol of fiscal freedom, and thus the protector of noble leagues, the Navarrese party, and the dual monarchy of the French and English. As a result his memory became a double-edged sword and, for a long time afterward, the favors that French royalty bestowed on him were tinged with ambivalence. This, however, did not prevent his cult from spreading slowly and steadily throughout the kingdom.

Saint Louis was the best known of the thirteenth-century kings of France: his personalization of power, the growing use and dissemination of writing, and hagiographic interests all combined between 1275 and 1309 to produce an important corpus of biographies, all of which resembled the genre of "Mirrors of Princes"—books of advice on how to rule well.[3] These became the touchstones for all later histories of the saintly monarch. But obsessed as they were with glorifying Louis and his royal house, they conveyed a very particular image of the king. Three of the four early biographies were written by members of the Mendicant orders to further Louis's canonization or to celebrate it. The Dominican Geoffroy de Beaulieu,[4] who had served as Saint Louis's confessor from 1250 to 1270, wrote the earliest of these laudatory accounts at the request of the pope sometime between 1272 and 1275, including in it a moving passage on Louis's second crusade and death, which he himself had witnessed. Shortly afterward, Guillaume de Chartres, the royal chaplain, produced a compilation of Louis's miracles to accompany Geoffroy's work.[5] Guillaume de Saint-Pathus, the Franciscan confessor to Louis's queen, Marguerite of Provence, wrote the third important biographical work in 1302–1303 for Louis's daughter, Blanche of France, a member of the Tertiaries.[6] He structured it around a list of Louis's virtues, and included long extracts from Saint Louis's canonization of 1297 (of which the full text has since been lost).

These three hagiographic works, which nearly attained the status of official biographies of the king, all came from the same Mendicant milieu. To them were added, in 1309, a fourth work from a very different sphere which, though the last, was certainly the most lively of all the biographies. Its author, Jean, lord of Joinville, had been seneschal of Champagne and a friend of Louis IX, and his story of a more secular and familiar Louis was shaped by changes in political attitudes during the reign of Philip the Fair.[7] Commissioned by Blanche of Navarre, Philip's wife, for the future Louis X, Joinville's account served as a kind of instruction book for the edification of the future king.

Other collections, most of them later, drew on the same sources, but they tended to be more selective. Both the *Mirror of History* of Vincent of Beauvais[8] and the *Life of Saint Louis* by Guillaume de Nangis, written around 1300 and incorporated into the *Great Chronicles*,[9] presented the official version of the life of Saint Louis, the version that Jacobus de Voragine later adopted in his widely circulated *Golden Legend*.[10] The origins and orientation of these works show that it was primarily as a spiritual ideal that Saint Louis served the last centuries of the Middle Ages. As Chancellor Gerson said in one of his great political discourses to King Charles VI and the court: "Have faith in God as did Saint Louis, bear up steadfastly under misfortune as did Saint Louis."[11] Louis was "the law and standard of good behavior"; he was "the mirror of the great," an aristocratic model of the true Christian—so royal ordinances proclaimed.[12] Books of *exempla*, sermons, and manuals for preachers all lauded him for his Christian virtues rather than for his strengths as a ruler, while their indexes listed him under "Faith," "Alms," "Blasphemy," and "Temperance," rather than under the political rubrics of "Justice" and "Good Officials," where Trajan, Philip Augustus, and Solomon appeared.[13]

SAINT LOUIS OF THE MENDICANTS

The mass of literature that the Mendicant orders produced about Saint Louis between 1275 and 1500 had a determinative effect on his official image. Louis had had strong ties to the Mendicants, whose orders were expanding rapidly during the thirteenth century because they so well served the new needs of the faithful. Franciscans, Dominicans, and Carmelites came in great numbers to the court, while members of the royal family joined their ranks in turn and asked to be buried in their convents.[14] Ambassadors and *enquêteurs* were often members of the Mendicant orders; so too were confessors and chaplains. Saint Louis lavished donations and endowments on the Mendicants; he placed the Sainte-Chapelle and its precious relics in their keeping and attended their chapter meetings; and, as did many of his contemporaries, he imitated them in his spiritual life, visiting the sick and the lepers, helping the poor, living an ascetic life. In consequence, Mendicant friars were more than willing to play an important role in his canonization.[15] Most of those who conducted the inquest and most of the witnesses belonged to the Franciscan order; after his canonization in 1297, Franciscans composed five of the six liturgies in his honor;[16] their convents became the primary centers for the diffusion of his new cult.

For this reason, Louis has come down to us through the ages as the most perfect of "mendicant saints," the very model of thirteenth-century virtue. The authors of his biographies and of the liturgies in his honor portrayed him following the path of God from the very moment of his birth, for he satisfied all their prerequisites for sainthood: his education was based on the Bible; he subordinated bodily needs to the world of the spirit; he practiced an ardent form of faith, monastic humility, and was greatly charitable toward the poor and sick; steadfast in misfortune and great in virtue, he desired to die for the faith.

Once this portrait had taken shape around 1300, the Mendicant orders began to select certain elements from it. By 1500, they had refined from the larger picture a simplified image of the saint, centered on three principal components: his hatred of sin and blasphemy, his clothing, and his role as a crusading saint.

HATRED OF SIN AND BLASPHEMY

The theme we encounter most often in the biographies of Saint Louis is his revulsion toward mortal sin, above all the sin of blasphemy. The *Alphabetical Table of Exempla*[17] attributed sayings and stories to Louis which had traditionally been associated with Blanche of Castile: the king, for example, saying to his three young sons, "He who strangles you in my presence will hurt me less than he who leads you to commit mortal sin." An imagined conversation between Saint Louis and Saint Bonaventure gives voice to the same theme: when the Angelic Doctor asks whether it is better to live in order to go to hell or not to live at all, Louis replies, "I would rather be reduced to nothingness a thousand times than live eternally in this world and indulge in royal power while offending my creator."[18] Though newly created, these exempla faithfully reflected what was known about Saint Louis's piety: it was motivated by his fear of hell.

Louis's aversion to blasphemy also gave birth to a variety of tales. An early story, told at Saint-Denis by Guillaume de Nangis,[19] showed Louis demanding that the lips of a burgher be pierced because the man had blasphemed. In reply to mutterings of opposition, Louis answered that he himself would rather have his lips pierced than commit a mortal sin as serious as blasphemy, or (in other versions) that he would give up his life if it would free his kingdom from blasphemy. The story of the pierced lips met with astonishing success, due in part to its inclusion in the work of Etienne de Bourbon.[20] It reappeared in many French sermons on blasphemy from the fourteenth through the seventeenth centuries[21] and in all the mystery plays and lives of the holy king. And it was no less popular in other countries, where (in Germany and England, for example) Louis's fear of blasphemy was often the only trait known.[22] Another version of this story probably originated in the sermons of Jacques de Vitry.[23] Here, a knight who had knocked out the teeth of a blaspheming burgher was brought before a ruler (Saint Louis in Spanish versions, a *podestà* in Italian versions), who promptly declared that his violence was justified.[24]

Though it may surprise us today to see how the Mendicants foregrounded the act of blasphemy, so inconsequential in our own world, it points clearly to the fact that blasphemy was hardly a minor offense in the Middle Ages. Until well into the fifteenth century, royal ordinances continued to forbid it—in memory of Saint Louis. Speech was to reflect the spirit and the will of God, for if it was false or blasphemous it would bring chaos and evil into the world. Behavior had to conform to a norm—the norm of Saint Louis—and the elite classes were to be the model: neither the king nor the nobles blasphemed, and they bore the responsibility of guaranteeing that the lower classes did not do so either.

The references to blasphemy are one example of how the Mendicants used Saint Louis to provide the ruling classes with a model of conformist moderation.

CLOTHING

The second theme of interest may seem at first glance to be as insignificant as blasphemy: it is the question of Saint Louis's clothes. But we must not forget that at the end of the Middle Ages appearance was an important indicator of social position. Colors and styles varied with the status and gender of the wearer, such that the inner cohesion of certain social groups as well as their worldly identity was established by what they wore. For this reason, royal clothing had progressively grown more intricate and ostentatious. After his first crusade, however, Louis had chosen to abandon the luxury of courtly fashion, hoping in this way to gain in purity, for the failure of his crusade had been attributed to the crusaders' sinfulness. From then on, Louis wore simple, plain-colored clothes and prohibited his subjects from wearing refinements such as rose bedecked hats on solemn liturgical occasions.[25]

Toward the end of the thirteenth century, this austerity gave birth to another *exemplum,* which appeared first in the sermons of Thomas de Cantimpré and remained popular throughout the Middle Ages:[26] when the squire or messenger of an anonymous prince (sometimes identified as Count Otto of Gueldre), on his way back from the Capetian court, mocked King Louis for wearing a monk's hood and a hairshirt rather than clothes worthy of his station, God grew angry and twisted the messenger's head around on his shoulders. Head-twisting was a traditional motif in popular folklore. He who offends the authority of the saints will be punished, for saints are both beneficent and terrible; and when an offender has turned the truth around, he himself will be "turned around" by God. A similar though rarer exemplum dealt with differences between the clothing of Saint Louis and Sultan Saladin II:[27] Saladin, "a pagan king" (and Louis's actual historical enemy), always wore beautiful clothes, the story went, but envied King Louis his informal and simple ways; when he died, he lost all his wealth and only his banner accompanied him to the grave. This story is a curious mixture; on the one hand, it is merely a variation on the well-worn theme that "you can't take it with you"; on the other hand, it shows how the thirteenth-century West misunderstood the differences between medieval Islamic and European funerary rites—for in Western Europe, a dead king was decorated with the material signs of royalty.

In other stories the attribution of worldly goods was reversed, and it was Louis who possessed the wealth. According to Etienne de Bourbon, when Louis fell gravely ill before his departure for the crusade, he was heard to say: "I, who was the richest and the noblest lord in the universe, cannot now pluck even one hour's respite from death." Something similar appeared at the end of the fifteenth century, when Jean Hérolt in his sermons depicted doctors telling Louis he could not be cured; Louis responded by gathering his nobles and clergy around him and saying that, though his riches were no longer of any use to him, his charitable acts might still have value in the eyes of God.[28] The story has changed a desire for life into a desire for the material things of life, but the didactic message has not changed. The English preacher John de Bromyard made a surprisingly archaic use of the same exemplum in recalling the joys of life: "I must leave the castles and the palaces I have loved so much, and go toward an unknown land."[29]

By then, however, the exemplum had become quite removed from the legend of Saint Louis, and Bromyard gave his king no name. For by the end of the Middle Ages, it was no longer possible for the bearer of Majesty to pattern his life on Saint Louis, and the theme slowly began to disappear. The university scholar Josse Clichthove,[30] for example, insisted that the king's clothing did in fact conform to the norm of royal dress: his humility was in his inner attitudes and not in his attitudes toward others. To the sixteenth century, royal moderation in dress seemed either heroic or unimaginable.

For the Mendicants, stories about clothing were a very concrete way to introduce the virtue of poverty—a virtue whose exact demands were hotly debated even within their own ranks. Saint Louis embodied the moderate position: his clothes were humble but not too humble, just as the Friars Minor were allowed few material goods but could legitimately possess those. Moderate poverty, they said, freed their time and energies for singing and for giving alms to the poor.[31] (It is interesting to note however that Mendicant writers rarely depicted Saint Louis's charity toward the poor and sick.) In general, the Mendicant evocation of

Louis's clothing complemented the theme of blasphemy: as a model of recommended behavior, Louis's simple dress was one of traditional moderation.

THE CRUSADER

The third topic that the Mendicant sermons popularized had to do with the Crusades, and it was here that a number of fantastic and extraordinary stories entered the legend of Saint Louis.

Before Louis departed on crusade, it was said, he had a vision of the defeat of the Christians at Chorasmini; he saw the Saracens throw the Christians into the sea and a voice came to him: "King of France, take revenge for this irreparable loss."[32] This vision paralleled that of the legendary Charlemagne before his own expedition to the Holy Land. The impact of this vision was powerful; at the end of the fifteenth century a confraternity manual, the poet Pierre Gringoire in his *Life of Saint Louis,* and the Venetian chronicler Marino Sanudo all referred to it.[33] In other stories, the news of Louis's crusade and capture came miraculously to holy men, especially, of course, to Franciscans. Thomas de Cantimpré saw a luminous cross set against the backdrop of a clear sky.[34] Etienne de Bourbon reported nocturnal images of recriminating demons, who alerted knights waiting to accompany Louis of the king's impending departure.[35] Boniface, bishop of Lausanne, heard while deep in prayer a voice that spoke of Louis's defeat, his capture, and the size of his losses.[36] A yet later story told how God himself sent word of the disaster to Gerard, a relative of John of Parma (Franciscan minister-general from 1247 to 1257). This particular affirmation of hierarchical propriety dates from the seventeenth century![37]

By contrast, news of Louis's death came only once via this kind of miraculous manifestation: the late-thirteenth-century *Great Chronicle of Limoges* reported that a blood-red sun and four days of darkness followed Louis's death abroad.[38] Perhaps the story of Louis's demise inspired French popular imagination less than did his imprisonment.

Another legend, which spread among the Fraticelli in early fourteenth-century Italy, placed Saint Louis in the Holy Land for the mystical number of seven years, leading a very private life, as Jesus had before his public ministry began, and visiting the great holy sanctuaries of Christianity. There the king engaged as well in silent, mystic conversation with Brother Gilles of Assisi, one of Saint Francis's companions.[39] A representation of this scene existed in the church of San Francesco in Perugia in

1500. The story showed up in France around 1400 and in England and Germany at the end of the fifteenth century.[40]

These legends also showed Louis adopting new forms of lay devotion during this voyage to the East: using the psalm-book and venerating the Holy Sacrament. Joinville reported that while Louis was being held captive he was greatly dismayed to discover that his psalm-book had disappeared,[41] a tale that Guillaume de Chartres turned into the story of a miracle.[42] As the story went, a monk was sitting with Louis in the room where he was being held prisoner, and the king told him how sorry he was not to be able to say his prayers at the canonical hours; miraculously, at this moment, someone appeared to return the psalm-book that had been in the baggage that the Saracens had captured. Boniface VIII in his canonization sermon of 1297 called this "the most beautiful of all the miracles that occurred during Louis's captivity."[43] All the liturgies of Saint Louis devoted a lesson to it,[44] and during the fifteenth and sixteenth centuries it became the theme of a popular exemplum and of many pictures, especially in Burgundy and Brittany.[45] The story had many variants: in the early fourteenth century, for example, Guillaume Guiart added an angel who interceded on Louis's behalf;[46] from then on, the angel was a required motif in all the lives of Saint Louis. Not surprisingly, by the end of the Middle Ages, King Louis's psalm-book had become the most famous relic housed at the Franciscan convent of Saint-Marcel in Paris. In 1500, the book of the confraternity of dry-good merchants of Paris interpreted the miracle of the psalm-book to mean that "Our Heavenly Father was anxious not to lose the regular devotion of his loyal servant."[47]

Louis also became a precursor of devotion to the Host of the Sacrament. His devotion to the cross and the body of Christ is, in fact, historically documented, and he needed no miracle to help him believe in the real presence of Christ in the sacramental bread and wine: he saw Him constantly in his heart. But legend rapidly embellished this devotion. The Florentine chronicler Giovani Villani and others referred to "a great miracle of the body of Christ in the heart of Paris":[48] at the moment when the Host was raised during mass in the chapel of the royal palace, a beautiful young child appeared. Fourteenth- and fifteenth-century writers emphasized the Host on board the ship that brought the saint back from the crusades: because Louis prayed to the Host, the ship was saved from shipwreck.[49] In Italy, the story was told of how Louis gave the reliquary of the Host to the sultan as security for his ransom.[50] The spread of these stories was the direct result of the growing liturgical practice of elevating the Host for adoration—a practice that in the thirteenth century had been a special privilege granted by the popes to crusading kings.[51]

This theme, then, encircled the image of Louis with the miraculous aura of the crusades. Further accounts added a few divinely inspired conversions: one Saracen converted by Louis was martyred for refusing to renounce his new faith;[52] several pagans were punished for insulting the cross. But none of these details were specific to the story of Saint Louis. Far more interesting was the way his death was presented in some rare accounts as a kind of martyrdom. Louis, the righteous victim, submitted patiently to his tormentors and in the end sacrificed his life for God.

SAINT LOUIS OF THE CARMELITES AND DOMINICANS

Thus far, we have looked at the Mendicant image of Saint Louis as a single entity. This image is primarily Franciscan, for the greatest number of books of exempla and sermons in which Louis appears are of Franciscan origin, whether French, English, or Italian. But there was also a specifically Carmelite Saint Louis, who in turn differed significantly from the Dominican Saint Louis, who we will look at in a moment.

The Carmelite order originated in Italy and came to France during the reign of King Louis, their benefactor. Already in 1280, Guillaume de Sanvico in his *Book on the Origins and Progress of the Carmelite Order*[53] had told the story of how Louis set off for Palestine, how the royal ship was carried by the wind to Mount Carmel—where a monastery had been built on the spot where Elijah had had his divine revelation—and how, because the king was received so well by the Carmelite brothers, he promised to help spread the order on his return. So he took a number of Carmelites back to Paris with him, where he established a convent for them. According to another story, Carmelite prayers protected Louis from shipwreck, and a miraculous fountain quenched the thirst of his army.[54]

The Carmelites, who wore a scapular, took Thomas de Cantimpré's description of Saint Louis's cowl and hairshirt and replaced the hairshirt with a scapular, evidently using it to justify their own practice.[55] Later, in the seventeenth century, Carmelite brothers employed the same argument to justify their inclusion of Louis in the ranks of their order.[56] Louis, however, was hardly one of the order's favorite saints. They only began to celebrate his cult in 1306, and they never instituted a major feastday in his name. Despite the existence of a Dominican liturgy of Saint Louis as well as three from the Franciscans, we do not know of a single Carmelite liturgy dedicated to him. The Carmelites limited themselves to demonstrating that in the frequent contacts Louis had with the order, he showed that he shared their spiritual concerns. It is particularly noteworthy, though the example is a localized one, that Carmelites in Brittany during the second half of the fifteenth century decided to throw their support to cults connected to the ducal families.[57] It was not the Carmelites but the Franciscans who nurtured francophile cults during this period—like the cult of Charles de Blois or the cult of Saint Louis—which may explain why French Carmelite texts had little to say about Louis.

As for the Dominicans, a number of writers from that order claimed that Saint Louis was born through the intervention of Saint Dominic. Ignoring the fact that Louis IX was not the first son of Blanche of Castille and Louis VIII, they told a story of how Dominic had advised the queen to recite the rosary because she was distraught at not having given birth to a successor to the throne.[58] Other Dominican accounts claimed that Louis had important ties to great thirteenth-century theologians of the order, even though (aside from his exchanges with Vincent of Beauvais) Louis apparently never frequented any of the masters of the order, not even Thomas Aquinas, who was teaching in Paris from 1253 to 1274.

Nonetheless, there were three exempla that claimed various associations of the king with Aquinas. One presented Aquinas as a frequent guest at the royal table, where one day, deep in thought, he suddenly hit on a way to counter the Manicheans; at this, he began to pound his fist on the table and King Louis, showing not the least sign of irritation, asked a clerk to take note of his argument.[59] (The story seems to have been designed to inspire kings and nobles to respect the university.) A second exemplum settled for a more distant connection, portraying a Louis who knew how to read and savor the texts of Saint Thomas, a person who indeed was better acquainted with them than anyone else. When a preacher in the story claims during a sermon on the passion of Christ that all candles should be extinguished in observance of Good Friday— because all the apostles had abandoned Christ on that day— Louis responds to the objections of those in attendance by sending for Aquinas's *Commentary on the Gospel of John,* where he finds support for the preacher's assertion.[60] The third exemplum was particularly unhindered by chronological veracity, as it turned Thomas into Louis's tutor.[61]

Dominican portraits were most original in the detailed way they presented Louis's connections with learned culture. The liturgies from the early fourteenth century, that of the Dominicans included, remained rather vague on the subject, going no further than to say that Louis's mother and Mendicant tutors gave him instruction "in the science of letters."[62] At the end of the fifteenth century, however, the question of Louis's education became far more important; it appeared in the Mystery and in the stained-glass windows of Champigny-sur-Veude.[63] Louis was now the perfect student not only of his mother but also of the Dominican scholars as well, and some even went so far as to describe him as a learned philosopher.[64]

The Dominicans also emphasized Louis's relations with the university, relations that were real enough. They presented the king as the protector of the Univeristy of Paris: "Louis created peace between the bourgeois and the masters and worked so hard at it that the parties aforesaid stayed on and set themselves to reading again, and the king arranged for the clergy and the knights to spend all their time together and in his company."[65] Louis, they said, had books of liturgy copied, and he criticized those who owned beautiful books but did not read them.[66]

Mendicant imagery was so powerful and so pervasive that Saint Louis was eventually identified with them. Italians in particular made him a secret member of the Carmelites,[67] or the Dominicans,[68] or most often, the Franciscans. Louis's contemporaries often blamed him for being "the king of monks."[69] Monastic life, with its virtues of humility, charity, and chastity, heightened numbers of masses and prayers, and sermons (both as listener and preacher) all attracted him. Yet, texts of his own day made no mention of any affiliation with the orders, nor did Louis's confessors or his Mendicant biographers, nor did the canonization process; nor, finally, did the papal bull of canonization. Only Richer de Senones's monastic *Chronicle*, dating from sometime before 1264, reported that Louis planned to become a monk: according to Richer, a Dominican had managed to seduce Louis into entering the order but, under the influence of the queen and his counselors, the king had eventually changed his mind.[70] Thomas de Cantimpré's story of Louis's cowl and hairshirt could lend itself to a similar interpretation.[71]

Most likely the legend of Louis's affiliation with a Mendicant order originated in the Angevin court at Naples in the latter half of the thirteenth century.[72] The papacy had set up the Angevin princes, the brothers, nephews, and grand-nephews of the Capetian kings of France, on

Italian territory, a move supported by the Franciscans, who chose two Louises as their dynastic saints—Louis, king of France, and Louis of Anjou, the son of Charles II, a Franciscan who eventually became the bishop of Toulouse.

Louis of Anjou had refused the throne and died at a young age in 1299. His canonization review began in 1306 and Pope John XXII officially proclaimed his sainthood at Avignon in 1317. Primary cult sites were dedicated to him in the Mendicant convents in southern Italy and in Provence—at Brignoles, Aix, and at his tomb in Marseille, which became a popular pilgrimage site for many believers, especially on August 19, his feastday. But confusion between the two was inevitable, for Louis of Anjou and Louis IX bore the same name, were canonized about the same time, came from the same lineage, and their feastdays fell only a week apart.

The confusion was heightened by the Angevin habit of portraying the two figures side by side on official monuments, so that gradually their images began to resemble each other; Louis of Anjou, who had given up the throne, appeared with a crown under his feet, in his hands, or beneath his miter, and his bishop's mantle was often decorated with lilies. King Louis wore the robe and corded belt of the Third Order—the clothes that Louis of Anjou had worn beneath his bishop's robe. Around 1330, Giotto depicted the two figures this way in the Bardi Chapel in the church of Santa Croce in Florence. (The donor, Ricardo Bardi, was a banker who represented Angevin interests in Florence.) Coupled images of the two figures, increasingly popular, began to spread gradually through northern Italy: at Montefalco, Benozzo Gozzoli painted King Louis with the corded belt of the Third Order, standing alongside Bishop Louis; Carpaccio painted the same image on the walls of the Accademia in Venice. During the Renaissance, though the wave of popularity lessened, the doubled image earned official sanction: in 1547, Paul IV officially enregistered Saint Louis in the Franciscan Third Order and, around 1550, the order's liturgy affirmed that "Louis joined himself with Saint Francis so that he might be led along the path of penitence."[73]

In France, however, this assimilation did not occur. Louis of Anjou, to be sure, was honored there—particularly in Toulouse, where he had served as bishop and in the Angevin patrimony of Bar, Lorraine, and Anjou; but the primary sites of his cult remained outside the borders of the kingdom until 1483. French kings were devoted to Louis of Anjou in part because of their alliances with Angevin princesses (Clemence of

Hungary was the wife of Charles IV, and Marie of Anjou was the wife of Charles VII) but also in part because they had an eye on the city of Marseille as a port from which they could launch a crusading expedition. Philip VI visited Bishop Louis's tomb in 1330 and again in 1336; John II went there in 1362; Marie of Anjou in 1443; and the future King Louis XI in 1447.[74] But since citizens of the kingdom considered this Louis a saint of the House of Anjou rather than of the House of France, few representations outside the Angevin territories depicted him in the company of King Louis. It also seems to have been unpopular to depict King Louis dressed as a Franciscan, bearded and wearing the corded belt of the Third Order: this type of representation appeared only rarely in France and only at the end of the Middle Ages.[75]

These late-thirteenth-century Mendicant images of Saint Louis obviously had both advantages and drawbacks.

They presented a threefold portrait of the king as a spiritual model for nobles to emulate. Louis taught that one should not blaspheme, should avoid ostentation and be generous with alms, and should fight in the crusades; all who did so would gain salvation. As these images proliferated and gained increasing popularity they contributed greatly to the growing prestige of the Capetian house; during the reigns of Philip III and Philip the Fair, Louis steadily developed into the saint who best filled the new needs of the monarchy, needs for which Saint Denis was ill-suited. Ordinances issued prior to 1315 on Jewry, blasphemy, and coinage automatically contained references to him; and Jean Favier has well demonstrated how the policies of Philip IV which led to the rupture in his relations with the pope were a logical extension of Louis's religious policy.[76] In consequence, the royal house did its best to stimulate the growth of the cult of their prized ancestor. They founded an abbey in the town of Poissy, where Louis was born; they arranged solemn ceremonies around the translation of the saint's head from Saint-Denis to the Sainte-Chapelle; they arranged to have a new liturgical service composed. Altars and chapels dedicated to him multiplied rapidly in places like Joinville and Maineville, where, at the request of Enguerran de Marigny, the sculptor made the statue of Louis look like Philip the Fair.[77] Pilgrims poured into the abbey of Saint-Denis, the Sainte-Chapelle, the abbey of Poissy, and the house of the Dominicans at Evreux. Miracles flourished at all of them.

But these images were nonetheless incomplete in one important way: they had no political statements to make, nor did those of the *Great Chronicles* which came in their wake. They offered no coherent account of the king's political accomplishments. For Guillaume de Saint-Pathus, "justice" was only seventeenth in the list of Louis's virtues.[78] He is silent on the peace Louis had achieved in the course of his reign, on his policy toward England, his restrictions on feuds and vendettas, his prohibition of dueling, and his relations with the papacy. Mendicant sermons also did not deal with the problems of the material and financial failure of Louis's two crusades. But how could the guardian of a nation already conscious of its own identity be more of a saint than a king? We may wonder if the Mendicants thought of such things. Perhaps their awareness came too late, only at the beginning of the fourteenth century, by which time they could only follow in the wake of a political movement led by the nobility, one in which they no longer had an important role. By then the Saint Louis of the nobility had succeeded to the Saint Louis of the friars.

For though the royal house possessed the archives necessary to create a coherent political assessment of Louis's reign, they left the task to others; and it was Joinville who began the politicization of Saint Louis in the interpretive memoir that he dictated around 1309. A Saint Louis dear to the nobles would dominate the perceptions of the generation 1310–1330.

SAINT LOUIS OF THE NOBILITY

During the reign of Philip the Fair, Saint Louis became the official patron saint of the royal house; its apologists referred to the "House of Saint Louis" and the "Crown of Saint Louis." On many matters King Philip drew his inspiration from his grandfather's policies. In the Great Ordinance of 1303, which reformed the organization and practices of royal officials, Louis's methods were a constant point of reference. Clerics and nobles no longer remembered that noble barons had once conspired against Louis, or that popes had had troubles in their relations with him. Public opinion now held that Saint Louis had been the protector of the nobility and the Church, a vision that Joinville expressed in his widely read *History of Saint Louis*.

This vision of Louis was also colored by recollections—some vague, others accurate—of the Ordinance of 1254,[79] which many now lauded: "The kingdom was greatly improved through this ordinance," said Joinville.[80] Even the mystery plays and the lives of Saint Louis at the end of the fifteenth century gave faithful summaries of it.[81]

Another text that helped memorialize the political policies of Louis

IX was the *Teachings* of Louis to his son Philip, written in 1267–1268.[82] This text was eventually incorporated into other works in French and Latin, including those of Guillaume de Saint-Pathus, Yves de Saint-Denis, Guillaume de Nangis, Joinville, and the *Great Chronicles*. Joinville inserted a series of interpolations into his version of the text, pious frauds composed in the reign of Philip the Fair, which bear particularly telling witness to the new political concerns of the time; they omitted all references to the deference the king owed to the pope and added a commentary on Louis's respect for local, provincial, and noble rights. They also mentioned Louis's acceptance of restrictions on taxation, other than "in dire necessity." Joinville's version of the *Teachings* was so popular that the manuscripts of the *Great Chronicles* commonly mistook it for the authentic text of Louis himself.

Beginning with the noble leagues of 1314–1316, Louis served as the guardian of a nobility that was increasingly menaced by the growing authority of the monarchy. The movement of revolt—in which Joinville participated—proclaimed Louis their hero.[83] The nobility's political agenda of "reform"—expressed in petitions of grievances, in royal ordinances, in the *Metrical Chronicle* of Geoffroy de Paris,[84] in the satirical *Roman de Fauvel*[85]—called for changes in fiscal policy, the reinstatement of older judicial practices, the right to wage private war, and guarantees of sound coinage, and always in the form of a return to the ways of Saint Louis.

In this way, Louis's reign became a political myth that had little to do with the realities of his rule. The image that prevailed from 1300 to 1340 caused the monarchy considerable embarrassment, and it was not until after 1340, when the nobles had been defeated and dishonored by the English, when they had stopped their contestatory tactics and begun to seek the support of the monarchy to preserve a place for themselves in the social order, that the power of this myth of Saint Louis began to wane.

Let us examine some of its main features.

SOUND COINAGE

To the nobility, Saint Louis stood above all for sound coinage and fiscal freedom; he was a ruler who had lived "of his own"—on the resources of his own lands and rights—and taken nothing from his subjects. At the end of the thirteenth century, however, due in part to wars, the burden of royal financial obligations greatly increased. To meet those obligations, two solutions were possible: either the king could devalue the coinage or he could raise taxes. Devaluation and tax levies were two different ways of arriving at the same end, but changing the value of money represented the more subtle and acceptable tactic, for coinage was the privileged domain of the kings. Philip the Fair often resorted to it, and his descendants alternated back and forth between devaluation and tax levy. As for Louis himself, despite the fact that taxes increased markedly during his reign while coinage remained stable,[86] legend turned the tale around and described his reign rosily as a blessed conjunction of solid money and fiscal freedom.

Let us first consider the question of sound coinage—primarily of the silver denier and gros that were struck from 1266 onward. (Since gold coinage was not used in everyday transactions, the times Saint Louis issued this type of money have left little impression.)

The nobility and clergy, who lived on fixed incomes vulnerable to devaluation, obviously had good reason to support the reputation of Louis's coinage[87] and, as early as 1295, they began to give it a special value, to hoard Louis's coins, leaving the weaker new issues in circulation. The weight and alloy of Louis's silver coins was considered "the true value and the true condition of the coinage," the one that was most just and conformed to God's plan for things. The first formulations of this idea appeared in grievances that the nobility put forth at the end of the reign of Philip the Fair. The roll of grievances from the bailliages of Amiens and Vermandois, for example, called for a return to the "good money of the king's predecessors."[88] Charters issued to the Burgundians, to the nobles of Champagne, and to the nobles of Berry promised a return to it.[89] Other sectors of the population whose investment in the strength of coinage was less evident were equally attached to it. As early as 1302–1303, devaluation gave rise to generalized discontent: "Philip the Fair was a counterfeiter . . . whose money was worth only a third its proper value, and for this he was castigated and cursed by all Christians," the Florentine chronicler Giovanni Villani later recorded.[90]

Continual devaluation, of course, was not possible and, when tax revenues did come in, it was preferable to return to strong money. Whenever the monarchy revalued coinage, it made use of the opportunity to remind people of Saint Louis's good money; in fact, royal ordinances remained faithful to the coinage of Louis for nearly a half century, from 1295 to 1343. This practice of referring to the money of Saint Louis began in 1295[91] and reappeared every time Philip the Fair altered his coinage between 1303 and 1310. Three ordinances on coinage in 1314 and 1315 bore traces of the Leagues[92] and, after the assemblies of 1329 and 1332, a brief return to strong money produced renewed references to Saint Louis.[93] But in 1343 an attempt to return to the "situation as it was under Saint Louis" had catastrophic consequences for the common folk; prices went up, and debts had to be paid back in strong money. After this, the monarchy resigned itself to allowing coinage to stabilize at a level lower than where it had stood in the thirteenth century, and though nostalgia for sound money continued, economists, politicians, and royal ordinances no longer referred to the good money of Saint Louis.

Yet for a half century, this was the aspect of Saint Louis's policies which ordinances pointed to most frequently; there were fifteen references to the "good money of Saint Louis" and only four to Louis's prohibitions on usury, five to his expulsion of Jews, three to his prohibiton of private war, and three to his prohibition of blasphemy. Aside from the occasional recollection of one of Louis's moralizing measures, coinage was the only aspect of his governance that remained an ongoing concern through the middle of the fourteenth century.[94]

Once the theme of Louis's coinage was taken out of the arena of concrete political activity, it became more and more fictionalized. At the end of the thirteenth century, the popular mind had already tied it to Louis's return from the first crusade and his ransom: Saint Louis had minted "a coin on one side of which appeared the chains of his imprisonment to commemorate this disastrous time, so that one day either he or his descendants would take revenge," said Villani.[95] The liturgy of 1298 onward already asserted that the ransom had been miraculously small: "Who could fail to see the miracle, that a savage people liberated him for such a modest ransom?"[96] A Benedictine liturgy from the first half of the fifteenth century was explicit: "Having been taken captive by misfortune, he was freed by a miracle."[97] The ransom actually amounted to 200,000 livres parisis, the equivalent of one year's royal revenues, which was hardly a negligible sum. But after the capture of John the Good at Poitiers in 1356 and the extraordinary size of his ransom, the ransom of Saint Louis appeared quite modest: "And it was only 8,000 besants of Saracen gold, not at all like the ransom for King John," wrote Etienne Leblanc at the beginning of the sixteenth century.[98]

A sum less than what the Saracens might have asked for was finally transformed through myth into something smaller still, until it became almost nothing at all. At the end of the fifteenth century the story was told that Charles of Anjou, Louis's brother, had asked the abbot of

Saint-Denis for a gold crucifix that a king of France had once given the abbey; the crucifix was to be melted down to make the coin for Louis's ransom. But when the minter had turned an arm of the crucifix into the besants needed to pay the Saracens and taken his own costs and profit, he discovered that enough gold was left to reconstruct the missing arm of the cross. And so the ransom was paid "without any other toil from the king's people."[99]

People soon began to use the good coins minted at the time of the ransom—coins that bore the pious inscription of "Blessed be the name of the Lord," with a cross set against ovals of fleurs-de-lys and Louis's prison chains—as amulets, for the inscription seemed to them to imply that the king had gone to prison for the sake of the cross. After Louis's canonization in 1297, mementos like these, readily available and easily carried, became enormously popular. Even as late as the seventeenth century, people continued to use them as talismans to ward off fever: Arthur du Monstier, a monk at the convent at Meaux, told how he had discovered a large tournois in the convent garden, which saved him after twenty-two days of fever.[100] "These coins are kept to this very day and used against fevers," reported Claude Menard, another seventeenth-century author.[101] Old people, he added, venerated these coins in a way that was not superstitious, for they did so in remembrance of the king-saint and of the crusaders who had died for their faith.

Though fictions surrounding Louis's money continued to flourish from the fourteenth to the the seventeenth century, enhancing the positive aura around the king, the populace of Paris seemed divided on the question. The story had a noble air about it that led some to reject it; common folk,[102] artisans, the poor, and women—all scorned and closed out of learned culture—were wary of it. And indeed it was surely illogical to mint new coins immediately on the heels of a financial disaster. To answer this doubt, both the liturgies and official policy of the time cleared Louis's name by lowering the ransom figure. But some among the people held Louis responsible nonetheless for minting bad money and inventing new taxes, such as the *tiers et dangier* on wood and even the infamous *gabelle,* the salt tax.[103]

Sometime after 1356, probably toward the end of the century, Saint Louis's "leather money" entered the picture, through a story that three of the extant texts on the subject tell in particularly interesting fashion. The first, a chronicle written in 1409, probably in the merchant milieu of Paris, tells how Louis had leather money made to pay his ransom because the kingdom was destitute.[104] The second, a history manual written around 1423 in Paris or Soisson whose political viewpoint is rather ambiguous (the author's sympathies are with the Navarrais and the English at Agincourt, but he criticizes the Burgundians for their excesses in 1418), recounts that "for ransom money, Louis circulated leather money."[105] The third text, from the beginning of the sixteenth century, was the work of Etienne Leblanc, secretary to Louise of Savoy; it bears the title *Demonstration that Saint Louis Did Not Destroy the Kingdom.*[106] Leblanc aimed one of his main criticisms at the myth of Louis's leather money: "No one has meant to suggest that Saint Louis impoverished the kingdom through his journey to the Holy Land because of his ransom. If the kingdom was so poor and so underpopulated that leather money had to be made, he would not have established a number of famous churches, nor returned to the Holy Land; the supposed money would have been of no use to him, for it has no exchange value here." Leblanc simply blamed Emperor Frederick II for this shameful deed.

Why did such a far-fetched tale—so far removed from reality—develop? Perhaps certain sermons[107] had taught attentive listeners that, according to Aristotle, the first method of exchange after the age of barter was based on livestock, that this is what preceded metal coinage; and learned etymologists of the time derived the word *pecunia* (money) from *pecus* (livestock). After his defeat, Louis might well have taken the step backward from minting to livestock exchange. After all, Pope Pius II (1458-1464) told the story that when Milan had risen in revolt against an Ottonian emperor, they had rejected his coins; as a punishment, when the town was taken, they were forced to use ancient leather money.[108] Perhaps people were no longer able to conceive of exchanges that did not involve money and therefore they simply began to believe that the money must have been made from some other material. Confusion might also have stemmed from the limited understanding listeners must have had of the Latin liturgical sequences dedicated to Saint Louis. They may have transformed *moneta cudi* (to mint coins) into *moneta cutis* (leather coins), or *moneta bove* (chain coins) into *moneta bovis* (leather coins), mistaking the rare word *boia* or *bove* (chain) for the more common *bos/bovis* (cow, leather). The Florentine chronicler Villani tells us Saint Louis's gros were called chain coins (moneta bove), a usage that remained current through the seventeenth century.[109] Or perhaps people remembered the cheap metal tokens that Louis's Parisian administration had used as aids to calculation and mistook the worthless tokens for real money.

What is particularly interesting about the legend of Louis's leather
money, regardless of the elusiveness of its sources, is that it clearly
contradicted what thirteenth-century historical works and royal ordinances had to say, as well as the propaganda spread abroad by the
nobility in the first half of the fourteenth century. Apparently in the
popular strata of Paris, where written culture was rare, people harbored
a considerable ambivalence toward Louis IX, which contrasted sharply
with the enthusiasms of the nobility and the prudent, political maneuver-
ing of the royal house.

FISCAL FREEDOMS

To the monarchy taxes were a second useful way to fill the coffers of
state and, early in the Hundred Years War, its levies became heavier and
more frequent as more and more military men had to be paid. In the
period from 1340 to 1360, cries of "fiscal liberty" supplanted those of
"good money." As the ruling house grew more imaginative, it created
more varied sources of "exceptional revenues"—tithes, forced loans
and gifts, salt taxes, and subsidies to finance the war and administrative
growth, all sustained by propaganda that asserted that a king who was
willing to wage war for his people should be helped by them in return.
The basic lines of this argument were assembled in the entourage of
Philip the Fair and widely broadcast during the first decade of the war.
Then the ransom for John II made taxation a way of life.

But the new taxpayers—most of whom did not hand over their
money willingly—began to look for ideological reasons to resist. They
found them principally in the reign of Saint Louis; and because the
nobility had been saddled with taxes from the end of the thirteenth
century to the reign of Charles V, fiscal freedom and limitations on
taxes were policies on which, for once, they could all agree.[110]

The historical vision that justified their resistance was simple: the
Franks had fought to ensure this freedom since the earliest days of the
nation; they refused to pay tribute to the Romans, to Charlemagne, and
to the Emperor Otto,[111] and the freedoms they managed to win by dint
of sword were respected by the highest authorities from Charlemagne to
Saint Louis. The disappearance of this privilege under Louis's successors
was thus a direct violation of the ancient rights and customs of the
country.

Such was the argument that emerged during the rule of Philip the
Fair. Joinville stressed the importance of fiscal freedom in his version of

the *Teachings of Saint Louis*,[112] and Geoffroy de Paris in his *Metrical Chronicle* set forth a comparison between Saint Louis and his son Philip III on the one hand and Philip IV on the other, a comparison that was harshly critical of the latter. Louis and his son, said Geoffroy, despite all their expeditions "took nothing, stole nothing, and seized nothing from their subjects," whereas Philip IV "levied so many taxes, carried so much off, that he will never be absolved." And he concluded:

> Ou nous serons tous francs en France
> Ou il viendra meschéance.[113]
>
> [Either we will all be free in France
> Or it is misfortune that will reign.]

The satirist Gervais du Bus expressed similar views in his *Roman de Fauvel* (1310–1316), when he described a Saint Louis who favored the freedom "of the beautiful garden of sweet France" (thus softening his allusion to a Saint Louis who promoted hostile designs against the Templars).[114]

Ordinances from the period of the noble leagues of 1314–1316[115] called for a return to the fiscal practices of Saint Louis, the reduction of customs and taxes to earlier levels, and the temporary suspension of all exceptional levies. The Norman charter was insistent: "Only the old taxes are to be collected, as they used to be in the time of King Louis."[116]

From 1316 to 1356, Saint Louis continued to be associated with the idea of fiscal freedom and local liberties, though with decreasing frequency. During the periods of unrest following Crécy and Poitiers the Estates of Languedoc drew attention directly to "the statutes of Saint Louis" when they resisted royal demands for money.[117] The need for reform in the kingdom—above all, fiscal reform—remained firmly implanted in peoples' minds;[118] singers nostalgically recalled the freedom of those who were happy though poor when there were no taxes to pay.[119] People criticized the rate of taxation and dreamed of returning to the thirteenth century, to the stability of its governments and the modesty of its taxes. At the beginning of the fourteenth century, the poet Jean Dupin lamented "that now the prince of hell has seized the city of Good Freedom, renamed it Unhappy Servitude, and broken its customs." But Dupin thought God would take revenge for these injustices: "He who seizes another will be punished in hell. He who takes from his subjects taxes that are too great, without considering the capacity of men, is a murderer, for he has taken the life away from the poor man and his children."[120] Guillaume de Machaut—musician, reformer, and member of the entourage of the king of Bohemia and of the future King John II—called this sorry state "being skinned alive." Louis IX, in contrast, he celebrated:

> Il y eut jadis un roi en France
> Homme vaillant, de grande puissance,
> Qui ne fut prenant ne louis,
> Mais véquit ades justement . . ."[121]

> [Once there was a king in France
> A valiant man, of very great force,
> Who was neither venal nor rapacious,
> and lived always justly . . .]

But when the crisis arrived in 1356–1358, Saint Louis was forgotten. Neither the Paris bourgeoisie when they demanded control of tax rates and collection by the Estates, nor Etienne Marcel, the provost of merchants, paid any attention to him. Saint Louis seemed destined to be forgotten as long as he was connected to freedom from taxes, for that freedom—except for the nobility—was illusory. One of the last sparks of Louis's influence in this domain flickered over Charles V's deathbed, when in his last moments the king abolished the hearth tax.[122]

It was not until the final decades of the fifteenth century that Louis as protector of fiscal liberties reappeared. Francisque Michel's *Mystery of Saint Louis* and Pierre Gringoire's *Life of Saint Louis* made tax limits the chief theme of Louis's Great Ordinance of 1254:

> Je veux, si plaît au roi divin
> Mauvaises coutumes mettre à fin
> Comme tailles, exactions
> Gabelles, impositions
> Que plus cette chose n'abonde . . .
> Que notre peuple ne soit point
> Mangé ne défoulé sous nous.[123]

> [I would like, if it please the heavenly king
> To abolish the bad customs
> Like *tailles*, exactions
> Salt taxes, imposts
> So that these thing no longer abound . . .
> So that our people are neither
> Devoured nor trampled beneath us.]

But by then it was no longer possible for taxation to disappear entirely. So Saint Louis became the symbol of moderate taxation and especially of specific exemptions such as that of the noble estate or those of localities he had founded or endowed.

Of the first the *Moralized Chess*[124] of Jacques de Cessoles is about our only witness, for noble exemptions had come into existence slowly, by custom rather than by statute, tied to the nobles' service in war, and few texts speak of it. Cessoles declared that knights and nobility were the only ones that Louis freed of these fiscal burdens, whereas the common people had the responsibility of feeding them and paying taxes. At the same time, however, Cessoles criticized the weight of taxation. The silence of other texts seems to cover a generalized belief that under the rule of Saint Louis nobles had not paid taxes and that they alone retained their old freedom. The word *franc* (free) began to take on the meaning "free from taxes" and, by the fifteenth century, had become a synonym for noble.

Of the second, the case of Neuville-les-Hez, a village in the county of Clermont-en-Beauvaisis, is instructive. In 1468 and again in 1475, Neuville's inhabitants announced that it was in their own town that Louis IX had been born, not in Poissy, where he had only been baptized. Furthermore, they said that Louis had exempted both towns from taxes as an expression of his gratitude.[125] Since the royal chancery raised no objections to their claims, the reigning king, Louis XI, had no choice but to reinstitute the "well-deserved exemptions." The era evidently still saw Saint Louis as the embodiment of fiscal freedom, both specific and general.

But it was the deputies of the Third Estate at the meeting of the Estates of 1484 who made the most original use of the legend of Saint Louis. The Estates had been summoned following the death of Louis XI, in the hope that they would refill the empty coffers of state.[126] They replied to the demands of the new king with the assertion that, "in accordance with the natural freedom of France and the doctrine of king Saint Louis—who in his instructions to his son ordered him neither to establish nor collect taxes from his people unless it was absolutely necessary—no such taxes should be instituted or required without first assembling the three estates and explaining the reasoning and needs of the king and kingdom, and without obtaining the consent of said estates, while respecting the privileges accorded to all regions." The reference to Louis's instructions directly followed Joinville and the league program of 1314–1316, but the Third Estate now transformed Saint Louis into the patron of a parliamentary monarchy, a government respectful of local rights and closely resembling the English system. Consequently, by the beginning of the sixteenth century, Josse Clichtove was able to hold that Saint Louis's government had been a model of moderate monarchy.[127]

Thus from 1314 to the very end of the Middle Ages, Saint Louis's associations with fiscal policy proved more cumbersome than useful to the ruling house. The myth of Louis's fiscal freedoms, which the nobles of the first half of the fourteenth century had launched in their call for reform, buried the realities of the king's historical fiscal policy, which had not in fact been very different from that of Philip the Fair. But Louis had become a kind of "anti–Philip the Fair." Though rulers could invoke his name any time they strengthened the value of the coinage or cut taxes, they did not have complete control over the force of the saintly image, and that lack of control could only pose a threat. As far as fiscal policy was concerned, the Saint Louis of the nobility triumphed over the Saint Louis of kings.

JUSTICE

Alongside the Louis of solid coinage and fiscal freedom, Joinville and later reformers also created Louis the Just, a ruler who surrounded himself with good officials and never leased offices for money. This Louis was less embarrassing to the monarchy than the Louis of fiscal freedom, for royal justice with its implied guarantees satisfied the public more than seignorial or church courts of justice.

The justice of Saint Louis appeared in a number of anecdotes in sermons and in Joinville. Three were particularly popular. The most famous was the story of Enguerran de Coucy, who had three Flemish noble youths hanged for poaching hare on his land. Saint Louis was unmoved by the lineage of the murderous Coucy and charged him to pay a large fine and go off to the Holy Land. Every life of Saint Louis devoted at least one chapter or book to this episode; it appeared in the *Mystery of Saint Louis* and the books of confraternity. It was one of the best loved of the many picturesque and moving anecdotes involving the king.[128] Another was the tale of Etienne Boileau, Louis's provost in Paris, who, unswayed by ties of kinship, condemned his nephew to death for the many misdeeds he had committed.[129] Guillaume de Chartres devoted the entire sixth book of his *Life of Saint Louis* to it, recounting in detail the execution and the despair of the nephew's mother. The third exemplum embodied the theme "be just at all times." Saint Louis was depicted here reading his psalm book on Good Friday when he was asked to pardon a criminal. As his finger fell on a passage in the book which said, "Be just at all times," Louis called for the provost of Châtelet and decided on his advice to have the prisoner executed that very day. This story first surfaced in the thirteenth century, though it was less widely known than the others.[130] It complemented the others well; Saint Louis judged the great and small alike and, though he did not treat them alike, the punishments he meted out were tailored to fit the status of the accused. The Louis of myth was always prepared to listen to a complaint; his judgment was impartial, swift, and always available, mindful of custom, and little swayed by friendships. It was, all in all, a very medieval brand of justice. He did not favor the poor at the expense of the rich and noble, nor did he create a "superior justice" that the social order would surely have rejected. His was not a combative justice, a justice of opposition; it was quite fitting that Saint Louis became the patron of the highest royal court, the Parlement of Paris.

But the image of Louis's justice varied considerably from one era to another. Throughout the Middle Ages it remained a secondary element of the legend: dispensing justice after all was a common task, one that fell to all kings, and there was nothing special in the particular justice that Louis meted out. Though the artists of the fifteenth century and after occasionally depicted Louis with the Staff of Justice in his hand,[131] not until the seventeenth century did he appear firmly seated in judgment beneath the broad oak of Vincennes.[132] Joinville made only one reference to Louis dispensing justice under the tree after mass,[133] and subsequent authors made none at all. The image did not really become popular until the eighteenth century, by which time real contact between the king and the people had grown rare, and a king dispensing justice to all comers could attain the status of myth.

The Oak of Saint Louis then was an ecological and patriarchal dream that the Middle Ages knew nothing about: three-quarters of the representations we have of it actually come from the nineteenth century, from the Restoration, when nostalgia was strong and the Romantics harbored particular affection for all that was Gothic.[134] By then, the idea of Louis's justice had begun to change from a coercive, repressive regime that severely punished those who infringed on divine or human laws to a more distributive kind of justice, capable of overcoming the small-mindedness and particularities of legal rules in a way that resembled the medieval notion of divine justice far more than it did the justice of the historical Saint Louis.

Good justice in the Middle Ages required good officials. The Great Ordinance of 1254 had so much to say on that subject that it was regularly referred to until 1303.[135] Then there was the reputation of Louis's officials—especially of Etienne Boileau, provost of Paris. "Boileau maintained and surveyed his jurisdiction so thoroughly that not a single criminal dared live in Paris . . . since neither relatives nor lineage nor gold nor silver could have protected him," Joinville reported.[136] An exemplum in an English translation of a *Mirror for Princes* that was composed for John II about 1347 made the point another way, when it described Saint Louis wearing a belt with little tablets that he had inscribed with the names of people he deemed competent and of good repute, so that he could name them to royal appointments when positions became available.[137]

This then was the Saint Louis of the medieval nobility: he stood for good coinage, fiscal privilege, and a sound judicial system administered by skillful officials who were mindful of local liberties. The monarchy had an easy enough time endorsing one or more of these myths; it made allusions to Saint Louis whenever it strengthened the coinage and when it issued ordinances that called for multiple reforms—even as late as the Cabochian Ordinance of 1413.

But the image of Saint Louis was not easy to manipulate, especially when war with the English made it necessary to tighten the fiscal reins and take a critical stand against Louis's concessions to Henry III of England in the Treaty of Paris of 1259. Louis, who had suffered military defeat, could hardly serve as patron saint to a country at war. From 1340 until Charles VII retook the country, authors made few references to Louis other than in spiritual contexts.

One exception, however, came under Charles V when he dared to resurrect Louis's memory during the triumphant final period of his reign, stealing the Louis of the nobility and implementing a large part of their program of reform: carefully chosen administrators, strong money, and tight controls on the alienations of royal rights. Christine de Pisan associated the wise King Charles with Saint Louis, particularly in fiscal matters,[138] by stressing his devotion to Louis: "Charles worshipped and revered Monseigneur Saint Louis of France and deeply respected his feastday . . . and there is no doubt that his devotion to the blessed Saint Louis made of him [i.e. Louis] his intercessor before God."[139] During this period, Saint Louis was occasionally summoned to support political arguments, as in an oration delivered to the Emperor Charles IV,[140] and in the famous ordinance of 1374 on the coming-of-age of French kings—"Our very holy ancestor and predecessor, our patron saint and special defender, the most fortunate Louis, the flower, honor, light, and mirror of our race and of all French people, he whose memory is blessed and will endure through the centuries . . . governed so well that his ways should serve as an example to us."[141]

But despite this pretense at reestablishing Louis's image, the knotty question of fiscal freedoms remained. Through the reign of Charles VI, entire villages and towns had invoked his name in support of their petitions for concessions.[142] English occupation exacerbated the problem, for Saint Louis was also very popular in England: Henry V and later the regent, the duke of Bedford, sought his protection. Because the English administration had few centralizing tendencies on the Continent and was generally underrepresented there, it soon developed a healthy respect for provincial freedoms. "Henry V," the monk of Saint-Denis reported, "induced several fortified castles to submit by tendering them promises: to all those he asked to surrender, he guaranteed exemption from taxes, total freedom in satisfying their agricultural and commercial needs, and the reestablishment of the ways and customs of the late king of France, Saint Louis."[143] The event in question was in fact Henry's promise to respect the 1316 Charter to the Normans—a century after it had originally been issued.

Henry also set up special provincial administrations in Normandy and Guyenne. Not surprisingly, his rival, the Dauphin Charles VII, felt obliged to make the same kinds of promises. In a letter dated 1429, he swore "that he would maintain the same freedoms that the king Saint Louis had established in his kingdom."[144] But when the need to expel the English and to reestablish social order, even at the expense of local freedoms, had permitted Charles to prevail at last, a variety of groups began to launch particular campaigns to protect their specific interests rather than the freedoms of all, and Saint Louis—once the guarantor of all freedoms, once a visible threat to the ruling house—now ironically became patron saint of these special-interest groups. Churches, monasteries, towns, and corporations of artisans all began to enjoy the new freedoms he guaranteed. By the second half of the fifteenth century, Louis no longer represented freedom in general; he had become the patron saint of particular freedoms.

THE PATRON SAINT OF SPECIAL INTERESTS

CONFRATERNITIES

By the end of the Middle Ages, Saint Louis had also become the patron saint of Parisian confraternities, small, orderly organizations that had almost no political power at all. The two most important were the confraternity of the sergeants of the Châtelet and the confraternity of dry-goods merchants. Other professions and groups also had confraternities dedicated to Saint Louis: the wheat porters,[145] the carpenters (who asked Gringoire to write a *Life of Saint Louis*),[146] the anglers (their fishing poles assimilated metaphorically to Louis's Staff of Justice), the blind of Paris, and many other small artisanal associations connected to the dry-goods industry.

The confraternity of the sergeants of the Châtelet was not really an artisanal group, for sergeants held royal appointments. We have already seen, in the exemplum "be just at all times," how unloved both they and the provost who commanded them could be, for it was the provost who had convinced Louis that a criminal should be executed on the holiest of days; and in the public mind, the post of sergeant, at the bottom of the official hierarchy, offered many opportunities for corruption and extortion, and thus for illegitimate wealth. The confraternity was created by ten sergeants in 1353 to help protect fellow officers in this world and the next, officers who were vulnerable "to the risks of the byways, attacks by robbers and murderers," and also to the rancor of a populace "who dislike them because of their official duties." They dedicated the organization to helping sergeants "carry out their actions in accordance with the grace of God" and be good officers. Dedicated initially to both Saint Martin and Saint Louis,[147] it later took the patronage of Saint Louis alone.[148]

The confraternity first began to meet at the church of Sainte-Croix-de-la-Bretonnerie and later moved to Sainte-Catherine-du-Val-des-Ecoliers, a church that Saint Louis had so richly endowed that, by the mid-fourteenth century, he was being claimed as its founder. Yet later the story spread that the sergeants had founded the church of Sainte-Catherine to fulfill the vow they had purportedly taken at the battle of Bouvines to build a church in Paris if they succeeded in defending the bridge successfully against the attacking Imperial forces.[149] Saint Louis, it was said, had given their project his financial support. This narrative undoubtedly emerged at the beginning of the fifteenth century, when the post of sergeant, which until that time had been a civil appointment, acquired a military character, as did nearly every administrative post in a kingdom permanently beset with war. (It is undoubtedly also the source of Saint Louis's modern-day patronage of associations of French war-wounded and military veterans.)

More surprising perhaps was the fact that several confraternities of dry-goods merchants also dedicated themselves to Saint Louis. Twenty-six merchants of the palace, whose shops were located in the commercial gallery next to the Sainte-Chapelle, dedicated their organization to him in the fourteenth century, probably because of where they were working. The confraternity of the dry-goods merchants of Paris was also dedicated to Saint Louis, though the date of this dedication is unknown: a reference to this "old confraternity of Saint Louis" appeared in 1470,[150] but neither the 1324 nor the 1408 statutes of trade mention its patronage. This confraternity met in the church of the Holy Innocents near the market of the Champeaux, where dry-goods traders had first displayed their wares in the twelfth century; around 1485, it moved to the chapel of Saint-Voult in the church of the Holy Sepulcher.[151]

Saint Louis was also very popular in Guelf commercial circles, to which the Parisian dry-goods merchants from Lucca and Florence belonged. Perhaps their choice of Louis as patron came as a fringe-benefit of their transalpine commerce. For it mattered little that all these dry-goods merchants lacked real homogeneity as a class, that rich traders in luxury cloth, such as Italian and oriental silks, rubbed shoulders with more modest traders who crafted or resold small items of dress such as purses, belts, hats, and gloves. They all had one very important thing in common: they all traded in luxury goods to clients from the court, the nobility, and the rich sectors of society.

The dry-goods merchants claimed to have chosen Louis as their protector because, they said, their privileges had been given to them in the days of that king (privileges that, though cited in 1324, have, alas, since been lost). Though Etienne Boileau devoted a chapter to them in his *Book of Crafts and Trades,* we do not know for certain whether Louis actually blessed them with any special favors. Mendicant literature, as we recall, portrayed the king dressed in somber clothes of simple cloth, saving the elegant, gold fabrics for the Church.[152] By contrast, Joinville tells how Louis advised his sons and son-in-law to dress well, in accordance with their status, so that their wives and subjects would love them all the more.[153] But word associations must have proved more powerful than historical fact for the dry-goods merchants. Perhaps they saw little difference between Louis's name and the word *luire* ("to shine")—for merchants like these were above all dealers in brilliant objects. And after Louis died, he was always portrayed in full glory. Master Dudon, the canon of Paris and Louis's royal doctor, had a vision of Louis "in a white robe embroidered with golden lilies."[154] A woman who saw him in a vision in the Sainte-Chapelle said he was "dressed in purple and gold and held a sceptre in his hand."[155] The iconographic tradition followed similar lines: his statues represented him dressed in luxurious cloth, embroidered with gold lilies, decorated with lace, collarettes, and furs. Perhaps the gloves that sometimes appeared in the sculpted hands were subtle allusions to the confraternities that sold them.[156] This Louis—whose brilliant clothing was exceptional for a saint who spurned adornment—was the saint whom the merchants claimed as their client and in a way their precursor: had he not received precious cloth from merchants in the Holy Land? He could therefore be entrusted with protecting the long-distance trade of their goods.

Another legend told how Saint Louis had saved his vessel from shipwreck by praying. Because fourteenth- and fifteenth-century France had little involvement in the sea, no saint was specifically dedicated to filling this role: usually either the Virgin Mary, Saint Michael, or Saint Louis filled in when needed. By the seventeenth century, however, the tokens, arms, and emblems of the confraternity of dry-goods merchants all carried images of sea vessels; on the reverse there always appeared the figure of Saint Louis, framed with the words: "You will support us in our hope of salvation. We will follow you throughout the land."[157]

From the fifteenth century onward, there were yet other trades related to dry-goods that dedicated themselves to Saint Louis. The makers of straps for breeches and harnesses, whose confraternity met at Saint-Eustache, was one such group; others included the used-clothing sellers, the lacemakers, upholsterers, and ropemakers.

In the sixteenth and seventeenth centuries, though affiliations with Saint Louis became more widespread, they changed little in nature. What greater luxury trade could one find than the gemcutters, whose confraternity is documented in 1554? All the new crafts linked to the expanding jewelry trade dedicated themselves to Saint Louis: fine-clothing designers in 1677, fan-makers in 1650, craftsmen of gold and silver embroidered cloth in 1665. The wig-maker's and hairdresser's trade appeared in 1616, formed a confraternity in the name of Saint Louis in 1653, and found an engaging justification for their profession while they were at it: when Louis lost all his hair on crusade, they said, his doctors advised him to keep his head covered by wearing a wig; but because his mother wanted the wig to remind him of the devotion and faithfulness of his loyal lords, she asked each of them to contribute a lock of hair to its manufacture.[158] Thus Louis's imagined wig symbolized the unwavering support of his devoted nobility.

During the period from 1350 to 1500, as Saint Louis increasingly became the patron saint of individual confraternities—the confraternities grouped around the manufacture of luxury goods—he moved further and further from the image the Mendicants had created. The saint who was guardian of the poor and dressed in simple, somber clothing was transformed into an ostentatious king, looking more like real kings do. He protected particular freedoms rather than freedom in general.

But around the year 1450, the earlier saint resurfaced: still serving as protector of a specific group, Louis nonetheless found himself the guiding light of an organization so powerful that its interests nearly coincided with those of the entire nation.

THE PRIVILEGES OF THE GALLICAN CHURCH

In the middle of the fifteenth century, the monarchy began to make particularly skillful use of the link between the king and special privileges. Saint Louis became the defender of the privileges of the Church of France, privileges that were important to the monarchy because they countered papal influence in the kingdom.[159]

When, in 1438, Charles VII issued the Pragmatic Sanction of Bourges after the clergy of France had assembled to enact the decisions of the Council of Basle, he faced strong opposition from southern clergy who were closely allied with the pope. Both Guillaume de Montjoie, bishop of Béziers, and Bernard du Rosier, the future archbishop of Toulouse, wrote treatises hostile to it; and though neither contained references to Saint Louis,[160] Bernard du Rosier was known to have lauded Louis as the guarantor of the fiscal immunity of the Church and towns in opposition to the power of the monarchy.[161] Then, in 1450, at a meeting of the clergy with the papal legate, the Cardinal d'Estouteville—a meeting first held at Chartres, later at Bourges—the monarchy had the idea to exploit a *Pragmatic of Saint Louis* to serve its own ends. When the text appeared, according to Thomas Basin[162] (the bishop of Lisieux whom certain nineteenth-century commentators suspected to have been the ingenious counterfeiter), it was displayed with an official seal for all the bishops to see. Whoever the forger was, he was certainly crafty, for the only thing that finally betrayed him—in the second half of the nineteenth century—were some mistakes in stylistic formulas. All the essential aspects of the false act corresponded perfectly with what was known of Louis's independent, though respectful attitude toward the pope.

The 1450 *Pragmatic of Saint Louis* met with great success. The Parlement incorporated it into its list of remonstrances to the king in

1461;[163] Elie de Bourdeille, archbishop of Tours, included it in his treatise *In Favor of the Abrogation of the Pragmatic Sanction;*[164] and some of the speeches of Jean Jouvenal des Ursins contained summaries of it. In the seventeenth century, the Pragmatic of Saint Louis became the war-horse of the Gallicans.[165] They apparently hesitated for a while before deciding which king had set the appropriate precedent: Clovis with his decisions before the Council of Orléans in 511; Philip Augustus and his testament; or Charlemagne, for as Elie de Bourdeille wrote: "Some say that Charlemagne also made a Pragmatic, and they display it."[166] But in the end they chose Saint Louis. The seven pages that Bourdeille devoted to the document in his tract of 1474 make clear why. Of all the kings, Louis's image had remained the most profoundly medieval: the Mendicant influence was still visible in representations of his virtue, his alms-giving, the foundations he established, and his relics, all of which were still elaborated in terms that had originated in the liturgy of 1298. But Bourdeille also emphasized Louis's military operations in such a way that they verged on conquests. And he devoted long passages to the prohibitions on dueling and private wars—things that were indispensable to public tranquility. Bourdeille's text conveyed a new set of concerns and pointed to the possibility of enlisting Saint Louis's image to support the cause of royal power.

SAINT LOUIS AND FOREIGN POLICY

Since, by the end of the fifteenth century, Louis had become the patron of the particular privileges that a king was supposed to guarantee rather than of the universal fiscal freedoms that he was obliged to oppose, he once again found himself candidate for election to dynastic sainthood. Only one obstacle remained, though it was a formidable one. Louis had supported entente with England. But from 1337 to 1435 the kingdom had been at war with England almost constantly. Louis had won at Taillebourg against the English and at Damietta against the Saracens, but he had been defeated in the Holy Land, and of this the French took a dim view. They needed glorious memories to sustain their resistance efforts and their dreams of future expansion.

Thirteenth-century authors had often referred to Louis's military losses and his friendly relations with England. In the 1330s people were still speaking of his good relations with England. Guillaume de Machaut, in his *Dit de l'Alérion,* mentions how Louis during his crusade chose one brave Englishman to perform a crucial mission, for which he gave him his favorite white horse. As we have already pointed out, Louis's cordiality had made his memory immensely popular in England—the favorite, above all, of the Franciscans. And he was the chosen guarantor of Henry V's and Henry VI's policy of decentralization, particularly in Normandy.[167]

But in late-fourteenth-century France, a tactful silence fell on the subject, and during the rule of Charles VII this aspect of Louis's royal policy drew outright criticism. "Saint Louis handed over and surrendered in payment to King Henry five hundred knights and their following for an entire year with the intention of mounting a crusade, all of which cost twelve hundred thousand écus . . .": so wrote an anonymous critic. "And for this Henry was paid even though he did not go . . . and the people of Périgord and their neighbors were so distraught about this that they never again loved the king. And because of this, to this very day in the lands of Périgord, Quercy, and round about, even though Saint Louis is a saint canonized by the Church, they do not consider him a saint, nor do they honor him as one does in other parts of France."[168] The author craftily took the blame for the war away from Louis, who had yielded Gascony in return for homage, and placed it instead firmly on the English, who had not honored their engagements. But the loss of faith in Louis is undeniable and demonstrates how painful the memories of surrender still were nearly two centuries later.

By the end of the fifteenth century, Louis's activities in the Holy Land also drew criticism, though they rarely had earlier, when people still thought the earthly losses represented mystical victories, that Louis had waged these wars for the love of God and Christianity. But the gradual distintegration of the ideal of the Crusades led to the belief that these were just like any other wars. And they were lost wars. Detractors now asserted that Louis should not have participated directly, for in doing so he had abandoned the kingdom and placed himself in danger of losing his life. As Georges Chastellain wrote, in a comment meant to be critical despite the implicit parallel with the last duke of Burgundy: "the king, Saint Louis, was defeated two or three times in Syria, dominated, martyred, and, along with his soldiers, tinted with, bathed in and inundated by their own blood, help captive and seized, his descendants left in tears."[169]

Paradoxically, Josse Clichthove managed an even more categorical condemnation—despite the fact he was supposedly writing a panegyric—when he admitted: "Many are those who criticize these dangerous and poorly managed operations."[170]

Around 1500, the strongest defense that authors could mount for Saint Louis still lay in the idea that his losses had actually been victories. They emphasized his capture of Damietta during his first crusade, the manner in which he fortified the towns of the Holy Land, and the reputation he won for his people while abroad. "Under the reign of Saint Louis, the glory of the French reached Africa and the East. . . . He conquered Palestine, Arabia, and Carthage (Damietta), whose empire stretched to the Ocean. He destroyed the city of Hannibal, who had conquered Rome. He fought the Numidians, the Moors, and the *Gétules,* exacting a tribute from them and imposing the freedom to preach Christianity. The African kings became the allies and tributaries of the Franks . . .": so boasted Christophe de Longueil;[171] the fame of Louis, heroic conqueror of peoples, who overthrew tyrants and guided Assyrian and Arab souls toward righteous laws, had spread along shores that had once, Longueil asserted, been those of Gaul![172]

We have seen how many difficulties blocked the election of Saint Louis as the single, incontestable patron saint of the monarchy during the two centuries that followed his canonization—prevented him from becoming the figure he eventually became in the reign of Henry IV or of Louis XIV. Louis's apotheosis had come up against two different obstacles. On the one hand, pervasive Mendicant imagery soon after his death had made him into a model Christian rather than a model king. On the other hand, movements of protest among the nobility joined his name to fiscal freedoms and later to special privileges. This had made it difficult for a centralizing monarchy without financial resources to profit fully from his legend.

Ambiguity continued to blight the memory and cult of Saint Louis until sometime in the sixteenth century. Although as early as 1300 he was called the "patron saint of the kingdom"—in accordance with the bull of canonization—he did not in fact take on that role. His aura was multiform and scholarly, and was affected only superficially by the power of folklore.[173] For a long time he remained chiefly a spiritual figure and, because he did not serve as a political model on earth (a few of his achievements aside), he hardly qualified to be a patron in the kingdom of Heaven.

Few figures so thoroughly sterilized by Mendicant imagery have managed to remain as intriguing as Saint Louis. He raises the question of what the nature of royal power really was at a time when so many certainties were crumbling and accepted ideas were undergoing such fundamental changes. Not until the ideal of the Christian ruler was created in the sixteenth and seventeenth centuries did Saint Louis become its model. In the meantime, other paths were sought.

CHAPTER 4

Sanctuaries and Festivals of the Kingdom of Bourges

The political entity now known to historians as the "Kingdom of Bourges"—the central and southern parts of France that remained faithful to the Dauphin Charles after his disinheritance by the Treaty of Troyes on May 21, 1420—played a key role in the French concept of nationhood. When the French royal house managed to rise from the nadir of its political and military fortunes and found itself safe from threat once again, its subjects viewed the process as a miracle. They little doubted that its cause was divine intervention. But they wondered who the intercessor had been. Traditional patron saints, who had lost their credibility because most of their sanctuaries had passed through the hands of the enemy, did not seem feasible choices. Saint Denis had served the English; Charles VII could not—or would not—make use of his oriflamme once it had been unfurled against partisans of the Valois cause. Saint Louis's major cult sites were all located in the area around Paris; and, in addition, he was the saint who had once made peace with the enemy. As for Charlemagne, he was associated with northern and eastern lands now lost and would have been a poor choice anyway, because his imperial aspirations seemed inappropriate to the current atmosphere of uncertainty.

For about a half-century after 1418, the kingdom seemed unwilling to adopt another official patron saint. The Dauphin Charles chose Saint Michael as his personal guardian; but since Mont-Saint-Michel was too isolated and far removed from the center of the kingdom, Saint-Michel-

en-l'Herm, north of La Rochelle, was too small, and all the other important sanctuaries dedicated to Saint Michael were outside the parts of the
kingdom that Charles controlled, his well-reasoned choice had to wait a
long time to become established as patron of the kingdom.

Meanwhile, in different localities of the kingdom, people were gathering to pay homage to a number of different saints, saints already long
venerated south of the Loire in the lands so vital to the Dauphin's
government: Saint Catherine at Fierbois, Saint Martialis at Limoges,
Charles of Blois, and a host of others. They came from the Limousin
and Poitou, and after 1450 above all from the Touraine. And though
their cults were essentially spontaneous phenomena, they enjoyed full
official encouragement, for they provided a reassuring line of defensive
holy ramparts around the borders of the dauphin's threatened territories. The protection that these saints afforded was of the most traditional sort—miracles in the name of the king and his partisans—and
though we generally find only isolated references to them today, there
are a few complete registers of these miracles still extant. In the first part
of this chapter we will examine three of them: one from Limoges dated
1388; one from Fierbois from 1375 to 1407, 1409 to 1429, and 1429 to
1475; and one from Noblat in 1409.

When Charles triumphed at last, his government commanded that
festivals be held to celebrate the grace that God had bestowed on him.
From these came a variety of local festivals that in turn provided the
models for a kingdom-wide festival that the king ordered in 1450 to
celebrate the monarchy's victory in Normandy. This was simply added
to the local festivals without suppressing them. The second part of this
chapter will describe the net of commemorations that spread outward
from the Kingdom of Bourges.

SANCTUARIES AND MIRACLES

First let us examine the most accessible texts from the miracle tradition:
the two long series from Fierbois and Limoges.[1]

FIERBOIS

The kingdom's primary sanctuary of Saint Catherine was located at
Fierbois, south of Tours in the valley of the Loire. There was nothing
intrinsic in the figure of this virgin to call for a francophile cult, and
indeed it had appeared on the scene very late: the church of Sainte-

Catherine in Rouen, built to honor the relic of her finger that the monk Syméon had brought back from the Holy Land,[2] dates back only to the twelfth century; Sainte-Catherine-du-Val-des-Ecoliers in Paris was only established in the thirteenth century; the earliest reference to Fierbois itself did not come until 1375.

But Saint Catherine cut an exotic figure. As Jacobus de Voragine tells the story in his *Golden Legend*,[3] she lived in Alexandria, was converted to Christianity, and refused the hand of the Roman emperor because she wanted to remain a virgin. After heated debate, she convinced fifty pagan philosophers to convert. In the end she was imprisoned, tortured on the wheel, and martyred, and in death her body was carried off by angels to the top of Mount Sinai, where a convent was established under her patronage.

Iconography traditionally associated her with the palm frond, the sword, the martyr's wheel, and the book. She was the Queen of the Virgins, her role elaborated in the vision of the Mystical Marriage, in which the infant Christ gave her a ring. The theme of the ring appeared around 1330, and probably grew out of a misinterpretation of the wheel;[4] it figured in Etienne Lansquelier's *Life of Saint Catherine*, written around 1391 for the duke of Berry, brother of Charles V,[5] as well as in the works of the Italian hagiographer Pierre de Natali and the Burgundian Jean Miélot.[6] As fiancée of Christ, Catherine was elevated to a rank nearly equal to the Virgin Mary. "Of no other female saint has such a wonder been told," wrote Vincent Ferrier.[7]

After 1418, this saint who had long enjoyed such popularity throughout the western world was assigned new roles by French texts—roles that profoundly altered an image that until then had always been free of national associations. Now Catherine became the patron saint of prisoners, a feminine version of Saint Michael. The eleventh and twelfth century *vitae* had already mentioned her imprisonment, but only these later texts took care to elaborate, emphasize, and embellish it so fully. During the imprisonment, they said, a dove appeared who gave Catherine food and drink; angels came to light her cell, give her comfort, and care for her wounds; and Catherine continued to carry on her mission while in prison. There she received visions of Christ and the Virgin.[8] Though this part of the legend had only enjoyed minor importance earlier, it gained enough stature in the fifteenth-century *Lives* of Saint Catherine to vie with the traditional scenes of her debate and martyrdom. As the numbers of war prisoners increased, this new role became increasingly important. The *Book of Hours of Charles d'Orléans* contained prayers for deliverance addressed to her;[9] and Marshal Boucicaut had a hospice built at Fierbois in 1400 to commemorate the help she had given him after the catastrophic crusade to Nicopolis (though this did not protect him from ending his life as a prisoner in England).[10]

But the challenge of making Catherine into the patron saint of the soldiers proved more difficult. Already in the thirteenth century, the main doorway of the Parisian church of Val-des-Ecoliers had been decorated with the story of the sergeants-at-arms of the king who during the battle of Bouvines promised to erect a church in Catherine's honor if they won,[11] but not until the fourteenth century did Catherine's military vocation as the sword-bearing saint become firmly established. A male companion, the knight Porphyre whom she converted to Christianity and who was later martyred along with two hundred of his companions, was invented for her. Though Jacobus de Voragine devoted only four lines to this episode, Miélot spent fully one-third of his *Life of Saint Catherine* on it. The military cast to the legend was due in particular to similarities between Catherine and Saint Michael, the Prince of Knights. Both appeared adorned with sword and crown; both were virgins who fended off heresy and evil; both served as protectors of youth—Michael of young men, Catherine of young women[12]—who often became intermediaries in divine revelations; both were intercessors on whom people called for help in times of danger or death.

Undoubtedly because of all these parallels, Saint Michael soon found himself assigned a role to play in the legend of Saint Catherine—as the angel at the scene of martyrdom. The angels, unnamed, whom Pierre de Natali and Saint Vincent Ferrier had written into the prison episode, Jean Miélot handily recombined and transformed into the single figure of Saint Michael, assigning him the role of leading Catherine to paradise in the final scene. The pairing became visible in more concrete ways: some of the sanctuaries dedicated to Michael were located near those dedicated to Catherine. Both saints seemed to have had a fondness for high places, and Mount Sinai, sacred to Saint Catherine, lent itself easily to association with Mount Gargano, sacred to Saint Michael.

Transformations such as these increasingly promoted the popularity of Catherine's cult. They also led to another change that is of particular interest to us, for her cult now became centered at Fierbois, in the vicinity of Sainte-Maure. Many of the other sanctuaries to Saint Catherine were Anglo-Burgundian. The cult's public also changed; worshippers no longer came to Fierbois for the same reasons they had done so earlier, nor did they come from the same regions.

The nature of these changes becomes apparent when we compare the miracles of Fierbois to those, for example, of a series from Rouen. Twenty-six miracles comprised the twelfth-century Rouen sequence, in each of which the beneficiaries came from Rouen or the surrounding region. They belonged to a variety of social groups, with proportionally more women to men, and traveled to Rouen seeking cures, especially cures for blindness and sterility. Only one of these miracles might conceivably have had anything to do with war, and even this is uncertain, for the story could as easily have been about someone possessed and the enemy simply the devil. By contrast, at Fierbois, we can be quite sure that people who journeyed there did so for reasons related to war. Of the 41 percent of the miracles involving some kind of cure, only 15 percent grew out of accidental injury. But fully 35 percent involved protection from the enemy (fifty-five cases). The pilgrims who came to Fierbois were predominantly male: 70 percent are identified as men, only 10 percent as women. Of the seventy-seven visitors who came to the sanctuary between the years 1375 and 1475, sixty-two were laymen, including forty-seven soldiers. We see then that soldiers made up about half the pilgrims at Fierbois.

Knights, squires, men at arms from the regular army—all journeyed to Fierbois to give homage to the saint whose rings could protect them from combat wounds and death. Not surprisingly, the kind of gifts these pilgrims left at Fierbois changed in telling ways over the years. Twelfth-century candles, masses, and property gifts give way in 15 percent of the cases to military objects like swords, lances, and arrows. Fully 6 percent of the gifts were prisoner's chains.

Yves Chauvin's maps[13] also tells us that Fierbois pilgrims began to come from a much wider geographical area. Admittedly, from 1375 to 1407, all but three came from within the bounds of the kingdom. Again from 1407 to 1429, only three were outsiders, and between 1430 and 1475 only fourteen came from beyond the frontiers. No more than 2 percent at any given time were foreigners. But the number of pilgrims who came from areas controlled by the Dauphin varied greatly. Between 1375 and 1407 they came from the west-central region. None were from the English lands in Gascony, whose proximity to Fierbois created an interesting phenomenon: the area where the miracles occurred formed a band from thirty to fifty kilometers deep, stretching all along the border. Between 1408 and 1429, however, though most of the pilgrims still originated from the west-central area, they no longer came primarily from the frontier. While Gascony continued to remain impervious to its lure, Fierbois was becoming attractive to other regions of Anglo-Burgundian France—one of many demonstrations of the clear superiority by this time of Valois propaganda. After 1430, the popularity of the sanctuary began to spread throughout the entire kingdom. Political unity had been reestablished and bore fruit in unified forms of worship.

Did Fierbois ever become a truly national sanctuary?

Joan of Arc made the journey there. Since early childhood she had been devoted to Saint Catherine, for the saint—so popular in the region of Bar from which she came[14]—had appeared to her in a vision accompanied by Saint Michael. Joan wore the ring of Saint Catherine[15] and came to Fierbois looking for the sword that voices had promised her she would find in the ground behind the altar. When she uncovered the weapon, the one she was destined to carry into battle, the rust—so her followers said—fell miraculously from its blade. It was a blessed sword, a sword that was

> Du temps des grands princes et rois . . .
> Qui est du temps d'Alexandre
> Et des hauts preux du temps jadis.[16]
>
> [From the time of the great princes and kings . . .
> That is the time of Alexander
> And the noble men of prowess of long ago.]

(Joan herself never identified the sword with any heroic figure from the past. Only in later legends did it become the weapon that Charles Martel had used against the Saracens at the battle of Poitiers in 732.) The influence of Joan of Arc, however, was not strongly visible in the miracles of Fierbois. Only one pilgrim, in 1430, made a vow to pray for the Maid of Orléans along with the kingdom.[17]

Kings may have set more successful examples. Charles VII may possibly have come to the shrine. Louis XI came twice to pray; the *Book of Miracles* of Fierbois was written for his wife, Charlotte of Savoy; and their son, Charles VIII, substantially endowed the church.

But the most convincing argument for Fierbois being a national sanctuary comes from the miracles themselves. With only one exception, no miracles spoke in favor of the English. They were the great nasty wolves of these stories. The English repudiated God and the truth of their own words; the English were merciless; the English waged war unjustly. It was from English prisons, from Alençon and Chaluceau, that French prisoners found it necessary to escape. Catherine was most certainly a partisan, if not quite a national saint. In the west-central lands of the kingdom, she was enlisted to support both the regular army and the population in resisting the English. Her sanctuary may not have enjoyed as large a public as did Mont-Saint-Michel's; people did not come from so far away (200 kilometers at the most) or in such large numbers. In 1443 and 1444, of the 225 people from Le Mans and Mayenne who requested safe-conduct from the English authorities to make a pilgrimage to a holy site, only 7.5 percent were going to Fierbois, whereas 30 percent were traveling to Mont-Saint-Michel.[18] The distance to either place would have been more or less the same, so the percentages are accurate indicators of differences in the rate of visits. But the cult of Catherine spilled over the borders of the kingdom. It was also popular in Flanders and in Burgundy. Though Catherine may not have been a national saint, clearly Fierbois was a national sanctuary.

THE BORDERS OF GASCONY

Along the border of Gascony, the abbey of Saint-Martial at Limoges played the same role as Fierbois, though its series of miracles was not quite so striking. There were only 72 miracles here as compared to 269 at Fierbois, and they occurred during a very limited time—either immediately before or after the abbey displayed the relics of Saint Martialis in 1388.[19]

Martialis, who was thought to be the apostolic evangelizer of Aquitaine, had been the subject of a number of *Lives*, including one by Adhemar of Chabannes at the beginning of the eleventh century.[20] Martialis was credited with working many miracles—making the blind to see, the lame to walk, and the dead to live. He was also a saint of prisoners; for he himself had been imprisoned, but lightning and earthquakes had quickly stirred the population to convert, and the count had wisely decided to free Martialis posthaste.

When, in 1388, the abbey decided to display Martialis's relics, which though housed at both Limoges and Bordeaux were not often shown, many miracles ensued. Their beneficiaries did not come from as far as did the pilgrims to Fierbois: the recruitment zone ran north to south along the line of frontier castles, and the most distant lived only seventy kilometers away. They also differed from the pilgrims of Fierbois in another important way: though forty-two of the seventy-two were men, only 14 percent of them were soldiers. Evidently their social status was lower than at Fierbois; many lived in Limoges itself, or were peasants from the surrounding area. As for the type of miracles Limoges inspired, unlike Fierbois, nearly one-third were cures. Forty percent had something to do with war but, by and large, Saint Martialis was not a helper in time of battle; he did not heal wounds. Instead, he saved civilians who had been innocently caught up in the fray. Nearly all the war miracles were stories about release from prison, or they lent themselves to being interpreted in this way, so it is hardly surprising that most of the people Martialis freed gave their chains to his sanctuary.

Only two of the miracles actually referred to soldiers. In one story, Martialis went to the rescue of forces who were fighting for the king when their plan to ambush the English at Chalusset failed. In the other, a squire in the royal army, having made the mistake of playing at the game of knuckle-bones with some Englishmen, fell ill, whereupon Saint Martialis came along and offered to cure him—provided he would promise to avoid henceforth all contact with the enemy.

Was the Abbey of Saint-Martial a national sanctuary?

It was in fact quite by accident that Saint Martialis came to play the role of resistance fighter against the English. Originally he had served more modestly as the everyday protector of Limoges and its surrounding region, mounting rescue missions in simpler ways. But after the outrage the king had suffered when the English temporarily regained possession of Limoges from 1372 to 1374, he took on a special significance. When the relics were displayed in 1388, barely fourteen years had passed since those events, and their memory was still fresh in people's minds; Martialis was transformed from a simple guardian into an anti-English savior. And so it was that the Limoges miracles of liberation conspired vigorously, defiantly against the English, who were no more fair to behold here than they were at Fierbois. The only exceptions were three miracles involving English beneficiaries of Martialis's good graces, of which one repented in the end and another vowed that "never again would he take up arms against any Christian," especially against troops of the king of France.[21]

Although registers of later miracles no longer exist, we know that, during the fifteenth century, relic displays at Limoges continued to be eminently francophile events. In 1424, people prayed "so that Saint Martialis might confirm the king's estate, give him prosperity and favor," and the display in 1458 included a special procession in honor of the recovery of Normandy and Gascony.[22]

Farther to the south, at the two Mendicant convents and at Saint-Front in Périgueux, the images of Charles of Blois—killed at the battle of Auray in 1364—likewise worked anti-English miracles.[23] Many other sanctuaries also attributed military or francophile tones to their titular saints for various periods of time, though only a few isolated references are extant: miracles of Saint Michael at Mont-Saint-Michel, Talmont, Saint-Michel-en-l'Herm, and La Rochelle; of Saint Leonardus at Noblat; Saint Radegundis at Poitiers; and Saint Evortius and Saint Anianus at Orléans during the siege of the city. They delineated the border between the French and English Gascony, and between the partisans of the Dauphin and the Anglo-Burgundians in northern France.

These saints of 1370 to 1435—all purportedly French, all relatives of the ruling house—resembled one another remarkably. Saint Radegundis was the daughter-in-law of Clovis, Charles of Blois was the nephew of Charles V, Saint Leonardus and Saint Julianus were also claimed by the royal house in the fifteenth century. Some of these were imaginary filiations, but there were few officially canonized saints from the royal family that people venerated in southern France. Admittedly, not all these saints were born in France, but one could certainly say they had lived their lives, been buried, or worked their miracles in France, or that one of their main sanctuaries was located there. Nearly all of these saints were men; for Joan of Arc would not ascend to sainthood until the twentieth century; Clotilda was hardly a candidate, for she was Burgundian; and Saint Genovefa (Sainte Geneviève) was too distinctly Parisian. And their functions were similar: they were not evangelists, they did not keep believers from temptation, nor were they particularly known for their cures (though they did heal from time to time) They were rather liberators—of individuals or groups. All of these saints had been harshly sequestered in the course of their lives; each had eventually been freed by divine intervention; every one became the savior of unfortunate prisoners. The real miracle was regaining freedom. The English occupation was seen as servitude or slavery, as oppression rather than theft; the loss of the kingdom's territory did not impinge on the consciousness of those who sought their intervention, and those saints who were famous for helping to recover lost objects were ignored.

The saints enlisted in the royal cause were French saints and liberating saints. They were also military saints; the moment of liberation would come through a miracle, but the addition of arms made it a sure thing. From 1370 onward, the heavenly stage filled with native-born saints, who acted as noble knights in defense of their prince alongside the liberating saints and the protectors who warded off violent death. For a society still so imbued with nobility and militarism, still so unstable, they embodied the very best hope for the future.

It is not easy to chart the geography and chronology of the nationalization of the celestial hierarchy. Few national sanctuaries and saints appeared prior to Charles V's campaigns of reconquest; their spread reached its high point in the somber years of the Kingdom of Bourges and followed closely the rhythm of the war. Royal sanctuaries in the strongholds and large towns behind the battle zone firmly marked the Gascon frontier. In contrast, the Anglo-Burgundian border was more fluid, perhaps because some of the pilgrims were themselves Burgundian; miracles rarely expressed hostility toward the Burgundians, nor did sanctuaries and festivals charged with anti-Burgundian feelings appear much before 1470. Nor was the Breton border clearly marked, for Breton beneficiaries figured in the registers of miracles, and some of them were allies of the king of England.

THE LOIRE VALLEY

After 1453, when the kingdom was finally freed from the English threat, the saints of liberation faded from view and, with the decision of the royal house to settle in the Loire Valley, the sanctuaries of Tours began to play an important role in the kingdom.[24]

Saint Martin was the city's patron saint. The Merovingians had found in him their protector, and the Capetians, who were lay abbots of Saint Martin's monastery there, had taken their dynastic name from Martin's cape (cappa), the subject of his most famous miracle. It was hardly surprising, then, that Charles VII stressed his predecessors' devotion to the saint when in 1433 he asked Martin for help "with the recovery of the kingdom and its other concerns,"[25] or that he buried one of his sons at the abbey. Louis XI made Saint Martin "the special guardian of the kingdom, he who so helped our predecessors,"[26] and in 1481 accorded new favors to ensure that Martin would contribute "to the maintenance and preservation of the kingdom . . . to its accord, peace, and union."[27] To the chapter he also gave stained-glass windows that recalled Clovis's reverence for its patron.

The convent of Saint-Julien in Tours also attracted royal favor.[28] Louis XI's nephew, Charles of Savoy, grew up under its protective roof, and Guillaume Danicot, the king's counselor and official historiographer, wrote his *Life* of Saint Julianus[29] at the queen's request, drawing on the saint's life attributed to Gregory of Tours and the *Book of the Virtues of Saint Julianus*. Julianus—imagined to have been a knight of high birth who was martyred at a very young age—was usually depicted with a falcon, a crown, a sword, and a short robe decorated with fleurs-de-lys. His specialty was combatting traitors. "My lord Saint Julianus protects from treason. . . . Seek help in him as in a special patron saint of your kingdom who belongs to the order of nobility and knighthood," wrote Danicot, "in order that in times of peace and war he may intercede with the divine majesty for the estate and the prosperity of the king, his house, and the whole kingdom. . . . Thus will enemies be punished as disloyal invaders of the Crown of France, nor will they be able to find the way out of their wicked undertakings." The enemies in question were either Spanish or Burgundian—for after the seizure of Roussillon from the Aragonese in 1463, the victorious banner of the seneschal of Saintonge was deposited at the church of Saint-Julien at Tours; and—as Danicot pointed out—the Burgundians had disliked Julianus ever since he blocked them when they attempted to seize Brioude. We do not know how the royal house reacted to the thought of Julianus as new patron saint, but we do know how very popular he was south of the Loire. By the middle of the fifteenth century, about as many pilgrims found their way to Saint-Julien-de-Vouvantes (between Nantes and Rennes), as they did to Catherine at Fierbois, though we have no extant records from the period that list his miracles there.[30]

The sanctuaries of the Virgin in the Loire Valley also enjoyed wide favor. Louis XI was particularly fond of Béhuard, where he had been saved from drowning, and Cléry, whose dedicatory Saint Andreas was eclipsed by the Virgin in the fourteenth century.

At Cléry a collegiate church had grown up on the spot where a miraculous statue was discovered around 1280.[31] The English pillaged the church in 1428; to those who knew of that desecration, the reconquest of Orléans became the Virgin Mary's revenge.[32] The sanctuary at Cléry belonged to Dunois, the companion of Joan of Arc, who chose it as his burial site. Louis XI acquired it by exchange in 1453, added to its endowment, had the building reconstructed, and—in a highly unusual move—turning his back on the abbey of Saint-Denis, ordered that two of his sons and he himself should be buried there. Louis spoke clearly of his expectations of the Virgin of Cléry, when he called her "our refuge, protectress of ourselves, our children, and our kingdom . . . that with her help, our kingdom might be saved, maintained, kept whole, despite the wars and division that have occurred."[33] Later he prayed "that she might defend us from the machinations and conspiracies wrought against us and the public, that she might contribute to the public good, make all our affairs prosper, and work for the destruction of our rebellious enemies and adversaries."[34] Charles VIII shared Louis's devotion to the Virgin of Peril. Thus was his heart interred at Cléry.

The second half of the fifteenth century had therefore witnessed the victory of saints with deep ties to the Loire Valley. The theme of miraculous liberation disappeared along with the orientation toward the border, as royal favor turned to sanctuaries in the very heart of the kingdom. Their military aura grew more faint. They offered protection less from foreign armies than from plots and treason—especially from the treacheries of Charles the Bold of Burgundy, Louis XI's most dangerous opponent, whom royal propaganda had managed to project not as a foreign ruler but as a French lord who had rebelled against his king and betrayed his duties. After 1477, French patron saints began to ensure the kingdom's expansionist interests, and themes associated with the growth of the kingdom finally triumphed during the Italian wars.

COMMEMORATIVE FESTIVALS

Clergy and people usually gave thanks immediately when a king or his allies benefited from a miracle; they also commemorated the event later with a procession of thanksgiving. This was a longstanding custom, but now it was enhanced with regular observance. At first the formal thanksgiving ceremonies occurred on the feastday of the saint who had worked the miracle. Special religious rituals of thanksgiving and secular rituals commemorating victory were simply incorporated into the traditional feastday observance. But eventually two different kinds of local patriotic festivals developed: the oldest were held on the regular feastday and were simply garnished with lay additions; the newer ones, by contrast, were largely secular and took place on the anniversaries of important military events.

Most of the former seem to date from the end of the fourteenth century or the beginning of the Kingdom of Bourges and were observed all along the border of Gascony. It is difficult to determine what events catalyzed these celebrations, for their popularity was limited to the modest sphere of small towns and semirural fortified areas; the question of their origins remains unanswered. The celebration of the battle of Orléans in 1430, however, is an example of the latter. (As it happened, in this case May 8 was both the anniversary of the battle and the feastday of Saint Michael, so the religious and secular festivals coincided.) The events such celebrations honored are generally easier to identify, for they were often major battles, and the celebrations themselves were far more visible. They tended to forge links between influential communities that had both sufficient financial means and will to organize them—when the reward was a promise of fortified municipal pride.[35]

NOBLAT

Saint-Léonard-de-Noblat is located twenty kilometers east of Limoges, on a promontory in the Massif Central looking out over the Vienne River. The town, whose lordship was shared by the king and the bishop of Limoges, was first seized by the English and then recaptured by Charles V in the summer of 1372. The fortress at Noblat had special significance for the kingdom of Bourges, as a pilgrimage tradition had been reinstituted there in 1403, when Saint Leonardus's long-hidden relics resurfaced.[36] A confraternity of Saint-Léonard, which dated back to around 1358—began mounting the ritual display once every seven years, and the occasion became one of the major preoccupations of the town. Since a short list of miracles from 1403—about ten cures in all— is all that remains of its registers of miracles,[37] more indirect sources of information about the role Noblat may have played as a frontier sanctuary must be used. We will examine the changes that occurred in the image of Noblat's Saint Leonardus, and the nature of Charles VII's devotion to him, and then turn to the patriotic aspects of the celebration that Noblat held every year on November 6.

Saint Leonardus lived the life of a hermit in the sixth century, converted the Limousin, founded a monastery at Noblat, and was buried there. He enjoyed the same degree of popularity as Martialis: "The entire universe sings his praise," wrote Bernard Gui.[38] According to tradition, Leonardus ministered to women when they were troubled by infertility, pregnancy, or the pangs of childbirth, such that in the 1403 register of miracles 60 percent of his beneficiaries were still women. But two other aspects of the Leonardus legend allowed a symbolic transformation to occur: he was also allied to the royal dynasty, and he also eventually became a saint who freed prisoners.

Carolingian lives of Saint Leonardus did no more than associate him with Saint Remigius (who had baptized him) and credit him with saving an unnamed Frankish queen from the complications of childbirth. In compensation, the king gave him as much of the forest of Pauvain as he could traverse on donkey-back in one day. This, they said, was how Noblat came to be. Then in the thirteenth century Jacobus de Voragine called Leonardus a figure "of noble race,"[39] Vincent of Beauvais gave him relatives "among the first of the palace of Clovis,"[40] and Bernard Gui made him the godson of the king (though he did not identify as Clotilda the queen whom Leonardus saved).[41] These affinities all foreshadowed the blood ties that were to come.

About 1400, the hagiographer Pierre de Natali took the important step of casting Leonardus as "the relative and god-son of Clovis."[42] Around 1470, this affiliation was recognized through royal privilege— "Saint Leonardus issued from and was born of the blood and the line of France"[43]—and his miracle on behalf of Clotilda earned his monastery exemption from taxation. Eymoutiers, Saint-Junien, and Saint-Michel in Limoges adorned Leonardus's dalmatic with fleurs-de-lys; the royal castle at Noblat took the name "Clovis's Castle."

Leonardus's association with the royal dynasty was destined to flourish. In 1432, the Noblat notary Bordas wrote a ballad that affirmed it in verse:

> Saint Léonard chacun de nous te prie
> Comme celui en qui a fleurs de lys
> Et ton parent le roi Charles se fie . . .[44]
>
> [Saint Leonardus we all pray to you
> Who is blessed with fleurs-de-lys
> And on whom your relative King Charles relies . . .]

This royal trust was based among other things on the saint's power to free prisoners by breaking their chains and forcing open their prison doors; those freed gave their chains in thanks to the church. This belief, dating back to the Crusades, was reinforced in the fourteenth century by the miracle of the Lord of Braqueville, who, when imprisoned in the Holy Land, found himself miraculously transported back to Normandy.

Charles of Orléans and Marshall Boucicaut were particularly devoted to this saint. The Dauphin's confidence in his ancestor was such that in 1422 he took a vow to Leonardus so that "through the prayers of this blessed saint, he might restore his kingdom to peace and be delivered from the war with the English." In 1423, he granted new favors, in the hope that Saint Leonardus "might tend to our needs and to those of our kingdom."[45] At the same time he promised Leonardus a new reliquary case to protect the holy head if the saint helped him and "gave him back his lordship." In 1439, Charles was able to keep his promise.[46] Bishop Pierre de Montbrun, joined by the officials of the town, transferred the relic into the new reliquary, which—as described in a proclamation of the city magistrates—was "a miniature castle shaped like the one in Paris called the Bastide Saint Antoine and a small chest bearing an image of the king kneeling, so that Saint Leonardus might give the king a good life and a restored lordship, and keep and protect him from his enemies and adversaries." The ballad of the Noblat notary leaves no doubt as to the meaning of this gift: as Charles had liberated the town, so Leonardus rewarded him by liberating the kingdom; Charles gave the reliquary in turn as a form of thanks. Because Saint Leonardus was obligated to Charles, it was in his honor that Paris was retaken. Only Normandy remained to be reconquered, and here too Leonardus would help Charles fulfill his duty of reconquest.

Louis XI later carried on this tradition of paying homage to Noblat; so too did Louis XII (1498–1515) and Francis I (1515–1547), who called on Leonardus, as a son of France, to intercede on their behalf during the Italian wars.

Through the years—and still today—on the first Sunday after November 6, the inhabitants of Noblat have joined in celebrating a ritual whose meaning has now grown obscure.[47] In a game they call *quintaine*—a game that dates back to eleventh-century military training exercises designed for youths of the nobility—two teams of horsemen engage in a mock battle whose objective is to break down the doors of a target constructed in the form of a castle. Until the nineteenth century, contestants in the fray battled one another with lances; today they carry only sticks. The most obvious way to interpret this celebration is to say that the people of rural Noblat are miming the exercises from which they were once excluded: they are either giving themselves the illusion of participating in the prestigious world of chivalry, or else they are making fun of it. Georges Duby has interpreted other games of quintaine in this way,[48] but it does not quite hold true for Noblat, where new elements were superimposed on the traditional form.

Noblat's quintaine begins and ends with a festival procession. Confraternity members launch the ceremony by bringing the relics and a statue of Saint Leonardus out of the church and wending their way through the town toward the mall beyond the ramparts, where the games will be held. When they are over, the procession returns to the church. The castle-shaped target leads the way. The most unusual aspect of the ritual is that the procession travels all the way to the ramparts—for, more typically, festival processions make a point of remaining within the bounds of the city walls as they travel from one religious site to another. Noblat, however, has always believed that Saint Leonardus must pass out of the city in order to witness the event that will take place under his protection. More than just a test of skills, Noblat's mock battle is the projection of a struggle between two armies to win control of a castle. Its castle-target is also very strange: patterned after the reliquary of 1439 that disappeared during the Wars of Religion, it is fitting enough that it be carried in a ritual procession but it is shaped like a *bastide* or a fortified town gate, with four towers, high curtain walls, and two gates.

Other aspects of the festival date back to the period from 1370 to 1439. Confraternity members wear swatches of white cloth draped from shoulder to hip, representing the white sashes once worn by Armagnac troops. These were such well-known badges that when the Burgundians entered Paris in 1418, they vengefully chose to execute the constable Armagnac by peeling away the skin from his right shoulder to his left hip, leaving a band of red blood in place of the ceremonial white sash: red was the color of the Anglo-Burgundians, white that of the French royal house. Dressed as they are, the horsemen in Noblat's festival procession are playing the role of the royal troops and partisans of the Kingdom of Bourges.

At Noblat's festival banquet, the victors of the games feast on hare— the timid creature popularly associated with the English, and the traditional symbol of impending misfortune. People believed an encounter with a hare, like a meeting with the English, was bad luck, but that by eating hare they could eliminate the threat and take on whatever virtues the animal possessed. At the ceremonial dinner, celebrants are, in effect, dining on the English, who have been killed, have fled, or, more likely, defected (for most of the English garrisons originally came from Gascony). The feast is a fitting symbol of their defeat.

The ceremonies at Noblat thus seem to be a reenactment of a battle between two armies for control of a town, a battle in which—with the help of Saint Leonardus—the king's supporters always win. It refigures, among other possible events, what happened on May 18, 1372, when the townsfolk chased away the English garrison and opened the gates to the royal troops of Louis of Sancerre. On this occasion, the people of Noblat apparently declared themselves French on their own, for there is no indication that any armed assistance came from outside the town; and every year on the night before the games, the church bells of the town ring out in what appears to be a symbolic call to nocturnal revolt.

These ceremonies might also recall some skirmish along the border sometime between 1418 and 1422, or even the liberation of Paris and Normandy, for which Charles VII ordered festive observances throughout the kingdom. One of the few things we know for certain is that Noblat's game target could not have assumed its definitive shape before 1439, when the reliquary was offered to the church. But regardless of whether the confraternity of Saint-Léonard is celebrating the town's own liberation or the whole kingdom's, the meaning of the ceremony is the same.

LE DORAT

The medieval fortification at Le Dorat, about fifty kilometers north of Limoges, was burned by the English in 1356 and passed again to French troops in June 1370.[49] Guillaume Lhermitte, counselor to Charles VII and the dean of the chapter, refortified the town extensively between 1420 and 1430, the provincial Estates met there in 1437 and 1446, and the king visited twice in 1438 and 1440. The collegiate church in the town was dedicated to Saint-Peter-in-Chains—a dedication that vowed it to the release of prisoners; it was also the privileged guardian of the relics of Saint Israel and Saint Théobald, two eleventh-century canons of Le Dorat, who protected the fever-ridden and the pregnant.[50] In the late Middle Ages, it claimed Clovis as its founder.

Le Dorat's festival in honor of its three saintly patrons, though not as picturesque as Noblat's, continued to be observed until about 1900. Every fall, the confraternity of the church organized a procession through the main streets of the town, carrying the reliquaries from the collegiate church to the church of Saint-Michel in the upper part of town. The collegiate church also celebrated a mass. Though in some respects this was a very ordinary religious celebration, it incorporated some interesting references to the monarchy. Participating members of the confraternity wore white. Fifteen neighboring villages generally joined in the observance as well, and when their delegates arrived for the beginning of the procession, someone from Le Dorat called out, "Who goes there?" The other villagers always answered, "France." Historically, such an exchange would only have taken place in the kind of closed border village that Le Dorat in fact was between 1370 and 1435. The town probably instituted the ritual of inviting fifteen parishes in order to symbolize the loyalties that developed during this period; only partisans of the king who had demonstrated their worth by coming to give thanks for their liberation to Saint-Peter-in-Chains, Saint Israel, and Saint Théobald merited the privilege of taking part.

ORLÉANS AND OTHER TOWNS

In larger towns the celebrations were far more elaborate; their religious nature is often also less clear. Probably the foremost of such celebrations was the "Fête aux Anglais" (Festival of the English), which Montargis celebrated on September 5, 1428, in commemoration of the day a year earlier when Warwick was defeated before the gates of the town.[51] The centerpiece of the observance was Warwick's banner, seized by the French during the fray, which the town now paraded around in mockery. Montargis continued with this ritual celebration until the French Revolution, but we have little information about it today.

Fortunately, the case of Orléans is more accessible. From October 1428 to May 1429, Orléans lay under siege, going through an ordeal that would make a ready vehicle for symbolic expression in years that followed. On May 8, 1429, the townsfolk—whose resistance had been exemplary—greeted the entering royal troops with great enthusiasm: "In the year 1429, the sun began to shine again," said one observer.[52] The following year, the municipality, the clergy, and the count of Dunois, acting in the name of his half-brother, the duke of Orléans, organized a commemorative procession to celebrate the event. Town accounts carry details of its organization, right down to the cost of making and carrying candles, painting the banners, and maintaining order; the *Diary of the Siege* also ends with a description of the ceremony.[53] The procession was led by the clergy bearing the reliquaries, followed by the twelve town procurators and then the entire population of the city, each person carrying a candle; it wound its way through the city from the Augustinian convent—where the battle had been fought on May 7—to the churches of Saint-Aignan and Saint-Euverte (for some citizens had reported seeing Saint Evurtius, the fourth-century bishop of Orléans, running along the ramparts on the day of the battle), and then to the cathedral, where a mass was said and a sermon preached. The festival thus linked the main sanctuaries of the town with the sites of the major military events of the siege. The following day, a mass for the dead was celebrated, and alms were given to the poor.

In 1435, a native son contributed a mystery play to these observances,[54] a play that was probably also performed in 1439 and 1440; with musical interludes, complicated episodes, and a hundred characters, the production called for huge sums of money. (Gilles de Rais was one of those who took on the financial responsibility.) The scenario of the play closely followed the account of events as it appears in the *Diary of the Siege.* It lauded the king, the duke of Orléans, and his brother Dunois, and praised the heroism of the citizens of the town; the English, as might be expected, were not flattered, for the Virgin Mary and the saints had "pity and compassion on France." The play culminated in the triumphal entry of Joan of Arc, who asks the town burghers to establish a processional to be held annually every May 8.

The bridge, the Augustinian convent, the fortifications of the Tour-nelles, the house that was thought to be Joan of Arc's, the banners that had been captured from the enemies—all these things stirred memories of the extraordinary event. The mother of Joan of Arc retired to Orléans to live out the rest of her days sheltered by the good graces of the town. And by 1500 the town had built a memorial on the bridge to commemo-rate the Maid. Joan stood there in sculptured effigy beside the duke of Orléans (whose statue strikingly resembled King Louis XII), as both offered fervent prayer to the Virgin of Pity. About 1512, the church of Notre-Dame-de-la-Recouvrance arose on the site of one of the old tow-ers of the city walls. The May 8 processional continued untouched through the centuries, until it was supplanted by a new ceremony in 1855—one in which the presentation of the banner was followed by a historical cavalcade that reenacted Joan of Arc's entry into town and moved along the same route she had taken. The cavalcade gained fur-ther importance following Joan's canonization in 1921, at the time of the quincentenary celebration in 1929, and again in 1947 when, by a twist of fate, it celebrated the May 8, 1945, liberation of France along with the anniversary of the liberation of Orléans.

Similar commemorative doublings occurred in more modest ways in other towns. The April 1436 liberation of Paris occasioned a procession called "the procession of the English." After 1594, it was conflated with the celebration of Henry IV's takeover of Paris, since the dates were more or less the same. It continued to be solemnized until 1735.[55] The "saving of Dieppe," when the Dauphin Louis wrested the town from the English in 1443, was also long celebrated: its processional and games reappeared year after year from 1443 until well into the seventeenth century.[56]

BEAUVAIS

The army of the duke of Burgundy laid siege to Beauvais in June and July 1472. On June 27 and July 9, his forces mounted direct assaults on the town, but Dammartin and Rouault led reinforcements into the city to bolster its weak garrison and help the general populace to play a role in the combat. At one point, a young girl from town, Jeanne Laisné, stole a Burgundian flag near the Bresles gate and placed it in the church of the Jacobins. The outcome of the story was a happy one, and Beauvais ultimately attributed its victory to Saint Angadrisma—virgin, abbess, and patron saint of Beauvais—for the citizens had brought her reliquary to the ramparts during the battle. Her feastday is October 14.

As for Jeanne Laisné, few documents of the day tell the story of her exploits.[57] Robert Gaguin, in his *Compendium*, reported only in passing that "a young girl grabbed a flag from a Burgundian soldier." There are financial accounts of the construction of Beauvais cathedral in 1473 that mention three flags the town captured from the Burgundians, but they go no further than to attribute the possession of one to the bravery of women. King Louis XI, however, was more explicit. In letters of 1472, 1473, and 1474, he confirmed the town's municipal liberties and exempted it from taxes to thank its citizens for the loyalty they had shown; and in those of 1473 and 1474 he specifically requested that Jeanne Laisné and her new husband be exempted from taxes "because of the good and virtuous resistance which she showed when she seized and kept a flag of the Burgundians."[58] Louis also relinquished some of the taxes collected in order to allow the town to pay for a celebration in honor of Saint Angadrisma on October 14. Beauvais made plans forthwith for a processional observance, starting from the church of Saint-Michel where Angadrisma's reliquary was housed; it also included plans for the young girls and women of town to march directly behind the clergy in the celebration—in front of the menfolk—for this would duly honor the courage they had shown at the time of the battle.

It was during the second half of the sixteenth century that Jeanne Laisné began to be transformed into a figure of legendary proportions. She was given both a new name (Fourquet, then Hachette), and a weapon (the *hachette*, though this weapon did not exist before 1600), and converted into a wool carder—an important occupation in a city renowned as the capital of tapestry making. In the fifteenth century the assault was always commemorated with a procession in honor of Saint Angadrisma on her feast day of October 14, sometimes with, sometimes without, the flag. A more specialized procession appeared in the following century, an overlay to the original one, and it was this transformed ceremony—its expenses paid partly by the king and partly by the municipality—that became the basis for the modern festival. After 1612, despite the fact that the procession commemorating the victory

had always been held on July 10, the town redated Jeanne's exploit to
June 27. The modern Parade of the Attack—a procession of young
women who carry a flag that represents the one taken from the Binchois
in 1554—though still celebrated on June 27, has been observed in its
current form only since the Second Empire.[59]

Important towns like Beauvais, Orléans, Dieppe, and Paris—all influential communities proud of their achievements—quickly created festivals on the date or at the site of some great historical event. The secular
nature of these celebrations was particularly evident, though the processional format, drawn from religious sources, was inevitably the one they
chose. Communities like these had the means to celebrate both the
festival of their patron saint and some important military exploit on its
own date as well. For a long time, the celebrations remained isolated
events, limited to specific towns, and they served as much to buoy up
local patriotism as they did to stir national sentiment. Only the monarchy, it seems, had the means to bring more widespread celebrations into
being.

ROYAL INITIATIVES

The monarchy waited quite a while before taking this step. Though
from the twelfth century onward most parts of the kingdom joyfully
feted royal victories from time to time, no widespread commemorations
were held on a regular annual basis. The first sign of change was the
celebration of the victory that ended the siege of Orléans, which
Bourges and Poitiers celebrated as well. Many other towns soon began
to commemorate the liberation of Paris on April 13. This was the model
that the king decided to follow on a far more vast scale after the recovery of Normandy.

To mark the end of the reconquest and of the war, Charles VII
consciously chose the "return of Normandy" rather than the recapture
of Paris—a city Charles hated and in whose liberation he himself had
not participated—or the conquest of Gascony, which had by then come
to appear as part of a foreign war. Normandy seemed a far more fitting
symbol, for Charles had played an important personal role in its recovery; his troops fought valorously at Formigny, and the people of the
province had contributed enormously to his success. Unlike Gascony,
Normandy had nurtured a strong resistance movement—marked by the
offensive thrusts of peasant bandits against the English, who in the end
showed themselves little capable of holding the countryside or control-

ling the cities where they were threatened from within by constant plotting. Norman nobles had been opting for the Kingdom of Bourges from the very first days of the occupation, and—in 1434 in the Bessin region, in 1435 in the Vire and Caux—the inhabitants mounted massive revolts almost unassisted by royal support.[60] The reconquest seemed to come easily then, with a facility that appeared miraculous to everyone: the campaign lasted only a year and six days.

Normandy was large and wealthy and graced with many churches. Before 1415 it had provided one-quarter of all the kingdom's taxes (but no one harped that tune at the time of the reconquest); its fortifications were strong—between 30 and 100 castles, depending on which chronicler one reads.[61] Yet the struggle to liberate it did not produce many casualties, and destruction was very limited.[62] Nor did rain and mud limit the operations: the French troops, who fought well, could live on the bounty of the Norman land. The enemy was quickly demoralized.[63]

The fall of Cherbourg on August 12, 1450, marked the definitive defeat of the English and the end of the "reconquest." Other terms used at the time were "recuperation" (récupération), "recovery" (recouvrance), and "return" (retour); all served the same purpose—to assert that the king was reestablishing an earlier situation that had been unjustly altered. The war was not a simple conquest: it fell instead into the most important category of just war—a war of defense. (Though Charles VII himself had initiated the war in 1449, following the murky affair of the capture of Fougères, about which, contemporaries felt, the less said the better.)

Who was to be thanked for so great and well deserved a miracle?

To some, it was the consequence of the jubilee year: God had let his indulgence pour down on Christendom through the open doors of Saint Peter's—for, with the end of the Schism, the pope had solemnly declared a jubilee and many pilgrims had flocked to Rome. In a stained glass window of the cathedral of Evreux, we can see a "Reconquest of Normandy" in which Charles VII and his captains stand face to face with the pope and the cathedral chapter: the end of the Schism coincided with the end of the estrangement between Normandy and the kingdom. Belief in the beneficent powers of the jubilee year was widespread;[64] it seemed to announce a period of optimism and great endeavors to come, a fitting culmination to the reign of the "most victorious king."

Though the French kingdom was not the only candidate for reward in this jubilee year—since, after all, the whole of Christendom stood to benefit—its benefits were surely most singular. Undoubtedly, it was thought, either Saint Michael (the patron saint of the king and his army, the saint honored by a Norman sanctuary), or Saint Radegundis, or the Virgin Mary had intervened to win His special grace. The patronage of the second two was suggested by a conjunction of dates: the festival of Radegundis was August 13, the Assumption of the Virgin on August 15, and as feastdays usually begin on the eve of the specified day—August 12 and 14 in this case—they coincided respectively with the dates of the capitulation of the English and their expulsion from Cherbourg.

Radegundis, who was Clovis's daughter-in-law and the guardian of Poitiers (one of the two capitals of the Kingdom of Bourges), had all the qualities needed to be guardian of the kingdom. She had ties to the dynasty, she had spent a long time in prison, she was known as a saint who freed prisoners. As patron saint of Poitiers, she was credited with having saved the town from the English in 1202,[65] for, as the story went, during King John's siege of the town, a clerk of the bishop, who had promised to give the keys to the English, found himself unable to do so when he couldn't find them: they had been hidden in the sculpted hand of a statue of the Virgin Mary in the church of Sainte-Radegonde. Thus the Virgin Mary and Saint Radegundis had chased away the invaders. In sixteenth-century Poitiers, clergy and municipal officials commemorated the event by processing along the town's ramparts; the procession had probably originated earlier, in the second half of the fifteenth century, as a way to demonstrate Radegundis's anti-English associations and to establish appropriate ancient roots for the festival of August 12 and 13, which had only recently taken on patriotic hues. Charles VII purportedly had written to bishop Jacques Jouvenal des Ursins in 1450, alluding to the role that the Virgin Mary and Saint Radegundis had played in the recovery of Normandy.[66] In any event, Charles baptized one of his daughters with the unusual name Radegonde; and after 1450, Marie of Anjou maintained a candle lit in perpetuity before the tomb of the saint in memory of the victory, an offering she planned to endow.

The success of this new form of veneration was limited to the area immediately around Poitiers, however, where Radegundis's cult was already well implanted. Elsewhere, the victory in Normandy was attributed to the Virgin Mary. At Cherbourg, to commemorate the siege and its fortunate ending, a confraternity of the Assumption was formed to construct a complicated mechanism for the cathedral, depicting the Virgin's ascension into heaven.[67]

It was the monarchy, however, that made the decisive step in launching a kingdom-wide celebration of the reconquest of Normandy. At the
end of September 1450, Charles VII ordered that henceforth a general
and solemn procession be held each August 12 in every cathedral of the
land—both in areas held in appanage and those directly subject to
him—to commemorate the grace that God had bestowed in allowing
him to recover Normandy.[68] His letters announcing this to the bishops
and archbishops of Paris, Poitiers, Chartres, Beauvais, Béziers, and
Chalon-sur-Saône still survive. The resulting festival spread to all royal
cities and good-sized towns, whether they were episcopal sees or not;[69]
abbeys such as Maillezais in Poitou and Mont-Saint-Michel also joined
in the observance.

The first year, since the festival was scheduled for October 14, there
were only about two weeks to organize it. What the specific content
would be became the subject of discussions between the bishop and the
chapter in Rouen, and the subject of memoranda in Bayeux.[70] For the
celebration in Paris and the festivals in the Norman bishoprics we have
surviving accounts of the processions as well.

In each of the Norman cities the procession went from the cathedral
to one of the four Mendicant convents; in Paris, the route began at
Notre-Dame and ended at the Sainte-Chapelle; at Cherbourg and
Mont-Saint-Michel, the procession went along the ramparts. In each
city, the clergy of the town gathered around the relics at the cathedral,
sometimes supplemented by those of neighboring churches or abbeys
(as at Poitiers, where those of Sainte-Radegonde were brought in for the
occasion); at each station, a bishop or one of the canons said a mass of
thanksgiving; officials, members of confraternities, and all the citizenry
attended the celebration, for half the workday was canceled, and many
amusements provided. In Rouen in 1451 the *Mystery of the Incarnation*
was performed; most of the added activities in the other towns were
religious as well, but no one composed a specific liturgy for the occasion. The mass of the patron saint of the cathedral, or a mass of the
Virgin Mary or the Trinity, was sung with the addition of a few prayers:
Stirps Jesse (To the glory of the chosen people), *Tua est* (To You, Lord,
goes the glory and the victory), and *Domine salvum fac regem* (God
save the king).

In his letters ordering the celebration, Charles VII had expressed two
expectations for the sermons: they were to give thanks to God and
perpetuate the memory of the *reductio Normaniae,* that is, they were to
be both religious and nationalist. Thomas Basin, who had often been

called on in the past to create such sermons while serving as bishop of Lisieux, understood what was needed in such cases: "one thanks God for such a great gift and prays to him and asks for the material and spiritual well-being of the king and the kingdom."[71] Fortunately one particularly beautiful text, composed by the Italian humanist Orlando dei Talenti for his bishop at Bayeux in 1451, has survived.[72] Talenti began with a historical account of the recovery of Normandy, devoting the largest part to the story of Bayeux itself. He included two antithetical portraits—one, of a courageous, merciful, and just Charles VII, and the other of the thieving, violent English—and drew his main theme from their opposition. We must remember this oppression and servitude, Talenti tells us, for by remembering the pillaging and the death, we can better thank God for the victories he gave us and we can avoid falling into such dangers in the future. Talenti's sermon was based on a wholly secular theme drawn from national rather than biblical history. It honored the dead without extolling their Christian virtues, for Talenti aimed to teach a lesson more useful to national than to Christian lives.

It is difficult for us to know how successful the festival of August 12 was. Aside from references in liturgical books, we have little detailed information beyond descriptions of the ceremonies in Rouen in 1451, Paris in 1450 and 1451, and Poitiers around 1500. Whatever happened in Tours or Reims, nothing survives to tell us, though these towns had strong ties to the monarchy.[73] Ceremonies were apparently very popular at Poitiers and in the Norman dioceses, where until the Revolution they were observed even at the simplest level of the rural parishes. It was also celebrated at Tournai in Flanders.[74] After 1638, when King Louis XIII dedicated his kingdom to the Virgin of the Assumption, the Norman festival was subsumed under that of August 15 and became a simple vigil on the eve of the festival of the Assumption.

The reconquest of Normandy was the only historical event of the fifteenth century that prompted the desire for a kingdom-wide festival, though the reconquest of Gascony, rugged and lethal as it was, generated its own commemorative festivals. The defeat of Charles the Bold at Nancy in 1477 yielded no such national celebration: the procession on January 5 and the ecclesiastical endowments that commemorated that battle were tributes rather to local Lorrainer patriotism—demonstrating allegiance to the duke rather than to the king.[75] The "Recovery of Normandy," therefore, was one of a kind and represents an exceptional effort on the part of the monarchy to create a national festival in celebration of a newly rediscovered unity.

Fifteenth-century patriotic festivals were both very old and very new. The habit of celebrating royal victories by holding processions or masses of thanksgiving was very old. In Tours, La Rochelle, and Poitiers, people were moved to thank God after the siege of Orléans just as they had been earlier all through northern France after the battle of Bouvines. The format of the festivals was also very traditional: the lay and regular clergy processed with reliquaries of the patron saints, and the local populace followed them, led by the young men and women of town. As in times past, they all paraded and prayed together, winding their way from one important sanctuary to the next, until they reached the cathedral where the mass was said and sermon preached. Yet there were obvious innovations. Though still seen as miraculous, the events they commemorated were now military victories above all. Because the desire to ensure remembrance was often more important than thanksgiving, processional routes grew rather more idiosyncratic. Some led to ramparts where battles had been fought—at Orléans, Mont-Saint-Michel, and probably also Cherbourg and Beauvais. Different kinds of ceremonial objects were involved—candles at Orléans, floral wreaths in Normandy, white sashes at Noblat, enemy flags at Beauvais and Montargis. And there were many different ways of reenacting the original event: through the quintaine at Noblat, the mystery plays at Orléans, or the mounted machinery of the cathedral at Cherbourg. Apparently, no one gave any thought before the sixteenth century to erecting special commemorative monuments in honor of an event, aside from the usual endowment of churches, chapels, and crosses. Memory—continuously revivified—rather than stone, was what they counted on.

The commemorative festivals were not theatrical occasions performed for the edification of passive audiences: they were fully participatory, designed above all for townsfolk to become involved in. Each person was invited to join. Interestingly enough, when the transformation to theatrical celebrations did come about, festivals like these, born during the wars of the fifteenth century—partly religious, partly civic— all died away, except for the festivals designed around events of particular local importance. And though a few local commemorations survived, they too were transformed.

CHAPTER 5

Saint Michael

THE CULT

THE CULT THROUGH THE THIRTEENTH CENTURY

From among all the saints who protected the very Christian nation of France, Charles VII chose as his particular favorite the Archangel Michael.

Michael was one of the three angels named in Scripture who as leader of the heavenly army and standard-bearer for God enjoyed a clearly defined role:[1] he had chased the fallen Lucifer all the way to Hell in a struggle he was destined to repeat at the end of time, when he would triumph over the Antichrist on Golgotha. All believers during the Middle Ages could expect to meet Saint Michael on at least two important occasions: on their deathbeds, when he would ward off temptation, welcome them, and lead them to the next world; and at the Last Judgment, when he would weigh their souls on his balance and intervene on their behalf before God. Michael was a dual-natured angel. He was both the warrior who conquered the dragon and the weigher of souls, the angel of death. In the Old Testament he had yet a third role: he was the Angel of Israel, the Angel of the Chosen People, the one of whom Yahweh said to Moses, "Behold, I send an angel before you to guard you on the way and to bring you to the place which I have prepared."[2] Michael protected both Joshua at Jericho and Gideon when he fought the Midianites; he crushed Sennacherib before Jerusalem; he fought alongside the Hebrews against nations who were protected only by lesser angels.[3] Although this Old Testament side of his character, unlike the others, certainly could have lent itself to nationalist interpretations, for a long time it was forgotten.

With the conversion of Constantine, the angel who began as the protector of the Hebrews became the guardian of the Christian people and of the imperial armies fighting against the barbarians. Pseudo-Denis's *De Hierarchia* ranked him among the archangels of the second degree of the third hierarchy—one of those who guided the multitudes. Such angels stood higher than those who looked after individuals, but they served only earthly missions. It was more powerful figures like dominions and seraphims who made up the heavenly court of God.[4]

The early Middle Ages was a period of marked regression in the history of Saint Michael. Though he continued to be venerated in Byzantium, in the Latin West his cult was at first confined to the Celtic fringe and Italian Lombardy.[5] The cathedral of Pavia, the coronation site of the Lombard kings, was dedicated to him and, by the end of the fifth century, the story that Michael had appeared near a cave of southern Italy's Monte Gargano had begun to inspire popular pilgrimages. Meanwhile, at the opposite end of Europe, Celtic hermits were spreading his cult on the Continent, where it seems to have been largely unknown.

Under the influence of Byzantium and the Anglo-Saxons, Charlemagne proclaimed in the year 813 that Michael's feastday should be observed throughout his Empire; Hrabanus Maurus, abbot of Saint Gall, wrote a liturgical office in his honor, and Alcuin dedicated a liturgical sequence to him as protector of both the Empire and the Church (for in Alcuin's mind, the two were the same).[6] Sanctuaries dedicated to the saint had already begun to multiply throughout Western Francia, where they met with growing success at Le Puy, at Saint-Michel-l'Herm (already toward the end of the seventh century), and above all at Mont-Saint-Michel.[7]

This is how, around 850, the *Revelation of Saint Michael* recounted the legendary beginnings of the monastery of Mont-Saint-Michel:[8] In the course of the year 709, Michael appeared several times in visions to Saint Autbertus, bishop of Avranches, asking him to build a church in his name on a mount where oratories dedicated to Saint Stephen and Saint Symphorianus already stood; Autbertus sent to Monte Gargano for relics, and on October 16 a new building housing twelve clerics was consecrated on the site, where soon a miraculous spring welled up. A pilgrimage was immediately organized, though the region was torn by rival Norman and Breton armies as the Normans pursued their settlement and slowly converted to Christianity.

Around this time, the sanctuary on the mount passed into the hands of the dukes of Normandy; in 966, Duke Richard sent Benedictine monks to serve there under the rule of Abbot Mainard of Ghent. The *Introduction of the Monks,* a short history of the dukes and their ecclesiastical policy, was written during the reigns of the abbots who succeeded Mainard.[9] Gradually Mont-Saint-Michel gained possession of the relics of the early monks of their monastery and of the bones of Autbertus, miraculously recovered sometime between 1010 and 1016.[10] The Romanesque building erected after 1023 gave visibility to the sanctuary's new importance.

Abbots of the Mont, protected as they were by the dukes, enjoyed a powerful patrimony whose influence soon spread throughout Brittany, Normandy, and England. They established a noteworthy scriptorium and a superb library, all the while continuing to maintain monastic discipline. Under the leadership of Abbot Robert de Thorigny (1154–1186), Mont-Saint-Michel experienced extraordinary material and spiritual prosperity, comparable to that of Saint-Denis at the time of Suger.[11] Abbot Robert directed monks to compose the cartulary, catalogues, and annals of Mont-Saint-Michel; and Guillaume de Saint-Pair wrote the *Roman du Mont,*[12] a text in the vernacular that would bring the *Revelation,* the *Introduction of the Monks,* and a large number of miracles that had been little known until then, within the reach of all pilgrims.

Guillaume de Saint-Pair told how the new church had originally been dedicated by angels, how a child in a cradle had rolled together the foundation stones, how an angel had perforated the skull of Autbertus. Two other miracles from earlier times that he recounted grew more popular and became emblematic of Mont-Saint-Michel. One, the vision of Norgod, was said to have taken place in the tenth century: Norgod, bishop of Avranches, thought he saw the sanctuary burning, but the flames were actually a sign that Saint Michael was making a visit to the church that bore his name. The second was the miracle of the shore, in which a poor pilgrim woman suffering the pains of childbirth was about to be carried off by the sea, when Michael appeared and held back the waves to save both mother and child. The *Roman du Mont* also described the abbey's new relics—the sword and the shield of Saint Michael,[13] giving twelfth-century pilgrims the opportunity to return home from the abbey and tell their neighbors that they had seen the very weapons Saint Michael used to fight the dragon, as well as stories about how the saint made himself manifest as flames and saved those who were in danger of the sea.

Elsewhere, writers were showing the same strong interest in the cult of angels, and most particularly in the cult of the Archangel Michael. Every theological *summa* written after the mid-twelfth century devoted long passages to him; Saint Bernard of Clairvaux and Abbot Hugh of Cluny both gave sermons about him; in the *chansons de geste,* he was often depicted welcoming the souls of dying warriors—he carried up the soul of Roland, who had offered him his glove; he did the same for Guy de Saint-Pol; he fought at the side of Girart de Roussillon and of crusaders lost in the desert.[14]

When Philip Augustus took Normandy in 1204, making the Mont the border marker of the kingdom, he thus laid claim to a rich and venerated sanctuary. Until then, Saint Michael had served as the guardian of the Empire and of the Plantagenet kings. His picture appeared on the banners of William the Conqueror, and Henry II made three pilgrimages to the Mont, whose abbots he had in large part selected. But beyond the Angevin lands, though the cult did exist, its imperial and English connections were too bothersome. There was only one church dedicated to Michael in Paris, a small chapel not far from the palace on a street called Barillerie; most likely founded by Louis VII, it was the site of Philip Augustus's baptism.[15] At the end of the fifteenth century, a poet claimed it was 600 years old, for he could not believe the cult of the guardian saint of Normandy could have waited so long to make its entry into the capital.[16] The church (which survived until 1781) became the namesake of the Pont Saint-Michel.

The Capetians nevertheless remained very reserved in their attitudes toward Saint Michael. Their protector was Saint Denis, a patron saint who enjoyed the prestige of ancient times and occupied a central place in the kingdom. Even after 1250, few links were established with the cult of Saint Michael other than those occasioned by war or pilgrimage. The *Philippide,* written by Guillaume Le Breton, chaplain to Philip Augustus, contained a fine description of Mont-Saint-Michel at the time of the conquest of Normandy. "There, on a vertical rock, a church that was built on the request of the Angel rises straight to Heaven."[17] Saint Louis made a pilgrimage to the abbey in 1256; so did Philip III and, in 1307, Philip IV.[18] All bore gifts of reliquaries and relics. Louis IX had a statue of Saint Michael placed on the spire of the Sainte-Chapelle in Paris; Philip the Fair gave the monastery fragments of the precious thorns and wood from the Cross belonging to the relics of the palace chapel and ordered a large statue covered with gold for the main altar.[19] But even though it received the attentions of the kings, the abbey began losing influence during the thirteenth century. The Mont stood in an outlying area, its sympathies were somewhat suspect, and it could not avoid jurisdictional disorders and conflicts—despite the power of the abbots who built the great Gothic church that still stands today.[20] Fewer and fewer pilgrims found their way there.

THE HOUSE OF VALOIS

Both Siméon Luce and Paul Perdrizet have argued that Saint Michael was the guardian of the House of Valois;[21] the change from one dynasty to the next was thus what led to a change in the kingdom's heavenly patron. Their conclusion was based above all on a congruence of dates: the Valois accession coincided with a resurgence of pilgrimages to the Mont. But doubts are permissible. Would it have been wise for royal newcomers whose legitimacy was still being questioned to create such a break? The Valois were careful to emphasize the continuity of the royal house of France, presenting themselves as successors of Saint Louis and, like him, devotees of Saint Denis. Furthermore, although the saintly attachments of a house were important, kings often limited themselves to the spiritual preferences of their subjects, for religious innovation was not well accepted. Finally, there is no direct proof that the Valois were devoted to Saint Michael before 1328.

Nor can an indirect argument for this change be made from the dates the Valois chose for marriages and knightings and the places they chose to be buried. Most Valois were buried in the family necropolis at the Jacobin church in Paris: Charles of Valois in 1325, Marguerite of Sicily in 1299, Catherine de Courtenay in 1307, and Charles (Catherine's son by Charles of Valois) in 1346. The viscera of Philip VI were also interred there. Other family members, such as Mahaut de Chatillon, the third wife of Charles of Valois, were buried at the Cordeliers. Furthermore, no marriage date nor any ceremony of knighthood coincided with the feastday of Saint Michael.[22]

Among the other branches of the royal line, the family of Blois-Penthièvre, whose patrimonial possessions were near Mont-Saint-Michel, had a special reverence for him. His image appeared on the white banners of Charles of Blois at the battle of Auray and, in 1363, Charles presented the Mont with a statue and with relics of Saint Evodius. A story later spread that Saint Michael had helped Charles during the siege of Quimper by keeping the tide from changing for six hours; so in 1388, Charles's son, Henry, gave the abbey the reliquary of Guingamp, containing, among others, the relics of his father, whose beatification had been under consideration since 1371.[23]

The family of Blois-Penthièvre were allies of the Valois. But the Evreux-Navarre, whose claims to the throne had been pushed aside in 1328, and whose enmity to the Valois was notorious, were also particularly devoted to Saint Michael. They had a strong foothold in southern Normandy. In 1360, Charles the Bad (1332–1387) gave Mont-Saint-Michel a candle weighing twelve pounds decorated with his arms and ordered that a perpetual mass be celebrated for his house;[24] his son, Charles III, repeated the gesture; Charles's brother, the Infante Louis, made a pilgrimage to the abbey in 1358 and sent the captain of Cherbourg there in 1368. It seems that both the region and the cult of Saint Michael were pro-Navarre, perhaps even pro-English, for in 1364 Abbot Geoffroy de Servon pledged fealty to a representative of Edward III.

As new miracles were reported at the abbey, the Valois kings waited and watched. John II, while duke of Normandy, was married there in 1331 and knighted there in 1332. He later minted gold coins, the "gold angels," with the Archangel Michael slaying the dragon on one side and, on the other, a cross decorated with fleurs-de-lys.[25] But all this occurred during one of the rare periods of good relations between the royal house and the Evreux-Navarre. Become king, John II soon relinquished the cult because it was associated with his rival and his son-in-law. The monarchy had to wait until the family of Evreux-Navarre was crushed in 1380, at the beginning of the reign of Charles VI, before it could feel free to entertain a relationship of its own with Saint Michael.

In 1393, when Charles VI momentarily regained his health after traveling to Mont-Saint-Michel, he took a vow to endow the Archangel's cult. He also had hidden political reasons for making the pilgrimage, for he wanted to strengthen the royal hold in Normandy and to reconcile the lords of Montfort, Penthièvre, and Clisson. Charles promised the abbey 100 pounds annually to celebrate a perpetual mass in his name and gave it many relics from Rome and the Holy Land.[26] He also dedicated one of the gates of the city of Paris to Michael, and, in a first for the royal family, had his child who was born in 1394 baptized with the name Michèle, a name rarely used outside the western parts of the kingdom.[27] Pierre Leroy, abbot of Mont-Saint-Michel from 1386 to 1411, served Charles in very important ways, as counselor to the king, judge in Parlement, and, as a moderate Gallican, as ambassador to

Rome, Hungary, Aragon, England, and the Empire to gain support for
the French position during the Great Schism. He was also an excellent
administrator for the abbey.[28]

But it was Charles VII who definitively transformed Saint Michael
into a royal and national saint by publicly choosing him as his protector. As early as 1418, when he was only thirteen, he put on his banners
the image of Saint Michael slaying the dragon, the emblem which would
continue to be regarded as his until 1440;[29] accounts of the royal stables
show that it appeared constantly on royal flags and uniforms—in 1418,
1422, 1430, 1437, and later. In 1430 it was accompanied by inscriptions such as "Saint Michael came to my rescue" and "Saint Michael is
my only defender."[30] It was such a banner that accompanied Charles at
his royal entries into Rouen and Paris.[31] Toward the middle of the
fifteenth century, when a representation of the banner of France was
placed on the "Rouen tapestry," it bore the same motif—Saint Michael
fighting the dragon.[32] Charles's banner had replaced the oriflamme of
Saint Denis, which he could not or would not use, and, from this time
on, it became the national banner.

The Archangel Michael was in turn most generous with the miracles
he bestowed on the young "King of Bourges," so much so in fact that
Jean Jouvenal des Ursins, the archbishop of Reims, avouched to Charles
on one occasion that, through this intermediary, God had worked
"more miracles for you than he ever worked for Charlemagne or for
Saint Louis."[33] The first of many miracles came at the time of Charles's
ascension to the throne in 1422. He had called together an assembly on
October 11 at the town of La Rochelle, which was then threatened by
the English. When the floor of the meeting hall suddenly collapsed,
there were many who were killed, but Charles was only slightly injured
(though rumors of his death circulated in Paris and Picardy).[34] Grateful
that his life had been saved, Charles established a foundation at Mont-
Saint-Michel on April 6, 1423, "so that thanks to the pious intervention
of the archangel whom we venerate and to whom we entrust the greatest confidence, we might earn the right to maintain the prosperity of our
kingdom and triumph over our enemies."[35] News of the miracle thus
accompanied Charles's ascension to the throne: just as the Archangel
had saved the king, so would he save the kingdom.

From September 1424 to June 1425, Mont-Saint-Michel was cut off
on both land and sea by the English. Abbot Robert Jolivet had passed to
the English side; all of Normandy had been occupied; following the
disaster of Verneuil, the Mont was the only place in the west still faithful

to king Charles. In 1434 when three attacks were launched against the garrison commanded by Louis d'Estouteville, they all failed, and the garrison's heroic resistance against the assaults was attributed to divine assistance: Saint Michael had held the rocky mount. In 1427, Michael appeared above Mont-Saint-Michel and caused a fierce storm to rage against England's ships. Again in 1434, the English claimed they saw the Archangel in the skies; this time, the English were beaten "while not a single person died on the Mont, which is an event that could be called miraculous, and they [the English] came back from there disconsolate and confused, the mercy of God and Monseigneur Saint Michael having always protected and protecting still this place."[36] One of the many chronograms in the chronicle of the Mont—that for 1434—read *Pardos JUgULaVIt CanCro, MICaeL, tUa VIrtUs* (By your virtue, Michael, you have tamed the leopards).[37]

Echoes of the resistance at the abbey rang loudly through the kingdom, skillfully amplified by royal letters. Joan of Arc, a young peasant from Lorraine, was one of those who heard it. Long passages about the siege also appeared in the *Chronicle of the Mont*, in Guillaume Cousinot's *Chronicle*, and in the work of the Burgundian Monstrelet.[38] The saint who was the guardian of city gates and regional borders had played his role so well that any sanctuary dedicated to him was thought inviolable. A telling plaque was placed at Saint-Michel-l'Herm around 1450: "Those who try to penetrate here will die on the spot with their heads turned round on their bodies."[39]

Michael was now the Archangel of Resistance. Soon he was to become the Archangel of the Reconquest. On June 25, 1429, following the liberation of Orléans and the victories of Jargeau and Patay, the garrison at Chien, near Talmont in the Poitou, caught sight of a rider in the sky . . . "midst a great fire . . . and he held an unsheathed sword in his hand . . . and rode on the air at such great speed that it seemed the whole castle was burning." Another account described the collective hallucination as follows: "People saw fully-armed men coming into these parts, riding through the air on a great white horse, and over their armor were large white sashes . . . they passed above two or three fortresses and went on towards Brittany . . . and because of this, those lands are terrorized and their people say they have seen their end in it."[40] The same thing happened twenty years later during the two hard-fought campaigns that ended with the reconquest of Gascony. On August 6, 1451, at the very moment when the English garrison of Bayonne was surrendering to the king, the sign of Saint Michael appeared in the sky "around the mid-day hour, a black cloud with a white cross inside it that stood over the town for a quarter of an hour, signifying that God wanted this land to be given back to the one who carried the white cross."[41] Others claimed they saw a crown and fleurs-de-lys hanging over the town.[42]

It is hardly surprising therefore that around 1446, Charles VII had a chapel built in the name of the Archangel at the Château d'Amboise. The following year, Marie of Anjou made a pilgrimage to the Mont. During those same middle decades of the century, the royal house bestowed a long series of favors on the abbey, favors that were useful to a monastery whose patrimony and pilgrimages had suffered the rack and ruin of war. In 1439 and 1446, royal ordinances exempted the abbey and town from all taxes, because, "though continually exposed, it has remained obedient to us . . . and suffered so much for its loyalty."[43] Royal contributions helped the abbey to reconstitute its patrimony and to reconstruct the choir of the church.

Nor is it surprising that Saint Michael played such a decisive role in the mission of Joan of Arc.[44] He was the principal figure in her visions from 1425 to 1428. While Joan was praying before his statue in the church at Domrémy, he appeared in the form of a "prud'homme" (a gentleman) and, though he wore no crown, he was radiant with light. He instructed, guided, and comforted her, told her of "the great misery that was the kingdom of France," and assured her that God would help with her mission. Because of this, Joan too put Michael's image on the banner that she carried when she led the assault on Orléans, and, during the last minutes of her life, it was Saint Michael whom Joan invoked, as she asked him to take her to the paradise he had promised her. The entire story was replayed in the *Mystery of the Siege of Orléans*, which showed Saint Michael coming before Joan to tell her of her mission ("to help France in her distress"), promising to protect her from danger and make her victorious, and comforting her in the last of her great trials.[45]

THE ORDER OF SAINT MICHAEL

Though Saint Michael performed only three miracles for Louis XI—far fewer than he had for his victorious father—it was this king who made official the conversion of the kingdom to Saint Michael's patronage. During a hunt in 1472, Louis was saved by the prior of Saint-Michel-en-l'Herm from the attack of a wild boar.[46] In gratitude for his escape, he instituted a ceremony of perpetual commemoration to be held each year on December 23 at the prior's sanctuary. On his command, Michel Colombe also fashioned a relief at the sanctuary depicting the king in prayer while a mounted Saint Michael killed the boar. The 1473, Louis gave to Mont-Saint-Michel a statue of the saint and the rock that had almost crushed the king when he was at Alençon, witness to yet another miracle. Word was also put about that the reconciliation between Louis and his brother, Charles of France, on the banks of the Sèvre, had been facilitated by the saint's intercession.[47] Louis made three pilgrimages to Mont-Saint-Michel, all of them to promote decidedly worldly as well as religious ends. In 1462 he forced his brother (then the duke of Berry), as well as the prince of Navarre and the malcontents who filled the royal court, to accompany him to the Mont in order to make a show of force against their ally, the duke of Brittany. It was on this occasion that Louis presented the abbey with the gold statue of Saint Michael that he had taken into exile, and favored the abbey with important exemptions. He also gave the fortress new heraldic arms with fleurs-de-lys and a powerful set of cannon. Later, in 1467, Louis celebrated at the Mont his seizure of Normandy from his brother Charles. He made one final political pilgrimage there in 1470 in connection with the situation in Brittany but, as he became progressively more involved in the conflict with Burgundy toward the end of his reign, his journeys began to lead toward the east rather than the west.

Before this, however, Louis XI had already undertaken in 1469 to create a royal order of Saint Michael. It was not the first time a French king had tried to establish a national order of knighthood: in 1351, John II had launched the Order of the Star in honor of the Virgin Mary as a response to Edward III's Order of the Garter. Its motto had been, "Stars show kings the way"; but the project had gone awry during the disasters of the early period of the Hundred Years War and soon withered away. Now Louis reinstituted it, while making important changes—he admitted few members, and the king was absolutely preeminent. With the end of the wars, the Order became a way to reinforce royal authority. By forcing the high nobility to participate, the king could attempt to control them: the first fifteen knights included the king's mistrusted brother, Charles of France, the Constable of Saint-Pol (who would later end his days on the scaffold), and most of the army chiefs. From each of them, the king required a pledge of "true love to Us and Our successors." And, unlike most other chivalric orders of the age, this one prohibited its members from joining any other. So strongly was the organization imbued with the idea of submission that in 1469 the duke of Brittany—

avowing that he did not wish to commit himself "to guarding, maintaining, and defending the glory and rights of the Crown and royal majesty and the authority of the order," as the statutes required[48]—refused to join its ranks. The king was much displeased.

The founding statutes of August 1, 1469, spoke eloquently of Saint Michael—"Archangel, first knight who in the cause of God struggled victoriously with the dragon . . . his place, his oratory has always been safely guarded, preserved, and defended by him without being taken, subjugated, or put into the hands of the ancient enemies of our kingdom." The order's motto alluded to Saint Michael unleashing and calming the fury of the ocean at will. The first seat of the Order was Mont-Saint-Michel. There the yearly chapter meetings and celebrations were to be held, to which the member knights were to come dressed in white damask linen embroidered with golden-shell motifs. But the Mont—too far away from the center of the kingdom—proved an impractical meeting place. We do not even know if the knights' hall constructed at the Mont was ever used for its intended purpose. On December 22, 1476, Louis XI transferred the order to the Sainte-Chapelle in Paris,[49] where he established a chapter of canons to pray to Saint Michael—the saint "who continuously, without interruption, conducts our affairs and those of the kingdom." Though additional articles were appended to complete the organizational aspects of the order, the annual pilgrimage around which the earlier statutes of the group had been conceived now disappeared. All the knights still wore chains of gold shells decorated with the image of Saint Michael's battle with the dragon—insignia they were never to remove—but they now began to lace ribbons with the colors of the royal house around the shells. References to the cult of the king were growing more pointed than those to Saint Michael.

Miniatures in manuscripts of the order's statutes confirm this. Little by little, images of the battles and manifestations of the saint gave way to images of the king who presided over the chapter meetings.[50] But the two sets of symbols were still linked in a copy of the statutes which Jean Fouquet made for Louis XI. In his illuminated frontispiece, Saint Michael's battle appears displayed on the walls of the chapter hall as a picture within a picture, while at the bottom of the parchment leaf two archangels in shell armor bear the shield of France, itself crowned and surrounded by the chain of the order. The "Rouen tapestry"[51] conveyed a similar message. Saint Michael's combat was relegated to only a small portion of the whole—it decorated one of the banners in the tapestry; but a crowned deer stood at the center of the enclosed field of lilies that represented the French kingdom, and the shield of France below was guarded by the leopards of Charles of France, the king's brother. Accompanying banderoles bore the inscription:

> Cet étendard est une enseigne
> Qui a loyal Français enseigne
> De jamais ne l'abandonner
> S'il ne veut son honneur donner.
>
> [This banner is a sign
> Which teaches the loyal Frenchman
> Never to abandon it
> Unless he is willing to give up his honor.]

The kingdom thus shielded itself under the protective wing of a saint who, bit by bit, evolved into a symbol of loyalty to a victorious monarchy.

When, at the beginning of the reign of Charles VIII, a knight of the order wrote a prosopopoeia of its membership,[52] he followed his description of the order's founding and the excellence of its principles with a heated attack on its decadence—material decadence (the order's revenues had collapsed) and spiritual decadence (its most noble members had become "flattering, jealous, and disloyal"). The order needed to "keep the kingdom together," he wrote, and assure internal peace "without disagreement," to create the esteem and support that all knights needed in order to be pillars of the kingdom. By guaranteeing the cohesiveness of the high nobility, the order could also secure that of the entire nation. Abroad, it would guarantee military success. As for Michael, the prosopopoeia portrayed him as "the greatest war chief, whose aid merits being called upon in all places. . . . He assures victory, honor, and recompense to all."

WHY SAINT MICHAEL?

The Order of Saint Michael was thus little more than a consecration of the royal cult that dated all the way back to Charles VI, a cult that had found affirmation in the resistance to the English. The facts are easy enough to establish. But why was Saint Michael chosen for the task?

AN ANTI-ENGLISH SAINT

The first reason lies in the fact that the dragon of Saint Michael symbolized England, a country that was every bit an intruder by sea as the fearsome beast had been. The isle kingdom, for its part, had enjoyed the special protection of Saint George ever since the time of Richard the Lionhearted (1189–1199). During the Hundred Years War, its armies had carried the Cross of Saint George (a straight red cross) as they marched. And as they went into battle, it was George's name that they cried out. In 1345, accounts of the English wardrobe estimated that 86 shields with red crosses would be needed for the royal ship and 800 for the soldiers. By the end of the century, Richard II (1377–1399) was ordering all English soldiers to wear the cross of Saint George, whereas foreign soldiers caught wearing it would be put to death. In 1415—about fifty years before France officially adopted Saint Michael as its guardian—Saint George, whose cult had been celebrated through-out the kingdom since 1222, was officially adopted as the patron saint of the English nation;[53] Archbishop Chichele of Canterbury ordered that April 23, the feast of Saint George, be celebrated throughout the English territories with all the solemnity of Christmas.

George had not always been so exclusively English. Up until the fourteenth century, he had been just as popular in France. As the holy horseman of legend who had fought off a dragon to save a princess, he had served as a model for French knights as well. In his name they were dubbed; by his name they swore.[54] The Crusades reinforced Saint George's popularity as a military cult-figure. Even as late as 1344, John II entertained plans to establish an order of Saint George and the Virgin Mary, a project that Edward III preempted by founding the Order of the Garter.[55]

Then all began to change. The cult of Saint George disappeared almost entirely in France; although existing cult sites were not debap-tized, no new ones were created, nor were any statues or confraternities dedicated in his name. Even French representations of Saint George were rare between 1350 and 1480: one miniature in the book of hours of the duke of Bedford, another in the book of hours of Anne of Brittany (whose Montfort origins tied her to England), and a fresco at Saint-Léger-d'Ebreuil (dating from the wars in Italy) which commemorated the knighting of the lord of Ternant. In the Anglo-Burgundian territo-ries, in contrast, the cult of Saint George remained alive; organizations such as the confraternity of archers, founded in Rouen sometime be-tween 1415 and 1450, dedicated themselves to him; so too did the Flemish confraternities of archers, particularly as this area reaffirmed its ties to the Empire, where in 1470 the Emperor Sigismond instituted an order of Saint George to unite the German princes together against the Turks.[56] But in France, there must have been a collective phenomenon, conscious or otherwise, that had worked to associate Saint George with

England. Why else would a figure traditionally seen as the patron saint of knights and crusaders have been cast off, despite the ongoing vitality of the ideas of knighthood and crusade which he embodied?

Saint Michael became the French Saint George. Differences between the two were still visible around 1300: George was a mounted figure, wearing armor and carrying a lance and a shield; Michael was an angel dressed in a dalmatic, who with his processional cross struck down the dragon without apparent struggle. Then, slowly, Michael began to take on all the characteristics traditionally identified with George—except for his horse. Between 1380 and 1440, French representations of Michael generally portrayed him in a suit of armor, carrying a sword, a shield, and a banner.[57] The sword and armor had appeared as early as the thirteenth century at Lutz-en-Dunois and at Montceaux-l'Etoile; by 1400, they were widespread. The shield, in contrast, presents a problem, for there were several different versions plus a number of fantasized forms.

The one that appeared most frequently was a shield with a raised center divided into four sections by a large central cross, with a small cross filling each quadrant. This was an exact representation of the relic of Mont-Saint-Michel[58] and appeared on most of the fifteenth-century pilgrimage banners and in a number of late medieval statues. But the shield sometimes bore another emblem, which though less common is more interesting. It was an upright white cross—white, the color of angels, the symbol of purity. Knights of the Order of Saint Michael were adorned with white, just as were the banners of pilgrims who traveled to the Mont. And from 1300 onward, white was also the color of the kings of France.

The royal white was either worn as a sash or worn as an upright cross. During the Flemish wars, French knights had worn white sashes: they fashioned themselves scarves of this color for good luck in 1304, it was said, just before the decisive battle of Mons-en-Pevèle. The white cross ap peared in 1355 in orders Jean d'Armagnac sent to his royal soldiers: he demanded that they wear it in their confrontations with the red-crossed English along the Gascon frontier.[59] So Cuvelier in his *Chronicle* of 1380–1387 described Du Guesclin transferring his allegiance to the French:

> La croix vermeille ôta comme Français gentil
> Et si mit la blanche croix au nom de fleur de lys.[60]

> [He took off his vermillion cross as a good Frenchman should
> And donned the white cross called the lily flower.]

In 1422, moreover, when the death of Charles VI was announced, the Dauphin's entourage renounced the sash of the Armagnacs and took up the white cross, "the true and ancient insignia of the kings of France."[61] With the Civil Wars, the idea that this cross represented all that was French and the red cross what was English became embedded in the habits of the people.

But how did the cross come to replace the sash? Perhaps, as Cuvelier thought, it represented a simplified fleur-de-lys, the white lily. (Around 1400, the missal of Charles VI handily transformed the four small crosses on the shield of Saint Michael into a set of fleurs-de-lys.)[62] Perhaps there was also an allusion to the legend of Saint Michael at work here. Michael often appeared armed with a white cross as a weapon, and, as we have seen, the coin commonly known as the "angel" showed him in this same way. Early in the fourteenth century, the cathedral of Coutances portrayed him fighting off the dragon with a shield bearing a white cross; elsewhere, the cross also appeared either on his shield or his banner; and by the beginning of the fifteenth century, pilgrims dedicated to Saint Michael all wore white crosses on their clothing.[63] Perhaps French royal troops were also pilgrims and worshippers of Saint Michael. But what path did the transformation take, what direction did it go in? Did the kings of France begin wearing the white cross because it was the emblem of Saint Michael, or did the saint's cross eventually grow white because the kings were wearing crosses that were white? We cannot yet answer this question.

The image of Saint Michael was sometimes accompanied by fleurs-de-lys on pilgrimage banners and royal coins. This was true of Philip VI's "angel" of 1341 and the triple gold "little angel" (angelot) of 1467.[64] Miniatures adopted similar solutions,[65] one of the most interesting of which depicted Michael holding a shield decorated with three lilies topped with a crown and surrounded by the chain of the Order of Saint Michael.[66] Late in the fifteenth century, the arms of Mont-Saint-Michel—to whose motif of shells Louis XI had added three fleurs-de-lys in 1472—also became part of Michael's iconography.[67] From there it was but a small step to the shield of France. The royal, pro-French connotations of Saint Michael cannot be demonstrated more clearly. He had been transformed from a figure whose sympathies merely ran counter to Saint George to a full-blown protector of the monarchy.

RESCUE IN TIMES OF DANGER

Though pilgrimages to Mont-Saint-Michel had died away during the thirteenth century, they were revitalized again after 1333 with an onslaught of new miracles—whirlwinds of fire and repeated miracles of the shore, all popularized by a mystery play.[68] The journeying resumed, undaunted by military operations, for the English went no further than to exact travel taxes. By 1368, the confraternity of Saint-Jacques in Paris was welcoming 16,700 pilgrims heading to or returning from Mont-Saint-Michel. Though the stream must have diminished somewhat during certain military operations, it remained quite heavy throughout the fifteenth century.

Pilgrims heading to the Mont were seeking deliverance from an ill-defined, multifaceted danger: sometimes it was childbirth, a fall, or in some cases a shipwreck; in others it was blindness or paralysis. If Saint Michael was assigned any specialized practice at all, it was in treating fever (because Michael's sign was fire) and wounds (because he had fought the dragon). Jean de Lesche, an unfortunate student, made a pilgrimage to Mont-Saint-Michel for both these reasons.[69]

Though the saint's role was not clearly defined, those who came looking for his services were. Whether shepherds, cooks' helpers from the court of Charles VI, or burghers and nobles, they were above all young.[70] Two regions in particular, regions that had not been very involved in pilgrimages up until this time, began to produce them in great numbers. In Languedoc, Pierre Soybert, bishop of Saint-Papoul, worried about the risks the pilgrimages posed to the youths of Montpellier, Villefranche-de-Rouergue, and Millau, who traveled to the abbey in groups. Germany and Switzerland were also sending large waves of single people between fourteen and twenty years of age. Youths of this age had already fought in the wars: Saint Michael, the knight who fought in just wars for the cause of the good, was the first to have done so. Perhaps Charles VI, ascending the throne as he did at twelve, and his successor Charles VII, who assumed power at the age of thirteen, also felt a kinship with the youthful Archangel Michael.

THE PERFECT GUARDIAN ANGEL

The Holy Scriptures and the Fathers of the Church had all made Saint Michael the angel of the Chosen People. From this he turned into the angel of the Church and the Carolingian Empire. Finally, from the eleventh century onward, Michael became the angel of Western Francia.[71] Simple mortals merited only the help of lesser angels; collectivities deserved more. And, by the end of the thirteenth century, Saint Thomas had clearly set forth what such an angel should be. Thomas, like Pseudo-

Denis many centuries earlier, believed that God had created a hierarchy of angels. The archangels were those who instructed man and inspired him to do good; they were responsible for all important prophecies and they protected the human multitudes and their collectivities.[72] Certain mortals however could be assigned angels of a higher rank, if they were very holy and their social position merited it. Mary, for example, had been given Gabriel, one of the principalities.

At the end of the fourteenth century, Denys the Carthusian modified the hierarchy.[73] He made the principalities into the guardians of king-doms, peoples, and provinces. Communities of a lesser order, such as towns, castles, and cities, were protected by archangels. Principalities looked over kings, prelates, and princes, whereas archangels watched over bailiffs, seneschals, and royal officers. According to Denys's vision, however, Saint Michael escaped categorization entirely. He was the guardian of the entire Church. But Denys was troubled by the possibil-ity that one of the principalities might be assigned as a guardian angel to a bad ruler. So he followed the lessons of Peter Lombard and Udalric d'Auxerre and disassociated the ruler's rulership from his person, assign-ing a principality or archangel to his public function and a lesser angel to his person.

Such ideas quickly gained popularity. Chancellor Gerson, author of four sermons on Saint Michael, three in Latin and one in French, fol-lowed Denys's lead.[74] His Saint Michael served as the angel of the Church, protecting it from schism, while each member of the Church, "each person, has a good angel and sometimes several if need be, for himself and for the religious offices he observes." For the Spanish preacher Vincent Ferrier, Saint Michael was the greatest of all collective angels. The ministry of the angels of collectivities, he wrote, would rejoice "when rectors become more concerned with the public good than with their own, when they make holy laws."[75] His angels of col-lectivities were responsible for defending communities against demons, sustaining them in the midst of temptation, interceding on their behalf before God, and leading them to glory both in this world and the next. Ferrier's Michael was probably still responsible for the protection of the Church rather than the kingdom.

The concept of the angel of collectivities and dignities evanesced in the fifteenth century, replaced by the growing notion of the individual guardian angel. The idea that there were angels who protected man in general had always been around; but it took a long time for people to accept the idea that every man, whether a sinner or not, was accompanied by an angel from the time he was conceived and baptized to the time he died and passed on to the afterworld. Peter Lombard asserted that each angel served several people; others thought that angels had several charges in the course of time; yet others that angels were assigned only temporary missions, at crucial moments in a person's life. Monastic circles, led by Saint Bernard, slowly evolved the idea that angels were the confidants of monks, constantly engaged in benevolent conversation with them and showing them the way to moral perfection. Although many late medieval sermons on the subject of angels were still addressed to monks, such beliefs also developed among the laity. In his French sermon on Saint Michael, Chancellor Gerson spoke of the ongoing assistance that angels offered every moment of one's lifetime, as they watched over little children and encouraged, instructed, and led adults. Gerson was one of the first to claim that angels were always present and that a mutual love attached believers to their protecting angels. But the fact that the notion of the guardian angel took so long to gain popularity explains why so few prayers were dedicated to them between the thirteenth and the fifteenth centuries, and why those few that survive all came out of the monastic milieu.[76] It was not until 1518 that the bishop of Rodez established in his diocese the first festival of the guardian angel.

Nonetheless, Saint Michael was soon considered the guardian angel par excellence, the most powerful intercessor at the moment of death— when he would shelter and protect the soul—and at the Last Judgment. This is how the Rohan *Hours* depicted him, and how he appeared in the "Play of the Little Soul" presented every year at Avignon during the reign of King René, in which a small child pursued by demons takes refuge in the arms of Saint Michael. By the end of the Middle Ages, many prayers to the Archangel Michael echoed with the hope that the saint would offer help at death and at the final judgment.[77] The book of prayers that belonged to Charles d'Orléans, cousin of Charles VII, addressed Saint Michael in just such a manner: "Prince of angels, leader of the souls that you save in Paradise, may I be united with you, protect me in the hour of my death, defend me at the terrifying judgment of my soul."

Michael was also expected to protect the nation and the king from death and the condemnation of God. He was the guardian angel of the king—though of his dignity, his public office, rather than of his person. He was also the guardian angel of the kingdom. As the most noble of angels, he was necessarily linked to the most noble of monarchs. The

Diary of the Estates-General of 1484 reaffirmed this,[78] as did the jurist Guillaume Benoit in his *Repetitio:*[79] "In France, it is Saint Michael who is the angel of royal dignity because he is the most powerful of all the angels, just as the King of France is the most Christian of kings. And by the will of God he is appointed to guard the kingdom; as sign of this protection he appeared in France at the Mont and the kings of France can say, as Daniel did, 'he is the first who came to my aid.' " The *Counsel to Charles VIII* offered verses on the subject:

> Faites donc prier sans espace
> Par votre patron saint Michel
> Afin que se maintienne
> Tout le royaume en paix et union . . .[80]
>
> [Therefore ask without delay
> That your patron Saint Michael pray
> So that that the entire kingdom may
> Be kept in peace and unity . . .]

Two things were expected of this "guardian of France." He was to protect the nation against a catastrophic English invasion and occupation, and to watch over it from its very foundation. The first task was reminiscent of the role Michael played for the dying and the resurrected when they were called before the tribunal of God. It was particularly emphasized in the reign of Charles VII, and again during the reign of Louis XI when the king had openly compared his enemy, Charles the Bold, duke of Burgundy, to Lucifer.[81] Michael guaranteed military victory to the king who fought a just war under the banner of the white cross, a war against evil-doing and obstinate demons. He also shared revelations with the king, allowing him to keep to the proper path. And as he would appear to Joan of Arc, so he had also appeared to Pierre Hug of Montpellier in 1388 and to Marie Robine from 1390 to 1392.[82] Saint Michael was, in effect, the special intermediary for transmitting divine revelations during the wave of prophetic events that ran through France from 1388 to 1435—a movement that was most likely an unconscious form of collective refusal in the face of two unacceptable threats, invasion and the Schism. He appeared again in a prophetic text in 1458, carrying the ring of victory to Charles VII. In this last, the notion of collective guardian angel was certainly not far off.

But to the people of the fifteenth century, the story of Michael's guardianship had in fact begun way back with the first conversion of the kingdom. Theologians of the time were not sure if people who had never been baptized had the right to guardian angels. As Nicolo Albergati, the papal legate, wrote in 1431: "The first chapel ever to be established in the kingdom of France in honor of and with reverence to Monseigneur Saint Michael is located there [near Rouen], and King Clovis founded it, the first Christian king, to whom God sent the Holy Ampulla with which he was consecrated by a certain angel, and because of the grace that Our Lord showed him at this time he founded this noble chapel."[83] Albergati comes close to asserting that the "certain angel" in question was either Saint Michael or one of his representatives. With this went the concurrent belief that Michael would continue to protect the kingdom until the Last Judgment. The kingdom would endure, it was said, as long as the fountain continued to bubble at Mont-Saint-Michel.[84]

In time, Michael's protection turned toward conciliation. During the reign of Louis XI, he was the guardian of the borders, just as he had been protector of city gates in the early Middle Ages; he watched over the territory of the nation just as he had watched over Mont-Saint-Michel, keeping it inviolable and assuring its obedience to the natural and legitimate king. Louis XI gave statues of the saint to border churches, such as the church at Belpech in the Pyrenees—neighbor to the count of Foix of notoriously wavering loyalty—whose statue was graced with a chain of the order. During the Roussillon campaign, he changed the name of Collioure, an important fortified stronghold, to Saint-Michel, to ensure that the Spanish would not recapture it. And when he wrested Dijon from the Burgundians, he immediately dedicated a church to Michael there.

Thus it was that the idea that Saint Michael offered help only in exceptional times, in times of mortal danger, was replaced with the notion that he could mount an ongoing and attentive watch over the integrity and the rights of the Crown. From this time on, he protected the king and the kingdom above all else, an assignment that would continue for several centuries. He had undoubtedly triumphed due to the will of the kings themselves, but theirs was a will that conformed to the growth of popular religious beliefs. Guardian angels had given birth to a patron saint of the kingdom. Religion had shored up politics, and the way these two spheres joined reflected something that was unique about this Most Christian nation.

CHAPTER 6

The Most Christian King and Nation

By the end of the Middle Ages, both the king of France and the kingdom were "most Christian." The etymology of the term will not tell us why, for nothing there singled out either France or its king for the honor. Its meaning and its force came rather from a careful nurturing of a long historical tradition, a tradition that made of its kings the true inheritors of Pepin and Charlemagne, founders of the estates of the Church; made them the defenders of the papacy; made their knights so central to the story of the Crusades that the people of the Holy Land gave the name *Franci* to all Westerners.

Already early in the thirteenth century, it was a commonplace to call the French king and his kingdom "most Christian," using the title the papal chancery had bestowed on him and a number of other rulers. By the end of that century, France, the pious and orthodox kingdom that had known neither schism nor heresy, had become a "most Christian" kingdom of God, a veritable heaven on earth, with the French as the Chosen People of the new alliance. The chorus of glory was heard continuously from Philip the Fair to Charles V, as the royal religion gradually comingled with religion pure and simple. Then, in the last decades of the Middle Ages, the idea was given a new twist. From an occasional reference, it became a regular title: "most Christian" became the sole property of the king of France and of his dynasty, an empowering justification for his independence, raising him and his kingdom above the claims of both Church and Imperium. Having turned the title to their own benefit, the kings of France succeeded in making "most Christian"—innately religious though the concept was—into a juridical privilege that graced the king with the authority to intervene in the affairs of the Church of France.

THE TITLE "MOST CHRISTIAN"

The Church wrote the first chapter of this story in the early Middle Ages when it rewarded the title "most Christian" to rulers whose favor it wished to curry. The papal chancery called Charlemagne and Pepin "most Christian"; bishops sometimes used the term to address less important rulers.[1] But it was only late in the twelfth century that writers began to assert that the *Franci* were superior to others because of their faith.

Faith, the primary virtue of the day, appeared as a major theme in crusading literature,[2] as it did in the speech of Pope Urban at Clermont as reported by Guibert de Nogent in his *Deeds of God Through the Franks* and by Robert the Monk in his *History of Jerusalem,* where praise for all Christendom was inextricably mixed with praise for its particular embodiment in the faith of the French. The *gens Francorum,* the people of France, devoted to the pope, had been transformed by God into a *beata gens,* a holy people; from the earliest days, they had been steadfast and persevering; their emperors had assisted the popes who sought refuge among them.[3] Because they were "chosen by God and distinguished from all other nations as much by the agreeableness of their land as by the fervor of their faith and their devotion to the Church,"[4] the divine plan included yet another role for them to play: from their midst would come martyrs, confessors, and crusaders to deliver the Holy Land. Late-eleventh-century texts like this used the term "most Christian" to describe the French people rather than the territory. They rarely assigned it to French kings, since none before Louis VII had personally taken part in the Crusades. Though Abbot Suger described how Louis VI and Louis VII continuously defended the interests of Christianity—protecting churches, the poor, and the orphaned—he chose the words "most devoted" to describe their leadership, not "most Christian."[5]

It was in the twelfth and thirteenth centuries that "most Christian" began to grace both the king and a kingdom that had finally gained a degree of territorial stability. The king of France became "the most

Christian of all kings," the best of rulers,[6] and acquired the radiant cloak of "the king of all earthly kings, according to the plan of God."[7]

> Le premier roi de France fit Dieu par son commandment
> Couronner par ses anges dignement en chantant
> Pour être en terre son sergent, tenir droite justice.[8]
>
> [The first king of France was crowned by God's command
> In dignified manner by his singing angels
> To be his sergeant on earth, to keep proper justice.]

The papal chancery agreed when in 1239 and 1245 it called Saint Louis a "most Christian prince, head of a very devoted people,"[9] as did Matthew Paris—despite his Englishness—when he asserted that "the faith is the most vibrant and the most pure" in France.[10] Jacques de Vitry concurred: "there are many Christian nations, but the first among them is France, and the French are pure Catholic."[11]

The churches of France were numerous and prosperous, blessed with a treasury of precious and highly venerated relics. When the author of the prologue to the *Great Chronicles* undertook to describe the French nation toward the end of the thirteenth century, what he praised above all was its most Christian identity. Through this official history the monarchy was merely repeating and amplifying an idea that foreign works, papal bulls, and national chronicles had already clearly established:

> It is not without reason that this nation grew famous above all other nations, for she was not enslaved to idolatry and faithlessness for very long. . . . Early did she show obeisance to her creator, offered God the first fruits and the beginning of her reign. . . . Because she was converted, there was no more fervent and strictly held faith in any other land. All is multiplied through her, sustained by her, defended by her. If another nation causes the Holy Church wrong or grief, she turns to France to register her complaint, turns to France for refuge and help; it is from France that comes the sword to avenge her. France, like a loyal daughter, helps her mother in all her needs. And so it continues for all time. France alone is in a position to aid the Church and help her.[12]

How longstanding was the faith of France, how fervent and righteous!

Then, early in the reign of Philip the Fair, the royal house began using the term "most Christian" for propaganda purposes.[13] Up until that moment, loyalty to the king had been intertwined with reverence for the Church—a confusion reinforced by the memory of Saint Louis—but, in 1296, Philip IV began a campaign of violent conflict with the papacy over his fiscal demands and the independence of the Church in France.[14] Philip, a sincerely pious man, mounted his defense of himself and his kingdom on his claim to be most Christian; in order to undermine Pope Boniface VIII, who at that moment was mired in controversy, he established a direct link between himself, his kingdom, and God. He was the first king of France to require his subjects to address him regularly as "most Christian king."

What did he wish to accomplish thereby? Certainly not to extoll the personal merits for which he was already known—"Philip, King of France, outshines all other rulers of this world in justice, truth, faith, charity, true hope, humility, devotion and religion," exclaimed Ramon Lull.[15] For this grandson of Saint Louis was wont to hide behind the mask of royal lineage and duty. His dynasty, he reminded his subjects, had given the Church its blood and suffered misery, pain, and many trials for the sake of Christendom; some of his kin had let themselves be captured for the sake of their faith; others had been wounded or killed.[16] His ancient ancestral tradition stretched back to Charlemagne, to Clovis, a tradition that made of the king of France more than just a mortal: he was a minister of God, "a shield for the faith and a defender of the Church."[17] It was Philip's duty therefore to fight heresy and wrest the Church from the hands of Boniface, for his was the side of God, and with him truth and justice reigned throughout the house of France.[18] At the heart of his claim to be "most Christian" was rather a super-christianization of French territory.

This idea had been developing since at least 1250, before definitively emerging in Philip's propaganda as a group of juridical arguments that demonstrated the kingdom's independence from both emperor and pope.[19] Some of Boniface's decisions gave the impression that the pope wished to subordinate the kingdom to the Empire. To combat such assertions, a number of theoretical treatises on the relationship between the spiritual and the temporal defended "the honor and the liberty of the kingdom of France";[20] they and other voices of royal propaganda maintained that France was held of God alone, its king recognized no superior in this world.[21] By virtue of its people and its clergy it was a most Christian kingdom: the French nation is "notably most Christian," said one;[22] the kingdom is "an example and a mainstay for Christendom," said another.[23] Between the kingdom and the Church there had always reigned a friendship, a union, a confederation that had worked to the benefit of both. France was "the principal and most venerable part of Christendom,"[24] the pillar that upheld the Church. Destruction of the kingdom could bring scandal and destruction to the whole Church, for the kingdom was like the biblical wall that protected the House of Israel from heretics and infidels; the king is the angel who raises his sword to confront the forces of evil and darkness.[25] But the pope did not respect this kingdom's fervent people who more than any other were partisans of the true faith, and so he stood accused of heresy.

But soon after these appeals against the pope, calls for unity between the kingdom and the Church practically disappeared, as memories of the conflict with Boniface VIII eventually combined with the Great Schism and then the tensions arising from the wars in Italy at the end of the fifteenth century to replace union with the hierarchical Church with an alliance directly with God. The first signs of this transformation were already apparent in the reign of Philip the Fair.

It was the summer of 1302—a difficult time for the king, who was in conflict with the pope, and whose army had just been beaten by the Flemish weavers—when the Mendicant friar Guillaume de Sauqueville first referred to the French as the people of God.[26] France was chosen just as Israel had been; it was the heavenly kingdom on earth and the land of the new alliance, the promised land, the holy land: "God chose the kingdom of France before all other people."[27] In 1312, King Philip used similar words to describe the kingdom:

> The Most-High Lord Jesus, having discovered in this kingdom more than in any other part of the world a stable foundation for the holy faith and the Christian religion and having decided that the greatest devotion to him, his vicars, and his ministers was to be found there, decided to honor it above all kingdoms and principalities with a number of prerogatives and singular favors.[28]

These prerogatives were the Holy Ampulla for the coronation, the power to cure scrofula (successful even during the crisis with the papacy),[29] the fleur-de-lys on royal arms, and the oriflamme (about which we will see more at the end of this chapter). Bowing to the inevitable, the papacy at last admitted that "God chose the kingdom of France above all other peoples."[30]

A second transformation came as people gradually forgot many of the heresies that had troubled the kingdom in the twelfth and thirteenth centuries. Though they still believed the kings of France were fighting heterodoxy, the battleground was somewhere else, on the terrain chosen by the crusaders. Struggles within were limited to anti-Jewish campaigns (for Jews were not considered part of the nation in the fourteenth century). Full-blown campaigns against heresy happened only beyond the borders. This historical amnesia, as we will see, became an ideological necessity in the reign of Charles V.

Aside from this instance of fantasy, publicists of the later fourteenth century were content to reiterate and spread abroad the themes invented by the propagandists of Philip IV. They innovated in one important respect however; they made of the term "most Christian" a specific title and ancient privilege rather than a transitory honor bestowed by others; it belonged exclusively to the Capetian king and kingdom.[31] The monarchy was bent on a monopoly. "You are and must be," Raoul de Presles wrote to his king, "the only principal champion of the Church, the most Christian prince."[32] That is what the monarchy achieved, eventually persuading others of its cause, persuading them indeed that the epithet had been there from time immemorial, that Clovis himself bore it, that it was bound up with the history of the nation. Eventually, Pope Paul II (1464–1471) introduced it into the formulary of papal letters to the king, explaining that "even if his predecessors had not made use of the title 'most Christian,' he had witnessed and read about so many proofs of devotion in the life of the kings of France, that he would feel he was shirking his duty if he did not call the king 'most Christian.' "[33] The wars of Italy did not touch the monopoly claimed by Charles V and confirmed under Louis XI. For by then the title had become much more than a chancery form of address; it had been given a wide range of connotations by the political theologians of Philip IV and the jurists of Charles V and his successors. We will now look at these in detail.

THE MOST CHRISTIAN KINGDOM

Proofs of the superiority of the kingdom's faith were numerous and diverse. The official version was grounded first of all in material indicators, in the kingdom's "wealth of relics and holy bodies."[34] Thirteenth-century authors dwelt on relics of the Passion of Christ which were linked to the memory of Saint Louis; the transfer of the Crown of Thorns from Byzantium to Paris, for example, was interpreted to mean that it was the French king who was the chief ruler of Christendom:

> Car Dieu aime sur toute cette maison
> Aussi sa croix et sa couronne d'épines
> Clous, fer et lance de la Passion
> Y sont gardées en excellente cure.[35]

> [For God loves this house above all
> Thus his Cross and his Crown of Thorns
> The Nails, Iron and Lance from the Passion
> Are kept here under excellent care.]

After 1415, the lists of relics enlarged to include contributions from the south. According to the *Debate of the Heralds-at-arms* the treasuries of the kingdom housed "the most beautiful relics of Christendom: the Nail, the Crown of Thorns, the Holy Shroud [of Cadouin], the Seven Saints of Toulouse."[36] (Cadouin and Toulouse are markedly south of the Loire.)

The ecclesiastical organization of the period, the buildings that embodied it, inspired further arguments. France was a Conciliar nation, according to an anti-English line that grew primarily out of the Council of Basle.[37] It was graced with 12 archbishoprics whereas England had only 2, between 88 and 104 bishoprics,[38] and 7 universities. It overflowed with sacred sites,[39] large abbeys, and immense cathedrals. And thanks to the generosity of its kings and many believers, its ecclesiastical livings were richer and more notable than anywhere else in Christendom. The numbers of clergy in France, their devotion and knowledge drawn from that brimming source, the University of Paris, all added to the case.

These material considerations tended to validate a longstanding historical tradition, which held that the French had been a people of faith long before their conversion. "Even during the time when they worshipped idolatry, there were many faithful among them. When they turned to the Christian faith, they were the first of the Christian nations to receive it," as Claude de Seyssel puts it, thereby summing up an entire medieval tradition.[40] The same tradition was enlisted against the English and Burgundians, latecomers to Latin Christendom.

To this sense of the past, religious fervor was added. The kingdom had given birth to many saints, martyrs, and crusaders; no heretic had ever lived there.

> Le royaume très chrétien
> Où la foi est enluminée
> Où n'habite ni juif ni païen . . .[41]
>
> [The most Christian kingdom
> Where faith is enlightened
> And neither Jew nor pagan abides . . .]

Just as the fleur-de-lys repelled serpents, so it repelled heretics. "Gaul knows no monsters," wrote Saint Jerome,[42] and others repeated the saying.[43] The strength of such authoritative voices produced both prudent claims ("the kingdom of France alone has known no widespread heresy")[44] and bold ones (it "has never known any heresy at all").[45]

This remained a visible theme through the end of the fifteenth century: "I am known to have always been Catholic, never to have harboured heretical thoughts, and I never will," were the words Georges Chastellain put in the mouth of France.[46] It had identified the kingdom with Catholic orthodoxy in all the schisms that had threatened Christendom: in its name, the kings of France had always strived to pacify the crisis in the Church.

From Brunetto Latini[47] at the end of the thirteenth century to Alain Chartier in the middle of the fifteenth,[48] the kingdom's aid to the Church was repeatedly evoked. The most complete list of such occasions appears in a manuscript from the abbey of Saint-Denis dating from the reign of Charles VIII[49] which commemorates the kings of the Crusades (Pepin, Charlemagne, Philip Augustus, Louis VII, and Saint Louis), lists the shipments of soldiers and money France sent to the Holy Land, the offers of shelter to exiled popes (Innocent II, Alexander III, and Urban IV), the Italian expeditions of Pepin, Charlemagne, and Charles the Bald, and even the unrealized crusading projects of Philip I, Philip IV, Philip VI, and Charles VI.

In the imagination of all these authors, the struggle against heretics always took place beyond the borders of the kingdom; thus the Albigensian heresy was quashed when the lands where it had flourished "returned" to France. Exceptions to the rule involved at most some minor groups of intellectuals, and in these cases it was not heresy that had been repressed but merely some sinful books.

This insistence on the kingdom's untarnished orthodoxy was hardly innocent of political purpose: it aimed its charge at England—which always took the side opposed to France during the Great Schism—and above all at the Empire.[50] "There have already been twenty-one antipopes and few that the emperors had not supported in their schism against the popes," wrote Etienne de Conti. "And all of the true popes have fled to France which has sustained them until they have been reestablished in their see. . . . And I have seen the stories of more than twelve emperors who were heretics and schismatics . . .," among them Frederick II and his descendants, who were crushed by the Capetian Charles of Anjou.[51] In his *Treatise on the Differences Among Schisms*[52] written for Louis XII at the beginning of the sixteenth century, Jean Lemaire de Belges devoted twenty-three chapters to the conciliatory and saving gestures that France had made toward the Church: one chapter per schism. The virtuous race of Frenchmen, he said, had often "saved the vessel of the Church, led it back to the port of salvation and the harbour of peace."

This glorious Christian past guaranteed the kingdom of France a special place in Christendom, the place God willed for all time to come. As the Hebrews were in the Old Testament, so the Christian Church was in the present age—the Chosen People; the French, as Christians, participated in this new race of the elect; and given the exceptional quality of their faith, they belonged to the highest order of Christendom. The French were God's people, the people of the New Alliance.

It was around 1300 that writers began to assert that God had given the French kingdom His particular benediction and approval, that He had sent visible signs of their selection: the Holy Ampulla, the lily, and the oriflamme. France had become the special claim of God, his heritage and patrimony,[53] its mission to defend the Church, carry out the Crusades, and serve as an example and shield for all Christians; the Franks had become "a special people dedicated to carrying out the commandments of God."[54] As a papal ambassador said to Charles VII, "To you who are the most Christian of rulers, we entrust the salvation of all, for by hereditary right you are the chief of the army of Christians, and all rulers look to you for the salvation of everyone."[55] God had taken care of the kingdom from its earliest days: "He planted you first on earth."[56] He had tended to it in stormy times: "God fights for you,"[57] "God shines his countenance upon you, the hand of God rests on the people he has chosen."[58]

This sanctification found its most forceful expression in the equation of France with the Kingdom of Israel. For this, as we have seen, Guillaume de Sauqueville and his contemporaries around 1300 set a precedent when they drew parallels between the kings of France and Israel, between the people of France and the Hebrew nation: the royal throne was like David's, the king himself the figure of Moses.[59] But of all the expressions of this idea, the most interesting is that presented by Jean-Ange de Legonissa in his massive *Opus Davidicum*,[60] dedicated to Charles VIII. Here we find the people of France described as descendants of King David who would one day return to Palestine. But a thesis as surprising as this was one of a kind, for the concept of the most Christian king was built on a platform of religious purity that depended on strong undercurrents of anti-Semitism and xenophobia.

Since the only way the royal house could conceivably resemble the Hebrews was in spiritual terms,[61] French historiographers set out to find a pact of divine inspiration comparable to the one God had made with Moses. Until the time of Charles V, they had done little more than assert that the virtues of the kingdom, its faith and above all its chivalry, guaranteed its safekeeping. Then, between 1370 and 1415, allusions to the promise of Saint Remigius began to surface, eventually to become the keystone of a theory of the eternal—though conditional—alliance of France with God.[62]

The starting point for this belief was the *Life of Saint Remigius* that Archbishop Hincmar of Rheims had written in 878.[63] "As this holy person was teaching." the archbishop had related, "a prophetic inspiration came to him, and he predicted that the kingdom would belong to the line of Clovis, which would reign most nobly, assist the Holy Church, and be clothed in the dignity of the Romans, and would be victorious over other nations as long as it remained in the path of truth and faith. For when kingdoms neglect the Church and offend God, they are overthrown and change hands." From this, the authors of the period of Charles V and Charles VI concluded that the kingdom would last forever, or as long as Christianity lasted, for it was the last Empire, transferred from the Romans to the Franks. If the kingdom suffered military defeat it was a sign that it had shown insufficient thanks for its privileges and had broken off the alliance unilaterally; but the blood that was spilled in these frays earned God's renewal of the pact. After 1435, there was general confidence that the promise had been validated once again, to last until the end of time: "France has succeeded Rome, and the Empire will nevermore be transferred . . . the monarchy of France has already lasted longer than that of Babylonia, of Macedonia, and of the Romans. The older it is, the more beautiful and flourishing it becomes."[64] The kingdom of the New Alliance would never die out; throughout time, it would remain faithful to itself and to its divine mission, for God had anchored His very being in it. All that was most Christian would be associated with it forevermore.

A SACRED DYNASTY

It was around 1300 that a political theology of the royal bloodline appeared, increasing in vigor and range until it reached its apogee between the reigns of Charles V and Charles VII. From the very beginning, propagandists proclaimed, a model line of royalty had sat upon the throne of France—a line as supremely Christian as the people it ruled; the blood of kings was the hereditary transmitter of all that was most Christian.

CONTINUITY

This bloodline was first of all a single hereditary line, stretching continuously through time from one heir to the next, despite all the changes in its fortunes.[65] The Carolingians claimed as early as the ninth century that they were descended from Blitilda, a sister they had invented for the Merovingian king Dagobert.[66] The eleventh-century legend of Saint Valery, however, foretold only seven generations of kings for the Capetians; though some commentators tried to replace *septem* (seven) with *sempiternae* (eternal), this legend, by questioning the line's continuity, seemed to question its legitimacy as well. Then, in the second half of the twelfth century, the marriages of Louis VII to Adela of Champagne and of Philip Augustus to Isabelle of Hainaut allowed the Capetians to assert that the kingdom had returned to the dynasty of Charlemagne.[67] And just in time it was, for Philip was the seventh in the generation of Capetian kings. By the mid-thirteenth century this idea of dynastic continuity from the Merovingians to the Capetians had triumphed: "Here fell the line of the great Charlemagne, and the kingdom descended to the heirs of Hugh Capet. . . . It was recovered in the time of the good King Philip, for he married Isabelle of Hainaut to reestablish the line of Charlemagne," wrote Vincent of Beauvais.[68] Late in the fourteenth century, Bishop Robert Gervais again evoked this "return to the line of Charlemagne" when he wrote in his *Mirror*, "Philip, the father of King Louis, married Isabelle, who descended from Charlemagne."[69]

This idea of "return" was problematic, however, for the first seven Capetians, not being Carolingians, might be accused of having claimed the kingship illegitimately. For this reason, some late-thirteenth-century authors linked Capetians to Carolingians through Havise, the mother of Hugh Capet, or Ermengarde—assumed to have been the daughter of the last Carolingian, Charles of Lorraine, and thus a distant ancestor of Isabelle of Hainaut, wife of Philip Augustus—in order to legitimate as Carolingians all the members of the dynasty.[70]

The idea became problematic after 1328 as well, because the link it created between Carolingians and Capetians went through the female line. This had not posed any problem, of course, before women were excluded from the throne, but the recourse to the Salic Law to hide the hiatus in succession in 1316 and 1328 retroactively called into question the legitimacy of the Capetian succession. But this inconsistency was easily avoided. "Three principal dynasties have been kings of France up until now," wrote Jean de Montreuil between 1409 and 1413. "The first was the Merovingians, the second was that of Pepin, the father of Charlemagne, and the third was that of Hugh Capet, whom some have claimed came from modest and lowly lineage. [The song of Hugh Capet, composed in the second half of the fourteenth century, had in fact presented the founder of the dynasty as the son of a butcher.][71] He was descended through his father from Charlemagne and through his mother from the ruling emperor, since his father, Hugh the Great, married the emperor's daughter."[72] Jean de Montreuil was here following genealogies of the mid-twelfth century, which had made Havise, Hugh Capet's mother, the daughter of Emperor Henry I. But it remains a mystery how he made Hugh the Great a descendant of Charlemagne; no other chronicler gives a solution. In the fifteenth century, writers simply avoided the problem by writing baldly, "Then the Capetians—who were related to the Carolingians—came to the throne."[73]

PURITY

Royal blood was pure and *clarissimus*—clear, transparent, luminous—and in contrast to normal blood, a somber red.[74] (References to blue blood come only in the modern era.)

A preacher who supported Philip the Fair in 1302 urged his listeners to believe that "the sacred blood of kings from one generation to the next, forty-eight kings since the time of Priam, has known not a single bastard."[75] Charles Martel, reduced in status to duke of the Franks, did not appear on this preacher's list. A contemporary suppressed all references to the scandalous conduct of the Frankish king Childeric, father of Clovis, as well; for, as he put it, "adultery cannot engender a king of France."[76] Philip, however, had sprung from "the race of Pepin,"[77] a birthright that placed him above suspicion. In point of fact, however, disagreeable rumors about Philip circulated within the kingdom, rumors brought to light at the trial of Bernard Saisset, bishop of Pamiers.[78] The bishop was accused of asserting that the king was not of true Carolingian stock, that his father had descended from the bastard Hugh Capet and his mother, Isabelle of Aragon, from a family well fortified with adulterers; doubly descended from the mire, the king was destined to lose the throne, for he was the tenth and last generation after Hugh Capet.

Thus when two knights, Philip and Gauthier d'Aunay, were condemned in 1314 for adultery with the three daughters-in-law of the

king, it came in an atmosphere thick with rumors.[79] Horrible fornica-
tion! Unheard-of adultery!—contemporary chroniclers wallowed in the
harshness of it all. The knights were executed; two of the three princesses were likewise removed from the scene—one froze to death, the
other was suffocated—leaving the king's sons free to remarry with the
hope of producing male heirs. But the political implications of the affair
could not be hid. Not only had the princesses "cast suspicion on all
noble ladies," they had brought "injustice and dishonor to the kingdom," and their lovers were "traitors."[80] The adultery—so it was
said—had continued for three years;[81] it thus cast a shadow over the
birth of Joan of France, the daughter of Louis X, and helped to block
her succession to the throne on her father's death. For, according to
Jean Desnouelles, "the queen had a daughter by King Louis, so she said,
but because of the misdeeds of the mother, the daughter lost her rights
over the lands."[82] The only defense the child's supporters could find was
to say that Louis X had recognized her as his daughter and heir.

Less than fifty years later there was another suspicious affair in the
royal family when Raoul d'Eu, constable of France, was suspected of
engaging in amorous dalliance with Bonne, wife of the future John II.
The story differed notably from that of 1314, for Bonne was the sister of
Emperor Charles IV, and Raoul belonged to a famous family that had
contributed sovereigns to the Crusader States; Raoul also enjoyed a
well-earned reputation as a courageous and loyal soldier. It is impossible to know exactly how far the affair actually went but, when in 1349
the princess died suddenly at a very young age, not everyone thought it
resulted from natural causes. It was "a hasty end," wrote Jean de Noyal,
abbot of Saint-Victor of Laon, rather evasively, "about which we defer
to Him who is ignorant of nothing."[83] "Many people said that the death
of Madame Bonne was precipitated, I do not know why, or whether this
was true or not," wrote Jean le Bel.[84] As for Constable Raoul, he had
been held a prisoner in England since 1346. Upon his return to France in
the fall of 1350, he was immediately decapitated and under most curious circumstances at that: he was executed at the Hôtel de Nesles with
neither delay nor judgment, in the presence of all the great men of the
kingdom and the members of his lineage. His body was buried at the
Augustinian house, outside rather than within the church, on orders of
the king, who summarily declared: "You will have his body, I will have
his head."[85]

As to the motives of this macabre episode a total silence reigned—
"not a word was spoken of the reason why the king had the Count of

Eu killed," noted a Norman chronicler.[86] "I do not know what was the reason for this death, for the king and his council hid it and kept it a secret," said Gilles le Muisit.[87] The official *Chronicle of John II*, held that it had been a case of treason,[88] but others thought it unlikely. "It was a great shame and pity," commented Froissart, "for he was too great and noble a knight to have considered treason."[89] Le Muisit thought it might have been because the constable had fraudulantly spent the monies the king had sent to England for his ransom.[90] Jean le Bel, by contrast bluntly spoke of a liaison between the queen and the constable, which had been discovered in letters exchanged back and forth between France and England, "some love episodes between Madame and the noble constable, which had been brought to the attention of the king."[91] Jean de Noyal also thought that the constable was killed because of the queen.

Whatever the scandal, succession to the throne was nonetheless assured, since the four sons of John II had all been born between 1337 and 1341, before the liaison had begun. If there had been any adultery, the bastard children that may have come of it were girls: Agnes who was born in 1345 and died young, and Marguerite who was born at the beginning of 1347 and put into the convent at Poissy. Thus all was soon forgotten. Or nearly so; for in 1387, Charles VI made a point of paying for the funerary rites of Raoul's nephew, Constable Jean d'Eu, which the entire court attended. With this ceremony, the memory of the house of Eu was at last cleansed of treasonous complicity with England.[92]

Once again, at the beginning of the fifteenth century, though writers continued to assert "that no Joachim would ever sit on the throne of David"[93] and that the "blood of France is passed on from generation to generation without intruders,"[94] rumors began to circulate about another royal personage: Isabelle of Bavaria, wife of the insane Charles VI. Her reputation was not the best: Louis XI described her to the Neopolitan ambassador as "a great whore,"[95] and popular imagination contrasted her to Joan, the Maid of Orléans: what was lost by one was regained by the other. Was her son, the Dauphin Charles, legitimate? By the time of the Treaty of Troyes in 1420, the Dauphin himself was "deeply worried that his father might abandon him, might disavow him as a bastard," a later Burgundian chronicler reported.[96]

It was, of course, the opposition that had spread this talk of the Dauphin's bastardy. During the reconquest, the inhabitants of Mantes were reluctant to surrender to the royal army because they risked being accused of "blasphemy, sacrilege and rebellion; they said things,"

Blondel reported, "about the purity of birth of the king and about his honor, things that were false, deceitful and shameful."[97] And as late as 1457, at a gathering at the tavern of a village buried in the heart of the Massif Central, an old peasant could recount that "the king [Charles VII] was not of the house, for when he was born, he did not bear the royal sign, he did not have a fleur-de-lys like a true king."[98] The royal birthmark in the shape of a fleur-de-lys had long been linked in the popular mind with the royal blood. Rumors of illegitimacy were still going around.

The secret that Joan of Arc brought from heaven was thus to affirm to the Dauphin that he was "the true heir of France and the son of the king."[99] The vast majority waited, however. "Bon sang ne peut mentir, adonc se montrera"—Good blood cannot lie; it will show itself—said a fourteenth-century poet.[100] The liberation of Orléans was thus far more important symbolically than it was militarily, for the Dauphin's victory and coronation appeared to doubters as the proof of his legitimacy.

Thus, three strikingly similar tales had grown up in little more than a century. It is unlikely, however, that the queens of France were exceptionally immoral between 1300 and 1420. The possibility of queenly adultery must therefore have carried implications in France that went far beyond the moral issue, for there were nothing like such worries in England. Though King Edward II (1307–1327) was a notorious homosexual and Isabelle of France his wife took power with her lover, no one ever seems to have questioned the legitimacy of Edward III her son, for royal blood was only one of the things that made a king in England.[101] French propagandists were acutely conscious of this and mocked the changes in the English dynasties, accusing them all of illegitimacy. For France had just created the idea of blood-right—a promising force for the future despite the immediate problems with its application. Insane or an infant, a French king still reigned by right of blood. Though the term "legitimacy" had not yet been invented, the idea had already come into being.

Did the monarchy allow concurrent legitimacies to exist? Or to put the question differently, did noblemen who were related to kings, who shared their blood, win privileged places on account of it?

The vocabulary is suggestive; the expression "princes of the blood" has had a rich history, still far from over. During the fourteenth and fifteenth centuries, equivalent expressions were numerous: princes of France, princes of the royal house, princes of the fleurs-de-lys, royal ones, our lords.[102] The expression "prince of the blood" seems to have appeared for the first time during the reign of Charles V. Baudoin de Sebourc used it in his *Song;* so did an ordinance of May 1368 prohibiting the barony of Beaujeu from being granted "to whomever might be of royal blood or lineage."[103] But it came into common use only during the civil wars, when the nobility used it in their manifestos and the king in his pacification ordinances. An ordinance of 1413 expressed the hope that love would reign among "the lords of royal blood" and that the resulting peace would be "to the honor of our blood."[104] On the other side, manifestos of the Orléanist faction declared, "How cheap do you want it to be, the murder of princes of royal blood? Never has the blood of your house been spilled in such a way."[105] The term "blood rights" was used to justify the princes' participation in government; the manifesto of 1410 was written in the name of "the body of those who are of your blood," who should serve the king more faithfully and serve as an example to his other subjects.[106] A sermon addressed to Charles VI in 1413 put things more precisely: "The lords of the blood are members of and belong to your body. They are the eyes of the body of the state, watching over it continually. They have a singular affection for it, and a nobility and a special perfection."[107] Care of the government belonged "to none other than those of royal blood."[108] The expression soon became commonplace; in 1431 the "Bourgeois of Paris" saw "All the blood of France at the side of the king—that is to say, the great lords."[109]

But eventually, the growth of royal power stood in the way of this concurrent and possibly competitive legitimacy. The princes did not succeed in using their bloodline to make themselves a part of the power structure, nor in capturing a place in the hierarchy above the other nobility, as did their counterparts in England. Although Burgundian writers remained faithfully attached to the phrase, the terminology of "lords of the blood" appeared less and less frequently in royal texts after 1430.[110] The Estates of 1484 briefly renewed its currency, though with reference only to men of royal blood through the male line and only according to the degree of kinship they enjoyed. Although some orators still proclaimed that "the lords of the blood are the heart, the sense, and the strength of this kingdom," others felt they were no more than "the footstool beneath the feet of the king."[111] By the sixteenth century, the phrase had become merely a title and no longer a designation of power.

PERPETUITY

The bloodline was also perpetual. This came to mean not only that succession to the throne passed from father to son. It meant as well that it could pass to collateral kin as long as they were related through the male line. Philip VI, who took the throne in 1328, was his predecessor's first cousin; when Charles VIII died in 1498, the line had to be traced back four generations to Charles V in order to find a male heir who was descended from a king entirely through males. To justify it, the jurist Cosme Guimier proposed that "the bloodline of France is perpetual to the thousandth degree":[112] the kingdom would pass to the nearest male heir, no matter how distant, as long as at least one drop of the blood of kings flowed in his veins. An heir would thus always be assured, all the more so because it was God who provided him: "God has loved the most Christian house of France so much that he has never been willing to leave it without heir."[113]

Indeed, on at least two different occasions, it was thought that the birth of an heir to the throne was a miracle.

Before Philip II was born in 1165, his father, Louis VII—who was already quite old—had had by his three wives "only a horrifying number of daughters."[114] But at length the prayers of the king, the queen, and the people brought a son who was therefore called Philip the Godgiven—Philippe Dieudonné. His father, the chroniclers reported, had a prophetic vision;[115] he saw his son holding a chalice filled with blood, which he offered in turn to each of his barons to drink, beginning with Blois and Burgundy, going on to Flanders, and completing the round with the king of England. It was an astonishing image, for the priestly king-to-be was imitating quite faithfully the gestures Jesus had made on Holy Thursday. Rigord seems to have seen in this vision a reference to the community of greats who, as they encircled the king, represented the mystical body of the state. Gerald of Wales thought it foreshadowed Philip's victories. "In just this order he conquered all those who turned against the rights of the Crown." Although Rigord and the *Great Chronicles* placed the vision before Philip's birth, Gerald placed it before his coronation, before his birth to the status of king. Even those who made no mention of Louis's vision believed a miracle had taken place: so wrote the bishop of Limoges in 1165, elaborating at length on the joy of all believers in the kingdom—their desire has been fulfilled: "God has visited his people and shown the entire kingdom his goodness."[116]

The same fervor surrounded the birth of Charles VIII in 1470. Louis XI was by then forty-six years old, and none of his second wife's children were the healthy male heirs he waited for. Louis's brother, Charles of Guyenne, whom the king detested wholeheartedly, was thus fated to take the throne, yet every action that Louis undertook vis-à-vis the great princes presupposed that he would have an heir of his own to take over the crown. Before Charles VIII was born, the king and queen made three vows.[117] Louis promised to give the church of Notre-Dame at Le Puy a silver statue of a child as large as his son would be when he reached the age of ten—a statue that turned out to cost 160,000 gold écus; he also offered 2,000 gold écus to the monastery of Saint Catherine on Mount Sinai. For her part, the queen made a pilgrimage to Le Puy to proffer a vow to the Virgin Mary and to Saint Petronilla. (Petronilla was the imagined daughter of Saint Peter. The chapel dedicated to her at Saint-Peter's in Rome was considered the chapel of the king of France, the eldest son of the Church; on this occasion, the king had it rebuilt, and her sarcophagus was reconstructed as a monument supported by the figures of four dolphins [dauphins].)[118] Thus the birth of Charles was a miracle,[119] a mystery, a gift of grace, fulfilling the prayers of all French people who had been waiting for "the child to be born for the salvation of France":

> Dieu a mis main au corps former
> Pour Marie complaire
> La Dame a les cieux ouverts
> Pour envoyer cette grâce pleuvoir.[120]
>
> [God put his hand on the body to form it
> To please Mary
> The Lady opened up the skies
> To send this grace raining down.]

The statue of the Virgin at Le Puy—said to have been carved by the prophet Jeremiah and brought back from the Holy Land by one of Clovis's successors—had watched over the kingdom well.

An only son, sent by the Virgin, Charles VIII became the Christ *unigenitus*. The miracle was loudly proclaimed in official speeches. Those attending the Estates-General of 1484 heard the proclamation, "O happy day that saw your birth. . . . Blessed be God who sent you. . . . Let us give thanks to God who did not leave us without a ruler, who gave us one who is, in addition, a model of all virtue."[121] When Charles made his royal entry into Paris, people alluded to the care God had shown in giving the kingdom an heir: King Louis XI was "almost beyond all hope of producing the lineage needed to carry on the Christian Crown of France," but "God never let us fall into ruin. He gave us a miraculous blessing through your birth."[122] Even the child's tutor called him "like a son of the true God,"[123] a comment already tinged with the messianism that soon surrounded the young prince and which would later serve to justify his military expedition to Italy.[124]

The period that saw the development of a cult of the blood of Christ throughout the Latin Christian world, also made the blood of kings "holy," "sacred," and "miraculous." The idea began when Philip Augustus proclaimed himself a Carolingian. Philip did not have his own son, the future Louis VIII, crowned during his own lifetime (as he and his ancestors had been crowned while their fathers were still alive). When Gilles of Paris dedicated the *Carolidus* to this royal son, he celebrated in him an "heir by blood, this blood whose virtue will make you king, offspring of a holy race, which like the good tree will give forth good fruit" and enable him to "keep the line of the kings of France from degenerating."[125]

HOLINESS

This "best blood in the world"[126] was sacred blood. Consequently it was taboo. No one could and no one dared touch it. The regicide English were contrasted to the French, who never killed or wounded members of their holy line.[127] The blood of France had never been spilled except in the name of God. It should never be spilled by murder. Yet in 1407, the duke d'Orléans, younger brother to Charles VI, was assassinated. This was deemed an act of lèse-majesté and high sacrilege. For the kings of France were "blessed with never being killed or slain in war, have never been killed or slain or expelled by their people." *Noli me tangere* applied to them just as it did to Christ after the resurrection, for that which was holy could not be touched.[128]

Thus the bloodline of the kings was holy. From Louis VIII onward, most were considered saints, their lineage sacred; the canonization of Louis IX only accentuated the belief. As Charles of Anjou testified during the canonization proceedings, Louis was most certainly a saint, but so were Blanche of Castille, Robert of Artois, killed on crusade, and Alphonse of Poitiers, a "martyr by desire."[129]

Guillaume de Nogaret, Philip the Fair's chancellor, and the Mendicant Guillaume de Sauqueville both affirmed this holiness: "It is a proven and well-known truth throughout the world that the kings of France are holy and most Christian princes."[130] And this holiness flowing in their veins led them little by little to show that they could do without any sacred quality conferred on them from outside. Although from Charles V onward, kings of France were knighted at the time of their coronations,[131] it was sometimes considered that "the sons of kings were knights at the baptismal font"[132] and there was no need for the celebration of an additional sacrament; they were born as knights in the service of God. Louis d'Orléans, who was son and brother to kings, forewent the ceremony of knighting entirely,[133] since, at the time of his baptism in 1372, Constable Bertrand Du Guesclin had touched him with a sword while pronouncing the ritual words "Sire, I give you this sword and pray God that you will be as good a knight as any king who ever carried a sword." The act linked his knighthood to his birth and blood—Christian birth and blood, of course, for pagans could not be knights.

Fifteenth-century kings, having found they could do without the traditional ceremony of dubbing to knighthood, found they could do without the coronation ritual as well. Hereditary succession had long since replaced election as the way to choose kings; the coronation now experienced a comparable eclipse. Philip Augustus, as we have said, was the first Capetian not to crown his heir in his lifetime. And from 1270 onward, the dates of each reign were calculated starting from the death of the father rather than on the coronation of the son. Charles VII adopted the title of king in 1422, before his coronation, and, though his adversaries continued to address him as Dauphin, he proceeded to fulfill all his royal duties; his entourage was convinced that though the coronation was useful to make a king, blood alone was essential. The son of a king, they argued, shared in the kingship even while his father was still alive, and no one could take away the bloodright that was his; he would be crowned if possible, but "many were made kings before their coronation, without the intervention of the Church. . . . The four who preceded Clovis wielded power and jurisdiction and they were not crowned and annointed, and Clovis was a true king before he was crowned and baptized."[134] Some kingdoms, moreover, knew nothing of such things and had true kings nonetheless; for the ritual, they concluded, was in fact merely a benediction, a festival, a solemn ceremony. Thus, by the end of the Middle Ages, the coronation—no longer constitutive in and of itself—had become nothing more than a declaration of what was already true.

The king's ability to work miracles did not come from the coronation either, for, if so, all the kings who had been crowned in any country would be able to perform wondrous feats. Nor did it come from the Holy Ampulla, though some insisted this was so. The king's power came from his blood. As early as 1300, the *Quaestio in utramque partem* held there was "an hereditary air about the capacity to work miracles."[135] And in 1376, the *Dream in the Pleasure Garden* attributed the king's thaumaturgic powers to his blood. At the end of the Middle Ages it was a legal certainty. "All the kings of France have the capacity to work miracles," wrote Cosme Guimier; "the power to make miracles is inherited by the eldest son," wrote Guillaume Benoit.[136]

As the Chancellor Jean de Rely said: "The best blood, the most pious, the surest that exists in the world, is that most noble blood of the house of France."[137]

Not surprisingly, this theology of the bloodline of France corresponded to a political agenda that was probably quite conscious. It avoided periods of interregnum; it clearly designated an heir who became the natural heir, spontaneously surrounded by the love of his subjects; and it did this with no interference from the outside. It functioned without the Church's intervention and without splitting loyalties. The crown passed down the line regardless of the personal sentiments of the king or the nobility.

Though England and the Empire adopted very different solutions, the French obviously thought their solution the best. This is not the place to make such value judgments. But we can still conclude that the theology of royal blood worked effectively to shore up the principle of hereditary succession. From it the institution drew its force and its legitimacy. In the sixteenth century, Henry IV would owe much to those medieval propagandists who made it their task to differentiate and classify the virtues of the blood of French kings.

This was how the French nation came to be "most Christian" for all eternity, took to itself a title that rather than working to the benefit of a universal Christendom, isolated and specified one collectivity alone: the kingdom of France. This kingdom's sense of nationhood was formed early in its history; in consequence it was inspired far more than other nations to draw its worth from its faith and its conformity to divine will. The term "most Christian" was applied without distinction to the French king, the people, and the territory. Little by little the title developed into a reason for their glory and pride, justified their very being, and brought with it the calming certainty that France would always play an important role in God's plan for the order of the world.

The process by which the sacred was specified proved to be a useful weapon in the hands of the monarchy. Wielded against the Empire and the papacy, it demonstrated the independence of the French nation. Brought into play against enemies, it guaranteed divine support. "All those who fight against the holy kingdom of France fight against King Jesus . . . and they will win nothing," Joan of Arc wrote to the duke of Burgundy at the time of the coronation of 1429.[138] Abbot Suger long before her had portrayed the enemies of his king as sons of Satan. Already in the thirteenth century, those who spoke ill of the king were accused of blasphemy and sacrilege. Should not the enormous quantity of legislation that, from Philip Augustus to Louis XI, attacked blasphemy as a political as well as religious crime be thought of as part of the slow, secret prehistory of lèse-majesté? Put simply, to curse the king, as to curse God, was to attack the sacred.

The secularization of values at the end of the Middle Ages did not touch this complex of ideas, perhaps because all felt that the French nation belonged to the realm of belief and faith rather than of fact and reason. The sacred blood of kings continued to flow, and the Crown continued to lay claim to privileges in which religion was intimately mixed with politics.

PART II

Introduction

Signs and symbols can carry enormous weight in a society where communication is primarily orally based and belief in appearances strong, often more meaningful than texts. Medieval France was no exception to the rule, for its notions of reality were rooted in the richest symbolic soil.

The lilies of France offer an excellent case in point. Although scholars have studied the early manifestations of this emblem, as it appeared from the mid-twelfth century onward in armorial bearings, seals, and royal coins, and have devoted attention to material aspects of its representation—great fields of them later supplanted by smaller groups of three—the profoundly medieval character of the symbol has remained largely unexplored.

The symbolic life of the lily began as a religious motif associated with the Christian virtue of purity and its incarnation, the Virgin Mary. Since the sacred lily and its counterpart, the royal trefoil, shared many characteristics, the Middle Ages often considered them interchangeable. This explains how the fleur-de-lys eventually became a symbol of the unity of faith, clergy, and chivalry, in which medieval people saw the explanation for the kingdom's power. By 1300, however, the royal lily began to distance itself from theology, as heraldry drew associations from the world of secular nobility. Blue and gold were unrivaled in the hierarchy of colors; so too the lily in the realm of noble forms, which, though originally merely an indication of lineage, now stood for dignity and

inalienable privilege, things that—barring sacrilege and lèse-majesté—
were absolutely inviolable.

Sometime before 1350, a story appeared at the abbey of Joyenval
which told how, before the battle of Tolbiac, an angel of God presented
the fleurs-de-lys to Clovis as a sign of heavenly selection. The court of
Charles V soon launched a popularizing campaign, creating miniatures
and engravings, staging festive royal entries, and encouraging large sectors of the population to make pilgrimages to Joyenval to view the
miraculous shield; all of these focused on the lilies of France. Frenchmen
of the late Middle Ages carried "lilies in their hearts"; during royal
entries, young girls presented the king with the fleur-de-lys hidden in an
emblematic heart of their town.

Though in the second part of the fourteenth century such heraldic
emblems began to give way to simpler figures such as the white cross, we
are less interested here in whether symbols became simplified than in the
fact that they all came from the same symbolic universe: they were all
emblems of the French nobility, and the notion of France that the nobility
entertained shone brightly within them. This symbolic France—the one
that the nobility had built upon the earlier rock of theology—was the first
France to make itself visible.

It made itself visible symbolically; it made itself visible historically as
well, in a pagan legend. The Trojan origin of France was invented in the
seventh century on the antique model of Aeneas leading his Trojan exiles
to Rome. Like the Romans who governed the world, the Franks/French
descended from the most ancient and most noble race. The fifteenth-
century versions of this legend took care to push the Trojan arrival further and further back in time. A wave of migration attributed to a legendary king Marcomir in the fourth century was preceded by earlier waves in
which Trojans had joined the Gauls, who—thanks to the discovery of
ancient texts—began to become part of French history. Valiant soldiers,
cultured and pious, and all the more believable because Caesar spoke of
them in his *Gallic Wars*, the Gauls had everything to make them acceptable ancestors. This was why at the very end of the century Jean Lemaire
de Belges transformed the myth of the Trojan origins of France into a
myth of the Gallic origins of Troy. The Gauls were the immemorial
inhabitants of the country, and a part of them went to found the city on
the Bosporus, from which Francio then returned with his band of refugees after its destruction. The Trojans also gave birth to the Franks.
Trojans, Gauls, and Franks were thus all one. A single and continuous
line, a pure blood, tied the population of France to its glorious origins.

Meanwhile, late in the twelfth and throughout the thirteenth century, another sector of society, the scholars, had busily occupied themselves with launching a France in their own image. Professional and amateur scholars alike, scholars from within and scholars from beyond the borders of the realm, all flocked to the University of Paris, the showcase of European theological training; for the "transfer of learning," the *translatio studii,* had made the French kingdom into a new Athens, endowing it with knowledge that, though still profoundly religious, was to become the touchstone of the very idea of French national culture. Use of the French vernacular had never been as sensitive an issue for scholars in France as it was in England, where French fell into disfavor when England lost her continental empire at the end of the Hundred Years War; but the mother tongue ("la langue maternelle" as it was called from 1300 on) was something they encouraged people to value, long before their sixteenth-century descendants found it necessary to insist on it.

Another subgroup in the kingdom—men of law and servants of the state, those who belonged to the royal entourage and filled the Parisian Parlement—had affinities with the scholars. Thanks to them, the Salic Law, yet another primary sign of French identity, also became an object of national pride. Prior to 1350, people had viewed the Salic Law from a distance, as an ancient, respected law whose contents were largely unfamiliar. But the jurists of Charles V transformed it into the French kingdom's primary law of succession. By the beginning of the fifteenth century, the law had come into the full light of day. As Charles VII's jurists did not have access to the manuscript copy of the law housed at the abbey of Saint-Denis, they scoured the Kingdom of Bourges for another, which once discovered, they copied, wrote commentaries on, and translated. They found earlier uses of the law in the reigns of Merovech and Hugh Capet and guarantors in Clovis and Charlemagne. The Salic Law, they said, had been affirmed in 1316 and 1328, and by the end of the century people had begun to accept it as the norm of royal succession and succession to great fiefs. Jurists began to interpret other juridical concepts as its offspring. Thus, the "Gallic Law"—as it came to be known—established the superiority and absolute independence of French legislation. The story of its coming of age, graced with the predictable time lapse between new perceptions and the institutionalization of statutes, reflected the growing importance of men of law and civil servants in this late-medieval kingdom.

The symbolic fields of France created by the imaginations of each of

these groups—the clergy and noblemen, the scholars, and the jurists—
proliferated in accordance with each of their interests and their relative
importance in the evolving political framework of the society. An over-
view might attempt to convey the idea that the noble, clerical France
was superseded by the vision of the intellectuals and later by that of
officialdom; but closer examination reveals that these diverse conceptions actually flowed into one another.

I have devoted the last chapter in this part of the study to some of the
larger images of France: to France-as-a-person, an entity that grew
beyond the name and its surround of simple attributes to become a
voice, and ultimately the allegory of a prince, sorely missed or vibrantly
remembered; also to France-as-a-territory, sometimes captured in the
image of a tree, its rising line of generations firmly rooted in the earth,
or figured at other times as a charming garden of paradise. Ultimately it
was this larger type of image, this more global vision of France, so
radiantly evocative, that drew people's love and devotion. This love was
expressed in the attentive reflections of thirteenth-century scholastic
philosophers, in grants of money at the beginning of the fourteenth
century, and in lives sacrificed during the Kingdom of Bourges.

Even in death the link between medieval France and its people endured, for as the poets said:

> Quand serai poudre devenu
> Encore France demeurera . . .[1]

and

> Et quand par l'ordonnance de Dieu définerai
> Es cieux: "C'est ma France"
> Mon esprit l'aimera . . .[2]

[When I am dust
France will remain . . .]

[And when by God's command I die,
In heaven I will say: "This is my France"
My spirit will love it . . .]

CHAPTER 7

The Lilies of France

"May the lilies multiply!" Chancellor Gerson exclaimed at the beginning of the fifteenth century, calling for God's blessing on the royal house; for in the late Middle Ages, devotion to the king and country was expressed less through abstract ideas than through symbolic objects. Among the most important of these were the heraldic lilies of the kings of France.

Historians have succeeded in laying out the facts about when and how the lilies of France originated and have tried—not always convincingly—to situate those origins in faraway places and distant times. I have chosen a different tack. The question of origins promises to be less elusive if we first examine the lily as symbol within its medieval context. All medieval symbols were nurtured in the cradle of theology, and as early as the eleventh century, clerics contemplated the meanings that the Bible and the Fathers of the Church had attributed to the lily. My own discussion will therefore begin with the story of "the theology of the lily." It will move on to the fourteenth century to look at the writings of the heralds, who sketched out a noble and secular version of the lily, one that, despite its theological base, was more heavily influenced by legal than by religious ideas. It will then turn to the official texts that from 1350 onward spread legends about the origins of the lily, and to the treatises on the symbol, treatises that were spurred on by an important event: in 1340 the king of England adopted the French coat of arms.

THE PROBLEM OF ORIGINS

Changes in armor first made heraldic signs necessary in the twelfth century. Helmet and hauberk by then had grown to cover the warrior's face and body almost completely, so that those who wore them could no longer readily be identified in the field. Signs were therefore painted on the shields that knights carried into battle. It was only in the second half of the twelfth century, however, that heraldic emblems came to be associated with hereditary lines and with particular fiefs and alods. And it was only late in that century that the kings of France adopted their own heraldic signs, for the royal seal of the king "in majesty" served everywhere to identify his acts, and the oriflamme served to rally his troops.

It is only the armorial bearings of younger lines of the Capetian house that allow us to suppose that azure and gold were already royal colors in the first half of the twelfth century: Raoul, Count of Vermandois from 1120 to 1152 wore "gold and blue checks" perhaps as early as 1135, certainly in 1147.[1] The fleur-de-lys appeared only slowly.[2] During the reign of Louis VI, the royal mint at Dreux produced pennies stamped with a cross adorned with fleur-de-lys, relatively similar to a number of other coins, such as those minted by the archbishop of Reims. The pennies of Louis VII carried the fleur-de-lys at the center, surrounded with the words, "Christ triumphs, Christ rules, Christ commands." A single lily appeared on the reverse of the seal of Philip Augustus. On their forays, crusading French knights carried banners with fleurs-de-lys, the same as the one unfurled at Bouvines, and abbeys under royal safeguard could also display them. Finally, Louis VIII (1223–1226) placed a shield with fleurs-de-lys on the reverse of his seal, and his coronation robes were strewn with lilies.

It was only around 1250 that the heraldic lily took on its definitive form: three-petaled, without pistil, standing on a trilobate base, and clasped at the center with a small crossbar. The simplification probably reflected both the need for heraldic economy and a reference to the mystical power of the number three.[3] The "old shield of France," whose flowers were randomly sown across its field,[4] continued to appear even at the end of the fourteenth century. As early as 1228, a shield bearing only three flowers occasionally appeared, though it was only Charles V who definitively decreed this simplified version to be the royal arms. Two rows of lilies continued to be carried by the younger lines of Anjou and Burgundy until the late fifteenth century.

In the thirteenth century the fleur-de-lys symbol spread. Beginning in 1238 it appeared on the seals of royal courts from simple tribunals of the bailliages to the high sovereign courts. Royal notaries in southern France started to use it around 1261. Towns annexed to the royal domain added it to their seals. In the fourteenth century, it appeared on weights and measures, on insignia of corporations, on royal buildings, and on jewelry and cloth. In short, it became the universal sign of public power.

Though we know when it appeared and how it spread, its origins remain a mystery. Heraldists and historians have done their best to push it far back in time.[5] Since there are no examples of its use as a royal emblem before the twelfth century, they have hypothesized that it evolved from an earlier medieval emblem. Seventeenth- and eighteenth-century historians thought it was a transformation of the head of a lance, a javelin, or a battle-axe. Following the discovery in 1653 of jewels in the shape of bees in the tomb of the Merovingian king Childeric (a motif copied by Napoleon for his imperial mantle!) it was claimed that these had eventually been transformed into lilies. Nineteenth- and twentieth-century theories have been equally diverse; some have claimed that the lily motif originated in the trident of Neptune, whereas others see in them the fasces of Rome, or some image from Assyria, Crete, or Egypt, depending on whether the authors favor Eastern or Western origins, ancient or medieval. The need to attach the lilies to the origins of the dynasty has added its own complications.

It is probably wise to remain prudent, to think of the lilies as a medieval creation whose possible ancient antecedents are, after all, of little consequence. This approach, pioneered by P. E. Schramm, has recently been followed by Sir Francis Oppenheimer.[6] After demonstrating how the word *fleur-de-lys* means "abundance of light," Oppenheimer identifies it with the dove of the Holy Spirit, which bears the same appellation. It was the motif, he says, on the Byzantine robes offered by Stephen II to Charlemagne for his coronation at Saint-Denis in 754. From there it spread to Carolingian symbols of power. Copies, he claims, were made for the coronation of Louis VIII, who wished to be seen as the successor to Charlemagne. Oppenheimer's theory has the advantage of stressing the medieval development of the symbol and of explaining the incontestable popularity of the lily flower on Carolingian scepters and crowns. ("Royal lilies cap their brilliant scepters," wrote a Carolingian poet.)[7] This, however, makes it a preheraldic symbol common to the entire Carolingian empire. His equation of the lilies with the dove, furthermore, is contestable, and the assertion that the coronation robes of 1223 were copied from those of 754 rests more on faith than on evidence.

For this reason, I will start from a different place. Taking for granted that the fleurs-de-lys are simply lilies, as all good people of the Middle Ages did, I will try to explain the motif in terms of medieval symbolism itself.[8] Conceived most simply, the fleur-de-lys is perhaps merely a form, one among many, that the human imagination has chosen from era to era to fill with its evolving fantasies. And as medieval symbolism sprang first from the rich earth of religious thought, I will begin there.

THEOLOGY AND THE SYMBOLISM OF THE LILY

To the medieval world, antiquity contributed only two legends, and those were contradictory. In one of them, the lily sprang from drops of Juno's milk that had fallen unnoticed to the ground, whereas the other attributed it to Venus's seeking revenge from a rival. Both goddesses sometimes appeared with the lily.[9] The symbolism was feminine and positive but hardly precise—it represented hope, beauty, or fertility. To this, ancient medicine added the belief that the lily had a magical capacity to protect people, especially from snake bites, and this may possibly have been the source of its more generalized role as a palladium in Roman funerary rites.

Rather than looking to antiquity, medieval clerics turned to the Hebraic tradition for their keys to this symbol. In the Bible they found the lily mentioned both in the Prophets and in Ecclesiastes:[10] a flower of the valleys, fields, and gardens, of brilliant color and delightful perfume; it grows abundantly, as did Israel on return from exile. The Song of Solomon compared it to the beloved: "as a lily among brambles, so is my love among maidens" . . . "my beloved is mine and I am his, he pastures his flock among the lilies." "Consider the lilies of the field, how they grow," said Christ on the Mount, "they neither toil nor spin; yet I tell you, even Solomon in all his glory was not arrayed like one of these." Such references did not add up to a single clear lesson: the lily was both masculine and feminine, a symbol of beauty and love, but also, in Christ's words, of royalty. Nowhere, however, does the Bible make it a symbol of virginity, a virtue whose merit was, in any event, unknown to the Old Testament.

The Fathers of the Church spiritualized the symbol,[11] associating it with the beauty of the soul rather than of the unworthy body. Their lilies grew from the virtues that prefigured the heavenly beatitudes. And who was more graced with virtue than Christ and the confessors who followed him. For Saint Ambrose, Christ was "the lily of the valleys and the crown of the virgins"; for Pseudo-Melito the lily was both the Savior and the saints who were imbued with the radiance of heaven. Paul the Deacon saw Christ as a lily, white on the outside because of his purity, and golden on the inside, as a sign of his power; the fragrance of the lily's virtues was sweet and its stem curved delicately, gracefully pointing the way toward God; it prevailed over surrounding brambles for all to see. By the tenth century, then, the lily had become the symbol of certain not yet fully defined spiritual values such as faith, justice, purity; it signified striving toward the heavenly beatitudes. It was the flower of paradise, perhaps because antiquity had associated it with death—death to this world, which was life in the next. The medieval world valorized the lily as both masculine—Christ—and feminine—the Church.

The eleventh and twelfth centuries renewed this theological symbolism. While the school of Saint-Victor continued to maintain the lily's traditional references to Christ and to the righteous, whose bright souls and upright faith brought them close to God and eternal blessing, changes in religious sensibilities elsewhere had turned its symbolic force toward the Virgin. Gradually, theologians were investing Mary with greater importance. From the time of Ambrosius Autpertus (d. 778) and Pascasius Radbert (d. 865), Mary became the prefiguration of the Church and therefore the bride of Christ. At the same time, the popular epithets for the Virgin began to proliferate, "Star of the Sea," "Queen of Heaven," "Stairway to Salvation," "Intercessor." But references to Mary as Lily did not appear until near the end of the tenth century when the Virgin Mother depicted with her child was described as "cradling the lily of chastity." As Christ had continued to be designated by the lily, the Virgin's association with the flower most likely came through him.

It was Fulbert of Chartres—the learned eleventh-century scholar who had grown up surrounded by pilgrimages honoring the Virgin— who finally bridged the gap, transferring the symbol from Christ to the Virgin. The shift was indicative of the religious sensibilities of the time, which tended to give more attention to the merciful mother of Christ than to a deity now perceived as too distant. Since Mary was blessed with chastity as well as all other virtues, she became the lily in the midst of the thorns, the promise of salvation. By the end of the century, Rupert of Deutz had challenged the traditional interpretation of the

Song of Solomon and equated Mary with the Church;[12] both represented the new Eve—virgin and fruitful, heavenly intercessors, bestow-
ers of grace on others. Mary became an essential actor in the economy
of redemption; she moved to the very heart of the Christian vision.

Where eleventh-century theologians innovated, those of the twelfth
found creative ways to formulate and disseminate their views. In the
Cistercian monasteries, all of which were dedicated to Mary, Saint Bernard and his disciples spread the image of the Virgin-Lily, Giver of
Grace;[13] Mary was an advocate for all, a universal mother; the pure
white of her lily expressed the radiance of her beauty and her virtues.
The Ave Maria of the rosary soon numbered among the litanies consecrated to her so that all might learn and come to believe in the equiva-
lence of *Virgo* and *Lilium*. By the end of the century, doubters had
completely vanished.

At the same time, these theologians extolled the virginity of Mary:
the virgin birth was first proclaimed around the fifth century, but it was
only later that the Church resolved the question of whether Mary was a
virgin prior to Christ's conception and whether she remained so afterward. Eleventh-century theologians proclaimed that she herself had
been conceived free of sin and therefore stood beyond the universal
blemish of original sin. In the middle of the twelfth century, the first
treatise on the Immaculate Conception appeared, a sublimation of the
notion of virginity that likewise appears to be linked to the equation of
Mary and the Lily.

Twelfth-century theologians spoke of the Virgin-Lily as a white
flower, normally without pistil, for pistil-less flowers represented the
feminine. When a golden pistil was present in her picture, this indicated
that the Virgin was with child. The flower consisted of three petals—
representing the triple virginity of Mary—bound by a ring, which signified that she was like an enclosed garden, a sealed fountain. The lily had
no stem and flowered even if its root was cut, just as Mary was conceived without human intervention.[14]

During the twelfth century, statues of the Virgin were cloaked in
mantles adorned with lilies, and episcopal heraldic arms and the coins
of churches dedicated to Mary came to bear the lily motif as well.
Archbishop Gervais of Reims coined pennies with a cross that contained
a lily in each of the four quadrants,[15] to which his successor later added
the words *Sancta Maria*. In the following century, Louis VI adopted the
Reims type for the royal penny. By its form, then, if not by its color, the
royal lily was the Virgin's lily.

French kings had quite early showed deep devotion to the Virgin Mary.[16] Starting with Louis VI, they founded many churches and bestowed gifts of land and a variety of privileges in her name. They dedicated the palace chapel to her and all the cathedrals of the royal domain (in contrast to the remainder of the kingdom, where cathedrals were dedicated to many other saints). Gothic art, an aesthetic nurtured by the royal house in the Ile-de-France, produced new images of the Virgin's glory: the Virgin crowned, the Virgin of the Tree of Jesse, and the Virgin of the Annunciation. The kings also did their best to protect the churches dedicated to her: Louis VI guarded Chartres from the strains of the war he was waging against the turbulent barons of his domain.

Exceptional family events are equally telling. The births of Philip Augustus, Louis VIII, and Saint Louis were all attributed to the intervention of the Virgin. In return, kings made pilgrimages in her honor: Louis VII traveled to Notre-Dame-de-Longpont in 1140, to Notre-Dame-du-Puy and Notre-Dame-de-Liesse in 1145. At his request, he was buried at a church he himself had founded in Mary's name, Notre-Dame-de-Barbeaux.

The Virgin succored the kings of France in this world and the next. Philip Augustus above all enjoyed her protection: she spared his army from thirst at the siege of Montrichard, helped him to escape drowning as he crossed the Epte at Gisors, caused the king of England in most miraculous fashion to accept negotiations at Déols, and brought Philip victory at last at Bouvines. For each of these deeds, a royal foundation was made in Mary's name: Notre-Dame at Nanteuil, the golden statue of Gisors, Notre-Dame-de-la-Victoire near Senlis. In 1185, Philip also presented the abbey of Saint-Jean-lez-Amiens with lily-bedecked arms inscribed with the words: "the honor of the lilies—a gage that has been entrusted to me,"[17] and had a statue of her erected on the ramparts of his capital.

In these many ways the monarchy shared and helped to spread a devotion to the Virgin that was becoming tinged with courtly conventions. They also set about to establish a potentially useful parallel between the ministry of the Virgin Mary and their own most Christian rulership. Albert the Great (1193–1280) called Mary "Queen" to evoke the qualities of gentleness and goodness, for "Empress" seemed to him terrifying and severe. She was mother and queen of Christians, a refuge to the poor. Just so, the kings of France as sacred leaders were healers who guided their subjects along the path to salvation, protecting the

weak and humble, dispensing mercy to their subjects. This alone sufficed to link their names.[18]

It seems likely that the kings of France adopted the emblem of the
Virgin in the second half of the twelfth century out of chivalric devotion
and with a clear awareness of the parallels between their temporal role
and the spiritual duties of the beatific mother. In so doing, they were
demonstrating their respect for her, as Louis VII did quite literally
around 1180 when he knelt before the portal of Saint Anne at the
cathedral of Notre-Dame of Paris. The Capetians may well have drawn
encouragement in their choice from the popularity of religious motifs in
twelfth-century armorial bearings as well as from from vague recollections of a preheraldic floret.

The common origin of the Virgin Lily and the Royal Lily were soon
forgotten, though throughout the Middle Ages they continued to be
perceived as intertwined. The lily's political symbolism sprang from the
same sacred texts, to which were now added Aristotle, heralds, and
scholastic masters. As a result the royal lily retained attributes that
really had nothing to do with it. It was white like the cultivated lily of
the gardens, even though the fleur-de-lys of the heraldic arms of France
was golden. Botanists of the period certainly knew that cultivated lilies
were white and wild lilies were golden. How then could the royal insignia have become gold? To solve the problem, the story developed that
the royal lily was a white lily that had subsequently been gilded in
recognition of the honors the kings of France acquired in their military
exploits.[19]

Other associations surrounding the royal lily were equally surprising.
It represented gentleness, sweetness, gracefulness, and tenderness—all
of which were considered feminine. In 1450, Jacques Millet saw it
radiating grace, amenity, and beauty;[20] toward the end of the century,
the Royaumont Cistercian Giovanni Lodovico Vivaldi was struck by its
innocence, purity of heart, and humility. As it was problematic to transfer these feminine virtues directly to the king, they were said to represent
his soul rather than his person.

The spiritual qualities called forth by the lily—justice, steadfast faith,
integrity—could apply equally well to the king and to the Virgin. Just as
the lily chases snakes and heals certain illnesses, nervous conditions,
poisonings, open wounds, and tumors, so Mary fights vice and the king
fights heretics and infidels. The lily (Mary? the king?) will cleanse the
world of the perversions of Mohammed. The Virgin Mary was born
among the Hebrews and sprang from the race of David. The king of

France was also chosen by God, separated from all the pagan kings. Both were lilies among the thorns.[21]

Were the people of the Middle Ages aware that the Marian and Capetian lilies were connected? Fourteenth-century authors noticed parallels: "The lily flower is carried to the churches and placed before God and the virgin . . . and God the Almighty sent it to the king of France, the most noble of all Christian kings," wrote Jean Corbechon.[22] During the fifteenth century, people went so far as to posit a literal relationship between the lily of France and the Virgin Mary, though it was only a kinship of symbols.

> Car jadis la Mère de Dieu
> Elut ce champ délicieux
> Pour avoir en celui lieu
> Beau service et mélodieux
> Et en cestui champ azuré
> Sema les trois fleurs de lys d'or.[23]
>
> [For in olden days the Mother of God
> Chose this delightful field
> So that this place would yield
> Beautiful and melodious service
> And in this azure field
> Sowed the three gold fleurs-de-lys.]

Whether consciously or not, the two were conflated. Collections of royal songs gave praise to the virginal and the royal lily together. At the end of the fifteenth century, Olivier Maillard proclaimed that though Satan—the English—had attacked the lily, through God's aid it continued to flourish in triumph and glory. This lily, said Maillard, blessed with grace and defender of all, was both the Virgin Mary, to whom all prayed, and the king, whose virtues would win him heavenly beatitude. The two would be reunited in Heaven before the astonished eyes of the faithful, witnesses to "the lily growing in triumph and glory."[24]

Occasionally people dreamed of unifying the two in the here and now. "Since the king carried the lilies on his shield as a symbol of the Virgin most pure, it is only fitting that he love and respect her and that by her grace, he guarantee the salvation of the people who have been entrusted to him," wrote Giovanni Lodovico Vivaldi.[25] The reasoning was the inverse of that which originally put the lilies on the shield of France: the royal lilies belonged to the Virgin, and thus the king and kingdom owed her a special form of devotion. A dialectical relationship had grown up between reality and symbol. The cult of Mary had led to the blossoming of the royal lilies; the flowers in turn reinforced the links between Mary and the kingdom. The fifteenth century often maintained that Mary loved and protected the lily. They attributed to Pope Urban II (1088–1099) the phrase, "Kingdom of Gaul, Kingdom of Mary." Thus, when Louis XIII dedicated France to her in 1638, his gesture was the fruit of a longstanding tradition, a tradition due in large part to the fleur-de-lys on the royal coat of arms.

HERALDRY AND THE SYMBOLISM OF THE LILY

After 1350 heraldry began to contribute to the symbolic understanding of royal arms. It provided a way of defining their particular dignity and a legislation appropriate to them. The lily became more than the emblem of the king; it came to represent the greatness of the royal house and of the entire kingdom.

The judicial science of heraldry developed in the process of arbitrating disputes over armorial bearings; in 1355, the famous jurist Bartolus published what may be considered its first code, his treatise *On Heraldry and Arms,* which was followed in the fifteenth century by a great many others. These treatises generally presented a history of armorial bearings, a discussion of the hierarchy of the "metals" (i.e. the metallic colors gold and silver), the colors, and the figured objects, and then some texts on the manner of proffering a challenge to battle and on the functions of heralds-at-arms. Their authors picked from Aristotle, Isidore, lapidaries, and other books the materials that might answer the curiosity of a lay, warrior society.

There were only a few simple colors that appeared in coats of arms: white, red (gules), azure blue, green (sinople), and black (sable), which were accompanied by two metallic hues, gold and silver; every treatise discussed them. This small selection, initially a gratuitous choice from among all possible colors, eventually became obligatory; these were the most noble.

The criteria that the heralds used did not correspond to Aristotle's discussion of colors in his *Natural History,* where they are divided into seven categories according to the prismatic diffraction of sunlight.[26] Nor did it correspond to the ecclesiastical hierarchy of five liturgical colors— white, red, green, black, and violet—which Pope Innocent III established at the beginning of the thirteenth century: white for the Virgin Mary, red for the martyrs of Christendom, violet for Advent, green for Epiphany and Pentecost, and black for death. Blue did not appear among the sacred colors until the very end of the Middle Ages when the Church began to associate it with the Feast of the Immaculate Conception.[27] Heralds, in contrast, ordered the colors according to their dignity, the more brilliant, violent, and rich the better.[28] Gold was the first, the color of the sun and of the raiment of kings; it symbolized the justice and charity of Christ and of great men; it was also the color of power, of joy, of festivity. Azure blue came next in French treatises[29] (but third in line in non-French texts, where it was preceded by purple). As the color of the sky, azure inspired spiritual greatness: all coats of arms of celestial origin were either azure or decorated with a cross. Blue therefore became extraordinarily popular at the end of the twelfth century.[30]

The blue and gold royal coat of arms therefore combined a regal metal with a divine color to establish a bond between the king and God. It was hardly by chance that the emblems of France combined the two most noble colors: the height of dignity merited the noblest representation, said French theorists; but in more realistic terms, the combination was probably also due to the prominence the French enjoyed in the field of heraldry and to the great numbers of heralds from the royal domain, whose voices eventually made triumph the colors of their sovereign.

Heraldic treatises had less to say on the subject of the lily. They simply affirmed that it was the most noble of figures. The Italian jurist Bonus de Curtilli reserved the lily, along with animals and crosses for those of noble blood, whereas those of common extraction had to settle for letters or decorative lines.[31] Most of the treatises written by people outside the French kingdom however maintained that such a scheme was illogical, that living motifs were nobler than images of inanimate things. Accordingly, their hierarchies of images began with the animals, descended to trees and flowers, and ended with inanimate objects such as the cross and various celestial signs. Italian and English heralds did not hold back from the opportunity this offered: "It is wholly fitting that lilies were sent to the king of France by God, because He wanted to indicate in this way the inconstancy and the instability that reigned in this kingdom, then as in our own day," wrote Nicholas Upton.[32]

All arms were first of all the possession of a man and his family before they came to be thought of as representing the family's prerogatives. The lilies of France were no exception. Their nobility did not spring from their own nature but from what they represented—the most Christian king.

The lilies were originally merely the personal arms of the king; they became arms of the family at the end of the thirteenth century. In the fourteenth century, all princes belonging to the royal family were obliged to bear the lilies, and no "lord of the fleur-de-lys" could renounce them. They were both a birthright and a sign of subjection. In 1477, Maria of Burgundy, who claimed the inheritance of the last duke, had to face the argument that inasmuch as Burgundy carried gold and azure (i.e. its duke bore arms of the royal colors) it should return to the kingdom from which its arms had come.[33] The eldest son of the royal house bore the lilies until 1349, and after that a divided shield of France and of Dauphiné, without brisure while his father was still alive; Philip Augustus, who, in the manner of his predecessors, had been crowned before his father's death, bore the lilies without brisure, and the practice continued afterward, even though from Louis VIII onward, sons were no longer crowned in their fathers' lifetime.[34] The custom was reenforced in the fifteenth century when Charles VII without opposition bore the lilies from 1422 to 1429.[35] There is nothing particularly noteworthy about the customs regarding the younger sons and their descendants, except that the family's system for indicating their junior status was slowly taken over by all the great families of the kingdom.[36] Bastards were theoretically excluded from bearing heraldic arms until the fourteenth century and, though the losses of war and the increasing number of aristocratic bastards began to challenge that restriction, the royal arms long remained inaccessible to royal bastards: the late fourteenth-century *Dream in the Pleasure Garden*, following Bartolus and Baldus, was categorical on the subject. But mid-fifteenth-century treatises no longer mention that restriction.[37] In between those dates, the bastard Dunois—count, marshall of France, and prince of the blood royal—appeared with three lilies and a bar, and others soon followed his example. Royal daughters could carry the lilies but did not transmit them to their offspring; arguments were drawn from this fact to exclude them from succession to the throne.

Having become the collective arms of the royal lineage in the first half of the fourteenth century, the lilies slowly became the symbol of the abstract Royal Dignity.[38] Bartolus introduced the idea of heraldry of dignities early in the fourteenth century, and in the second half of the century it spread to France, prompted by the heraldic conflict between France and England. With the encouragement of his Flemish allies, Edward III had taken the title King of France in 1340 and quartered his English arms with those of France. According to Nicolas Upton the English argument for this move ran something like this: "Edward is justified in wearing the arms of France, because he is the son of Queen

Isabelle, heiress of France, and because he triumphed over King John and made him his prisoner."[39] And although it was generally accepted that sons did not wear the arms of their mothers, jurists on the Continent had a hard time proving that the lily, unlike other arms, could not be lost in battle. They had to establish that the arms of France were arms "of dignity," which could not be captured.[40] An envious neighbor, so their argument went, who took arms of dignity without the permission of the prince who bore them of right, did so by deceiving the people; he should be opposed with open war.

The issue remained a heated one until the end of the fifteenth century: "And in this regard, the king of England has done the king of France great wrong by carrying his title and his arms; he has also committed an outrage against the people, for some of the simple subjects of the king might be misled by these arms while others who show ill will towards the Crown of France might take it as an excuse not to observe their oaths to the king and Crown."[41]

Since arms of dignity could not be acquired by capture (a common way to acquire arms in the thirteenth century), they could only be acquired by gift. Already in the reign of Charles V armorial bearings received as gifts were considered more noble than those acquired in another way; it is therefore not astonishing that the legend about the origins of the lilies was itself a legend of gift—of gift by the King of Heaven. How then could these arms be lost? Not by extinction of the line, because the blood of France was perpetual. Loss by alienation or by renunciation was unthinkable;[42] for if the kingdom could not be alienated, neither could its "sign," for such would be contrary to the order of Providence and a great disturbance of the public weal. The arms of France belonged to the rights of the Crown that each king at his coronation swore to preserve; to give them away, the consent of all would be necessary, and even then it would not be possible as long as there exists a male of the same blood.

For all these reasons, an attack on the lilies became a horrible crime,[43] a case of lèse-majesté, because its victim was the Royal Dignity even more than the person of the king: in 1412, the duke of Lorraine was declared guilty of lèse-majesté for having attached a shield of lilies taken from the city of Neufchâtel to the tail of his horse.[44] Bernard du Rosier went even further: the lilies were "arms of the Crown," arms of the Royal Dignity belonging to all its holders past and future, that is to say arms whose bearer never dies. This idea reflected major changes in the royal funeral rituals of the House of France: from that of Charles

VII in 1461 onward, neither the crown nor the banner with the lilies
was buried with the royal corpse; at the funeral of Charles VIII and at
those of his successors, the banner with three lilies was simply lowered
before the tomb, for the lilies never died.

Kings therefore found it necessary to keep a closer watch over these
precious armorial bearings[45] and to demand from those who bore them
either a formal authorization or proof that their families had done so
from time immemorial. New grants of the three lilies became extremely
rare: one or two lilies were given to individuals or towns, but only
exceptionally. When they were part of an escutcheon, lilies had to have
the honorable position. By the end of the fifteenth century within the
kingdom only the king bore a shield *azur aux trois lys d'or en armes
pleines*.[46]

HISTORICAL LEGENDS AND ABSTRACT SYMBOLISM IN THE FOURTEENTH AND FIFTEENTH CENTURIES

The onset of the wars against the English, conflicts that threatened the
legitimacy of the House of Valois, compelled the French kings to defend their rights, chief among them being the armorial bearings of
France. Some of the propaganda—such as the newly created legends
about the origin of the arms of France—was quite direct; other propaganda was more abstract and developed slowly as discourses and treatises on the symbolism of the lily were composed. Through these
works, the victorious House of Valois after 1450 proclaimed its desire
to rule the West.

THE ORIGINS OF THE LILIES

First came the legends that recounted the origins of the lilies.[47]

It is not clear what origin people attributed to the fleur-de-lys prior to
1350. The thirteenth century quickly forgot that the arms of France
were a recent invention; the trouvère Adenet le Roi, in *Les Enfances
Ogier* (1275), claimed unhesitatingly that Charlemagne carried a shield
decorated half with a field of lilies and half with the imperial eagle[48]
and, not surprisingly, when Charlemagne became one of the Nine Worthies, this fantastical coat of arms came along with him. At the beginning of the fourteenth century, Clovis also acquired the arms of France;
a charter of Philip the Fair attributed arms with three lilies to the
Merovingian king (in contrast to the shield of scattered lilies that Philip

himself bore).[49] *Beautiful Helen of Constantinople*—a poem that probably dates from the same period—tells us how Clovis received them:

> Lui envoya Jésus qui fit ciel et rosée
> Un ange benoît de sa gloire loée
> Qui lui a prestement sa targe transmuée . . .
> C'étaient trois crapauds portraits d'ordre dorée
> Mais Dieu veut qu'il n'eut telles armes portées
> Aussi lui envoya par miracle ordonnées
> Trois fleurs de lys d'or en champagne azuré
> De par Jésus lui fut cette enseigne donnée.[50]

> [To him Jesus who made heaven and dew
> Sent an angel blessed with his resounding glory
> Who in an instant transformed his buckler . . .
> It had been three toads figured in gold
> But God did not want him to carry such arms
> And so sent him a miraculous set
> Of three gold lilies on a field of azure blue
> An emblem delivered to him by Jesus.]

If the poem does indeed date from the last quarter of the thirteenth
century, it gives us the base on which future legends were built.

Clovis, who stood here for all the kings of France, was already the
beneficiary of a well-known miracle—the gift of the Holy Ampulla.
The story of the lilies followed the same pattern, with an angel replacing the dove of the Holy Spirit. It was set against the backdrop of the
battle of Tolbiac, mentioned by Gregory of Tours, where Clovis defeated the "pagan" Goths, whose king Alaric personified all the infidels and heretics against whom it was the task of the Most Christian
Kings to do battle. The lily shield thus appeared at exactly the moment
when God showed his preference for Clovis and all his successors who
would be kings of France. It was the material form of divine help.

At the beginning of the fourteenth century, some writers were satisfied with the legend as a simple story of a gift of God, given through
the intermediary virtues Grace, Wisdom, and Reason.[51] But monks of
Joyenval saw an opportunity to add embellishments.[52] The story they
told was the following. Clovis had been warring against King Conflat,
who was trying to take over the kingdom. The decisive battle took
place near Conflans-Sainte-Honorine, between a fountain and the hill
of Montjoie. A hermit who wanted to escape the war was taking
refuge in this valley when he received a shield with three lilies from an
angel of God. When Clotilda urged Clovis to accept the gift, he did so
in order to show his gratefulness for his victory. He converted to

Christianity and established the abbey of Joyenval at the place where the miracle occurred.

This monastic tale is, of course, a classic example of a legend invented to exalt the founding of an ecclesiastical house; its author sought to bring renown to a monastery that, although powerful, was still quite young.[53] But it also bears noting that the miracle took place in the heart of the royal domain near Saint-Denis, the monastery that had asserted its rights to be sole guardian of the regalia of the coronation and sole home to the tombs of the royal family. The historical battle of Tolbiac was forgotten, to be replaced by the imaginary battle of Conflans, which was given the same role: it was waged against a pagan enemy just before the ceremony of baptism and sacring. This legend—so useful to the sacralization of royal power—was popularized by the court of Charles V. It appeared without modification in Raoul de Presle's translation of the *City of God*, in Jean Golein's *Treatise on the Coronation*, and in the *Dream in the Pleasure Garden*.[54]

Others felt the need to turn the anonymous hermit into Saint Denis, possibly finding their inspiration in Philip de Vitry's strange assertion that it was Saint Denis and his companions who brought science, faith, and chivalry from Athens to Gaul in the time of Clovis.[55] Etienne de Conti (d. 1414) and Chancellor Gerson identified the unnamed hermit of Joyenval with the Areopagite, along the way inventing the Château of Montjoie, whose name became the royal battle cry, and a lengthy speech by the angel explaining the meaning of the gift and promising God's grace.[56] It is not hard to understand why they transformed the story in this way: the two monasteries were near each other, and Saint-Denis claimed to control all the regalia of the coronation ceremony, a ceremony which by the late-fourteenth century included the blessing of the fleur-de-lys banner.[57] It is also not hard to understand why Saint Denis disappeared from the story after 1415. The disfavor into which the great abbey fell after the capture of Paris by the Burgundians probably accounts for the return of the hermit to the uncompromised anonymity from which he had come.

As for the angel of God, he too was usually anonymous, though some may have imagined him to be Gabriel, the angel of the Annunciation and therefore of the lilies, while others may have chosen Saint Michael (who often appeared with a fleur-de-lys banner), protector of France and angel of the Royal Dignity.[58]

The Joyenval legend passed nearly unchanged into the histories of Nicole Gilles, Robert Gaguin, and Guillaume Crétin.[59] It was the official version, and the most popular one as well. But there was also another, more peculiar version. In 1350 Evrard, abbot of Fontenay, used his funeral oration for Miles de Noyers to defend the right of the Noyers family to bear the oriflamme of France. He told the following story: a Miles de Noyers had been Clotilda's Christian squire; on the eve of battle, he had admonished Clovis to believe in Christ and brought to him both the oriflamme and the lilies which God had given him; as the first bearer of the oriflamme, he passed that privilege on to all the Noyers lords to come, by "hereditary and natural right."[60] In this familial version of the legend we find the first pairing of the lilies and the oriflamme. What audience the story may have had beyond the family we do not know, but the Noyers family retained the right to carry the oriflamme from 1304 to 1369, relinquishing it only when the sole remaining heirs were three girls.

Sometime after 1400, the author of an historical manual changed the legend of Joyenval to add the oriflamme (which until then had been attributed to Charlemagne) to the shield with three lilies.[61] Now it was Clotilda who in a dream on the eve of the battle saw an angel carrying the shield; he promised to her the life of her child and to Clovis his victory over the king of the Goths. She then asked the hermit of Joyenval to offer the shield to the king, but in vain. When Clovis prepared for battle, the angel reappeared with both the shield and a vermilion banner, the oriflamme, so dazzling that at the crucial moment it blinded king Alaric, who fled from the field. We can see the conscious shaping of this story to point up the intervention of God and the meaning of the gifts: victory over the Goths but also the survival of the lineage of France.

This story was popularized toward the end of the reign of Charles VII and continued to reappear here and there until the beginning of the sixteenth century. It is another example of how the disfavor of Saint-Denis brought about the eclipse of its Carolingian oriflamme; the object itself, it was said, had disappeared, but it was really its function that had been lost to the fleur-de-lys banner.[62] The abbot and monks of Joyenval had no difficulty gaining recognition for their "true oriflamme," the oriflamme of Clovis, still preserved in their church. The conflation of the oriflamme and the fleur-de-lys banner favored the mixing of the traditions of Saint-Denis and Joyenval. At the beginning of the fifteenth century, Saint-Denis still predominated, and its patron was identified with the hermit; after 1415 Joyenval won favor and was able to capture the oriflamme.[63] At this point, the lilies, associated with Clovis and the oriflamme, the Holy Ampulla, and even the royal healing touch,[64] joined a mythic entity that went far beyond them.

SYMBOLISM OF THE LILIES

Late-medieval authors also elaborated abstract explanations of the lilies; their symbolism, moral and religious in earlier centuries, became charged with politics. By the end of the fifteenth century, people were composing treatises exclusively devoted to their symbolic meaning.

Thirteenth-century authors had limited their symbolic explorations to the traditional ones linking the lilies to Christian virtues. To Guillaume de Nangis[65] they signified faith, wisdom, and chivalry, all of which the kingdom possessed in abundance; faith was at the center, wisdom on the right—the honorable place, and chivalry on the left; the union of these second two maintained the faith, assuring the salvation of the kingdom in both the temporal and spiritual worlds. This interpretation retained its popularity until the end of the fifteenth century, with only minor modification, such as the replacement of "wisdom" by "science" or *clergie;* and as the practice of dubbing to knighthood fell by the wayside, nobility took the place of chivalry.[66] At the end of the century, the list began to grow more secular, justice replacing wisdom, honesty replacing chivalry, and peace replacing faith at the center.[67] The fundamental idea of the emblem had not changed however: the kingdom earned its honor and peace because it practiced virtues that were fundamentally religious; and as the fleur-de-lys was both triple and unitary, so those virtues had to be conjoined.

Two of the virtues in question were the special domain of the nobles and clergy.[68] Accordingly, a monk at Chaalis, Guillaume de Digulleville (d. 1358), conceived of the lily in terms of three different statuses: the barons who protected the borderlands were on the left, the prince—a living sword of justice—was in the center, and to the right were the clergy and counselors. The base of the flower motif, he said, represented the mass of common humanity upon which all this was founded. Thus the coat of arms of France stood for the mystical body of the kingdom, whose different parts worked together to promote justice. Despite the interest of Guillaume's idea, its complexity did not serve to make it popular: it was rarely imitated, and even then, only in a greatly simplified form.[69]

Meanwhile, the court of Charles V found the lily indispensable in its struggle to prove its contested legitimacy, and the Joyenval legend helped to demonstrate that God was the guarantor of the monarchy. The founding royal charter of the monastery of the Celestines at Limay in 1376 turned the lilies into the symbol of the entire kingdom; they embodied its flourishing virtues; they made the greatness of the kingdom shine around the world; they were the Holy Trinity, which "manifests itself to such a degree in the dignity and supremacy of the royal house that the two seem to be identical."[70] This was more than just a clichéd affirmation that all power came from God. If the House of Valois carried the lily "as a sign of the Holy Trinity" or "in honor of it,"[71] it was because the kings of France were part of the order of God, as were their arms. Through his attachment to the lily, Charles V consecrated his own power. In the same manner Louis XI would later assert that his nobility and dignity "were graced by the fleur-de-lys with the countenance and the mark of Heaven."[72]

In the imagination of these late-medieval kings, the conjunction of Royal Dignity, the Holy Trinity, and the lily had a variety of meanings. First, it meant that the French monarchy enjoyed the special approval of God: through his gift of the fleur-de-lys, God "constituted, approved, and confirmed the crown, the jurisdiction, and the power of the kings of France."[73] And through history God continues to intercede on their behalf. "The fleur-de-lys was given and sent by God as a sign of love and alliance, a love and alliance that grows daily and will continue to grow, if it please God, without end."[74] As long as the lily fights against infidels and heretics, God will assure it protection.[75] It triumphs over tempests, thorns, and winter's cold, to bloom again when springtime comes, as the Bible says.[76] "Enclosed within the fleur-de-lys lies a grain and seed like gold, so that never will any conflict or any foreign power cause it to die out. . . . The fleur-de-lys is enriched and designed in such a way that it grows in floods and tempests; the older it is, the more beautiful and embellished it becomes; already the monarchy of France has lasted longer than any other."[77]

With the second half of the fifteenth century came the promise of temporal greatness, even the domination of the world. Such was the primary theme of the two great treatises on the lily from the end of the Middle Ages.

In his *Opus Davidicum*,[78] written for Charles VIII, the Italian Giovanni Angelo de Legonissa summarized all the meanings and properties of the lily as the tradition had reached him; he then went on to assert that it would escape any and all threats that might come its way and would therefore grow to dominate the three sectors of the world that God had promised to it; both the papacy and the imperial eagle would eventually stand beneath its protective banner. Fittingly, the frontispice of Legonissa's manuscript displayed a prince with lilies holding the papal tiara in one hand and the closed crown of emperors in the other.

A few years later, Giovanni Lodovico Vivaldi wrote his *Triumph of the Three Lilies* for Louis XII. This little-known text devotes 188 pages entirely to the symbolism of the lily. Though its organization is somewhat simplistic—the meaning of the lilies, the number three, gold, azure—it is an interesting work nonetheless. It begins with a very accurate account of the theological associations of the lily: Christ, the Virgin Mary, the royal virtues such as clemency, magnanimity, and mercy. The number three is of course associated with the Holy Trinity; gold stands for the enduring nature of the Crown; azure is for heavenly gifts. Vivaldi concluded his work with the assertion that the king of France is the champion of God, who would crush all forms of tyrannical barbarism in an unparalleled reign of glory.[79]

The lily also figured in very simple poems. Here for example it comes to tell the French . . .

> Que sur tous autres seraient victorieux
> Qu'ils germeraient en si haute abondance
> Qu'ils peupleraient le royaume de France
> Et outre plus par bataille et guerre
> Seraient doutés plus qu'autres de la terre.[80]

> [That they would be victorious over all others
> That they would spring up in such great abundance
> That they would populate the kingdom of France
> And what is more, by waging battle and war
> They would be more roundly feared than any other on earth.]

In this way the abstract symbolism of the lily passed through three principal phases, each overlapping the next. The thirteenth century elaborated a moral and religious interpretation that remained close to the theological origins of the emblem and celebrated the union of faith, wisdom, and chivalry. The fourteenth century developed the historical legends of the lily's divine origin and identified the flower with the Royal Diginity and the Trinity. Finally, the fifteenth century discovered in the lily the alliance of France with God which would justify its newfound imperial ambitions.

THE POPULARITY AND DIFFUSION OF THE LEGEND AND SYMBOLISM OF THE LILY

By what intermediaries did the king's subjects enter in contact with these legends and theories?

THE PILGRIMAGE TO JOYENVAL

The history of Joyenval offers one way into this subject, for in the fourteenth and fifteenth centuries the abbey gradually became one of the important centers of the royal religion.[81] Joyenval, a Premonstratensian convent originally dedicated to the Virgin Mary, was built between 1204 and 1224 in the forest of Yvelines. Its founder was Barthélemy de Roye—chamberlain of France, comrade in arms of Philip Augustus at Bouvines in 1214 and one of the executors of his will—who helped it gain many privileges from the king, including its heraldic arms with the three lilies. Later in the century, Philippe de Montfort—a relative of Barthélemy de Roye and a companion to Charles of Anjou, king of Sicily from 1266 to 1286—brought back so many relics of Saint Bartholomew from Southern Italy that Joyenval gained the reputation for being the saint's burial site.

The thirteenth-century church, which was restored in the fifteenth century, carried the mark of the lily: the French coat of arms appeared above the main doorway and on the central lintel. The jubé, altar, choir screen, and all the windows and reliquaries were likewise embellished with lilies. The mystical heart of the monastery however—aside from the reliquary of Saint Bartholomew—was the famous Fountain of Lilies. This is how it is described in a seventeenth-century inventory: "Also outside the church, near the Chapel of the Virgin Mary, is a covered fountain, which is known today as the fountain of the fleurs-de-lys, and around it is an enclosure in the form of a niche for arms, a bronze shield displaying the arms of France, and above as if in a frontispiece there is a stone relief representing a shield, decorated in turn with the coat of arms of France supported by the figure of an angel."[82]

Joyenval enjoyed the favor of the royal family through the end of the thirteenth century. It celebrated the anniversaries of the deaths of all the kings and queens of the kingdom.[83] During the first half of the fourteenth century, activities such as these increased, with the result that the abbey grew richer and acquired surrounding lands as well as houses in

Paris. The number of monks swelled: in 1224 there had only been twelve; by 1340 there were thirty, in addition to lay brothers and novices. Doubtless those responsible for managing the abbey were skillful administrators, but Joyenval's growing prosperity was most probably due to its development as an important pilgrimage site on the feastday of Saint Bartholomew, August 24.

Papal bulls from Urban V (1362–1370), Clement VII (1378–1394), and Martin V (1417–1431) sang the praises of the faithful who came in such great numbers. Indulgences were declared, first for the feastday itself and then for the entire year. But pilgrimages to Joyenval were also royal pilgrimages. The most important royal relic was probably the bronze shield held by the angels above the fountain, which inspired a local legend about how the shield had come to be, while the recent foundation of the monastery was forgotten.

Joyenval's own version of the fleur-de-lys legend probably first appeared long before it became official in 1350, for by then the abbey's prosperity was already well established. As early as 1328, Philip VI alluded in a benefaction to the abbey to "the salutary example set by his predecessors." From a purely local pilgrimage in the thirteenth century, it became a national site in the reign of Charles V, its popularity assured by a number of miraculous cures. At the beginning of the fifteenth century, however, the trend was reversed. The abbey, attacked several times by the Burgundians, did not regain its prosperity until around 1440. It was fortunate, however, in its election of two abbots who succeeded each other at this time: John VI Toppet and John VII of Hainaut both held high positions in the Premonstratensian order and traveled all over Europe to promote monastic reform. They quickly reaped privileges for their abbey from both the king and the pope. Charles VII visited there in 1440 and gave the monks the right to use the lily arms, which up until then had been reserved for the abbots alone. Popes Eugene IV (1431–1439) and Felix V (1439–1449) gave it new indulgences and graced the abbots with the right to carry the crosier and to wear the episcopal ring.

The key to this reestablishment of Joyenval's reputation was a new royal relic, the oriflamme of Clovis. In a letter dated October 6, 1480, the bishop of Beauvais wrote of the "sacrosanct flag of the oriflamme, the lilies, the skull of Saint Bartholomew, and all the other relics of the abbey,"[84] bringing together in one sentence the royal religion and the Christian religion. For the first time, characters began to appear in literature who had heard of the Joyenval pilgrimage or who had made the journey themselves. Robert Gaguin, for example, knew that inhabitants of the town always showed visitors the fountain of the miracle.[85] Symphorien Champier and Jean Bonaud knew of the relics and could situate the abbey quite exactly.[86] Guillaume Crétin spoke of the fountain, the hill, and the monastery of Saint Bartholomew, and dreamed of building there a temple to the monarchy made of white marble and porphyry and bearing representations of all the exploits of the kings of France, from the time of Clovis onward.[87]

And yet it was above all a popular pilgrimage. The monarchy, in any event, gave no support to the new relic. But this did not stop the oriflamme of Joyenval, a banner reserved for war against the infidels, from finding popularity among souls who were sensitive to the prestige of crusades and to the problems of European warfare. At the end of the fifteenth century Joyenval remained the center of a pilgrimage to the shield of France, before which (and with an intensity that is impossible to measure) people adored the greatness of the God who had given it and of the kings who had received it.

MINIATURES

Illustrations, the miniatures of manuscripts and engravings of early printed books, were another form of diffusion, especially those in the many copies of Raoul de Presles's translation of the *City of God* of Saint Augustine and the later fourteenth-century *Sea of Histories*.[88]

Illuminators favored two types of representation. The first figured the legend of Joyenval quite faithfully. It originated in a Parisian manuscript made for John, duke of Bedford around 1430, a manuscript that told the story of Clotilda through a series of small episodes: we see the queen visiting the hermit who, having received the shield from the angel, gives it to her; she talks persuasively to Clovis, who then raises it against the Saracens. The fountain, the hermitage, and even the church of Joyenval are represented, but the oriflamme is absent: Clovis carries only his shield and a fleur-de-lys banner into battle. This series of pictures spread through the royal domain and was distributed widely by the printed editions of the *Sea of Histories*, from which the woodcuts then passed to many other books. This series triumphed in the sixteenth century.[89]

The second type developed from the illuminations in a Lille manuscript of about 1420 from which scribes copied many times for the libraries of the dukes and other important Burgundians. It was more literally faithful to the text of Raoul de Presles than were those of the first type. Here Clovis is depicted in royal garb, watching as the angel brings the shield from heaven; the scene is a wooded valley overshadowed by the abbey of Saint-Denis; in the sky, the dove of the Holy Spirit bears the Holy Ampulla, as an eagle keeps his eyes fixed on the sun; the red oriflamme embroidered with a gold ornament appears in the middle of the scene, and the hermit and Clotilda are absent.[90]

It is possible that the differences between these two forms of representation stemmed from two different ways in which people thought about the legend. The royal domain remained faithful to the fourteenth-century version: the shield went with Clovis at Joyenval, the oriflamme with Charlemagne at Saint-Denis. The Burgundian territories in contrast, continued to hold the abbey of Saint-Denis in high esteem as it remained under Burgundian influence. It is possible that the conjunction of Clovis with the oriflamme is only a coincidence forced by the necessities of laying out the page, but we must recall that, at least until 1436, Burgundian texts were more favorable than those of the rest of the kingdom to the legend that linked Clovis and the oriflamme through the intermediary of Saint Denis. The union of Clovis and Clotilda seemed to guarantee that the hoped-for alliance between the duke and the king would materialize; glorifying Clovis's role by giving him the oriflamme may have been politically useful.

ROYAL ENTRIES

The legends of the lilies were also portrayed in flesh and blood. During the fifteenth century, whenever the king made his first entry into one of his favored towns, the lily played a central role in the ceremonies.[91] The town would be draped in blue and gold velvet, and the canopy above the king, like the one that in earlier times had been suspended over the Holy Sacrament during the feast of Corpus Christi, was covered with lilies. Fountains sculpted in the shape of lilies overflowed with wine for the pleasure of passersby, and mystery plays were performed along the parade route. Although for a long time the plays dealt only with religious subjects, during the reign of Louis XI their topics expanded so that they afforded anyone and everyone the opportunity to come into close contact with the symbolism of the lily, a recurrent motif in all celebrations of this kind.

The most frequent and least original of these tableaux vivants represented the religious and political virtues necessary for good government.

When Charles VIII made his entry into Paris, figures of Science, Justice, and Peace greeted him perched on lily petals; further along, the Poor and Sick lay on the ground and raised their hands toward the Lily, alluding to the flower's healing powers and to the hopes people invested in the new sovereign. This imagery was clearly religious. A more abstract form of symbolism was embodied in the Lily Tree, a kind of living genealogy of the princes of the fleur-de-lys from the first—Saint Louis, the most glorious of Capetians—to the newest king. It was inspired by the studies heralds had made of the lily emblems of the royal line. Even more interesting was the lily rendered as the Royal Dignity, as distinct from the royal person, which appeared at the entry of Charles VII into Rouen in 1449, and later in all the Parisian entries. Royal Dignity was embodied by a white horse that bore a seal with three lilies and preceded the king under a canopy. Thus, the new ruler appeared twice—once as Dignity, once as himself. The concept was probably taken from royal funeral rites in which, from 1422 onward, a figure of Royal Dignity had also doubled the royal personage:[92] the casket was accompanied by an effigy decorated with all the insignia of the royal house—a symbolic king who would never die. These spectacles, whether they were entries or funeral observances, all afforded people direct experience with the most abstract political forms of the lily symbolism (the symbolism of Royal Dignity), a symbol that could avoid the wastage of time and advance through the centuries toward the higher destiny that God had promised.

There is thus no reason to try to explain the lily in terms of anything other than the realities of medieval France. From the beginning, its religious component was determinative. The lily of the Virgin Mary gradually evolved into the lily of the royal house and in so doing sanctified the monarchy and assured its legitimacy. All the myths that surrounded it seemed easy to believe. And this kind of commonly held belief—in the myths, and their power to legitimate—a belief that was both religious and political, worked to reinforce the unity of the nation. The France of clergy and heralds formed the first stratum of this belief, but it was not the only stratum. The France of jurists and lawyers was also part of it, a more abstract and learned France, which attached itself to other symbols.

CHAPTER 8

The Political Uses of the Trojan Myth

The Trojan origin of France and its dynasty was everywhere in later medieval French literature. Despite the central position of the so-called "matter of France" of the chansons de geste (for, since the twelfth century, that was what interested the public),[1] in all the histories of France the story of the kingdom began with the migration of the refugees from Troy.[2] The *Great Chronicles* devoted its first chapter to the Trojan legend;[3] so did the history manuals and summaries that appeared in ever increasing numbers after 1300. The genealogies of the kings of France also began with the Trojan legend:[4] their first miniature always showed the open gates of burning Troy from which grew the great genealogical tree of France.[5] Often genealogies of the great families of France did the same: "From Scythia came the kings, dukes and all kinds of great persons," wrote the chronicler Roric.[6] After 1080, most comital and princely families claimed Trojan origins, and by the end of the Middle Ages there was hardly a noble who had not been allotted his own Trojan ancestor.[7] As Philip Mouskès said, "We are all Trojans."[8]

The most useful aspect of the Trojan myth was its capacity to root national solidarity firmly in a thick soil of blood ties; everyone—nobles and non-nobles alike, whether they were from the north or the south— was blessed with the same pure and illustrious blood. And although changes did occur in the myth, out of a need to take account of newly gained historical perspectives, it continued to be enlisted in the cause of preserving the unity and continuity of the French race. In this respect, the myth of Trojan origins was very different from the myths invented during the seventeenth century, which—in order to establish a biological justification for the social hierarchy—made the nobility the descendants of the Franks whereas the common people were made descendants of the conquered Gallo-Romans. For, although writers of the early Middle Ages were concerned to link patriotism to the glorification of the Franks and their inherent ethnic traits, those of the later Middle Ages were far more preoccupied with the bond between the territory of France and its immemorial inhabitants, the "Gallo-Franks."

Two things were deemed imporant: to come from somewhere else, from an elsewhere that was illustrious (as in the myths of origin of nomadic tribes such as the Franks), and at the same time to be indigenous—so necessary for the mythology of a territorial state. Thus a myth that justified possession of the land by those born there gradually replaced an older set of stories that justified conquest of the land by force, for it was no longer believed that might alone could justify the right to rule. The clear purpose of these changes was to create a right to possess the national territory and, at the same time, to anchor in ties of blood the solidarity among different regions and social groups. All of this was necessary in a society shaken by civil wars, one where the legitimacy of the dynastic line had been challenged. Those who witnessed the disasters of the first part of the Hundred Years War could hardly admit that simple conquest was sufficient to secure rights to the kingdom, whereas, paradoxically, the generation of 1450 saw in its successful reconquest of the national territory a sign of divine approval.

At length, a simple myth of origin of a territorial state became a myth about the ennoblement of a collectivity. As little by little this most Christian kingdom gained an eminent position among other kingdoms, it felt the need to find its superiority in the story of its national origins. In the Trojan myth, all the elements needed to justify its ennoblement were present: the military exploits of its ancestors against the Alans and the Romans, the exemption they had won with their blood from all obligations to pay tribute, and the land they had been given by God.

The motif of fiscal exemption was the most tangible sign of the kingdom's eminence. In the second half of the fourteenth century, when the nobility was slowly being exempted from fiscal obligations, the story of exemption from tribute was told in this way: "Valentinian sent them a charter of freedom and ennobled them, and each one was called Frank, that is French."[9] Trojan blood was also the noblest blood in the world; it carried exceptional virtues, virtues that justified

France's place in the world. The myth of national origin reflected the same concerns as the genealogies of the nobility that were its contemporaries: it gave the nation a famous ancestor who was far removed in time, a story of great ancestral military feats, a tie to a specific land, and a continuous and pure blood line. By the end of the Middle Ages, the Trojan myth had become a collective genealogy of nobility. It guaranteed the unity of the nation and its high rank among the other nations of the world. It also served more concrete ends, most particularly in issues of foreign policy. There it allowed the kingdom to confront its crises head on and to project a fitting role for itself in the larger game of European politics.

THE EUROPEAN CHESSBOARD AND THE TROJAN MYTH

THE FRENCH CRISIS

Between 1300 and 1500 the Trojan myth served mainly to bolster internal unity against the English threat. The siege of Troy showed how empires had fallen and been transformed, it gave a historical demonstration of the turn of Fortune's wheel. Between 1380 and 1450, in particular, many authors used the Trojan story to reflect on the unhappiness of the times: Martin Lefranc, Christine de Pisan, Alain Chartier, and others.[10] By citing an exemplary model, they were able to express far more freely their thoughts about the causes of the kingdom's troubles, and they could put forward their ideas about the proper solutions while at the same time remaining safely shielded behind the glorious ancestors of the nation. The collapse of the city of Troy, usually credited to the army of Agamemnon, was now explained as the result of internecine conflict. "Never do empires and kingdoms disappear because of wars with foreigners, even if such conflicts inflict great damage. Only civil war can lead a great monarchy to its downfall," wrote Alain Chartier.[11] Troy had been punished for its sin (the kidnapping of Helen), for its excessive wealth, and for its inordinate pride; because of its sins, God and fortune allowed it to be betrayed—for all these writers, the treason of Troy was a principal preoccupation. The ancient texts of course did not have much to say on the subject; Virgil did not speak of it. But the ancient romances of Dares and Dictys of Knossos, Benedict of Saint-Maure (c. 1180), the *Ancient History to the Time of Caesar*, and Boccaccio all affirmed that Troy had been handed over to the Greeks by Calchas,

Aeneas, and Antenor, the last of whom, according to some traditions, was the ancestor of the French.[12]

This betrayal was explained in two ways. Those authors who were interested in comparing the fall of Troy to the Anglo-Burgundian capture of Paris in 1418 claimed that the Parisians and the Trojans alike had betrayed their own kings and nobility; the Parisians, they said, were responsible for the forced flight of their king and noblemen, as the Trojans had been before them. The English, like the Greeks, were the punishment that the people through their sins had brought on themselves.

> Paris, rappelle-toi de Troie
> Le Grant qui fut détruite.
>
> [Paris, remember Troy
> The Great, which was destroyed.]

So warned Robert Blondel.[13] The Dauphin and the Armagnacs, urged Martin Lefranc, should be as courageous as their ancestors in achieving the much-desired reconquest:

> Souvenez-vous de vos ancêtres
> Dont la valeur qui n'a seconde
> Fit triompher nos puissants sceptres
> Aux quatre coins du monde.[14]
>
> [Remember your ancestors
> Whose merit has no rival,
> Who made our powerful scepters victorious
> Throughout the four corners of the world.]

Another set of authors assigned responsibility for the misfortunes of Troy (which they identified with the whole of France rather than Paris alone) to the factionalism of the nobility and the betrayal of the Trojan king Priam by some among them. Although the treason of Chalcas (identified with the Church) was scarcely whispered, Benedict of Saint-Maure made Antenor and Aeneas, who treated with the Greeks, into vassals who had broken their oaths. Later authors made them traitors to their country; motivated by excessive pride, by jealousy, by deceitful malice and personal interest, these men had repudiated their ruler and their country and conspired in the deaths of their comrades. They should themselves have been killed! In Jacques Millet's *History of the Siege of Troy* and Christine de Pisan's *Epistle of Othea to Hector of Troy,* Antenor and Aeneas appeared as incarnations of evil; like Judas, they refused to repent even after they had committed their crimes.[15] In the same way, Isabelle of Bavaria was sometimes equated with Helen, whose beauty and loose ways had caused the downfall of Troy; like Troy, the French kingdom risked being lost for a woman.[16]

Yet these transformations of the Trojan myth emphasized that the story of Troy also held the secret of salvation. Troy was not dead, for the kingdom of France was its reincarnation. Here men still extolled the glory of the ancient city.[17] France could yet manage to protect itself from the same destiny if it used the virtues it had inherited from Troy, the courage and valor of its men. Already at the beginning of the twelfth century Guibert de Nogent had proclaimed Hector a brave soldier and a symbol of true devotion to his country. Robert Blondel was still doing so at the end of the fifteenth. Many other Trojans had also endured the ten years of siege without losing faith and willingly died for their country. Jacques Millet's Priam cried:

> Défendez votre terre que vos ennemis anciens
> Veulent conquerre . . .
> J'ai volonté de mort souffrir
> En défendant ma liberté . . .
> Que je meure avant que je visse
> Exterminer mon pays. . . .[18]
>
> [Defend your land that your ancient enemies
> Are trying to conquer . . .
> I want to die
> Defending my freedom . . .
> May I die before I see
> My country exterminated. . . .]

For Alain Chartier, Hector fighting to save his kingdom was the model of Joan of Arc fighting to save hers.[19] Valor, unity, and patriotism—all these could save the French kingdom as they had that other Troy. In the prologue to his *Chronicles* (written c. 1419–1422), the Burgundian Chastellain interpreted the resurrection of Troy as a promise given to his own country, which he likewise thought of as an offspring of that great city.[20] In Millet's *Mystery,* the king of Troy, shortly before his death, has a vision of the Castle and Wheel of Fortune in which he sees far into the future: his heir Charles VII triumphs over his misfortune and regains his honor, building the city of Troy once again.[21]

During the second half of the century, these comparisons disappeared. But when Philip the Good, duke of Burgundy, chose the Golden Fleece as his emblem, the subjects of Charles VII may have seen the implied threat—for the theft of the legendary Fleece was the work of

Jason and Hercules, who had been responsible for the second destruction of Troy.

TROY, THE PAPACY, AND THE EMPIRE

Originally created to demonstrate the right of the Franks to a certain portion of the ancient Roman Empire, from the late-thirteenth century onward the Trojan myth served as well to justify the independence of the kingdom from the papacy and the Germanic Empire—the two powers that claimed to be the successors to Rome. In the early thirteenth century, when arguments were raised about that independence, French jurists generally went no further than to proclaim that the king of France recognized no superior power in the temporal sphere, that the king of France was "emperor in his kingdom." They quoted Innocent III's bull *Per venerabilem* of 1202 in which he recognized the independence of the kingdom, though he did not seek to defend it.[22]

It was in the course of Philip the Fair's conflict with Pope Boniface VIII[23] that the group of historical questions raised by that claim to independence—questions that would be raised continuously until the sixteenth century—finally appeared: Did the Donation of Constantine include the French kingdom? What conclusions could be drawn from the approval that Pope Stephen II gave in 754 to the deposition of the last Merovingian king? What was the status of the *regnum Franciae* in Charlemagne's empire? What did the kingdom's Trojan origins prove?

The pamphlet *Rex pacificus* (The Peaceful King) launched the debate. The holy kings of France, it asserted, had been independent for more than a hundred years, indeed for time immemorial, without anyone calling their right into question. This was the argument by prescriptive right; but such arguments were not always recognized with respect to the regalia, the rights belonging to the king, and so it was necessary to look elsewhere. The *Quaestio in utramque partem* (The Question on Both Sides) of 1303 built its argument on the symbolism of the two swords and the sun and moon, on the bull *Per venerabilem*, and on the Trojan origins of France to demonstrate the antiquity of French independence.[24] John of Paris in his treatise *On Royal and Papal Power* made especially skillful use of this last argument.[25] When the first great Troy fell, he wrote, the *Franci* left for Sycambria where they enjoyed undisputed independence for several centuries. When Constantine made his donation to the pope, the Franci were not subordinated to Rome; the donation therefore did not apply to them. It is true, he admitted, that the *Galli* had fallen under the Roman yoke for a brief period, but might cannot make right, and the Franks themselves were never subjected to Roman power. When at last some did submit voluntarily they nonetheless continuously rebelled against the injustice of the Roman monarchy. Original independence thus guaranteed contemporary independence; never to have been subordinated was felt to be a more convincing argument than one based on prescription, even of time immemorial.

This historical argument was a radically new proposition, for the prologue to the *Great Chronicles* of Saint-Denis had maintained that the Franks were subjected to Rome.[26] From 1300 to 1500 authors repeated both sides of the argument. The *Dream in the Pleasure Garden* stated that the Franks had never been subject to the Roman yoke and that the Roman Empire had been founded on force and born of murder.[27] Honoré Bonet picked up the same thread in the eighty-fourth chapter of his *Book of Battles*. After developing arguments from the Scriptures and the history of the Hebrew people, he went on to the Trojan origins of France: the conquest of Troy preceded the founding of the Roman Empire and took place far away from it; the kings of France could not possibly have been subordinated to an empire such as this, founded on force and often racked by schism and heresy.[28]

Fifteenth-century authors argued in a similar way. Both the little-known Pierre Desgros and the famous jurist from the Dauphiné, Guy Pape (1402–1476), dealt with the question in more or less the same way.[29] First they recalled *Per venerabilem* and the conflict between Philip the Fair and Boniface VIII. To this they added that "insofar as the emperor is concerned, the French are not his subjects and legally never were, as the chronicles about the origin of the French make clear." Next came the traditional rendition of the Trojan origins of the French, demonstrating that "the Romans subjugated them by force and for only a short time," from the time of Constantine to the time of Valentinian, that is to say for far less than a century. "And against the pope and the emperor prescription of a hundred years suffices." From that time on, they maintained, for a time "to which memory runs not to the contrary," the holy kings of France had ruled peacefully over their kingdom, holding their power from no one else. These authors clearly were walking a fine line between historical reality and the argument they had to make.

Early sixteenth-century authors, however, proved themselves less prudent. They asserted the independence of both Franks and Gauls. When the jurists Jean Feu and Guillaume Benoit took up the famous scholastic question *An rex franciae recognoscat imperatorem?* ("Does the king of France recognize the emperor as his superior?"), they argued that thanks to their Trojan origin the Franks had avoided subjugation by the Romans;[30] they had fought against Valentinian; they had conquered their territory by the force of their own swords. As for the Galli, though they were subjected by the might of the Romans (whose reputation had darkened with the Wars of Italy), they had defeated the armies of Rome more often than they had been defeated by her. Brennus eclipsed Vercingetorix.

RELATIONS ACCEPTED, RELATIONS REFUSED: ENGLAND, THE CELTIC LANDS, HUNGARY, AND MORE FAR-OFF ADVENTURES

The anti-English function of the Trojan myth is evident in two famous texts of the fifteenth century, a memorial of 1420 and the *Debate of the Heralds at Arms* of 1450,[31] but it predates these texts by over a century. The *Chanson de Perceforest,* from the beginning of the fourteenth century,[32] is graced with a prologue that is an extraordinary bit of anti-English propaganda. Brutus, sprung from the blood of Troy—"that most noble blood, full of valor and courage"—appears as ancestor of the Bretons, the first inhabitants of the great island. Brutus is both a parricide and a regicide, making the English into killers of kings.[33] (In the same vein, Jacques Millet would later make the traitorous Antenor the ancestor of the English.[34]) The Breton-Trojans, however, no longer ruled England, having been killed "with great cruelty" by invading hoards of Saxons. Those who escaped went to Brittany. Thus the English were hardly in a position to glorify the great exploits of either Brutus or King Arthur. The English were not a pure line; and mixed as they were, they were capable of any and all evil deeds. As for the dynasty of Norman extraction, whose origin protected it from these reproaches, they were not Trojan either. Unlike Dudo of Saint-Quentin, who at the beginning of the eleventh century had claimed that the Norman dukes were descended from Troy, the sixteenth-century jurist Guillaume Benoit insisted that they had been little more than Germanic chiefs, related to the Goths and suffering from the same inadequacies— a weakness for drinking, murder, and fathering bastard children; only later had they invented glorious (and deceitful) origins for themselves; their name, in fact, proved this was so—a Norman was "a man of the north." And Normandy, under its Carolingian name of "Neustria," had now returned to its rightful place in the French kingdom.[35]

The same kind of reasoning could also be applied to Brittany to demonstrate that it was a part of the kingdom because of its Trojan roots, or that its traditional alliances with Scotland, Wales, and Ireland were justified by a shared Trojan origin. This theme appeared as early as the fourteenth century in the *Chanson de Cyperis de Vignevaux*.[36] Cyperis, a Trojan prince (identified with the Merovingian king Childeric III) who also claims descent from the Hungarian royal house, conquers England; he marries three of his seven sons to the queens of Wales, Ireland, and Scotland. The poet Alain Chartier made a similar assertion in a discourse addressed to the king of Scotland:[37] the Scottish and French peoples are fraternally bound by their common heritage; their blood endows them with the same bravery and loyalty.

Most likely, the Franco-Hungarian alliance, strengthened by the marriage of Madeleine of France to Ladislas I (1446–1453), was justified in the same way.[38] Though the official speeches from the wedding of Madeleine to Ladislas I in 1453 and the wedding of Anne of France to Ladislas II in 1502 have been lost, leaving us without direct evidence for propagandistic use of the Trojan legend on these occasions, the city of Buda had been equated with Sycambria as early as the beginning of the fourteenth century. The wedding of Anne to Ladislas II included a staging of the judgment of Paris and the kidnapping of Helen of Troy, the banquet hall was hung with tapestries telling the story of Troy, and the herald Pierre Choque, Anne's escort, went touring the ruins of Aquincum.[39]

Thus the myth of the Trojan origins of France justified the kingdom's exalted claim to independence from other states and anchored in those origins the political attractions and repulsions of the fifteenth century, endowing them with fitting and apparently solid reasons for being.

But the most obvious way in which the legend was used for political ends was to justify exotic adventures, above all wars in the Holy Land. Theoretically, the Crusades aimed at recovering Christian lands taken over by the infidels and at liberating the Holy Land; neither aim suggested that the myth of Troy might be useful. But Byzantium, where the idea of the Crusades did not exist, had made the recovery of its own territory one of the primary justifications of just wars, using it to demand homage from the hands of the crusading rulers in the eastern Mediterranean. The crusaders could hardly ignore this demand; Troy thus became their sought-for validation against these Byzantine claims to power.

The site of Troy was supposedly lost, though a later town, Ilion, was thought to have been built on more or less the same spot; Alexander visited it; Caesar awarded it many privileges. In time, hurried medieval travelers and writers who based their accounts on hearsay identified Troy with a variety of places—with Cyzicus or with Pera-Galata (as did the Herald Berry, for example, because it was near Galatia),[40] or with Abydos, a mistake more readily understood.[41] But there were also examples of more precise sitings, accurate descriptions, and accounts of visits to Troy itself. Geography manuals, such as the twelfth-century *Imago mundi* written by Honorius of Autun and Pierre d'Ailly's manual from about 1411, devoted as much as a full paragraph to Troy;[42] so too did dictionaries such as Giovanni Balbi's *Catholicon*.[43] One localization came from a work *On the Names of Places* attributed to Saint Jerome and from Isidore of Seville's *Etymologies:*[44] Troy was located in Phrygia Minor, across from the island of Tenedos. Such was also the information of Vincent of Beauvais in the mid-thirteenth century.[45] But as a result of the Crusades, descriptions of Troy might include references to the Byzantine town situated between Dardanos to the north and Alexandria Troas to the south, near the customs post of Abydos; it was the seat of a bishopric within the archbishopric of Cyzicus or of Mitilini, according to the thirteenth-century monk Aubrey de Trois Fontaines.[46] By the end of the century, the Catalan Ramon Muntaner, having spent his entire life in the Middle East, knew far more. Troy, he said, was located across from Gallipoli: "near Cape Artaki was part of the city of Troy, the other part being a port in the middle of the strait of Abydos graced with a sturdy castle which Paris had built after abducting Helen from the island of Tenedos, five miles out to sea. Troy was 300,000 [*sic*] miles in circumference. Another section of its gates was located at Cape Edremit."[47]

As travel to the Middle East increased, the sitings grew more precise; at the same time, the psychological and political importance of Troy was expanding. Empress Eudoxia went there in 1071;[48] Godfrey of Bouillon and Tancred stopped there during the First Crusade; so did Emperor Frederick I in 1190 during the Third Crusade. From 1204 to 1306, the entire area by and large lay under the control of the West. At the same time, the siege of Troy became an increasingly frequent metaphor to meet a whole range of needs.

On the simplest level, the image of Troy was an expression of Western admiration for the great fortifications of the Middle East. Artasia became "a citadel like unto that of Ilion, work of the Gods."[49] To Baudri of Dol and Henry of Huntington, the siege of Nicea seemed longer and harder than that of Troy.[50] To Radulf of Caen and Guibert de Nogent the crusaders' capture of Antioch was like the Achaean capture of Troy.[51] In all of these texts, the crusaders were assigned the role of the Achaeans, not that of the Trojans; they were Westerners who had come to the East. At the same time, the Trojan theme was to attain political ends. Some of those who would become the heroes of the Crusades enjoyed Trojan genealogies even before their departure: that of the counts of Boulogne dates from 1080–1087 and continued to be carefully elaborated after they had ascended to the throne of Jerusalem. The counts of Flanders, future Latin emperors of Constantinople, had enjoyed Trojan ancestry since as far back as 1120.[52] The bravery of Godfrey of Bouillon, it was said, was equal to that of Achilles, that of Tancred equal to that of Alexander.[53] Radulf of Caen asserted that the very blood of Alexander and Hector flowed in the veins of Bohemond of Antioch and his nephew, Tancred.[54]

Three texts in particular demonstrate the progressive development of this kind of political use of the Trojan myth. Here is Abbot Guibert de Nogent on the siege of Antioch: "In the stories of all sieges of towns, what people can be found who endured so many miseries and obstacles so far from the land of their fathers? Even during the ten years that Troy was besieged, the Trojans enjoyed many periods of truce and they did not suffer famine. They fought for their life and for their country. Our people fought for God, for the Church, they endured famine, fear, rain, cold, much more than the besieged of earlier times . . . as if they were suffering for their own lands."[55] Here the Trojans were the model for the crusaders. Guibert also asserted that Bohemond had justly deprived the Emperor Alexis of his territory, for it had been prophesied that this emperor "being of Frankish origin, these same people would take away his power and his empire."[56] Since the Comneni emperors in fact had sprung from the military nobility of Asia Minor and it was not until Manuel I (1143–1180) that one of them married a Western woman, Guibert's strange assertion can only be explained by assuming that he was giving both Alexis and Bohemond a common Trojan ancestry; for elsewhere Guibert had tried to prove that the Norman Bohemond was a Frank, and he firmly believed that the Franks had descended from the Trojans.

Guibert's allusions remained relatively vague. Others were far clearer. Fulcher of Chartres (1059–1127), describing the passage of the crusading army by Abydos on the Dardanelles, where

Ultra non magis intervallis
Arva jacent Phrygiae Minoris
Praeclaro nomine Troia . . .[57]

[Not far away in Phrygia Minor,
Lay the ploughed-over walls
Of brilliant Troy . . .],

went on to give a summary of the Trojan War and then to recount different stories of the migration of the Franco-Trojans, whose travel finally brought them to France where destiny held in store a future of glory and fame. For Fulcher, the victories of the crusaders in the east seem to have been the realization of that destiny—all the more so as he had just traced the itinerary of Godfrey of Bouillon from Germany to Pannonia and Byzantium as exactly the reverse of the one which had brought the Trojans north and west.

Radulf of Caen, for his part, described Bohemond and his nephew challenging the count of Toulouse in 1098 for control of the Troiad, Bohemond wanting to hold on to the fortification at *Ilion Trojae suae—* Ilion his Troy.[58] Had he not succeeded, said Radulf, he would have been but half the prince of Antioch. Was he thinking of the real strategic importance of the area or of its political and mythic significance? In the *Deeds of Tancred* he included many comparisons with the classical world, as we have seen, equating Tancred with Alexander and Hector, Tancred's adversaries with Ulysses and the perfidious Aeneas—possibly an allusion to the claim of the count of Toulouse to descent from a Tolosus or Tolosanus, another companion of Aeneas.

But it was the Crusade of 1204 that transformed the crusaders definitively into Trojans, as their battle with the Greeks which ended in the plundering of Byzantium and the creation of the Eastern Latin Empire became a fitting revenge for the pillage of Troy. The Franco-Trojans were exacting retribution from the Greeks by taking back the lost lands of their ancestors. Thus the chronicler Robert of Clari makes Pierre de Bracheux boast to Johanissa, king of the Blachs and ally of Byzantium, "Troy belonged to our ancestor, and those who escaped from it came to live in the country which we have come from. It is to regain what once belonged to our ancestors that we have come here to conquer the land."[59] Describing the sack of his city—of which he was an eye-witness—and the crusaders' destruction of the statue of Helen, the Byzantine Chronicler Nicetas Choniates exclaimed, "And these barbarians, . . . descendants of Aeneas, were they trying because of ill-feelings toward you to condemn you to the flames that your beauty once lit within Ilion?"[60] Byzantine mythological history had Constantine the Great move the Palladium of Troy from Rome to Constantinople, the same Palladium that Aeneas had carried with him when he fled from his burning city.[61] This symbol of the transfer of empires now had fallen into the hands of the Westerners; until that moment, it had guaranteed that the Byzantine capital would be unassailable. And so Robert of Auxerre saw the assault on Byzantium as a transfer of empire, a punishment for the sins of the Greeks.[62]

Strangely, though medieval historians and chroniclers made wide use of the Trojan theme as a way of justifying the Crusades, the authors of epics and romances indulged in it far less. The texts belonging to the cycle of the Crusades[63] made few references to the myth of Troy. Godfrey of Bouillon was equated with Hector or Alexander; the town of Edessa—the possession of the counts of Saint-Gilles/Toulouse—was said to have been founded by Antenor; the conquest of Acre was comparable to the taking of Troy—

> Quand Acre la cité fut prise
> Telle destruction ne fut ouïe
> Depuis Troie la Grant qui fut exilée.[64]
>
> [When the city of Acre was taken
> There was destruction such as had never been heard of
> Since the exile of the great city of Troy.]

But despite such occasional references, these authors seem far more taken with Godfrey's maternal descent from the Knight of the Swan, of romance fame, than with his paternal descent from Troy, derived from the learned tradition. The thirteenth-century *Romance of Landamata*, however, focused almost entirely on the reconquest of the ancient lands of Troy from the Greeks and the Turks by Landamata, son of Hector, who had been raised in Europe. His conquests took him all the way to Syria and Palestine, prefiguring the Crusader States to come. The entire romance announced the desire to reclaim ancestral lands and avenge the blood that the accursed Greeks had spilled.[65]

From very earliest times,[66] the Trojan myth had also carried with it a sense of kinship with the Turks, one readily admitted in the epics that made up the cycle of the Crusades. In the later Middle Ages, however, as Ottoman power increased, this kinship became a burden that had to be dealt with as political needs required. When Crusades were in the offing, the Trojan ancestry of the Turks was denied; for William of Tyre

(d. 1190) and many after him, they were nothing more than Scythian barbarians.[67] So they were as well in the fifteenth century for Pope Pius II and Jean Lemaire de Belges.[68] By contrast, when the Turks were considered allies in the war against the Paleologues, their Trojan origins were affirmed: they were waging a just war to recover their inheritance. One could at least negotiate with them. Early in the sixteenth century, for example, Liquainus of Tours could depict the fall of Constantinople as a revenge for the Greek destruction of Troy.[69]

Even though the Franks had to share the inheritance of Troy with the Turks, the story remained quite popular. It reappeared in full force at the time of the Wars of Italy, when the eastern conquests of the Gauls, as told by Strabo and Justin, were added to the memory of Troy. The Wars of Italy were thus doubly justified.

Italy was normally the springboard for the Crusades; it was also the starting point for the conquest of the world that would be accomplished by the emperor-king of the Last Days. Between 1507 and 1510, Louis XII, who claimed to inherit Milan from the Visconti, used the Trojan legend with full force. The propagandists Martin Dolet, Valerand de Varannes, Christophe de Longueil, and Jean Pyrrhus Angleberme all told the same story: the Gauls, having left for the East, founded Galatia and "Gallo-Greece" and then went on to settle Troy and make all Asia tremble before them. The Trojan War culminated with the flight of the exiled, who made their way back to their ancient lands. They lost none of the virtuous spark of their ancestors and forgot nothing of their stay in the East. The Crusades, then, were the fitting means to recover the lost ancestral land.[70] Godfrey of Bouillon, Bohemond, the Lusignans, and the kings of France had all collaborated on the same pious work. Charles VIII followed in the footsteps of Brennus when he crossed the Alps; he captured Rome, as Brennus had done, and reclaimed the towns of Cis-Alpine Gaul that had been founded by Trojan hands. The Gallic monarchy was the legitimate heir to the foundations of its ancestors; the branch of the family descended from Aeneas had brought dishonor on itself by murdering and plundering. The king of France was the rightful descendant of Hector, who counseled him from the land of the dead to undertake this policy of political expansion.[71]

The Trojan myth served as well to justify the rights of the dynasty and the Frankish race to rule over an empire of worldwide dimensions. This argument was enlisted only rarely, since dynastic messianism tended to seek its rationale in Christian motivation rather than in its ancient, pagan inheritance. Two examples are interesting nonetheless.

At the beginning of the fifteenth century, Christine de Pisan wrote her *Path of Long Study* for Duke Louis of Orléans, consecrating a very lengthy passage to the story of the Trojan origins of France; alluding to the duke's imperial ambitions, she concluded, "His high lineage makes him worthy of any royalty and any empire."[72] Nearly a century later, the jurist Guillaume Benoit, as he traced the descent of the royal house from Priam, remarked, "the race of Priam, already endowed with the dignity of royalty, merits the imperial title."[73] Louis XII and Francis I both dreamed of building an empire; Louis's favorite motto, *Ultus avos Trojae*—Avenge our Trojan ancestors—may have been a sign of excessive piety, but it was also a rich expression of imperialist hopes. Jean Lemaire de Belges had a vision of the king of France, who had conquered and converted the Turks and who went on to dominate Europe and the Middle East, establishing an empire and earning the supreme reward—a vision of the walls of Troy:

> Dont si ainsi fut, que Dieu qui tout octroie
> Nous donna voir la grande terre de Troie
> Et là endroit nos fleurons embellis
> Fussent plantés nos armes et nos lys,
> Lors en rendant à sa hautesse grâces,
> Nous enquerrions des grandes ruines basses
> De ta cité, en contemplant le tout
> En souhaitant qu'elle refut debout,
> Même le lieu de ta très riche tombe (celle d'Hector)
> Illec jadis par merveilleux exemples
> Furent dressés riches autels et temples
> Aux vertueux héros . . .
> Ayant vaincu de Fortune la roue. . . .[74]
>
> [And so it came to pass that God who rules over all
> Let us see the great land of Troy
> And there our florets were embellished
> And our arms and our lilies planted,
> Then, paying homage to his greatness,
> We searched the great low ruins
> Of your city, looking at everything
> And wishing it could be raised again,
> Even the site of your very rich tomb (Hector's tomb)
> Here once stood like marvelous models
> The rich altars and temples
> Dedicated to the virtuous heroes . . .
> Who conquered the Wheel of Fortune. . . .]

Mythic time is cyclical: every story ends where it begins.

CULTURAL PRESTIGE

One last theme remains to be examined. The myth of Trojan origins also served to prove that the nation was intrinsically Hellenistic, that it was attached through its valor and its culture to a chronologically distant but still very prestigious ancient world.

The earliest texts, to be sure, did not view the Trojans as civilizing missionaries, though some did credit them with establishing the Salic Law[75] or building towns and castles such as Sycambria on the Danube and Dispargum on the Rhine. But first and foremost, the Trojan heroes were soldiers; they were images of the chivalric ideal. It was the generation of the mid-twelfth century who were most responsible for changing that view, authors of romances rather than of histories. Thus the Merovingian prince Partonopeus de Blois is made to say of his ancestors,

> Troy had much great nobility, great honor, great wealth, and abounded with knights. . . . France, then called Gaul, had neither castles, nor towers, nor noble cities, nor beautiful towns. Thus, everyone lived very much spread out. The countryside of France was uncultivated, covered with woods. There were no kings nor dukes nor counts. Marcomir made them establish rich castles and strong cities and taught them to live together.[76]

The author's vision of the Trojan contribution was of a feudal polity, in which people were grouped together within walls; it is a curious example of the medieval process of settlement–nucleation projected backward into the ancient world. These Trojans were the ancestors of the lords who settled the land in the twelfth century, those who were responsible for new lordships and fortified villages.

The same idea does not seem to appear in chronicles before the beginning of the thirteenth century. Rigord and Guillaume le Breton, historians of Philip Augustus, when telling how the king rebuilt the walls of Paris and paved its streets, compared these actions to the building of Troy.[77] Vincent of Beauvais established the image firmly in people's minds. It appeared again in the *Great Chronicles:*[78] the Trojans, who knew well the art of arms and fortification, were welcomed warmly in Gaul, in part because of the superiority of their civilization; they brought the Gauls from anarchy to a unitary monarchy—the best system of government according to Aristotle. From 1300 onward, the newly discovered merits of French culture were attributed to this civilizing mission of the Trojans.

This civilizing role was particularly manifest in three areas: the founding and fortifying of towns, the superiority of legislation, and the language they brought with them.[79]

Although at least a hundred Italian towns traced their establishment to the migration of Aeneas and Antenor, France had far fewer examples. French towns were more likely to have been founded by the epic heroes of the Charlemagne cycle or to spring from Gallic cities. Only towns that were closely linked to the ruling dynasty paraded their Trojan roots: Paris, Reims, Tours, and Metz.[80] Reims was probably the first to be endowed with a Trojan founder. Through the efforts of Archbishop Hincmar in the ninth century and Flodoard's *History of the Church of Reims* in the tenth, Reims could claim as its founder Remus, the brother of Romulus, and his Trojan companions.[81] Metz, the cradle of the Arnulfian family, displayed the same sort of Carolingian predilection for Trojan roots.[82] In the twelfth century the Englishman Geoffrey of Monmouth attributed the founding of Tours to Turnus, the friend of Brutus. In the thirteenth century, such founders multiplied: Nimes, Narbonne, Troyes, Toulouse, and Clermont all claimed Trojan ancestry and created their own eponymous heroes—Troïlus, Tolosanus, and the like. At Metz, texts from Hugues de Toul to the *Rhymed Chronicle* and Philippe de Vigneulles, present the Trojan Arenus and Serpanus building two of the city's gates, accompanied by other ancestors of noble lineage, each of them named;[83] the city's Trojan foundation was used to explain the existence of specific toponyms already in place and ancient monuments whose origin was unknown. It also justified the social structure of the town.

As it was with towns such as Metz, so it was with the entire kingdom. Trojan origins were invented either for towns that were closely tied to the monarchy, or for city-states, like Metz and Toulouse, cities sure of themselves and anxious to establish themselves as the equals of Rome. These myths, inspired by a kind of homophonic association, had to have appeared relatively early; for after 1300 French authors came to prefer as ancestors the "Gallo-Trojans," whose civitates Caesar had enumerated in his *Gallic Wars*.

Trojan laws were likewise slowly being made the origin of the Salic Law. This, of course, did not begin to happen until the reign of Charles VII when the Salic Law itself became the law of royal succession, with a definitive author, date, and interpretation. Jean Jouvenal des Ursins could not have been more certain: "When the Trojans came to France, they made the Salic Law."[84] The Salic Law was different from Roman and imperial laws; it was also different from feudal customs, and it demonstrated the originality and independence of the nation. It applied to the kingdom alone and was in fact consubstantial with it. The law first appeared with the earliest days of the kingdom, in the time of Pharamond; it was applied forthwith, during the reigns of Clodion and Merovech; it would last as long as the kingdom did. The Salic Law was the new palladium of the kingdom.

The French language was also sometimes graced with Hellenistic origins. Since the days of Fredegar, writers had affirmed that *franc* meant audacious, wild, or free "in the Attic language." Isidore of Seville linked the term *Gallia* or *Galatia* with the Greek word *gala;* the word *Gallogreci* used in geography manuals inspired similar connections; the names of some French towns—Paris for one—were claimed to be Greek in origin. Greek was one of the three sacred languages, and it was free of the negative associations that came from ties to Italo-Latinate culture. To Italian ears, French was little more than a barbaric corruption of Latin. By claiming Greek origin for their language, the French could fend off such denegration. And so they did, from a sermon of 1302 on the wars with Flanders to Jean Lemaire de Belges in the sixteenth century—using, to be sure, historical rather than philological arguments.[85] It was, they said, a noble and beautiful language, worthy of those who spoke it. As philological knowledge developed, Celtic roots were conjoined with the Greek.[86]

The Trojan heroes had thus in the short span of a little more than two centuries passed from exemplars of the warrior ideal to the bearers of civilization, reflecting a new concern with the cultural prestige of the nation.

Trojan ancestors long remained useful. No longer merely guarantors of the great age and prestige of the nation, they had also become defenders of its ethnic purity and a form of national solidarity that was rooted in the bloodline. They guaranteed the kingdom's preeminence within the community of European nations and its high rank in the face of the power of the Church and the Empire. Alliances and wars alike found their explanation in this Trojan protectorship. All foreign adventures were linked to it—from the Crusades to the Italian Wars and the ambitious striving toward imperial domination of the world. Finally, the Trojans became the kingdom's civilizing heroes. France, initially without political power, had taken its time in becoming concerned with its cultural identity. But at last the soldiers of Troy also became the founders of its cities, the creators of its laws and words. They became the guarantors at birth of the originality of its culture. The Trojan myth during the late Middle Ages adapted well to the interests of the growing nation. It did not hesitate to incorporate the whole of the history of Gaul. The myth became the mirror of all the hope and anguish of a troubled time, a time when many of the old values were crumbling. It became irreplaceable, not because it was true but because it was alive and evolved in response to needs.

There was however one aspect of national history that it could not take care of—the Christian religion—where the kingdom already claimed primacy. The Trojans could not serve the kingdom's needs in this regard, for they were pagans, regardless of the efforts made to demonstrate that the Galli were most pious people, even before their conversion to Christianity. Clovis continued to be placed in the balance against Pharamond. When Charles VIII made his entry into Reims in 1484, he was greeted by two figures: on one side of the town square was Pharamond, creator of the Salic Law; on the other was Saint Remi as he baptized Clovis. The nation at birth, like any member of the faith, retained its dual character, natural and spiritual. The Trojan myth could not absorb both of them. Thus France developed two myths of origin: the Trojan myth justified the Franks, and later the Gauls, while the myth of Clovis justified the nation's status as "most Christian," holder of the Holy Ampulla, guardian of the secret cure to scrofula, and beneficiary of the royal lilies. All of these symbols were far too strongly linked to the Christian vision of the world to be attributed to ancestors who were pagan.

CHAPTER 9

The Salic Law: First Law of the French People

The *lex Salica*, the law of the Salian Franks, was one of the many Germanic laws written down in Latin between the sixth and eighth centuries;[1] it dates from the end of the reign of Clovis. The compilation was drawn principally from the traditional forms of oral law, when (so the text itself relates) "during the reign of the first Christian king of the Franks," Hisogast, Arogast, Salegast, and Hidogast, four great figures of the kingdom, all of them selected from the tribes of the Franks, had set down the content of the law in the course of three meetings in the villages of Ratheim, Saleheim, and Widoheim, east of the Rhine. At some later date a prologue was added that began with the words, "Vivat Christus, qui Francos diligit"—Long live Christ who loves the Franks. Yet later, Charlemagne added thirty-five articles, increasing it in size from sixty-five to a hundred.

In its earliest form, the lex Salica was essentially a compilation of private law; later versions added provisions that made it into something resembling a political pact. Among its many articles was one destined for a great political future. Entitled *De allodis*, it concerned the inheritance of goods within the family clan.[2] Male blood-relatives, it stated, received the landed property called *terra salica* or *hereditas aviatica*—the heritage of the ancestors, whereas women received only personal property. There are two versions of this article:

> De terra vero salica, nulla in muliere portio hereditatis est, sed ad virilem sexum qui fratres gerunt, tota terra pertineat.

[Concerning salic land, women have no part in the inheritance of it, but all
this land belongs to the heirs of the male sex, that is, to the brothers.]

and,

De terra salica, nulla portio hereditatis mulieri veniat, sed ad virilem sexum
tota terrae hereditatis perveniat.

[Concerning salic land, no part of it may go as an inheritance to a woman;
but rather all hereditary land passes to the heirs of the male sex.]

It is clear that the sole concern of this article was to safeguard the
integrity of the family patrimony—a most important matter in a society
where land constituted the sole form of wealth and where possession of
land allowed one to go to war and thus belong to the privileged class of
free men.

In 1316, when Philip V pushed aside his infant niece to succeed his
brother Louis X, and in 1328, when Philip of Valois took the throne,
not a word was breathed of this text. On both occasions, these men
were simply the strongest candidates at moments of ill-defined succession; and when, later on, it became necessary to justify their seizures of
power, the "customs of the kingdom" were invoked, not the Salic Law.[3]
For, as we have seen, the text itself concerned family inheritance, not
succession to the kingdom. Likewise, the *Great Chronicles* of Saint-
Denis (like the texts they followed—Roric and Aimoin de Fleury) were
silent about the Salic Law both in their account of Pharamond, "the first
Frankish king" (who later would be made the author of the Law), and
in their story of the succession of Philip V and Philip of Valois.[4] Vincent
of Beauvais guarded a similar silence in his *Mirror of History*, the most
widely used historical encyclopedia of the thirteenth century.[5] Yet at the
end of the fourteenth century and the beginning of the fifteenth, the
Salic Law was erected into a major political myth. It became the first
law of the French and the first law of succession to the kingdom. It is
with this myth that this chapter will be concerned.

The historical fortunes of the Salic Law began with Fredegar's *History of the Franks* composed around 660.[6] To liven up the reign of the
shadowy Pharamond (most likely a creation of his own), Fredegar recounted how the Salic Law was set down in writing by four great figures
of the kingdom, meeting east of the Rhine. In this way he established a
strong and entirely original link between the first king of the Franks and
the first law of the kingdom. Without ever presenting Pharamond as

personally responsible for composing that law, he made the beginning of the monarchy and the beginning of Frankish legislation coincide.

In the eighth century, the *Deeds of the Frankish Kings* told essentially the same story, modifying it only to the extent of transforming the four great personages of the kingdom into royal counselors.[7] After this, however, the Salic Law went into an eclipse from which it was rescued only in the twelfth century by Sigebert of Gembloux, who in his *Chronographia*—one of the best universal chronicles of the time— devoted a long paragraph to it, including all of Fredegar's details and a large part of the prologue, quoted word for word. He added new elements to the story as well: a discussion of its juridical nature, and the statement that it was drawn up *per tres mallus*—by three separate meetings of the court.[8] Bernard Gui most likely borrowed much from Sigebert for his *Flowers of Chronicles*.[9] Like his predecessor he told how the Salic Law had been drafted as a judicial code by Pharamond's four councilors.

What did Gui's contemporaries—the men of the early fourteenth century—know then of the Salic Law? Both a great deal and very little.

They knew little, because their official texts, national history, and juristic treatises were not familiar with it. It is noteworthy that Bernard Gui himself seems not to have thought of using the law to explain the exclusion of women from the throne in 1316 and 1328. It was the "custom of France" alone that all used to explain the history of the succession. Even theologians, always quick to comment on the political inferiority of women, knew nothing of it. Though the jurist François Meyronnes around 1320–1328 wrote a defense of the Roman *lex Voconia*, the law that excluded women from inheriting, and brought together almost all the arguments that would be used later on to exclude women from the throne of France, he made no reference to the Salic Law in doing so.[10]

By contrast, people at this time knew a lot about the Law. They knew that it existed, and they knew more or less its value. They knew it had all the prerequisites needed to make a valid law: it conformed to natural law and to divine law because it aimed to secure justice and order in the early days when political organization was completely unknown; it emanated from a sovereign power acting with good counsel; it was ancient and respected. Because it had been born with the monarchy it embodied a Frankish power that was separate from the power of the Roman Empire, one that could legislate in defense of its own interests. Finally, the Salic Law represented a pagan form of authority. It injected the story of the origins of the monarchy with the wishes of thirteenth-century kings of France who would submit to neither emperor nor pope. The Salic Law held the promise of a rich future.

THE SALIC LAW IN THE STRUGGLE BETWEEN FRANCE AND ENGLAND

From the beginning, the Valois kings were strongly challenged on their own territory by kings of England who had taken over the title and arms of France. War forced them to enlist every possible argument in defense of their own legitimacy. They needed to establish a legal basis for excluding women and descendants through the female line from the throne. Edward III (1327–1377), whose mother was a daughter of Philip the Fair, claimed to be "closer in line" to the throne than Philip of Valois, who was merely a cousin of the last Capetian. The succession of women was part of normal usage in some kingdoms and great fiefs and, up until then, the Capetians had accepted it freely. In 1316, furthermore, many powerful people had supported Joan of Navarre, the daughter of Louis X, who only later, in 1318, officially renounced her rights (which of course presupposed that these were rights she had originally enjoyed). And even where feudal law did not allow women themselves to succeed to land, it frequently allowed them to pass rights of inheritance to their heirs. Thus, neither custom nor feudal law came down very clearly in favor of the Valois cause, and it was a delicate matter to have to depend on the Lex Voconia, a Roman imperial law, for an unambiguous statement excluding women from inheritance and supporting exclusive succession by agnates.

THE DISCOVERY OF THE SALIC LAW

It was the jurists and clerics in the entourage of the future Charles V, we are commonly told, who were primarily responsible for turning the Salic Law into a law of succession that would exclude women and their descendants from the throne of France. The Parisian coterie who gravitated around the Dauphin and the abbey of Saint-Denis were the magicians who created the new dynastic mystique at a critical moment when both Edward III of England and Charles "the Bad" of Navarre were laying claim to the throne.

This commonplace needs to be partially modified. For the argument had not yet been formed when, around 1340, the English addressed a memorial to the pope challenging "the custom of the kingdom" as a weak basis for judgment on the right of succession and chastising the French for not producing "an edict or a statute" in their defense.[11] The French, on their side, defended themselves in the name of "the approved and legitimate custom of the kingdom of France." And indeed a later English memorial, dating from sometime between 1380 and 1396, apparently put the Salic Law to work for the Plantagenets.[12] The memorial has been lost, but we have the French reply: "Again, according to the statute of the Salic Law *which the defenders of the king of England wish to put forward*, the land should fall to the masculine sex." A pro-French interpretation of the Salic Law was not necessarily self-evident, and it remains entirely possible that the English themselves played a large part in bringing the Law to people's attention.

On the French side, the historian Richard Lescot (1329–1358) was the only author who was familiar with a manuscript copy of the Salic Law in the second half of the fourteenth century.[13] (We shall look more closely at this manuscript and Lescot's rediscovery in a moment.) But others knew about the Law as well. One of these authors, though he was neither a jurist nor a historian, wrote a splendid passage on the subject that, despite the popularity of his work in the fourteenth century, has long escaped the notice of historians. Sometime between 1337 and 1350, Jean de Vignay translated Jacques de Cessoles's *Moralized Chess* for John, duke of Normandy, the father of Charles V. In the chapter devoted to the chess queen, de Vignay interpolated a remark on the rule that denies women the right to succeed to the throne.[14] "This institution," he wrote, "was established long before Charlemagne and was respected by all the kings since that time. . . . The kings of France can make laws like this . . . and this ordinance is certainly worthy of praise." To be sure, de Vignay was hardly precise here; he mentioned neither the Salic Law nor Pharamond; but he was indeed referring to the Salic Law, and he knew well that the Law could be used to determine royal succession. Moreover, he then went on in this passage to talk about the independence of France vis-à-vis the Empire, an independence he found exemplified by the independence of its legislation. De Vignay shows us clearly how the resurrection of the Salic Law took place at the junction of the two principal preoccupations of fourteenth-century French jurists: the relationship between France and England on the one hand, and between France and the Empire on the other.

Several others who belonged to the circle of Charles V also referred directly or indirectly to the Law. Two passages in the translation that Raoul de Presles prepared for Charles V of Saint Augustine's *City of*

God show how the argument from the Law slowly emerged at this time, largely by borrowing provisions from feudal and Roman law that served to exclude women.[15] Raoul dated the Law to the reign of Pharamond and understood it to justify a special rule of succession in their kingdom; like the monarchy, the Salic Law was also sanctified.[16] The *Dream in the Pleasure Garden*[17] and Nicholas Oresme[18] made similar assertions, though they did not specifically mention the Salic Law. Thus, it was indeed the authors around Charles V who discovered and publicized the content of the Salic Law, though the spirit that infused this resurrection was far more religious than juridical.

It was really only in the first half of the fifteenth century that French jurists gave precision to the Salic Law, establishing its text, finding precedents, resolving difficulties, and establishing an interpretation. In their hands, the arsenal of related arguments grew larger and larger, while the Salic Law itself was slowly transformed into an official truth.

ESTABLISHING THE TEXT

The first known manuscript of the Salic Law, indeed until 1418 the only known manuscript, was one belonging to the abbey of Saint-Denis. The abbey enjoyed one of the most prestigious libraries of the period and one of the most perfectly arranged collections.[19] The intrinsic merits of the monastery, home to the tombs and regalia of the kings of France, added luster to its manuscripts, which were thought therefore to offer stronger testimony than others; Saint-Denis's copy of the *Great Chronicles*, for example, was considered the official, the normative version;[20] the same was true of the Salic Law. And it was in the library of his own abbey that the monk Richard Lescot, historiographer of France, discovered the text of the Law around 1358, for though the memory of its existence had survived, its exact contents had been forgotten. Lescot decided to use the law in a genealogy of the kings of France that he was writing in order to validate the rights of the Valois against the Evreux-Navarre. "I will demonstrate it [their rights] by means of the Salic Law," he wrote.[21]

What manuscript did Lescot use? Latin manuscript 4628A of the Bibliothèque Nationale, which belonged to Saint-Denis from the thirteenth to the fifteenth centuries, is the only one from the abbey to survive, but the abbey may have possessed others. Fortunately, Lescot summarized the contents of the manuscript he had under his eyes.

It[s text] was issued by the first kings, who were still pagan, and then amended by Clovis—the first Christian king of France, who was baptized by Saint Remigius—and by Childebert and Clotaire. These three kings added a prologue to it: "Long live Christ who loves the Franks!" Charlemagne, the king of the Franks and Roman emperor, added thirty-nine chapters to it. Louis the Pious, his son, added many others.[22]

This tells us that the manuscript he had before him included the great prologue, the capitulary added by Charlemagne in 803 (numbered differently than what is now considered standard), and the one added by his son Louis—whose addition comprised "many others" because, though the text of his capitulary was very short, he appended the long capitulary on the *missi* to it.[23] There were only three manuscripts of the Salic Law arranged in this way; two may be excluded;[24] the third is Latin manuscript 4628A, which therefore must be the one that Richard Lescot used. It is quite possible that it was the structure of this particular manuscript which gave him the idea of transforming the Salic Law into a law of royal succession. The title "The Salic Law" appears on the first sheet. It is followed by two Merovingian genealogies, the prologues, the *Liber legis salicae,* and appended laws. The last sheet bears the words "Here ends the Salic Law." The entire sequence is presented in such a way as to give the impression that it constitutes a single, continuous work. The Law and the royal genealogies appear to be related and not simply juxtaposed; they seem to be bound together as effect and cause. And in the *Genealogia* Richard Lescot would place the passage on the Salic Law in the same position as it was in this source—after the genealogy of the kings of France.

Lescot also wrote a *Treatise Against the English* in the vernacular, of which the opening sentence and two passages on the events of 1316 and 1328 are all that survive. This treatise—either a first draft or a summary of the *Genealogia*—remained very popular and was often still cited in the later fifteenth century.[25] Although we do not know for certain if it went further in its argument than the *Genealogia*, it is possible that it incorporated a version of the article *De allodis* guaranteeing the throne to male heirs alone. Between 1380 and 1396, when writers referred to "the statute in a Salic Law that says the land should descend to the masculine sex,"[26] they seem to have been quoting "tota terra ad virilem sexum perveniat," which Lescot had probably given word for word. When the same writers said that "it excludes women from the monarchy entirely" they seem to have been loosely translating "mulier vero nullam in regno habeat portionem." Lescot must have discovered the

Saint-Denis manuscript and understood well how it could be put to use; the text he put into circulation seems to have been a version of *De allodis* that he had altered to suit the needs of his day. Nor did the approximate nature of his version seem to disturb anyone. When Charles VI and Richard II were attempting to negotiate a settlement, the English do not seem to have accused the French of corrupting the original text (though since manuscripts of the Salic Law were most likely extremely rare in England and Gascony, it would have been difficult for them to verify the text before they took possession of the abbey of Saint-Denis themselves).

At the beginning of the fifteenth century, the humanist Jean de Montreuil consulted the Saint-Denis manuscript on several occasions.[27] He had not cited the Salic Law in his *On Kingly Descent* in 1408, but, thanks to the efforts of the precentor, Michel Pintouin, historiographer of France,[28] he had a chance to see Lescot's *Treatise*. He was interested in this work because he himself was in the process of putting together a compilation on the same theme. Lescot must have provided him with the false version of the Law: "Mulier vero in regno nullam habeat portionem"—No woman shall have hereditary rights to the kingdom—which he used in *To All the Knighthood* and in his *Treatise Against the English*. At a later date, either Jean de Montreuil or Michel Pintouin went back to Lescot's source, Latin manuscript 4628A, and Montreuil then reproduced a faithful, though shortened, version of the article, "Nulla portio hereditatis mulieri veniat sed ad virilem sexum tota terra perveniat"—A woman shall have no share in the inheritance; all land passing to those of the male sex—but then in his translation/interpretation turned it right back into the reworked version of Lescot: "No woman shall have any part of the monarchy"!

Until the English occupied Paris and the abbey of Saint-Denis, then, only one manuscript was known. It gave the Carolingian version of the Law, preceded by two historical prologues that made it possible to identify its authors and its date, and it was followed by the added capitularies of Charlemagne and Louis the Pious. For a partisan of the king of France, therefore, the Salic Law embodied a number of historical and juridical texts, whose scope went far beyond the *Liber legis salicae*.[29] When Paris and the abbey library were lost to the government, that unique manuscript was replaced by several others (see app. A to chap. 9); but as soon as access to the abbey manuscript was reestablished, it again became the normative version.

Meanwhile, aside from identifying and copying various versions of the text, people were also trying to situate it in time and to interpret it.

ESTABLISHING THE DATE AND AUTHOR; SHOWING THE LAW'S CONTINUED USE

Slowly but surely, the date of the Salic Law was fixed in terms of papal and imperial reigns, the traditional chronological benchmarks in works of universal history: in the reign of Pope Boniface I (418–422), during the ninth or eleventh year of the reign of Emperor Honorius (395–423), and in the first or last year of the reign of Pharamond. All these put it around the year 420; few authors of the later Middle Ages used this absolute chronology, though Jean Jouvenal des Ursins placed it in 422 or 424[30] (since Pharamond was supposed to have ruled from about 420 to about 430), putting the composition of the Law exactly 1000 years before the Treaty of Troyes.

The identity of the author caused far more discussion. From Fredegar to Sigebert of Gembloux, writers attributed it to Pharamond, about whom they had little else to say. Others left it anonymous, made before there were Christian kings in France: "It was the first kings, still pagans, who established it," wrote Lescot.[31] Though Raoul de Presles opted for Pharamond, other candidates were also possible—Clovis, supposedly the first to have it written down, or Charlemagne, who had issued the longer version. Partisans of one theory or the other continued to raise their voices. "The law of Charlemagne the Great, *et dicitur lex salica,* is consonant with the custom of France (whereby women are excluded)," wrote someone who called himself "a good and loyal Frenchman."[32] Both Jean de Montreuil[33] and Jean Jouvenal des Ursins[34] agreed: not only did this emperor sanction the Law, he also "proclaimed it more amply and more explicitly; for he ordered as well that any male heir of royal blood descended through the female line should not ascend the throne."[35] Jouvenal des Ursins was also aware that according to the chronicles it was in 803 that the emperor added thirty-five chapters (thirty-three in his version of the manuscript) to the Law, which he ordered "to be respected always"—a solid defensive weapon against the English.

Others assigned to Clovis the role of "augmentor" of the Law. Richard Lescot posited that it was Clovis who had revised the Law and added the prologue "Vivat Christus."[36] Noël de Fribois could not decide between Clovis and Charlemagne.[37] Robert Blondel made it a divine gift to Clovis: "For when God, the sovereign Emperor of Heaven, gave the arms, the fleurs-de-lys, the oriflamme, and the Holy Ampulla to France, he gave them to King Clovis alone and to all those who would descend from him through the male line, so that this kingdom would be like the celestial monarchy which is continually governed by male providence."[38] Yet others wanted to have it all ways and claimed "the law was made by Pharamond, Clovis, and Charlemagne."[39] In the second half of the century, Clovis slowly began to win out over the others—he alone was named in the *Great Treatise* of 1450 and by Guillaume Crétin and the jurists Guillaume Benoît, Vincent Cygault, and Claude de Seyssel[40]—whereas after 1500, Pharamond was the man of choice, indeed he owed his popularity solely to the Salic Law. Clovis found himself with a partner; for, as the Salic Law necessarily harkened back to a pagan social order, and Clovis, the first Christian king, could not be a part of it, he had to make room for an imaginary first legislator in the story of the origins of French national life. French legitimacy came to stand on the firm pedestal of both religion and law; it found its source in the work of a legislator and a saint.

Last of all, jurists and historians showed that the Salic Law had always been in force, had always been respected, and thus enjoyed full validity. Thanks to the Law, Merovech had succeeded to Clodio the Hairy, Hugh Capet had followed the last Carolingian in 987, Philip V his brother in 1316, and Philip VI his cousin in 1328. Jean Jouvenal des Ursins was the first person to proclaim this truth. By 1450, all agreed. Thus, in the span of a century, all memory of the real events of 1316 and 1328 had disappeared.

The jurists of Charles VII managed to do their job very well. Although the Salic Law was not yet very popular in the mid-fifteenth century, everything had been put in place for it to become so. A definitive text had been established, the interpretive difficulties resolved, and the supporting arguments had been constructed which would serve unchanged for a long time to come. During the next half century, the text of the Salic Law would circulate in ever wider circles as its myth became increasingly grand.

FIXING THE INTERPRETATION: A CUSTOM OR A LAW?

The decisive moment when *terra salica* was taken to mean "kingdom" came between 1435 and 1450. Since no text used the words *in regno,*

someone had to demonstrate that "salic lands" were in fact synonymous with the kingdom, including all its dependencies and apanages.
Jean de Montreuil already suggested it; Jean Jouvenal des Ursins established it as a truth: "now the kingdom was governed by the Salic Law
and could be called a Salic land."[41] Similarly, the *Great Treatise* of 1450
declared, "The Salic land is the kingdom, and the royal power—in
contrast to all others—is neither dependent on any other nor subordinate to anyone else,"[42] a sovereign union of land and rights.

In contrast, it was in a quiet, almost indetectable way, that between
1350 and 1450 the law changed from a transcription of a custom into a
royal statute. When it was introduced as the law of succession to the
kingdom, it merely took on the role of a long-standing custom of the
kingdom, and for a long time the custom of France and Salic Law were
equated, their conformity to each other lauded. Women were excluded
from the throne in accordance with "the custom of France . . . with
which the Salic Law agrees," wrote the "good and loyal Frenchman."[43]
More than that, to all authors before Raoul de Presles,[44] the Salic Law
was accepted as being a transcription of the customs of the Franks
before their conversion to Christianity (as in fact was the case). At the
beginning of the fifteenth century, Aimery de Peyrac, abbot of Moissac,
stood by this history of its composition. The Salic Law, he wrote, consists of "customs used by the Salian Franks much earlier, when they
lived in the area of Cologne."[45] According to both Guillebert de Metz[46]
and Jouvenal des Ursins[47] it had been written down under uncon-
strained, fully democratic circumstances; as the ancestors of the French
or their barons were in the habit of electing counselors whose task it
was to interpret everyday problems of law, and their opinions were little
by little codified in writing. Noël de Fribois praised the French who
"after mature deliberation, concluded that they wanted laws . . . and
had a very beautiful book called the Salic Law drawn up by four of the
most noteworthy men, who had been elected to make decisions on the
disagreements among the French."[48]

The mid-fifteenth century, however, marked a turning point. The
anonymous *Great Treatise* of 1450 made a distinction between the Salic
Law and custom, and spoke of the process of codification in different
terms: "the Salic Law, was first dictated by Wisogast, Arogast, Salegast
and Hidogast . . . who were commissioned by King Pharamond, and
nominated and elected by the nobles."[49] The *Great Treatise*, as a transi-
tional text, combined two conceptions. Although it allowed Guillaume
Benoît, for example, to assert at the end of the century that the Law had

been established "according to the ancient customs and the interpretations of the four wise men," and to speak of "the custom contained in
the Salic Law,"[50] it nonetheless affirmed an important distinction. The
Law had been dictated by the central authority; it was a norm transmit-
ted from the upper level of power rather than from the people themselves. Writers begin to call it a statute, an edict,[51] a constitution,[52] an
ordinance[53]—all terms implying legislative power concentrated more
and more completely in the hands of a single figure, the king, whose
decisions were permanent and universally valid for the community he
ruled. One person alone was now responsible for having instituted it,
promulgated it, constituted it, requested it by command;[54] he did so in
consultation with advisers, but fewer and fewer texts bothered to mention this detail. Eventually, its very customary character was denied. In
the years before the invention of the Salic Law, ambassadors from the
king of England had declared, "The question of whether women accede
or not is a custom, not a statute; but a custom which is not founded in
law cannot be accepted."[55] And in 1450, English and French emissaries
alike had agreed that in some cases it was best to put both custom and
imperial law aside, "for custom could not contain a clear enough reason
for such an important matter."[56] So the Salic Law became a law, the
first law of the French, a law separate from the laws of the Empire and
the laws of other kingdoms. It was no longer simply a custom.

The stage was now set for it to be widely circulated.

DIFFUSION OF THE LAW FROM 1450 TO THE SIXTEENTH CENTURY

Once the Law was invented, making it known involved more than
getting the text into libraries. It was far more a matter of using it
effectively in royal propaganda. To believe in the Salic Law came to be
the test for being a partisan of the king of France, for supporting him in
his war.

The earliest forms of propaganda to mention the Salic Law were legal
memorials of the Anglo-French war, texts written by professionals who
sometimes enlarged their public by preparing summaries in French.
Then, sometime between 1450 and 1464 an anonymous author composed the *Great Treatise* on the Salic Law, giving the second half of the
century its classic statement of all there was to know about the Law.
The popularity of the *Treatise* is demonstrated by the number of surviving manuscripts, at least ten—half of which belonged to members of the

high nobility, and by the repeated printed editions in the sixteenth century and after. At the same time, summaries of the Law began to appear in accounts of the reign of Pharamond in historical manuals, which likewise, in passing, "corrected" earlier accounts of the royal successions in 1316 and 1328. Thus from 1475 onward, royal officers and members of the urban middle class either directly or indirectly knew that the Law existed and something about its contents. The audience of the Salic Law had grown larger.

The first propaganda vehicles for the Salic Law were legal memorials connected to the great Valois-Plantagenet conflict, the work of clerks, lawyers, and royal secretaries assigned to plumb the depths of the royal archives for arguments to use in negotiations. On each of these occasions they created new versions of the Salic Law, shamelessly changing and extending the previous ones. Copies were made of these memorials in Latin or French, depending on what public was being targeted. These texts were most often working copies rather than polished literary productions, and it would be not only difficult but fruitless to attempt to date them and identify their authors. Despite the mechanical nature of their production, however, their number and the fact that many were written in French meant that they had substantial influence.[57]

In 1449, Robert Blondel listed eleven treatises on Anglo-French relations since the wars had begun, to which he then added his own.[58] We can in fact identify twelve, beginning with one in 1340.[59] Three of these treated the Salic Law at length: those of Jean de Montreuil and Jean Jouvenal des Ursins, and a third which remains anonymous.[60] It was the last that was the most influential.

The anonymous *Great Treatise* of mid-century contained a long and detailed passage on the Salic Law, written in vibrant French. At least ten manuscript copies have survived; some of these belonged to people closely linked to the royal house, but others show it circulated well beyond this narrow circle. There were also numerous printed editions beginning in 1488.[61] Their existence shows that knowledge of the Salic Law was spreading beyond the circles in power during the latter part of the century. The *Great Treatise* probably did the most to accomplish this, especially because of the clarity of its writing and its lively style.

In the ten or more folios it devoted to the subject (in comparison to earlier texts that devoted at most ten lines to it) the *Treatise* presented a very special view of the Salic Law. It began by rewriting history, presenting a debate that supposedly had taken place in 1328 before the Estates-General convoked to hear the advocates for Philip of Valois and Edward III. The two parties in the debate first agree that neither imperial laws nor custom can govern the succession to the throne, that the Salic Law alone was to be used. They then talk of Pharamond and his four wise counselors on the banks of the Rhine composing the Law, and Charlemagne, king of France, amending it. The discussion dates its composition to 420–422 and explains that *terra salica* means both the kingdom and the rights of the Crown. "The Salic Law presents the manner of succession and ruling in the royal land";[62] it also excludes sons through the female line, since, if this were not the case, Charles the Bad, king of Navarre, would have better right than Edward III. These rules had always held, ever since the time of Clodio, the grandfather of Clovis, who succeeded to Merovech because he was the closest male heir. "Of all the descendants of Charlemagne and Hugh Capet, nowhere is there to be found a woman who succeeded to the crown or a man who succeeded to it through the female line."[63] This law was justified, said the treatise, by the unstable nature of women, their capacity to take a low-born individual or an enemy for their husband, and their inability to rule and to make war. They could not serve as most Christian kings, could not be annointed by the Holy Ampulla, could not carry the oriflamme or the royal lilies, could not cure scrofula. Finally, the treatise held that since the custom of Paris did not recognize the right of seniority among daughters, the kingdom risked being divided by female succession if women were allowed to succeed to the throne. This was wholly unacceptable. The treatise succinctly summarized in this way all the myths that had been invented during the reign of Charles VII.

Around 1450, the Salic Law also began to appear in historical compilations written in French for a very broad audience. A good example is the first great historical encyclopedia to speak explicitly about it, the *Mirror of History* of Noël de Fribois, composed in 1459–1461, and a later text related to it,[64] where the Law is called the law of succession to the kingdom, a law detrimental to the English cause. Here again we find the date of the law, the place it was made, its authors, details about the manuscripts, its revisions, and a plea for it to be translated. The points are abbreviated in the manner of contemporary legal memorials. The next example of such historical presentation—the *Annales* of Nicolas Gilles—did not appear until the end of the fifteenth century.[65]

More interesting than these stereotyped abbreviated presentations of the Salic Law, however, are the passages that rewrote the history of the succession crises in 1316 and 1328. The Salic Law had in fact played no role whatsoever at these moments. But the *Great Treatise* had done its work well. No reader, to be sure, imagined "correcting" the manuscripts of the *Great Chronicles* at those passages where they recounted the successions of Philip V and Philip VI, nor the story of Pharamond as it appeared there or in manuscripts of Vincent of Beauvais's *Mirror of History;*[66] these texts were too well known to be tampered with. But other historical manuals and encyclopedias were fair game. Shortly after Louis XI died, a reader of one of these manuscripts made the following notation alongside the account of the accession of Philip V: "for he could only do this by the law of France which was made by Pharamond, first king of pagan France, Clovis and Charlemagne."[67] This rewriting of the history of France was so successful that the role of the Salic Law in the succession of Philip V and Philip VI remained a commonplace until the very end of the nineteenth century, when Emile Viollet finally showed it had played no role at all.[68]

THE CREATION OF THE MYTH OF THE SALIC LAW AROUND 1500

What did the lex Salica mean to someone in the days of Louis XI or Charles VIII? To answer this question, we must first look into the etymologies authors gave for the word "salic"—a word they found highly problematic, for it had no evident resonances.

ETYMOLOGIES

To the best of my knowledge, the real etymology of the word "salic" appeared only once: "Salic" and "Salian" mean Germanic, Aimery de Peyrac, abbot of Moissac, wrote in his *Tragic Miscellany of Charles the Great*. "The law is not called Salic because of its author Salegast, but rather because those who made use of it were the Salian Franks, who lived in the area of Cologne."[69] The abbot was writing in the late fourteenth century, when it was still permissible to say that the Franks were Germanic. In the next century, all references to the Germanic origins of the Law disappeared; though it was promulgated at Saleheim, east of the Rhine, its makers were presented as French.

A second group of explanations grew up around the word "Salic" as a designation "of the place where the Law was created." This was the explanation given in the *Great Treatise* and by Guillaume Benoît: "It was called this because of Saleheim in Germany, where the Gauls then lived."[70] The jurist Jean Ferrault adopted the same etymology in his

Insignia pecularia at the end of the fifteenth century;[71] so did Guillaume Crétin.[72]

There were also more far-fetched etymologies. Raoul de Presles, inspired by the popular fourteenth-century etymology of "Frank" as noble or free, claimed the Law was named Salic "because the people of the country were a noble people."[73] In 1434, Guillebert de Metz gave the same etymology.[74] For other authors, "Salic" meant reasonable; it indicated that the Law had been the work of sages—Salian priests, Roman priests dedicated to the war god Mars!—for the Gauls, grown warlike, had become avid followers of this god.[75] Classical antiquity had clearly not yet been fully mastered.

Another etymology was even more imaginative. "Salic" came from *sal*, meaning salt. *Jus salicum* (*jus* like *lex* can mean "law") was a salty juice. Amazingly awkward as this joke was, it was a very popular etymology. The law, like a kind of salt, would conserve the kingdom and preserve it for all time to come. The Salic Law was *licita condita*, it was well seasoned with just the right ingredients. Such an explanation appeared in the *Great Treatise* and in the works of Guillaume Crétin, Nicole Gilles, and Guillaume Benoît. As Gilles wrote: "Some say that just as salt maintains and preserves, so the Salic Law is designed to maintain, direct and govern the French, who are virtuous in their ways."[76]

At the same time, the Salic Law was being made into "the law of France," "the royal law." We have already seen the annotations from shortly after the death of Louis XI which "corrected" the stories of the accessions of Philip V and Philip VI in order to coincide with the new conception of "the law of France."[77] Jean Divry wrote of "the law of France, that we call Salic."[78] The sense that the Salic Law was the "law of the kingdom" grew directly out of the notion that *terra salica* meant "the kingdom." Since the jurists of Charles VII had made this connection, it took but a small step of reasoning to conclude that the Salic Law had been so named because it applied to the Salic land, to the kingdom itself rather than to alods and fiefs. Salic Law thus meant the law of succession to the kingdom. "The Salic Law concerns only the administration and succession to royal land . . . *id est lex salica vel regni*,"[79] wrote Jean-Pyrrhus Angleberme.

Lex regni itself was often translated as *la loi royale*, the royal law—a satisfying translation that, of course, coincided well with recent historical developments. This royal law differed very little from the *lex regia* of Roman law, by which the emperor, at the time of his succession, received power from the people and henceforth became the sole legislative power. Lex salica and lex regia were equated at the beginning of the sixteenth century: "Only the king can make statutes and pass legislation, for in the ancient *lex regia*, which is our own Salic Law, all powers and all rights are given to him."[80] In this way the writers of the early sixteenth century arrived at an explanation that was the exact opposite of Raoul de Presles's etymology in the fourteenth. The law of the noblest and freest people was replaced by a law that took the freedom to legislate away from the people:

> On ne dit pas que Pharamond fit grande prouesse,
> Touchant bataille, mais il fit sans réplique . . .
> La loi salique pour mettre gens en ploye,
> Auparavant avaient été sans roi.[81]
>
> [No one claims that Pharamond achieved great things
> As far as battles go, but he did most certainly make
> The Salic Law, to bend a people
> Who until then had gone without a king.]

The reason was that the nature of the Salic Law itself had changed.

THE KINGDOM'S LAW OF SUCCESSION

The advantages of the Salic Law were most visible in matters of internal rather than of foreign policy. It gave a juridical base to the practices of royal succession that had existed de facto since the tenth century: the crown was kept within a single family; the preferred heir was the oldest son; and, finally, women were excluded from the throne—this last practice originating in the successions of 1316 and 1328. These practices had early eliminated the election of kings and eventually reduced the coronation itself into a ritual whose function was only declarative. Yet though these practices had long existed, no one had ever bothered to give them a theoretical foundation.

Already in the thirteenth century, French university discussions of the relations between king and emperor had argued that hereditary monarchy was preferable to elective monarchy. The hereditary principal, it was asserted, selects a specific heir, who will have the natural affection of his subjects; it avoids disputed succession and the rivalries of princely families. But these discussions did not consider the possible succession of women. For this issue, the fourteenth century was a period of transition from one argument to another.

As we have already seen, the case for male succession in 1316 and 1328 was built upon "the customs of the kingdom" or else on the approval of the peers of the realm and the Estates (thus running the risk of reintroducing the dangers of elections).[82] The arguments in defense of this custom were for the most part religious; Raoul de Presles, for example, cited the biblical story of the daughters of Shephatiah, as did Jean de Montreuil and Jean Jouvenal des Ursins, and stressed that the kingship was a dignity almost sacerdotal in nature. And as women were neither allowed to be priests nor to give the sacraments, so they could not be anointed in the sacring and crowning of a ruler. It was by sanctifying the royal throne that these authors justified the exclusion of women. The advantage to this argument was that it made the exclusion of women a special trait of the French monarchy, one not necessarily characteristic of others. Thus, by the time the Salic Law was introduced, a groundwork of justifications was already in place.

Jean de Montreuil fit the Salic Law to this groundwork, making whatever changes were necessary to turn it into the law of succession to the kingdom. But he did not stop there. For the Salic Law came to exclude as well the descendants of kings through women. For this part of his argument Jean de Montreuil made use of Roman Law, which favored agnatic kings, and of feudal law, where—except in the Paris region!—women generally could not pass rights to others which they themselves did not enjoy.[83] Jean Jouvenal des Ursins and the *Great Treatise* attributed this rule to the Salic Law as well.[84]

Above all, the Salic Law justified the principle of primogeniture and prevented the disinheritance of a child of France. In May 1420, the jurist Jean de Terre-Vermeille argued that the crown of France was public patrimony and therefore did not fall under the control of ordinary rules of succession; it was not dependent upon the good will of the king, for the king was merely the provisional administrator of the Crown; he who stood to inherit the throne could not lose his rights; neither his father nor his younger brothers could take them away because, even before the death of his father, he was already coadministrator of the Crown.[85] Though Jean de Terre-Vermeille never actually mentioned the Salic Law by name in his argument, he furnished material that Jean Jouvenal des Ursins later used in his discussion of the Law. As a result, primogeniture and protection from disinheritance were soon thought to be part of the Salic Law itself. Jurists after 1500, such as Guillaume Benoît, insisted on it.

Thus, by the end of the fifteenth century, the Salic Law enjoyed an unquestioned prestige. It may have been responsible for persuading Charles VII not to block the accession of an eldest son of whom he was not very fond. Thanks to the Law, in 1498 Louis XII and in 1515 Francis I—each of them only a distant cousin of his predecessor— inherited the throne. It was likewise in the name of the Salic Law that criticism rained down on the regents Anne de Beaujeu (1460–1522) and Louise de Savoie (1476–1531), as the literature on the Law had taught all its readers that the power of women, from Clotilda to Isabelle of Bavaria, had always led to catastrophe.[86] Some attempts were even made to apply the Law to the inheritance of apanages and certain great fiefs, even though women had never before been excluded from inheriting them (Jean de Montreuil himself had accepted female succession to apanages with little hesitation): the Salic Law was enlisted against Marie of Burgundy in 1477 and in the disputed succession of Anjou-Provence in 1483.[87] Little by little, it spoke to every issue.

THE KINGDOM'S PRIVILEGE

The Salic Law was soon fully sanctified. It guaranteed that the English could be defeated: "It has in fact been said that the Salic Law was the palladium of France, for just as the Trojans thought that their kingdom was firm and stable as long as they possessed their statue of Pallas, which if lost would lead to the destruction of their kingdom, so too the observance of the Salic Law meant the state was saved and that if it happened that the Law was abolished or removed, it would lead to the ultimate ruin of the state," wrote Laurent Bouchel.[88] The Salic Law guided the kingdom, maintained it, and kept its honor and authority, for it prevented conflicts and partitions.[89] Just, holy, inviolable, and good for the king and the kingdom, it exalted the name of Gaul.[90] It had raised the French from barbarism and anarchy;[91] it caused their virtuous ways to grow and prosper, encouraging them to invest their talents peacefully in literature and the arts while they enjoyed the calm of a stable political order.[92]

It is hardly surprising that—from the days of Charles VII onward— the Salic Law appeared in lists of the *privilegia regni*. Already in 1406, Pierre d'Ailly, when speaking of the quasi-sacerdotal nature that unction gave the king, included among the signs of divine favor the hereditary succession to the Crown, freed of any dependency on another ruler.[93] Around 1430, an anonymous work, *Concerning a Certain Maid*, linked the lily, the Holy Ampulla, and the cure for scrofula to the

fact that there was no female succession in France.[94] After 1461, drawing inspiration from Jean de Terre-Vermeille, the *Garden of Nobility*
gave the same list, adding "the hereditary succession through the oldest
male which has been observed since Pharamond," and extolling its great
advantages.[95] Ferrault's contemporary, Jean Feu, agreed.[96] For them,
the Salic Law stood for the independence and the specificity of the
kingdom. Succession by the eldest male and the impossibility of disinher-
iting an heir (even if he should be incapable of ruling) were by then fully
rooted in the law, and those who conspired against the king were guilty
of lèse majesté; this too had become a part of the Salic Law. Little by
little, almost every basic principle of French public law, in fact, had been
made part of the Salic Law.

By 1500 the myth of the Salic Law was complete. A law that had still
been relatively unknown around 1450, but which had been the object of
intense legal comment and increasing popularization in the last half of
the century, had finally established itself as the fundamental principle of
the political structure of the kingdom. The Salic Law became one of the
privileges of the kingdom, the premier monument to its special genius
and juridical independence. It had become the law of succession to the
kingdom, destined to ensure its stability and permanence. It would help
preserve the kingdom from its birth to its very end. On occasion, the
four wise counselors of Pharamond were thought of as the founders of
the Parlement and the royal council; the Salic Law, far more than the
model of the Roman Senate, gave pride to a Parlement whose esprit de
corps was beginning to affirm itself.[97] All these ideas reflected the growing importance of jurists and royal officials in the political structure of
the kingdom and reflected their awareness of the juridical and political
originality of their nation.

Jean-Pyrrhus Angleberme summed up the whole development in his
work *On the Salic Law and the Law of Succession to the Kingdom*,
published in 1517. It was wholly devoted to a discussion of the Law,
differing in this way from the *Great Treatise* in that it was not a memorial on the Anglo-French conflict in which the Law figured merely as
one of the arguments. Angleberme began with a prologue about the
author, date, and etymology of the Salic Law and then went on to
develop arguments both in favor of and against recourse to it. He concluded, of course, in favor if its use, and ended his book with a celebration of the endless merits of the Law. Angleberme's twenty arguments in
favor of the Law led to the conclusion that it is just and in conformity
with Holy Scriptures, with Canon law, feudal law, and natural law.

Through its promulgation, Pharamond had launched France on a most favorable course. Every people has its own rites, its own laws, and its own privileges, says Angleberme, and, as a special privilege, the Salic Law reflected French identity and the honor of the kingdom. Through his defense of the Salic Law, he concludes, he has experienced what it is like to "fight for his country, like a Roman soldier."[98]

The idea of France and its privileges was fully set by 1500, when the Salic Law had finished traveling the road from reality to myth.

CHAPTER 10

Language and Culture

At a first glance, the role of language and culture in the making of the French nation appears problematic. Most medieval nations were multilingual, like the Swiss cantons and Burgundy, both of which included both Romance- and Germanic-speaking peoples. France used at least five languages—the "langue d'oil," the "langue d'oc," Basque, Breton, and Flemish. In addition, the lanque d'oil varied significantly from region to region. Superimposed on these vernaculars was Latin, the language not only of sacred texts and the liturgy, and therefore of clerics, but also of students and (at least until 1300) of the royal admnistration. Latin was an international language, the language of the well-schooled, the language of works in both law and theology, and, by the end of the Middle Ages, the growing prestige of classical antiquity added additional numbers to its public. There was thus little to bring together language and nation.

Culture likewise seems not to have been concerned in any central way with the nascent idea of French nationhood. Culture was viewed in the Middle Ages as a stepping stone toward acquaintance with God. The Seven Liberal Arts laid the foundation for universalistic theological knowledge. The schools of Paris, which had become full-fledged universities by the beginning of the thirteenth century, attracted students and professors from all over the Western world. They formed in turn a large proportion of the bishops of Latin Christendom. For this reason, from its very earliest days the University of Paris was the spiritual child of the pope rather than of the king. The knowledge that it disseminated was supranational and Latin.

In the last two centuries of the Middle Ages, although Latin retained its role as sacred language, as the language of Western Christendom, the French language slowly developed into a sacred language with perceived strengths of its own. The mystique that began to surround it eventually led people to affirm—against all reality—that French was spoken throughout the kingdom, that the language coincided with the nation. As it became "the mother tongue" it came to be the object of great affection. Wars could now be overlaid with linguistic rivalry.

At the same time, the idea of French culture slowly emerged from that favorite medieval theme summed up in the phrase *translatio studii*, the "transfer" of learning from Athens to Rome to Paris. This transfer was first attributed to Alcuin (735–814), then to Saint Denis, and eventually to Charlemagne himself. In this way the university at last became the spiritual child of the king. And university culture, which had at first been thought of as a replication of that of Athens and Rome, came to be celebrated for its own uniqueness; Parisian theology had replaced Greek philosophy and Roman law. When later the Italian humanists identified culture with rhetoric and poetry, unsettling Parisian complacency, defenders of the French tradition—with varying success—sought to demonstrate its own continuous development of these as well as theology. Yet still, at the very end of the Middle Ages, though an image of French cultural continuity was firmly established, it was a culture that remained both Latin and French. One could without paradox sing the praises of France in both languages.

THE FRENCH LANGUAGE

To people of the Middle Ages, the origin and diversification of languages was a theological question whose answer was to be found in the Bible.[1] At the beginning of human history, they believed, only one language existed, invented at the moment when Adam named the things of this world. This primordial language was usually thought to have been Hebrew, the language of Paradise, the language in which God had spoken to the Hebrew people. Linguistic unity had continued until the Tower of Babel, when God, enraged by the inordinate pride of men, punished them by inflicting a confusion of languages upon them.[2] Linguistic diversity was thus the fruit of sin; and Pentecost, when the

Apostles earned the gift of tongues, was the inversion of the story of Babel, a sign of redemption (though only the Apostles enjoyed its reward). Furthermore, it was long believed that languages had not changed since the Tower of Babel. Those of Europe were all related, for all the Europeans were descendants of Noah's son Japheth.

Abelard in the middle of the twelfth century was the first to assert that language was a creation of humankind.[3] God, he argued, had permitted man to name things for himself and, although all languages manifest the unique and identical rational structure of the human mind, they change in the course of time. Abelard's argument was the essential first philosophical step toward the nationalization of language. Dante took the second when he asserted that every language is the creation of a group of human beings whose particular characteristics and story it reflects.[4] It would still be some time, however, before these arguments bore fruit.

Three languages were thought to play particularly important roles—Hebrew, Greek, and Latin, all of them sacred languages, the languages of the Holy Scriptures. Other languages were less noble than these, corrupted forms of one of these sacred languages, some of them even barbaric corruptions. French was but one of the seventy-two languages that thirteenth-century scholars listed on the basis of the Bible. They divided European languages into "families" (languages that were Greek, Latin, Germanic, or Slavic in origin, according to Bishop Ximenes de Rada around 1250) and, within each of these families, developed more refined typologies.[5] Dante, for example, divided the Latin languages into three groups: the languages that use *si* for "yes", those that use *oc*, and those that use *oui*. But vernacular languages continued to be viewed as inferior to the sacred languages, good enough for poetry and epics but not for serious subjects.

ORIGINS

French had to be given value before it could be identified with the French nation, and that took a long time. As with all phenomena in the Middle Ages, that was done first of all by searching for its ancestors. Latin was its most obvious source, and non-French scholars of the twelfth and thirteenth centuries held firmly to it.[6] But within France itself, support for this idea was not so strong. To be sure, Adhemar de Chabannes (988–1030) and Guibert de Nogent (1053–1124) inferred that this was so from the fact that France belonged to Latin Christendom;[7] and in the middle of the fourteenth century, the chronicler

Etienne de Conti reasoned along the same lines when he asserted that all people of Christian Europe shared Latinate languages, whereas Christian Byzantium's languages were Greek in origin.[8]

The Latin origin of French, however, carried with it the inconvenient implication that it was subordinate to Rome's successor, the Holy Roman Empire, or else to Italy. For this reason, some French scholars began to canvas the possibility of finding its source in Greek. After all, Isidore of Seville had said of Greek that it was "more illustrious, older, and sounded more pleasant" than Latin.[9] The Trojan origins of the country also suggested this possibility, since the Greeks could only have had a Greek form of speech. Writers began to seek Greek etymologies for the names of the people and places that were key to the French historical tradition. *Franc* became the word for noble or valiant in the "Attic language." Well before the *Great Chronicles* affirmed this etymology, it was formulated by the monk Aimoin of Fleury (965–1008),[10] who claimed to find it in Fredegar and in classical texts; hadn't Caesar reported that the Gauls used Greek letters in their writing?[11] At the beginning of the thirteenth century, Robert of Auxerre affirmed that French was a Greek language,[12] while Guillaume le Breton in his *Philippide* told how both the Gauls and Franks came of Greek stock; when they arrived in Gaul they had given "Greek names" such as Paris to the towns that they founded.[13] In 1302 a sermon on the war in Flanders sang the praises of France's "Attic language,"[14] Later in the century, Nicholas Oresme, more nuanced, asserted that French was both Greek and Latin: Greek because the Franks were Trojans, and Latin because that language also derived from Greek.[15] Greek origins were ideologically more useful.

A far more complicated historical derivation was invented by Jean Lemaire de Belges early in the sixteenth century when he asserted that the Celts were the fathers of the Trojans. This made Celtic the origin of Greek, which in turn gave birth to French. French, in effect, had engendered itself. His *Concord of the Two Languages* extolled "your natural Breton tongue, which is the true Trojan language."[16] Thus, the sixteenth-century linguists who built theories of the Greek origins of French enjoyed the support of a long historical tradition, while those who were partisans of the idea that French was an indigenous language owed much to the work of Lemaire de Belges.[17]

The idea that Hebrew influenced the development of the French language also occurred from time to time, though less frequently, drawing its strength from the assumed primordial nature of Hebrew and from the political idea that the French were the new Chosen People. All those who believed that the Franks were descendants of King David also implicitly believed French came from Hebrew: Nicolas of Lyra, Pierre Desgros, and Jean de Legonissa.[18] But, apart from French Jews (who were all expelled in 1394), few scholars followed their lead.

INNATE QUALITIES

The qualities of a language were thought to derive from the nobility of its origins. Already in the thirteenth century, French was called "harmonious" and "beautiful," words also used to describe France. French was "the most beautiful language in the world,"[19] "the sweetest sounding," "the most charming to listen to." "Sweet French is the most beautiful and graceful language and the most noble speech in the world, the most prized and loved, because God made it sweet and attractive in honor and praise of himself; it is like the speech of the heavenly angels."[20] People also found in it a nobility and pride reflective of the qualities of the nation as a whole. Both the sermon on the war in Flanders and Nicholas Oresme declared it to be a "noble tongue," even "the most noble language in the world."[21]

For a long time, French comments on the language were far more a mystique than a linguistic analysis. Before 1350, the technical aspects of the language were hardly attended to. The poverty of their working language was the despair of many fourteenth-century translators, who compensated by introducing a great number of Latin neologisms into French. Oresme, however, stood out as one who thought that French was the richest and most precise language of the age, well-equipped to render even the most complex thoughts and to play a role equivalent to the one that Latin had played in antiquity.[22] The humanist Jean de Montreuil echoed Oresme's sentiments, as he sang the praises of French (though paradoxically he chose to do so in Latin).[23] French had sprung from a single, pure source, whereas English and German had come from mixed stock and were consequently unclear and confused forms of expression; French was sweet to listen to, tempered and equilibrated. The poet Alain Chartier (1380–1433) and the Burgundian historian Georges Chastellain (1416–1475) lauded its supple and harmonious nature,[24] and Lemaire de Belges extolled its virtuous fidelity, its precision, and its great capacity of expression: "The French language is noble, gracious, elegant, and polished."[25]

USE

The language's merits, it was believed, had led to its widespread use, though wide use was itself sometimes taken as a sign of its merits. French, said Brunetto Latini, is "common to all people."[26] Foreigners ought to learn it: "he who does not speak French," sneered Pierre Dubois, "is taken for a barbarian."[27] These remarks, however, hid a paradox.

The international success of French in the thirteenth century is clear; the Crusades had established it as the language of the Latin States in the eastern Mediterranean and of the Latin Empire of Constantinople, a success that the French recognized and applauded, proud to point out that in the East, all Westerners were called *Franci*.[28] Italians such as Brunetto Latini, Martino da Canale, Marco Polo, and Philippe de Novare wrote their major works in French, as did thirteenth-century authors in other countries. French was also the language of the cultivated classes and of the courts of England, Germany, and Flanders. Many conversation manuals of the thirteenth and fourteenth centuries, designed to teach French to the people of these countries, have survived. In England, even the primary schools taught in French, despite the fact that university instruction was in Latin.

By contrast, however, Parisian French only slowly established itself within the kingdom, despite the support of the royal chancery and the rest of the royal administration. From the time of Philip the Fair, French was employed in royal documents addressed to places in northern France. In southern France, in contrast, Latin continued to be the language of royal administration, while urban cartularies, private accounts, and testaments there were written in Old Provençal. And although the southern nobility was becoming bilingual, in 1444 John IV of Armagnac carried on negotiations with the English in Latin, since, as he said, "I don't know French very well, especially how to write it." The transition to French came at different rates, which varied from one region to another: it had reached Auvergne by 1400, Bordeaux by 1500, the Landes by 1550, and the Pyrenees by 1600. Royal officials converted first to its use. The popular classes, in contrast, remained untouched for a long time.[29] The governments of Charles V and Charles VII had no linguistic policy (such as Francis I would have in the sixteenth century) and though the southern lands were incorporated into the kingdom, this did not signal a shift to French either as the official language or the commonly spoken language of the region. Though the installation of royal government south of the Loire during the "Kingdom of Bourges" had a significant lingustic impact, it was not consciously orchestrated.

How was this linguistic mixture perceived? Some spoke quite clearly about it. The Parisian Guillaume Guiart (d. 1316), for example, listed Norman, Picard, and Flemish as languages spoken within the kingdom.[30] Etienne de Conti conceived of them hierarchically: "In this kingdom," he wrote, "there are three languages: the French of the north, which is the most common, Breton, and Flemish." To him, this showed the kingdom's superiority because of its size; he mocked the tiny kingdom of England, with only one language.[31] Bernard du Rosier, updating this linguistic map in accordance with the rules of the royal chancery, wrote that the France of 1450 enjoyed "two specific idioms or languages, Gallic [i.e. northern French] and Occitan."[32] But hardly anyone suggested the possibility that there was only one language in the kingdom or that French was understood throughout the land. At most, people spoke of "those of our language," meaning the French, and "those of their language," meaning the English; and Jean Jouvenal des Ursins thought it intolerable that some of the speakers of "our language" could throw their allegiance to those of the other.[33]

Yet linguistic unity was beginning to seem essential to nations. Already in the middle of the twelfth century Hugh of Saint-Victor could write, "Just as animals of the same idiom live together in peace, so too men who share the same language more easily lead a life in common with each other."[34] And around 1300, Pierre Dubois could write of the desirability of regular training in foreign languages, in order to reestablish the unity of Christian nations; having a language in common, he asserted, would lead Christians to show "pure love and confederation" toward each other.[35] In the Dialogue Between a Frenchman and an Englishman, written around 1420, the Frenchman is made to claim that differences of language explain why he and his fellow French could not "obey you English, whose language we do not understand."[36] (The Englishman responds, quite reasonably, that in earlier times there were many multilingual polities, not the least of which was the French kingdom itself.) At about the same time, Gerson went so far as to assert that Philip of Valois had been chosen king "because we understood his language."[37] And at the beginning of the sixteenth century both Claude de Seyssel and the Lyonnais physician Symphorien Champier pointed out that a people needed administrators who shared their own language, with whom they had natural affinities.[38] Joan of Arc meanwhile had cast these beliefs into the realm of the supernatural: when asked in what language Saint Margaret spoke to her, she answered that she spoke in French, "For how could she have spoken English, since she was not on the English side?"[39]

Thus, as early as 1300, the French language had become one of the distinguishing characteristics of the nation. Above all, it was greatly loved. Whereas in the early Middle Ages, clerics referred to vernaculars as the languages of "the people" (vulgus), a term that did not imply great fondness for them,[40] toward the end of the twelfth century the spoken languages became "mother tongues."[41] Around 1300, Dante and Pierre Dubois began to use this expression in something like its modern sense; for Dante, the "mother tongue" was natural to man and much loved for that reason, whereas for Dubois it was the creation of each group of human beings and arose from sharing a native land.[42] In the second half of the fourteenth century the translator Laurent de Premierfait, using the same term, called himself "French by birth and conversation."[43] And at the end of the century, the grammarian Henri de Cussey defended the study of mother tongues by introducing the term into the technical domain of grammar.[44] Growing usage of the term reflected increased valorization of the language itself. The sentiments of the poet Robert Blondel (1390–1461) were not exceptional: it was the duty of everyone "to die to save France its name."[45]

The obverse of this idea was that both God and nature willed that people of a given language should be united in a single state. Every military conflict found itself shadowed by a linguistic conflict, and vice versa; if people spoke French, they should be annexed. Already in 1287 a chronicler of eastern France included the count of Montbéliard among the French because that was the language he spoke.[46] Midway through the fifteenth century, the Herald Berry noted that French was spoken in both Burgundy and Savoy, two counties of the Empire; as they had belonged to the kingdom, he asserted, they would return to it.[47] His contemporary, Philippe de Commynes, claimed Lorraine for the kingdom "since they speak French there and not German."[48] Commynes never lost the opportunity to proclaim the inherent weakness of an army or a state where a number of languages were spoken and to emphasize the antipathy that existed between the Burgundians and their mercenary Germans and Italians.[49] (Though such arguments would have been quite out of place at the court of Charles the Bold, who himself spoke seven languages. It was hardly by chance that the Tower of Babel, an image nearly absent in French art, became one of the favorite themes of the art of Burgundy.)

Yet the Hundred Years War did little at first to develop in French minds a dislike for the English language. English armies were largely recruited in Gascony, and the English soldiers who made up perhaps 20 percent of those armies were long able themselves to speak French: the Black Prince wrote his letters to his wife in French. Thus the mockery directed at the English was aimed at their accent rather than at their ignorance of the language. But the defeats of the later fourteenth century brought increasing attention to the contrast between the French and the English; and to this the growing nationalization of the French language added its color. It was in the fifteenth century that the English came to be known in France as the *godons* ("God damns") and English described contemptuously as "dissonant" and "mixed."[50]

In contrast, no voices were raised in criticism of the regional tongues that competed with the language of the court within the kingdom, nor did anyone accuse them (or Latin) of collusion with foreign powers. A speaker of Limousin might be the butt of ridicule in medieval France, but so were those who spoke the dialects of Normandy or Picardy.[51] Breton was also viewed favorably, as we can see in the story of the siege of Fougères, when it was recaptured by a Franco-Breton army in 1449.[52] In order to mislead the English about the origins of the besieging army, the soldiers all pretended to speak only Breton; the Breton nobility knew the language, and the French troops did not find it demeaning to pretend to speak it. Paradoxically, Breton autonomy in the mid-fifteenth century was promoted in French;[53] and when the Breton language came to be valorized at the end of the century as a pre-Trojan form of Celtic, it happened too late to be of any use to the independent-minded dukes.

One of the languages of the kingdom, however, did raise violent negative reactions throughout these last two centuries of the Middle Ages. That was Flemish, which was recognized as a Germanic language. The Flemish "brayed" and "yelped," wrote Guillaume Guiart;[54] to Etienne de Conti it seemed that the Flemings at Roosebecke had "clamored."[55] For Georges Chastellain, Flemish was the vile language "of bestial stuttering swamp-dwellers, covered with dung."[56] The hatred was mutual. During the revolt of 1302 known as the "Mâtines of Bruges," all those who spoke French were killed; and in 1382, Philip van Artevelde wanted to take the young Charles VI to Ghent to force him to learn Flemish.[57] The Flemings, however, were the only linguistic minority in the kingdom to arouse such animosity. It was but one of the many forms of hostility toward a region that was very different from the rest of France—highly urbanized, ruled by artisans rather than by noblemen, and strongly tied by its wool trade to its English suppliers. The enmity was fundamentally not linguistic.

Elsewhere in the kingdom French was favored but not exclusive, either in point of fact or in terms of ideology. In 1500, French had not yet won the field. It is not certain that anyone would have thought such a triumph desirable either, for the victory of French had not yet become a coveted goal of French national sentiment.

FROM THE "TRANSFER OF LEARNING" TO THE IDEA OF AN INDIGENOUS CULTURE

TRANSLATIO STUDII

Translatio studii was the somewhat paradoxical term used by medieval scholars for their cultural inheritance.[58] Among other things, it expressed the great prestige of the schools of Paris from the twelfth century onward. Modeled on the older Carolingian idea that the Empire had been transferred from the Greeks to the Romans and then to the Franks,[59] whose political and cultural center at Aachen was successor to Rome, illumined by the Palatine Academy and by Alcuin, John Scotus Erigena, Hrabanus Maurus, and their fellow scholars, the term had served first to embody the idea that the empires of thought—of wisdom and science—had moved from the East to the West.[60] Paris was the new Athens and the new Rome: its wisdom shone forth like a flaming candelabrum that lit up the world.

A tradition of praise developed for the schools of Paris, a tradition that was in large degree the work of successive generations of students and professors. The best known were those of Guy de Bazoches, writing in Champagne toward the end of the twelfth century, of the English encyclopedist Bathelemy de Glanville around 1230 (still copied by Jean Jouvenal des Ursins in the fifteenth century), and of Jean de Jandun in 1323.[61] Within this tradition, the terms "science" and "wisdom" quickly gave way to others. *Clergie,* used by the courtier poet Chrétian de Troyes in his *Cligès* and by thirteenth-century writers including the authors of the *Great Chronicles* of Saint Denis,[62] enjoyed a momentary popularity but eventually disappeared. Other terms referred much more precisely to the organization of the Parisian schools: the city was illustrious for its "letters," its "liberal arts," and above all its most frequently mentioned "philosophy."[63] Theology, the university term for *clergie,* appeared rarely before Guillaume le Breton, who like Helinand de Froidmont in 1210 wrote in detail of the University of Paris.[64] Ideology quickly incorporated the way the Parisian schools had developed into a regularly organized *studium* early in the thirteenth century, as well as the dominant influence of the arts students by their sheer numbers and of the theologians because of their great prestige.

At this point it became possible to put in parallel the passage from Athens to Rome to Paris of *clergie* and *chevalerie* (a term that fit the kingdom much better than the term "empire," which had been used by Carolingian publicists). This parallel appeared everywhere: in *Cligès,* in the *Great Chronicles,* and in the fifteenth century in the work of Alain Chartier.[65] Not until the trying years of the Hundred Years War was it prudently forgotten, though Anseau Choquart's talk of the glorious tradition of Parisian studies continued to allude indirectly to it.[66]

In the twelfth century, no one put a precise date on this transfer of culture, though the transfer of the Empire to Rome was attributed to Caesar, and that to the Franks attributed to Charlemagne. It was therefore possible to imagine that the transfer of culture had also occurred deep in the past—at least once the recent origins of the Parisian schools had been conveniently forgotten. At the beginning of the thirteenth century, Helinand de Froidmont made Alcuin and his companions the scholars responsible for the great deed.[67] To Vincent of Beauvais it seemed a good story,[68] as it did to many others, though late in the century it underwent an interesting transformation. In 1290, the Dominican Martin de Troppau (who had attended the University of Paris) wrote of Alcuin, "he was the professor of Charlemagne, who transferred the studium to Paris,"[69] making the emperor himself the founder of the schools. The popularity of Martin's chronicle quickly spread this idea throughout Europe.

Meanwhile, the story had reached the abbey of Saint-Denis, where it gave Guillaume de Nangis the idea of a new way to promote his abbey. The abbey had always considered its patron Saint Denis to have been a great philosopher, accompanied on his mission by a number of very learned disciples. What better than to have them bring to Paris at the end of the first century the faith, knowledge, and wealth of science, whose unity had since then guaranteed the stability of the Most Christian kingdom.[70] Although the beginning of the prologue to the *Great Chronicles* remained faithful to the role of Alcuin, the end of the prologue adopted this new version of the founding of the schools.

It was a daring story, but also problematic. Was there a studium in

Paris in the first century? Guillaume de Nangis was expressly vague on this point. And if clergie had been transferred, what about chevalerie? It was, after all, well known that the Empire had not been transferred to the Franks at so early a date, since the Merovingians had never held the imperial title. But Guillaume de Nangis's tale was attractive at the same time, for it helped negate the claim of the University of Bologna that it was older than the University of Paris; it also transported the kingdom's cultural prestige back to the very beginnings of its nationhood. The kingdom from its birth had everything it needed to transform itself into an empire—both chivalry and science.

Yves de Saint-Denis adapted this story with skill and the appearance of verisimilitude.[71] Denis the Areopagite, he wrote, had brought both faith and philosophy, but the latter soon fell into eclipse. Charlemagne then reestablished the studium in Paris and enlarged it by bringing from Rome the four Faculties of the University; in this way he unified the Empire and the studium and reestablished the ancient alliance among faith, chivalry, and philosophy, which had characterized the kingdom from its earliest days. Yves's version of the story circulated widely in the first decades of the fourteenth century. It appeared, for example, in the work of Thomas of Ireland as well as in the *Chapel of the Fleurs-de-lys*.[72]

But Martin de Troppau's attribution of the founding to Charlemagne was not forgotten. The great emperor finally triumphed during the reign of Charles V. Charles chose Charlemagne because Alcuin and John Scotus Erigena, as men of the British Isles, were now out of favor.[73] Already in 1300 the university, which had been the "daughter of the pope," was given the title "daughter of the king." In the reign of Charles VI it drew from this epithet both increased prestige and a heightened capacity for political activity. When the university was dispersed in 1418, it seemed to prefigure the ruin of the monarchy, so intimate had the university and the royal house become.[74]

As the product of the university, with its great theological prestige, Parisian culture could now be distinguished from that of antiquity because it was a Christian culture; in 1384, in the course of a trial between the chapter of Notre-Dame and the law faculty, the chapter pointed out that there could not have been a theological faculty at either Athens or Rome, nor could there have been any Canon law.[75] And this culture was the superior one; for although Athens excelled in philosophy and mathematics and Rome in law, Paris stood out in theology. Thus, the transfer of learning no longer involved a simple passing on of the same body of knowledge.[76] Each people, it now appeared, had their own area of specialization; the Chaldeans and the Egyptians had astromony, Rome had its law, and theology was the domain of the French.[77]

The cultural affinity the French felt with theology, moreover, was attributed to earlier and earlier times. Guillaume de Nangis placed it in the first century. Others did not stop there. In 1367, the king's orator, Anseau Choquart, remembered that Caesar had described the druids of the first century B.C. as learned and pious men.[78] The author of the *Dream of the Pleasure Garden*, Raoul de Presles, and the entire generation of the beginning fifteenth century accepted them as the founding fathers of Parisian learning. This story was so persuasive that during the 1384 trial mentioned above, the chapter of Notre-Dame was forced to admit that the seven liberal arts and medicine had been taught in Paris since well before the Incarnation of Christ.[79]

Thus the cultural prestige of France dated back to the time when the Franco-Trojans first established themselves on the nation's territory. Since then, it had boasted three different moments and places of greatness: among the druids of Gaul, in the Carolingian studium, and in the University of Paris since the twelfth century. Of the lesser periods between these, prudently little was said. The essence of this culture remained always the same, however: it was a religious, a theological culture, one well adapted to serve the Most Christian nation. And the university that provided it had become a focus of national pride.[80] Though it spread its light and knowledge throughout Latin Christendom, little by little that light and knowledge had begun to lose its anational character.

THE CONFLICT WITH ITALIAN CULTURE

Unfortunately, at the very moment when this very gratifying notion of national culture first appeared, it came into conflict with the new perceptions of Italian humanism. Taught by antiquity, the Italians were now insisting on the primary role of rhetoric and poetry.[81] The clash began in 1367 when Pope Urban V decided to abandon Avignon and return to Rome. While Anseau Choquart urged him to stay in France,[82] the Florentine poet Petrarch wrote him "that outside of Italy, it is fruitless to seek either orators or poets."[83] French pride was deeply wounded, for Petrarch was much appreciated in France. His letter drew a biting reply from Jean de Hesdin, published in 1372; following some aggressive remarks about the inconstancy, treacherousness, and lying nature of the Romans, Hesdin refuted Petrarch's claim first by citing two Gallo-

Roman poets, Statius and Claudian, and then asserting that after them the true orators were scholars. Late antiquity supplied him with Salvian, Hilary, Photinus, Eucherius, Vincent of Lérins, and Prosper of Aquitaine; then, following a gap from the sixth to the eleventh centuries, came a list of university scholars—Petrus Comestor (d. 1179), Alexander of Hales (d. 1245), Guillaume d'Auxerre (d. 1230), and Henry of Ghent. It was a meritorious effort to resurrect the memory of Parisian theological superiority. A year later, Petrarch answered by saying that the French were barbarians whose superficiality allowed them to write nothing more than summaries and textbooks.[84]

The debate broke out again in 1394, with a letter by Cardinal Pietramala that occasioned one response from Jean de Montreuil and two from Nicolas de Clamanges. In his replies Clamanges—who thought of himself as a poet and rhetor—composed a very different list of the cultural glories of France. Late Latin antiquity, he said, had contributed Statius and Hilary (whom Jean de Hesdin had already named), Sulpicius Severus, Ireneus, Gennadius, and Gregory of Tours (all of whom Hesdin had forgotten); he then leapt forward to Yvo of Chartres and to the school of Saint-Victor, adding Saint Bernard and the outstanding member of the humanist circle of the twelfth century, Hildebert of Lavardin. To Clamanges, however, the masters of the thirteenth and fourteenth centuries represented little more than a scholastic decadence of knowledge and manner; all of the Parisian theologians of whom Hesdin had been so proud disappeared. Of French orators and poets from the late-twelfth century to his own generation, there were none. Jean de Montreuil's answer to Pietramala, by contrast, was very brief. He simply accused Petrarch of presumptuousness. But a look at the indexes of the recent edition of Montreuil's works reveals that, aside from Scripture and classical texts, he had recourse to the same authors whom Clamanges had listed: Statius, Claudian, and Aulus Gellius from late antiquity, Saint Bernard and Helinand from the twelfth century; he drew on no later authors.[85] Thus, the Italianate notion of culture reigned supreme in these first manifestations of Parisian humanism. The result was a fragmentary notion of French culture itself, one whose history was punctuated by many long pauses.

In the second half of the fifteenth century, Robert Gaguin raised the question again, first in a letter to François Ferrebouc in 1468 and then in his *Compendium*,[86] meant as a national history of rhetoric and thus as a challenge to Petrarch. Gaguin asserted France's cultural equality with Italy, but his idea of French culture was really not very different from that of Clamanges; his chronology passed from the Gallo-Romans and Gregory of Tours to Carolingian writers such as abbot Hilduin of Saint-Denis, then to Saint Bernard and the school of Saint-Victor, and ended with a period of decadence that started, he said, about 1240 and continued to his own day. The early humanists, Montreuil and Clamanges, were missing completely; but Gaguin did retain the Carolingian authors, insisting that Charlemagne had founded the University of Paris (destroying, in the process, the legend that Saint Denis had been the one to do it). It was the downfall of culture, faith, and morals around 1240, he said, that required his generation to reform and reconstruct.

The argument sprang up yet once again at the end of the fifteenth and beginning of the sixteenth century, fed by the wars in Italy. Three lists of cultural heroes survive from this period: one from Christophe de Longueil and two from Symphorien Champier.[87] Longueil began by extolling the wealth, piety, and courage of the French as well as their cultural prestige; he repeated the familiar list of Gallo-Roman poets and orators—Statius, Aulus Gellius, Sidonius Apollinaris, Prosper of Aquitaine, Hilarius, Ireneus, Gennadius, Sulpicius Severus—as well as a newcomer, Saint Remigius; he told the story of Charlemagne's "transfer of learning" from Rome to Paris; but then he jumped directly to the late-fifteenth century, to Gaguin, and the humanists Guillaume Fichet and Guillaume Budé.

Champier returned to the debate between Petrarch and Jean de Hesdin in his *Defense Against a Calumniator of Gaul*, citing most of the authors mentioned by Hesdin in an effort to integrate medieval theology and the traditional version of the translatio studii into the humanist vision. In 1507 he returned to the subject in his *On the Writers of Gaul*,[88] a work in imitation of classical and medieval models, such as Saint Jerome's *On Ecclesiastical Writers*, and Sigebert of Gembloux's *Book of Ecclesiastical Writers*, which remained very popular around 1500. But where these earlier writers had ranged over all of Christianity, or had (like Petrarch in his *Book of Famous Men*) mixed together military heroes and writers, or had confined their attention to particular religious orders, Champier consecrated his *Gallic Writers* entirely to the glory of French intellectuals.

The work contained the names of nearly a hundred writers, with descriptions of their works and evaluations of the most important among them. Champier arranged them more or less in chronological order, but their distribution over time differed remarkably from the lists of Hesdin, Clamanges, Gaguin, and the others. He listed many late-

Latin writers, three Merovingians, ten Carolingians, about twenty from the twelfth and thirteenth centuries, and as many from the fourteenth century and the fifteenth. It thus contained no gaps at all; even the eighth and tenth centuries were accounted for. The French genius was continuous. In terms of subjects, he listed sixty-three theologians, most of whom lived from 1100 to 1500, eight poets, three jurists, and nine scientists, among whom were musicians, astronomers, cosmographers, and mathematicians. The importance that Champier assigned to the sciences was a reflection of his own training as a physician. To these he added thirteen historians, ranging from Gregory of Tours to Gaguin—writers of universal histories and historical encyclopedias, of biblical histories, crusading histories, and national histories. In this way, Champier presented a complete vision of the history of France: Gregory of Tours spoke for the Merovingians, Freculf of Lisieux, Einhard, and the Pseudo-Turpin for the Carolingians, Sigebert of Gembloux and Robert the Monk for the tenth, eleventh, and twelfth centuries, Vincent of Beauvais for the thirteenth, and Robert Gaguin for the fourteenth and fifteenth. Champier's conception of French culture was far more global and chronologically complete, far less Parisian, than what had preceded it. Its only drawback was that, though its subject was French culture, the authors it extolled had all written in Latin.

It was only later that Jean Lemaire de Belges provided in his *Concord of the Two Languages* a description of vernacular French literature—set against the Italian literature of Dante, Petrarch, and Boccaccio.[89] The two principal works he cited were the *Romance of the Rose* and Alain Chartier's *Quadrilogue,* both of them still greatly admired in the first half of the sixteenth century.[90] The task of conflating these lists of French and Latin writers in such a way as to make of them the bearers of a single French culture was not undertaken until Thévet did so in the second half of the sixteenth century.[91]

WAS FRANCE TO BE PRAISED IN FRENCH?

In which language—Latin or French—were the glories of France to be celebrated? Jean de Montreuil and Gaguin sided with Latin, the appropriate language for serious matters, the one which guaranteed that "the fame of France would not be limited to the confines of its language";[92] evidently, the humanist vision blocked any shift in favor of French. Chancellor Gerson, who often wrote in the vernacular for those unschooled in Latin, held the opposite opinion, "since of matters so important, I choose to speak in French rather than Latin."[93] In his *In Praise of Writers* he praised the translations made for the royal library, comparing them to the Septuagent.[94] Similarly, Alain Chartier and Chastellain both wrote much of their most important works in French. But it was not until the end of the fifteenth century that Seyssel would argue (in his prologue to his translation of Justinus)[95] that all classical authors should be translated into French in order to nourish French culture, which would then spread its light across both France and Italy. Seyssel followed his own advice, writing his *Great Monarchy* in French. Champier likewise insisted that the exploits of French heroes should be written "in our French tongue, for they always sought the public welfare of the French nation [and therefore] have always been loved by all French people."[96] (This however, did not keep Champier from writing *On Gallic Heroes* in Latin.)[97]

The idea of an indigenous language and culture developed very slowly in France. The foundations were first laid by thirteenth-century writers who lauded both the French language and the theologians of the University of Paris. The views of fourteenth- and fifteenth-century authors were ambiguous, however, for the French kingdom was multilingual, and Latin was still held in high esteem. French national sentiment had many other foundation stones on which to build its identity. Language and culture were only two, and far from being cornerstones at that.

In this respect, France was very different from England, where the language question was a major national concern. There the flow and ebb of French were linked to expansion and losses of Continental possessions and to the growth of isolationism and English patriotism.[98] In Germany and Italy as well, the need for a commonality of language was strongly felt because political unity was weak or nonexistent. It is hardly surprising then that scholars in these two countries were in the vanguard of research on vernacular grammar and philology at a time when the French were hardly concerned with these questions at all.[99]

CHAPTER 11

France and the French

It was not until two centuries after the creation of Western Francia at the Treaty of Verdun in 843 that people finally began to speak of "France." At first only a vaguely defined term of political geography, it finally came to refer to the Capetian kingdom. "France" then attracted a number of stereotypical attributes, most of them derived from its etymology. She became Lady *Francia*, portrayed in the vivid colors of clerical and chivalric culture. The thirteenth century added learned France to Noble and Christian France, in recognition of its cultural prestige, while the fourteenth century created France the Best Governed in appreciation of the originality of its institutions. Around 1350, these images of a human France began to give way to allegories of a France in-and-of-itself, allegories that both summed up the essence of its people and at the same time remained quite distinct. France became first a voice, then a sorrowing mother, and finally, during the reconquest, a radiant princess. Religious theater adapted these images; miniaturists elaborated their typology, modeling it on the standard types of the Virtues.

France the real and France the allegorical had long since been assigned an idealized space. The Garden of France was an earthly paradise, with its own special character. The Tree of France flourished there with the help of God. Bonds of love had been knit between the people of France and the land where they had lived since time immemorial, a love first voiced in the twelfth century and justified philosophically in the thirteenth. In the late Middle Ages, this love brought poets to sing of its sweet life and others to insist that it justified any sacrifice. The defense of the realm gave birth to taxes; it also resurrected Horace's old maxim, *Dulce et decorum est pro patria mori*—How sweet and proper it is to die for one's country.[1]

IMAGES OF THE COMMUNITY

FROM THE NAME TO THE IMAGE

France at first was little more than a name, a name that referred either to the Ile-de-France or to the kingdom as a whole, more geographical in resonance that political.[2] During the early Middle Ages, *Francia* designated first the Merovingian kingdom, then the whole of Charlemagne's empire, and finally one or another of the three kingdoms created by the Treaty of Verdun—Western Francia, Middle Francia or Lotharingia, and Eastern Francia. Only in the late-eleventh century did it begin to take on its modern geographical connotation. In 1083, the chancery of King Philip I dated one of his diplomas *Philippo regnante in Francia*—Philip reigning in France. About the same time, Hugh of Fleury wrote in his *Universal Chronicle* that the treaty of 843 gave birth to *Francia, Italia,* and *Alemania,* and called Charles the Bald the first king of Francia.[3] Hugh of Fleury also used the term *Francia* in a limited way to mean the country between the Loire and the Seine, but within a political framework that was Carolingian rather than Capetian. In the twelfth century Francia was still rarely used to refer to the kingdom as a whole and, when it was, it was commonly accompanied by a modifier: *Francia tota*—all of France. "This western area is specially named France," wrote both Sigebert of Gembloux and Suger.[4]

But in the voices of preachers and the work of chroniclers it was all of France—a Capetian France now—who cheered the birth of the crown prince Philip, the son of Louis VI, and it was all of France who mourned his death. It was this France that Louis VI invoked in 1124 before his decisive encounter with the forces of the emperor. Finally, from the reign of Philip Augustus onward, Francia was commonly used to mean the kingdom as a whole; the royal chancery wrote of the *regnum Franciae*—the Kingdom of France—and in 1254 its usual title for the king, *rex Francorum*—King of the French—was officially changed to *rex Franciae*—King of France. Thus in the middle of the thirteenth century, Francia was finally accepted by all to mean the whole of the kingdom, a specific territory, a land in which the race of the Franks had lived since time immemorial.

In the twelfth and thirteenth centuries little by little this France gained substance; its name acquired ritual qualifiers, stable, precise attributes that enabled authors to sketch their portraits of France. These attributes fell into two categories. The earliest originated in the chansons de geste. Around 1100 the *Song of Roland* portrayed Roland remembering *douce France*—sweet France—as he lay dying, the first occurrence of this qualifier, and in a decidedly Carolingian context;[5] William of Orange was given the words "Land of France, you are a very sweet country,"[6] as centuries later Du Guesclin announced "Ah! France sweet love, I will sing of you briefly."[7] The adjectives varied little. *Douce*—sweet—and *belle*—beautiful—were the most popular, for France was the knight's beloved, his gracious and faithful lady, indeed, for Abbot Suger, she was the *domina terrarum*—the lady of all lands.[8] France was the ideal, the perfect female counterpart to the male models of the day, faithful, loyal, courtly, merciful, and generous like a knight, of unstained reputation and perfect faith like a cleric.

Other qualifiers were more learned; they were derived from the imagined etymology of Francia. *Francia*, Fredegar told his readers, was Germanic in origin;[9] it meant free, for the Franco-Trojans had never abased themselves by paying tribute to anyone. Up to the very end of the Middle Ages, this etymology was enlisted to combat papal and imperial claims to hegemony, to answer the famous question, *an rex Franciae recognoscat imperatorem*—whether the king of France recognizes the emperor as his superior—a question debated in the faculties of law even at the beginning of the sixteenth century. The etymology gave rise to the well-known adage, *Le roi est empereur en son royaume*—the king is emperor in his kingdom.[10]

In the Middle Ages, however, the freedom that was more highly valued was freedom from taxation rather than national independence.[11] The two concepts indeed were closely connected:

> Ceux du royaume par nature
> Treu aux Romains n'ont pas payé . . .
> Pourquoi ils sont francs
> Ce qui veut dire sans redevance.[12]
>
> [Those who are naturally of the kingdom
> Paid no tribute to the Romans . . .
> For this reason they are free
> Which is to say they owe no taxes.]

When he awarded temporary tax exemptions, the king made skillful use of this preconception: "Noting that the kingdom is called free [franc], and desiring to act in accord with the name. . . ."[13] But as the king's subjects paid taxes more frequently than they were exempted from them, between 1300 and 1500 this derivation of "France" from "free [of taxes]" was more likely to show up in antitax protests. Fauvel, hostile to the levies of Philip the Fair, exclaims

> France soulaie être, or suis serve.[14]
> [France/free I should be, but am enslaved.]

A century later, Nicolas de Clamanges lamented that France had lost its freedom to "taxes and tribute without protection for its inhabitants,"[15] while Jean Jouvenal des Ursins boasted "The French are free in spirit [ont coeur franc] and do not choose to be serfs, nor are they in the habit of being held in servitude or under tyranny," a sentiment later echoed by Bernard du Rosier.[16] The same was heard at the Estates-General of 1484: "Who would ever have imagined seeing this poor people once called free [franc] treated in such a fashion. . . . Now, we see them called lower than serfs. . . . This freedom that your ancestors worked so zealously to defend, suffer it not to be threatened. . . ."[17] Though the kings of France enjoyed the support of public opinion in their struggles to defend the *libertas Franciae* beyond the borders,[18] within the country that liberty could lay in ambush for them.

Yet other etymologies offered by Fredegar grew in popularity after 1400. *Franc* meant barbarous or ferocious, which were now converted to valiant, courageous, and faithful, in recollection of the military glory of the Gauls and the crusaders.[19] History was brought in to support the etymology: France was well endowed with soldiers and brave men; its reputation reached throughout the world; it was "protector of the good, the refuge of the unfortunate, the shield of the poor, the standard for those who are valiant."[20] Chivalry found a permanent home there when it left Greece and Rome.[21] Daring, courage, and loyalty characterized it; so too did fidelity. In England, kings were slandered, betrayed, and killed,[22] but in France the king enjoyed steadfast and constant obeisance from his subjects. Such etymologies, produced by a society militarized by the Hundred Years War and later reinforced by the imperialism of the ending fifteenth century, submerged the older derivation of France from (fiscal) freedom, which now seemed but a vain and outdated protest against taxes. That older etymology would only reemerge at the end of the sixteenth century in the work of the Protestant historian, François Hotman, who would give it a radically new meaning.

Among these attributes, none were negative. The idealized France had no failings. When by chance someone admitted that the French had a few weaknesses (and only rarely did a writer do so), these weaknesses never reflected on Francia itself. Caesar and Strabo had attributed numerous failings to the ancient Gauls: they were excessively emotional and impulsive, they lacked shrewdness and could not follow through on an idea, their lack of sobriety made them quarrelsome and faction ridden.[23] These criticisms were not forgotten.[24] Others remembered their love of money, their pride, and their self-satisfied air.[25] But these negative qualities were merely the inverse of all the most illustrious characteristics of Francia.

Thus the attributes of France created an image of great complexity, one which was entirely positive. From these, authors could draw "portraits" of France. Guy de Bazoches was the first to do so at the end of the twelfth century. His *Apologia*[26] began by describing the borders of ancient Gaul, then bypassed those of the Carolingian Empire to come quickly to Capetian France, which, he said, had been created by "the division among the sons of Louis the Pious." This land was *franc*—free—because its virtuous men were skilled in arms; the ways of the people were as temperate as the land itself; it was for this reason that the country had come to be called "sweet France." Bazoches concluded with a quotation from Saint Jerome, "Gaul alone has no monsters."[27]

Primat's portrait a century later in the prologue to the *Great Chronicles* is far more elaborate: "and even though this nation is proud and cruel toward its enemies, as its name signifies, it is merciful toward its subjects and those it dominates. . . . Thus, it is not without reason that this lady is renowned above all other nations, for . . . she received the Christian faith with great devotion. . . . Learning and chivalry came to France from Greece and Rome."[28] Primat used etymologies in the same manner as had Bazoches; his portrait harbored the same tension between lady France, sweet France, and warlike France. But his vision of *domina Francia*—lady France—and of the uniqueness of this Most Christian nation gave it a very different character than the images created a century earlier. As culture shaped by faith had as its ultimate goal the study of sacred texts, the "transfer of faith, knowledge, and chivalry," and the "transfer of empire"—themes that had been unknown to Guy de Bazoches—here took pride of place in justifying French cultural superiority. A France that was both learned and Christian took its place alongside warlike France and sweet France. It became the France of Saint Louis and of Robert de Sorbon.

We will end this brief survey with two portraits of France created by Bernard du Rosier around 1450 in his *The Glory of the French* and *Wonders in Praise of France*.[29] Here the expected themes appear: the borders of ancient Gaul (borrowed as always from Isidore of Seville), the etymology of the name, and the merits of the country's Most Christian king. Du Rosier quickly passes beyond them, however, to include reflections on the country's language and on the uniqueness of its political institutions, going well beyond the single matter of the Salic Law. He defined the French kingdom as a tempered monarchy, with Parlement, the twelve Peers, and three Estates; because of those institutions, justice and right reigned throughout its fertile, tranquil, and contented land. Such meditations were forerunners of those that would be written by early sixteenth-century jurists. Earlier writers had boasted of the superiority of French institutions, but not of their uniqueness. France was different, and its writers now became conscious of what made it so. Reflections on the Salic Law had begun to produce institutional patriotism that had not existed before.

In this way each century added something to a fundamental image that was firm and immutable. The twelfth-century military and Christian France was enlarged in the thirteenth to include its cultural prestige; in the fifteenth and sixteenth centuries it acquired an institutional identity. Yet for long these were images rather than portraits of a personified nation; they were not yet distinct from the collectivity and the land they represented.

FROM IMAGE TO PERSONIFICATION

Only slowly was France personified.

From 1350 to 1420 it was a disembodied voice, a voice of lament and a call to duty, borrowing its forms of rhetorical complaint from the Church and from cities. As a rhetorical form based on antique models, the lament was the opposite of the speech of praise. It was constructed on the contrast between a happy past and the misfortunes of the present, a contrast that was supposed to bring about a return to virtue and therefore a return to happiness. The genre was already utilized in the *Tragic Argument on the State of the French Kingdom*[30] and the *Lamentations of France* by the poet Eustache Deschamps, both written in the mid-fourteenth century:

> Je plains et pleure le temps que j'ai perdu
> Vaillance, honneur . . .
> Mon nom se perd et tourne en moquerie
> Je périrai et c'est pourquoi je crie.[31]
>
> [I lament and cry for the times I have lost
> Valor, honor . . .
> My name is spent and is turned to ridicule
> I will perish and this is why I cry out.]

The loss of a name symbolized the loss of identity, perhaps even of the essence of life itself.

Such passionate pleas to the parties in conflict characterized many of the laments of the beginning of the fifteenth century as well. The *Lament Over a City which Turns Its Sword Upon Itself*,[32] addressed to the city of Paris following the massacres of 1418, portrayed France crying over her children who had been cut down in the tumult, her lament cast in terms borrowed entirely from classical poetry. Such a faceless, unreal voice came again from the quill of Jean de Montreuil, who attributed it to the Crown and to *politia nostra* (our system of government).[33] Sick and starving, the voice recalled her past glories and called on her children to remember their responsibilities toward her. At about the same time, Nicolas de Clamanges presented Francia, the mystical body of the state, deformed and wounded by what her children have done, seeking help in vain. Although Clamanges claimed only to give speech to "the voice and tongue of the land," he did so through the image of a person—a weakened mother, eyes blindfolded, who has lost both her scepter and her crown, and is no longer able to nourish her own sons, who have brought ruin on her and on themselves as well.[34]

Alain Chartier's famous *Invective in the Form of a Quadrilogue* is the masterpiece of the genre.[35] It combined brilliance of language with a rich depth of culture and an ardor of national feeling. Here, the voice of France found its definitive embodiment. She becomes a lady of high title and lordship and excellent lineage, wearing a royal crown atop her fine blond hair, and bearing on her shoulders a cloak adorned with lilies, the emblems of kings, and the symbols of the different sciences; on the border of the cloak are portrayed various aspects of the nation's political, cultural, and economic identity and the flowers, fruits, and animals that render her beautiful and fertile. Sorrowing, disconsolate, she stands before the ruins of a palace (the Palais Royal) and rails at her three children, the three Estates, who prefer to live in comfort rather than fight for her. The *Quadrilogue* enjoyed a popularity that was well deserved, for it projected a complex image of France as an ensemble of things given by nature (climate, flora, and fauna) and things given by ideology (national symbols and cultural patrimony) toward which each inhabitant had the same responsibility as a child toward its mother; the three Estates should act as brothers, for they shared the same blood.

The *Quadrilogue* provoked many imitations: the *Listen to Heaven of which I Speak* of Jean Jouvenal des Ursins,[36] the *Champion of Ladies* by Martin Lefranc,[37] and the *Book of Lament* of Robert Blondel.[38]

> Jadis si puissante dame
> Errant sans sentier et sans voie
> En habit de povre meschine
> Criant le meurtre et la famine
> Jettée aux mâles aventures . . .
> De mon sang rougit Loire et Seine . . .
> Le ciel ne me peut tant arroser . . .
> A France Aidez![39]
>
> [Once so powerful a lady
> Wandering without path or way
> Dressed like a poor young waif
> Lamenting murder and famine
> Thrown to violent adventures . . .
> By my blood the Loire and Seine have grown red . . .
> The heavens themselves cannot wash me clean
> Bring help to France!]

So laments the France of Martin Lefranc.

From the mid-fifteenth century on, such poetic lamentations grew increasingly rare. Although at the end of the century Chastellain would still sing the misfortunes of this unhappy, unfortunate lady—a most beautiful princess, crowned with glory, her head adorned with lilies, seated on a throne of splendor, whom wars had wrongly turned into a poor, languishing mournful lady, a "princess now changed in color and degraded."[40] And the wars in Italy at the end of the century would provide another example in a poem of 1494, in which France addresses her son, King Charles VIII, and the Estates, as the king is about to leave for Italy;[41] here she is a grave and magnificent lady, beautiful but sorrowful, dressed in a cloak of fleurs-de-lys, who calls on everyone to do his duty while the king is absent from the realm.

While such lamentations became rare as the century drew to a close, France increasingly appeared as a theatrical persona, most especially in religious plays; no longer limited to monologues, she became an actor or a witness to events. She is the partially evoked heroine of the *Mystery of the Siege of Orléans* and of the *History of the Destruction of Troy the Great;*[42] she also appears in three mysteries attributed to Georges Chastellain. In the *Mystery of the Death of King Charles VII* there is a dialogue between the king, surrounded by his servants, and France "in the form of a person speaking to the king of his exploits, praised around the world"; in the second part, knights talk to her, recalling their devotion, and in the final scene, France sings their praises to God.[43] The *Entry of the King into His New Reign* compares the accession of Louis XI to the birth of Christ; France figures as the Virgin Mary—the one true and perfect lady, chaste and inviolate, and filled with every perfection—who rejoices at the birth of her child, King Louis; Saint Joseph is identified with the duke of Burgundy![44] In the *Mystery of the Council of Basle,* France in the presence of the Church and Peace defends her orthodoxy against Heresy.[45] She also appears as the silent though principal character in the *Vigils of King Charles VII* of Martial d'Auvergne, a piece written just after the king's death, describing his reign and his virtues. Here the three Estates speak with France as she presents her sons—Pepin, Charlemagne, and the new king—to God.[46]

Only later did France appear in satirical drama as well; in farces and *sotties* her role was played by "the World," "the People," or the "Poor Commoner." When at last she made her appearance in Pierre Gringoire's *Play of the Prince of Buffoons* in 1511, it was not to play the part of the buffoon but to accuse the others of not behaving as they should.[47]

Thus during the fifteenth century the character France finally outgrew her earlier allegorical abstractness. Meanwhile, manuscript illuminators depicted her in two ways, both of them idealized: one as a lady, the other as the Garden of Eden.

At first, illuminators were at a loss to decide on her distinctive attributes as a lady and refrained from portraying her in the prosopopoeias of France, even in manuscripts of texts that were metaphorically very rich. The illuminator who worked on the *Champion of Ladies* for the duke of Burgundy, Philip the Good,[48] seems to have taken the easy way out: he depicted a royal shield, crowned with a vase of three lilies, speaking to two characters. Later artists vacillated between two pictorial solutions. Some of the illuminators of Alain Chartier's *Quadrilogue* chose to remain faithful to his text, portraying France as a blond princess with a golden crown and a scepter; her long cloak, with its lilies, flowers, fruit, and emblems, represented the kingdom, while a palace in ruins symbolized the royal house.[49] But this type of representation never really gained wide acceptance.

The second type was far more popular. Here, France appeared clothed in a white dress (white being the color of royalty) occasionally wearing a blue cloak decorated with fleurs-de-lys; she was surrounded by her children (the Estates, the kings); her long blond hair was haloed with a crown or a widow's veil, depending on whether she was associated with eternal youth or the maturity of her long motherhood.[50] This representation, not yet fully set, was modeled on the typology of Charity, who in the sequence of the Virtues also figured as a white-robed mother surrounded by children. In the eyes of medieval scholars, as we will soon see, *amor patriae* was one of the primary subclasses of charity, binding each inhabitant to his country and to all his fellow inhabitants, guaranteeing harmony and peace.

Other virtues could have provided just as fitting an analogy, of course: *Justicia* with her sword or *Libertas* with her Phrygian bonnet. But the idea of liberty as it was proclaimed in 1789 did not yet exist as a medieval ideal; it would not be until the French Revolution that Marianne would make an appearance with her celebrated bonnet. France could also have been depicted as a queen, replete with all the emblems of power. But this did not happen, for even if France coincided with the Capetian state, her representational power was greater; she was as much a part of the order of values as of the order of reality. In illuminations, she occupied the most central position. Only God stood above her. Her children, the king among them, surrounded her and honored her with respect.

All this changed in the sixteenth century. France, dressed in classical robes and playing the part of warrior or queen, now knelt in reverence before the king, who from this point on became the father rather than the son of the nation.[51] France was no longer first; her symbolic place had been subordinated to his as the monarchy was transformed into an absolute state.

METAPHORS OF TERRITORY

THE GARDEN OF FRANCE

The story of the metaphor of the Garden of France is rich and complex. It began when writers attempted to conceptualize the nation as a clearly defined territory, endowed with boundaries and with specific characteristics. As this presupposed a kingdom with stable territorial frontiers, and that did not exist before about 1300, the first descriptions of the

Garden of France did not appear in literature until the beginning of the fourteenth century.

> En toute chose je plains
> Le beau jardin de grâce plein
> Où Dieu par especiauté
> Planta le lys de royauté . . .
> Tel jardin fut à bon jour né
> C'est le jardin de douce France.[52]

> [Above all I lament
> The beautiful garden full of grace
> Where God of his special will
> Planted the lily of royalty . . .
> Such a garden on a good day was born
> The garden of sweet France it was.]

The image quickly gained popularity; both Chancellor Gerson and Robert Blondel made systematic use of it.[53] After 1450 it became a commonplace of official speeches.[54] The poet André de la Vigne (d. 1527) transformed it into an orchard of honor.[55] But the complete iconographic set of representations took more time to develop. By the middle of the fifteenth century, it had begun to appear in both tapestries and in manuscript illuminations,[56] and in the sixteenth century in theater.[57] It persisted throughout the sixteenth century.

The Garden of France has obvious heraldic sources. It continued to be referred to as a "field," a clear reference to the heraldic "field" of a shield.

> Le noble champ fleuri sans pair . . .
> Cil noble champ fleuri de France . . .[58]

> [The noble flowering field without equal . . .
> This noble flowering field of France . . .]

The shape the garden took—either round (the form of perfection), or polygon- or diamond-shaped like the shields of noble ladies, surely owed more to heraldry than geography.[59] Its colors and objects also came from heraldic iconography. The Garden of France was azure or celic (sky blue); green rarely appeared before 1400.[60] Lilies, either gold or white, the ornaments on the Arms of France, held the place of honor among its flowers.

It would be a mistake to imagine that the image came only from musings on heraldry. The Garden of France also had literary sources. It was related to the *locus amoenus* that medieval poetry had inherited from Ovid, Virgil, and Theocritus.[61] Beginning in the twelfth century, this idealized landscape began to invade French literature. A parklike orchard or a garden, with a bubbling brook, shaded by many trees, it was located out in the open, beyond the forest of adventures. There it was always spring, filled with color, the air gentle and warm; the birds sang, the fruit was plentiful, and all the senses were satisfied. Latin and French poetry, chansons de geste, courtly romances, such as *Cligès* and *Flore et Blanchefleur,* and late-medieval political dreams,[62] all chose the Garden of France as their setting.

The Garden of France also had many specific associations. Some of the motifs (its enclosure, its central fountain, its four rivers) came from the Christian image of Paradise. According to the biblical account,[63] the Garden of Eden is in the East. Through the hedges or walls surrounding it, the four rivers flow out to irrigate the rest of the world.[64] The Fountain of Grace stands at its center, beside the Tree of Knowledge and the Tree of Good and Evil.

Every biblical commentary on the garden looked for its deep meaning. For some, it represented the soul that remained faithful to God, nurtured with grace as it cultivated the roses of virtue and weeded out the thorny vines of vice; it was the Church, with Christ or the Virgin of the Immaculate Conception serving as its careful gardener; it was an enclosed garden, a sealed spring. Some collections of prayers carried the title "Garden of the Devoted Soul" or "Garden of Roses." This garden bloomed when God's benediction fell upon it; it dried out when it deserved His wrath.

It was, however, the association of the garden with the Church or the Virgin Mary in particular that determined this metaphor. For France was the most Christian of nations, the best part of the Church; it was the Garden of Christ[65] where all virtues bloomed. God rested there [66] in the midst of his faithful flock, delighting in this "other earthly paradise."[67] Chancellor Gerson devoted an entire sermon to the comparison between the Garden of France and the Garden of God that shone forth with pleasure and virtue.[68] The dew of benediction watered it generously; the just laws that enclosed it protected it from being trampled by earthly and spiritual enemies. Lambs—the righteous—grazed around its fountain of wisdom and grace—an image that he probably took both from the Garden of Eden and from the *Romance of the Rose,*[69] where lambs pastured around the good shepherd amidst an idyllic, protected countryside. The Garden of France was a spiritual garden that was difficult to find, different from the gardens of pleasure of the here and now.[70] It united faith and charity in a way that made it possible for souls of the righteous to gain access to God. The popularity of medieval political pastorals and the widespread dissemination of the theme of the Mystical Lamb may also have contributed to the success of this image.

But this was not only a garden of God; it was also the privileged place of the Virgin. Artists of the fourteenth and fifteenth centuries produced many representations of the Virgin seated in the enclosed garden or next to a bush, allusions to the dogma of the Immaculate Conception which was then gaining prominence. France, we have seen, knew nothing of heresy, just as the Virgin knew nothing of carnal sin; as the mother of God had been born through the will of God, so too had France. The association of the royal lily with the lilies of the Virgin carried these same connotations.

> Car jadis la mère de Dieu
> Elut ce champ délicieux
> Y sema les trois lys d'or . . .[71]
>
> [For long ago the mother of God
> Chose this wonderful field
> And there sowed the three golden lilies . . .]

Though the Garden of France had always remained in the realm of the ideal, rarely situated in a specific time and place, during the fifteenth century it began to take on a secular character and the common attributes of the real kingdom. The king became the cultivator of the garden;[72] he cleared the stones and thorns, maintained the enclosures; his efforts allowed useful plants to flourish unhampered by weeds. The gardener-king paralleled the heavenly shepherd.

There was continuity in this evolving set of images. But the garden soon came to represent the soil of France, the real land that was so fertile and abundant because of the excellence of its climate. Geographers maintained the kingdom belonged to the seventh climate, the most moderate one and the most apt to produce fertile lands and intelligent and vigorous men. For a long time, such claims remained hidden in the manuscripts of technical treatises; then, around 1300, Pierre Dubois introduced them into his political propaganda, adding new claims for the kingdom's wealth and resources, and the diversity and abundance of its produce.[73] Etienne de Conti extolled France's excellent wheat, grains, vines, and oil, its waters that abounded with many different kinds of fish, its fields grazed by many flocks, its woods filled with wild game.[74] Jean Gerson likewise alluded to the richness of the French soil, irrigated by many rivers and abundant rainfall. The theme reappeared in the *Debate of the Heralds at Arms of France and England* and the *Book of Descriptions of Countries;*[75] the Garden of France was superior to England in the delightfulness of its châteaux and its forests full of game, its land rich in grains, olives, fruit, salt, and animals. For the Herald Berry, the Garden of France was the most graceful, the best proportioned, the most temperate, and the richest of all. After 1450, this became the refrain of all official discourses; it was useful in defending needed fiscal measures. In 1484, the chancellor of France asserted, "the beauty of the country, the fertility of the soil and the healthiness of the air outdo all the other countries of the world." No other country was better supplied with necessary riches and "all the treasures of human delight."[76]

The garden drew praise for its aesthetic qualities. "France is the jewel of the earth," said Chastellain.[77] Real gardens served as models for its beauty. Its attractions also grew directly from its own meanings. The Garden of France resembled the royal gardens described by the Italian theoretician Pietro de Crescenzi (1230–1316), whose work was translated for Charles V.[78] The royal gardens were regular in form, surrounded by enclosures decorated with heraldic arms (such as those at the Hôtel Saint-Pol in Paris); they were carpeted with grass and planted with lilies, roses, violets, and sweet-smelling herbs. Yews, boxwood, and fruit trees provided shade. There were fountains and arbors as places for conversation, rest, and receptions. In a manuscript of Guillaume de Nangis at the Walters Art Gallery in Baltimore, the garden is a many-sided space where eight kings of France are seated; it is surrounded by stakes or low walls, and has a lily-bearing tree in the center and flower beds that set off the fountain and the rivers. In a Paris manuscript of the same chronicle the garden appears simply as a flowered lawn.[79] The Garden also appeared in royal entries as a flowered, sweet-smelling lawn, enclosed by wicker stakes, with a central fountain (representing the university, or the fountain of grace);[80] its flowers were all symbolic—the lilies and roses stood for love and virginity, the violets for humility, the daisies for immortality, the flowering strawberries were the Trinity; here again a variety of people might appear—the king's ancestors, figures of the Virtues, allegories such as Peace, God's Grace, Good Counsel, and France.[81] The Garden of France stood halfway between the real world and the symbolic.

We can learn many things from this idealized image, full of praise for the "best of the ninety kingdoms that God made in this world."[82] It was

absolutely unique: the Flemish and Italian city-states projected themselves symbolically into urban landscapes, bristling with ramparts, tow-
ers, and belfries. For France, in contrast, the imagined space was entirely rural. The existence of Paris was alluded to only at the center of
the garden, with its fountain of faith and royal throne. The rest was all
field or garden, earth that showed intense signs of human cultivation
and transformation, lands that were well-ordered, enclosed, and delim-
ited. Though in reality the kingdom had already acquired important
maritime frontiers, the Garden of France was not bounded by water. It
was not in the least like Shakespeare's England. All of its boundaries
were Continental or closed to the outside and, where borders were in
the process of definition,[83] they were indicated by moveable stakes or
less sturdy enclosures,[84] occasionally decorated with the lilied arms.
This image conveyed the notion of a land of one's own, a land endowed
with particular virtues; it represented the maintenance of all that was
good, beautiful, and orderly. It was also a religious image. The crowned
lady France, dressed in blue and gold, either standing, or seated like the
Virgin in an enclosed garden, *inviolata,* having submitted neither to a
tyrant nor to a foreign prince, faithful to her own natural prince—what
image could resemble a religious symbol more closely?[85]

THE TREE OF FRANCE

The dead tree that leafs again was another image that served to symbolize the kingdom, its new life—like the fertility of the Garden—a sign of
divine benediction. It too derived ultimately from biblical imagery, with
a strong admixture of folklore.

Already in the mid-twelfth century, legends began to appear in the
West of the bare tree that stands on the boundary of the world.[86] Other
texts placed it in the center of the world in Palestine, the great green tree
of Nabuchadnezzar's dream, which reached to heaven until an angel of
God hewed it down and left it a dry stump.[87] Mandeville, in his *Voy-
ages,* placed the tree in the Hebron Valley; when the Holy Land was
freed, he said, it would blossom again.[88] It was tempting to portray
France as a tree of this kind,[89] for was it not the center of the earth, a
second Holy Land in the eyes of God?[90]

The theme of magical blossoming was also very popular. The
Pseudo-Turpin told how the Crown of Thorns had bloomed in the
hands of Charlemagne, how the lances of the brave men who were
doomed to die had flowered; the Grail story told of the castle of the

Fisher-King, where all burst into flower in the hand of the Chosen One.[91] The writers of saints' lives were fond of it as well.[92] The calamities of the Hundred Years War set the stage for its appearance in political contexts. The Tree of France became either a giant lily or a green tree with white flowers: in 1386, the bishop of Sénez, Robert Gervais, referred to the green tree, threatened by drought; Martin Lefranc, Chastellain, and Molinet picked up the image.[93]

When Charles VIII made his royal entry into Rouen, he was greeted with a representation of the "French People" in the form of the tree.[94] But the lily tree functioned more frequently as a dynastic representation. It appeared in the *Lament on the Death of Charles VII*, in the illuminations to Guillaume de Nangis's *Abbreviated Chronicle*, and at the entry of Queen Claude de France into Paris in 1515. Heavenly anger and disgrace in the eyes of various social groups could cause it to languish, dry out, and become twisted, or it might be overrun when briars—the English—threatened to choke it.[95] After 1435, however, the tree was once again green and beflowered, renewed by God's grace; it shone forth and embellished the world.

The tree and the garden complemented each other as two possible ways of symbolizing France. One referred to the land itself, the other to the people. From 1300 onward it became difficult to distinguish between these images of the land and the people, for the links that had long since joined them were now gradually becoming visible.

TO LOVE THE FATHERLAND AND DIE FOR IT

BEFORE 1300

In classical Greco-Roman culture, those who died for their country were deified as heroes, their shades destined for the Elysian fields while their memories were revered in glory among men.[96] The Church fathers broke with this tradition and tried to discourage devotion to the pagan state. And even after the conversion of Constantine, love for one's country was less important than love of God. Saint Augustine recounted examples of patriotism only as an encouragement to martyrdom: if pagans could die so courageously for the state, he argued, how could we hesitate to do the same for God? The disappearance of the Roman Empire helped further to accelerate the obsolescence of the idea of *patria*, of the fatherland, for the barbarian kingdoms were based on private ties of man to man.

During the early Middle Ages, the term *patria* and the secular values associated with it, were forgotten.[97] It came to mean nothing more than land or region; its emotional connotations were Christianized, as the Heavenly City took its place as an object of desire and love. "The patria that we hope for is the heavenly Jerusalem. In these lands of Babylon we do no more than wait in exile," sang Abelard in the twelfth century.[98] Gerson could still echo this in a sermon preached before Charles VI: "Your patria is there in heaven, the quiet harbor, the triumphal hall of the saints, your ancestors and future companions."[99] For a long time, then, crusaders and martyrs alike might die for God and for their celestial patria, but the fatherlands of this world were not worthy of such sacrifice. Before 1300, the word rarely appeared in its modern sense; and when it did it was a term of learned men, fervent worshipers of antique texts. In common usage, *pagus*—region—tended to be used instead. Not until the Pléiade in the sixteenth century would *patria* pass into common usage.

Yet though the word was not in current usage, devotion to the fatherland nonetheless existed. Traces of it can be found in administrative and philosophical texts of the thirteenth century.

"The defense of the realm" was invoked in France from 1124 onward when levying troops, and from 1250 onward when levying taxes. Abbot Suger used the expression—rare at his time—when he described the invasion of 1124;[100] it was the king's personal responsibility, closely resembling his duty to defend the Church. Loyalty to the king was likewise still a personal duty. Only during the reign of Philip Augustus did the defense of the kingdom, of its rights and territory, begin to appear with any frequency in royal documents. Philip spoke of the "integrity of the kingdom," which he was duty-bound to protect, and several times enlisted the "defense of the Crown" to justify taxes that were more or less modeled on crusading taxes.[101] As the thirteenth century wore on, the royal chancery invoked the theme with increasing frequency. The jurist Beaumanoir (1246–1296) insisted that "the king must defend his land for the common good,"[102] and Philip the Fair placed it at the very heart of his politics, enlisting it to justify all his military levies of troops and the taxes he demanded from the goods of the Church. "All are obligated to fight to defend their native soil," he said. "This is a service demanded of each one of you." His propagandists were quick to follow. All were to "pay what the king asks for the common defense,"[103] for each was responsible for protecting the kingdom with his own arms or with the money in his pocket whenever necessity required it. Guillaume de Nogaret defended his brutal actions at Anagni by evoking the kingdom to whose defense he was duty-bound.[104] But such patriotism, insistently promoted by the royal administration, probably met with little enthusiasm. The future of the patria lay elsewhere, not in the realm of fiscal duty.

Thirteenth-century scholars laid the philosophical and moral groundwork for the reappearance of the idea of the patria. Around 1240, men who belonged to the Parisian university world were meditating on amor patriae—love of the homeland—in the context of their typologies of virtue. Love of self was mere egotism and vice, they asserted; love for others was a virtue, though it ranked below the love of God, which was the root of all virtue. Love for others was meritorious because it went beyond the family to encompass the collectivity. Henry of Ghent devoted some of his *Quodlibeta* to one's duties to his country. He argued that to show the faith and charity that ties fellow citizens to one another, one must be willing to die in war, provided the war is justified by defense of "one's life, country, liberty, and laws."[105] God approves of such a death, which, far from being shameful or sorrowful, shows virtuous courage and magnanimity, and is a duty that applies not only to knights but to all—great and small, laypeople and clerics, commoners and women—for everyone shares these responsibilities, "because we are not born for ourselves, but for others and for our country." Natural and divine law in this case agreed.

Saint Thomas and his disciple Ptolemy of Lucca saw the problem somewhat differently.[106] They sought to retain the Aristotelian idea of the common good, while subordinating it to the individual's responsibilities toward God. For them, the charity that one owed to God and the pious respect due the family were the most important; yet at the same time good Christans had an obligation to defend the public good. One had to be willing to confront death for the sake of the public authority, for it was worthy of reverence and support. Those who were willing to make this sacrifice would earn honor in this world and salvation in the next, provided they had fought fairly in a war that was just. But for Saint Thomas and Ptolemy these duties were less important than those owed to God and to Christendom.

The reasoning of Raymond de Sebonde at the beginning of the fifteenth century was fundamentally Thomist,[107] but the attention he devoted to amor patriae and the tone of his argument is markedly different. For him, *amor* or *caritas* is the primary Christian virtue. Though love of individuals leads to sadness and darkness, love of others is a form of love of God, to the extent that it leaves the personal and particular behind to focus on one's Christian fellows or one's compatriots; for all human communities, patriae as well as the Christian Church, are similarly founded on the love of God and the reciprocal love of their members. "This love is perfect, good, lasting, and permanent," he said, for it is directed toward something beyond the individual. The good Christian loves his country, for love of God nurtures the desire to live in a godly land "and to sacrifice oneself if necessary."[108] Neither gold, silver, nor honor could provide consolation to someone who had abandoned his own country (patria propria). This kind of love was universal, and it led to eternal life.

In this way the theories of amor patriae oscillated between two poles—Christian reflections on the hierarchy of the virtues, most particularly on love, and Aristotelian political reasoning that glorified the common good and the community of men as the product of natural law. But had it not been for the slow revival of the classical tradition, this reasoning would not have come to fruition, would not have led to the rebirth of the ideal of sacrificing oneself for one's country.

When Vincent of Beauvais took up the subject in his classification of the virtues in the *Mirror of Doctrine*,[109] he considered love of the patria to be a moral question. It was higher than devotion to the family, but lower than love of humanity in general. Though he did not attempt to justify this schema in theoretical terms, it is evident that he drew on three different groups of sources. All of the examples he gives of devotion to country come from the *Memorable Deeds* of Valerius Maximus and the *City of God* of Saint Augustine.[110] The authors he specifically cites are from the first century A.D.—Cicero, Ovid, Horace, and Cato. Vincent's knowledge of classical culture was thus quite limited; his examples came from two well-known texts and the rest most probably from some anthology.

About fifty years later, Giles of Rome, the tutor of Philip the Fair, demonstrated more extensive knowledge of the classical treatments of this subject.[111] Like Vincent of Beauvais, he brought together Saint Thomas's commentary on amor patriae and examples from classical culture drawn from Valerius Maximus and the *City of God*. But he knew all of Cicero and Sallust, whose works on the subject he summarized, and he skillfully added biblical and Christian examples drawn from Deuteronomy, the Maccabees, and Luke. Christ himself, he reminded his readers, gave his life to save others. Dying for God and the faith and dying for the state were thus equivalent; the valiant peers who died at Roncevaux did so for one another; they deserved both heaven and the immortality of their names in heroic song.

Essentially, then, classical influences had come along two different paths: some passages came from Valerius Maximus and Saint Augustine, who led their readers to be hostile toward Roman virtue; others came from the first century A.D., a period when the spirit of Roman patriotism was changing from the austere, masculine duty of the Republic into a more emotional virtue. Fourteenth- and fifteenth-century patriotism in France would speak more often of love than of duty toward the patria, a patria that was far more feminine in character than masculine.

Was that late-medieval patriotism then simply a rebirth of classical love of country? In fact, deliberate choices were made to retain some aspects of classical patriotism and to discard others. Writers rarely referred to exile, for example, though this was one of the great themes of antiquity; only Charles d'Orléans and Robert Blondel devoted passages to the pain of "living in other houses."[112] The need to protect the tombs of ancestors also disappeared, for Christianity did not grant much importance to the physical remains of the deceased.[113] And one's patria was not eternal Rome; its longevity was contingent on divine will. From the classical tradition writers took the words they used to connote sacrifice and duty toward one's country and words that expressed love for one's native soil. But even here, usage changed those words in ways that carried them away from their classical resonance. They applied to *tota Francia*—the entire fatherland—those words that classical poets had used only to speak of their lands of origin, their birthplaces. French patriotism thereby gained a new element of emotional warmth, of passionate commitment. It was not an abstract, institutional obligation; for the state at the end of the Middle Ages had neither the force nor the structures to impose such obligations. It was a sentiment commonly shared.

FROM 1300 TO 1500

The many wars that plagued the kingdom from 1300 to 1500 also revived Horace's maxim, *Dulce et decorum est pro patria mori*—It is sweet and fitting to die for one's country. In order to follow the chronological development of this phenomenon, we will examine both a body of literature and a body of facts. The production of military literature increased enormously during the Hundred Years War; it gives us the theoretical insights of experts on battle. By contrast, a study of deaths that occurred in the wars between 1350 and 1525 gives us a more concrete view of what was going on.

Military Literature   The increasing frequency of wars at the beginning of the fourteenth century prompted an increasing number of translations of the classical treatises on tactics and strategy by Vegetius Renatus and Frontinus; it also brought forth a series of instruction manuals for noble youths, the military class par excellence.

At mid-century, Geoffroi de Charny's *Book of Chivalry* and *Questions on the Joust*—both written for King John II—achieved the status of quasi-official statements.[114] In these works, Geoffroi, a member of the Order of the Star and bearer of the oriflamme, sought among other things to discourage soldiers from dishonorable flight; for him, a knight's only duty was to remain at the scene of action. He willingly accepted the possibility of capture and ransom, which were normal occurrences in the military encounters of the day, but he was not preoccupied with death. Death in battle was not valued; it was merely a risk. And only a crusader could expect heaven as a reward for that risk.

> Si tu n'es mort, pris seras-tu!
> [If you do not die, you will be taken!]

Geoffroi himself was killed while carrying the oriflamme at the battle of Poitiers.

Around 1393 or 1394, Honoré Bonet took an even more reserved stance on the issue in his *Tree of Battles*.[115] He was not certain that it was better to die than to run away, for death was such a terrible and fearful thing. "He who dies in battle dies in a state of mortal sin, angered against others and in bad temper. And those who die in mortal sin go to Hell, except for those who die on crusade or in a just war," he wrote. Such soldiers could not be buried in sanctified ground nor in a church cemetery. As both the kings of France and of England claimed their side was just in their wars with each other, it was unclear whose side Heaven was on. This was why Bonet sanctioned running from the scene of battle; for in any battle between Christians, the only ones on the losing side who were obliged to stay until the end were mercenaries and vassals under oath; it was feudal service and loyalty to one's employer that obligated a fighter to risk possible death, not an abstract notion of obligation to his country. The only war in which Bonet encouraged fighting to the death was in war against the Saracens, for in that case the warrior was assured his entry into Heaven, and immortality was certainly worth more than earthly life. Yet even here, Bonet considered it permissible to run away from battle if this would change nothing in the eventual outcome. Death was a risk to be avoided if possible; for this author as well it was not a thing of value. Bonet, a cleric from the Midi, embodied the vision of a regional social group that remained apart from the particular contingencies of the age.

Members of the court of Charles V at the time of the reconquest had very different ideas on the subject. If the edition of 1514 is correct, and a work called the *Banner of Wars* was actually written by the knight of La Tour Landry to whom it is attributed,[116] this text predates Bonet's *Tree of Battles*. Strongly Aristotelian and full of ideas about the common good and the wise and learned king, this work speaks explicitly of patriotic duty. "No one should fear dying in defense of the common good, for there is merit in it. One has the duty to fight for his country. . . . It is a good and charitable act to expose one's life this way. . . . For the good of the country one must not be afraid to spill his blood." But this duty applies only to a small number of professional soldiers; in battle, the untrained multitudes only get in the way.

These views triumphed in the last half of the fifteenth century. The *Banner* was the principal source for the *Rosebush of Wars*, written in the entourage of Louis XI for the education of the future Charles VIII.[117] It repeated in its entirety the passage just quoted, adding that the common good was the responsibility of all Estates, even though the knights were those whose principal role was to protect the state. The author is evidently not yet certain whether a professional army or the support of the entire population was what was needed. At about the same time, Jean de Bueil wrote in his *Jouvencel*, "One must give up his body to guard his sire's right and protect the little people from trial and invasion. The peers of France did this who died on the plains of Roncevaux. . . . God loves him who risks his body for others in a just conflict."[118] Here were crusaders depicted as patriots and promised entry into paradise for that reason, a paradoxical reversal of the views of Honoré Bonet. Even more explicit was the *Doctrine of the Nobility*, written at Metz toward the end of the century: "Everyone should devote himself to the defense of his land. Honor and true glory crown those who die for their country. Nothing is too difficult to save the place of one's birth."[119]

These theoretical discussions fall into three distinct periods. Up until the fourteenth century, only crusaders went to Heaven; death was a risk incurred in battle, not a meritorious deed, and it concerned only a small number of professionals. Then, during the fourteenth century, writers began to complicate the issue. Although some continued to see death as a possible risk tied to a specific job, others began to see it as a general duty and a valuable act that afforded entry into heaven. Finally, in the fifteenth century, the urgent necessities of the time made death for one's country a duty that was imposed on all, and generally accepted. "May it please the heavens that I die not with the public good but for it. Every evil may befall me and my family, but may God save France." "May it please God that we fall with you in this very holy death rather than living in captivity." Dying for one's country was a sacrifice, a death that was willingly accepted so long as the country was threatened with annihilation or occupation.[120] Yet, this was still far removed from the kind of fervor for one's country expressed by Corneille in the seventeenth century:

> Mourir pour la patrie est un si digne sort
> Qu'on briguerait en foule une pareille mort.[121]
>
> [To die for one's country is such a worthy fate
> That one would compete with many for the chance.]

The medieval conception was in fact much closer to a Christian view. Dying for one's country was a form of redemption, a sacrifice like Christ's. The sacrificial blood earned God's pardon along with victory and peace. It became the guarantor of entry into paradise as well as of glory and fame on earth.

Practice   Did this development in theory have any counterpart in reality? In the fourteenth century we find even greater ambiguity in actions than in theory. Fear of violent death is everywhere. "It is better to die in your bed and know your sins than to die in war for the sake of glory," said one proverb.[122] "Who in your agony will call you forth to the Catholic faith and who will close your eyelids?" asked a preacher.[123] In the dances of death, knights confronted the reaper with the same repulsive horror as did the men and women of other Estates.

Death in battle took a very long time to acquire its specific meaning. In 1350, French and English soldiers in the *Combat of the Thirty* were not sure they would gain access to Heaven:

> Prions Dieu pour tous les combattants
> Qu'ils ne soient damnés au jour du Jugement.[124]
>
> [Let us pray God for all the soldiers
> That they might not be damned on Judgment Day.]

At about the same time, a peasant, Grand Ferré, organized his village to resist the English and, when he died in the effort, his death was mourned by everyone in the village and in the region of Compiègne,[125] but nothing was said of any greater duty, nor of his fate in the afterlife. The death of Du Guesclin at Chateauneuf-de-Randon in 1380—the death of a constable of France rather than a simple peasant—was no different. Knights throughout the West lamented the loss of this valiant man; he had died bidding farewell to France and his king, as Roland had done at Roncevaux. God may well have greeted him in paradise but, if so, it would have been because he was a model of knighthood rather than a patriot.[126]

It took the invasion of 1415–1416 to shock people sufficiently to convince them that it was a duty to die for their country. One example presents this transformation in a vivid way.

An offspring of the petty nobility of the Pyrenees, the Bastard of Vaurus—a vassal of Bernard VII, constable d'Armagnac—on occasion served as a mercenary. The fortunes of war had made him captain of Meaux for the Dauphin when the English laid siege to it between October 1421 and May 1422. Meaux was an important fortified post isolated in Anglo-Burgundian northern France, and the Bastard mounted a resistance that rankled and brought bloody reprisals from Henry V when he finally captured the town: the Bastard was executed along with his half-brother, the bailiff of Meaux, and several others. The event fired the imagination of many who heard about it.

There are two versions of the Bastard's death, and they have little in common. In the eyes of contemporaries, it was highly unusual to execute prisoners in this way. A wartime military leader, when captured, usually had the choice of going to prison or paying ransom, or, if the opportunity was offered, of changing sides, for only an oath was necessary to "make French" or "make English." Writers on the Anglo-Burgundian side, therefore, made the Bastard into a killer, who was rightfully punished for misdeeds that had nothing to do with resisting the English. The "Bourgeois of Paris" told a terrifying story of how he had tied a laborer's pregnant wife to a tree in the forest and left her to be eaten by wolves.[127] Pierre de Fénin told how the Bastard was hanged to the tree where he had hanged poor laborers, his banner attached to his chest.[128] The "Monk of Saint-Denis" claimed that his head was "impaled on the end of a pike attached to the tree where he had hanged poor laborers."[129] Yet this same chronicler recognized that "the law of nature demands that one should fight for his country." Partisans of the

Dauphin saw the event very differently. Jean Jouvenal des Ursins, in his *Chronicle of Charles VI*, acknowledged that the Bastard may have been too expeditious with the Parisian and Anglo-Burgundian partisans he discovered in the fields, but he died "because he was a brave fighter and a gentleman, because he had loyally served his lord."[130] Monstrelet shared his opinion, though he was Burgundian; he emphasized the heroism of the people of Meaux who resisted though they had neither food nor arms.[131] The *Declaration of Freedom of Normandy* is the most interesting text on the subject. It turns the Bastard's sentiments at the moment of his execution into an example for Frenchmen of all generations to come.[132] When the Bastard was captured, this chronicler relates, Henry V threatened to hang him and to dishonor his banner if he did not agree to change camps. The Bastard is made to reply: "I prefer to die unjustly to keep my faith than to live having broken with it. No death one dies for the state is shameful or miserable." This beautiful example of a death that was accepted, that was freely chosen for the sake of his country, in many ways presages the death of Bayard in 1524 as the later sixteenth century would remember it: "My lord, I die as a good man, but I pity you who are in service against your prince and your country," the knight says to the constable of Bourbon, who had passed over to the Spanish side.[133] The ideal of such a death, of a death on the field of honor (even though this phrase was not yet spoken), was born during the dark years of the Kingdom of Bourges.

If we now compare what we have seen of reality and what we have seen of theory, it is clear that though the ideal of sacrifice for one's country was affirmed theoretically by writers in the court of Charles V, it was not accepted until after 1415, and even then accepted within Armagnac circles far more readily and profoundly than elsewhere. The Armagnac nobility had risked their lives at Agincourt in 1415 and at Verneuil in 1424, and they were willing to do so because they believed such sacrifice was necessary. Later, they would come to celebrate the idea and do what they could to justify it.

There are similarities between this development in the peace that followed Charles VII's reconquest and the secular cult of "death for the *patrie*" which followed World War I in France. It was quite normal during the Middle Ages to bury the dead after a battle and celebrate masses in their honor, establishing a chapel if need be on the battleground itself, whether clergy were present or not. After Bouvines in 1214, Philip Augustus founded Notre-Dame-de-la-Victoire near Senlis. The same happened just about everywhere in the late Middle Ages.

Prayers were offered for the dead; military leaders who had been killed by the enemy were buried as a matter of right at Saint-Denis. It would be interesting to make a systematic study of the epitaphs of soldiers who died under such circumstances; a review of those in the Paris area suggests that, after 1415, their death in battle was considered worthy of inscription on their tomb, as it was for Pierre d'Orgemont and for Béraud de la Tour.[134] This seems to confirm our earlier conclusions. Jean de Bueil's epitaph, celebrating his death in 1477, though somewhat later and unclearly dated, is more explicit on the subject:

> Priez pour moi bonnes gens,
> Pour les sires de Bueil occis à la grant guerre
> En bataillant pour la France et pour vous.[135]
>
> [Pray for me, good people,
> For the lord of Bueil killed in the great war
> Fighting for France and for you.]

We are very close here to our own twentieth-century *mort pour la France*—died for France.

The duty to risk one's body, to put it on the line for the state, was nevertheless always considered exceptional, a duty that arose from the urgent necessities of a war that was both just and defensive, a war with consequences for all. Wars fought elsewhere did not call for such great sacrifices.

FERVOR AND LIMITS OF AMOR PATRIAE

To these lugubrious meditations the closing Middle Ages normally preferred instead their songs of the sweetness of life in France, songs that foreshadowed those of the sixteenth century. Nothing was dearer to man than the land where he was born; it was more precious to his heart than gold. It was a delight to be able to live peacefully on the land of one's birth, beside brothers and friends. A natural love tied such a person to the earth to which his body would finally return. In that land lay the security, peace, refuge, and the last resting place of every person.[136] This was the common heritage and promise given to all French. France is "our land," Suger was already saying in the middle of the twelfth century,[137] the mother of us all, of the king and of the commoner. The land gives us life and everything associated with it. We are all born French of France, all "from the same womb,"[138] part of one and the same flesh, protected by this earth and this sky.[139] We all owe it therefore our love and support.

The family model, so omnipresent in medieval society, cannot be missed. What one owed to his father and mother or to his heritage, one also owed to his country, which was likewise a *parens*—a blood relative. Obligations to one's country were indeed considered more important than those owed to ordinary families. During the first half of the fifteenth century, the Parlement of Paris decided that children of French mothers and English fathers had no rights of inheritance, nor did the fathers.[140] For France was one big family, and it was more important than others that were more perishable and less perfect. Just as the French people were a pure and ancient race, whose descent had been mapped in the manner of noble genealogies, love and duty to mother Francia were projected onto an enlarged, idealized family. One was bound to defend her honor, her life, and the territorial patrimony shared by all.

France was a "land and the image of a land." It was inseparable from the people. It shared the characteristics of the people over the course of time: warlike, pious, learned, and well governed. In the end, it took the form of an allegorical abstraction based on the image of *Caritas*. For France was the mother, and this family role justified the demands she made on her collective children, as it validated also the sentiments the community felt toward her, the fact that they accepted to sacrifice themselves for her. France became "our land," "our motherland," surrounded with a patriotism that was more emotional than juridical. Of this land the fertile minds of the closing Middle Ages created a range of images, to which each century made its contributions in accordance with its own preoccupations, and without removing anything that had come before. The image of France was composed of accumulated layers, which gave it complexity and plasticity. Each social group could find what it needed there. There was a France for the knight, a France for the cleric, for the scholar, for the legal-minded; there were many Frances rather than a single France. And all these Frances told their own tales, through myths and stories, embodied in the signs and symbols of a unique and evanescent entity in which they nonetheless believed.

Conclusion

What was the France of the late Middle Ages? What were the sources of the "incomprehensible and natural love" its inhabitants held for it? It was the awareness its people had of being a particular human community, unique in its origins and history, a people who imagined themselves linked to this specific valued land for all time. Its difference was imagined to be a superiority, for it was willingly xenophobic. In order to see itself as good, it had to project an evil outside itself. The English played this role. French national sentiment was both ethnic and territorial; it rose from the conjunction of a given people and a given countryside. It was consciously constructed by successive generations. It did not simply happen.

France was first of all a composite of the French past, present, and future. Though made up of the three Estates of the nobility, clergy, and commoners, the traditional components of a medieval polity, it encompassed all of them. For the Middle Ages, nation and race were identical. The vitality of the Trojan myth shows this; it was unity of blood that gave the people their innate and common qualities, their military strength and purity of faith. The history of France revealed its characteristics over time and justified the exceptional prerogatives the kingdom enjoyed.

Group memory tended to privilege some moments over others: the reigns of Clovis, of Charlemagne, the battle of Bouvines in 1214, the crusades of Saint Louis. This common history had a specific meaning:

the nation was born, won battles, gave way to sin and earned redemption. But history did not *create* the nation; for the nation preexisted its history. It was a gift of God revealed over time. He approved it and gave it a role and a destiny. It was a teleological history, like that of the Jewish people. The shield of faith, free of heresy, the land of the saints, the Most Christian kingdom fought to preserve and extend the faith. It was the last of the Chosen People.

This community had been promised a land of its own. Just as the early Middle Ages praised the qualities of the people—"Long live Christ who loves the Franks," trumpeted the Salic Law—so the late Middle Ages, the era of territorial states, exalted the idea of national territory. The history of France, which Hugh of Fleury still imagined in a Carolingian frame at the beginning of the twelfth century, became Capetian in the historical works of the monks of Saint-Denis. Their France was a space bounded by four rivers (the Escaut, Meuse, Saône, and Rhône), centered on Paris, and endowed with special properties, some of which were real, some not. This terrestrial paradise was an ideal land, safe from occupation and from government by strangers. Already for Suger it was "our land."

For a long time, the precise nature of the bond between the people and the country was not examined at all. The early Middle Ages accepted the idea that the people had conquered the land; the twelfth century covered over the conquest by emphasizing the will of God and predestination; at the beginning of the thirteenth century, the monk Rigord invented the rights of those who were native to the land: the Gauls were Trojans who had come to an empty country, centuries before the Franks. But his invention took long to catch on. Not until 1400 did it become commonplace to assert that the French had sprung directly from French soil.

This conception of nationhood accurately reflected the values of the society that had created it. It was monarchist, clerical, and aristocratic. Its history was entwined with the history of the dynasty. Although, in the name of the king who never dies, the human king was sometimes roundly blamed for his fallibility and mortality, the form of government itself was never questioned. Freedom was not a cherished value in the Middle Ages.

France was also a Christian France, which drew meaning from its role in a larger plan, the plan of God; everyone in the kingdom shared the same faith and prayed for the success of the same king; what few Jews there were did not count as French. France was conceived of as a homogeneous religious space, where theology supported political power. The idea that the offices of the Church "never die" provided the model for the distinction between the two bodies of the king—the physical king who is mortal and the political king who never dies—and thus for the perpetuity of France through its undying dynasty. The Immaculate Conception inspired the Garden of France; Saint Michael, as his cult grew popular, became its guardian angel. Pre-1500 France was neither a secular value nor one that was becoming secular.

France was also strongly aristocratic and profoundly hierarchical. It gave no thought to equality nor did it wish to destroy the equilibrium among the three Estates. It saw itself in terms of seignorial lineage, as a race of warriors earning ever greater privileges from one generation to the next, privileges that the oldest in line held as the common patrimony. France was a knight errant, sprung from fantastical origins, glorying in high adventure, winning for itself heraldic arms.

The promised land of France was field or garden, for, after 1415, Paris never regained status as the *communis patria* of all the French. France was a cultivated land, the cultural ideal of the nobility. In this it differed markedly from the chosen images of mercantile countries such as Flanders and Italy, whose piazzas and battlements bore the emblems of urban dominance.

The idea of France, then, was of a monarchic, aristocratic, and clerical nation. At first glance this does not suggest any of the innovations of the times: the push toward democratic ways in the fourteenth century, the growing presence in places of power of administrative officials alongside the nobles. All forms of ideology distort the relations between seminal facts and the discourses produced from them, for they belong to the realm of that which is preestablished and that which is commonly held to be true. The ideology of France was no different; it accumulated successive strata of images without consciously correcting them. France experienced the normal gap that exists between reality and its image.

French national sentiment took shape slowly throughout the course of the Middle Ages. Every era made its contributions, but periods of crisis made the greatest ones. Each symbol that composed it went through three distinct phases: each was invented or discovered, then acquired a variety of meanings, and finally was incorporated into a coherent and well-ordered myth.

The early Middle Ages left behind only the images of Clovis and the Salic Law, both of which were long forgotten, and the story of the Trojan origins of the Frankish race. The Carolingians were great innovators. Usurpers of the throne, they invented a holy royalty whose right was sanctified by the Holy Ampulla. The kings of the twelfth century created new sacred objects: the oriflamme was raised for the first time between 1124 and 1126, the lily appeared on the arms of Kings Louis VII and Philip Augustus. A territorial state composed by the chance conquests of the Capetian kings took on borders that ideology made necessary. In the thirteenth century France became the Most Christian nation, crowned by the memory of Saint Louis. When Primat of Saint-Denis finished the *Great Chronicles of France* around 1274 on orders of the king, he provided a coherent and laudatory vision of the national past, one written in French. This made it possible at the end of the century to draw portraits of a France that was now unique in its history, its boundaries, and its character. The struggle between Philip the Fair and Pope Boniface VIII, rather than leading to a secularization of this national idea, created instead a direct link between France and God, bypassing the Church of the world, a mystique of nationhood that was tied to the royal blood of the kings.

The events of 1314 and 1328, amplified by the coming of the Hundred Years War, confronted the Valois with the same problems as the Capetians had faced in the tenth century: they were kings whose legitimacy was both questionable and questioned. Rather than basing their defense on law, an unsure foundation on which to build, the Valois kings developed a vibrant form of national propaganda designed to counteract their real loss of maneuverability. History provided them with the arguments they needed: a story of national origins that allowed them to reabsorb the Gauls by identifying them with the Franks, a Salic Law to rediscover and transform into a law of succession for the kingdom, a story of Clovis in which he was given the heavenly lilies at Joyenval.

The reign of Charles VI put in question all that had been created. The "Kingdom of Bourges" seemed condemned to failure: the reigning king was a child, a suspected bastard, a child who was disinherited after the murder of Montereau. "Woe to you, O land, when your king is a child, and your princes feast in the morning!": the blast from Ecclesiastes was widely broadcast by Burgundian progaganda. The Kingdom of Bourges was obliged to invent new images to save itself. France changed its moorings, and national ideology, which up until then had been centralized and oriented toward the north, rapidly turned toward the south and became more diffused. From the south it borrowed relics, new sanctuaries like Bourges, Poitiers, and the frontier churches like those of

Gascony and the Loire. All the heavenly guardians of the Kingdom of Bourges came from the south of France. They grew up on French soil and were often related to the royal house; they were the youthful liberators of a country at war. Saint Michael, the personal guardian of the dauphin-king, became the model of all, though there were many local variants. The bond with Saint-Denis and Paris was loosened.

National sentiment had become self-conscious. The nation had a countenance of its own. It was now the mother for whom all her children were bound to give up their lives if necessary. National ideology had won a new coherence and unity. Between 1370 and 1430, all the many different royal symbols that had originated haphazardly over time were brought together to form the double myth of origin, centered on both Clovis and Pharamond. Clovis, now a saint, was credited with the lily and the oriflamme, which joined the Holy Ampulla. The angel who brought him these gifts became identified with Saint Michael, the guardian angel of the Crown. The pagan Pharamond stood beside him, though little was known of him other than that he was linked to the Trojan origins of the Gauls and Franks, and that he issued the Salic Law, which itself had been increasingly made the source of all the nation's most fundamental political principles. It was perhaps with Pharamond, an image of a royalty that was legitimate though neither sacred nor Christian, that the secularization of the myth of national origin began. Around 1500, however, Pharamond still paled beside the much-glorified Clovis.

French national sentiment was composite. Its slow evolution was far from continuous or unrelenting; there were moments of stasis, failure, and impasse, as well as progress; only from this distance does its path look like a straight line.

Later eras would see different values in France. The sixteenth century emphasized its cultural distinction, which by then most considered to be a fully secular culture, as in the famous phrase of Du Bellay:

> France, mère des arts, des armes et des lois.
> [France, mother of the arts, of arms and of laws.]

Religion and country had begun to go their separate ways. The seventeenth century then invented a new and dangerous biological justification for the social hierarchy: the nobility had descended from the Franks, the common people from the Gauls. The eighteenth century converted the country into the land of liberty; the Revolution spread abroad the celebrated ideals of *Liberté, Egalité, Fraternité*—"eternal values," two of which had only recently appeared and been put into practice in France. There was no single France, but rather many; no single national sentiment, but many, of varying composition and degrees of intensity.

Once we have recognized the multiplicity of these images of France, we are forced to redefine many old problems. In this way, I hope this work may inspire future research. The historiography of the nation, the history of the history of France, has yet to be fully explored. The figure of Pharamond, the once colorless legislator who (with the social rise of the nobility of the robe) began to take on life in the sixteenth century, could be brought more completely into focus. Brennus and his deeds— the only Gallic hero known to the Middle Ages, and the archetype of all kings who waged wars in Italy—could also be studied more closely. Vercingetorix continues to hold a more significant place in ancient history than in the history of the nation.

France's history is not as simple as that of younger nations that were founded with the Christian conversion of king-saints, nations that are certain of their birth dates. Even if we overlook the fact that the story of France is the story of the intermingling of the traditions of several different peoples, we cannot avoid the plurality of the founding heroes. Literal plurality and typological plurality: there was the warrior, who, king or not, either opposed or stood alongside the saint and the legislator. This is why the legends of the founding of France are so ambiguous. When one wished to describe the creation of the kingdom as a new order torn from the dissolution of the guilt-ridden old, one chose the traitor Antenor, founder of Sycambria—in imitation of the Romans who had chosen Romulus, the man who had killed his brother Remus before the walls of new Rome. On other occasions one chose the blood that was spilled willingly, when rebirth sprang from the martyrdom or suffering of the leader. Vercingetorix, like the heroes of the myths of Scandinavia and the Slavic cultures, was sometimes preferred, his failure taken as the sign of new birth. But there was also a more straightforward plot: France had been given birth by the victory of a great general, a general who was the right arm of God. In this case one chose Clovis.

Confronted with such a wealth of choices, each era reacted differently. Each generation of historians made choices more or less consciously from this historical material, privileging some, assigning others to oblivion, according to the preferences of their age for a given social group or a particular seminal event. After a while there were no longer any questions about who the heroes were. The Third Republic extolled "our ancestors, the Gauls," ancestors of republican France, whereas after 1940, the People gave way to the Masses, and the birth of France became impersonal and anonymous. (This last tendency has been detrimental to a major genre of historical writing, that of biography, because the very idea of famous men no longer has any meaning, even less so the historiography of the saints, kings, and heroes, even though these long comprised the essence of popular manuals of history, a vital form of memory that was accessible to the largest number of people.)

Our study of Saint Louis could easily lead to a sequel that would follow the evolution of his image up to the French Revolution, a far more real demarcation point in the trajectory of this subject than the beginning of the sixteenth century. The memory of the saint-king proved difficult to exploit. The Jansenists of Port-Royal objected to the pomp and absolutism of his reign. Yet Henri IV used it to justify his own legitimacy, since the House of Guise could only claim descent (quite falsely) from Charlemagne. And every French schoolchild knows that Louis XVI's confessor called from the foot of the execution scaffold, "Son of Saint Louis, ascend to heaven!" There are historical studies waiting to be done on many other medieval figures as well. Though work has been done on the historiography of Dagobert, Hugh Capet, and Joan of Arc, little exists for Blanche of Castille, Jacques Coeur, or Anne of Brittany. How did Anne become the "duchess in wooden shoes"? Each era, one after the other, has shaped their images of national glory according to their own options. These images, rather than constituting a fixed Pantheon, make up a vast collection of changing, fleeting myths.

As medieval writers conceived it, the history of France went beyond the past they were constructing, beyond the present with whose uncertainties they had to contend, and spoke of the future as well; for the medieval historian was also part prophet. The messianism of the French dynasty, unlike that of Germany, has never been made an object of study. Yet messianism existed in France, even if it came later than that across the Rhine. From the beginning of the twelfth century to the end of the sixteenth, many people believed in a glorious common destiny, a destiny in which the king of France—following a certain number of initiation trials—would become emperor first of the Western world, and then of the East and Jerusalem. Then would come the end of time. The dynasty had the potential to guarantee happiness, peace, and prosperity to all in a holy millennium that was the more ardently desired the more difficult life became. With each event, each crusade, each great victory—from Bouvines to the reconquest of Normandy—these same dreams returned.

This messianism played in two arenas. Among the educated the king disseminated prophecies in Latin that gave positive resonance to his power, sometimes even using them to formulate his policies: Charles VIII's Italian campaign followed the route that had been laid out in prophetic visions as early as the thirteenth century. But there was also a popular, folkloric form of messianism. The Children's Crusade of 1212 and the Pastouraux of 1251 set out to find and save the king in order that he might fulfill his messianic destiny. Since nothing like this occurred after 1320, it might seem that skepticism was then on the increase; but we need only look at popular literature and village festivals from 1450 to the beginning of the seventeenth century to discover a messianism personified by the allegorical *Bon Temps*—"Good Time"— whose adventures and future reign they celebrated. Next came utopia, when hope had been lost, when a dynasty no longer could bring happiness and peace, and the only hope lay in an imaginary world. Messianism was not absurd; it was the medieval equivalent of the idea of progress in the Third Republic or the rule of the proletariat in Marxism. The role was the same: to create a common project and to give assurances of stability and durability to a society that imagined itself to be both unique and representative of the whole of humanity. The belief that a state can guarantee happiness tomorrow, in consolation for the miseries of today, is a powerful legitimizer. For five centuries, the kings of France controlled that imagined future.

The nation also existed outside of time, as a symbol. In this book, I have followed the development of several symbols, above all those taken from heraldry. But medieval emblems formed a para-heraldic constellation that was far richer than heraldry itself. It is quite unfair to devote little more than vague introductions to this subject, as is usually done, on the premise that the first great books of emblems only appeared around 1510–1520. Medieval devices were not printed and are therefore more difficult to capture, but they were more than a simple intellectual game; they signaled the existence of power. Political parties and governments recognized one another by their colors and devices, representative of entire programs, reflective of the concerns of the times. Some that merit detailed study are *the sun*, symbol of imperialistic ambitions, which appeared from the reign of Charles V onward; the *flying deer*, symbol of the immortality of the king, used from Charles VI to Francis I. Though white was not a royal color in heraldry, it was in the realm of devices. The deer, cross, and band were all white, and white was the royal color of every generation since Charles V. The origin of the white flag probably lies somewhere in the story of emblems, though the white flag, we are usually told, did not appear until the war in the Vendée in 1793. The medieval source of the *coq gaulois*—the Gallic rooster—is another major candidate for study. It came very late to the scene, even though the pun on *gallus,* Latin for both "Gaul" and "cock," was widely known. Medieval bestiaries tell us why it took so long for this bird to become the emblem of France, for they associate the cock with the sin of lust—a most unedifying representation for the Most Christian nation. That sinful association began to disappear in the course of the fifteenth century, however, allowing this emblem to take on prominence as the ancestral Gauls displaced the Trojans. We need to recover for political history what has been rashly abandoned to art and literary history; for figurations of power have a power of their own.

This process of creating France was enormously successful; it was one of the most precocious and solidly unified nations of the West, capable of surviving devastating blows. Yet because it has been impossible to measure this strength directly, historians have usually been reduced to giving little more than a simple list of individual patriots. It would be far better to study the reason for that success in terms of media and public.

The first form of media the historian immediately thinks of is the text, in French or Latin. Any written document can bear the mark of national aspirations; the language of the text or its technical aspects only rarely make examination of it difficult. But prior to 1400, it was rare for national ideals to constitute the only topic in such texts. Studying such texts in and of themselves is therefore not particularly useful for our topic; rather, we should look at the size and the social and geographical spread of the audiences that they touched in successive generations. We already know quite well what the "best sellers" were: the 103 manuscripts of the *Great Chronicles of France* demonstrate that this text was the most popular. It was followed by Raoul de Presles's commentary on the *City of God,* which survives in fifty manuscripts. Next came three texts in French, with from thirty to forty surviving manuscripts for each: Alain Chartier's *Invective in the Form of a Quadrilogue,* the anonymous *Dream in the Pleasure Garden,* and Honoré Bonet's *Tree of Battles.* The success of technical texts can be measured by their more modest rate of survival: there are sixteen manuscripts for Jouvenal des Ursins's most popular work, *Listen to Heaven,* the same number for the Latin works of Alain Chartier, and ten manuscripts for the *Great Treatise* on the Salic Law. Then there are those texts whose audience was limited to readers in the royal library but which are very rich sources for us: Jean Golein's *Traité du sacre* or Etienne de Conti's chronicle. But we need to be careful. In some cases, we may find particular notions in only a very few manuscripts, whereas the ideas themselves seem to be widely known. The paucity of manuscripts could hide for us their transmission through another medium.

Some of these texts were officially commissioned: the histories composed at the abbey of Saint-Denis, for example. Others were dedicated to the king, and we do not know if they were written on royal commission or not. Still others were produced independently. Some kings, like Philip the Fair, Charles V, and Charles VII, made it a point to carry out an active campaign of national propaganda. From 1300 to 1500, the targeted public was first and foremost the nobility and those in service to the state. The nobility made up the largest group of owners of the *Great Chronicles,* the *Dream in the Pleasure Garden,* and the *Great Treatise.* Royal officials shared their interests. We know that notaries and secretaries to the king often composed treatises on political questions and works of national history, subjects to which they were led by their education, their professional activity, and the easy access they enjoyed to the archives. Jean de Montreuil, Alain Chartier, Guillaume Cousinot, Noël de Fribois, and Nicole Gilles all served in such capacities. The Parlement also played an important role. All those charged with tracking down manuscripts of the Salic Law in 1430 were or had been members of that court. After about 1450, servants of the state began to replace the nobility in this important role.

There is one other source not to be overlooked, a surprising one. During the late Middle Ages, Italy produced specialists in language, in fiscal matters, and in rhetoric. The celebrated historian Paulus Aemilius Veronensis wrote a history of France and a work *On the Antiquities of Gaul;* Orlando dei Talenti, a Milanese humanist and secretary to two bishops of Bayeux from 1434 to 1473, wrote the first discourse we have on the national holiday, July 14. Were we to study not the text itself in each case but the history of the text (who commissioned it, who owned it, who cited it), we would be better able to define the learned public that was touched by the national feelings it expressed. We could make greater room alongside our histories of events and people for histories of texts, treating their degree of success and their transformations over time.

But the written text was neither the most commonly used nor the most effective way to spread national feelings. In a society that was still primarily an oral culture, writing could only hope to touch a small elite group. In the written texts themselves, furthermore, the discourse was secondary to the symbolic images that existed independently. Generally, these texts appeared after the fact, and sought to explain the sense of a given image or the link between certain images. They presented explanatory schemas that were quite reductive: battle/victory, gift of a sacred object/victory, loss/recuperation, infection/purification. The characters described were stereotypical: the English were traitors, the king or France was the hero, God was the benefactor or the protector, the thing sought was national salvation or a worldwide empire. The narrative structure in these texts was equivalent to that in popular oral literature; they sought to reach a public much larger than could be reached by writing alone and reflected that public's mental categories. They owed their success to their simplicity and to their skill at incorporating the aspirations shared by all. We need to turn our attention therefore to forms of media that were far more humble, but whose emotive appeal was broad-based.

Images of the king and the nation were spread abroad in many different ways. The complex images of luxury manuscripts and tapestries, with their intricate allegories, enjoyed only limited audiences; only a limited number of workshops linked to the court won princely and royal commissions, indicative of prestige and rank. But an illumination could be reproduced in a church painting, an engraving, a printed pamphlet, or a drawing for a stained glass window, and in this way become very popular; the illustration of the Clovis cycle, painted in all probability by Henri de Vulcop, which appeared at the beginning of Raoul de Presles's *City of God,* was copied in many editions of the *Sea of Histories.* Heraldic shields, seals, and coins were visible for all to see.

The most popular images were those that appeared on coins. Though they did not present antique-style portraits of the king until the reign of Louis XII, they were nonetheless important vehicles of propaganda. The lilies on the coins of Louis VIII and Philip Augustus glorified the kingdom of Mary; those on the gros of Louis IX were interpreted as signs that the chosen people were protected by God (people continued to use the coins as talismans through the seventeenth century); Philip VI's ange d'or with its image of Saint Michael striking down the dragon was very much in keeping with the king's preoccupations at the beginning of the Hundred Years War. Coinage played the same role as medals did later in royal propaganda of the sixteenth and seventeenth centuries. From the second half of the fourteenth century onward, these images were protected by special legislation, and those who mocked them were quickly accused of lèse-majesté. Some of these images were imagined to have been relics belonging to Clovis, Charlemagne, Saint Louis, or other dynastic saints. They inspired collective visions and miracles and helped spread national abstractions as if they were sacred truths.

The primary means of touching the greatest number of people during the Middle Ages was without a doubt religion. Only the Church had the means to offer the royal house free dissemination of information across the entire territory, conveying a set of national ideas that themselves were very close to theology or mysticism. Though each village certainly did not have the benefit of a representative of the state, it did enjoy the presence of a representative of God. The parish's weekly sermon could convey a great deal of political news. It managed, in fact, during times of normalcy, to guarantee that people participated in national life. Every church could have a statue of Saint Louis, Saint Michael, or Saint Catherine. Of course, their clergy did not all react to royal demands in the same way. Some individuals and some religious orders tended to side with England, whereas others (such as the Celestines) supported the king. On the whole, however, the clergy were loyalist, and national propaganda was able to reach its public thanks to their help. Sometimes the king gave a special boost to their efforts: Belpech's statue of an armed Saint Michael confronting the states of Foix-Béarn in 1469 was hardly there by chance, and the same was surely true of a similar statue at Domrémy on the eastern border of the kingdom around 1415. It would be interesting to study the situation in each border zone: Saint Charles of Blois stood watch over the Breton border; Saint Julianus and Saint Nicholas guarded at the border of Burgundy. In addition to these statues, we need to pay attention to the confraternities dedicated to national saints; the statues and confraternities together assured that information would be communicated at the parish level.

There was also a rather complicated network of national and provincial sanctuaries which relayed both information and national feeling. From the early twelfth century to 1415, the communicative power of the abbey of Saint-Denis made itself felt throughout the kingdom and across the borders as well. Joyenval took up the baton during the second half of the fourteenth century. After 1330, Mont-Saint-Michel also wielded great influence, outside as well as within the kingdom. A network of influential regional centers existed as well, at Fierbois, Limoges,

Noblat. More limited were local centers such as Le Dorat, whose sphere comprised only about ten villages.

The nature of the public in each case varied according to the sanctuary in question. We can hypothesize that the audience they reached was more rural than urban; Parisian sanctuaries retained their influence through the early fourteenth century, but those that grew up after 1350 were almost all rural. The tendency became more pronounced during the fifteenth century: there was no town at Joyenval or Cléry or Béhuard, nor at Mont-Saint-Michel or Saint-Michel-en-l'Herm. Were the peasants won over? Joan of Arc offers one kind of answer, but it is an answer to a specific situation; we have another in the lists of peasants who were executed for pillaging in Normandy during the English occupation between 1416 and 1450. The English were at first rather well received but, after 1430, the population began to resist. More than 90 percent of those executed came from rural areas: they represented peasants of all kinds, some relatively well off, some village artisans. The hundreds of names listed with professions and dates offer the finest testimony available to the degree of national feeling that had developed among them.

In addition to the social effectiveness of the propaganda, we must also consider its geographic effectiveness. National feeling first saw the light of day in Paris and at the abbey of Saint-Denis. For a long time the phenomenon was restricted to the Paris basin, for a longer time in fact than was the state that had given birth to it. Neither Vienne nor Clermont, nor even Orléans nor Chartres, believed that Saint Denis had been the Areopagite; until the end of the twelfth century this notion was confined to Paris and Reims. When in 1317 Yves de Saint-Denis claimed the whole kingdom had been converted by the Areopagite, it was still the north of France that he was really talking about; the south barely figured among his evangelizers. And Georges Duby has pointed out that the decisive battle of Bouvines in 1214 was hardly mentioned south of the Loire River. Some regions that belonged to the kingdom were not yet integrated ideologically. With few exceptions, national feeling was a delayed response to Capetian annexation.

The Parisian area continued to play a decisive role in the story until 1415, harboring most of the royal sanctuaries. The frontier zones also had an important part to play: the eastern frontier where Jean de Montreuil and Joan of Arc were born; the fluctuating, much disputed Gascon border above all, where from the thirteenth century onward the inhabitants nurtured a hardy hostility toward the English. After 1415, the situation changed. The Parisian region disappeared from the scene almost altogether. For a century, the Loire Valley became the center of the kingdom. Different areas of France were moved by national ideology at different times. Were there some that missed it entirely? Until 1453, Gascony remained quite estranged from the kingdom. The Pyrenees and Roussillon were relatively unmoved, and Béarn and Navarre by tradition were quite hostile. From the Montfort accession in Britanny in 1365 and the reign of Philip the Fair in Burgundy, those provinces had other options. As for Flanders, it had very mixed feelings toward the kingdom. Though its patricians were *leliaert*—"lilied," pro-French—the artisan guild-members favored autonomy.

Studying the relative success of the idea of nationhood in terms of the media clarifies how the nature of its public changed over time, both socially and geographically. Integrating the images of the nation with the national sanctuaries allows us a more global and also a more refined grasp of the subject. Would this approach be applicable to more recent periods as well? The cult of Notre-Dame-des-Lumières may be related to the appearance of the sun motif as a royal emblem after 1663. It spread further with each annexation and thus seems to parallel the phenomenon of border sanctuaries in the fifteenth century. Although the influence of written, secular forms increased after 1500, folk versions of the royal religion continued underground until the French Revolution dismantled all these old networks of communication. It is therefore quite unfair to conclude, as Eugen Weber has done, that the French peasants of the nineteenth century were untouched by national feeling until the Third Republic. In fact, there was a passage from one France to another, from one medium to another. Though the Third Republic fashioned a particular kind of France through its compulsory schooling delivered in a single language and designed to imbue all children with a particular vision of the history of France—a France that was abstract, secular, and unified—this was in fact only one version of France among many. It was not the first and will probably not be the last.

In the fifteenth century, the form of national discourse that enjoyed status as the official discourse, the voice of the majority, was not the only one heard in the kingdom. The ideal of the nation in the Middle Ages did not have the imperialism of the nineteenth century. It was one ideal among many. The Church continued to remind the individual that his first duty was to love and serve God. Next came love of all men, especially all Christians. On the scale of virtues, love for humanity and for one's neighbor was intermediate between love for God and love for one's country. Even if some were worried about meeting the English in heaven, the king and his people had greater responsibilities toward Christianity than toward the nation. And below the value of national duty stood various regional attachments, which were especially strong in the larger principalities. These were not very different from the national feelings that the monarchy promoted, though they appeared later; and partisans of the king insisted that they should be balanced among one another, each in its own place, rather than that one should exclude all the others. Medieval national ideology was by and large not capable of centralizing. One could be French and Breton at the same time, and, though one loved his place of birth very much, one owed primary allegiance to the most important community. So said the Church, and the king took up the refrain. In real terms, of course, life was not so simple.

Aside from this national discourse, opposition discourses were created by different political parties. For a long time, historians have believed that medieval parties were merely factions of clients without any ideological base. But the words produced by these parties, though difficult to interpret, can indeed be recovered, and they tend to privilege other values than that of the nation: the reformation of the kingdom, fiscal justice, the choice of good officers, and peace with England. They body forth images of an ideal time in the past, a time when their major ideas were actualized: the days of Saint Louis, perhaps, or later of Charles VII. It would certainly be possible to study temporal dreamworlds like these in a systematic way. They are no less real or fictive than the geographical other-worlds that were so dear to leftists during the 1960s. The eras of Lord Charlemagne and of good King Henry IV still have much to teach us.

The ideal of France occupied a large portion of the realm of values, but not all of it, for France depended on God. The ideal created faithful and fervent solidarities, reunited a divided community by promoting love and accord and expelling the enemy beyond the borders—into chaos, the deep forest, and the night. It was an ideal based on emotions, one which spoke of love more than of duty. Yet it succeeded in persuading people to accept the changes that were needed to ensure the survival of the group and to pay the regular taxes and to support the permanent army to defend it. The people agreed to pay, and the nobility agreed to die; the clergy awarded entrance into paradise for goods contributed and for death in battle. The uniqueness of this ideal merits recognition: it was founded on race, on religious feeling, on respect for hierarchies—

varied and unified. It was very different from the Frances that have come since: neither egalitarian nor secular, neither grounded in the idea of the land of liberty nor in the idea of linguistic unity or literary genius. But this earlier France was the consoling mother who sustained hope for each of her sons, from the king down to the humblest of the fold. It was an ideal whose powers worked. In that age of great catastrophes, it was this France personified who saved the France of history.

APPENDIXES

APPENDIX TO CHAPTER 3: THE CULT OF SAINT LOUIS

As far as I know there is only one partial study of the cult of Saint Louis, based on a survey of the parishes that are now dedicated to Saint Louis, data that are difficult to interpret historically.[1] Saint Louis is the patron of only 0.5 percent. The reasons for this tiny number are easy to undertand. Most parishes already had titular saints by the thirteenth century, so Louis could only replace saints who had the same feastdays as his—Saint Bartholemew (24 August) or Saint Genesius (25 August)—or become the patron of new towns such as Montjoie, Saint-Louis-d'Aude, or Saint-Louis-de-Dordogne. His patronage was very unevenly distributed through the kingdom: relatively frequent in the Parisian basin, the lands of Alphonse of Poitiers, and in the Atlantic provinces, it was completely absent from ten modern departments in the Massif Central, Champagne, Burgundy, Franche-Comté, and Lorraine. Given that the monarchy in the seventeenth and eighteenth centuries undertook to distribute the centers of the royal cult more evenly throughout the kingdom (Saint-Louis-de-Brest, -de-Lorient, and -de-Rochefort all date from the seventeenth century), the cult more certainly was very unevenly spread in the late Middle Ages and must have been above all a Parisian phenomenon.

Since parish dedications are not particularly revealing, it seems more profitable to examine the religious offices dedicated to Saint Louis and references to his feastday in manuscript breviaries. In an effort to generate a geography and chronology of his cult, we will try to relate the results of this survey to information on the distribution of statues of Saint Louis. The work has already been done on the religious offices, though the results are not very encouraging for us.[2] There are five offices specifically dedicated to Saint Louis, written between 1298 and 1450. Only one, entitled *Louis, the Honor of*

Sovereigns, which the Dominican Arnaud Duprat wrote on commission for Philip IV in 1298, was widely used for the feast of August 25. It seems that celebrants often chose simply to recite the normal office of confessors, inserting the king's name, for the other offices were not often used. *Exultamus omnes* appeared occasionally in Paris and Rouen for the feastday of May 8, the anniversary of the translation of the skull of Saint Louis to the Sainte-Chapelle in 1306. Elsewhere this occasion was not celebrated. September 30, the date when Charles V raised the relics of Saint Louis, was celebrated only at the Sainte-Chapelle. At this church then, there were three observances for Saint Louis, documented for example by the breviary of Charles VIII: May 8, August 25, and September 30.[3]

The fact that we have material on only a very small number of offices dedicated to Saint Louis, the fact that only one predominated, prevents us from drawing clear conclusions, though the breviaries provide us with a large series: their number lessens only toward the end of the fifteenth century when breviaries began to be printed.[4] Relics also provide a test of the spread of the cult. Most were in the Parisian area centered on the Sainte-Chapelle and Saint-Denis; there were also many secondary centers such as Poissy, Le Lys, Maubuisson, Evreux, and Meaux. Louis's psalter, clothing, hairshirt, and judicial staff were venerated at the mendicant convents of the Parisian basin. Other relics were in England at the chapel at Windsor Castle, in Italy, at Monreale and Bologna, and at Malta (Louis XII gave the saint's crusading sword to the Order of Malta in 1504). The royal house and the abbey of Saint-Denis helped spread the cult when they distributed these relics. In 1392, for example, Charles VI gave packages of relics to the dukes and the pope; they were to become the focal point of the cult of Saint Louis at Dijon, Moulins, and Avignon.

Mendicant convents also had a founding role in this story, convents that may have celebrated the memory of Saint Louis in dioceses unfamiliar with his feastday. Also, the personal preferences of the great personages, of abbots, bishops, and princes, made important contributions. Some families threw their unquestioning support to the cult, either because their lineage could be traced back to Louis and they felt it beneficial to their own prestige to broadcast the fact, or because some of their family members were named Louis. The families of Anjou, Lorraine-Vaudémont, and Laval, the dukes of Bourbon (whose line went back to Saint Louis's son, Robert de Clermont), and Louise de Savoie all celebrated the cult of Saint Louis.[5]

Despite the papal bull proclaiming Louis a saint and despite decisions taken by various national assemblies asking for celebrations of the feastday of the king-saint throughout the kingdom, the realities of cultic practice varied considerably from place to place. During the fourteenth century there were many allusions to celebrations of Saint Louis in Paris and its region. Celebrations appeared at the royal chapel, from the reign of Philip the Fair to Charles V, and also at the great convents and most of the Parisian parishes. Maubuisson, Royaumont, Le Lys, Poissy, and Evreux became cult centers and eventually developed into sites of pilgrimages and miracles. Towns in the valleys of the tributaries of the Seine (Beauvais, Meaux, Senlis, Laon) also played an important part; they supported the revolts of 1358 and then became followers of the Burgundian party. This zone, where the cult of Saint Louis appears to date back to the beginning of the fourteenth century, was limited to the areas north of Arras and Corbie in the Artois and south of the border of French Flanders, which itself seems to have remained untouched by the phenomenon. In the southern and southeastern regions the cult extended to Orléans and Sens. Normandy, one of the hotspots of French patriotism since its conquest by Philip Augustus in 1204, was also well represented at Bayeux, Rouen, and Sées. There were also two areas outside the greater Parisian basin. In the southeast, in Languedoc and Provence, the cult was first introduced by Louis's brother, Alphonse of Poitiers, and by the house of Anjou; there both Saint Louis of France and Saint Louis of Toulouse were celebrated. The cult also came to French-speaking parts of Brittany at Nantes and Saint-Méen.[6] The Franciscan's love for all things French and the influence of the Penthièvres explain why royal cults for Saint Charles of Blois and Saint Louis developed there. Both the exile of Duke Jean IV and Charles V's near incorporation of Brittany to France reinforced these tendencies.[7] But at the end of the century, whole areas of France still remained untouched: there was no cult in Burgundy; nothing in the southwest, an area that we know did not cherish the memory of Saint Louis (aside from one inconclusive reference to Louis along with four other saints, entered at Limoges for the date August 25). Thus, aside from Orléans and Moulins after 1292, Saint Louis did not appear in the ecclesiastical calendar of the Kingdom of Bourges.

In the fifteenth century, however, while Paris and its immediate surroundings (Chartres, Evreux) remained the center of devotion, the cult began to spread. The importance of the valleys of the Oise and Aisne continued: Compiègne and Noyons joined the ranks of worshippers. In the north, the borders of the cult moved to the edge of the Empire—at Boulogne, Cambrai, and Thérouanne—and took hold in French enclaves such as Tournai. But the biggest changes came in the south. The entire kingdom of the Dauphin Charles began to pray to the great Capetian saint: at Bourges, at Tours, Loches, Poitiers, and at Saintes; the Duchy of Bourbon feted him at Moulins and Clermont. To the southwest and in French-speaking Brittany, however, little changed. Thus during this period the untouched areas were reduced to Gascony, the Pyrenees, Burgundy (except for Dijon and Cluny), Dauphiné, and Celtic Brittany. But they were still palpable exceptions.

The distribution of various kinds of material memorials to Saint Louis (stained-glass windows, frescoes, and above all statues) supports this testimony.[8] In the fourteenth century, the Parisian area and the western region were particularly well represented in this regard; they were the only areas where important cycles were displayed (most notably at the Sainte-Chapelle and at La Trinité in Fécamp). There were many statues, the most famous being the one at Maineville, commissioned by Enguerrand de Marigny. There were others in the regions of the Oise, the Marne, and the Eure, where they could be found even in the smallest of parishes. The southeast however had very few, and Brittany none.

In the fifteenth century, Paris and the western area continued to be leaders:

there were the windows at Carentan, Le Mans, and especially at Saint-Saens. The Kingdom of Bourges did not participate in this phenomenon, for the war did not permit the luxury of construction. The Bourbonnais, however, was very active, with its Palais de Justice, the Sainte-Chapelle at Riom, the cathedral at Moulins, and the church at Aigueperse. There were also two regions to which the breviaries do not testify which actively portrayed Saint Louis in stone, paint, and glass. In Celtic Brittany, statues of Saint Louis fashioned in a popular and simple way now began to show up all over: at Loc Maria, Pléherel, Moreac, Chateauneuf-du-Faou, and Pont-Aven. Most appeared after the duchy had been absorbed into the kingdom and bore witness to the growth of French influence in the area, but Saint Louis also appeared at Nantes, on the tomb of Francis II, the last duke of independent Brittany. In Burgundy and Franche-Comté, there were fifteenth-century statues at Arc-sous-Montenot, Flavigny, and Venarey-les-Laumes, and sixteenth-century statues at Arley, Lavans-les-Dole, Menotet, Gredisan, and even in the areas that had not yet been reclaimed at the death of Charles the Bold. The expanding political influence of France toward the eastern regions and the lands of the Empire thus manifested itself in religious terms. But nothing like this appeared in either Lorraine or Alsace, though we know that there was a statue of Saint Louis at Domrémy.

The Burgundian and Breton statues were rare variants of the statues found in the Parisian centers where the iconographic canon of Saint Louis had been set. Whereas the Parisian examples represented the king with the scepter, the Crown of Thorns, or the Sainte-Chapelle, the outlying regions portrayed him holding a book, most likely his psalter. Sometimes he held gloves in one hand.[9] Perhaps in the latter case, these were statues of the confraternity of cloth merchants, or perhaps they bore allusions to an exemplum that has since been lost: the gloves may have represented the sacerdotal gloves (Saint Louis apparently traveled with numerous relics), or they may have been the gloves that the French kings from Charles V onward wore for their coronation, or, then again, they may have been a judicial symbol, representing the idea of commitment, or a challenge to the infidels.[10]

We do not know how to interpret the rise of the cult of Saint Louis in areas where he had been little heeded. On the one hand, perhaps it was indicative of a realignment with the dominant ideology of royalty and the nation. On the other hand, the king may have been given the role of supporting provincial freedoms.

APPENDIX TO CHAPTER 6: THE LISTS OF PRIVILEGES OF THE KING AND THE KINGDOM

To late-medieval writers both the king and the kingdom enjoyed a certain number of privileges by the simple fact of being Christian. Varied in origin, some were inherent, others conferred; and as early as the thirteenth century, efforts were made to classify them in meaningful ways.

One way was to consider them to be divine gifts—called "celestial signs," "dignities," "perfections," "recommendations," or "approbations." Another was to think of them as giving a particular kind of superiority—as special honors, the preeminence of the king, or the preeminence of the kingdom.[1] But whether they emphasized the king's link to God or his position as head of Christendom, the items they listed were few in number and varied little in terms of order: the sacring of the king with the Holy Ampulla and his power to cure scrofula were ranked in the highest category by Guillaume Guiart around 1300, by Raoul de Presles in the second half of the fourteenth century, and by the jurist Guillaume Benoit at the beginning of the sixteenth.[2] These two privileges were generally tightly linked: one was the result of the other. To these, the publicists of the reign of Charles V added God's gift of the royal insignia—the fleurs-de-lys and the oriflamme, the group as a whole signifying that the kingdom was held of God alone (though "the independence of the kingdom" was sometimes listed as a fifth privilege in the lists of the end of the fourteenth century and the beginning of the fifteenth).[3]

In the period of Charles VII the schema was radically revised into lists of seven or nine privileges, a change that sprang directly from the political situation at the time. First the Salic Law took a place of honor often coming just after the unction and before the fleurs-de-lys and the oriflamme, a rampart raised against the English. It was of divine origin and unique to France. The law first appeared in lists drawn up by Chancellor Gerson and Pierre d'Ailly and reached its fullest development in the works of the jurists of Charles VII.[4]

Later, following the Pragmatic Sanction of Bourges of 1438, the king's prerogatives with respect to the Church of France were added to the list in the form of either two or three "privileges." These "privileges" had in part originated during the Schism, when the repeated removals from and returns to obedience to the popes had allowed the monarchy to intervene directly in the life of the Church. In part they had originated in papal concessions. And publicists pointed to both the king's sacred character—half layman, half cleric—and to these papal concessions in defending the royal control that the Pragmatic Sanction affirmed.

The king's ecclesiastical prerogatives had long been the subject of particular attention in the royal archives.[5] Between 1307 and 1324, Pierre d'Etampes had assembled all 800 papal bulls conserved there. As this collection was quite unwieldy, Charles V ordered that it be replaced by summaries of the sixty-three most important bulls of perpetual privilege. (The list drawn up by Pierre de Gonesse has since been lost.) And between 1375 and 1391, Gerard de Montaigu the younger assembled for the royal library a chronological collection—with French summaries—of about eighty bulls, a collection known throughout the fifteenth century as the *Liber liliorum*—the *Book of Lilies*.[6] The jurist Jean Ferrault was not the first to appreciate its usefulness.[7] The "spiritual privileges" that eventually appeared in the lists were thus already a selection from a selection. The list dating from before 1461 which appeared in the *Miranda de laudibus Franciae* (The Wonders in Praise of France) of the Archbishop of Toulouse, Bernard du Rosier, shows what was retained.[8]

Bernard, who favored a moderate and balanced form of monarchy (foreshadowing the ideas of the theoretician Claude de Seyssel), composed his *Miranda* in the form of a list of "privileges," with a chapter devoted to each—nine privileges, nine chapters, nine justifications for the epithet "Most Christian." He began with the personal privileges of the king—those related to unction, scrofula, the fleurs-de-lys, and the oriflamme. Next came the general privileges, drawn from the papal bulls in the *Liber liliorum*: the right to be a cathedral canon, to give Church prebends, to appoint papal legates, to be free from excommunication and interdict. Last came the most original privileges: the king of France had no superior in the world and, finally, France was better organized than any other state, because of its Salic Law, its Parlement, and the twelve Peers who guided the actions of its kings.

A list similar to, though more succinct than, Bernard's can be found in the chancery formularies of Charles VII and Louis XI,[9] sometimes adding indulgences for those who prayed for the king and the king's right to tax the property of the Church.

The reign of Louis XI brought no innovations. But the wars of Italy, with their attendant tensions in the relations between the French king and the emperor and pope, brought a renewed need to define precisely the place of the king and the kingdom in the divine order of things, and with it a fresh spate of lists, composed between 1485 and 1510.[10] The jurists Cosme Guimier, Etienne Aufreri, and Jean de Selve laid the groundwork for the classical and, for the most part, definitive version—Jean Ferrault's list of twenty privileges of the kings of France (composed around 1509 but not published until 1520).[11]

Ferrault's treatise was more a recapitulation of medieval thought on the *privilegia regni* than the announcement of a new approach to the subject. The celestial signs of the thirteenth and fourteenth century are all there—the title "Most Christian," the unction, scrofula, the holy lineage, the Salic Law, the recognition of no superior in this world. Ferrault asserted that he had drawn his inspiration from the *Liber liliorum* and asked Louis XII to shelve his work alongside it in the royal library. In fact his third privilege and his fifth through ninth came from the *Liber,* including indulgences for those who prayed for the king, the right to receive revenue from vacant bishoprics, protection from excommunication and interdict, the right to be a cathedral canon, as well as others.

Ferrault's innovativeness did not lie here, but rather in his privileges fifteen through nineteen, which defined royal sovereignty in the civil sphere, such as the right to ennoble and the sole right to summon assemblies. Much of this too was old. The Salic Law had taken its place among the *privilegia* by 1400; Bernard du Rosier had introduced the idea that Parlement, the twelve Peers, and an independent legislative power were privileges of the kingdom; the *Allegations* of Vincent Cygault and the 1496 *Treatise Concerning Parlement*[12] contributed their definitions of "royal cases" which tended to enlarge the rights of the king yet further. But althought the *jura regni*—"the rights of the kingdom"—were steadily growing more secular toward the end of the fifteenth century, no efforts were made to clarify the nature of royal sovereignty itself. Interest concentrated rather on establishing those rights that other kings did not have, rather than the rights that were in and of themselves attributes of sovereign power. The secularization of the notion of jura regni was therefore a relative thing.

Jean Ferrault's compilation enjoyed an enormous success throughout the first half of the sixteenth century. Complemented by the works of Barthélemy de Chasseneuz and Charles de Grassaille, it inspired the Chancellor Duprat's policy of accord between Church and State, following the Concordat of 1516. As the culmination of the medieval tradition, it slowly erased the memory of the complex path the evolving lists of royal privileges had taken in the course of the Middle Ages and became, instead, one of the founders of the modern list of fundamental laws of the kingdom. Henceforth, references would no longer be made to celestial signs or to privileges; the composite whole became jura regni, the rights of the kingdom, with their own unique origins, rights that were specific to the convergence of this particular royal line and a particular people on one and the same land.

APPENDIX TO CHAPTER 8: TROJANS AND GAULS IN THE FIFTEENTH AND SIXTEENTH CENTURIES

It is generally thought that the legend of the Trojan origins of France first appeared in the seventh century and continued unchanged into the latter half of the sixteenth,[1] as "the Trojan heroes continued to be the mythical ancestors of the new states."[2] The legend ran as follows: Francio and his companions fled burning Troy and founded the city of Sycambria. At the request of Emperor Valentinian, who granted them ten years exemption from tribute, they decimated the Alans who had taken refuge in the Meotide Swamps. Ten years later, refusing to take up the burden of tribute, they withdrew to Germany. Then, in the fourth century, from their base on the banks of the Rhine, they penetrated into Gaul with Marcomir. The legend, then, concerned the origins of the Franks. Of the Gauls it said not a word, for they belonged to ancient history not to the history of the Franks.

We know, however, that the Italians abandoned their own legendary Trojan origins around 1450, and the Germans did the same seventy years later, replacing them with claims to indigenous roots. We have to suppose that French historiography remained unchanged, proved quite impervious to outside influences, despite the wars in Italy and the invention of printing. Was that true? The sources are varied and widespread, for those written in the kingdom in the fifteenth century sprang from a long and complex tradition and a peculiar typology. Within that tradition, early fifteenth-century authors made decisions about who had been the leader of the Trojan migration, about the geography and chronology of their move, and the manner of their settlement in Gaul. These represented new concerns. And from 1450 onward, doubts about the whole story appeared, sometimes leading to outright negation. At the same time, a Gallo-Hebrew tradition was growing, which culminated in the works of Jean Lemaire de Belges soon after 1500.[3] And with this reappearance of Gaul, the story of the Trojan origins of France shrank to a single, secondary episode in the larger story of Gaul. For the story of Gaul was just as long, just as glorious, and it was better documented. After 1500, people were no longer concerned with the question of the origin of the Franks; they had taken up the problem of the origin of the Gauls, and in the course of the century, that story grew increasingly distinct from both biblical and Trojan history.

THE TYPOLOGY OF FIFTEENTH-CENTURY VERSIONS

The French legend, based on the antique model of the founding of Rome by Aeneas, sprang from two texts from the end of the seventh and beginning of the eighth centuries.[4] These texts were very different from each other. Around 660, Fredegar introduced Francio, the son of Friga and brother of Aeneas, in his *History of the Franks.* Francio, who was related to the Turks and Macedonians, established, he said, a powerful kingdom between the Rhine and the Danube, fought off the Alans, and earned the name of *Frank,* meaning ferocious. The second text, the *Deeds of the Frankish Kings* of 727, placed Antenor and the young Priam at the center of the story. It was they who founded Sycambria on the Danube and fought off the Alans, earning a ten-year exemption from tribute. When they later refused to make tribute payments, they moved on to Germany. *Frank* in this version meant "free from tribute."

Carolingian texts added little that was noteworthy in the way of new details, and most of the twelfth-century universal chronicles merely integrated these two versions into one, Rigord adding only one important element at the beginning of the thirteenth: Ybor, he said, left Sycambria and founded Paris in the ninth century B.C.[5] During the thirteenth century, historical encyclopedias like the *Great Chronicles*[6] and Vincent of Beauvais's *Mirror of History*[7] popularized this compromise version, which from then on was the most common account. But this was never the only account; it was admittedly a composite, and did not do away with its own sources, which continued to offer possibilities for other mixed variants. Thus fifteenth-century texts were hardly stereotypical; there were important divergences among them on a number of fundamental issues. Many of them, however, avoided making choices and merely juxtaposed various options, using expressions like "some say . . . others say . . ." This gives us some perspective on knowledge of earlier texts during this period, but not on current preferences.

The identity of the leader of the migration was hotly disputed. Fredegar created Francio for this role and attributed to him a kingdom free of Roman rule between the Rhine and Danube. Around the year 1000 Aimoin of Fleury[8] adopted his story, and it passed from Aimoin to the *Great Chronicles.* Rigord and Guillaume le Breton[9] invented a far more prestigious genealogy: the leader was the son of Hector and the cousin of Turcus, the son of Troilus. The Franks were therefore descended from the royal family of Troy, from the heroic Priam and Hector (the latter one of the Twelve Worthies of chivalric legend). By the fifteenth century, it was at most out of habit that the epithet "son of Friga" continued to be appended to Francio's name.

This new genealogy, however, had its problems. Most ancient authors gave only one son to Hector—Astyanax, who died when Troy was taken. As the king of France had to be descended from the eldest son,[10] one was created who softened Greek hearts with his beauty; he was surnamed Francus, in honor of his courage. Others built their stories around Laodamas,[11] the creation of the ancient "Dictys of Knossos." This particular variant was popularized by Benedict of Sainte-Maure around 1180,[12] and a fourteenth-century chanson de geste described his conquests and revenge.[13] But around 1450, there were already some, like the Provost of Lausanne, Martin Lefranc,[14] who knew that the existence of Francio was not supported by the ancient texts. Then there were those who hypothesized about a bastard son of Hector,[15] or about a son born of Andromache in another marriage.[16] Francio, after all, was burdened with an inconvenient parentage: he was traced back to the Turks, through the intermediary Turcus, and to the English through Brutus. But the English and the Turks were the enemies of the most Christian king. By the end of the century, those versions that still told of Francio had eliminated both of these other Trojans.

In opposition to the hero Francio, who had neither substance nor any other intrinsic interest aside from the fact he served as an eponym for France, there often stood a character who was less well suited etymologically for the task but far more solidly attested by the texts. Antenor was Virgil's creation,[17] endowed with a happy fate: he founded Padua and Venice and gave his name to their people. "Dares"[18] and "Dictys"[19] completed the story of the uprooted exile, attributing to him a role in the Trojan War parallel to that of Aeneas: Antenor was one of the powerful leaders of Troy; disliked by Priam, he tried to defend himself and his possessions but ended by betraying his city when he brought the Trojan Horse within the gates. When Troy was taken, he handed over Polyxena and left with twelve thousand Trojans. In the eighth century, the *Deeds of the Frankish Kings* made him a hero and added a third part to the story: accompanied by the young Priam, he went on to establish Sycambria on the Danube.[20] The story met with enormous success. Around 1180, Dudo of Saint-Quentin adopted Antenor as the ancestor of the Normans;[21] Aimoin of Fleury and Sigebert of Gembloux claimed him as ancestor to the French.[22] In contrast, Vincent of Beauvais and the *Great Chronicles* made him simply one of the barons who escaped from Troy. The fourteenth and fifteenth centuries kept sight of him: for La Bouquechardière, Noël de Fribois, Martin Lefranc, and the *Antonine History,* he was the forefather of the French.[23] He took on human dimensions for Jacques Millet, who chose him to be the hero of the *History of the Destruction of Troy the Great.*

The appearance of Antenor brought both difficulties and rewards. He was more fully documented than Francio. Benedict of Sainte-Maure and Guido da Columna (d. 1276) cast him as the hero of their Trojan cycles;[24] Burgundian histories of Troy all included him. He was also linked to Italy, and these links took on added value when alliances were strong with Venice or with other towns of Northern Italy he was said to have founded. But Antenor was hardly an attractive figure; most texts called him a "nasty traitor,"[25] though some did credit him with having called for peace and with demonstrating "reason and good government."[26] He did not enjoy blood ties to the royal family of Troy, nor did his name provide a possible etymology for the name of the nation. And the legends of other places also laid claim to him.

MIGRATION AND ARRIVAL IN GAUL

The period the Trojans spent between the Rhine and the Danube gave rise to little disagreement. Though some early writers identified the setting of this part of the story as Thrace, or Scythia, or the marshes of Guelderland, by the end of

the thirteenth century most accounts had settled on Pannonia.[27] People imagined it to have been near Germany, where the Alans, it was said, lived in the
vicinity of the Lahn.[28] In the fourteenth century, Sycambria was first identified
as the capital of Pannonia, then with Buda (Budapest), which fifteenth-century
authors favored almost exclusively. At the end of that century, the great ruins of
the Roman town of Aquincum, near Buda, were identified as those of Sycambria; it is possible that the Hungarian delegation to the court of France in 1457
had described them, for at the beginning of the sixteenth century the herald
Pierre Choque, escort to Anne de Foix, bride to a king of Hungary, made a point
of visiting ancient Sycambria and singing the praises of its high walls and its
warm water springs.[29]

Since the Trojan's stay in Germany was thought to have lasted no more than
one or two generations, a very long period spent at Sycambria was automatically implied: a period stretching from the fall of Troy in the twelfth century
B.C. to the struggle with Valentinian in the fourth century A.D. Yet there were
few names to fill the void, so most accounts went no futher than to say there
were several dukes who were either unknown or who shared the same name.
Because fifteenth-century authors had a predilection for long chronologies, few
of them condensed the entire migration into only a few generations.[30]

Versions of the story might differ elsewhere, but they all agreed on the battle
against the Alans at the time of Valentinian. The details came primarily from
Fredegar: how at the emperor's request the Sycambrians fought the Alans, who
had taken refuge in the Meotide Swamps. The *Deeds of the Kings of the Franks*
added the story of the ten-year exemption from tribute (which everyone afterward remembered) and a story of the murder of two Roman legates (which later
writers prudently forgot).[31] Thanks to the *Great Chronicles*, the battle against
the Alans appeared automatically in all later tellings of the tale; but fifteenth-
century authors chose to emphasize even more the story of a second battle, this
time against the Romans in Germany, when the Sycambrians refused to pay
tribute after their ten-year exemption had ended.[32] Some accounts glossed over
the question of tribute and recounted the battle against Valentinian in a way
that implied that the Franks had never been subordinated to the Romans, a
"fact" of which sixteenth-century writers were convinced.[33]

The part of the story that changed the most from one account to another was
that of the Trojan's arrival in Gaul; it became a primary point of concern. Some
told how a massive goup of migrating peoples came into an unpopulated land,[34]
whereas others told of a single conquest[35] or of two or more waves of immigrants
arriving at a very early period. Rigord, invented this last remarkable idea, though
he failed to make full use of its potential.[36] As he told it, in 895 B.C., Duke Ybor
(whose name was the same as a Lombard leader mentioned by the fifth-century
Prosper of Aquitaine), led 23,000 Trojans toward Gaul, where they settled in the
area around Paris and the Romans subjugated them; they then welcomed
Marcomir, a later Trojan, with open arms. Guillaume le Breton told almost the
same story,[37] stressing the cordiality and unity that reigned between these two
groups of Trojan immigrants. The story then passed to the *Great Chronicles*, and
on to fourteenth- and fifteenth-century writers—to the poet Jean de Paris,[38]
Honoré Bonet,[39] and the chronicler Guillaume Cousinot.[40] But where thirteenth-

century writers had used this chapter of the story to establish a prestigious and ancient past for Paris while avoiding any reference to a conquest, those of the fifteenth century made it a way to think of all the "Gallo-Trojans" as natives or, if not that, at least as a people who had been in France for a long time. Marcomir arrived in Gaul earlier and earlier, until finally he became a contemporary of Francio.[41] The founding of Paris was set in the eleventh-century B.C., sometimes attributed to an anonymous individual,[42] sometimes to Francio.[43] Others thought the Trojans' arrival had been gradual, that there had been a first wave in the time of Francio, another with Ybor, and yet another with Marcomir.

Not only did people insist on setting an early date for the arrival, they also envisioned a kind of fusion between the two peoples, the natives and the new Trojan arrivals; together they formed a single harmonious people. The advantages of this consolidation were mutual. The Sycambrians contributed their knowledge of warfare and fortification; they freed the natives from the burdens imposed on them by bandits and Romans.[44] In return they were allowed to settle in a beautiful, fertile, well-bounded country, populated and peaceful, where they established themselves permanently and harmoniously. One unique variant delightfully illustrated this idea: Marcomir was raised and nurtured in Gaul by a native wet nurse; he married there, was crowned king, and eventually had a son, Gallus. Imagined history could hardly go further.

For Rigord, these Gauls had lived in the Golden Age. Fifteenth-century writers made them simple folk, holding everything in common, who each year chose councilors from among the wisest of their numbers; no wars threatened the open villages and fertile lands. When the Romans arrived they submitted peacefully.[45] Jean d'Outremeuse named their dukes, who were the eponymous founders of most of the towns and some of the provinces of France.[46] Most authors, however, credited them with neither monarchic rule nor written laws prior to the arrival of the Franks.

Just when did this people take on the real historical characteristics of the Gauls? From Rigord onward, they were called Galli. Jean de Paris—with his stories of Brennus and other leaders of pre-Roman Gaul—was probably the first to attribute specific exploits to them.[47] Raoul de Presles added a description of the government of the Druids.[48] In the fifteenth century, their identity grew clearer. Jean d'Outremeuse credited to his mythical dukes all that he knew of the deeds of Brennus, the wars against Caesar, and the revolts of Gaul under the Empire. Although many abbreviated chronicles continued to consider them a peace-loving people,[49] others began to allude to their military skills: "The Gauls' great reputation as knights was known by people throughout the world. . . . Like the Romans, they were descended from the Trojans . . . and were proud and disdainful of all subjugation."[50]

In this way, around 1475, the story of the Gauls began to add itself to the history of France;[51] the "Gallo-Trojans" had been in France since time immemorial and little by little became the historical Gauls. At one and the same time, then, parallel legends developed about the Trojan origins of the Franks—origins that were very far away and very foreign, but glorious—and about the Trojan origins of the Gauls, preoccupied with making the Trojans "indigenous," even though they were not glorious enough to eclipse the Franks.

The accounts of the Trojan origins written in the fifteenth century differed markedly from one another. Though they tended to place the preliminary stop-over in Pannonia and all elaborated a lengthy chronology, they disagreed on who had been the leader. Marked by the wars with Italy, those of the end of the century made the Franks into opponents of the Romans rather than their allies. Their war with the Alans as Valentinian's ally became a battle against him. The Gauls reappeared with a common Trojan origin. Yet from this time on, histori-ans joined a new concern with historicity and with establishing the people's roots in the land itself to their earlier preoccupation with the nation's distant and glorious origins.

FROM CRITICISM TO REHABILITATION

Meanwhile, in Italy, humanism was reviving the classical genre of historical writing, imposing on it certain formal traits drawn from Latin rhetoric as well as a secular, patriotic flavor.[52] Those who came under its influence now viewed with skepticism the legends of which earlier centuries had been so fond. The rediscovery of Homer, Diodoros of Sicily, Greek geographers, and Tacitus, and the publication of many translations and critical editions, began to change scholars' vision of the origins of nations.[53] Rome, now rediscovered, was ex-alted, by reaction devalorizing the barbarian peoples who had brought about its downfall—all the more so because texts now seemed to demonstrate that they were of more recent origin than the Romans.

Flavio Biondo (1388–1463) included no story of Trojan origins in his *De-cades*, the earliest of humanist universal histories,[54] and the Franks made their appearance only in the fourth century, in the context of Valentinian's wars. Biondo's patron Pope Pius II took a more complex approach.[55] In his earliest works, he accepted the classical version of the Trojan origins of the Franks; but in the "Asia" section of his *Cosmography*, he criticized the claims of all those who sought to establish ancient and glorious origins for themselves, whether it was the Germans, the French, or the English.[56] Troy was too small to have populated the entire earth. Pius retained the story of the Trojan origins of Rome, which had been attested from ancient times. But the other European peoples, he said, had descended either from the Germans or the Scythes, who were also the ancestors of the Turks. He drew his conclusions from a solid knowledge of the historical literature of France as well as from Homer, whose works Lorenzo Valla had recently translated. Though late-fifteenth-century his-torical works in Italy prudently said nothing more,[57] well before the French invasion of Italy historical writers there had stopped believing in the story of the Trojan origins of France. For them, the Franks were barbarian invaders, inferior to the Romans, who had first appeared in the fourth century. This attitude would bear rich fruit in subsequent polemics.

What effect did these writings have in France? Though the *Cosmography* found its way into French libraries, in the last decades of the fifteenth century only Robert Gaguin and Jean Lemaire de Belges were familar with Flavio Biondo and Marco Antonio Sabellico and with the translations of Lorenzo Valla. Around 1500, the jurist Jean Feu and the physician Symphorien Champier joined them. I have found no references to the Italian critics of the story of the Trojan origins of France prior to 1480, and no direct citations of Italian texts before 1500. It seems likely that what vague knowledge of Italian writings on the subject existed in France was brought by the Italian scholars who took up residence there in the last decades of the century: Paulus Aemilius Veronensis, Faustus Andrelin, and Michael Riccio of Naples all wrote histories of France, bringing to their works the new humanist conception of history and the changing Italian perception of the Franks. Their works were official commissions, and they presented only softened versions of the Italian critiques: Michael Riccio pointed out that Homer said nothing of Francio but quickly added that the name was perhaps a surname;[58] all peoples quite excusably tend to embellish the story of their origins, he added. Paulus Aemilius wrote indulgently of the genealogical pretensions of the Franks, while pointing out that Saint Jerome and Cicero had both considered these people to be of Germanic stock.[59]

Whatever the Italian influence may have been, French writers of the late-fifteenth century began to have doubts of their own about the story. The first objection they saw came from the many different versions in circulation, a problem that Rigord had already pointed out at the end of the twelfth century.[60] No official version ever succeeded in suppressing the others, and many complained with Nicole Gilles (d. 1503) of the "multitude and confusion of stories."[61] Fifteenth-century authors either simply listed all the versions they knew, or else tried to create a synthetic version that would somehow reconcile them all. Those who chose the first solution usually stuck with Fredegar and the *Deeds of the Kings of the Franks* or else the *Great Chronicles*. But some writers knew many others: around 1430, la Bouquechardière listed five.[62]

Unease with this situation appeared in learned circles around 1450. In the epilogue to his *History of the Destruction of Troy,* Jacques Millet wrote that, judging from the accounts he had read, the existence of Francio was not attested by any classical text. Robert Gaguin's doubts were more fully formulated.[63] He knew for certain that no classical authors had referred to the Trojan origins of the Franks, nor had Gregory of Tours. Jean Lemaire de Belges was also certain that there were "errors" in the French historical tradition, that its corruption made it seem laughable to knowledgeable people.[64] The silence of the ancients, some thought, could be explained: Roman historians were enemies of the Franks and therefore tended to minimize their accomplishments;[65] they were interested only in the history of Rome, while the Franks themselves produced few historians of their own, thus leaving their own beginnings in the dark.[66] Perhaps new texts, they thought, would be unearthed. But doubts remained.

At least three authors, indeed, went beyond such doubts to reject the Trojan story entirely.

At the end of the reign of Louis XI the Franciscan Pierre Desgros composed an encyclopedic work of theological and political knowledge, in the course of which he labeled the Trojan story "not truthful."[67] The Trojans, he said, were pagan and lacked in nobility; they worshipped idols and were rewarded with none of the Four Empires; thus even to claim kinship to them would be shameful. Furthermore, even if the kings of France were originally descended from the Trojans, there had been many breaks in the royal line since then. In any event, the story was not necessary to demonstrate that France was independent of the Empire; for Roman rule had been founded on conquest, not on right.

Early in the reign of Charles VIII, the Italian scholar Giovanni Candida expressed grave uncertainties about the story in the summary of the history of France that he wrote for the king.[68] The origins of the Franks, he said, were surely very noble, but all people want to enhance the glory of their ancestors, and this renders all human genealogies only plausible at best. Although some thought the story was a fable, he went on, it was surely conceivable. He admitted that he had no alternative to put in its place.

In the *Opus Davidicum*[69] yet another Italian Franciscan labeled the story a "poetic fable." He went further to assert that all claims to Trojan origins, even those of the Romans themselves, were false. Between the fall of Troy and the appearance of the Franks, many centuries had elapsed; a single race could not endure for such a span of time. Furthermore, ancient authors had shown that all the sons of Priam had died without offspring.

Thus the story of Troy increasingly seemed inadequate. The need for an ancient and noble inheritance was still there. But the tale of Trojan origins—of pagan and foreign ancestors whose very existence was poorly attested—had originated in the need to defend the independence of France from the Empire. By the end of the fifteenth century that was an obsolete problem.

JEAN LEMAIRE DE BELGES AT THE CROSSROADS OF TWO TRADITIONS

Just before 1500, Jean Lemaire de Belges resurrected the legend with his *Illustrations of Gaul and Particularities of Troy*. He had three concurrent goals. First, he wanted to replace the myth of the Trojan origins of the Franks with something else, or rather, he wanted to make a new adaptation, for the inadequacies of the old one had begun to appear quite clearly. He also wanted to incorporate the Gauls into the myth, for the substantial new knowledge of Gaul that had developed in the fifteenth century had given them new luster. In the twelfth century, Rigord had made the Trojans the ancestors of the Gauls. Lemaire de Belges now made the Gauls into the ancestors of the Trojans. He also tied them to the biblical tradition: the Gauls, he said, had issued from the sons of Noah; their religion, though pagan, was pure and spiritual; it foreshadowed the coming of Christianity.

The Traditions from Antiquity   What was the acquired classical learning on which he drew?

Until 1480, knowledge of ancient Gaul was limited to a small number of classical texts. In his abridgment of Trogus Pompeus, Justin described the expansion of the Celtic peoples across Germany, Hungary, Greece, and Asia Minor.[70] Livy described how Brennus and his Gallic forces swept down from Northern Italy and forced Rome to pay a heavy tribute in gold, weighed out on trumped-up scales.[71] But Caesar's *Gallic Wars* remained the primary source.[72] Here were two well-known passages: one on the borders of Gaul and its settlements, and the other on the habits and customs of its people. Caesar claimed to value druidic knowledge and religion and the wealth and military skill of the Gallic soldiers (for had he downplayed his adversaries, he would have devalued his own victories). Finally there was Isidore of Seville's description of Gaul, which identified the natural boundaries of the country and described the strengths of its people: they were famous for the whiteness of their skin, for their ferocity and resilience; some had settled in Cisalpine Gaul, others in Galatia in Asia Minor.[73] Greek sources on the subject, by contrast, (principally Diodorus Siculus and Strabo) remained unknown.

Justin and Livy appeared in many medieval libraries. Pierre Bersuire translated Livy for King John II in 1341. Justin was finally translated by Claude de Seyssel in 1520. Yet those who could only read French could find information from them in fourteenth-century French compilations of classical history,[74] especially the *Ancient History to the Time of Caesar*,[75] a much reduced, epic version of Livy, which contained, among other things, the story of the martyrdom of Rome at the hands of the "excessive legions" of Brennus. Its aim was to sing the praises of Roman exploits, overlooking anything that did not give the Roman point of view. It hardly lent itself to nurturing the story of Gallic origins.

The age of the Gallic Wars was more familiar terrain. In school, students read *The Gallic Wars*, Suetonius's life of Caesar, and Lucan's *Pharsalia*. Caesar was one of the Nine Worthies and found a place in every universal chronicle. His skill as a strategist and administrator made him a model of princes. Petrarch and Poggio Bracciolini had followed Cicero and castigated Caesar for burying Roman liberty,[76] but until the last quarter of the fifteenth century such criticism fell on deaf ears in France. Knowledge of Caesar through classical works, however, was rarer than knowledge derived from the *Deeds of the Romans*,[77] a very popular compilation drawn from Suetonius, Sallust, Lucan, and Caesar, which told the story of the Gallic Wars through Caesar's eyes; it did not give much of an account of the Gauls and added some false geographical information of its own. Around 1450, one reader made marginal notes on a thirteenth-century manuscript citing newer geographical references and reproaching the old account for its use of toponyms.[78] And after 1470, the work was no longer consulted.

Meanwhile, in 1473, Jean Duchesne translated Caesar for the duke of Burgundy, Charles the Bold.[79] Here, Gaul became illustrious, fertile, well populated, proud, and disdainful of any form of subjugation. Vercingetorix, blessed with a proud countenance, fought for the common good of Gaul, of which he was the guardian and good shepherd. "And to give them back healthy fortune, he offered his life and his death, if perchance his body might satisfy the Romans." It was only Caesar's triumph over the Gauls that enabled him to become emperor. Some time later, Robert Gaguin translated the same text for Charles VIII under the title *The Deeds of the Romans*. Any work that "acquaints us with the many things serving the glory of Gaul," he wrote in the prologue, is to be praised (though his own translation remained faithful to the letter of the text and to its pro-Roman bias).[80] This translation remained popular throughout the sixteenth century.

Thus, until the middle of the fourteenth century, real knowledge of Gaul was minimal, even in the most learned circles. Although works on ancient Roman history all mentioned Gaul, none of those that dealt with the history of France did so. It was only in descriptions of France inspired by Isidore of Seville that one could find some information—a list of its borders, praise of its abundant rivers, fertile lands, and healthful climate. *Gallia*, nevertheless, remained merely a geographical term.[81]

Over the following century, however, the Roman story of the Gauls began to become familiar, as authors drew on Raoul de Presle's prologue to his translation of Augustine's *City of God*, where they found a full translation of Caesar's account of the customs of the Gauls, the story of the siege of Paris, and an attempt to locate Gallic cult sites in the Paris region.[82] In the first half of the fifteenth century, Guillebert de Metz copied his material, to which he added a long passage from book 25 of Justin, containing an account of the eastern conquests of the Gauls.[83] And in 1467, Jehan Mansel's second version of his *Flowers of History*, composed for the duke of Burgundy, put together Livy's story of Brennus with Caesar's story of Vercingetorix.[84]

Soon afterward, authors began to go beyond mere compilation of Roman texts. Bernard du Rosier and Noël Fribois introduced their histories of the French people with stories of Gaul.[85] Jehan Massue, in his *Pearls of History*, praised the skills and habits of Gallic soldiers;[86] while Jean Germain wrote of the Druid senate at Chartres that meted out prompt and effective justice.[87] The praise that Robert Gaguin lavished on Gaul in his *Letter Against the Arrogance of the Castillians* of 1468[88]—citing its fertility, its prosperity, its soldiers whom the Romans were able to conquer only because of divisions among them— expressed a common sentiment of the time. For the rediscovery of ancient texts led more and more of the French to become familiar with Gaul and to see themselves as descendants of its ancient peoples. By 1480 a Frenchman was almost certain to boast of Gallic ancestors he would not have known he had around 1400.

The last two decades of the century witnessed the completion of two works that were particularly representative of this new tendency, both written by Italian scholars, one for the duke of Burgundy, the other for the cardinal of Bourbon.

In his *Index* to Caesar's *Gallic Wars*, written in 1475, Robert Marlian listed all that Caesar had reported about the Gauls.[89] He not only identified the geographical location of the peoples Caesar mentioned but also described what had happened in their provinces from then until his own time. He devoted half the articles to the story of the Belgians, whom he considered the ancestors of the subjects of Duke Charles. He also introduced a wealth of details about the Greek towns of Provence, which had been little known until then.

Paulus Aemilius Veronensis began his *Antiquities of Gaul* sometime before 1485,[90] the first work entirely devoted to the history of Gaul. In a rather gradiloquent prologue, he deplored the darkness that had so long enshrouded the history of its peoples, doers of great deeds, pious men and great soldiers, but without memorialists to sing their praises. He described how the Scythians had migrated from the Black Sea, sending some of their people to Gaul, and from thence to Germany, Spain, England, and northern Italy. At the time, he said, there were many Greek towns in southern Gaul, and when Hercules married

Galatea, the daughter of the Gallic king, Celtus, he gave many Greek customs to his new subjects. This led him to a description of Gallic institutions and religion, and, finally to a chronology of the various Gallic expeditions to Italy. A second volume was begun, wholly dedicated to the story of the heroic Brennus, the model of civic and military virtue, but with the death of his patron, the cardinal of Bourbon, he stopped abruptly in the middle of the siege of Rome. Paulus Aemilius introduced many innovations into his work. Its style obeyed the rules of classical history; the speeches—such as that of Brennus to his troops before the battle of Allia—followed the model of Cicero. He also drew on new sources: his story of the Celtic migration was based on Diodorus Siculus and Strabo, which he knew through late-fifteenth-century Italian translations.[91] Above all, his work was the earliest example of the particular kind of national pride that was coming into existence around 1500. He made the Gauls an indigenous population, settled on the land for a very long time, valiant warriors, deeply religious, and possessed of a brilliant civilization. With his elaboration of Gallic relations with Greece, he promoted the idea that these two civilizations were akin, an idea that would eventually give rise to Gallic Hellenism.[92] Gaul could be glorified at the expense of Rome. In these several ways, Paulus Aemilius prefigured the achievement of Jean Lemaire de Belges.

The Tradition of King David   As the Trojan story of the Franks was one of pagan origins, however, it ill suited the needs of a most Christian king. To meet those particular needs, other authors created a rival tradition that made the king of France a descendant of King David.

The origins of this myth are not clear. King David, with his lily crown and his blue and gold arms, served as a model for many rulers, including the Carolingians.[93] After Pepin's coronation, Pope Stephen II celebrated this "new David," protector of the Church. Charlemagne, Charles the Bald, and Frederick II were likewise called David, who became the model of the Christian prince: since the Christian Church had succeeded the Hebrews as the Chosen People, the emperor-in-chief of the Christians succeeded their kings; the king, the image of David, was his spiritual son, just as Christ was the image of and the son of God.

It is difficult to determine exactly when the kings of France first introduced these claims. In the *ordines* of the royal coronations of western *Francia*,[94] and most particularly the text from 877, the unction of the Hebrew kings was equated with the Holy Chrism of the kings of France. Around 1300, many prayers called upon the king to imitate David.[95] Guillaume de Sauqueville gave the title *Hosanna filio David* to a sermon he preached to Philip the Fair,[96] justifying this spiritual filiation with the assertion, first, that the Christians were the successors of the Hebrews, second, that France was the most noble and the freest of all Christian kingdoms and, third, that it was a prefiguration of celestial Jerusalem. Using the Holy Chrism, the king could work cures just as Christ and David had done. Guillaume recognized, nonetheless, that the king was bodily the son of earth, the son of a real family.

Following France's seemingly miraculous recovery from the English invasion in the fifteenth century, a notion of real kinship with David began to emerge. Pierre Desgros traced "the most noble line in the world" from Adam to Jesus;

then, he said, the empire was taken from the Jews because of their sins and transferred to the most Christian kingdom. He seemed to think of this as a real line of descent, rather than one that was purely spiritual, because at the same time he criticized the rival tradition of descent from the Trojan royal house.[97]

Finally, in 1491, a lengthy exhortation addressed to Charles VIII detailed the theme in precise terms.[98] The king, it claimed, descended directly from Adam and the divine creation of the world. The beginning of the line was clear: Adam, Abel, Noah, and Eber; it then continued through the line from Abraham and Moses to David and Solomon; Christ descended from David. With the diaspora of the Jews, some found themselves in Gaul, where they were the first to be converted to Christianity. Constantine was one of them; but the truly glorious rebirth of the race came when Pepin and Charlemagne took the throne from obscure Germanic barbarians who could not even claim Trojan origins. It was certainly advantageous for French kings to be able to trace their lineage directly back to Genesis, to the beginnings of the human race; theologically, it was preferable to the Trojan line, for it conformed to the traditional image of the most Christian king, heading the forces of Christendom in alliance with the pope, playing for all intents and purposes the role of an emperor.

Jean Lemaire de Belges   Historians have not given *The Illustrations of Gaul and Particularities of Troy*[99] the attention it has merited, most likely because of its anomalous form. It is a love story, a primer of princely education, an epic in classical style, and a work of history—a dense, complex book. Though very successful during the first half of the sixteenth century, it subsequently fell into disregard, in part because it was a compilation, in part because it was naive and marred by errors. Yet these are exactly the characteristics that allow us to determine what the French of the early sixteenth century expected from a myth of national origins.

Jean Lemaire de Belges wanted to restore to health a version of French history that he thought had grown corrupt and decadent. He wanted to erase mistakes in order to reestablish its credibility among men of letters. To accomplish this, he drew on a number of classical texts: on Homer in Latin translation, on Cato and Caesar. He also worked with fragments from classical historians recently unearthed (or, more likely, invented) by Annio of Viterbo. Lemaire was familiar too with numerous late-medieval Italian sources: Boccaccio's *Genealogy of the Gods*, Pope Pius II's *Cosmography*, Fra Jacopo Filippo of Bergamo's *Supplement to the Chronicles*, and Michael Riccio's histories.[100] Among French authors, his preference was for Robert Gaguin. Broadened by travels in Italy, Lemaire de Belges brought a number of humanist traits to his version of the story.

Drawing inspiration from these new sources, he transformed the story of the Trojan origins of France completely. He reduced it to a simple subplot in the larger narrative of the Gallic origins of France. Following Homer and two late-Latin forgeries by "Dictys of Crete" and "Dares the Phrygian," he described the Trojan War and the flight of Hector's son, Francus-Laodamas, to Gaul where he settled. On his way west, Francus founded Sycambria on the Danube, where his descendants built a great empire. Won over by the goodness of Octavian, these later Trojans were induced by the Romans to emigrate to Germany, from which they slowly penetrated into Gaul. There the Gallic descendants of Francus awaited them.

This version in some ways resembles those we have already seen. Lemaire de Belges took pains to establish the Trojans' early arrival, to eliminate the battles under Valentinian, and to symbolize the fusion of Trojan and Gallic populations by having Francus marry the daughter of a Gallic king. He chose, however, to incorporate it in a larger story that focused on the Gauls. This was his primary story.

In this new version, Gaul (which stretched from the Pyrenees to the Rhine and Alps) was first peopled by Samothes, fourth son of Japheth, who was himself the third son of Noah. Samothes's successors ruled over an educated people who were well-disciplined in their laws and dignified by their religion. They built cities and created universities. Hercules, husband of Samothes's distant descendant the beautiful Galatea, founded Alesia (the site where Caesar would later defeat Vercingetorix). A later descendant, after killing his brother, fled to Asia where he founded Troy, thus bringing Gallic culture to Greece. While war raged around Troy, the Gauls carried on their succession of kings and continued to bring honor to themselves in struggles against the Romans until the return of their own Trojan, Francus. They distinguished themselves not only through their skills at warfare but also through cultural wealth that they passed on to Greece and Rome. The originality of Gallic culture lay in its being pre-Christian. These sons of Japheth, who believed in the immortality of the soul, prohibited human sacrifice. They were not barbarian in the least.

Lemaire de Belges's revised version of the early history of France is thus centered on the Gauls, indigenous since biblical times, who surpassed the Greeks and Romans in war and culture. As a humanist interpretation, it made Gaul the source of all great actions and all civilization. As a Christian interpretation, it carefully linked the chosen nation to the Bible and to evangelical virtues. It thus joined two rival traditions, one secular and Trojan, the other Davidic and Christian. At the same time, it incorporated new knowledge about ancient Gaul. It established a coherent outline of events in a way that pleased a cultivated public. It corresponded precisely to what was expected from a myth of national origins in the fifteenth century: a story of glory rooted in the reality of the country.

Consequently, the story of the Gallic-Trojans replaced that of the Frankish-Trojans. The French nation, having grown in maturity and confidence, now became its own progenitor. Trojans and Frankish-Trojans were both of Gallic stock. Lemaire de Belges's skillfully reworked version, at once encompassing and reversing the old myth, met with tremendous success, which it continued to enjoy throughout the sixteenth century.

APPENDIX A TO CHAPTER 9: MANUSCRIPTS OF THE SALIC LAW

Up until 1418, only the manuscript of the abbey of Saint-Denis was used, though it was not the only one known. We have discovered by chance that Charles VII's confessor, Gérard Machet, saw and read a manuscript of the Salic Law at the library of Saint-Remi in his hometown of Reims before 1418.[1] This manuscript was, he reported, "similar" to the other. And in fact, there was a manuscript at the library of Saint-Remi in the fifteenth century which was so similar to manuscript *latin* 4628A that it was most probably the original for it:[2] it is Bibliothèque Nationale manuscript *latin* 10758. We do not know when or by the command of whom Machet took on his search; but he demonstrated his talents well, for these two manuscripts are the only ones of their kind that we know.

When the Burgundians captured Paris, and the duke of Bedford set up rule in the capital, the Dauphin had to retreat hastily to Bourges and Poitiers, forming a government essentially without archives. For a long time it had no access to the two known manuscripts of the Salic Law. Writers of memorials for the Dauphin between 1420 and 1425 knew the Law only by word of mouth.[3] This enormous gap explains how the legend of the text *Mulier in regno* persisted for so long. It appears in particular in the work of Jean Jouvenal des Ursins. In *Listen to Heaven of which I Speak* and the *Compendious Treatise on the Disputes Between France and England*[4] he asserted that one article of the Law entirely excluded both women and males descended through the female line, for, he said, many respectable authors claimed the Salic Law contained this clause and "they could not have done it without having seen it and known it was true"; some among the English who now hold Saint-Denis and its manuscript say that this clause does not literally appear in the Salic Law; but perhaps, he added, it does appear in other manuscripts.

The need to find a manuscript of the Salic Law and the hope of finding one with the *Mulier in regno* clause in it, pushed the government of Charles VII to try to locate other manuscripts, to have them read and copied so they could be used as proof against the English. Around 1430, at the time when the trilateral negotiations that would culminate with the Treaty of Arras were in the offing, Charles's government began to pursue this project in earnest.[5] A group of the king's trusted councilors received the charge: Christophe de Harcourt, Geoffroy Vassal, Renaud de Chartres, Gérard Machet, and the king's Norman secretary who wrote the *Mirror of History* of 1451. The members of this group resembled one another: all except for Machet were nobles; almost all had studied law or theology; all had practical experience dealing with charters—since Renaud de Chartres was the chancellor of France, Gérard Machet was the vice-chancellor of the university, and Christophe de Harcourt and Geoffroy Vassal were members of Parlement. All had been members of delegations to assemblies, to the pope, to the duke of Burgundy, or to the king of England. To fulfill their mission they visited the Benedictine abbeys near Poitiers; they did not seek elsewhere because their assignment was not to find *all* manuscripts of the Salic Law that might exist in the Kingdom of Bourges but, rather, to find one "good" manuscript that conformed to a predefined standard. They were to find the manuscript that most resembled those of Saint-Denis and Reims. In other words, they looked not for all the manuscripts of the Salic Law but only for what was thought to be the true text. Thus, it was enough to locate just one manuscript. In fact, it seems they found two, but ultimately only one was used: Geoffroy Vassal found it at Savigny in Poitou, and Gérard Machet transcribed it.

This manuscript raises several problems. First of all, which Savigny did it come from? Saint-Pierre de Savigny was a Benedictine priory, located thirty kilometers to the north of Poitiers. Notre-Dame de Savigny was located near Châtellerault, twenty kilometers northeast of Poitiers. The latter was probably where the manuscript was found, because its discovery was linked to the name of Christophe de Harcourt, and the Harcourts were the lords of Châtellerault, where the eldest branch of the family had lived since they had been forced out of their Norman fiefs. Their castle, no longer standing, but which remained in the family until 1447,[6] stood alongside the priory of Notre-Dame whose patrons they were. Unfortunately, we have no information about the library at Saint-Cyprien in Poitiers, the abbey to which Notre-Dame de Savigny belonged, and even less about the one at Savigny. As for the manuscript itself, we do know, thanks to Jouvenal des Ursins,[7] that it contained the Carolingian version of the Salic Law. Did it contain the appended texts that appeared in the manuscripts of Saint-Denis and Reims? We have no way to know.[8] After it was discovered, Gérard Machet went to Savigny to "translate this manuscript for the king,"[9] that is to transcribe it, to make an "authentic" copy, one that conformed exactly to the original and could serve as proof in the diplomatic dossiers to be prepared for the Treaty of Arras.

It is possible that Gérard Machet later worked on the Saint-Denis manuscript in the same way, around the end of 1440. "I stayed in Paris by orders of the king and I went to the monastery of Saint-Denis to see the earlier writings. Three times I went to see the king about these chronicles [he asked us] to examine or see concerning the work he has requested of us . . . ," he wrote in a letter to Pierre de Versailles.[10] The letter specified that what he was doing included work with chronicles, with anti-English memorials, and with *documenta*, original documents. The Salic Law could have been part of this last category of papers that the king was interested in.

Thus, the era of the kingdom of Bourges was a decisive one. Despite the obstacles in locating a manuscript of the Salic Law, the text of Article 62 was made available in both French and Latin, exactly as it appeared in the Carolingian text.[11] Around 1444, after Gérard Machet made his copies, Jouvenal des Ursins reintroduced what was in fact the *De Terra salica* in his *Compendious Treatise*. From then on, the text was definitively set. No translations were made of it, however, despite the fact that some thought of doing so: "This book is in Latin, at the Abbey of Savigny, and it was the king's wish to have it reworked into French in a clear translation, by a man of learning, for it could be very important in proving the story of Charles VII."[12] A complete translation would have been difficult and unwieldy. It was easier to give a page-length summary of the essence of the historical prologues, to add a translated version of Article 62 (the only important one), and in this way to popularize the most important elements that Charles's subjects needed to believe. The royal secretary Noël de Fribois launched this project in his second version of the *Mirror*.[13] It took its definitive shape in the *Great Treatise* of 1450.[14]

Three fifteenth-century copies survive of the Carolingian text of the Salic Law. Are they the results of the work of Charles's jurists? Manuscript *latin* 4631 was produced in the middle of the fifteenth century.[15] It includes genealogies, prologues, and the capitularies of Charlemagne and Louis the Pious that appear in both the manuscript of Saint-Denis and that of Reims. It is easy to demonstrate that these are copies of the Saint-Denis manuscript. The substitutes that appear there for difficult Germanic words have been traced back to the Saint-Denis manuscript, and this would seem to imply that the two manuscripts were at least temporarily housed together at Saint-Denis. In the manuscript, *De allode* appears under the rubric *de successione ab intestato*. As the author most certainly believed as did all others of his generation that the kingdom and "Salic land" were one and the same, the question of royal succession was synonymous with a case of succession without will, for the king can leave his kingdom only to his eldest son. Such an interpretation can only be traced to the reign of Charles VII and to attacks mounted against the Treaty of Troyes in 1420. This copy does not have a Saint-Denis library number from the second half of the fifteenth century but, as it was produced for the king, there is no reason why it should have remained at the Abbey. The only difference between it and the original is that it did not number the articles. Nonetheless, it did retain the subdivision of the Salic Law into three books. Is this the copy that Gérard Machet made around 1440? It is at the very least a copy of manuscript *latin* 4628A dating from the middle of the fifteenth century, a work that has had a long history, the work of a specialist. The copy is an excellent one; the equivalences most judicious.

There is also another copy that dates from about the same period. Curiously, it was joined to the 1451 *Abbreviated Mirror of History*, which referred to the need to transcribe the Savigny manuscript. But unfortunately, the beginning and end of this copy of the Carolingian Salic Law have been destroyed. It stops before Article 62. As a result, we cannot determine whether or not the original came from Savigny, Saint-Denis, or Reims. At the end of the fifteenth century, this manuscript was housed at an Augustinian convent of Saint-Pierre *Monasteriensis*, which we cannot precisely identify.[16]

The last copy appears in manuscript *latin* 4630. It dates from the end of the fifteenth or beginning of the sixteenth centuries and includes the Carolingian Salic Law with seventy articles, no prologue, and no later capitularies. Article 62 is underlined in red. This copy was probably made in Reims on the basis of either *latin* 10758 or *latin* 4789. It includes *De terra salica*, as do both of the others. Yet this was an unusual error. It is likely, therefore, that manuscript *latin* 4630 followed the manuscript of Reims.

It appears then that between 1430 and 1500, three complete copies of the three manuscripts of the Carolingian Salic Law were made and that these earlier manuscripts were those located in three different Benedictine libraries. Saint-Denis and Reims had been preserving objects sacred to the monarchy since the early Middle Ages. Their copies were complete, long, and very specialized. Savigny was a very small abbey. There, only the most essential part of the Carolingian text was copied, and this was a copy that may even have been cut to be included in a diplomatic dossier. After 1451, no one spoke any longer of the Savigny manuscript. All trace of it seems to have been lost. Pieces stayed in the possession of the Harcourt family. In 1470, the manuscript of Saint-Denis again became the standard version of the Salic Law.[17]

APPENDIX B TO CHAPTER 9: MANUSCRIPTS AND EDITIONS
OF THE GREAT TREATISE ON THE SALIC LAW

J. M. Potter has catalogued with great care the printed editions of the Great Treatise.[1] They include an anonymous one from Rouen dated 1488, another joined with the works of Pierre Rogier from Paris in 1522, a third published under the name of Claude de Seyssel in Paris in 1507, and two more, in 1541 and 1556, which were included in editions of Seyssel's *La Grande Monarchie de France.* Yet another was published in Hanover in 1700 in a volume of Leibniz's *Mantissa Codex Juris Gentium.* Each of these gives the same text, the 1507 Paris edition dating the original to 1464 and placing it under the general rubric *The Salic Law, First Law of the French.*

The manuscript versions of the treatise however present certain difficulties. J. M. Potter and R. E. Giesey[2] cite only a single manuscript, housed at the Bibliothèque Mazarine.[3] That there should be but one manuscript seems odd, given that so many printed editions of the treatise appeared in the sixteenth century; we should expect to find a number of manuscripts dating from the late-fifteenth century when handwritten texts were first being reproduced in print. The apparent absence of manuscripts presents a more formidable problem than one might think since, if the diffusion of this text began with the printed versions, then the spread of knowledge about the Salic Law would seem to begin very late, as late as 1488.

Searching for manuscript versions is hindered by the way manuscripts are catalogued. The catalogue of manuscripts at the Bibliothèque Nationale, for example, lists nothing under the names of Pierre Rogier or Claude de Seyssel, nor does it list the rubric "The Salic Law, First Law of the French."[4] But if we bear in mind that the anonymous treatise is organized around three successive sections—the right of the kings of France and England to the Crown of France, English rights to various seignories, and complaints about the violation of the truces of 1449—then the manuscripts become easier to find.

There are in fact at least ten manuscript copies of the treatise dating from the second half of the fifteenth century. P. S. Lewis has listed seven of them;[5] variations in the incipit have kept others hidden from view.[6] The title differs in different manuscripts: in one it is *Livre de la querelle de France et d'Angleterre,* in others it is *Traité des droits que le roi Charles a à la couronne* or *Justification de France contre Angleterre* or *Décision des différents qui ont été entre France et Angleterre* or *Discussion de France et d'Angleterre.*

It is difficult to date the text. Obviously it appeared sometime after the violation of the truces of 1449. Although the title suggests it was written for Charles VII, the only manuscripts we know of date from the reign of Louis XI, two of which are dedicated to this king.

Aside from King Louis, three other owners can be identified: Louis of Bruges,[7] Joan of France,[8] and Jacques d'Armagnac, duke of Nemours—owner of the one once housed at the library at the castle of the Carlat:[9] the manuscript bearing the arms of the House of Nemours must date from 1462–1477 when Jacques d'Armagnac held this title. Louis of Bruges, lord of Gruthuyse, was one of the great bibliophiles of his age; he was also an experienced diplomat and took part in negotiations with France and England for the Burgundian dukes, favoring an alliance with France. Joan of France, the wife of John II, duke of Bourbon, was a daughter of Charles VII; she received her manuscript in 1470, the year of the great reconcilation between Louis XI and the princes, including the duke of Bourbon, who thereafter remained loyal to the king.

The owners of these manuscripts comprised a small group of important people, people closely linked to the royal house. The fact that they owned copies of the treatise was symbolic of their ongoing or renewed allegiance to the monarchy. But these luxury manuscripts of the nobility made up only a third of those we have today. The remaining are common manuscripts, without illuminations, dedications, or armorial bearings. The owners therefore are difficult to identify.

LIST OF
ABBREVIATIONS

AA.SS.	*Acta sanctorum* (Antwerp, 1643–).
BN	Bibliothèque Nationale.
CCNF	J. A. C. Buchon, ed., *Collection des chroniques nationales françaises* (Paris, 1824–1828).
GC	J. M. E. Viard, ed., *Les Grandes Chroniques de France* (Paris, 1926–1953).
MGH	*Monumenta Germaniae historica.*
nouv. acq.	nouvelles acquisitions
Ordonnances	E. de Laurière et al., *Ordonnances des Rois de France de la troisième race* (Paris, 1723–1849).
PL	J. P. Migne, *Patrologiae . . . series Latina* (Paris, 1841–1864).
RHC	*Recueil des historiens des croisades. Historiens occidentaux* (Paris, 1844–1895).
RHGF	*Recueil des historiens des Gaules et de la France* (Paris, 1869–1880).

Notes

GENERAL INTRODUCTION

1. The most recent works that summarize the history of the question are: Hans Kohn, *The Idea of Nationalism: A Study in Its Origins and Background* (New York, 1944); Boyd C. Shafer, *Nationalism: Myth and Reality* (New York, 1955); J. M. Leclercq, *La Nation et son idéologie* (Paris, 1979). In general, most of these works pay little attention to the Middle Ages, especially because the bibliography on the subject is uneven and widely dispersed.

There is one French thesis in medieval history on the subject, but with a narrow geographic focus: J. Lejeune, *Liège et son pays: naissance d'une patrie (XIII–XIVe siècle)* (Liège, 1948). The French case has only been studied extensively for the sixteenth century: M. Yardeni, *La conscience nationale en France au XVIe siècle* (Paris, 1971). Several works of popularization are worth attention: M. François, *La France et les Français* (Encyclopédie de la Pléiade) (Paris, 1972); P. Chaunu, *La France et les Français* (Paris, 1982) (concerned above all with the modern period); and F. Braudel, *L'identité de la France* (Paris, 1986). An excellent summary of the issues as they concern medieval France and Germany can be found in K. F. Werner, "La nation et le sentiment national dans l'Europe médiévale," *Revue historique* 244 (1970): 285–304.

2. G. Guibal, *Histoire du sentiment national en France pendant la guerre de Cent Ans* (Paris, 1875); C. Lenient, *La poésie patriotique en France* (Paris, 1891); M. M. Martin, *Histoire de l'unité française* (Paris, 1948); F. Lot, "La formation de l'unité française," *Revue des deux mondes* (1950): 256–278, 418–435.

3. P. Vidal de la Blache, *Tableau de la géographie de la France* (Paris, 1903); C. Seignobos, *Histoire sincère de la nation française* (Paris, 1933).

4. Marc Bloch, *Les rois thaumaturges* (Paris, 1927) (English trans., *The Royal Touch: Sacred Monarchy and Scrofula in England and France* [London, 1973]).

5. R. Cazelles, *La société politique et la crise de la royauté sous Philippe VI de Valois* (Paris, 1958); *Société politique, noblesse et couronne sous Jean le Bon et Charles V* (Paris/Geneva, 1982).

6. B. Guenée, *Tribunaux et gens de justice dans le bailliage de Senlis à la fin du moyen âge* (Paris, 1963). See also his *L'Occident aux XIV et XVe siècles: les Etats* (Paris, 1971) (English trans., *States and Rulers in Later Medieval Europe* [Oxford/New York, 1985]), and Guenée and F. Lehoux, *Les Entrées royales françaises* (Paris, 1968).

7. F. Autrand, *Naissance d'un grand corps de l'Etat: les gens du Parlement de Paris* (Paris, 1981). See also her *Charles VI* (Paris, 1986).

8. J. Krynen, *Idéal du prince et pouvoir royal en France à la fin du Moyen Age* (Paris, 1980).

9. P. S. Lewis, *Later Medieval France: The Polity* (London, 1968); M. Vale, *English Gascony (1399–1453)* (Oxford, 1970); M. Vale, *Charles VII* (Berkeley, Los Angeles, London, 1974); C. Allmand, *Lancastrian Normandy (1415–1450): A History of Medieval Occupation* (Oxford, 1983).

10. E. Kantorowicz, *The King's Two Bodies: A Study in Medieval Political Theology* (Princeton, 1957); R. E. Giesey, *The Royal Funeral Ceremony in Renaissance France* (Geneva, 1960); L. R. Bryant, "La cérémonie de l'entrée à Paris au Moyen Age," *Annales, E.S.C.* 41 (1986): 513–542; S. Hanley, *The Lit de Justice of the Kings of France* (Princeton, 1983).

11. G. Spiegel, *The Chronicle Tradition of Saint-Denis: A Survey* (Brookline, Mass., 1978); E. R. Brown, "La notion de légitimité et la prophétie sous Philippe Auguste," in *La France de Philippe Auguste* (Paris, 1982), 77–111; A. Lewis, *Royal Succession in Capetian France: Studies on Family Order and the State* (Cambridge, Mass., 1981).

12. M. Lugge, *Gallia und Francia im Mittelalter: Untersuchungen über den Zusammenhang zwischen geographisch-historischer Terminologie und politischen Denken vom 6sten bis 15sten Jahrundert* (Bonn, 1960); G. Dupont-Ferrier, "Le sens des mots patria et patrie en France au Moyen Age," *Revue historique*, 188 (1940): 89–104.

13. Suger, *Vie de Louis VI le Gros*, ed. H. Waquet (Paris, 1929), 224.

14. Quoted in J. Huizinga, *Im Bann der Geschichte* (Basle, 1943), 101.

15. H. Kohn, *The Idea of Nationalism*, 107–109 and 604, n. 62.

16. *Oeuvres de Georges Chastellain*, ed. J. Kervin de Lettenhove (Brussels, 1863), 1: 63.

17. G. Duby, *Le Dimanche de Bouvines* (Paris, 1973).

18. B. Guenée, "Les limites de la France," in M. François, ed., *La France et les Français*.

19. Autrand, *Naissance d'un grand corps*, and the same author's *Pouvoir et société politique en France (XIVe–XVe siècle)* (Paris, 1974); also the two articles by A. Bossuat, "L'idée de la nation et la jurisprudence du Parlement de Paris," *Revue historique* 204 (1940): 54–59, and "Le Parlement de Paris durant l'occupation anglaise," *Revue historique* 229 (1963): 19–40.

20. A. Baldit, "Sur la souveraineté des évêques de Mende," *Bulletin de la Société d'agriculture de la Lozère* 10 (1859): 72–124.

21. On this text see Spiegel, *The Chronicle Tradition*, and more generally, B. Guenée, *Histoire et culture historique dans l'Occident médiéval* (Paris, 1980).

22. Concerning attitudes toward the English, see P. Rickard, *Britain in Medieval French Literature (1100–1500)* (Cambridge, 1956), and G. Ascoli, *La Grande Bretagne devant l'opinion française depuis la Guerre de Cent Ans jusqu'à la fin du XVIe siècle* (Paris, 1927). On attitudes toward the Germans, M. Schmidt-Chazan is preparing a thesis, *L'Allemagne et les Allemands dans l'historiographie française au Moyen Age*. C. Gauvard is preparing a general survey of this problem in his thesis, *L'opinion publique en France sous le règne de Charles VI*.

23. P. S. Lewis, "War, Propaganda and Historiography in Fifteenth-Century France and England," *Transactions of the Royal Historical Society*, 5th series, 15 (1965): 1–21.

PART I: INTRODUCTION

1. R. Giesey, *The Royal Funeral Ceremony in Renaissance France* (Geneva, 1960); R. Giesey, "Modèles de pouvoir dans les rites royaux en France," *Annales, E.S.C.* 41 (1986): 579–599; R. E. Jackson, "Les manuscrits des ordines de sacre de la bibliothèque de Charles V," *Le Moyen Age* 82 (1976): 67–88.

2. B. Guenée and F. Lehoux, *Les entrées royales françaises de 1328 à 1515* (Paris, 1968); L. Bryant, "La cérémonie de l'entrée à Paris au Moyen Age," *Annales, E.S.C.* 41 (1986): 513–542; Robert Sainceriax, *Sermon en vers*, RHGF, 23: 124–130; sermon on the war in Flanders in BN MS latin 16495 fol. 96v and ff.; sermons of Gerson preached before the king, in Jean Gerson, *Oeuvres complètes*, ed. E. Dupin (Antwerp, 1706), 2: 141 ("Vivat rex") and 4: 625 ("Veniat pax"); C. Liebman, "Un sermon de Philippe de Villette," *Romania* 66 (1945): 444–470.

3. One could study what happened in the wake of the battles of Castillon or Formigny, just as Georges Duby has done with Bouvines: G. Duby, *Le Dimanche de Bouvines* (Paris, 1973).

4. Charles was the son of Guy de Chatillon and Marguerite, sister of Philip VI. He was killed at the battle of Auray and declared Blessed in 1371.

5. L. Theis, *Dagobert* (Paris, 1982).

6. A. Tardif, *Privilèges accordés par le Saint Siège à la couronne de France* (Paris, 1855), 12, 16, 30; B. Barbiche, *Les actes pontificaux des Archives Nationales* (Vatican City, 1975–1978), 1: 299, 312; 2: 3.

7. B. M. Reichert, *Monumenta ordinis fratrum praedicatorum* (Rome, 1898), 3: 66.

8. Thomas Aquinas, *Opera omnia*, ed. S. Fretté (Paris, 1884), 10: 576–577.

9. N. van Paulus, *Geschichte des Ablasses im Mittelalter* (Paderborn, 1923), 2: 18, 126.

10. See the 1406 testament of Gérard d'Athis, archbishop of Besançon, in W. Paravicini, "Moers, Croy, Burgund," *Annalen des Historischen Vereins für den Niederrhein*, 179 (1977): 20, and W. Paravicini, *Guy de Brimeu* (Bonn, 1975), 574–575.

11. "Psalter of Louis XI": BN MS latin 1080; C. Auchier, "Charles de Melun," *Le Moyen Age 5* (1892): 80–87 and 106–110.

12. V. Advieille, *Histoire de l'ordre des Antonins* (Paris, 1883), 101.

13. "Psalter of Charles V": BN MS latin 1082; see V. Leroquais, *Les psautiers manuscrits des bibliothèques publiques de France* (Paris, 1940), 1: ii–lxiii.

14. Robert the Monk, *Historia hierosolymitana*, PL, vol. 155, col. 670.

1. SAINT DENIS

1. Hilduin, *Passio sanctissimi Dionysii*, PL, vol. 106, cols. 23–50.

2. Eusebeus of Cesarea, *Opera omnia*, ed. H. Grapin (Paris, 1905), 2: 233–235.

3. *Acts*, xvii, 34.

4. Gregory of Tours, *History of the Franks*, trans. L. Thorpe (Harmondsworth, 1974), 87.

5. AA.SS., October, 4: 925–928.

6. Bede, *Expositio super actu Apostolorum*, PL, vol. 91, col. 981.

7. Bede, *Martyrologia*, PL, vol. 94, col. 1067–1068.

8. According to R. Loenertz, "La légende parisienne de Denis," *Analecta Bollandiana* 69 (1951): 217–237, another *vita* "Post beatam et gloriosam . . ." dating from 817, already put forward the inventions that Hilduin would make his own.

9. MGH, *Epistolae aevi carolini*, 3: 383.

10. MGH, *Auctores antiquissimi*, 4: 383.

11. Contrary to the views of G. Théry, "Contribution à l'histoire de l'aréopagitisme au IXe siècle," *Le Moyen Age*, 2d series, 25 (1923): 111–123.

12. Dom J. Dubois, *Le Marytrologe d'Usuard* (Brussels, 1965).

13. Aelius Aristides, *The Apology*, ed. J. R. Harris (Cambridge, 1893).

14. John Scotus Erigena, *Opera omnia*, PL, vol. 122, col. 1032.

15. AA.SS., November, 1: 49–50.

16. Letaldus of Micy, *Vita sancti Juliani*, PL, vol. 137, col. 783.

17. Adhemar of Chabannes, *Epistola sancti Martiali*, PL, vol. 141, cols. 87–111.

18. Fulbert of Chartres, *Opera omnia*, ed. C. de Villiers (Paris, 1608), 72; AA.SS., October, 1: 22–26.

19. Fulbert of Chartres, *Decretum*, PL, vol. 161, cols. 55, 288.

20. Sigebert of Gembloux, *Liber de scriptoribus ecclesiasticis*, PL, vol. 160, col. 548.

21. Hugh of St-Victor, *Expositio in hierarchiam coelestem Sancti Dionysii*, PL, vol. 175, cols. 925–1154.

22. Peter Abelard, *Historia calamitatum*, ed. C. Charrier (Paris, 1934), 129–133.

23. Peter Abelard, *Epistola 11*, PL, vol. 178, cols. 341–344.

24. B. Guenée, *Histoire et culture historique dans l'Occident médiéval* (Paris, 1980), 129–133, 147–164.

25. MGH, *Epistolae aevi carolini*, 3: 325–330.

26. Hincmar, *Epistola 23*, PL, vol. 126, col. 154.

27. AA.SS., October, 4: 722.

28. J. Doublet, *Histoire chronologique pour la vérité de Denis l'Aréopagitique* (Paris, 1646), 367.

29. L. Hausherr, "Doutes au sujet du divin Denys," *Orientalia christiana periodica* 2 (1936): 112–134.

30. E. Martène, *Veterorum scriptorum . . . amplissima collectio* (Paris, 1724), 5: 919–920.

31. AA.SS., October, 4: 797.

32. C. Liebman, *Etudes sur les vies en prose de saint Denis* (New York, 1942).

33. BN MSS français 2090–2092 and MS latin 5286.

34. BN MS latin 5286 fols. 57–60.

35. Jerome, *Liber de viris illustribus*, PL, vol. 23, col. 625.

36. Lorenzo Valla, *Opera omnia* (Basle, 1553), 852.

37. L. Levillain, "Les origines du Lendit," *Revue historique* 154 (1927): 241–263.

38. GC, 5: 64–69.

39. C. Liebman, "La consécration légendaire de Saint-Denis," *Le Moyen Age*, 3d series, 6 (1935): 252–264.

40. H. F. Delaborde, "Le procès du chef de saint Denis en 1410," *Mémoires de la Société de l'histoire de Paris et de l'Ile-de-France* 11 (1884): 297–409.

41. In shaping their own argument, the canons of Notre-Dame overlooked the evidence offered by the work of Robert de Thorigny (1128–1186) and made use instead of Jean de Saint-Victor's *Memorial of Histories* (written from 1308–1322) and Guy de Castres's *Sanctilogium*. They also enlisted supporting evidence from the iconography of Parisian churches.

42. Le Religieux de Saint-Denis, *Chronique de Charles VI*, ed. and trans. L. F. Bellaguet (Paris, 1839–1852), 3: 436–444.

43. R. Bossuat, "Traditions populaires relatives au martyre et à la sépulture de saint Denis," *Le Moyen Age* 62 (1956): 479–509.

44. F. H. Bateson, *La Chanson de Floovant* (London, 1938).

45. A. de Reiffenberg, ed., *La Chronique rimée de Philippe Mouskès* (Paris, 1836), 1: 15.

46. BN MS français 5706 (*Chanson de Florent et Octavien*).

47. J. H. Baltzell, "Un poème sur saint Denis," *Le Moyen Age* 62 (1956): 331–334.

48. J. H. Baltzell, *The Octosyllabic Life of Saint Denis* (Geneva, 1958).

49. GC, 5: 276–277.

50. GC, 6: 203–205.

51. Guillaume de Nangis, *Vie de Saint Louis*, RHGF, 20: 346–347.

52. GC, 9: 148–150.

53. Le Religieux de Saint-Denis, *Chronique*, 2: 23, 35, 94, 557, 771.

54. *Ordonnances*, 11: 181; 4: 137–140; 18: 561; 19: 82, 86–87; L. Theis, *Dagobert* (Paris, 1982), 38–40.

55. L. Theis, "Dagobert, Saint-Denis et la royauté française," in B. Guenée, ed., *Le Métier d'historien* (Paris, 1977), 19–30; B. de Gaiffier, *Etudes critiques d'iconologie et d'hagiographie* (Brussels, 1967); BN MS latin 17361 (Goezwin

Kemp); BN MS français 5706; Nicole Gilles, *Les très élégantes . . . Annales de France* (Paris, 1525).

56. MGH, *Capitularia*, 2: 432.

57. MGH, *Scriptores rerum merovingiacarum*, vol. 7, pt. i: 51.

58. E. de Certain, ed., *Les Miracles de saint Benoît* (Paris, 1863), 36.

59. MGH, *SS. rer. merov.*, vol. 7, pt. i: 54.

60. Flodoard, *Historia remensis ecclesiae*, PL, vol. 135, col. 116.

61. BN MS latin 12710 (*Gesta Francorum usque 1180*), fol. 1; BN MS latin 6295 (anonymous chronicle of Bethune), fol. 35; *Chronique rimée de Philippe Mouskès*, 1: 79.

62. BN MS latin 5286 (Yves de Saint-Denis), fol. 166.

63. MGH, *Scriptores*, 10: 370.

64. MGH, *Poetae aevi Karolini*, vol. 2, pt. ii: 301–303.

65. C. Meredith-Jones, *Historia Karoli Magni et Rothlandi ou Chronique du Pseudo-Turpin* (Paris, 1936), 228–230. The basic components of this vision were adapted from one composed soon after the death of the Holy Roman Emperor Henry II (1002–1024).

66. BN MS latin 12710 (*Vita et actus sancti Dionysii* [1233]), fols. 133–135; BN MS latin 5286 (Yves de Saint-Denis), fols. 180–181; GC, 3: 290–292.

67. Rigord and Guillaume le Breton, *Oeuvres*, ed. H. F. Delaborde (Paris, 1882–1885), 2: 375–377; Richer of Sens, MGH, *Scriptores*, 25: 297; *Chronicon Turonense*, RHGF, 18: 304–305. See J. Le Goff, *La naissance du purgatoire* (Paris, 1982).

68. BN MS latin 2447, fols. 151–152; *Chronique rimée de Philippe Mouskès*, 2: 435–440.

69. BN MS latin 2447, fol. 152.

70. GC, 6: 370; BN MS latin 5286, fol. 202.

71. J. Le Goff, "Philippe Auguste dans les exempla," in *La France de Philippe Auguste: le temps des mutations* (Paris, 1982), 150–151.

72. Le Goff, *Purgatoire*, 324–332.

73. Hariulf of Saint-Riquier, *Chroniques*, ed. F. Lot (Paris, 1894), 144–148; MGH, *Scriptores*, 10: 457–458.

74. Helinand of Froidmont, *Chronicon*, PL, vol. 212, col. 868; BN MS latin 4998 (Guy de Bazoches, *Chronographia*), fol. 540.

75. BN MS latin 2827, fols. 145–149.

76. G. M. Spiegel, "The *reditus regni ad stirpem Karoli*," *French Historical Studies* 7 (1971): 145–174; B. Guenée, "Les généalogies entre l'histoire et la politique; la fierté d'être capétien en France au Moyen Age," *Annales, E.S.C.* 33 (1978): 450–477.

77. Helinand of Froidmont, PL, vol. 212, col. 870.

78. BN MS latin 12710, fols. 1–2. On this manuscript see G. Spiegel, *Chronicle Tradition*, 41–51.

79. BN MS latin 2447, fols. 187–190; GC, 4: 247–253.

80. BN MS latin 5286, fols. 190–193.

81. R. A. Jackson, "The *Traité du sacre* of Jean Golein," *Proceedings of the American Philosophical Society* 113 (1963): 304–324.

82. BN MS latin 17361 (Goezwin Kemp, *Recueil*); BN MS latin 14117 (Guillaume Lemaire, *Papiers*), fol. 134.

83. BN MS français 5706, fols. 8v–18.

84. Helgaud of Fleury, *La Vie de Robert le Pieux*, ed. R. H. Bautier (Paris, 1965), 133–135; Suger, *Vie de Louis VI le Gros*, ed. and trans. H. Waquet (Paris, 1929), 271–285.

85. Louis IX: GC, 7: 280–282; H. Guéraud, ed., *La Chronique de Guillaume de Nangis* (Paris, 1843), 1: 236–237; Jean, sire de Joinville, *L'Histoire de Saint Louis*, ed. N. de Wailly (Paris, 1868), 280–283. Philip IV: BN MS latin 5286, fols. 212–215. Charles V: BN MS latin 8299, item 2 (*Relation anonyme de la mort de Charles V*); Christine de Pisan, *Le Livre des fais et bonnes meurs du sage roi Charles V*, ed. S. Solente (Paris, 1936), 2: 277–288; Jean de Roye, *Journal dit Chronique scandaleuse*, ed. B. Mandrot (Paris, 1894–1896), 2: 120, 252–255.

86. BN MS latin 5286, fols. 212–225.

87. M. Félibien, *Histoire de l'abbaye royale de Saint-Denis* (Paris, 1706), lxxxiv, pièce cx.

88. *Ordonnances*, 11: 181.

89. G. M. Spiegel, "The Cult of Saint Denis and Capetian Kingship," *Journal of Medieval History* 1 (1975): 43–69; E. A. R. Brown and M. W. Cothren, "The Twelfth-century Crusading Window of the Abbey of Saint-Denis," *Journal of the Warburg and Courtauld Institute* 49 (1986): 1–40; A. W. Lewis, "Suger's Views on Kingship," in P. L. Gerson, ed., *Abbot Suger and Saint-Denis* (New York, 1986), 49–54.

90. BN MS français 2090, fols. 82–86, 92–96.

91. Above, p. 25.

92. H. Morétus-Plantin, *Les Passions céphalophoriques de saint Lucien et leurs dérivés* (Paris, 1953), introduction.

93. See above, pp. 22–25.

94. Morétus-Plantin, *Passions céphalophoriques*. It is unclear whether the second *Life* of this saint dates from before or after Hilduin's *Life* of Saint Denis.

95. Spiegel, *Chronicle Tradition*.

96. BN MS nouv. acq. latine 1509, fol. 102; Mathew Paris, *Chronica majora* (Rolls Series, London, 1892), 5: 480; 6: 99–100.

97. This was taken from an eleventh-century *Life of Saint Regulus*. The first life of Saint Regulus, from the tenth century, was derived in turn from a life of Saint Lucianus, which had linked Regulus's mission to that of Saint Denis. AA.SS., March, 3: 820–824.

98. BN MS français 2090, fols. 82–86, 92–96.

99. *Vita sancti Juliani*, PL, vol. 137, col. 783.

100. Martène, *Veterorum scriptorum*, 5: 919–920.

101. *History of the Franks*, bk. 1, chap. 31 (Thorpe trans., p. 87).

102. AA.SS., August, 2: 11–12.

103. Ordericus Vitalis, *Historia ecclesiastica*, bk. 2, chap. 5, PL, vol. 188.

104. A. Fliche, *Les Vies de saint Savinien et saint Potentien* (Paris, 1912).

105. J. B. Driot, *Senonensis ecclesiae querela de primatu Galliarum adversus Lugdunensem et de metropolico jure adversus Parisiensem* (Sens, 1657).

106. *Vita sancti Juliani*, PL, vol. 137, col. 783; *Vita sancti Piatonis*, AA.SS., October, 1: 22–26.

107. Morétus-Plantin, *Les Passions céphalophoriques*.

108. Baltzell, *The Octosyllabic Life*; the *Life* of Saint Exuperius is in AA.SS., August, 1: 52–55.

109. Doublet, *Histoire chronologique*.

110. Jean Masselin, *Le Journal des Etats généraux de 1484*, ed. A. Bernier (Paris, 1835), 169; *Ordonnances*, 19: 82.

111. L. Olschki, *Der ideale Mittelpunkt Frankreichs im Mittelalter* (Heidelberg, 1913).

112. *Ordonnances*, 4: 137–140.

113. A Leroux de Lincy and L. M. Tisserand, *Paris et ses historiens aux XIVe et XVe siècles* (Paris, 1867); M. Yardeni, "Le mythe de Paris . . . à l'époque de la Ligue," *Mémoires de la Société historique et archéologique de Paris et de l'Ile-de-France* 20 (1969): 49–63.

114. P. C. Timbal, "Civitas Parisius, communis patria," *Economies et sociétés au Moyen Age. Mélanges offerts à Edouard Perroy* (Paris, 1973), 661–664.

115. GC, 5: 240.

116. A. Longnon, *Paris pendant la domination anglaise (1420–1436)* (Paris, 1878); J. W. MacKenna, "Piety and Propaganda: The Cult of King Henry VI," *Chaucer and Middle English Studies in Honor of Rossell Hope Robbins* (London, 1974), 78–88; E. Carleton Williams, *My Lord of Bedford* (London, 1963).

117. BN MS latin 5332, fols. 81–82.

118. E. Griffe, *La Gaule chrétienne à l'époque romaine* (Paris, 1964), vol. 1.

119. For all that follows see P. Contamine, "L'oriflamme de Saint-Denis aux XIVe et XVe siècles," *Annales de l'Est* 25 (1973): 179–245; C. Liebman, "Un sermon de Philippe de Villete abbé de Saint-Denis en 1414," *Romania* 78 (1944–1945): 444–470.

120. Suger, *Vie de Louis VI*, 229.

121. Félibien, *Histoire de Saint-Denis*, lxxxiv, pièce cx; D. Gaborit-Chopin, "Les couronnes de sacre des rois et des reines au trésor de Saint-Denis," *Bulletin monumental* 133 (1975): 165–181.

122. H. Pinoteau, "L'ancienne couronne française dites de Charlemagne," *Bulletin de la Société archéologique, historique, et artistique du vieux papier* 26 (1972): 305–312, 351–362, 381–396.

123. Leroux de Lincy and Tisserand, *Paris et ses historiens*, 548–549; D. Godefroy, *Le cérémonial français* (Paris, 1649), 1: 474.

124. Guglielmus Benedicti, *Opera omnia* (Lyon, 1582), fol. 26.

125. Gaborit-Chopin, "Les couronnes de sacre."

126. GC, 8: 39; le Religieux de Saint-Denis, *Chronique*, 1: 31.

127. J. Quicherat, *Procès de condamnation et de réhabilitation de Jeanne d'Arc* (Paris, 1841–1850), vol. 4.

128. Quicherat, *Procès*, 5: 185.

129. R. A. Jackson, "Les manuscrits des *ordines* de couronnement de la bibliothèque de Charles V," *Le Moyen Age* 82 (1976): 67–88.

130. Quicherat, *Procès*, 4: 453; and 5: 184–185.

131. J. Varin, *Archives administratives de la ville de Reims* (Paris, 1840–1845), 2: 559–579.

132. Varin, *Archives administratives*, 3: 505.

133. Quicherat, *Procès*, 5: 185.

134. P. Tarbe, *Les Trésors des églises de Reims* (Reims, 1843), 177.

135. B. Guenée and F. Lehoux, *Les Entrées royales françaises de 1328 à 1515* (Paris, 1968), 73 and 78.

136. D. de Montfaucon, *Les Monuments de la monarchie française* (Paris, 1731), 3: 275.

137. Thomas Basin, *Histoire de Charles VII*, ed. C. Samaran (Paris, 1933–1944), 1: 145.

138. P. E. Schramm, *Der König von Frankreich* (Weimar, 1960), 2: 92, and 141, n. 5.

139. Félibien, *Histoire*, 364.

140. F. Tuetey, *Journal d'un bourgeois de Paris (1405–1449)* (Paris, 1881), 377.

141. Godefroy, *Le cérémonial*, vol. 2.

142. MacKenna, "Piety and Propaganda"; J. H. Rowe, "King Henry VI's Claim to France," *Library*, series 4, vol. 14 (1933): 77–88.

143. Tuetey, *Bourgeois de Paris*, 274–279; Godefroy, *Le cérémonial*, 1: 169–172; Carleton-Williams, *Bedford*, 201–210.

144. Tuetey, *Bourgeois de Paris*, 377.

145. Leroux de Lincy and Tisserand, *Paris et ses historiens*, 548–549.

146. G. Peyronnet, "Rumeurs autour du sacre de Charles VII," *Annales de l'Est*, series 5, vol. 33 (1981): 151–165.

147. Jackson, "Manuscrits des *ordines*," 67–88.

148. Religieux de Saint-Denis, *Chronique*, 1: 611–615.

149. Félibien, *Histoire*, 315.

150. H. F. Delaborde, "Notice sur les ouvrages de Guillaume Rigord," *Bibliothèque de l'Ecole des Chartes* 45 (1884): 585–614.

151. Christine de Pisan, *Livre des faits*, 2: 96; Religieux de Saint-Denis, *Chronique*, 5: 743–747.

152. G. S. Wright, "A Royal Tomb Program in the Reign of Saint Louis," *Art Bulletin* 56 (1974): 224–243; E. Erlande-Brandenbourg, *Le Roi est mort: études sur les funérailles, les sépultures et les tombeaux des rois de France jusqu'à la fin du XIIIe siècle* (Paris, 1975).

153. GC, 5: 35.

154. The queens, like the kings, were also often honored by secondary tombs (tombs where the heart or other vital organs were buried), which were established for them in the mendicant convents of the Parisian area.

155. R. Branner, "The *Montjoies* of Saint Louis," *Essays in the History of Architecture Presented to Rudolf Wittkower* (New York, 1966), 1: 13–17; A. Lombard-Jourdan, "Montjoies et Montjoie dans la plaine Saint-Denis," *Mém-*

oires de la Société de l'histoire de Paris et de l'Ile-de-France 25 (1974): 143–181; 27 (1976): 141–181.

156. M. Barroux, "Suger et la vassalité du Vexin en 1124," Le Moyen Age 63 (1958): 1–26; Erlande-Brandenbourg, Le Roi est mort.

157. Doublet, Histoire, 1028–1032.

158. E. Kantorowicz, The King's Two Bodies: A Study in Medieval Political Theology (Princeton, 1957), 87–96.

159. Félibien, Histoire, xciii.

160. Barroux, "La vassalité du Vexin."

161. Spiegel, "The Cult of Saint Denis."

2. SAINT CLOVIS

1. See G. Kurth, Clovis (Paris, 1901); G. Tessier, Le Baptême de Clovis (Paris, 1964); C. Beaune, "Saint Clovis: histoire, religion royale, et sentiment national à la fin du Moyen Age," in B. Guenée, ed., Le Métier d'historien au Moyen Age (Paris, 1977), 139–156.

2. GC, 1: 58.

3. "At that time," wrote Gregory of Tours (History of the Franks, bk. 2, chap. 27), "many churches were plundered by the troops of Clovis, for he still held fast to his pagan idolatries. The soldiers had stolen an ewer of great size and wondrous workmanship. . . . The bishop of the church sent messengers to the King to beg that . . . this ewer might be restored. . . . They came to Soissons and all the booty was placed in a heap before them. King Clovis pointed to the vessel in question and said, '. . . you should agree to grant me that ewer over and above my normal share.' . . . As they spoke one of their number . . . raised his battle-axe and struck the ewer. 'You shall have none of this booty,' he shouted, 'except your fair share.' . . . The King took the vessel and handed it over to the envoy of the church; but in his heart he resented what had happened. At the end of that year he ordered the entire army to assemble on the parade ground. . . . The King went round inspecting them all and came finally to the man who had struck the ewer. 'No other man has equipment in such a bad state as yours,' said he. . . . He seized the man's axe and threw it on the ground. As the soldier bent forward to pick up his weapon, King Clovis raised his own battle-axe in the air and split his skull with it. 'That is what you did to my ewer in Soissons,' he shouted. The man fell dead." (Trans. L. Thorpe [Harmondsworth and Baltimore, 1974], 139–140.)

4. Vincent of Beauvais, Speculum quadruplex (Douai, 1606), 4: 819.

5. BN MS français 24976, fol. 12.

6. BN MS latin 5366 (Life of Saint Maximinus), fol. 3.

7. BN MS français 5692, fols. 61–62v.

8. BN MS français 17160 (Bernard Gui, Flores cronicorum), fol. 67; BN MS nouv. acq. française 6853 (Miroir historial) fol. 69; BN MS français 1965 (Le rosier des guerres), fol. 44.

9. BN MS français 4924 (Origo regum Franciae), fol. 212v; H. Beaune and J. d'Arbeaumont, Mémoires d'Olivier de La Marche (Paris, 1883), 1: 51–64; Mer des Histoires (Paris, 1517–1518), fol. 87; C. Bruneau, ed., La Chronique de Philippe de Vigneulles (Metz, 1927), 1: 98–101.

10. R. Bossuat, "Un poème latin sur l'origine des fleurs de lys," *Bibliothèque de l'Ecole des Chartes* 101 (1940): 80–101.

11. Hugh of Fleury, *Historia ecclesiastica,* ed. B. Rottendorf (Münster, 1638), 129.

12. BN MS français 820 (*Les miracles de la Vierge par personnages*), fols. 262–280.

13. BN MS français 1965, fol. 44.

14. BN MS nouv. acq. française 6853, fols. 53 ff.

15. BN MS français 56 (Jehan Mansel, *La fleur des histoires*), fols. 257–260; BN MS français 17274 (Guillaume Crétin, *Chroniques de France rimées*), fol. 47.

16. BN MS latin 4991A, fol. 104.

17. Vincent of Beauvais, *Speculum,* 4: 819.

18. BN MS français 24976, fol. 12.

19. BN MS français 5692, fols. 61–62.

20. BN MS français 20793, fol. 317.

21. BN MS nouv. acq. française 6853, fol. 82v.

22. N. Gilles, *Les Trés Elégantes . . . Annales* (Paris, 1525), 14–17.

23. Robert Gaguin, *Compendium de origine et gestis Francorum* (Paris, 1511), fol. 11; GC, 1: 58; BN MS français 17274, fol. 26.

24. BN MS nouv. acq. française 6853, fol. 82v.; BN MS latin 5366, fol. 1.

25. BN MS français 20124 (Jehan de Courcy, sire de la Bouquechardière, *Chronique universelle*), fol. 1.

26. Paulus Aemilius Veronensis, *De rebus gestis Francorum* (Paris, 1548), 6.

27. *Ordonnances,* 15: 200.

28. BN MS nouv. acq. française 6853, fol. 44v; BN MS latin 5366, fol. 1; BN MS latin 9670, fol. 105r–v.

29. BN MS latin 9670, fols. 105 and 158; BN MS français 820, fols. 262–280.

30. BN MS français 849 (*Petit traité sur le triomphe de France*), fol. 7v.

31. BN MS nouv. acq. française 6853, fols. 53 ff.

32. J. Krynen, *Idéal du prince et pouvoir royal en France à la fin du Moyen Age* (Paris, 1981), 228–241.

33. BN MS nouv. acq. française 1410 (*Le Livre des chroniques abrégées*), fol. 165.

34. BN MS français 20793, fol. 317.

35. BN MS français 15457 (Nicolas Boivin, *Miroir historial*), fol. 54v.

36. P. Contamine, "L'Oriflamme de saint Denis aux XIVe et XVe siècles," *Annales de l'Est* 25 (1973): 179–245; A. Héron, *Oeuvres de Robert Blondel* (Rouen, 1891), 1: 402; L. Pannier and P. Meyer, eds., *Le Débat des hérauts d'armes de France et d'Angleterre* (Paris, 1877), 12.

37. BN MS français 6017 (Gaspar Marin, *Histoire des sires des Noyers*), fol. 15; BN MS français 9866 (*Chronique universelle*), fol. 31v. In 1463, this manuscript was in the possession of Tristan L'Hermite, counselor to Louis XI.

38. Contamine, "L'Oriflamme"; Jean Bonaud du Sauset, *Commentaires du Traité de Jean de Terre Vermeille* (Paris, 1525); BN MS français 1371 (*L'Histoire antonine*), fol. 35; BN MS français 5692, fols. 61–62.

39. E. Roy, "Philippe le Bel et la Légende des fleurs de lys," *Mélanges de philologie et d'histoire offerts à Antoine Thomas* (Paris, 1927), 383–388.

40. Bossuat, "Un poème latin."

41. P. S. Lewis, "Two Pieces of Fifteenth-century Political Iconography," *Journal of the Warburg and Courtauld Institute* 27 (1964): 317–320.

42. See the discussion of manuscript miniatures at the end of chap. 7.

43. Adrevald of Fleury, *Les miracles de saint Benoit*, ed. E. de Certain (1858), 19.

44. BN MS latin 4991A, fols. 102v, 105, 116–122, 140, 170v.

45. BN MS latin 3184 (*De hierarchia subcelesti*), fol. 26v.

46. Jean Gerson, *Oeuvres complètes*, ed. P. Glorieux (Paris, 1962), 5: 151–168.

47. Gerson, *Oeuvres*, 4: 113–114.

48. *Ordonnances*, 18: 744.

49. *Ordonnances*, 4: 203.

50. Boniface Symoneta, *De christiane fidei* (Paris, 1509), fol. 6.

51. Jacques Almain, *De potestate ecclesiastici et laicali* (Antwerp, 1706), 1: 872.

52. Paulus Aemilius, *De rebus gestis*, 6.

53. Bibliothèque Mazarine, MS 1733, fol. 47v: "Incipit vita beati Ludovici."

54. BN MS français 10142 (*Recueil de portraits de rois de France*), fol. 5.

55. Tessier, *Baptême de Clovis*, 157–161. The church of Bethléem in the modern department of the Loiret, was a dependent of Ferrières-en-Gâtinais.

56. BN MS latin 5366, fol. 1.

57. E. Maffei Volterranus, *Commentariorum urbanorum libri* (Basle, 1530), 18.

58. *Ordonnances*, 8: 487; 20: 58.

59. RHGF, 23: 199; but most of the pertinent passages are available to us only in the manuscript: BN MS latin 4991A. A later version of the legend (between 1484 and 1492) is in Archives départementales du Tarn-et-Garonne, G 356. On the abbey's archives see E. Rufin, *L'Abbaye et les cloîtres de Moissac* (Paris, 1897).

60. A. Lagrèze-Fossat, *Etudes historiques sur Moissac* (Paris, 1874), 3: 495; Archives Tarn-et-Garonne, G 774, n. 1.

61. BN MS latin 4991A, fol. 104v.

62. E. Rufin, *L'Abbaye de Moissac*, 24.

63. Archives Tarn-et-Garonne, G 356.

64. Clearly, if the scene had been the more typical Last Judgment, this confusion would not have occurred. See Froment de Beaurepaire, "La légende de Moissac," *Bulletin archéologique du Tarn-et-Garonne* 23 (1895): 72–73.

65. BN MS latin 4991A, fol. 104.

66. BN MS latin 4991A, fols. 104–105.

67. *Ordonnances*, 9: 122 (1281), 123 (1370); 8: 131 (1397 and 1407); 5: 305 (1425); 16: 474 (1466); 18: 744 (1481).

68. A. Leymarie, *Histoire de Limousin* (Limoges, 1845), 341. The act is dated February 5, 1495.

69. The fortifications at Dorat date from 1420.

70. *Ordonnances,* 9: 122 (1281), 123 (1370); 8: 131 (1397 and 1407); 5: 305 (1425); 16: 474 (1466); 18: 744 (1481).

71. BN MS français 5902.

72. This church was in fact of relatively recent foundation, its organization modeled on the Sainte-Chapelle of Paris, founded by Saint Louis. Cf. J. M. Grandmaison, *L'Eglise Sainte-Marthe de Tarascon* (Avignon, 1957).

73. In addition to Grandmaison, cited above, see L. Dumont, *La Tarasque* (Paris, 1951), and L. Inard, *Tarascon, cité de Sainte-Marthe* (Aix, 1960).

74. *Ordonnances,* 18: 744.

3. SAINT LOUIS

1. Jean de Roye, *Journal dit Chronique scandaleuse,* ed. B. Mandrot (Paris, 1894–1896), 2: 62.

2. J. Quicherat, *Procès de condamnation et de réhabilitation de Jeanne d'Arc* (Paris, 1841–1850), 3: 6 (testimony of Dunois); R. Folz, *Le Souvenir et la légende de Charlemagne dans l'Empire germanique médiéval* (Paris, 1950); R. Folz, "Aspects du culte liturgique de Charlemagne en France," in W. Braunfels, ed., *Karl der Grosse: Lebenswerk und Nachleben* (Bonn, 1964), 4: 67–78; J. Monfrin, "La figure de Charlemagne dans l'historiographie du XVe siècle," *Annuaire-Bulletin de la Société de l'Histoire de France* (1964–1965): 67–78. L. Carolus-Barré, "Les armes de Charlemagne dans l'héraldique médiévale," *Bulletin de la Société nationale des antiquaires de France* (1964): 61–65.

3. D. O'Connell and J. Le Goff, *Les Propos de Saint Louis* (Paris, 1974).

4. Geoffroy de Beaulieu, *Sancti Ludovici . . . vita et conversatio* (Paris, 1617).

5. Guillaume de Chartres, *De vita et actibus sancti Ludovici* (Paris, 1617).

6. Guillaume de Saint-Pathus, *La Vie et les miracles de Monseigneur Saint Louis,* ed. M.-C. d'Espagne (Paris, 1971).

7. Jean, sire de Joinville, *L'Histoire de Saint Louis,* ed. N. de Wailly (Paris, 1868).

8. Vincent of Beauvais, *Speculum quadruplex* (Douai, 1624), 4: 1277–1315.

9. GC, vol. 7.

10. Jacques de Voragine, *La Légende dorée,* ed. G. Brunet (Paris, 1942), 2: 134–140.

11. Jean Gerson, *Oeuvres complètes,* ed. P. Glorieux (Paris, 1963), 5: 151–168, 179–190, 229–235.

12. *Ordonnances,* 7: 520.

13. J.-C. Schmitt, "Recueils franciscains d'*exempla* et perfectionnement des techniques intellectuelles," *Bibliothèque de l'Ecole des Chartes* 135 (1977): 5–23.

14. M.-T. Laureilhe, "Saint Louis et les franciscains," *Amis de saint François* 12 (1971): 8–16; M.-H. Vicaire, "Les ordres mendiants au XIIIe siècle," *Le Siècle de Saint Louis,* ed. J. Babelon (Paris, 1970), 245–280.

15. L. Carolus-Barré, "Les enquêtes pour la canonisation de Saint Louis," *Revue d'histoire de l'Eglise de France* 57 (1971): 19–31.

16. R. Folz, "La sainteté de Saint Louis d'après les textes liturgiques," *Revue d'histoire de l'Eglise de France* 57 (1971): 31–45. A. Vauchez, *La Sainteté en Occident aux derniers siècles du Moyen Age* (Paris and Rome, 1981).

17. J.-T. Welter, *La "Tabula exemplorum secundum alphabeti"* (Paris, 1927).

18. J. Babelon, ed., *Le Siècle de Saint Louis*, 93–99; P. Fedele de Fanna, *Ratio novae collectionis venturae* (Turin, 1874), 220.

19. GC, 7: 188–189; Geoffrey de Beaulieu, *Sancti Ludovici vita*, 57; Guillaume de Saint-Pathus, *Vie et miracles*, 80; Joinville, *Saint Louis*, 290.

20. Etienne de Bourbon, *Anecdotes historiques, légendes et apologies tirés du recueil inédit d'Etienne de Bourbon, dominicain du XIIIe siècle*, ed. A. Lecoy de La Marche (Paris, 1877), 341.

21. BN MS français 13754 (*La Sainte vie et les hauts faits dignes de mémoire de Monseigneur Saint Louis roi de France* [circa 1500]), fol. 45v; *La Fleur des commandements de Dieu* (Paris, 1510), lxii; Pierre Gringoire, *Oeuvres complètes*, ed. C. d'Héricault and A. de Montaiglon (Paris, 1877), 2: 221–231; Francisque Michel, *Le Mystère de Saint Louis* (London, 1871), 279; D'Averoult, *La Fleur des exemples* (Lyon, 1608), 1: 497–498.

22. P. Gottschalk Hollen, *Sermonum opus exquisitum* (Haguenau, 1517) (unpaged); Jean Hérolt, *Sermones cum promptuario exemplorum* (Lyon, 1483), 227; J. de Bromyard, *Summa praedicantium* (Lyon, 1608), 1: 424.

23. T. Crane, *Les Exemples de Jacques de Vitry* (London, 1890), 91.

24. A. Morel-Fatio, "El libro de los exemplos," *Romania* 7 (1878): 514; *Novelette, exempli morali e apologhi di Bernardino da Sienna*, ed. F. Zambrini (Bologna, 1868), 18.

25. Y. Deslandres, "Le costume du roi Saint Louis," *7e Centenaire de la mort de Saint Louis, Actes des Colloques de Royaumont et Paris 1970* (Paris, 1976), 105–115.

26. Thomas de Cantimpré, *Bonum universale de apibus* (Douai, 1605), 1: 591, and *Magnum speculum exemplorum* (Douai, 1605), 1: 347.

27. Etienne de Bourbon, *Anecdotes historiques*, 63; C. Stolfi, *Corona dei monachi* (Prato, 1862), 145; J. de Bromyard, *Summa*, 2: 79; P. Gottschalk Hollen, *Sermonum*, sermon 22.

28. Hérolt, *Sermones*, 383.

29. Bromyard, *Summa*, 2: 62.

30. Josse Clichthove, *De laudibus sancti Ludovici* (Paris, 1516), 14.

31. Welter, "*Tabula exemplorum*," p. 41, n. 141; Etienne de Bourbon, *Anecdotes historiques*, 443; *Magnum speculum exemplorum*, 1: 284.

32. L. d'Achery, *Spicilegium veterorum scriptorum* (Paris, 1723), 2: 632.

33. Gringoire, *Oeuvres*, 2: 101; BN MS français 13754, fol. 170v.; Marino Sanudo, *Liber secretorum fidelium crucis* (Paris, 1611), 217.

34. Thomas de Cantimpré, *Bonum universale*, 136.

35. Etienne de Bourbon, *Anecdotes historiques*, 89–90.

36. AA.SS., February, 3: 154.

37. L. Wadding, *Annales minorum* (3d ed., Florence, 1931), 3: 214.

38. *Grande chronique de Limoges*, RHGF, 21: 775–776.

39. P. Sabatier, *Actus beati Francisci et sociorum ejus* (Paris, 1902), 144–146.

40. BN MS français 9688 (*Chronique universelle jusqu'à la mort de Charles VI*), fol. 41v.; Wadding, *Annales*, 4: 209–210; Denys the Carthusian, AA.SS., August, 5: 449; A. du Monstier, *Martyrologe franciscain* (Paris, 1638), 366–375.

41. Joinville, *Saint Louis*, 2: 128–130.

42. Guillaume de Chartres, *De vita et actibus*, 93.

43. Geoffroy de Beaulieu, *Sancti Ludovici vita*, 149.

44. BN MS latin 911 (*Ludovicus decus regnantium*), fol. 12, lesson 5; BN MS latin 1288 (*Francorum rex magnificus*), fol. 492, lesson 3; BN MS latin 13239A (*Lauda celestis regio*), fol. 384v, lesson 8.

45. P.-M. Auzas, "Essai d'un répertoire iconographique de Saint Louis," *7e centenaire . . . de Saint Louis*, 156; S. M. Crist, "The Breviary of Saint Louis: The Development of a Legendary Miracle," *Journal of the Warburg and Courtauld Institute* 28 (1965): 319–323.

46. Guillaume Guiart, *La Branche des royaux lignages*, CCNF, 8: 48.

47. BN MS français 13754, fol. 25.

48. Giovanni Villani, *Chronica*, ed. F. Dragomanni (Florence, 1844), 1: 285; H. de Sponde, *Continuation des annales de Baronius* (Paris, 1641), 1: 264–265.

49. Guillaume de Saint-Pathus, *Vie et miracles*, 31; GC, 7: 175.

50. This was a fiction created by Panormitanus at the end of the fifteenth century, but it met with little success in France. We find only one later reference to it there. AA.SS., August, 5: 428; du Monstier, *Martyrologe*, 376.

51. BN MS français 13754, fols. 37–38; BN MS français 5715 (Etienne Leblanc, *Les gestes de la reine Blanche*), fols. 1–21.

52. Etienne de Bourbon, *Anecdotes historiques*, 338–340.

53. AA.SS., August, 5: 442.

54. BN MS français 24954 (Battista Mantuanus, *Carmen de sancto Ludovico*), fols. 230–231.

55. Thomas de Cantimpré, *Bonum universale*, 1: 591.

56. J. B. Lezana, *Annales sacri ordinis beatae Mariae Virginis de monte Carmeli* (Rome, 1654), 4: 338.

57. H. Martin, *Les Ordres mendiants en Bretagne* (Paris, 1975).

58. André de la Roche, *De psalterio* (Cologne, 1480) (unpaged); Seraphino Razzi, *Hortulus exemplorum* (Florence, 1594), n. 26; AA.SS., August, 5: 285; du Monstier, *Martyrologe*, 390. There was possibly confusion here with a popular story about the birth of Philip Augustus.

59. Clichthove, *De laudibus*, 7; C. Franchet, *Saint Louis roi de France* (Paris, 1954).

60. Thomas Aquinas, *Opera omnia*, ed. S. E. Fretté (Paris, 1884), 21: 292–293.

61. P. Mestreus, *Oratio de laudibus sancti Ludovici* (Paris, 1551), 4v.

62. BN MS latin 911 (*Ludovicus decus regnantium*), fols. 1–9v, lesson 1.

63. F. Michel, *Mystère de Saint Louis*, 1–2; C. Tesseyre, "Le prince chrétien aux XVe et XVIe siècles à travers les représentations de Charlemagne et de Saint Louis," *Annales de Bretagne* 87 (1980): 409–414.

64. P. Desagroux, *De divi Ludovici praeconis oratio* (Paris, 1516), A iv.

65. BN MS français 5869 (*Compilation en l'honneur de Louis XII sur Saint Denis*), fol. 4.

66. AA.SS., August, 5: 466; Humbert de Romans, "Expositiones super regulam Augustini," in M. de LaBigne, *Maxima bibliotheca veterum patrum* (Paris, 1677), 25: 631.

67. J. B. Lazana, *Annales*, 338.

68. L. d'Achery, *Spicilegium*, 2: 645.

69. L. d'Achery, *Spicilegium*, 2: 645.

70. Guillaume de Saint-Pathus, *Vie et miracles*, 82–83; Wadding, *Annales*, 2: 85.

71. Thomas de Cantimpré, *Bonum universale*, 591.

72. E. Bertaux, "Les Saint Louis de l'art italien," *Revue des deux mondes* (1900): 616–644.

73. AA.SS., August, 5: 447. This liturgy was published in Paris in 1650 but is very difficult to find.

74. M.-H. Laurent, *Le Culte de saint Louis d'Anjou à Marseille au XIVe siècle* (Rome, 1954), vol. 2.

75. Auzas, "Répertoire iconographique."

76. J. Favier, *Philippe le Bel* (Paris, 1978), 98, 250–254.

77. Auzas, "Répertoire iconographique."

78. Guillaume de Saint-Pathus, *Vie et miracles*, 86–92.

79. L. Carolus-Barré, "La grande ordonnance de 1254 sur la réforme de l'administration et la police du royaume," *7e Centenaire de la mort de Saint Louis*, 85–96; *Ordonnances*, 1: 65–75.

80. Joinville, *Histoire*, 388.

81. Michel, *Mystère de Saint Louis*, 271–272; Gringoire, *Oeuvres*, 2: 255–256.

82. D. O'Connell, *The Teachings of Saint Louis* (Chapel Hill, 1972).

83. C. Dufayard, "La réaction féodale sous les fils de Philippe le Bel," *Revue historique* 54 (1894): 241–272; and 55 (1895): 241–250; A. Artonne, *Le Mouvement de 1314 et les chartes provinciales de 1315* (Paris, 1912); P. Contamine, "De la puissance aux privilèges, les doléances de la noblesse française envers la monarchie," in P. Contamine, ed., *La Noblesse au Moyen Age: Essais à la mémoire de R. Boutruche* (Paris, 1976), 235–257.

84. Geoffroy de Paris, *La Chronique métrique*, ed. A. Diverres (Paris, 1956).

85. Gervais du Bus, *Le Roman de Fauvel*, ed. A. Langfors (Paris, 1914–1919).

86. J. Favier, "Les finances de Louis IX," *7e Centenaire de la mort de Saint Louis*, 133–141.

87. R. Cazelles, "La stabilisation de la monnaie par la création du franc: Blocage d'une société?" *Traditio* 32 (1976): 296–311; R. Cazelles, "Quelques réflexions à propos des mutations de la monnaie royale française," *Le Moyen Age*, series 4, vol. 21 (1960): 83–105, 251–278.

88. Artonne, *Mouvement de 1314*, 198–204.

89. Artonne, *Mouvement de 1314*, 189; *Ordonnances*, 1: 573–576, 557–567.

90. Villani, *Chronica*, 2: 70.

91. *Ordonnances,* 1: 325.

92. *Ordonnances,* 1: 400 (Dec. 1303), 407 (May 1304), 431 (May 1305), 442 (June 1306), 452 (Sept. 1308), 477 (Jan. 1310), 536 (1314), 615 (Jan. 1315), 559 (April 1315).

93. *Ordonnances,* 2: 45 (March 1329), 34 (Sept. 1329), 83 (March 1332).

94. J. Babelon, "La monnaie de Saint Louis," in *Le siècle de Saint Louis,* 83–88.

95. Villani, *Chronica,* 1: 259.

96. BN MS latin 911, fol. 11v., lesson 5.

97. BN MS latin 13239A, fol. 383v.

98. BN MS français 5719 (*Probation de ce que Monseigneur Saint Louis ne détruisit point le royaume*), fols. 23–30.

99. BN MS français 13754, fols. 30–31. This story was probably told to visitors of the royal tombs at Saint-Denis and associated perhaps with the solid-gold cross given the abbey in 1205 by Philip Augustus: G. Millet, *Le Trésor de Saint-Denis* (Paris, 1612), 86.

100. Du Monstier, *Martyrologe,* 383.

101. C. Ménard, *Histoire de Saint Louis* (Paris, 1617), 338.

102. BN MS français 5719, fols. 23–30.

103. BN MS français 5719, fols. 23–30; BN MS français 9688, fol. 41v; Clichthove, *De laudibus,* 29v: "He established new taxes to pay that ransom, which was very high. These taxes continued afterwards, but that was the fault of his successors and not his. Besides, it is normal that the people pay the ransom of its king."

104. C. Gauvard and G. Labory, "Une chronique rimée parisienne écrite en 1409: 'Les aventures depuis 200 ans,' " *Le Métier d'historien au Moyen Age,* ed. B. Guenée (Paris, 1977), 182–231.

105. BN MS français 9688, fol. 41v. This text also includes a number of previously unknown legends about Clovis and Philip Augustus, but its primary focus is the fourteenth century.

106. BN MS français 5719, fols. 23–30. The author was a clerk or jurist in the service of the Bourbons. When he was disgraced, he entered the service of Louise de Savoie and there wrote this text and a history of Blanche of Castille (BN MS français 5715, a text with striking resemblances to the book of the confraternity of dry-goods merchants, BN MS français 13754).

107. Gottschalk Hollen, *Sermonum,* vol. 2, sermon 96.

108. Aeneas Sylvius Piccolomini, *Rerum memorabilium commentarii* (Rome 1844), 1: 259–260.

109. Du Monstier, *Martyrologe,* 383.

110. R. Cazelles, "Une exigence de l'opinion depuis Saint Louis: la réformation du royaume," *Annuaire-Bulletin de la Société d'Histoire de France* (1962–1963): 91–99.

111. Jacques de Cessoles, *Les Echecs moralisés* (Paris, 1504), fols. 8r–v, 18v, 24.

112. O'Connell, *Teachings.*

113. Geoffroy de Paris, *Chronique métrique,* 212–214.

114. Gervais du Bus, *Fauvel,* 1: 40, 45; 2: 115.

115. *Ordonnances*, 1: 551 (Norman charter), 559 (Burgundian charter), 562 (charter for Vermandois), 558 (charter for Forez), 613 (charter for Auvergne), 636 (charter for Languedoc): the first four from 1315, the last two from 1316.

116. Artonne, *Mouvement de 1314*, 199.

117. *Ordonnances*, 2: 129 (28 July 1338), 139 (15 Feb. 1345); 3: 112 (Feb. 1356).

118. Cazelles, "Réformation du royaume."

119. Philippe de Vitry, *Oeuvres*, ed. P. Tarbé (Reims, 1850); A. Piaget, "Le Chapel des fleurs de lys et le dit de Franc Gontier de Philippe de Vitry," *Romania* 26 (1898): 55–92.

120. Jean Dupin, *Le Champ vertueux de bonne vie appelée Mandevie* (Paris, no date), D ii and G iv.

121. Guillaume de Machaut, *Oeuvres*, ed. E. Hoeppfner (Paris, 1911), 2: 311; 3: 114; "Le Voire dit," ed. B. Ten Brink, *Chaucerstudien* (Munich, 1870), 222–224; *Oeuvres complètes*, ed. V. Chichmaref and L. de Mas Latrie (Paris, 1909), 1: 251; C. Gauvard, "Etude sur les idées politiques de Guillaume de Machaut," *Colloque Guillaume de Machaut* (Paris, 1982), 23–39.

122. H. Miskimin, "The Last Act of Charles V: The Background of the Revolts of 1382," *Speculum* 26 (1963): 433–442.

123. Michel, *Mystère*, 270; Gringoire, *Oeuvres*, 2: 256.

124. Cessoles, *Echecs*, fols. 24, 50.

125. AA.SS., August, 5: 287–289.

126. Jehan Masselin, *Le Journal des Etats généraux de 1484*, ed. A. Bernier (Paris, 1835), 679.

127. Clichthove, *De laudibus*, 23: "D'administrer sagement, d'être un monarque prudent et modéré."

128. D. Barthélmy, *Les Deux Ages de la seigneurie banale: pouvoir et société dans la terre des sires de Coucy* (Paris, 1984): 475–484; GC, 7: 190–193; Gringoire, *Oeuvres*, 2: 221–231; BN MS français 13754, fol. 45v.

129. Lecoy de La Marche, *L'Esprit*, 98–100.

130. BN MS français 13754, fol. 17; D'Averoult, *Fleur des exemples*, 1: 497.

131. Auzas, "Répertoire iconographique."

132. BN MS français 20064 (*Panégyrique de Saint Louis*, 1681), fol. 260.

133. Joinville, *Histoire*, 22.

134. Auzas, "Répertoire iconographique."

135. *Ordonnances*, 1: 321 (1291), 402 (1303).

136. Joinville, *Histoire*, 299; B. Mahieu, "Le livre des métiers d'Etienne Boileau," in Babelon, ed., *Siècle*, 64–75.

137. J. P. Genet, *Four English Political Tracts of the Later Middle Ages* (London, 1977), 203–204.

138. Christine de Pisan, *The "Livre de paix,"* ed. C. Willard (The Hague, 1958), 160.

139. Christine de Pisan, *Le Livre des fais et bonnes meurs du sage roi Charles V*, ed. S. Solente (Paris, 1936), 1: 86.

140. R. Delachenal, *Chronique des règnes de Jean II et de Charles V* (Paris, 1916–1920), 2: 252.

141. *Ordonnances*, 6: 26–30.

142. *Ordonnances*, 2: 128 (1338 in Languedoc), 28 (1350 at Mâcon); 6: 619 (1380 at Bruère); 7: 781 (1390 at Lère).

143. Le Religieux de Saint-Denis, *Chronique de Charles VI*, ed. and trans. L. F. Bellaguet (Paris, 1839–1852), 6: 165.

144. Quicherat, *Procès de condamnation*, 4: 295.

145. *Ordonnances*, 9: 518 (1410).

146. Gringoire, *Oeuvres*, 2: xii–xv. The confraternity, founded in 1478, was located in the church of Saint-Blaise-et-Saint-Louis on the rue Galande.

147. *Ordonnances*, 5: 559 (1353 and 1372).

148. *Ordonnances*, 9: 238 (1407).

149. G. du Bois, *Historia ecclesiae parisiensis* (Paris, 1690), 2: 325; *Ordonnances*, 9: 541 (1410). On the incident, see G. Duby, *Le Dimanche de Bouvines* (Paris, 1973), 182–230.

150. R. de Lespinasse, *Les Métiers et corporations de Paris* (Paris, 1892), 2: 242–257.

151. *Ordonnances*, 19: 478.

152. Thomas de Cantimpré, *Bonum universale*, 1: 591.

153. Joinville, *Histoire*, 15. Some of Louis's personal possessions were kept as relics by Parisian churches: his ring and crusading sword at the Sainte-Chapelle, and a hairshirt at the church of the Trinitaires.

154. AA.SS., August, 5: 648–649.

155. Guillaume de Chartres, *De vita et actibus*, RHGF, 20:37.

156. Auzas, "Répertoire iconographique." Saint Louis appears with gloves in the chapel of Saint-Sépulcre, at Bouquetot, Roman, Champigny-sur-Veude, and Marigné. Another possible explanation for this iconography is the legend that Louis wore gloves at his coronation.

157. De Lespinasse, *Métiers*, 2: 241.

158. L. Carolus-Barré, "Saint Louis dans l'histoire et la légende," *Annuaire-Bulletin de la Société de l'Histoire de France* (1970–1971): 37–49.

159. G. Dufresne de Beaucourt, *Histoire de Charles VII* (Paris, 1881–1891), 213–220; V. Martin, *Les Origines du gallicanisme en France* (Paris, 1939), 1: 67–68; N. Valois, *Histoire de la Pragmatique Sanction de Bourges* (Paris, 1906), 139, 141, 193–194.

160. Dufresne de Beaucourt, *Charles VII*, 213–220; BN MS latin 4242 (Bernard du Rosier, *Accensus veris luminis*), fols. 213–407; J.-L. Gazzaniga, *L'Eglise du Midi à la fin du règne de Charles VII* (Paris, 1976), 67–68.

161. BN MS latin 4242 (Bernard du Rosier, *Harangue faite devant le roi Charles pour les habitants de Béziers*), fols. 555–561.

162. Thomas Basin, *L'Apologie de Thomas Basin*, ed. C. Samarin and C. Groer (Paris, 1974).

163. *Ordonnances*, 15: 195–208 (Nov. 1461), articles 5 and 41.

164. BN MS latin 10045, fols. 304–316.

165. BN MS français 2701 (Jean Jouvenal des Ursins, *Verba mea*), fol. 101; P. de Marca, *De concordia sacerdotii et imperii* (Paris, 1663), 2: 301; Jean Bouchet, *Annales d'Aquitaine* (Paris, 1527), bk. 4: 100.

166. BN MS latin 10045, fols. 304–316.

167. Le Religieux de Saint-Denis, *Chronique*, 6: 165.

168. BN MS nouv. acq. française 6214 (*Cy commence le traité des droits que le roi Charles VII a à la couronne*), fol. 12v.; C. Ménard, *Histoire de Saint Louis* (Paris, 1617), 295.

169. *Oeuvres de Georges Chastellain*, ed. J. Kervyn de Lettenhove (Brussels, 1863–1866), 1: 24.

170. Clichthove, *De laudibus*, 28v, 29.

171. Christophe de Longueil, *Oratio de laudibus sancti Ludovici* (Paris, 1510), C 3v and C 4.

172. BN MS français 24954, fols. 230–231.

173. P. Morel, "Le culte de Saint Louis," *Itinéraires* (1970): 127–151.

4. SANCTUARIES AND FESTIVALS OF THE KINGDOM OF BOURGES

1. They have been the subject of much recent work: Y. Chauvin, "Le livre des miracles de sainte Catherine de Fierbois," *Bulletin de la Société des Antiquaires de l'Ouest* 13 (1975): 282–311; the same author has published an edition of BN MS français 15538 in "Le livre des miracles de sainte Catherine de Fierbois," *Archives historiques du Poitou* 60 (1972); J.-L. Lemaître, "Les miracles de saint Martial lors des ostensions de 1388," *Bulletin de la Société historique et archéologique du Limousin* 102 (1975): 67–139.

2. L. Cellier, "Sanctae Catarinae translatio et miracula," *Analecta Bolland-iana* 22 (1903): 423–438; R. Fawtier, "Les reliques rouennaises de sainte Catherine d'Alexandrie," *Analecta Bollandiana* 41 (1923): 357–368.

3. Jacques de Voragine, *La Légende dorée*, ed. and trans. T. de Wyzewa (Paris, 1929), 3: 769–776.

4. H. Varnhagen, *Zum Geschichte der Legende der Katherine von Alexandrien* (Erlangen, 1891), 18–23.

5. A. Langlois, "La vie de sainte Catherine par le peintre Etienne Lansquelier," *Romania* 39 (1910): 54–60.

6. Pierre de Natali, *Catalogus sanctorum* (1521), fols. 182v–183; M. Sepet, *La Vie de sainte Catherine de Jean Miélot* (Paris, 1881).

7. Vincent Ferrier, *Oeuvres complètes*, ed. P. Fagès (Paris, 1909), 1: 113–122.

8. Jacques de Voragine, *Légende dorée*, 3: 769–776.

9. P. Champion, *La Librairie de Charles d'Orléans* (Paris, 1910), 79–80.

10. J. B. Fourault, *Sainte-Catherine de Fierbois* (Tours, 1887), 14.

11. G. Duby, *Le Dimanche de Bouvines* (Paris, 1973), 184.

12. S. Luce, *Jeanne d'Arc à Domremy* (Paris, 1887).

13. Chauvin, "Le Livre des miracles," in *Arch. hist. Poitou*.

14. Luce, *Jeanne d'Arc*, 127.

15. J. Quicherat, *Procès de condamnation et de réhabilitation de Jeanne d'Arc* (Paris, 1841–1850), 1: 185.

16. F. Guessard and E. de Certain, *Le Mystère du siège d'Orléans* (Paris, 1862), 412–415.

17. Fourault, *Ste-Catherine*, 20.

18. Chauvin, "Le Livre des miracles," *Arch. hist. Poitou,* 284–285, 302.

19. F. Arbellot, *Miracula sancti Martiali parata anno 1388* (Brussels, 1882); Lemaître, "Miracles de Saint Martial."

20. AA.SS., June, 5: 535–573.

21. Miracle 1 in J. L. Lemaître, "Les miracles de saint Martial lors des ostensions de 1388," *Bulletin de la société historique et archéologique du Limousin* 102 (1975): 67–139.

22. A. Perrier, "Une manifestation populaire de religiosité: les ostensions limousines," *Bulletin de la Société archéologique et historique du Limousin* 101 (1974): 119–156; M. Ardent, *Les Ostensions limousines* (Limoges, 1835).

23. A. Vauchez, *La Sainteté en Occident aux derniers siècles du Moyen Age* (Paris, 1981), 660.

24. B. Chevalier, *Tours, ville royale* (Paris, 1975).

25. *Ordonnances,* 13: 192.

26. *Ordonnances,* 18: 158 (Dec. 1475).

27. *Ordonnances,* 18: 716 (Jan. 1481).

28. *Ordonnances,* 15: 313–316.

29. BN MS français 2099 (*La Translation de la légende de monseigneur saint Julien*).

30. J. Lespinasse, "Le Culte de saint Julien de Brioude," *Almanach de Brioude* (1934): 25–27.

31. E. de Torquat, *Histoire de Cléry* (Orléans, 1856).

32. Guessard and de Certain, *Mystère d'Orléans.*

33. *Ordonnances,* 18: 135 (Sept. 1475).

34. *Ordonnances,* 18: 725 (Jan. 1481).

35. G. Duby, *Fêtes en France* (Paris, 1977), 184–187; A. Chédeville, J. Rossiaud, and J. Le Goff, *La Ville médiévale* (Paris, 1980), 591–603.

36. L. Guibert, *Saint-Léonard-de-Noblat au XIIIe siècle* (Paris, 1881).

37. F. Arbellot, *La Vie de saint Léonard solitaire en Limousin: ses miracles et son culte* (Paris, 1863).

38. BN MS latin 5407 (Bernard Gui, *Speculum Sanctorale*), fol. 210.

39. Jacques de Voragine, *Légende dorée,* 1: 134.

40. Vincent of Beauvais, *Speculum majus* (Douai, 1624), 4: 821–822.

41. BN MS latin 5407, fol. 210. Etienne Maleu (canon of Saint-Junien from 1282 to 1322), by contrast, remained content with having Leonardus baptized at the same time as Clovis: *Chronique d'Etienne Maleu, chanoine de Saint-Junien,* ed. F. Arbellot (Saint-Junien, 1847), 13.

42. Pierre de Natali, *Catalogus,* fols. 182–183.

43. *Ordonnances,* 17: 336–337 (Oct. 1470).

44. L. Guibert, "Une ballade au roi Charles VII," *Bulletin de la Société archéologique et historique du Limousin* 42 (1894): 556–558.

45. *Ordonnances,* 15: 115 (Jan. 1422), 116 (Oct. 1423).

46. A. Leroux, "Don par Charles VII d'un reliquaire à Noblat," *Bulletin du Comité des travaux historiques* 25 (1906): 110–115.

47. M. Robert, "La quintaine limousine," *Bulletin de la Société d'ethnographie du Limousin* 13 (1965): 193–197.

48. Duby, *Fêtes.*

49. E. Aubugeois, *Histoire du Dorat* (Paris, 1880).

50. E. Rougerie, *Vie de saint Israël et saint Théobald* (Le Dorat, 1871).

51. C. T. Allmand, *Lancastrian Normandy (1415–1450)* (Oxford, 1983), 305; F. Dupuis, *Mémoire sur le siège de Montargis en 1427* (Orléans, 1853).

52. Quicherat, *Procès*, 5: 4.

53. P. Charpentier and E. Cuissard, *Le Journal du siège d'Orléans* (Paris, 1896), 150–155, 240 ff.

54. Guessard and de Certain, *Mystère*.

55. Allmand, *Lancastrian Normandy*, 660; P. Champion, *Splendeurs et misères de Paris aux XIVe et XVe siècles* (Paris, 1934), 164.

56. Allmand, *Lancastrian Normandy*, 305; L. Vitet, "Fragments historiques: le siège de Dieppe," *Revue de Rouen* 1 (1833): 83.

57. H. Fromage, "Jeanne Hachette, histoire et légende," *Bulletin de la Société de mythologie française*, no. 101 (1976): 41–63.

58. *Ordonnances*, 27: 529 (July 1472), 530 (July 1472), 531 (June 1473), and 583 (Feb. 1474).

59. J. Chastenet, *Beauvais: vingt siècles d'histoire* (Paris, 1972).

60. Allmand, *Lancastrian Normandy*; R. Jouet, *La Résistance à l'occupation anglaise en Normandie* (Caen, 1969).

61. Jacques Duclerq, *Mémoires*, CCNF, 37: 83.

62. Jean Chartier, *Chroniques de Charles VII*, ed. A. Vallet de Viriville (Paris, 1858), 2: 233.

63. For what follows, see E. Le Mâle, "La Fête de la *Reductio Normaniae*," *Baiocana* 3 (1911): 49–70; 4 (1912): 193–242; suppl. 1 (1913): 61–78; suppl. 2 (1914): 60–70.

64. Jacques Duclercq, *Mémoires*; Orlando dei Talenti, quoted in Le Mâle "La Fête," *Baiocana* 3 (1911), 60–70; Thomas Basin, *Histoire de Charles VII*, ed. C. Samarin (Paris, 1933–1944), 2: 155–157.

65. Jean Bouchet, *Annales d'Aquitaine* (Paris, 1527), 258–259.

66. J. Filleau, *Les Preuves des litanies de sainte Radegonde* (Paris, 1878), 184–190.

67. J.-T. Voisin, *Histoire de Cherbourg* (Cherbourg, 1835).

68. A. Mirot and B. Mahieu, "Cérémonies officielles à Notre-Dame de Paris au XVe siècle," *8e centenaire de Notre-Dame de Paris* (Paris, 1967), 263–290.

69. Bouchet, *Annales*, 258–259.

70. Le Mâle, "La Fête."

71. Basin, *Histoire*, 2: 155–157.

72. Talenti, in Le Mâle, "La Fête," *Baiocana* 3 (1911): 60–70.

73. Chevalier, *Tours*; P. Desportes, *Reims et les Rémois aux XIIIe et XIVe siècles* (Paris, 1975).

74. Accompanying the festival at Tournai was a *puy* or poetry competition for patriotic verse, similar to the *puys* at Tournai during the Feast of the Assumption: F. Smet, *Recueil des chroniques de Flandre* (Brussels, 1880), 3: 469.

75. C. Pfister, *Histoire de Nancy* (Paris, 1902), 1: 566–575; H. Tribout de Morembert, "Une pieuse fondation de la municipalité de Metz: la chapelle de la Victoire dite des Lorrains, 1476–1754," *Bulletin philologique et historique*

de la Comité des Travaux historiques (Congrès de Montpellier, 1961) (1963): 235–247.

5. SAINT MICHAEL

1. *Dictionnaire d'archéologie chrétienne et de liturgie,* 1: 2080; *Dictionnaire de spiritualité,* 1: 579–626; *Dictionnaire de théologie catholique,* 1: 1189–1271. Daniel X, 13; XII, 1; Eccl. XVII, 17; Exodus XXIII, 20–23; Maccabees XV, 23; Kings XIX, 35; Apocalypse XII, 1–10; Deut. XXII; Jude IX.

2. Exodus XXIII, 20.

3. Daniel X, 13; XII, 1.

4. Pseudo-Dionysus, *De hierarchia angelorum,* PL, vol. 3, cols. 120–370.

5. O. Rojdestvensky, *Le Culte de saint Michel et le Moyen Age latin* (Paris, 1922); M. Baudot, "La diffusion et l'évolution du culte de saint Michel en France," *Millénaire monastique du Mont-Saint-Michel* (Paris, 1967), 3: 99–112.

6. Hrabanus Maurus, PL, vol. 112, col. 1659; Alcuin, MGH, *Poetae aevi carolini,* 1: 307.

7. J. Hourlier, "Le Mont-Saint-Michel avant 966," *Millénaire,* 1: 13–28; M. Lelegard, "Saint Aubert," *Millénaire,* 1: 29–52.

8. Hourlier, "Mont-St-Michel"; T. Leroy, *Curieuses recherches* (Paris, 1878), 1: 407–419.

9. Leroy, *Recherches,* 1: 419 ff.

10. Lelegard, "Saint Aubert."

11. A. Dufief, "La vie monastique du Mont-Saint-Michel au XIIe siècle," *Millénaire,* 1: 80–126; R. Foreville, "Robert de Torigny et Clio," *Millénaire,* 2: 141–153.

12. Guillaume de Saint-Pair, *Le Roman du Mont,* ed. E. de Beaurepaire and F. Michel (Caen, 1856); R. Herval, "Un moine jongleur au Mont-Saint-Michel: Guillaume de Saint-Pair," *Millénaire,* 2: 397–411.

13. J. Laporte, "L'Epée et bouclier dits 'de saint Michel,' " *Millénaire,* 2: 397–411. They were referred to as well by the poet Baudry de Bourgueil.

14. *Roland,* I, ll. 196, 200, 295; II, ll. 214, 216, 217, 2394; *Covenant Vivien,* l. 4; *Les Aliscans,* l. 11; *Ogier le Danois,* l. 10995; *Huon de Bordeaux,* l. 4; *Esclaramonde de Foix,* l. 854; *Aiol,* l. 9407; *Galien,* l. 8002; Richard le Pèlerin, *La Chanson d'Antioche,* ed. E. de Sainte-Aulaire (Paris, 1862); Guillaume de Tyre, *Histoire de Jérusalem,* ed. P. Paris (Paris, 1880), 2: 109. R. Lejeune, "Le Mont-Saint-Michel au péril de la mer, la chanson de Roland et le pèlerinage de Compostelle," *Millénaire,* 2: 411–433.

15. P. Morel, "Saint Michel dans la titulature et le patronage des lieux de culte en France," *Millénaire,* 3: 127–234; C. Rémy-Lassale, "Les sanctuaires consacrés à saint Michel en France," *Millénaire,* 3: 113–127.

16. BN MS français 2365 (*L'ordre royal de France*), fol. 19.

17. Rigord and Guillaume Le Breton, *Oeuvres,* ed. H.-F. Delaborde (Paris, 1882–1885), 2: 214.

18. E. R. Labande, "Les pèlerinages au Mont-Saint-Michel," *Millénaire,* 3: 237–250.

19. J. Dubois, "Le trésor des reliques de l'abbaye du Mont-Saint-Michel," *Millénaire,* 1: 501–503, nn. 22 and 22A.

20. J. Chazelas, "La vie monastique au Mont au XIIIe siècle," *Millénaire,* 1: 127–150.

21. S. Luce, *Jeanne d'Arc à Domrémy* (Paris, 1887), 87; P. Perdrizet, "Anges et Saluts," *Revue numismatique* 35 (1932): 189–197.

22. Le Père Anselme, *Histoire généologique et chronologique de la maison royale de France* (Paris, 1726–1733), 1: 99–104.

23. Dubois, "Trésor des reliques," 501–503, nn. 10 and 10A; G. Lobineau, *La Vie des saints de Bretagne* (Paris, 1836), 3: 92–93.

24. Baudot, "La diffusion et l'évolution."

25. Perdrizet, "Anges et Saluts."

26. Dubois, "Trésor des reliques."

27. Anselme, *Histoire généalogique,* 1: 115.

28. M. Reulos, "L'organisation et l'administration de l'abbaye par Pierre Leroy," *Millénaire,* 1: 191–209.

29. A.N., KK 53, fols. 21 and 85v.

30. M. Gasnier, *Saint Michel archange* (Paris, 1940), 120.

31. B. Guenée and F. Lehoux, *Les Entrées royales françaises de 1328 à 1515* (Paris, 1968), 77, 275; Martial d'Auvergne, *Les Vigiles de Charles VII,* ed. E. Coustelier (Paris, 1724), 1: 159.

32. J.-B. de Vaivre, "Les cerfs ailés et la tapisserie de Rouen," *Gazette des Beaux-Arts* 87 (1982): 93–108; E. Picot, "Notes sur une tapisserie à figures symboliques," *Bulletin de la Société de l'histoire de Normandie* 111 (1911): 111–120.

33. BN MS français 2701 (Jean Jouvenal des Ursins, *Discours politiques*), fol. 87; Jean Jouvenal des Ursins, *Ecrits politiques,* ed. P. S. Lewis (Paris, 1978), 2: 190–191.

34. G. Dufresne de Beaucourt, *Histoire de Charles VII* (Paris, 1881–1891), 1: 240–241.

35. Luce, *Jeanne d'Arc,* 87–92.

36. S. Luce, *Chronique du Mont-Saint-Michel* (Paris, 1879), 1: 34–35.

37. A chronogram is a Latin verse in whose text a date has been encoded, represented here by bold capitals. Putting them together gives MCCCLLVVVVVIIII (1434). The text is given in S. Luce, ed., *Chronique de Saint Michel,* 35.

38. Guillaume Cousinot, *Chronique,* ed. A. Vallet de Viriville (Paris, 1859), 219–220; Jean Chartier, *Chronique de Charles VII,* ed. A. Vallet de Viriville (Paris, 1858), 38–39; Enguerrand de Monstrelet, *Chronique,* ed. L. Douet d'Arcq (Paris, 1857–1862), 4: 275–276.

39. L. Brochet, *Histoire de Saint-Michel-en-l'Herm* (Fontenay-le-Comte, 1891), 46.

40. J. Quicherat, *Procès de condamnation et de réhabilitation de Jeanne d'Arc* (Paris, 1841–1850), 5: 122–123.

41. Chartier, *Chronique,* 2: 320.

42. Dufresne de Beaucourt, *Histoire,* 5: 52.

43. *Ordonnances,* 19: 301; 13: 497; S. Luce, *Jeanne d'Arc,* "pièces justificatives," 95–96, 132–133.

44. Luce, *Jeanne d'Arc,* 108–112; R. Delaruelle, "L'archange saint Michel dans la spiritualité de Jeanne d'Arc," *Millénaire,* 2: 363–367.

45. F. Guessard and E. de Certain, *Le Mystère du siège d'Orléans* (Paris, 1862), 273.

46. Brochet, *Saint-Michel-en-l'Herm.*

47. B. Sébillot, *Le Folklore de la France* (Paris, 1907), 2: 18; and 4: 356; A. de Barante, *Histoire des ducs de Bourgogne* (Brussels, 1839), 9: 239.

48. *Ordonnances,* 17: 236–237.

49. *Ordonnances,* 18: 217–223; Cossé-Brissac, "L'ordre de Saint-Michel," *Amis de Mont-Saint-Michel,* no. 79 (1969–1970): 7–17.

50. BN MS français 5746, fol. 3; BN MS français 14361, fol. 6; BN MS français 19819 (MS illuminated by Jean Fouquet), fol. 1; BN MS français 19815, fol. 11; BN MS français 25190, fol. 1. All are statutes of the order.

51. W. R. Staehlin, "Symbolischer Wandteppich zum Gedächtnis an die Stiftung des Sankts Michael Orden," *Archives héraldiques suisses* 39 (1925): 80–82; de Vaivre, "Les cerfs ailés."

52. BN MS français 2365, fols. 1–18.

53. E. O. Gordon, *Saint George, Patron of England* (London, 1907), 69–85; B. Riehl, *Sankt Michael und Sankt Georg in der bildenden Kunst* (Munich, 1883).

54. P. Deschamps, "La légende de saint Georges dans les peintures murales du Moyen Age," *Académie des Inscriptions et Belles-lettres. Fondation Piot. Monuments et mémoires* 56 (1950): 109–123.

55. Y. Renouard, "L'ordre de la Jarretière et l'ordre de l'Etoile: étude sur la génèse des ordres laïcs de chevalerie et sur le développement progressif de leur caractère national," *Le Moyen Age* 55 (1949): 281–300.

56. W. Paravicini, *Karl der Kühne* (Göttingen, 1968), 48–49.

57. C. Rémy-Lasalle, "Les représentations du combat de l'Archange en France," *Millénaire* 3: 53–64; Rémy-Lasalle, "Les sanctuaires."

58. Laporte, "L'épée."

59. P. Contamine, *Guerre, état et société à la fin du Moyen Age* (Paris, 1972), 668–670.

60. J. Cuvellier, *Chronique de Bertrand Duguesclin,* ed. E. Charrière (Paris, 1839), 1: 31, ll. 784–786.

61. Contamine, *Guerre,* 669.

62. A. A. Germain, P. M. Brin, and E. Corroyer, *Saint Michel et le Mont-Saint-Michel* (Paris, 1880), esp. p. 88: reproduction from the missal of Charles VI.

63. U. Gabler, "Die Kinderwahlfahrten aus Deutschland und Schweiz zum Mont-Saint-Michel," *Zeitschrift für Kirchengeschichte* 63 (1969): 221–231.

64. *Millénaire,* 3, plates 28 and 31.

65. BN MS français 5748, fol. 3.

66. BN MS français 14363, fol. 6.

67. L. Bosseboeuf, "A propos des armoiries du Mont," *Revue de l'Avranchin* 17 (1913): 207–227.

68. E. Beaurepaire, "Les miracles du Mont-Saint-Michel," *Mémoires de la Société archéologique d'Avranches* 4 (1873): 17–41.

69. BN Reserve Ye 1311 (undated) (*Le testament de Jenin de Lesche qui s'en va au Mont-Saint-Michel*).

70. E.-R. Labande, "Les pèlerinages au Mont-Saint-Michel," *Millénaire* 3: 237–250; V. Chomel, "Pèlerins languedociens au Mont-Saint-Michel à la fin du Moyen Age," *Annales du Midi* 70 (1958): 230–239; Gabler, "Kinderwahlfahrten."

71. Leroy, *Recherches* 1: 69–81.

72. Thomas Aquinas, *Opera omnia*, ed. S. E. Fretté (Paris, 1884), *Summa theologiae*, pt. 1, quaes. 111–113.

73. Denys le Chartreux, *Opera omnia* (Tournai, 1906), 15: 351–355, 421–438; 21: 491–493, 549.

74. Jean Gerson, *Oeuvres complètes*, ed. P. Glorieux (Paris, 1963), 5: 292–309, 309–324; vol. 7, pt. 2: 622–639.

75. Vincent Ferrier, *Oeuvres complètes*, ed. P. Fagès (Paris, 1909), 2: 726–734.

76. J. Wilmart, "Les prières médiévales à l'ange gardien," *La Vie spirituelle* 13 (1925): 18–40.

77. BN MS latin 1131 (*Breviary*), fols. 93–99; BN MS latin 1300 (*Breviary of Coutances*), fol. 473; BN MS latin 1065 (*Breviary of Limoges*), fol. 70v.; BN MS latin 1196 (*Book of Prayers of Charles d'Orléans*), fol. 67.

78. Jehan Masselin, *Le Journal des Etats généraux de 1484*, ed. A. Bernier (Paris, 1835), 621.

79. Guglielmus Benedicti, *Repetitio contra Raynutium* (Lyon, 1611), fol. 218v (*Adjectio impuberi*, a. 46–48).

80. BN MS français 2365, fols. 9 and 11.

81. *Ordonnances*, 18: 396–402 (1478).

82. Chomel, "Pèlerinages languedociens"; N. Valois, "Conseils et prédictions adressés à Charles VII par un certain Jehan Dubois (1445)," *Annuaire-Bulletin de la Société de l'Histoire de France* 46 (1909): 201–238.

83. A. Fouré, "Le prieuré de Saint-Michel près de Rouen," *Millénaire*, 3: 309.

84. Germain, Brin, and Corroyer, *Saint Michel*, 113.

6. THE MOST CHRISTIAN KING AND KINGDOM

1. N. Valois, "Le roi très chrétien," in M. Baudrillart, ed., *La France très chrétienne dans l'histoire* (Paris, 1885), 314–327.

2. L. Boehm, "Gedanken zum Frankreichs Bewusstsein im frühen Jahrhundert," *Historisches Jahrbuch* 74 (1955): 681–687.

3. Guibert de Nogent, *Gesta Dei per Francos*, PL, vol. 156, cols. 699–702.

4. Robert the Monk, *Historia Hierosolymitana*, PL, vol. 155, col. 671.

5. Suger, *Vita Ludovici sexti*, ed. and trans. H. Waquet (Paris, 1964).

6. Rigord and Guillaume le Breton, *Oeuvres*, ed. H.-F. Delaborde (Paris, 1882–1885), 2: 21.

7. Matthew Paris, *Chronica majora* (London, Rolls Series, 1892), 5: 480.

8. Jean Bodel, a twelfth-century author, quoted in M.-M. Martin, *Histoire de l'unité française* (Paris, 1948), 157.

9. L. Gauthier, *La Chevalerie* (Paris, 1895), 64–65; Clement V, *Registres pontificaux*, ed. A. Tosti (Rome, 1885–1892), n. 7501.

10. Matthew Paris, *Chronica*, 5: 480.

11. Cited by Martin, *Histoire*, 157.

12. GC, 1: 4–5.

13. J. R. Strayer, "France, the Holy Land, the Chosen People and the Most Christian King," in Strayer, *Medieval Statecraft and the Perspectives of History* (Princeton, 1971), 300–314.

14. J. Favier, *Philippe le Bel* (Paris, 1978).

15. Quoted in K. Wenck, *Philipp der Schöne* (Marburg, 1905), 11–12.

16. G. Picot, *Documents relatifs aux Etats généraux et assemblées réunies sous Philippe le Bel* (Paris, 1901), 12.

17. Picot, *Documents*, 34.

18. Picot, *Documents*, 34.

19. H. Wieruzowski, *Von Imperium zum nationalen Konigtum* (Berlin, 1933).

20. Picot, *Documents*, 8.

21. A. Bossuat, "La formule 'Le roi est empereur en son royaume': son emploi au XVe siècle devant le Parlement de Paris," *Revue historique de droit français et étranger*, series 4, vol. 39 (1961): 371–382.

22. Picot, *Documents*, 40.

23. Picot, *Documents*, 41.

24. P. Dupuy, *Histoire du différend d'entre le pape Boniface VIII et Philippe le Bel* (Paris, 1655), 241–243.

25. Picot, *Documents*, 30.

26. H. Kempf, *Pierre Dubois und die geistigen Grundlagen des französischen Nationalbewusstsein um 1300* (Hildesheim, 1972), 111–114.

27. Clement V, *Régistres*, n. 7501.

28. Wenck, *Philipp der Schöne*, 72.

29. M. Bloch, *Les Rois thaumaturges: étude sur le caractère surnaturel de la puissance royale* (Paris, 1961), 110.

30. Clement V, *Régistres*, n. 7501.

31. Valois, "Le roi très chrétien," 321.

32. Valois, "Le roi très chrétien," 325.

33. Charles d'Orléans, *Oeuvres complètes*, ed. J. Guichard (Paris, 1842), 182.

34. Martial d'Auvergne, *Les Vigiles de Charles VII*, ed. E. Coustelier (Paris, 1724), 2: 131.

35. L. Pannier and P. Meyer, *Le Débat des hérauts d'armes de France et d'Angleterre* (Paris, 1877), 34.

36. Pannier and Meyer, *Débat*, 39–40.

37. J.-P. Genet, "English Nationalism: Thomas Polton at the Council of Constance," *Nottingham Medieval Studies* 28 (1984): 60–78.

38. BN MS latin 11730 (Etienne de Conti, *Brevis Tractatus*), fol. 31v; P. Contamine, "Une interpolation de la Chronique martinienne: le *Brevis Trac-*

tatus d'Etienne de Conti," *Annales de Bretagne et des pays de l'Ouest* 87 (1980): 367–386; Jean Ferrault, *Tractatus jura seu privilegia regni Franciae continens* (Paris, 1545).

39. Jean de Montreuil, *L'Oeuvre polémique,* ed. E. Ornato and N. Grevy-Pons (Turin, 1963), 1: 297; Nicolas de Clamanges, *Opera omnia* (Lugduni Batavorum, 1613), *Traités,* 47–48, *Lettres,* 4.

40. Claude de Seyssel, *La Grande Monarchie de France,* ed. J. Poujol (Paris, 1961), 115.

41. Martial d'Auvergne, *Vigiles,* 2: 34.

42. Jerome, *Ad vigilantium,* PL, vol. 23, col. 339.

43. Jean Gerson, *Oeuvres complètes,* ed. P. Glorieux (Paris, 1962), 7: 522–523; A. Vernet, "Le *Tragicum argumentum de miserabili statu regni Franciae* de François de Montebelluna (1357)," *Annuaire-Bulletin de la Société d'Histoire de France* (1962–1963): 133; Robert Blondel, *Oeuvres complètes,* ed. A. Héron (Rouen, 1892), 2: 402–403; Seyssel, *Grande monarchie,* 115; BN MS français 23428 (Pierre d'Ailly, *Proposition au concile de 1406 et autres discours au même concile*), fols. 48 and 430.

44. *Ordonnances,* 15: 195 (1438).

45. BN MS français 2831, fols. 2–14 (*Réponse du dauphin aux ambassadeurs de Charles VII*).

46. Georges Chastellain, *Oeuvres,* ed. J. Kervyn de Lettenhove (Brussels, 1863–1866), 6: 1–48.

47. Brunetto Latini, *Le Livre du Trésor,* ed. P. Chabaille (Paris, 1863), 84–85, 100–101.

48. Alain Chartier, *Les Oeuvres latines,* ed. P. Bourgain-Heymerick (Paris, 1977), 177. And between these two authors: Etienne de Conti, *Brevis Tractatus,* BN MS français 2831, fols. 2–14; Martial d'Auvergne, *Vigiles,* 2: 131; Pannier and Meyer, *Le Débat,* 34.

49. BN MS français 5869.

50. Honoré Bonet, *L'Arbre des batailles,* ed. E. Nys (Brussels, 1883), 188; J. L. Brunet and P. Dupuy, *Traité des libertés de l'Eglise gallicane* (Paris, 1645), 1: 156; 2: 204–205; Robert Blondel, *Oeuvres,* 2: 402–403.

51. Etienne de Conti, *Brevis Tractatus,* BN MS français 11730, fol. 32.

52. Jean Lemaire de Belges, *Oeuvres complètes,* ed. J. Stecher (Louvain, 1885), 3: 231–359.

53. Vernet, "*Tragicum argumentum* . . . de F. de Montebelluna," 138; Blondel, *Oeuvres,* 2: 403; Guglielmus Benedicti, *Opera omnia* (Lyon, 1582), 17v.

54. BN MS nouv. acq. française 6853 (*Miroir historial* and *Liber legis Salicae*), fol. 30v.

55. BN MS latin 8537 (Orlando dei Talenti, *Discours au roi Charles VII*), fol. 34.

56. Chastellain, *Oeuvres,* 6: 136.

57. Charles d'Orléans, *Oeuvres,* 101.

58. Chastellain, *Oeuvres,* 6: 133–138; BN MS latin 16495 (Sermon "Hosanna filio David" on the war of Flanders [1302]), fols. 96v–98; Chartier, *Oeuvres latines,* 217–218.

59. Philippe de Mézières, *Le Songe du vieil pèlerin,* ed. G. W. Coopland (Cambridge, England, 1969), 1: 110.

60. BN MS latin 5971.

61. A. Linder, "L'expédition italienne de Charles VIII et les espérances messianiques des juifs," *Revue des études juives* 137 (1978): 179–186.

62. Bonet, *Arbre des batailles,* 188; Bibliothèque Mazarine, MS 3524 (Robert Gervais, *Speculum morale regium*), fol. 84v; Gerson, *Oeuvres,* 72: 519–538 (*Adorabunt eum*), 1015–1030 (*Rex in sempiternum vive*), and 1137–1183 (*Vivat rex*).

63. MGH, *Scriptores rerum merovingiacarum,* 3: 239–349.

64. BN MS français 2831 (*Réponse du dauphin*), fol. 6v.

65. B. Guenée, "Les généologies entre l'histoire et la politique: la fierté d'être capétien en France au Moyen Age," *Annales: E.S.C.* 33 (1978): 460.

66. L. Theis, *Dagobert* (Paris, 1982), 79–80.

67. E. A. R. Brown, "The Quest for Ancestry in Later Medieval Europe: Myths of Origins and Genealogies in Capetian France and Angevin and Norman Dominions," unpublished paper presented at the *Colloque "Legitimation by Descent: Myths of National Origin and Descent"* (*Paris, 1982*); Gabrielle Spiegel, "The *Reditus ad stirpem Karoli,*" *French Historical Studies* 7 (1971): 145–174.

68. Vincent of Beauvais, *Speculum Majus* (Douai, 1624), 4: 995; GC, 5: 1–2.

69. Bibliothèque Mazarine MS 3524, fol. 3v.

70. BN MS latin 5286 (Yves de Saint-Denis), fol. 195; BN MS latin 3826 (Yves de Saint-Denis), fol. 77; BN MS latin 4918 (Guillaume de Nangis), fol. 315. See G. Spiegel, "The *reditus regni ad stirpem Karoli,*" *French Historical Studies* 7 (1971): 148.

71. E. de Lagrange, *La Chanson d'Hugues Capet* (Paris, 1864).

72. Jean de Montreuil, *Oeuvre,* 2: 89.

73. BN MS latin 5971A, fol. 27.

74. Chartier, *Oeuvres,* 177.

75. J. Leclercq, "Un sermon pour les guerres de Flandres," *Revue du Moyen Age latin* 1 (1945): 169.

76. Bibliothèque Sainte-Geneviève, MS 1994, fol. 2.

77. Wieruzowski, *Von Imperium,* 14.

78. Favier, *Philippe le Bel,* 319; Dupuy, *Histoire du differend,* 635–638, 639–651, 658.

79. P. Lehugueur, *Philippe V le Long* (Paris, 1897), 17–18.

80. Jean de Saint-Victor, *Memoriale historiarum,* RHGF, 21: 658–659.

81. Guillaume de Nangis, *Chronique,* ed. H. Guéraud (Paris, 1843), 1: 404–405.

82. Jean Desnouelles, *Chronique,* RHGF, 21: 197.

83. R. Cazelles, *La Société politique et la crise de la royauté sous Philippe de Valois* (Paris, 1958), 247–252; A. Molinier, "La Chronique de Jean de Noyal," *Annuaire-Bulletin de la Société de l'Histoire de France* 21 (1883): 254.

84. Jean le Bel, *Chronique,* ed. J. Viard and E. Déprez (Paris, 1904–1905) 2: 183.

85. Gilles le Muisit, *Chronique et annales,* ed. H. Lemaître (Paris, 1906), 279–282.

86. A. Molinier, ed., *Chronique normande du XIVe siècle* (Paris, 1882), 96–97.

87. Le Muisit, *Chronique*, 279–282.

88. R. Delachenal, ed., *Chronique des règnes de Jean II et de Charles V* (Paris, 1916–1920), 1: 28–30.

89. Jean Froissart, *Chroniques*, ed. S. Luce, G. Raynaud, L. Mirot, and A. Mirot (Paris, 1869–1967), 4: 124–125.

90. Le Muisit, *Chronique*, 279–282.

91. Jean le Bel, *Chronique*, 2: 198–200.

92. This was probably the first occasion that a representation of the deceased was used in a funeral ceremony at the royal court. AN, series KK, n. 19 (1387–1388), fols. 103–105.

93. Vernet, "Le *Tragicum argumentum*," 138.

94. Blondel, *Oeuvres*, 2: 85.

95. P. S. Lewis, *Later Medieval France*, 114.

96. Dufresne de Beaucourt, *Histoire de Charles VII* (Paris, 1881), 1: 8.

97. Blondel, *Oeuvres*, 2: 85.

98. Bloch, *Rois thaumaturges*, 208.

99. J. Quicherat, *Procès de condamnation et de réhabilitation de Jeanne d'Arc* (Paris, 1841–1850), 4: 279–281.

100. L. Boca, *La Chanson de Baudouin de Sebourc* (Paris, 1845), 251, 256.

101. C. T. Wood, "Queens, Queans, and Kingship," in *Order and Innovation in the Middle Ages: Essays in Honor of Joseph R. Strayer* (Princeton, 1976), 385–400.

102. S. Luce, *Chronique des quatre premiers Valois (1327–1393)* (Paris, 1862), 289; R. A. Jackson, "Peers of France and Princes of the Blood," *French Historical Studies* 7 (1971): 27–46.

103. Boca, *Chanson . . . B. de Sebourc*, 320; *Ordonnances*, 5: 113.

104. Enguerrand de Monstrelet, *Chronique*, ed. L. Douet d'Arcq (Paris, 1857–1862), 2: 388.

105. Monstrelet, *Chronique*, 2: 128.

106. Monstrelet, *Chronique*, 2: 82.

107. Monstrelet, *Chronique*, 2: 377 and ff.

108. S. Solente, "Christine de Pisan, *L'Epitre de prison de vie humaine*," *Bibliothèque de l'Ecole des Chartes* 75 (1924): 282.

109. A. Tuetey, *Journal d'un bourgeois de Paris (1405–1449)* (Paris, 1881), 276.

110. Jean Le Fevre de Saint-Remy, *Chronique*, CCNF, 32: 279; Jacques Duclercq, *Mémoires*, CCNF, 39: 371; Monstrelet, *Chronique*, 2: 388.

111. Jehan Masselin, *Le Journal des Etats généraux de 1484*, ed. A. Bernier, (Paris, 1835), 169, 236–237.

112. Cosme Guimier, *Commentaire sur la Pragmatique Sanction* (Paris, 1546), fol. 140.

113. BN MS français 5869, fol. 1v.

114. Rigord, *Gesta Philippi Augusti*, RHGF, 17: 4.

115. GC, 6: 89–90; Rigord and Guillaume le Breton, *Oeuvres*, 2: 376–377; Gerald of Wales, *De instructione principis*, RHGF, 18: 124.

116. RHGF, 16: 128, item n. 394.

117. Y. Labande-Mailfert, *Charles VIII ou la jeunesse au pouvoir* (Paris, 1975), 14.

118. See L. Réau, *Iconographie de l'art chrétien* (Paris, 1959), 3: 1063–1065.

119. BN MS français 2222 (*Congratulations et grâces de la nativité de Charles*), fols. 1–8.

120. BN MS français 2222, fol. 4r–v.

121. Masselin, *Journal*, 45, 61, 170.

122. BN MS français 1192 (*Harangue de la France au roi Charles VIII*), fols. 3, 5.

123. BN MS latin 10909 (Johannes Candida, *Speculum historiale*), fol. 4r–v.

124. Labande-Mailfert, *Charles VIII*, 178–190.

125. Gilles de Paris, *Carolinus*, RHGF, 17: 289–290.

126. Masselin, *Journal*, 217.

127. Masselin, *Journal*, 39; P. S. Lewis, "Two Pieces of Fifteenth-century Political Iconography," *Journal of the Warburg and Courtauld Institute* 27 (1964): 317–320.

128. BN MS français 5104 (*Discours à la reine Marie d'Angleterre de la part de l'Université*), fol. 6.

129. P. Riant, "Déposition de Charles d'Anjou," in Société de l'Histoire de France, *Notices et documents publiés à l'occasion du cinquantième anniversaire* (Paris, 1889), 155–180.

130. E. Boutaric, *Documents relatifs à l'histoire de France sous Philippe le Bel* (Paris, 1861), 68; Kempf, *Pierre Dubois*, 111–114.

131. P. Contamine, "Points de vue sur la chevalerie en France à la fin du Moyen Age," *Francia* 4 (1976): 255–285.

132. Jacques Duclerq, *Mémoires*, CCNF, 37: 178–179; Jehan de Wavrin, *Anciennes Chroniques de France et d'Angleterre* (London, 1891), 399–400.

133. E. Jarry, *La Vie politique de Louis d'Orléans* (Paris, 1899), 1–2.

134. Jean Feu, *An rex Franciae recognoscat imperatorem* (Lyon, 1541), fol. 73v; BN MS français 193 (Pierre Dubois, *Le jardin des nobles*), fol. 181v.

135. Bloch, *Rois thaumaturges*, 129–130.

136. Guimier, *Commentaire*, fol. 2v; Benedicti, *Opera*, 97–98.

137. Masselin, *Journal*, 217.

138. Quicherat, *Procès*, 5: 127.

PART II: INTRODUCTION

1. BN MS français 12476 (Martin Lefranc, *Le Champion des Dames*), fol. 5v.

2. BN MS français 1716 (*Complainte sur la mort de Charles VII*), fol. 416.

7.   THE LILIES OF FRANCE

1. M. Pastoureau, "La diffusion des armoiries et les débuts de l'héraldique," in *La France de Philippe Auguste: le temps des mutations. Colloque du C.N.R.S.* (Paris, 1982), 737–765; H. Pinoteau, "Les origines de l'héraldique

capétienne," *Actes du 3me Congrès international de généalogie et d'héraldique* (Madrid, 1955), 483–511.

2. G. Saffroy, *Bibliographie historique et nobiliaire* (Paris, 1964), 1: 102–105, 547–549; E. Rosbach, "De la fleur de lys comme emblème national," *Mémoires de l'Académie des sciences, inscriptions et belles-lettres de Toulouse,* series 8, vol. 6 (1884): 136–172; G. Braun von Stumm, "L'origine de la fleur de lys des rois de France du point de vue numismatique," *Revue numismatique* 13 (1951): 43–58.

3. Guillaume de Nangis, *Chronique,* ed. H. Guéraud (Paris, 1843), 1: 182.

4. M. Prinet, "Les variations du nombre des fleurs de lys dans les armes de France," *Bulletin monumental* 75 (1911): 469–488.

5. Lacurne de Saint-Palaye, *Mémorial sur l'ancienne chevalerie* (Paris, 1759–1760), 1: 294; J. Mabillon, *De re diplomatica libri sex* (Paris, 1681), 419; J. J. Chifflet, *Anastasis Childerici* (Antwerp, 1655), 165–166; I have not been able to consult A. Wulf, *Vaser lilier og kroner i heraldiken* (Copenhagen, 1966).

6. P. E. Schramm, *Der König von Frankreich* (Weimar, 1960), 1: 208–214; F. Oppenheimer, *Frankish Themes and Problems* (London, 1952), 171–235.

7. MGH, *Poetae aevi Carolini,* 3: 230–231.

8. Compare Marc Bloch, *Les Rois thaumaturges: étude sur le caractère surnaturel de la puissance royale* (Paris, 1961), 230–233, 285.

9. G. M. Spiegel and S. Hindman, "The Fleur-de-lys Frontispieces to Guillaume de Nangis's *Chronique abrégée:* Political Iconography in Late Fifteenth-century France," *Viator* 21 (1981): 381–407; J. Rey, *Histoire du drapeau, des couleurs et des insignes de la monarchie française* (Paris, 1887), 2: 8–13.

10. Song of Solomon, II, 2; VI, 3; Ecclesiastes XXXIX, 13; Hosea XIV, 6; Luke XII, 27; Matthew V, 28.

11. Saint Ambrose, *Hymni attributi,* 80, "De Virginibus," PL, vol. 17, col. 1221; Pseudo-Melito, in J. B. Petra, *Analecta sacra spicilegio solesmensi* (Paris, 1874), 2: 41; Hrabanus Maurus, *De universo,* chap. 8, PL, vol. 111, col. 528; Paul the Deacon, *Sermo in Assomptione Mariae,* in E. Martène, *Veterum scriptorum amplissima collectio* (Paris, 1733), 9: 268; Ambrosius Autpertus, *Sermo in festo beatae Mariae Assumptionis,* PL, vol. 139, cols. 2129–2134; Paschasius Radbert, *Expositio in psalmum XLIV,* PL, vol. 120, cols. 994–999; Hugh of Saint-Victor, *Explanatio in Cantica,* PL, vol. 196, col. 474; Fulbert of Chartres, *Sermo de nativitate beatae Mariae,* PL, vol. 141, cols. 320–324; Saint Anselm, *Hymni attributi,* "Ave celeste lilium," PL, vol. 158, col. 1042.

12. A. Salzer, *Die Sinnbilder und Beiworte Mariens* (Linz, 1893), 163–168; H. Coathalem, *Le Parallélisme entre la sainte Vierge et l'Eglise jusqu'à la fin du XIIe siècle* (Analecta Gregoriana, vol. 74) (Rome, 1974).

13. P. Bernard, *Saint Bernard et Notre Dame* (Paris, 1953).

14. Guibert de Nogent, *Liber de laudibus Mariae,* PL, vol. 156, col. 576.

15. Braun von Stumm, "L'origine de la fleur de lys"; Oppenheimer, *Frankish Themes,* 203–204, 218–219.

16. A. Latreille, J. Palanque, E. Delaruelle, *Histoire du catholicisme en France* (Paris, 1963), 14–16; Rigord and Guillaume le Breton, *Oeuvres,* ed. H. F. Delaborde (Paris, 1882–1885), 1: 91; 2: 128–142; GC, 6: 162–165, 344–365.

17. H. Dusevel, *Histoire de la ville d'Amiens depuis les Gaulois* (Amiens, 1832), 1: 171.

18. Albert the Great, *Summa de laudibus Virginis Mariae quea incipit "Missus est Gabriel"* (Cologne, 1509), fols. 92v–93v.

19. BN MS français 2228 (Benard, *Rubis rayant, saphir oriental*), fols. 3v–4.

20. Jacques Millet, *L'Istoire de la destruction de Troie la Grant,* ed. E. Stengel (Leipzig, 1883), 12.

21. Giovanni Lodovico Vivaldi, *Elogium de laudibus et prerogativis sacrorum liliorum in stemmate regis Gallorum existentium* (Paris, 1608), 56–61, 75–79.

22. Barthélemy de Glanville, *Le grand propriétaire de toutes choses,* trans. Jehan Corbechon (Paris, 1518), fols. 94v, 138.

23. Robert Blondel, *Oeuvres complètes,* ed. A. Héron (Rouen 1892), 1: 88, 123.

24. Olivier Maillard, *Oeuvres françaises,* ed. A. de la Borderie (Nantes, 1877), 46–48.

25. Vivaldi, *Elogium,* 45–46.

26. R. Mugnier, *Petits traités d'histoire naturelle d'Aristote* (Paris, 1953), 29, 35.

27. *New Catholic Encyclopedia,* 3: 1034.

28. Bartolus, *De insignis* in Jean Faure, *Breviarium in codicem* (Paris, 1499) (pages not numbered); Honoré Bonet, *L'Arbre des batailles,* ed. E. Nys (Brussels, 1883), 240–241; M. Schnerb-Lièvre, *Le Songe du verger* (Paris, 1982), 1: 290–293.

29. Guglielmus Benedicti, *Solemnis et perutilis repetitio contra Raynutium* (Lyon, 1522), 22.

30. M. Pastoureau, "Et puis vint le bleu," *Europe* 61 (1983): 43–50.

31. R. de Curte and Bonus de Curtili, *Tractatus de jure patronatus* followed by *Traité sur la noblesse de Bonus de Curtili* (Lyon, 1526), fol. 27r–v.

32. Nicolas Upton, *De militari officio* (London, 1564), 35–36, 256.

33. R. Chabanne, *Le Régime juridique des armoires* (Lyon, 1954), 297.

34. R. Marchand, "Les brisures des armes de France," *Bibliothèque de l'Ecole des Chartes* 83 (1921): 79–83.

35. BN MS français 193 (Pierre Dubois, *Le jardin des nobles*), fols. 181v, 182.

36. BN MS français 1968 (Jacques Lefèvre de Saint-Remy, *Traité de blason*), fols. 159–162v.

37. *Le Songe du verger,* 292; BN MS latin 6020 (Bernard du Rosier, *Miranda de laudibus Franciae* and *Gloria francorum*).

38. E. Kantorowicz, *The King's Two Bodies: A Study in Medieval Political Theology* (Princeton, 1957), 383–450; R. E. Giesey, *The Royal Funerary Ceremony in Renaissance France* (Geneva, 1960), 138–139.

39. Upton, *De militari officio,* 145–146.

40. *Le Songe du verger,* 1: 290–293.

41. BN MS français 11463, fol. 43.

42. Jean Bonaud du Sauset, *Commentaire du traité de Jean de Terre-Vermeille* (Paris, 1526), fol. 121.

43. Jean Gerson, *Oeuvres complètes,* ed. P. Glorieux (Paris, 1962), 4: 113.

44. Jean Jouvenal des Ursins, *Histoire de Charles VI roi de France,* in J. F. Michaud and J. J. F. Poujoulat, eds. *Nouvelle collection des mémoires* (Paris, 1836), 2: 479.

45. BN MS français 2776 (*Traité de blason*), fol. 52r–v.

46. R. Mathieu, *Le Système héraldique français* (Paris, 1946), 1–11.

47. Bloch, *Rois thaumaturges,* 230–233; L. Carolus-Barré, "Les armes de Charlemagne dans l'héraldique médiévale," *Bulletin de la Société nationale des antiquaires de France* (1952), 46; E. Roy, "Philippe le Bel et la légende des fleurs de lys," *Mélanges de philologie et d'histoire offerts à Antoine Thomas* (Paris, 1927), 383–388; A. Piaget, "Le *Chapel des fleurs de lys* et le *Dit de Franc Gontier* de Philippe de Vitry," *Romania* 26 (1898): 55–92; R. Bossuat, "Un poème latin sur l'origine des fleurs de lys," *Bibliothèque de l'Ecole des Chartes* 102 (1940): 80–101.

48. Carolus-Barré, "Les armes de Charlemagne."

49. Roy, "Philippe le Bel," quoting Archives Nationales, JJ 88, n. 71.

50. Cited in Roy, "Philippe le Bel," 385.

51. Piaget, "Le *Chapel des fleurs de lys.*"

52. Bossuat, "Un poème" following BN MS latin 14663, fol. 34.

53. A. Dutilleux, "L'abbaye de Joyenval au diocèse de Chartres," *Mémoires de la Société historique et archéologique de l'arrondissement de Pontoise* 13 (1890): 41–63.

54. Raoul de Presles, *La Cité de Dieu de saint Augustin* (Abbeville, 1486), fols. A3v–A4; R. A. Jackson, "The *Traité du sacre* of Jean Golein," *Proceedings of the American Philosophical Society* 113 (1969): 304–324; *Le Songe du verger,* 1: 132–133.

55. Piaget, "Le *Chapel des fleurs de lys.*"

56. BN MS latin 1730 (Etienne de Conti, *Brevis tractatus*), fols. 30–31; P. Contamine, "Une interpolation de la chronique martinienne: le *Brevis Tractatus,*" *Annales de Bretagne* 87 (1980): 367–386; Gerson, *Oeuvres,* 4: 113–114.

57. Jackson, "The *Traité du sacre* of Jean Golein."

58. Guglielmus Benedicti, *Opera omnia* (Lyon, 1522), 218.

59. Nicole Gilles, *Les très élégantes Annales de France* (Paris, 1538), fol. 15; Robert Gaguin, *Annales de Francorum regum gestis* (Paris, 1521), fol. 9v; BN MS français 17274 (Guillaume Crétin, *Chroniques de France rimées*), fol. 37.

60. BN MS français 6017 (Gaspar Marin, *Histoire des sires de Noyers*), fol. 15.

61. BN MS français 9688 (*Chronologie universelle jusqu'à la mort de Charles VI*), fol. 31v; Blondel, *Oeuvres,* 1: 402; L. Pannier and P. Meyer, eds., *Le Débat des hérauts d'armes de France et d'Angleterre* (Paris, 1877), 1.

62. BN MS français 17274, fol. 38.

63. BN MS français 9688, fol. 31v; Bonaud du Sauset, *Commentaire,* fol. 121; Benedicti, *Repetitio,* 85; Symphorien Champier, *De monarchia Gallorum* (Paris, 1537), bk. 3, chap. 7, fol. 1v.

64. P. S. Lewis, "Two Pieces of Fifteenth-century Political Iconography," *Journal of the Warburg and Courtauld Institute* 27 (1964): 317–320.

65. G. de Nangis, *Chronique,* 1: 182; Piaget, "Le *Chapel des fleurs de lys,*"

72: BN MS français 5869 (*Compilation sur saint Denis*), fol. 3v; BN MS français 2776 (*Traité de blason*), fol. 52.

66. Gilles, *Annales*, fol. 15.

67. BN MS latin 5971A (Jean de Legonissa, *Opus Davidicum*), fol. 66.

68. Piaget, "Le *Chapel des fleurs de lys*," ll. 445–456, 601–605, 900–905.

69. A. Piaget, "Un poème inédit de Guillaume de Digulleville, le *Roman des fleurs de lys*," *Romania* 62 (1936): 317–358.

70. P. Paris, "Le *Dit des Alliés* de Geoffroi de Paris," *Annuaire historique de la Société de l'Histoire de France* 1 (1837): 157–171; A. Moutie, "La charte de fondation du couvent des Célestins de Limay près de Mantes," *Bulletin du Comité de la langue, de l'histoire et des arts de la France* 4 (1857): 239–249; P. Lefébure, "Le monastère des Célestins de Limay," *Mémoires de la Société historique et archéologique de Pontoise* 44 (1935): 7–106.

71. Raoul de Presles, *Cité de Dieu*, fol. A3v; *Songe du verger*, 1: 133.

72. BN MS français 2831 (*Réponse du dauphin aux ambassadeurs de Charles VII*), fols. 2–14.

73. Piaget, "Le *Chapel des fleurs de lys*," ll. 1035–1046; BN MS français 20793 (*Remontrances sur Lorraine et Barrois*), fol. 316.

74. Jehan Corbechon, *Le Grand Propriétaire*, fol. K 4.

75. BN MS latin 5971A, fols. 71v–72.

76. Blondel, *Oeuvres*, 1: 148.

77. BN MS français 2831, fols. 2–14.

78. BN MS latin 5971A, fols. 65–71; A. Linder, "L'expédition italienne de Charles VIII et les espérances messianiques des juifs," *Revue des études juives* 137 (1978): 179–186.

79. Vivaldi, *Elogium de laudibus*, 18, 35.

80. Jean Divry, *Les Triomphes de France et l'origine des Français* (Paris, 1508), fol. E 7r–v.

81. Dutilleux, "L'Abbaye de Joyenval"; Archives départementales des Yvelines, series 48 HI.

82. Inventory of 24 July 1670, Arch. Yvelines, series 48 HI, liasse 3.

83. A. Molinier, *Obituaires de la province de Sens* (Paris, 1906), 2: 283–309.

84. Dutilleux, "L'Abbaye de Joyenval," 41.

85. Gaguin, *Annales*, fol. 9v.

86. Champier, *De monarchia*, fol. K 1v; Bonaud du Sauset, *Commentaire*, fol. 121.

87. BN MS français 17274, fols. 38–39.

88. A. de Laborde, *Les Manuscrits à peinture de "La Cité de Dieu" de Saint Augustin* (Paris, 1903); P. Contamine, "A propos du légendaire de la monarchie française à la fin du Moyen Age," *Texte et image: Actes du colloque de Chantilly (1982)* (Paris, 1984): 201–214.

89. British Museum add. MS 18850 (Bedford manuscript from around 1430); Bibliothèque municipale, Mâcon, MS 1 (*Cité de Dieu* around 1470); *Mer des Histoires* (Paris, 1488, and Lyon, 1491).

90. Brussels, Bibliothèque Royale, MSS 9005, 9015, 1445; British Museum, MSS français 14, 1465; Turin, MSS français 49, 1466. R. E. Giesey, "Modèles de pouvoir dans les rites royaux en France," *Annales: E.S.C.* (1986): 579–599;

L. M. Bryant, "L'entrée royale à Paris au Moyen Age," *Annales: E.S.C.* (1986) 513–542.

91. B. Guenée and F. Lehoux, *Les Entrées royales françaises de 1328 à 1515* (Paris, 1968), 111–114, 129–130, 160.

92. Giesey, *Royal Funeral Ceremony,* 138–139.

8. THE POLITICAL USES OF THE TROJAN MYTH

1. B. Guenée, *Histoire et culture historique dans l'Occident médiéval* (Paris, 1980), 58–65.

2. BN MS français 4924 (*Histoire de France*), fol. 119; C. Beaune, "L'utilisation politique du mythe troyen à la fin du Moyen Age," in *Images médiévales de Virgile* (Rome, 1982), 331–355.

3. B. Guenée, "Les Grandes Chroniques de France," in P. Nora, ed., *Les Lieux de Mémoire* (Paris, 1984–1987), 2: 189–215.

4. E. A. R. Brown, "The Quest for Ancestry in Capetian France and Angevin and Norman Dominions," unpublished paper presented at the *Colloque: "Legitimation by Descent: Myths of National Origins and Descent"* (Paris, 1982); B. Guenée, "Les genéalogies entre l'histoire et la politique: la fierté d'être capétien en France au Moyen Age," *Annales: E.S.C.* 33 (1978): 450–477.

5. A. W. Lewis, "Dynastic Structures and Capetian Throne-right: The Views of Gilles de Paris," *Traditio* 33 (1977): 225–252.

6. Roric, *Gesta Francorum*, PL, vol. 139, col. 590; L. Genicot, *Typologie des sources du Moyen Age. Les généalogies* (Turnhout, 1975).

7. Though many of these genealogies have not survived for us to see. L. Genicot discusses the families of Boulogne, Namur, Brabant, and Flanders in his *Etudes sur les principautés lotharingiennes* (Louvain, 1975), 217–310; G. Raymond, *Les Cent Ballades* (Paris, 1886), 1: 208–209.

8. P. Mouskès, *La Chronique rimée*, ed. A. de Reiffenberg (Brussels, 1836), 1: 8.

9. BN MS français 20124 (Jehan de Courcy, *Chronique universelle*), fols. 157–160.

10. BN MS français 600 (Martin Lefranc, *L'estrif de vertu et fortune*), fols. 34, 37, 56, 58v; Christine de Pisan, *La Mutation de fortune*, ed. S. Solente (Paris, 1959), pt. 6; Christine de Pisan, *L'Avision Christine*, ed. M. L. Towner (New York, 1932), 102, 120, 134–135; Christine de Pisan, *Le Chemin de longue étude*, ed. R. Puschel (Berlin, n.d.), 152–153. Both Alain Chartier and Jacques Millet in his *Istoire de la destruction de Troye la Grant*, ed. E. Stengel (Marburg, 1883), also touch on this theme.

11. Alain Chartier, *Oeuvres latines*, ed. P. Bourgain-Heymerick (Paris, 1977), 216, 228.

12. Alain Chartier, *Oeuvres,* 228, n. 6.

13. Robert Blondel, *Oeuvres complètes*, ed. A. Héron (Rouen, 1892), 1: 12–13.

14. Martin Lefranc, *Le Champion des dames*, ed. A. Piaget (Lausanne, 1968), 108.

15. Millet, *L'Istoire de la destruction de Troie la Grant*, ed. E. Stengel

(Marburg, 1883); Christine de Pisan, *The Epistle of Othea to Hector of Troy*, ed. G. Warner (London, 1904).

16. J. Quicherat, *Le Procès de condamnation et de réhabilitation de Jeanne d'Arc* (Paris, 1846), 2: 447; 3: 431.

17. Rigord and Guillaume le Breton, *Oeuvres*, ed. H. F. Delaborde (Paris, 1882), 2: 7; Guibert de Nogent, *Gesta Dei per Francos*, RHC, 4: 199; Blondel, *Oeuvres*, 1: 136.

18. Millet, *Istoire*, 251, 351.

19. Alain Chartier, *Oeuvres*, 329.

20. Georges Chastellain, *Oeuvres complètes*, ed. J. Kervyn de Lettenhove (Brussels, 1886), 1: 1–12.

21. Millet, *Istoire*, 385.

22. R. Bossuat, "La formule *Rex Franciae est imperator in regno suo* et son emploi devant le Parlement de Paris au XVe siècle," *Revue historique de droit français et étranger*, 4th series, 39 (1961): 371–381.

23. J. Fournier, *Le Problème de l'Eglise et de l'Etat sous Philippe le Bel* (Louvain, 1926).

24. Fournier, *l'Eglise et l'Etat*, 268, 279.

25. M. Goldast, *De Monarchia* (Frankfurt, 1668), 140–141.

26. GC, 1: 12.

27. M. Schnerb-Lièvre, ed., *Le Songe du verger* (Paris, 1982), 1: 53–57.

28. G. W. Coopland, ed., *The Tree of Battles of Honoré Bonet* (Liverpool, 1949), 175–179.

29. Guy Pape, *Decisiones* (Lyon, 1554), *quaestiones* 114 and 239, pp. 152, 334; BN MS français 193 (Pierre Desgros, *Le Jardin des nobles*), fols. 176–178, 180–181.

30. Jean Feu, *Commentarii* (Lyon, 1541), 17, 41, 64–67, 227; Guglielmus Benedicti, *Solemnis repetitio in cap. Raynutium . . .* (Lyon, 1575), 16–22 at *Duas habens.*

31. A. Bossuat, "Les origines troyennes: leur rôle dans la littérature historique du XVe siècle," *Annales de Normandie* 8 (1958): 187–197; L. Pannier and L. Meyer, eds., *Le Débat des hérauts d'armes de France et d'Angleterre* (Paris, 1878), 7–11; Bibliothèque Sainte-Geneviève, MS 1993–1994, fols. 80–81v.

32. H. Vaganay, ed., *La Chanson de Perceforest* (Paris, 1907), 14–17.

33. P. S. Lewis, "Two Pieces of Fifteenth-century Political Iconography," *Journal of the Warburg and Courtauld Institute* 27 (1964): 317–320.

34. Millet, *Istoire*, 409.

35. Guglielmus Benedicti, *Solemnis repetitio*, 23: "Tractatus de ducatu Normaniae."

36. W. S. Woods, ed., *Cyperis de Vignevaux* (Chapel Hill, 1949).

37. Chartier, *Oeuvres*, 211–217.

38. A. Eckardt, *De Sycambria à Sans-Souci* (Paris, 1943).

39. G. Dufresne de Beaucourt, *Histoire de Charles VII* (Paris, 1891), 6: 160–173; A. Leroux de Lincy, ed., "Pierre Choque, *Discours des cérémonies du mariage d'Anne de Foix*," *Bibliothèque de l'Ecole des Chartes*, 5th series, vol. 2 (1862): 437.

40. Gilles le Bouvier dit le Héraut Berry, *Le Livre de la Description des pays,* ed. E. T. Hamy (Paris, 1908), 93.

41. Robert de Clari, *La Conquête de Constantinople,* ed. P. Lauer (Paris, 1924), 40.

42. Honorius of Autun, *Imago Mundi,* PL, vol. 172, col. 129; E. Buron, *L'Imago Mundi de Pierre d'Ailly* (Paris, 1930), 1: 311.

43. Giovanni Balbi, *Catholicon* (Paris, 1499), *s.v.* Palladium, Pergama, Troja.

44. Jerome, *De nomine locorum,* PL, vol. 23, col. 1300; Isidore of Seville, *Etymologiarum,* bk. xiv, secs. 3, 38–42, PL, vol. 82, cols. 502–503.

45. Vincent of Beauvais, *Speculum Historiale* (Douai, 1624), 4: 619.

46. Aubry of Trois-Fontaines, *Chronique,* RHGF, 18: 770.

47. Ramon Muntaner, *Chronique,* CCNF, 6: 169–170.

48. E. Zellwecker, *Troia: drei Jahrtausende des Ruhms* (Zurich/New York, 1947).

49. Radulf of Caen, *Gesta Tancredi,* RHC, 3: 672.

50. Baudri of Dol, *Historia hierosolymitana,* RHC, 4: 28; Henry of Huntington, *De captione Antiochiae,* RHC, 5: 374.

51. Radulf of Caen, RHC, 3: 672; Guibert, *Gesta Dei,* RHC, 4: 199.

52. Genicot, *Etudes . . . lotharingiennes,* 217–306.

53. Baudry of Dol, RHC, 3: 28; Radulf of Caen, RHC, 3: 702.

54. Radulf of Caen, RHC, 3: 702.

55. Guibert, *Gesta Dei,* RHC, 4: 199.

56. Guibert, *Gesta Dei,* RHC, 4: 133–134.

57. Fulcher of Chartres, *Historia gestorum,* RHC, 5: 715.

58. Radulf of Caen, RHC, 3: 675.

59. Robert de Clari, *Conquête,* 102.

60. RHC, *Historiens grecs,* 1: 509–510.

61. Nicetas Choniates, RHC, *Historiens grecs,* 1: 376–377; and 2: 574. This is probably the same statue that Robert of Clari speaks of: *Conquête,* 88.

62. Robert of Auxerre, *Chronicon,* RHGF, 18: 272.

63. M. Duparc-Quioc, *Le Cycle de la croisade* (Paris, 1955).

64. A. de Reiffenberg, *La Chanson de Godefroi de Bouillon* (Monuments pour servir à l'histoire des provinces de Namur [Brussels, 1848]), 4: 215; 5: 157, 215, 267.

65. BN MS français 821, fols. 267 ff.

66. Fredegar, *Liber historiae francorum,* MGH, *Scriptores rerum merovingiacarum,* 2: 46.

67. William of Tyre, *Historia hierosolymitana,* RHC, 1: 21–23.

68. Aeneas Sylvius Piccolomini (Pius II), *Commentarii,* II, 115, in *Opera omnia* (Basle, 1551), 383–386, 394–395, and his *Cosmographia,* in *Opera omnia* (Basle, 1551), 349; Jean Lemaire de Belges, *Oeuvres,* ed. J. A. Stecher (Louvain, 1882), 3: 72–73.

69. Zellwecker, *Troia,* 96, quoting Liquianus's *Fall of Constantinople.* This has also been a topic of interest to more recent scholars: T. Spencer, "Turk and Trojan in the Renaissance," *Modern Language Review* 48 (1952), 330–333; R. Schwoebel, *The Shadow of the Crescent* (London, 1967).

70. Martin Dolet, *De parta ab invictissimo rege victoria* (Paris, 1508); Christophe de Longueil, *Oratio de laudibus divi Ludovici* (Paris, 1508); Valerand de Varannes, *Carmen de expugnatione genuensi* (Paris, 1508); Faustus Andrelin, *La Victoire sur les Vénitiens* (Paris, 1508); Faustus Andrelin, *De captivitate Ludovici Sforzae* (Paris, 1508); Jean-Pyrrhus Angleberme, *Militia Francorum* (Paris, n.d.); Pierre Pontanus, *De invictissimo rege* (Paris, 1515).

71. Jean Lemaire de Belges, *Oeuvres*, 3: 68–86.

72. Christine de Pisan, *Le Chemin*, 152–153; G. Ouy, "Humanisme et propagande politique en France au début du XVe siècle: Ambrogio Migli et les ambitions impériales de Louis d'Orléans," *Culture et Politique en France à l'époque de l'humanisme et de la Renaissance (Convegno, Turin 1971)* (Turin, 1974), 13–42.

73. Guglielmus Benedicti, *Solemnis repetitio*, 18v, at *Duas habens*.

74. Jean Lemaire de Belges, *Oeuvres*, 3: 84.

75. Fredegar, *Liber historiae francorum*, MGH, *Scriptores rerum merovingiacarum*, 2: 244; Sigebert of Gembloux, *Chronicon*, PL, vol. 160, cols. 77–78.

76. A. Crapelet, ed., *Partonopeus de Blois* (Paris, 1835), 13–14.

77. Guillaume le Breton and Rigord, *Oeuvres*, 1: 54–59.

78. Vincent of Beauvais, *Speculum historiale*, 3: 68; 4: 619; GC, 1: 18–19.

79. A. Chédeville, J. Le Goff, and J. Rossiaud, *Histoire de la France urbaine* (Paris, 1980), 2: 394–396.

80. Barroux, "Les origines légendaires de Paris," *Mémoires de la Société historique et archéologique de Paris et de l'Ile-de-France* 7 (1955): 9–11; P. Desportes, *Reims et les Rémois aux XIIIe et XIVe siècles* (Paris, 1979), 530–534; A. Prost, *Etudes sur l'histoire légendaire de Metz* (Metz, 1865).

81. Flodoard, *Historia remensis ecclesiae*, PL, vol. 106, cols. 956–958.

82. *Gesta episcoporum mettensium*, MGH, *Scriptores*, 2: 261–264.

83. J. F. Huguenin, *Les Anciennes chroniques de la ville de Metz* (Metz, 1838); Philippe de Vigneulles, *La Chronique*, ed. C. Bruneau (Metz, 1927–1933), vol. 1.

84. Jean Jouvenal des Ursins, *Ecrits politiques*, ed. P. S. Lewis (Paris, 1978), 1: 156.

85. BN MS latin 16495, fols. 95–96; Jean Lemaire de Belges, *Oeuvres*, 3: 69.

86. Jean Perionius, *Dialogorum de linguae gallicae origine libri* (Paris, 1554).

9. THE SALIC LAW: FIRST LAW OF THE FRENCH PEOPLE

1. K. A. Eckhardt, ed., *Pactus legis salicae*, MGH, *Leges*, 1: 4; see in general, M. Conrad, *Deutsche Rechtsgeschichte* (Karlsruhe, 1962), 159–163 and M. Scovazzi, *Le origine del diritto germanico* (Milan, 1957).

2. N. 59 in the early versions, n. 62 in the revision of Charlemagne.

3. E. Viollet, "Comment les femmes ont été exclues en France de la succession à la couronne," *Mémoires de l'Académie des sciences, inscriptions et belles-lettres* 34 (1894): 125–178; M. Roblot, *Examen des circonstances dans lesquelles se sont dégagées quelques règles de la dévolution du trône de France*

(Paris, 1945); J. M. Potter, "The Development and Significance of the Salic Law of the French," *English Historical Review* 52 (1937): 235–253; R. E. Giesey, "The Juristic Basis of Dynastic Right to the French Throne," *Transactions of the American Philosophical Society* 60 (1961).

4. GC, 1: 20; 9: 72–73.

5. Vincent of Beauvais, *Speculum majus* (Douai, 1624), 4: 619.

6. MGH, *Scriptores rerum merovingiacarum*, 2: 244.

7. *Gesta regum Francorum*, PL, vol. 96, col. 1424.

8. Sigebert of Gembloux, *Chronographia*, PL, vol. 160, col. 78.

9. BN MS latin 4985 (Bernard Gui, *Flores chronicarum*), fol. 45.

10. François de Meyronnes, *Flores beati Augusti* (Cologne, n.d.), A 9v; P. de Lapparent, "L'oeuvre politique de François de Meyronnes," *Archives d'histoire doctrinale et littéraire du Moyen Age* 15 (1940–1942): 5–151.

11. BN MS Moreau 699 (*Discours des ambassadeurs anglais . . .*), fols. 98–99, 117.

12. BN MS Moreau 306 (*Réponse du roi de France aux raisons et moyens du roi d'Angleterre*), fol. 79.

13. Richard Lescot, *Chronique (1328–1344) et continuation (1344–1364)*, ed. J. Lemoine (Paris, 1896), 173–176.

14. BN MS français 1728 (Jean du Vignay, *Les échecs moralisés de Jacques de Cessoles*), fol. 165r–v.

15. R. Giesey, "Juristic Basis."

16. BN MS français 171 (Raoul de Presles, *La Cité de Dieu de saint Augustin*), fols. 147, 262v; A. Leroux de Lincy and L. M. Tisserand, *Paris et ses historiens aux XIVe et XVe siècles* (Paris, 1867), 135.

17. M. Schnerb-Lièvre, *Le Songe du verger* (Paris, 1982), 1: 248–255.

18. R. Bossuat, "Nicole Oresme et *Le Songe du verger*," *Le Moyen Age*, 4th series, vol. 2 (1947): 114–116.

19. C. Samaran, "Etudes sandionysiennes: notes sur la bibliothèque de Saint-Denis au XVe siècle," *Bibliothèque de l'Ecole des Chartes* 104 (1943): 110.

20. B. Guenée, *Histoire et culture historique dans l'Occident médiéval* (Paris, 1980), 137–138; C. Beaune, "Histoire et politique: la recherche du texte de la loi salique de 1350 à 1450," *104e Congrès des Sociétés Savantes, Bordeaux 1979. Section de philologie et d'histoire* (Paris, 1981), 25–35.

21. Lescot, *Chronique*, 173–176.

22. Lescot, *Chronique*, 176.

23. K. A. Eckhardt, *Pactus*, xx.

24. Only BN MSS latin 4628A, 10758, and 4632 have this arrangement. MS 10758 belonged to the library of Saint-Rémy of Reims from the tenth to the fifteenth century. The location of MS latin 4632 before the eighteenth century is unknown, but it dates the additional capitulary to 819, a date of which Lescot seems to have been ignorant.

25. BN MS français 4950 (*Miroir historial jusqu'à 1380*), fol. 11r–v; BN MS nouv. acq. française 1858 (Noel de Fribois, *Miroir historial*), fol. 13.

26. BN MS nouv. acq. française 1858, fol. 79; BN MS français 4950, fol. 11r–v.

27. Jean de Montreuil, *L'Oeuvre historique et polémique,* ed. E. Ornato and N. Grevy-Pons (Turin, 1975), 2: 132, n. 220; 168, n. 222; 226, n. 223; 274, n. 224.

28. E. Ornato and N. Grevy-Pons, "Qui est l'auteur de la Chronique de Charles VI dit du religieux de Saint-Denis?" *Bibliothèque de l'Ecole des Chartes* 134 (1972): 85–102.

29. And this text was known only in the version of 803, the K group of manuscripts in Eckhardt's edition: BN MS latin 4628A and BN MS latin 10758 are K35 and K33 respectively.

30. Jean Jouvenal des Ursins, *Ecrits politiques,* ed. P. S. Lewis (Paris, 1978), 1: 156, 345.

31. Lescot, *Chronique,* 173–178.

32. "Réponse du bon et loyal Français," in Dom des Salles, *Mémoires pour servir à l'histoire de France et de Bourgogne* (Paris, 1729), 1: 319.

33. BN MS français 10920 (Jean de Montreuil, *Veritatis praesens testimonium*), fol. 5v.

34. BN MS français 1751 (Jouvenal des Ursins, *Traité compendieux*), fol. 3.

35. Jouvenal des Ursins, *Ecrits,* 1: 93–281.

36. Lescot, *Chronique,* 174–176.

37. BN MS français 5026, fol. 43.

38. R. Blondel, *Oeuvres complètes,* ed. A. Héron (Rouen, 1891–1892), 1: 402.

39. BN MS nouv. acq. française 1417 (*Miroir historial jusqu'à l'année 1382*), notes on fols. 161 and 170v.

40. Claude de Seyssel, *La Grande monarchie de France* (Paris, 1556) (which contains the *Great Treatise* on fols. 81–153), fols. 84–85; BN MS français 17274 (Guillaume Crétin, *Chroniques de France rimées*), fol. 12v; Guglielmus Benedicti, *Opera omnia* (Lyon, 1575), 1: 196; 2: 115; Vincent Cygault, *Allegationes supra bello italico* (Paris, 1512), fols. 29–30; Claude de Seyssel, *La Grande Monarchie de France,* ed. J. Poujol (Paris, 1961), 113.

41. J. Krynen, *Idéal du prince et pouvoir royal en France à la fin du Moyen Age* (Paris, 1980), 292.

42. BN MS français 5026, fol. 3.

43. "Réponse du bon et loyal Français," in des Salles, *Mémoires,* 1: 319.

44. BN MS français 171 (Raoul de Presles, *La Cité de Dieu*), fols. 147, 162v.

45. BN MS latin 5944 (Aimery de Peyrac, *Stromatheus Karoli Magni*), fol. 24.

46. Leroux de Lincy and Tisserand, *Paris et ses historiens,* 135.

47. Jouvenal des Ursins, *Ecrits politiques,* 1: 156.

48. BN MS français 5026, fol. 43.

49. *Grand Traité* in Seyssel, *Grande Monarchie* (Paris, 1556), fols. 84–85.

50. G. Benedicti, *Opera,* 1: 196; 2: 115.

51. BN MS Moreau 306, fol. 79.

52. BN MS français 1728, fol. 165r–v; BN MS latin 10920, fol. 5v.

53. BN MS français 1192 (*Harangue de la France au roi Charles VIII*), fol. 18.

54. BN MS français 17274, fol. 12v.

55. BN MS Moreau 699, fols. 98, 117.

56. Seyssel, *Grande monarchie* (Paris, 1556), 84.

57. P. S. Lewis, "War Propaganda and Historiography in Fifteenth-century France," *Transactions of the Royal Historical Society*, 5th series, vol. 15 (1965): 1–21.

58. Blondel, *Oeuvres*, 1: 402–404.

59. BN MS Moreau 699; R. Lescot, *Chronique*, 173–176; BN MS français 15490, *Pour ce que plusieurs . . .* , fols. 2–15, and *Mémoire abrégé*, fols. 32–43; BN MS nouv. acq. française 6215, *Memoire abrégé*, fols. 32–43; BN MS français 17182, *Mémoire abrégé*, fols. 1–31; Montreuil, *L'oeuvre historique*, 2: 65–82 (*Regali ex progenie*), 89–135 (*A toute la chevalerie*), 159–311 (*Traité contre les Anglais*), and 316–330 (*Sophisme que les Anglais*); Jean Gerson, *Oeuvres complètes*, ed. E. Dupin (Antwerp, 1706), 4: 850–859; BN MS français 5059 (*Après la destruction de Troie la Grant*), fols. 41–55; Jean Bonaud du Sauset, *Commentaire du Traité de Jean de Terre Vermeille* (Paris, 1526); "Réponse du bon et loyal français"; R. Blondel, *Oeuvres*, 1: 402–404; Lewis, "War propaganda."

60. For the work of Jean de Montreuil on the subject composed in 1415–1416, there are four manuscripts and a printed edition appended to the c. 1503 Paris edition of Robert Gaguin's *Chronique martinienne*. (See the survey of the MSS in Montreuil, *L'Oeuvre historique*, introduction.) For the *Traité compendieux* of Jean Jouvenal des Ursins, there are three or four manuscripts of the fifteenth century. For his popular vision-speech of 1436, *Audite celi, quae loquor*, there are thirteen manuscripts and a recent edition. (See the edition of his *Ecrits politiques* by P. S. Lewis.)

61. For a discussion of the manuscripts, see the appendix to this chapter.

62. BN MS français 5056, fol. 3.

63. BN MS français 5056, fol. 4.

64. BN MS français 5026, fol. 43; BN MS nouv. acq. française 6853, fol. 39.

65. Nicole Gilles, *Les très élégantes . . . Annales de France* (Paris, 1525), fol. 11v. Other historians who included the Salic Law in their texts at this time were Robert Gaguin (in his *Compendium super Francorum gestis* [Paris, 1501]), Paulus Aemilius Veronensis (in his *De rebus gestis Francorum* [Paris, 1516]), and Guillaume Crétin in his *Chroniques de France rimées* (BN MS français 17274).

66. GC, 1: 20; and 9: 72–73; Vincent of Beauvais, *Speculum*, 4: 614.

67. BN MS nouv. acq. française 1417, fols. 161, 170v.

68. Viollet, "Comment les femmes ont été exclues . . . ."

69. BN MS latin 5944, fol. 24.

70. G. Benedicti, *Opera*, fols. 16–17 ("Duas habens").

71. Jean Ferrault, *Tractatus jura seu privilegia regni Franciae continens* (Paris, 1545), 349–351. On this work see J. Pougol, "Jean Ferrault on the King's Privileges," *Studies in the Renaissance* 5 (1958): 15–26.

72. BN MS français 17274, fol. 12v.

73. BN MS français 171, fols. 147, 262v.

74. Leroux de Lincy and Tisserand, *Paris et ses historiens*, 135.

75. Jean-Pyrrhus Angleberme, *De lege salica* (Paris, 1517), fols. M 4v–8v.

76. Gilles, *Annales*, fol. 11v.

77. BN MS français 1417, fols. 161–170v.

78. Jean Divry, *Les Triomphes de France et l'origine des Français* (Paris, 1508), fol. 1v.

79. Angleberme, *De lege salica*, fols. M 4v–8v.

80. H. Morel, "La place de la *lex regia* dans l'histoire des idées politiques," *Etudes offertes à Jean Macqueron* (Aix-en-Provence, 1970), 544–555.

81. Divry, *Triomphes de France*, fol. 1v.

82. Krynen, *Idéal du prince*, 282–302.

83. Krynen, *Idéal du prince*, 284–287.

84. Jouvenal des Ursins, *Ecrits politiques*, vol. 2.

85. Krynen, *Idéal du prince*, 297–303.

86. BN MS latin 3340 (*An mulieres non ut ab hereditate regni sic ab ejus procuratione gallico jure accedant*), fols. 194–197.

87. C. T. Wood, *The French Apanages and the Capetian Monarchy* (Cambridge, Mass., 1966).

88. Laurent Bouchel, *Bibliothèque de droit françias* (Paris, 1615), 3: 399.

89. BN MS français 1192 (*Harangue de la France au roi Charles VIII*), fol. 18.

90. Vincent Cygault, *Allegationes supra bello italico* (Paris, 1512), fols. 29–30; Angleberme, *De lege salica*, fols. M 4v–8v.

91. G. Benedicti, *Opera*, vol. 1, fols. 16–17 ("Duas habens").

92. BN MS français 17274, fol. 12v; Divry, *Les triomphes*, fol. 1r–v.

93. BN MS français 23428 (Pierre d'Ailly, *Proposition au concile de 1406 et autres discours au même concile*), fols. 48, 430. See Bernard Guenée, *Entre l'Eglise et l'Etat* (Paris, 1987), 125–301.

94. Gerson, *Oeuvres complètes*, vol. 4, cols. 850–851.

95. BN MS français 193 (Pierre Dubois, *Le Jardin des nobles*), fols. 181–183.

96. Jean Feu, *Opera omnia* (Orléans, 1541), fol. 73.

97. G. Dupont-Ferrier, "Les institutions françaises du Moyen Age vues à travers les institutions romaines," *Revue historique* 71 (1933): 281–298.

98. Angleberme, *De lege salica*.

10. LANGUAGE AND CULTURE

1. L. Kukenheim, *Histoire de la grammaire* (Amsterdam, 1932); A. Borst, *Der Turmbau von Babel* (Stuttgart, 1957–1963), vols. 2 and 3 (paged continuously); P. Wolff, *Les Origines linguistiques de l'Europe occidentale* (Paris, 1970); N. Pons, "Latin et Français au XVe siècle: le témoignage des traités de propagande," in *5e Colloque international sur le moyen français* (Milan, 1985), 64–81.

2. Genesis XI, 1–9.

3. Borst, *Turmbau*, 632–637.

4. Dante, *De vulgari eloquentia*, ed. S. Rhéal (Paris, 1858), 6: 198.

5. G. Bonfante, "Ideas on the Kinship of the European Languages from 1200 to 1800," *Cahiers d'histoire mondiale* 1 (1954): 679–699; Dante, *De vulgare eloquentia*, 6: 196.

6. Borst, *Turmbau*, 728.

7. Adhemar of Chabannes, *Chronique*, ed. J. Chavanon (Paris, 1897), 1: 5; 2: 65–69; Guibert de Nogent, *Moralia in Genesim*, PL, vol. 156, cols. 68, 108.

8. BN MS latin 11730 (Etienne de Conti, *Brevis Tractatus*), fols. 30v, 32v.

9. Isidore of Seville, *Etymologiarum*, IX, 1: PL, vol. 82, col. 325–326.

10. Aimoin of Fleury, *De gestis regum Francorum libri IV*, PL, 139, cols. 635–638.

11. Caesar, *De bello gallico*, I, 29, 1 and VI, 14, 3.

12. Robert of Auxerre, *Chronique*, ed. M. Camusat (Troyes, 1608), 4.

13. Rigord and Guillaume le Breton, *Oeuvres*, ed. H. F. Delaborde (Paris, 1885), 2: 11.

14. H. Kämpf, "Pierre Dubois und die geistigen Grundlagen des französischen Nationalbewusstsein," *Beiträge zur Kulturgeschichte des Mittelalters und Renaissance* 54 (1935): 1–114 (reprinted Hildesheim, 1972), at pp. 111–114.

15. A. D. Menut, *Le Commentaire de l'Ethique d'Aristote par Nicole Oresme* (New York, 1940), 100, 364, 513.

16. See also other statements of this sort in M. Jones, *The Creation of Brittany: The Late-Medieval State* (London, 1988), 284.

17. Kukenheim, *Histoire*, 176–181; D. Droixhe, *La Linguistique et l'appel de l'histoire* (Paris, 1978).

18. Borst, *Turmbau*, 894.

19. Brunetto Latini, *Li Livres dou Tresor*, ed. P. Chabaille (Paris, 1863), 3.

20. F. Brunot, *Histoire de la langue française* (Paris, 1903), 1: 358.

21. Kämpf, "Pierre Dubois," 111–114; Oresme, *Commentaire de l'Ethique d'Aristote* (Paris, 1488), fol. Aiiiv.

22. Borst, *Turmbau*, 987.

23. Jean de Montreuil, *L'Oeuvre polémique*, ed. E. Ornato and N. Grevy-Pons (Turin, 1963), 1: 176.

24. Alain Chartier, *Les Oeuvres*, ed. Duchesne (Paris, 1617), 1–2; Georges Chastellain, *Oeuvres*, ed. J. Kervyn de Lettenhove (Brussels, 1863–1866), 1: 11–12.

25. Lemaire de Belges, *Concorde*, 3–5.

26. Brunetto Latini, *Li Livres dou Tresor*, 3.

27. Borst, *Turmbau*, 886.

28. Brunot, *Histoire de la langue*, 1: 358 ff.

29. M. Brun, *Recherches historiques sur l'introduction du français dans les provinces du Midi* (Paris, 1923).

30. Guillaume Guiart, *La Branche des royaux lignages*, CCNF, 8: 199–200.

31. BN MS latin 11730, fols. 30v, 32v.

32. BN MS latin 6020 (Bernard du Rosier, *Miranda de laudibus Franciae*), fols. 1–2.

33. Jean Juvenal des Ursins, *Ecrits politiques*, ed. P. S. Lewis (Paris, 1978), 1: 153.

34. Borst, *Turmbau*, 718.

35. Pierre Dubois, *De recuperatione Terrae Sanctae*, ed. C. Langlois (Paris, 1891), 106.

36. Jean Gerson, *Oeuvres complètes*, ed. E. Dupin (Antwerp, 1706), 4: 851.

37. Gerson, *Oeuvres*, 4: 855.

38. Claude de Seyssel, *La Grande monarchie de France*, ed. J. Poujol (Paris, 1961), 218; BN MS français 1959 (Symphorien Champier, *Le Régime d'un jeune prince*), fol. 14.

39. Borst, *Turmbau*, 2099.

40. Hincmar of Rheims, *Expositio super ecclesiae libertatum defensio*, PL, vol. 125, col. 1037; Hugh of Fleury, cited by Borst, *Turmbau*, 440; W. von den Steinen, "Das mittelalterliche Latein als historische Phänomen," *Revue d'histoire suisse* (new series) 7 (1957): 1–27.

41. Borst, *Turmbau*, 898.

42. Dante, *De Vulg. eloq.*, ed. S. Rhéal, 6: 193; Dubois, *Recuperatione*, 109.

43. Laurent de Premierfait, *De casibus de Boccace* (Paris, 1494), fol. 1v.

44. Borst, *Turmbau*, 897.

45. R. Blondel, *Oeuvres complètes*, ed. A. Héron (Rouen, 1892), 1: 7, 65.

46. B. Guenée, "Les limites de la France," in M. François, ed., *La France et les Français* (Paris, 1972), 50–69.

47. Gilles le Bouvier dit le Héraut Berry, *Le Livre de la description des pays*, ed. E. T. Hamy (Paris, 1908), 52.

48. Memorial on Lorraine and the Barrois addressed to King Louis XII, cited by de Pange, *Le patriotisme français en Lorraine* (Paris, 1889).

49. BN MS français 146 (*Dialogue du chevalier et de chrétienté*), fol. 10; Borst, *Turmbau*, 994–995.

50. BN MS latin 11730 (Etienne de Conti), fol. 32v.

51. Borst, *Turmbau*, 993, referring to the *Farce de maître Pathelin*.

52. Blondel, *Oeuvres*, 2: 33.

53. M. Jones, "Mon pays, ma nation: Breton Identity in the Fourteenth Century," in C. T. Allmand, ed., *War, Literature and Politics in the Late Middle Ages* (Liverpool, 1976), 144–168.

54. Guiart, *La Branche*, 268, 296.

55. BN MS latin 11730, fol. 38.

56. Chastellain, *Oeuvres*, 1: 11–12.

57. Jean Froissart, *Chroniques*, ed. S. Luce, G. Raynaud, and L. and A. Mirot (Paris, 1869–1967), 11: 40.

58. A. G. Jongkees, "*Translatio studii*: les avatars d'un thème médiéval," *Miscellanea medievalia in memoriam J. F. Niermeyer* (Groningen, 1967), 41–61; D. Gassman, *Translatio studii: A Study in the Intellectual History of the Thirteenth Century* (unpublished Ph.D. thesis, Cornell University, 1973).

59. W. Goez, *Translatio imperii* (Tübingen, 1958).

60. Hugh of Saint Victor, *De arca noe morali*, PL, vol. 176, col. 677D; Otto of Freising, *Historia de duobus civitatibus*, MGH, *Scriptores rerum germanicarum*, 8.

61. Guy de Bazoches, *Epistolae*, ed. W. Wattenbach, *Neues Archiv* 6 (1891): 72–73; Jean Jouvenal des Ursins, *Ecrits*, 1: 356–358; A. Leroux de Lincy and L. M. Tisserand, *Paris et ses historiens aux XIVe et XVe siècles* (Paris, 1867), 23–79.

62. Jongkees, "Translatio studii"; Chrétien de Troyes, *Cligès*, ed. W Foerster (Halle, 1899), 191; "Cligès, poème du XIIe siècle," *Histoire Littéraire de France,* 18: 304; GC., 1: 5–6; 7: 61.

63. Baudry of Dol, "Vie de Robert d'Arbrissel," AA.SS., February 25, 604c; Alexander Neckham, *De natura rerum,* ed. T. Wright (London, 1863), 308–309; Guy de Bazoches, *Epistolae,* 72–73.

64. Guillaume le Breton, *Oeuvres,* 1: 230; Helinand, quoted in H. Grundmann, "Sacerdotium, regnum, studium," *Archiv für Kulturgeschichte* 34 (1952): 14, n. 19.

65. Jongkees, "Translatio studii"; Neckham, *De natura rerum,* 308–309; GC, 1: 5–6; 7: 61; Guillaume de Nangis, *Vie de Louis IX,* ed. H. Géraud (Paris, 1843), 1: 182–183; Guillaume de Nangis, *Chronique abrégée,* RHGF, 20: 320; Alain Chartier, *Oeuvres latines,* ed. P. Bourgain-Heymerick (Paris, 1977), 277; BN MS latin 13836 (Yves de Saint-Denis), fols. 30v, 101; BN MS latin 5286 (Yves de Saint-Denis), fols. 174–175, 204; BN MS latin 15966 (Thomas of Ireland, *Flos duplex Achaie*), fol. 7r–v; BN MS français 5869 (*Compilation sur saint Denis*), fol. 3v.

66. C. E. du Boulay, *Historia universitatis parisiensis* (Paris, 1668), 4: 408–409.

67. See Grundmann "Sacerdotium, regnum, studium," 14, n. 19.

68. Vincent of Beauvais, *Speculum majus* (Douai, 1624), 4: 960.

69. Jongkees, "Translatio studii," 45.

70. G. de Nangis, *Chronique abrégée,* RHGF, 20: 320.

71. BN MS latin 5286, fol. 62v.

72. BN MS latin 15966 (Thomas of Ireland, *Flos duplex Achaie*), fols. 7–8; A. Piaget, "Le *Chapel des fleurs de lys* et le *Dit de Franc Gontier* de Philippe de Vitry," *Romania* 27 (1898): 55–92.

73. R. Folz, "Aspects du culte liturgique de Charlemagne en France," in W. Braunfels, *Karl der Grosse: Lebenswerk und Nachleben* (Bonn, 1966–1968), 4: 77–99.

74. Chartier, *Oeuvres latines,* 226; Gerson, *Oeuvres,* 4: 786–787; Blondel, *Oeuvres,* 1: 58–59, 72, 87; Jouvenal des Ursins, *Ecrits,* 1: 358.

75. E. Gilson, *Les Idées et les lettres* (Paris, 1932), 182–196.

76. Christine de Pisan, *Le Chemin de longue étude,* ed. R. Puschel (Berlin, 1881), 150, 262.

77. BN MS latin 5971A (Jean de Legonissa, *Opus davidicum*), fols. 4, 7.

78. Caesar, *De bello gallico* VI, 16–18.

79. Choquart, in du Boulay, *Hist. univ. paris.,* 4: 408–409; *Le Songe du verger,* ed. M. Schnerb-Lièvre (Paris, 1982), 1: 334–335; Leroux de Lincy and Tisserand, *Paris et ses historiens,* 112–113; Gilson, *Idées,* 182–196.

80. Choquart, in du Boulay, *Hist. univ. paris.,* 4: 408–409; M. Goldast, *De monarchia* (Frankfurt, 1668), 1: 226.

81. F. Simone, *Il rinascimento francese* (Genoa, 1961); E. Gilson, *La Philosophie au Moyen Age* (Paris, 1962), 747 ff.; P. Renucci, *L'Aventure de l'humanisme européen au Moyen Age* (Paris, 1953).

82. G. Ouy, "La plus ancienne oeuvre retrouvée de Jean Gerson," *Romania* 83 (1962): 435–492; M. Schmidt-Chazan, "Histoire et sentiment national chez

Robert Gaguin," in B. Guenée, ed., *Le Métier d'historien au Moyen Age* (Paris, 1977), 233–300.

83. Petrarch, *Opera omnia* (Basle, 1551), 2: 397 (*Seniles*, IX, 1).

84. E. Cocchia, "Magistri Johannis de Hesdinio contra Franciscum Petrarcham epistola," *Atti della reale Academia di Archeologia, Lettere, et Belle Arti di Napoli* 7 (1920): 112–139.

85. N. Mann, "Humanisme et patriotisme en France au XVe siècle," *22e Congrès de l'Association internationale d'études françaises* 23 (1971): 51–84, 335–336; Montreuil, *Oeuvre*, 1: 135–136; Nicolas de Clamanges, *Opera omnia* (Leyden, 1613), letter 4, pp. 20–23; letter 5, pp. 24–30.

86. Schmidt-Chazan, "Histoire et sentiment national"; Robert Gaguin, *Epistolae et orationes*, ed. L. Thasne (Paris, 1903), letter 5, vol. 1: 185–208.

87. Christophe de Longueil, *Oratio de laudibus sancti Ludovici* (Paris, 1510); Symphorien Champier, *Apologia in Gallia calumniatorem* (Lyon, 1507). See also Valerand de Varannes, *Carmen de expugnatione genuensi* (Paris, 1507); Guillaume Bude, *De asse* (Paris, 1514); Jean-Pyrrhus Angleberme, *Militia Francorum* (Paris, 1519).

88. Symphorien Champier, *Tropheum Gallorum* and *De viris illustribus necnon scriptoribus Galliae* (Paris, 1507); Symphorien Champier, *Duellum epistolare* (Venice, 1519).

89. Lemaire de Belges, *Concorde*, 4.

90. Thomas Sebillet, *Art poétique français* (Paris, 1548), 14; Joachim Du Bellay, *La Défense et illustration de la langue française*, ed. H. Chamard (Paris, 1904).

91. Nicolas Thévet, *La Cosmographie* (Paris, 1582), 2: 641–644.

92. Montreuil, *Oeuvre*, 1: 177–178; 2: 244; Schmidt-Chazan, "Histoire et sentiment," 248.

93. Ouy, "La plus ancienne oeuvre," 435–492.

94. Jean Gerson, *De laude scriptorum* (Cologne, n.d.).

95. Claude de Seyssel, *Les Histoires universelles de Justin* (Paris, 1559), fols. 1v–2.

96. Symphorien Champier, *Les gestes et la vie du preux chevalier Bayard* (Lyon, 1525), fol. 2v.

97. Champier, *De viris illustribus*.

98. H. Suggott, "The Use of French in England in the Later Middle Ages," *Transactions of the Royal Historical Society*, 4th series, vol. 28 (1946): 61–83; B. Cottle, *The Triumph of English (1350–1400)* (London, 1969); J. Coleman, *English Literature in History* (London, 1981).

99. Kukenheim, *Histoire de la grammaire*.

11.   FRANCE AND THE FRENCH

1. Horace, *Odes*, III, 2, 13.

2. M. Lugge, *Gallia und Francia im Mittelalter: Untersuchungen über dem Zusammenhang zwischen geographisch-historischer Terminologie und politischen Denken vom VIsten bis XVsten Jahrhundert* (Bonn, 1960).

3. Hugh of Fleury, *Chronicon*, ed B. Rottendorf (Münster, 1648), 180.

4. Sigebert of Gembloux, *Gesta abbatem Gemblacensium*, MGH, *Scriptores*, 8: 539; Sigebert of Gembloux, *Chronicon*, PL, vol. 160, col. 161; Suger, *Vita Ludovici sexti*, ed. and trans. H. Waquet (Paris, 1929), 220, 267.

5. *Chanson de Roland*, ll. 1867, 1895.

6. In the *Couronnement de Louis*, quoted by F. Lot, "La Formation de l'unité française," *Revue des deux mondes* (1950): 273 (where Roland and Du Guesclin are also cited).

7. J. Cuvellier, *Chronique de Bertrand Duguesclin*, ed. E. Charrière (Paris, 1839), 2: 320.

8. Suger, *Vita Ludovici sexti*, 223.

9. Fredegar *Liber historiae francorum*, MGH, *Scriptores rerum merovingiacarum*, 2: 93–95.

10. A. Bossuat, "La formule 'Le roi est empereur en son royaume,' son emploi au XVe siècle devant le Parlement de Paris," *Revue historique de droit français et étranger*, 4th series, vol. 39 (1961): 371–382.

11. J. Favier, *Finance et fiscalité au bas Moyen Age* (Paris, 1971).

12. Guillaume Guiart, *La Branche des royaux lignages*, CCNF, 7: 14.

13. *Ordonnances*, 1: 583 (1315).

14. Gervais de Bus, *Le Roman de Fauvel*, ed. A. Langfors (Paris, 1914–1919), 1: 45.

15. Nicolas de Clamanges, *Opera omnia* (Leyden, 1613), *Epistolae*, 192.

16. Jean Jouvenal des Ursins, *Ecrits politiques*, ed. P. S. Lewis (Paris, 1978), 1: 156, 359; BN MS latin 6020 (Bernard du Rosier, *Miranda de laudibus Franciae*), fol. 76.

17. Jehan Masselin, *Le Journal des Etats généraux de 1484*, ed. A. Bernier (Paris, 1835), 673.

18. J. Favier, *Philippe le Bel* (Paris, 1978), 352–353.

19. Honoré Bonet, *L'Arbre des batailles*, ed. E. Nys (Brussels, 1883), 185.

20. Georges Chastellain, *Oeuvres*, ed. J. Kervyn de Lettenhove (Brussels, 1863–1866), 1: 7.

21. GC, 1: 4.

22. P. S. Lewis, "Two Pieces of Fifteenth-century Political Iconography," *Journal of the Warburg and Courtauld Institute* 27 (1964): 317–320; Jean Gerson, *Oeuvres complètes*, ed. E. Dupin (Antwerp, 1706), vol. 4: 857.

23. Caesar, *Gallic Wars*, VI, 24; Strabo, *Geography*, IV, 4, 2, 5.

24. BN MS français 601 (*La forge des hommes belliqueux*); Masselin, *Journal*, 63, 245–254.

25. Jouvenal des Ursins, *Ecrits*, 1: 241–248.

26. BN MS latin 4998 (Guy de Bazoches, *Chronographia*), fol. 40v.

27. Jerome, *Ad vigilantium*, PL, vol. 23, col. 339.

28. GC, 1: 14.

29. BN MS latin 6020, fols. 1–4, 76–77. It seems worthwhile spending time with these texts, for they are far less well known than the contemporary *Apologie* by Thomas Basin (ed. C. Samaran [Paris, 1974], 19–35).

30. A. Vernet, "Le *Tragicum Argumentum de miserabili statu regni Franciae* de François de Montebelluna (1357)," *Annuaire-Bulletin de la Société d'Histoire de France* (1962–1963): 101–163.

31. Eustache Deschamps, *Oeuvres complètes,* ed. de Queux Sainte-Hilaire and G. Raynaud (Paris, 1878–1903), 2: 93.

32. G. Ouy, "Le *Deploratio super civitatem aut regionem quae gladium evanginavit super se,* Gerson est-il l'auteur?" *Divinitas* (1967): 747–783.

33. Jean de Montreuil, *L'Oeuvre polémique,* ed. E. Ornato and N. Grevy-Pons (Turin, 1963), 1: 79–80.

34. Clamanges, *Opera,* 1: *Epist.,* 180–182, 301.

35. Alain Chartier, *Les Oeuvres,* ed. Duchesne (Paris, 1617), 402–454.

36. Jouvenal des Ursins, *Ecrits,* 1: 146 ff.

37. Martin Lefranc, *Le Champion des dames,* ed. A. Piaget (Lausanne, 1968).

38. Robert Blondel, *Oeuvres,* ed. A. Héron (Rouen, 1892), 1: 1–42.

39. Lefranc, *Champion,* 103–104.

40. Chastellain, *Oeuvres,* 1: 37 ff.

41. A. de Montaiglon, *Anciennes poésies françaises du XVe et XVIe siècles* (Paris, 1855–1866), 8: 74–90.

42. F. Guessard and E. de Certain, eds., *Le Mystère du siège d'Orléans* (Paris, 1862); Jacques Millet, *L'Istoire de la destruction de Troie la Grant,* ed. E. Stengel (Leipzig, 1883).

43. Chastellain, *Oeuvres,* 6: 437–457.

44. Chastellain, *Oeuvres,* 7: 1–35.

45. Chastellain, *Oeuvres,* 6: 1–48.

46. Martial d'Auvergne, *Les Vigiles de Charles VII,* ed. Coustelier (Paris, 1724).

47. Pierre Gringoire, *Oeuvres complètes,* ed. C. d'Héricault and A. de Montaiglon (Paris, 1877), 1: 244–269.

48. BN MS français 841, fol. 25v.

49. BN MS français 24441, fol. 5v.

50. BN MS français 1133, fol. 7; BN MS français 19127, fol. 5v; BN MS français 5054, fol. 35v.

51. W. M. Jones, *The Royal Tour de France by Charles IX and Catherine de Médicis* (Toronto, 1979), 181, 273; W. M. Jones, *The Paris Entries of Charles IX* (Toronto, 1974).

52. Gervais de Bus, *Fauvel,* 2: 115.

53. Jean Gerson *Oeuvres complètes,* ed. P. Glorieux (Paris, 1963), 5: 151–168; Blondel, *Oeuvres,* 1: 86–88.

54. BN MS français 600 (Martin Lefranc, *L'Estrif de vertu et fortune,* fols. 33v–34v; Masselin, *Journal,* 39.

55. André de la Vigne, *Le Verger d'honneur* (Paris, n.d.).

56. G. M. Spiegel and S. Hindman, "The Fleur-de-lys Frontispieces to Guillaume de Nangis's *Chronique abrégée:* Political Iconography in Late-fifteenth-century France," *Viator* 21 (1981): 381–407; E. Picot, "Notes sur une tapisserie à figures symboliques," *Bulletin de la Société de l'histoire de Normandie* 11 (1911): 111–120.

57. B. Guenée and F. Lehoux, *Les Entrées royales françaises de 1328 à 1515* (Paris, 1968), 261–263, 271–276, 290, 297.

58. Blondel, *Oeuvres,* 1: 88.

59. Lefranc, *Champion*, 102; Blondel, *Oeuvres*, 1: 1–42, 86–88; Gerson, *Oeuvres*, 5: 151–168.

60. E. T. Hamy, *Le Livre de la description des pays du Héraut Berry* (Paris, 1908), 38.

61. E. R. Curtius, "Rhetorische Naturschilderung im Mittelalter," *Romanische Forschung* 56 (1942): 219–256; D. Thoss, *Studien zum locus amoenus im Mittelalter* (Vienna/Stuttgart, 1972).

62. C. Marchello-Nizia, "Les songes politiques à la fin du Moyen age," *Revue des sciences humaines* 55 (1981): 39–53.

63. Genesis, II, 15 and III, 23–24; Ecclesiastes, XXIV, 30–32; Song of Solomon, IV, 12–13, 15.

64. C. Deluz, "Le paradis terrestre, image de l'Orient," *Sénéfiance*, 11 (1982): 145–61.

65. Guglielmus Benedicti, *Opera omnia* (Lyon, 1582), 17 ("Duas habens").

66. Benedicti, *Opera*, 17v.

67. Lefranc, *Le Champion des dames* (Paris, 1530), 110.

68. Gerson, *Oeuvres*, 5: 151–168: *Considerate lilia agri* ("Consider the lilies of the field . . .").

69. *Romance of the Rose*, vv. 19931–20667.

70. D. W. Robertson, "The Doctrine of Charity in Medieval Literary Gardens: A Topical Approach Through Symbolism and Allegory," *Speculum* 26 (1951): 24–49.

71. Blondel, *Oeuvres*, 1: 86–88.

72. Blondel, *Oeuvres*, 1: 1–42; Gerson, *Oeuvres*, 5: 151–168; BN MS français 1240 (*Le Rosier des guerres*), fol. 6v.

73. Pierre Dubois, *De recuperatione Terrae Sanctae*, ed. C. V. Langlois (Paris, 1891), 139.

74. BN MS latin 11730 (Etienne de Conti, *Brevis Tractatus*), fol. 30v.

75. L. Pannier and P. Meyer, *Le Débat des hérauts d'armes de France et d'Angleterre* (Paris, 1877); Herald Berry, *Le Livre de description*, ed. Hamy.

76. Masselin, *Journal*, 39.

77. Chastellain, *Oeuvres*, 7: 188; 6: 28.

78. F. Crisp, *Medieval Gardens* (London, 1924); Pierre de Crescent, *Le Livre des profits champêtres et ruraux* (Lyon, 1530).

79. Spiegel and Hindman, "The Fleur-de-lys Frontispiece."

80. Guenée and Lehoux, *Entrées*, 261–263, 271–276, 290, 297; G. Guigue, *L'Entrée de François Ier à Lyon en 1515* (Lyon 1899), 16.

81. M. Levy d'Ancona, *The Gardens of the Renaissance: Botanical Symbols in Italian Painting* (Florence, 1977).

82. E. Langlois, ed., *Le Couronnement de Louis* (Paris, 1920), 1.

83. C. Gauvard, "L'opinion publique aux confins des Etats et des principautés," *Les Principautés au Moyen Age* (Congrès de la Société des historiens médiévistes [Bordeaux, 1973]) (Bordeaux, 1979), 127–152; B. Guenée, "Les limites de la France," in M. François, ed., *La France et les Français* (Paris, 1972), 50–68.

84. Guigue, *L'Entrée de François Ier*, 16.

85. J. Krynen, *Idéal du prince et pouvoir royal en France à la fin du Moyen Age* (Paris, 1980), 255–256.

86. Deluz, "Paradis terrestre"; Marco Polo, *Le Devisement du monde* (Paris, 1980), 19–25.

87. Daniel, IV.

88. *The Book of John of Mandeville,* ed. M. Letts (London, 1953), 2: 264–265.

89. L. Réau, *Iconographie de l'art chrétien* (Paris, 1957), 2: 129–139, and bibliography, 150.

90. Du Boulay, *Historia universitatis parisiensis* (Paris, 1668), 4: 396–412.

91. C. Meredith-Jones, ed., *Historia Karoli Magni et Rothlandi ou Chronique de Pseudo-Turpin* (Paris, 1936), 117–300; E. Hucher, *Le Saint Graal* (Paris, 1878), 3: 466; Du Boulay, *Hist. univ. paris.,* 4: 404.

92. It appears in the legends of Saint Elizabeth of Hungary, Saint Fina, Saint Rosalia of Palermo, Saint Casilda, and Saint Diego of Alcala. All imitate a passage in the *Historia Karoli Magni,* "De bello . . . ubi astae floruerunt": C. Meredith-Jones, *Historia Karoli magni,* 109–113.

93. Bibliothèque Mazarine, MS 3524 (Robert Gervais, *Speculum morale regium*), fols. 5v, 6v; BN MS français 600 (Martin Lefranc), fols. 34 ff.; Chastellain, *Oeuvres,* 6: 133; BN MS français 12490 (Jean Molinet, *France est gracieuse, non fière*), fols. 103–104.

94. Guenée and Lehoux, *Entrées,* 261–263.

95. BN MS français (*Complainte sur la mort de Charles VII*), fols. 303–307, 415–419; Spiegel and Hindman, "Fleur-de-lys Frontispieces"; BN MS français 5750 (*L'Entrée de Claude de France*), fols. 39v–40v.

96. M. Bonjour, *Terre natale: étude sur une composante affective du patriotisme romain* (Paris, 1975); F. Paschoud, *Roma aeterna: études sur le patriotisme romain à l'époque des grandes invasions* (Neuchâtel, 1967).

97. G. Dupont-Ferrier, "Le sens des mots *patria* et patrie en France au Moyen Age," *Revue historique* 89 (1940): 89–104; E. Kantorowicz, "*Pro patria mori* in Medieval Political Thought," *American Historical Review* 56 (1951): 472–492.

98. Quoted in E. Kantorowicz, "Pro patria mori," 475.

99. Gerson, *Oeuvres,* 1, p. 846.

100. J. R. Strayer, "Defense of the Realm and Royal Power in France," in his *Medieval Statecraft and the Perspectives of History,* (Princeton, 1971), 291–299; Suger, *Vita Ludovici sexti,* 221: "regnum defendere."

101. Strayer, "Defense of the Realm."

102. Philippe de Beaumanoir, *Coutumes de Beauvaisis,* ed. C. Beugnot (Paris, 1842), 2: 260.

103. M. M. Martin, *Histoire de l'unité française* (Paris, 1948): 151–158; Lot, "La formation de l'unité française," 429.

104. Duc de Levis-Mirepoix, *L'Attentat d'Anagni* (Paris, 1969): 345.

105. P. de Lagarde, "La philosophie d'Henri de Gand et Geoffroi de Fontaines," *Recueil de travaux d'histoire et de philologie,* 3rd series, vol. 18 (1943): 80–87; Henri de Gand, *Quodlibeta* (Paris, 1518), XV, 16, XII, 13.

106. S. E. Fretté, ed., *Oeuvres attribuées à Thomas d'Aquin* in *Opera Omnia* (Paris, 1871–1880), 27: 384 ff.; Thomas Aquinas, *Opera omnia* (Rome, 1897), 8: 245; 9: 485–486.

107. Raymond Sebonde, *Theologia naturalis* (Nuremberg, 1502), *quaestiones* 125, 126, 127, 142.

108. Sebonde, *Theol. nat., quaestio* 142.

109. Vincent of Beauvais, *Speculum majus* (Douai, 1642), 2: 109.

110. Valerius Maximus, *Facta memorabilia*, et. P. Constant (Paris, 1935), 443–447; Augustine, *De civitate dei*, V, 17–18.

111. Aegidius Romanus, *De regimine principum*, ed. J. Mathis (Rome, 1948), 41.

112. Charles d'Orléans, *Oeuvres complètes*, ed. J. Guichard (Paris, 1842), 139; Blondel, *Oeuvres*, 1: 306–307.

113. Lefranc, *Champion tes dames*, 107: "Regardez les os de vos pères épars . . . ."

114. A. Piaget, ed., "*Le Livre de chevalerie* de Geoffroy de Charny," *Romania* 26 (1897): 396–411 (a partial edition of the text in BN MS français 25447; there is no edition of the *Demandes sur la joute*).

115. Bonet, *L'Arbre des batailles*, III, 32.

116. Chevalier de la Tour Landry, *Le Guidon des guerres* (Paris, 1514), which discusses these issues on fols. 86v–87, 92, 99v.

117. BN MS français 1240, fols. 4r–v, 12r–v.

118. Jean de Bueil, *Le Jouvencel*, ed. J. Lecestre (Paris, 1889), 1: 51.

119. BN MS français 10017 (*Doctrinal de noblesse*), fols. 30, 71, 94.

120. Alain Chartier, *Les Oeuvres latines*, ed. P. Bourgain-Heymerick (Paris, 1977), 265; Blondel, *Oeuvres*, 1: 307.

121. Corneille, *Horace*, II, v.3.

122. Symphorien Champier, *Les Proverbes des princes* (Lyon, 1502), fol. 22v.

123. BN MS latin 6221 (Albert de Bontesten, *Sermon en vers sur la mort du Téméraire*), fol. 22v.

124. G. A. Crapelet, *Le Combat des Trente* (Paris, 1827), 34–35.

125. Jean de Venette, *Continuatio chronici Guillelmi de Nangiaco*, ed. H. Géraud (Paris, 1843), 2: 288–293.

126. Cuvellier, *Bertrand Duguesclin*, 2: 320.

127. A. Tuetey, *Journal d'un bourgeois de Paris (1405–1449)* (Paris, 1881), 656–657.

128. Pierre de Fénin, *Chronique*, ed. Michaud and Poujoulat (Paris, 1836), 2: 612–613.

129. Le Religieux de Saint-Denis, *Chronique de Charles VI*, ed. and trans. L. F. Bellaguet (Paris, 1839–1852), 6: 451–453.

130. Jean Jouvenal des Ursins, *Chronique de Charles VI*, ed. T. Godefroy (Paris, 1614), 487–489.

131. Enguerrand de Monstrelet, *Chronique*, ed. L. Douet d'Arcq (Paris, 1857–1862), 4: 71, 91, 96.

132. Blondel, *Oeuvres*, 2: 198–199.

133. The meeting with the constable of Bourbon and the remark appear only in texts written after 1550, such as "Le Loyal Serviteur": J. Roman, *Bayard par le Loyal Serviteur* (Paris, 1878), 223. Earlier versions of the death are in Symphorien Champier, *Les Gestes et la vie du preux chevalier Bayard*

(Lyon, 1525), where he says nothing, and Aymar Rival, *De Allobrogibus libri novem* (reprinted Lyon, 1844), 577–578, where the speech has begun to take shape.

134. E. Raunie and M. Prinet, *Epitaphier du vieux Paris* (Paris, 1890–1894), 2: 290; 3: 360.

135. De Bueil, *Le Jouvencel*, 1: cccv.

136. Chartier, *Oeuvres*, 410.

137. Suger, *Vita Ludovici sexti*, 222.

138. Chastellain, *Oeuvres*, 1: 32.

139. Lefranc, *Champion des dames*, 108.

140. A. Bossuat, "L'idée de la nation et la jurisprudence du Parlement de Paris," *Revue historique* 204 (1940): 54–59.

APPENDIX TO CHAPTER 3: THE CULT OF SAINT LOUIS

1. P. Morel, "Le culte de Saint Louis," *Itinéraires* (1970): 127–151.

2. R. Folz, "La sainteté de Saint Louis d'après les textes liturgiques," *Revue d'histoire de l'Eglise de France* 57 (1971): 31–45; R. Folz, *Les Saints Rois du Moyen Age en Occident (VIe–XIIIe siècles)* (Brussels, 1984).

3. BN MS latin 1370 (*Psautier du roi Charles VIII*), fols. 212, 216.

4. V. Leroquais, *Les Bréviaires manuscrits des bibliothèques publiques de France* (Paris, 1934).

5. V. Leroquais, *Les Livres d'heures manuscrits de la Bibliothèque Nationale* (Paris, 1927).

6. V. Leroquais, *Les Psautiers manuscrits des bibliothèques publiques de France* (Mâcon, 1940).

7. H. Martin, *Les Ordres mendiants en Bretagne* (Paris, 1975).

8. P. M. Auzas, "Essai d'un répertoire iconographique de Saint Louis," *7ème Centenaire:* 156.

9. He appears with a book at Vitrac, Flavigny, Angicourt, Chateauneuf-du-Faou, and with gloves at La-Chapelle-Saint-Sépulcre, Bouquetot, Roman, Champigny-sur-Veude, Marigné.

10. AA.SS., August, 5: 473.

APPENDIX TO CHAPTER 6: THE LISTS OF PRIVILEGES OF THE KING AND KINGDOM

1. BN MS latin 6020 (Bernard du Rosier, *Miranda de laudibus Franciae*), fol. 4v; BN MS français 193, fols. 182–183; Benedicti, *Opera*, fols. 16–17 at "Duas habens"; BN MS latin 11730, fol. 31; A. Leroux de Lincy and L. M. Tisserand, *Paris et ses historiens aux XIVe et XVe siècles* (Paris, 1867), 148.

2. In addition to the texts listed in the previous note, see Kempf, *Pierre Dubois*, 111–114; Guimier, *Commentaire*, fol. 2v; Benedicti, *Opera*, fols. 95–97 at "Uxorem nomine"; Guillaume Guiart, *La Branche des royaux lignages*, CCNF, 7: 13.

3. Bonet, *L'Arbre*, 184–190; BN MS français 23428 (Guillaume Jouvenel,

Proposition à l'assemblée du clergé en 1406), fol. 83v; Jean Gerson, *Oeuvres complètes*, ed. E. Dupin (Antwerp, 1706), 4: 850–851; BN MS français 193, fols. 182–183.

4. Jean Bonaud du Sauset, *Commentaire du traité de Jean de Terre-Vermeille* (Paris, 1526), fols. iii, 5; Jean Jouvenal des Ursins, *Ecrits politiques*, ed. P. S. Lewis (Paris, 1978), 1: 136–160.

5. A. Tardif, *Privilèges accordés à la maison de France par le Saint-Siège* (Paris, 1855); B. Barbiche, *Les Actes pontificaux originaux des archives nationales* (Vatican City, 1975), fol. 1.

6. BN MS latin 9814.

7. It had also been used by the authors of BN MS nouv. acq. française 6853, fol. 30, BN MS latin 6020, fol. 13.

8. On Bernard, see J. L. Gazzaniga, *L'Eglise du Midi à la fin du règne de Charles VII* (Paris, 1976), 67–68; Abbé Cayre, *Histoire des archevêques de Toulouse* (Toulouse, 1871), 271–282.

9. BN MS français 1965, fol. 42v.

10. Guimier, *Commentaire*, fol. 140; Etienne Aufreri, *Opusculum avidissimus cumulus* (Lyon, 1533), p. 22, fols. 110v–116; Feu, *An rex Franciae*, fols. 62–79v.

11. J. Poujol, "Jean Ferrault on the King's Privileges," *Studies in the Renaissance* 5 (1958): 15–26.

12. Vincent Cygault, *Allegationes supra bello italico* (Paris, 1512); BN MS français 4515 (*Cy après s'ensuivent aucuns privilèges et droits royaux*), fols. 117–206.

APPENDIX TO CHAPTER 8: TROJANS AND GAULS IN THE FIFTEENTH AND SIXTEENTH CENTURIES

1. G. Uppert, "The Trojan Franks and Their Critics," *Studies in the Renaissance* 12 (1965): 227–241; J. P. Bodmer, "Die französische Historiographie des Spätmittelalters und die Franken," *Archiv für Kulturgeschichte* 45 (1963): 91–118; A. Bossuat, "Les origines troyennes: leur rôle dans la littérature historique du XVe siècle," *Annales de Normandie* 8 (1958): 187–197.

2. Uppert, "The Trojan Franks."

3. Jean Lemaire de Belges, *Oeuvres*, ed. J. A. Stecher (Louvain, 1882), vols. 1 and 2.

4. M. Klippel, *Die Darstellung der frankischen Trojanersage in Geschichtsschreibung und Dichtung vom Mittelalter bis zur Renaissance in Frankreich* (Marburg, 1936), 71.

5. Rigord and Guillaume le Breton, *Oeuvres*, ed. H. F. Delaborde (Paris, 1882), 1: 55–59.

6. GC, 1: 12–20.

7. Vincent of Beauvais, *Speculum historiale* (Douai, 1624), 4: 619.

8. PL, vol. 139, cols. 638–639.

9. Rigord and Guillaume le Breton, *Oeuvres*, 2: 9–14.

10. Jean Divry, *Les Triomphes de France* (Paris, 1508), unpaginated. Chap. entitled "L'origine des Français."

11. BN MS nouv. acq. française 11338 (*Chronique universelle*), fol. 37.

12. A. Joly, *Benoît de Sainte More et le roman de Troie ou les métamorphoses d'Homère et de l'épopée gréco-latine au Moyen Age* (Paris, 1870).

13. BN MS français 821 (*Roman de Landamata*), fols. 261–269.

14. Jacques Millet, *L'Istoire de la destruction de Troie la Grant*, ed. E. Stengel (Marburg, 1883), 1–5.

15. BN MS nouv. acq. française 11330, fol. 37.

16. Michael Riccio, *De regibus Francorum libri tres* (Basle, 1517), fol. 3.

17. *Aeneid*, I, 242–249.

18. Dares of Phrygia, *De excidio Trojae historia*, ed. F. Meister (Leipzig, 1873).

19. Dictys of Crete, *Ephemerides belli trojani libri sex*, ed. F. Meister (Leipzig, 1872).

20. MGH, *Scriptores rerum merovingiacarum*, 2: 241–246.

21. J. A. Lair, "Le *De moribus et actis primorum Normanniae ducum* de Dudon de Saint-Quentin," *Mémoires de la Société des antiquaires de Normandie*, 3rd series, vol. 3 (1865): 129–130.

22. Sigebert of Gembloux, *Chronica*, PL, vol. 160, cols. 59–60.

23. BN MS français 20124 (Jean de Courcy, *Chronique universelle*), fols. 157–160; BN MS français 1371 (Noël de Fribois, *Miroir historial*), fols. 42–43; BN MS français 1371 (*L'Histoire antonine*), fols. 10v, 35.

24. Guido da Columna, *Historia destructionis Trojae* (Cologne, 1477), 8.

25. BN MS français 59 (Raoul Lefèvre, *Le recueil des troyennes histoires*), fol. 314.

26. BN MS français 53 (Jean Mansel, *La fleur des histoires*), fol. 9v.

27. BN MS français 24430 (*Chronique de Tournai*), fol. 166.

28. A. Leroux de Lincy and L. M. Tisserand, *Paris et ses historiens aux XIVe et XVe siècles* (Paris, 1867), 99–106.

29. A. Leroux de Lincy, "Pierre Choque, *Discours des cérémonies du mariage d'Anne de Foix*," *Bibliothèque de l'Ecole des Chartes*, 5th series, vol. 2 (1862): 437.

30. BN MS français 1371, fol. 37; Olivier de la Marche, *Mémoires*, ed. H. Beaune and J. D'Arbaumont (Paris, 1883), 1: 18–20; BN MS latin 6238 (*Regum Francorum stemma*), fol. 14v; BN MS latin 9670 (*Histoire universelle s'arrêtant à l'année 1428*), fol. 86v; BN MS français (*Histoire de France depuis 367 av. Chr. jusqu'à la mort de Louis XI*), fol. 119.

31. BN MS français 1371, fol. 10v, is an exception.

32. Already told by Guillaume le Breton: Rigord and Guillaume le Breton, *Oeuvres*, 2: 9–14.

33. BN MS français 1493 (*Résumé d'histoire universelle depuis la création du monde jusqu'au XVe siècle*), fols. 4–15; M. Schmidt-Chazan, "Histoire et sentiment national chez Robert Gaguin," in B. Guenée, *Le Métier d'historien* (Paris, 1977), 233–300.

34. Sigebert of Gembloux, PL, vol. 160, cols. 59–60.

35. BN MS français 17180 (Bernard Gui, *Fleur des chroniques*), fol. 66.

36. Rigord and Guillaume le Breton, *Oeuvres*, 1: 55–59.

37. Rigord and Guillaume le Breton, *Oeuvres*, 1: 170–173; 2: 13.

38. Jean de Paris, ed. A. Duchesne, *Historiae Francorum Scriptores* (Paris, 1636), 1: 128–133.

39. Honoré Bonet, *L'Arbre des batailles*, ed. E. Nys (Paris, 1883), 184–187.

40. BN MS français 5699 (*La geste des nobles français de Guillaume Cousinot*), fols. 13–15.

41. *La Mer des histoires* (Paris, 1488), fol. 130v.

42. BN MS français 9688 (*Chronologie universelle jusqu'à la mort de Charles VI*), fol. 19.

43. Olivier de la Marche, *Mémoires*, 1: 18–20; BN MS nouv. acq. française 1493, fols. 14–15; BN MS français 5696 (*Cy s'ensuivent les lignées des rois de France*), fols. 3–7.

44. BN MS nouv. acq. française 1493, fols. 14–15.

45. BN MS français 9688, fol. 19.

46. Jean d'Outremeuse, *Ly Myreur des histors*, ed. A. Borgnet and S. Bormans, in *Collection des chroniques belges*, vol. 29 (Brussels, 1864), 45–46.

47. Jean de Paris, in Duchesne, *Hist. Franc. SS.*, 1: 128–133.

48. Raoul de Presles, *La Cité de Dieu de Saint Augustin* (Paris, 1531), fols. 169–179.

49. BN MS nouv. acq. française 1493, fol. 14–15; BN MS français 24976 (*Les actes des François et les actes des Troyens et des Grecs*), fols. 3–7; BN MS français 5696, fols. 3–7; BN MS français 9688, fol. 19.

50. BN MS français 38 (Jean Duchesne, *Les Commentaires de César en français*), fol. 65.

51. M. Barroux, "Les origines légendaires de Paris," *Mémoires de la Société historique et archéologique de Paris et de l'Ile de France* 7 (1955): 9–11.

52. E. Fueter, *Geschichte der neureren Historiographie* (Berlin, 1936), 128–135.

53. R. Bolgar, *The Classical Heritage and Its Beneficiaries* (Cambridge, England, 1958), 13–58.

54. Flavio Biondo, *Historiarum romanarum decades tres* (Venice, 1483).

55. G. Voigt, *Aeneas Sylvius Piccolimini als Papst Pie II und sein Zeitalter* (Berlin, 1930), vol. 2.

56. Aeneas Sylvius Piccolimini: *Opera omnia* (Basle, 1551); *Cosmographia: De Europa*, chap. 38 (p. 433); *De Asia*, chap. 67 (p. 349).

57. Marco Antonio Sabellico, *Enneades ab orbe condito ad inclinationem imperii Romani* (Venice, 1498).

58. Michael Riccio, *De regibus*, fol. 3.

59. Paulus Aemilius Veronensis, *De rebus gestis Francorum* (Paris, 1517), vol. 1, fol. 3.

60. Rigord and Guillaume le Breton, *Oeuvres*, 1: 55.

61. Nicole Gilles, *Les très élégantes, très véridiques et copieuses Annales* (Paris, 1525), fol. 1r–v.

62. BN MS français 20124, fols. 157–160: in addition to stories derived from Fredegar, the *Deeds*, and the *Great Chronicles*, he knew two that are traceable to Freculph, a ninth-century author.

63. Robert Gaguin, *Compendium super Francorum gestis* (Paris, 1500), fol. 1v.

64. Lemaire de Belges, *Oeuvres*, 1: 4.

65. BN MS latin 10909 (Jean Candida, *Abrégé de l'histoire de France*), fol. 4.

66. Gilles, *Annales*, fol. 1r–v.

67. BN MS français 193 (Pierre Desgros, *Le Jardin des nobles*), fol. 240.

68. BN MS latin 10909, fols. 4, 7.

69. BN MS latin 5951 (Jean de Legonissa, *Opus Davidicum*), fol. 27; A. Linder, "L'Expédition italienne de Charles VIII et les espérances messianiques des Juifs," *Revue des études juives* 137 (1978): 179–186.

70. O. Seel, *M. Iuniani Iustini Epitoma historiarum Pompei Trogi* (Leipzig, 1935), 192–205.

71. Titus Livius, *L'Histoire romaine*, ed. J. Bayet (Paris, 1969), 5: 54–77.

72. Caesar, *La Guerre des Gaules*, ed. L. A. Constans (Paris, 1937), 1: 2–3; 2: 183–190.

73. Isidore of Seville, *Etymologiarum*, PL, vol. 82, col. 508.

74. P. Meyer, "Les premières compilations françaises d'histoire ancienne," *Romania* 14 (1885): 1–181.

75. BN MS français 246.

76. F. Gundorf, *Caesar: Geschichte seines Ruhms* (Berlin, 1925).

77. L. F. Flutre, *Les Faits des Romains dans les littératures françaises et italiennes du XIIIe au XVIe siècles* (Paris, 1932); B. Guenée, "La culture historique des nobles: le succès des *Faits des Romains*," in P. Contamine, ed., *La Noblesse au Moyen Age* (Paris, 1976), 261–288.

78. BN MS français 23083, fol. 20v.

79. R. Bossuat, "Les traductions françaises des *Commentaires* de César à la fin du XVme siècle," *Humanisme et Renaissance* (1943), 253–411.

80. BN MS français 728.

81. See Bartholomew de Glanville, *De proprietatibus rerum*, XV, 66 (Basle, 1475), fol. 123v; BN MS latin 4976 (Bernard Gui, *Descriptio Galliarum*), fol. 261; Leroux de Lincy and Tisserand, *Paris et ses historiens*, 117–236.

82. Leroux de Lincy and Tisserand, *Paris et ses historiens*, 110–115.

83. Leroux de Lincy and Tisserand, *Paris et ses historiens*, 117–236.

84. BN MS français 53, fol. 273.

85. BN MS latin 6020 (Bernard du Rosier, *Miranda de laudibus Francie*), fol. 1v; BN MS nouv. acq. française 6853 (*Miroir historial jusqu'au règne de Louis XI*), fol. 28.

86. BN MS français 955 (Jean Massue, *Marguerites historiales*), fol. 149.

87. BN MS français 69 (Jean Germain, *Dialogue du Chrétien et du Sarrazin*), fol. 29v.

88. Robert Gaguin, *Epistolae et orationes*, ed. L. Thuasne (Paris, 1900), 233–300; see Schmidt-Chazan, "Histoire et sentiment national."

89. Caesar, *Commentarii cum index Raimundi Marliani* (Lyon, 1508).

90. BN MS latin 5934.

91. Poggio Bracciolini, *Diodor Sicilii Bibliotheca e greco traducta* (Bologna, 1472); *Strabonis Geographiae libri XVII* (Rome, 1469).

92. For example in Jean Perionius, *Dialogorum de linguae gallicae origine libri* (Paris, 1554).

93. H. Steger, *David rex et propheta* (Nuremburg, 1961).

94. P. E. Schramm, *Der König von Frankreich* (Weimar, 1960), 1: 208–214.

95. T. Godefroy, *Le Cérémonial français* (Paris, 1659), 1: 19 (Ceremonial of 1223).

96. BN MS latin 16549, fols. 95–96.

97. BN MS français 193, fol. 24v.

98. BN MS latin 5971A.

99. In Jean Lemaire de Belges, *Oeuvres,* vols. 1, 2.

100. Giovanni Nanni Viterbensis, *Commentarii fratris Aenii Viterbensis* (Rome, 1498); Jacopo Filipo Forest Bergamensis, *Supplementum chronicarum* (Brescia, 1485); Michael Riccio, *De regibus Gallorum* (Basle, 1505).

APPENDIX A TO CHAPTER 9: MANUSCRIPTS OF THE SALIC LAW

1. N. Grevy-Pons, "La propagande de guerre française avant l'apparition de Jeanne d'Arc," *Journal des Savants* (1982): 191–214; P. S. Lewis, "War Propaganda and Historiography in Fifteenth-century France," *Transactions of the Royal Historical Society* 15 (1965): 1–21; BN MS nouv. acq. française 1858 (Noël de Fribois, *Miroir historial*), fol. 13; BN MS français 4950 (*Miroir historial jusqu'à 1380*), fol. 11r–v.

2. C. Samaran and R. Marichal, *Catalogue des manuscrits datés des bibliothèques de France* (Paris, 1965), vol. 5; L. Delisle, *Le Cabinet des manuscrits de la Bibliothèque nationale* (Paris, 1868–1881), 2: 411.

3. Jean Bonaud du Sauset, *Commentaire du traité de Jean de Terre-Vermeille* (Paris, 1526); BN MS français 5058 (*Fluxo biennale spatio*), fols. 49–56; BN MS français 5059 (*Après la destruction de Troie la Grant*), fol. 46v; "Réponse du bon et loyal français," in L. de La Barre, *Mémoires pour servir à l'histoire de France et de Bourgogne* (Paris, 1729), 1: 319; P. S. Lewis, "War Propaganda"; N. Grevy-Pons, "La propagande de guerre."

4. Jean Jouvenal des Ursins, *Ecrits politiques,* 1: 156; BN MS français 2701 (*Traité compendieux*), fol. 58.

5. BN MS nouv. acq. française 1858, fol. 13; BN MS français 5026, fol. 43.

6. L. Redet, *Dictionnaire topographique du département de la Vienne* (Paris, 1881), 209.

7. BN MS français 2701, fol. 58.

8. It is certain that they looked for a manuscript that included them. Perhaps the Savigny manuscript only included the seventy sections, like BN MS nouv. acq. française, fol. 6853 (*Miroir historial avec le Liber legis salicae*).

9. BN MS français 4950, fol. 11v; BN MS français 5026, fol. 43.

10. BN MS latin 8577 (Gérard Machet, *Epistolae*), fol. 99v.

11. Jean de Montreuil, *L'Oeuvre historique.* In a first version of the text, "Mulier vero nullam in regno habeat portionem" (2: 132); the three later versions (pp. 168, 226, 274) give the true text.

12. BN MS français 5026, fol. 43.

13. BN MS français 4943, fol. 36.

14. BN MS français 5056 (*Décisions des différents qui ont été entre la France et l'Angleterre*), fol. 2v.

15. MS K36 of Eckhardt's edition.

16. BN MS nouv. acq. française 6853, fols. 1–25 (a manuscript unknown to Eckhardt).

17. BN MS français 25159, fol. 36v.

APPENDIX B TO CHAPTER 9: MANUSCRIPTS AND EDITIONS OF THE GREAT TREATISE ON THE SALIC LAW

1. J. M. Potter, "The Development and Significance of the Salic Law of the French," *English Historical Review* 52 (1937): 235–253.

2. R. E. Giesey, *The Juristic Basis of Dynastic Right to the French Throne* (Philadelphia: Transactions of the American Philosophical Society, 1961), vol. 60.

3. MS 2031, fols. 1–53.

4. The catalogue lists them under the words *Angleterre, différents avec l'*: see L. Delisle, *Catalogue du fond Libri et Barrois* (Paris, 1880), 241–244.

5. BN MSS français 5056, 5058, 12788; BN MSS nouv. acq. françaises 6214, 20962; Bibliothèque de l'Arsenal, MS 3434; Bibliothèque Mazarine, MS 2031. See P. S. Lewis, "War Propaganda and Historiography in Fifteenth-century France," *Transactions of the Royal Historical Society*, 5th series, vol. 15 (1965): 1–21.

6. Bibliothèque municipale de Lille, MS 322; BN MS français 15490; BN MS nouv. acq. française 7006.

7. BN MS français 5059, fols. 41–55.

8. BN MS français 5056.

9. BN MS nouv. acq. française 20962.

Index

413

Designer: U.C. Press Staff
Compositor: Huron Valley Graphics
Text: 10/12 Sabon
Display: Sabon
Printer: Braun-Brumfield
Binder: Braun-Brumfield